CHANCELLOR ROBERT R. LIVINGSTON

OF NEW YORK

1746—1813

Other books by George Dangerfield

BENGAL MUTINY

THE STRANGE DEATH OF LIBERAL ENGLAND

VICTORIA'S HEIR

THE ERA OF GOOD FEELINGS

CHANCELLOR ROBERT R. LIVINGSTON

Painting by John Vanderlyn, Paris, 1804
Courtesy of The New-York Historical Society, New York City

CHANCELLOR

ROBERT R.

LIVINGSTON

OF NEW YORK

1746—1813

GEORGE DANGERFIELD

HARCOURT, BRACE AND COMPANY

NEW YORK

first edition
Library of Congress Catalog Card Number: 60-10924
Printed in the United States of America

To Hilary and Tony, with my love

FOREWORD

This book is primarily a study in aristocracy. Henry Adams has written that New York society in 1800, "in spite of its aristocratic mixture, was democratic by instinct." If one accepts this instinctual interpretation, it follows that the democratic instinct of New York was always working to purge society of its aristocratic mixture: a study of the early statehood of New York certainly supports this obvious inference. The life of a New York landed aristocrat, brought up in privileged colonial circles and afterward exposed to the emergence of popular government in the Revolution and post-Revolution, could this then show the other side of the process—the resistance of the aristocratic mixture to the attempted purge? I have not, I trust, committed myself to the fallacy of making the life of Robert R. Livingston (1746-1813) a paradigm of aristocratic experience in New York: but I have suggested that his private aversion to popular politics, which made him *politically* both an unpopular and an unreliable figure, may offer a clue here and there to the failure of aristocracy to resist the purge—even when, as was the case with the Livingstons, aristocracy went over to the popular side.

My thanks are due to the New-York Historical Society, where much of the reading for this book was done: especially to Dr. R.W.G. Vail, Director; Dr. James J. Heslin, Assistant Director and Librarian, and now Director; Miss Geraldine Beard, Chief of the Reading Room; Miss E. Marie Becker, Reference Librarian; and Mr. Wilmer R. Leach, Curator of Manuscripts. To that happy mingling of consideration and expert knowledge which one encounters everywhere in the Society, I cannot be too grateful. To Howard H. Peckham, Associate Professor of History and Director of the William L. Clements Library, University of Michigan, and to Mr. William S. Ewing, Curator of Manuscripts, I am indebted for many acts of kindness and of help during my brief stay at Ann Arbor.

I wish to thank the Head of Special Collections, Columbia University Libraries, for permission to quote from the John Jay and the De Witt Clinton Papers.

I am deeply grateful to Princeton University, for awarding me the Benjamin D. Shreve Fellowship for 1957-58, so that I was able to pursue my researches in the University Library, and in a fruitful and happy milieu.

I wish to take this opportunity to express my deep appreciation of the kindness and hospitality of Mrs. John Henry Livingston, who permitted me to visit Clermont on two occasions.

I am most grateful to General John Ross Delafield, who allowed me to visit Montgomery Place.

My warmest thanks go to Coburn Gilman, whose fine intelligence assisted me in many lines of research when I was away from New York and whose geniality remained unimpaired throughout the ordeal; to Miss Helen Burr Smith, who prepared the genealogical chart; to John Smith, Librarian of the Santa Barbara Public Library, for obtaining books for me on various occasions; to Burdette Dunn, for advice and instruction on the early steamboat; to Phyllis Plous, for her expertness in deciphering and typing my manuscript; and to Wayne Andrews, who first suggested that I should undertake this book, in the days when he was Curator of Manuscripts at the New-York Historical Society.

GEORGE DANGERFIELD

Carpinteria, California
March, 1960

CONTENTS

PART ONE

BACKGROUND

CHAPTER ONE

On Saturday, October 11, 1794, an Englishman named William Strickland came to visit Robert R. Livingston, Chancellor of the State of New York, at his country seat, called Clermont, situated on the Hudson, some hundred and ten miles from New York City.

Strickland was an agriculturalist, a friend of Arthur Young and of Sir John Sinclair; and, like most English visitors in the immediate post-Revolutionary era, he came in a spirit of more or less friendly inquiry—to explore, rather than to expose, to criticize, more than to cavil: even, it may be, to learn, and not to teach. He was primarily interested in types, not idiosyncrasies. No physical or personal impressions mar his careful pages. He does not apply to his host any of those epithets with which students of the Chancellor's life are familiar, and which are sometimes so contradictory as to suggest that they belong to two different men: such as tall, graceful, genial, fascinating, vain, plain, pompous. As far as Strickland's journal is concerned, the Chancellor had no shape. He describes Mr. Livingston as "one of the richest, & in respectability [*i.e.*, in social standing] one of the first characters of his country . . . our hospitable and intelligent host."

What interested Strickland was the fact that Chancellor Livingston was a great landlord, with estates on both sides of the Hudson, and that he had dedicated himself to the advancement of scientific farming. And it is no doubt true that at Clermont the Chancellor assumed—whenever his audience permitted it and because it was a favorite and possibly a controlling one with him—the benevolent mask or persona of an enlightened farmer. He was president of the New York Society for the Promotion of Agriculture, Arts and Manufactures, which had recently been incorporated; he had published in the Society's *Transactions* an article on the transcendent virtues of gypsum as a manure; and he had done some experiments on his own, and very successful they were. He had a field of clover (wrote Strickland) "above a yard high, thick as it can stand; such a field I never saw before." He had even built a mill on the other side of the Hudson, where he ground his plaster for himself, his neighbors, and his tenants.

Moreover, he was a copious fountain of information: facts and statistics gushed from him, and the dazzled Strickland wrote them down without questioning their authority. Was it not for this, chiefly, that he had come to Clermont?

II

After traveling through drab pine barrens, Strickland had plunged into a world of clear autumn. Trees burned with "the brightest yellow & orange . . . the most brilliant scarlet or purple. Europeans accustomed to the sober brown of their autumn, can form no idea of the splendor of that season, while the sun shines upon the woods." The house itself, he says, "was only finished the last year; it is built of brick and covered with stucco, & being planned in the form of an 'H', that is having a recess in the center, both in the front & in the back, has all the advantages of a single house for the purposes of ventilation, of shade, & a thorough draft of air. . . . It is situated upon a natural terrace about 30 or 40 feet above the level of the Hudson, & distant from the edge of it about 100 yards, backed by a narrow ridge covered with wood, beyond which are the fields and domains of Mr. Livingston." Some quarter of a mile to the north stood an older mansion, the residence at that time of the Chancellor's mother, Mrs. Margaret Beekman Livingston. It also was called Clermont. In the matter of family names, the Livingstons, as genealogists have discovered to their delight, and historians to their consternation, were apt to practice a pious redundance.

Strickland's description is a little pedestrian, but is far the best that has survived, and visitors to the ruins of the Chancellor's mansion will find it at any rate recognizable. Concerning the interior and its routine, the journalist grows more explicit. "The principal rooms which are of good dimensions are hung with french papers, which are chiefly used in this country, the patterns being more beautiful and elegant, & lively, than what are manufactured in, & exported from England, & much cheaper in proportion to their merrit; the whole house is handsomely & commodiously finished & furnished." One rose, he says, at six in the morning, and walked about for two hours before sitting down to breakfast at eight. Dinner was at three, supper at nine. The profusion, variety, and excellence of the dishes were quite remarkable; and when the cloth was drawn after dinner, what exquisite pastries and confectionaries appeared! Only the fruit, he thought, for in his opinion the Chancellor's gardens were not well kept up, was below the most exacting standards. Otherwise, there was nothing—and here he evidently intended an immense compliment—"that might not have graced the best English table."

His account of the Sunday breakfast begins, however, to show how little one could actually rely upon English analogies. The meal, to be sure, had everything or nearly everything that was to be seen at the best English tables, and some delicacies that were not, such as scraped beef, red herrings, "& other relishes." But it was rather casually served by four boys, aged from five to twelve, barefooted, but dressed in clean green livery turned up with red. Their chief function, apart from hanging around the table, was to carry off one by one, into some small adjoining room, the tea things which Mrs. Livingston, "a polite, well-bred, sensible woman . . . almost imperceptibly washed & wiped," while the guests still lingered conversing in their seats. He noted that there was not a single bell in Clermont and that two of these four boys always accompanied the master and the mistress of the house, lounging by the doorway of any room they happened to be in, or even tumbling and frolicking on the carpet behind their chairs, "& were spoken to familiarly & treated with great good humor by both of them." All this was of a simple, a charming, a pastoral oddity; but the four boys were Negro slaves.

Mr. Strickland had not reached that period in history when Englishmen, having emancipated their own colonial slaves, were apt to speak severely about the slaveholding habits of others: his journal registers surprise, not indignation. But there were other occasions, too, upon which he felt that he was getting a little out of his depth. The Chancellor took him to a nearby farm which he had leased to a family of "German" descent, "as I believe are most of Mr. Livingston's tenants"—a farm of sixty acres, so orderly and prosperous that "I have seen nothing to equal it in America." But then he led him to the banks of the Hudson, to a spot that commanded a full view of the opposite shore. It appeared to be a settled country, well wooded, but broken by cultivation. Some twelve miles away (in Strickland's estimation) rose the Catskills in all their majesty, covered with a primal forest of deciduous trees mixed with pines—a long range of mountains and deep valleys, scarcely explored, and inhabited (said the Chancellor) chiefly by bears, elk, deer, panthers, wolves, and wildcats. The Chancellor pointed out a frontage of some five thousand acres and said "that he has 200,000 acres beginning at these woods which he is just beginning to settle." As for the human dwellers in this savage wilderness, the Chancellor spoke of the terms of their leases with a singular—one might almost have said with an innocent—candor. He spoke of so many bushels of wheat per hundred acres, of so many fowls per year, of reserved milling and mining rights, of fines for alienation, of one day's labor annually for the landlord with horses or oxen, until his guest hardly knew what century he was in. "These are seemingly very extraordinary terms," he wrote, "& mark more of the spirit of feudal aristocracy, than might be supposed to be harboured in the breast of one of the *stanchest republicans* in the U:SS:, of one who is thought by many to entertain principles too highly democratic."

Thus Chancellor Livingston's politics entered the journal at last, but only as one of those anomalies and contradictions which, it would seem, everywhere underlay the placid, hospitable surface of life at Clermont.

III

In the Strickland journal, in fact, Robert R. Livingston was a man looking in two directions—forward as a scientific farmer, backward as a landlord, forward as a republican, backward as an aristocrat. A Livingston of Clermont, in 1794, had some difficulty in adjusting the demands of contemporary history to that past which hung about him, visible and even palpable in his way of life. The Chancellor was a man living simultaneously and conspicuously on two planes, which could not be brought into focus, so that Strickland's account of him becomes blurred and puzzled, and, in a later footnote, angry. Years afterward, rereading the Clermont entries in his journal, Strickland felt compelled to write in the margin:

In 1802 Mr. L: went Ambassador to France & negotiated with Bonaparte for the purchase of Louisiana, & made himself conspicuous in March & April 1804 for an infamous libel on the English respecting the forged correspondence imputed to Mr. Drake our Minister at Munich; which in servility to Bonaparte exceeded the reply of the Minister of any other State.

Of the justice of this passage, it will be necessary to say something in due time. But it is no more than just to Mr. Strickland to observe that his journal managed to suggest, in a few pages, a background, an attitude, and a career.[1]

[1] The notes will be found on pages 451 to 516.

CHAPTER TWO

Of Chancellor Robert R. Livingston's life from his birth until his graduation from college almost nothing is known. His family life was a happy one: so much can be fairly deduced from scattered letters and memories, and a psychologist would give it its due importance. He was also, as an eldest son, the heir to a large estate and to a name that was famous in the annals of provincial New York; famous or notorious—the annals of provincial New York were such that, with any great family, the two words were almost interchangeable and always coexistent.

It is, indeed, impossible to separate the Chancellor's mature personality, as it develops in his correspondence and is revealed in his career, from his family background and from the curious ambiguity that hangs about it. A member of a family that had been prominent in New York long before the Revolution, and had then survived it, the Chancellor inherited something more than a position and a name. He inherited a certain kind of self-consciousness, at once proud and sensitive, accepting respect as a matter of course but preternaturally quick to detect a slight or a sneer, as if ingratitude and adulation were equally to be his lot, not because of his character, but because of his name.

II

The founder of the American Livingstons was Robert Livingston, the Chancellor's great-grandfather.

There is a portrait of this Robert Livingston, painted apparently at the height of his career, in which the unknown artist—perhaps because he was unable to reconcile a notable quarrel between a noble forehead and a jutting aggressive chin—has rendered his subject's face almost in three-quarter view. But the disparity thus given to the two sides of Robert Livingston's face is not merely one of proportion. One side, the larger, is all persuasiveness, elegance, and, even, charm; the other, the foreshortened side, is cold and rapacious: and the two are united by a wide thin-lipped mouth. The total effect is one of extreme obliquity. Whether the painter achieved this effect through incompetence or through intuition— what Robert Livingston's face was really like—are questions that obviously cannot be answered: but since the portrait has survived, we may assume that Mr. Livingston did not object to this representation of himself. It is the representation of a man whose known career, again in a very oblique way, does justice and more than justice to his family motto: *Si Je Puis*. Except as an ironical coda to the troubled theme of his life, the other family motto—*Spero Meliora* (I Hope for Better Things)—is altogether less appropriate.[1]

Robert Livingston, the Chancellor's great-grandfather, was born in the year 1654, in Ancrum, Roxburghshire, Scotland. His father was the Reverend John Livingston, a Presbyterian divine, who fled or was exiled from his native land in 1663 because he opposed the episcopalian tendencies of the Stuart Restoration. The fact that the senior branch of the Reverend John Livingston's family (which was an old one) rose to eminence through its support of the Stuarts gives an added luster to his resolution, faith, and originality: and his reputation must have preceded him to his exile in Holland, for he established himself at once as the pastor of a congregation of Scottish refugees in Rotterdam. There he was joined by his wife, one of his daughters, and his youngest son.

In Rotterdam, young Robert Livingston received his training in the best business school of the seventeenth century—that is to say, in a Dutch countinghouse. He became as fluent in Dutch as in English, and in that cosmopolitan city he may well have acquired, and it has been asserted that he did acquire, a working knowledge of French. Perhaps from restless energy, or from a longing to reach some wider spiritual atmosphere, or because of the menace of Catholic France, his father twice attempted to sail for the New World; twice he was turned back; and it was not until after his death in 1672, that his son Robert, less spiritual but even more energetic, set out for America by way of Scotland. In the spring of 1674, he arrived in Charlestown, Massachusetts, stayed long enough to raise a small capital on the strength of his letters of introduction and his father's reputation, and reappeared in the fall of that year in Albany, a frontier community of colonial New York.

Good fortune is one of the elements of success, and the good fortune of Robert Livingston in this instance was conspicuous—the year, the place, his training, and his accomplishments all worked together to the same end. That year, 1674, was the year when the Province of New York, after a brief return to its former Dutch masters, fell once again into the hands of Great Britain and under the proprietorship of the Duke of York. Albany was a wealthy Dutch village, the center of certain profitable exchanges of Indian furs for English woolen goods. As an intermediary between the Dutch burghers and the Duke of York's agents, or between the Duke of York's agents and the Indians, whose interpreters usually spoke Dutch, a linguist like Robert Livingston would clearly be useful. In 1675, Governor Sir Edmund Andros appeared at Albany to negotiate a treaty with the Iroquois; and there is a fairly clear connection between this event and Livingston's appointment to the secretaryship of the colony's Board of Indian Commissioners and the clerkship of the Albany General Court, at a salary of four hundred guilders for both offices.[2] Within two years, this salary was raised to six hundred guilders.[3] He also secured a commission of 4 per cent on tax collections in the Albany area, which tends to show that he was not too interested in popularity.[4]

Albany was the unofficial capital of the vast patroonship of Rensselaerwyck, which was nearly fifty miles long from east to west and fully forty wide at its greatest width from north to south; and there was a traditional connection between the Albany clerkship and the office of secretary to Rensselaerwyck. In 1675, Livingston was appointed to the latter office, at a salary of two hundred guilders, by Dominie Nicholas Van Rensselaer, the manager of the patroonship.

These three offices were, no doubt, intended to be merely clerical— fit occupations for a diligent, unassuming young man who wrote a fair hand and kept a neat set of books: but they had fallen into the hands of one who, while diligent enough, was anything but unassuming. He proposed to use them as the fulcrum of the lever with which he would turn the world of Albany. As a self-taught attorney, he could, for example, collect fees for giving advice in the very court of which he was a salaried officer. As secretary to the Indian Board, he had special information which—since the Iroquois were middlemen between the Albany merchants and the tribes farther west—he could use with advantage as a private fur trader. The secretaryship to Rensselaerwyck he reserved for a more sensational exploit. In 1679, having accumulated a decent capital from his salaries, commissions, and from loans to the Proprietary Government, and from a contract to supply the royal garrison, he married Alida Schuyler Van Rensselaer, the widow of his first patron.

The young widow was related by birth or marriage to the Schuylers, the Van Rensselaers, and the Van Cortlandts, three of the greatest families in the province, whose influence—so harsh and yet so drowsy, so acquisitive and so backward—extended to every corner of it. They maintained this influence by intermarriage; and it would, one might conjecture, have taken something more than such modest prosperity as Livingston enjoyed in 1679 to unlock the heavy doors that gave admittance to their world. Decent birth, an unexceptionable religious background, capability, cunning, the impalpable aura of success—who knows what keys were used or if these were they? One thing is certain: with his marriage to Alida Van Rensselaer, Robert Livingston's status became that of parvenu aristocrat, in a land where all aristocrats were parvenus, and where there was the closest tactical connection between aristocracy and success.

In 1686, when Albany received its charter under Governor Thomas Dongan, Livingston was further appointed to the lucrative offices of clerk of the peace and clerk of the Common Pleas; there followed soon after, the posts of sub-collector of the excise and receiver of the quitrents for Albany County.[5] It was, of course, customary for the Provincial Government to borrow from the province's capitalists in advance of taxes, a situation that naturally increased the flow of favors; in 1689, Governor Dongan was £3,000 in debt to Livingston; in 1686, he had already granted his well-connected creditor a manorial patent for his estates on the Hudson and in the Taconic Mountains, an event that must be separately noticed.

Only the Revolution of 1688, which expelled James II and shook the British Empire, was seismic enough to impart a violent wavering to this upward line. The fall of James II provoked a rebellion in New York, not against William III, but against mercantile monopolies: it was a popular rebellion, its leader was Jacob Leisler, its focus the City of New York, and, from Albany, Livingston resisted it as long as he could. Long after the judicial murder of Leisler in 1692, the Leislerian party survived to make trouble for the anti-Leislerians. In 1695, accused of misappropriation of the public funds and threatened with the sequestration of his estates, Livingston fled to London to plead his case before the servants of the Crown. With an extraordinary adroitness, he turned the tables on his enemies. It was an easy task to blacken the character of Governor Benjamin Fletcher, Dongan's successor and an official notably blind to the distinction between public duty and private advantage, and to whiten his own perhaps not too difficult. But to convince the Lords of Trade and the Privy Council that the Indian aspect of the town clerkship of Albany was too burdensome for one man; to show them how important it was for this work to be undertaken by a separate official who could give his whole time to it; and then to obtain a royal patent confirming him in his town clerkship and other offices and at the same time creating him secretary for Indian Affairs—this, indeed, required a charm, a persuasiveness of no ordinary kind.[6]

On his return in 1696, his enemies assailed him more bitterly than ever. They condemned his new office of secretary for Indian Affairs as a mere invention, designed only to enrich the secretary. They had him suspended from it and from its emoluments. They sequestrated his estates. At length, he was forbidden to perform any duty but that of the town clerk at Albany. From this office, in the heart of his own country, he could not be dislodged; and there he bided his time. In 1698, the Earl of Bellomont became governor of New York, and Bellomont had been Livingston's friend in London. Although he was inclined to look at New York through Leislerian spectacles, Bellomont restored Livingston to his secretaryship—the two men saw eye to eye on Indian affairs—and made him, for a while, a member of his Council. But Bellomont was the rare phenomenon, an incorruptible governor; Livingston was, as regards the public finances, apparently incorrigible; and before his death in 1701, the Governor was obliged to remove his friend from the collectorship of excise at Albany. In April, 1702, he was suspended from the Council by Lieutenant Governor John Nanfan for committing "great frauds in relation to his Majes revenue."[7]

The arrival of Lord Cornbury, Bellomont's successor and in every way his opposite, only made matters worse; the province returned to its former turmoil; and in 1703, in circumstances even more perilous than those that had compelled him to flight in 1695, Livingston sailed for England. Once again, this singular man, after months and, indeed, years of labor, refuted the charges against him; once again, in 1706, he returned with a patent from Queen Anne fully as comprehensive as the one he had been given by King William. In 1708, Lord Cornbury with reluctance accepted it. And so the secretaryship for Indian Affairs was established, with all its circumambient local offices, never to be questioned again in Livingston's lifetime.[8]

This remarkable victory put it out of his enemies' power to destroy him. The granting of a new manorial patent in 1715, with the added and extremely significant privilege of one seat in the Provincial Assembly, completed that arduous and persistent battle: the graph of his success, which fate had plotted with two apparently insurmountable declivities, now climbed securely upward. In 1716, he became the manor's representative in the Assembly; in 1718, he was elected speaker, and he held this office until his retirement in 1725. In 1721, with the help of Governor William Burnet, all his other offices were permitted to devolve upon his eldest

living son, Philip. In 1728, he died. Officeholder, merchant, landed magnate—he seems like some eccentric, provincial counterpart of the Whig-
gish aristocracy then ruling in England.

III

To judge by the bitter reflections made upon him by his contemporaries—upon some of whom, in turn, and with equal bitterness, history has
been only too glad to reflect—the most noticeable element in Robert
Livingston's character was avarice. "Never disbursing six pence," said Governor Fletcher, "but with the expectation of twelve pence, his beginnings
being a little Book keeper, he has screwed himself into one of the most
considerable estates in the province. . . . He had rather be called knave
Livingston than poor Livingston." Fletcher, to be sure, as a character witness or as an official, was nothing if not impeachable: but Bellomont was
an upright man, and Bellomont once complained, in a moment of ex-
asperation over Livingston's handling of his military contracts, that he
had "pinched an estate out of the poor soldiers' bellies." Even Governor
Robert Hunter, who gave him his new manorial patent in 1715, had previously denounced him as "the most selfish man I know."[9]

The absence of favorable comments from the record does not mean,
of course, that they were not made; it is an assumption only, but still
almost an inescapable one, that Livingston could be charming when he
pleased; and if avarice were his ruling passion, as it certainly seems to have
been, the unrelenting pursuit of wealth was the ruling passion of the upper
class into which he had climbed. In this respect, he was merely *primus
inter pares*.

As for his methods, they are most readily discovered in the story—
a curious one even for provincial New York—of the founding of the manor
itself. A landed estate in the province was not only a source of potential
wealth or an object of frantic speculation: it was also an emblem of status,
as it was everywhere in Western civilization. In the New York oligarchy
of wholesale merchants or the Albany oligarchy of fur-trading magnates,
it represented full membership. Livingston began by claiming a portion
of the huge Van Rensselaer properties, as his wife's guardian. The claim
was sternly resisted, though the sternness was mitigated by the payment
of a sum of money in compensation—a tacit admission that the claim was
more unfamilial than unfounded. He then followed the usual course for
a man with standing. He petitioned Governor Andros for permission to
buy two thousand acres from the Wappinger Indians; the petition was

eventually granted; and on July 12, 1683, the purchase was made.[10] The estate lay on the east bank of the Hudson, some forty miles below Albany, where Roeliff Jansen Kill flows into the great river. The price—three hundred-odd guilders' worth of wampum, guns, powder, and a curious miscellany of manufactured goods—presumably satisfied the Wappinger Indians, whose notions as to the value of their land were not immoderate. The whole transaction was then confirmed by Governor Thomas Dongan, who granted a royal patent on November 4, 1684.[11]

In 1685, Dongan sanctioned a further purchase of land—some six hundred acres of Indian land upon the Massachusetts border, which Livingston represented as "lying upon ye same [*i.e.*, Roeliff Jansen] Kill called by the Indians Tachkanick behind Patkook about Two or 3 hund: acres." The price was six hundred guilders' worth of wampum and assorted goods.[12] On July 22, 1686, by royal patent, the two tracts were united into one Lordship or Manor of Livingston, "with full power and authority at all times for ever hereafter in the said Lordship and Manor one Court Leet and one Court Baron to hold and keep." The annual quitrent to the Crown was in the extremely modest sum of twenty-eight shillings.[13]

In other words, 2,600 acres had been increased to 160,000—a feat of multiplication beyond the scope of any patent or the reach of most imaginations. Yet no other construction seems possible. A tract of land on the banks of the Hudson and a tract of land many miles to the east, in the Taconic Mountains, had been blandly described as contiguous: sandwiched between, lay nearly 158,000 acres of land which had never been bought and the Indian title to which had never been extinguished.[14] Almost two hundred years later, an attorney general of the State of New York was to express his amazement at this transaction, which, however, a judge of the State Supreme Court pronounced free of fraud on the face of the record; and time and again in the years between, it troubled the repose of the proprietors of the manor and their descendants.[15]

Whatever his financial relations with Mr. Livingston may have been at this time, Governor Dongan was committed to the Jacobean policy of supporting, one might almost say of creating, a provincial upper class; and to grant a patent without requiring an adequate survey might not have struck him as impolitic. Moreover, if he had any knowledge of the geography of his province, it was unquestionably deficient; and this deficiency would scarcely have been diminished by Livingston's habit of using Indian place names to describe the bounds of his purchase. Indian place names had the great merit, for one who wished to throw dust in the eyes of authority, of referring to natural objects of a transient or perishable nature

—such as heaps of stones or trees of a peculiar shape—objects that were difficult to identify in the first place and that were apt to vanish altogether, except from the wandering memories of the Indians themselves. In any case, the Governor's Council, in those pre-Leislerian days, would have espoused rather than opposed the ambitions of a man of wealth and family influence: and the Council's advice was paramount. If the patent were fraudulent, it was by no means unique in that respect: if the patentee was far from blameless, so too was the system.

With the issuance of this manorial patent, at any rate, Robert Livingston attained an eminence in provincial society which, but for the Revolution of 1688 and the consequent Leislerian turmoil, might have been secure. As for the manor, it was at first, and for some time, only a social asset. A manor house arose in 1692; in 1698, it was enlarged and improved. But the manorial lands lay vacant. Governor Dongan's patent declared that Livingston was receiving his manor because of "vast Charges and Expences in purchasing said Tracts and Parcells of Land from the Indians and also in settling and Improveing the same and for Encouraging the future settlement."[16] The vast charges amounted to some nine hundred guilders' worth of wampum and assorted goods; or, to employ a more generous estimate, nine hundred guilders in wampum plus the cost of the goods: and as for settling and improving the lands, it is a matter of reasonably accurate record that in 1700 there were but four or five families on all that vast estate. Nor was their condition, strange to say, such as to encourage future settlement. As Lord Bellomont put it in a report to the Lords of Trade: "Mr. Livingston has on his great grant 16 miles long and 24 broad, but four or five cottages, as I am told, men that live in vassallage under him and are too poor to be farmers having not wherewithal to stock a farm." "What man," asked his lordship, "would be such a fool as to become a base tenant of Mr. Delius, Colonel Schuyler, Mr. Livingston when, for crossing Hudson's river that man can for a song purchase a good freehold in the Jerseys?"[17]

The title "Lord of the Manor" is not, of course, a title of honor, but indicates a peculiar kind of land tenure; and the question of whether or not the New York manorial patents were "feudal" has been the subject of learned and ingenious debate. But "feudal" is a term that presupposes the existence of a set of extinct relationships which could not have been revived, even on the remote colonial border of Christendom. "Quasi-feudal" is a better description. This implies that there was a good deal in the legal and social aspects of manorial life in New York which carried now an echo, now a sharp reminder of the feudal past. The quitrent to the

Crown was one such reminder. The right to a Court Leet and a Court Baron,[18] though there is no evidence that the former right was ever exercised, is such an echo. From the printed conveyances that began to appear around the middle of the eighteenth century, one can deduce that, from the beginning, many tenants held their farms for one, two, or three lives, or (this was known as "fee-farming") in fee simple "for ever" with a reserved annual rent; that their rents were paid in kind—so many skipples of wheat, so many fat fowls per annum—with the additional requirement of one or two days' "riding" for the landlord with their team of horses or oxen; that the landlord reserved for himself all milling and mining rights; that he had the right of distraint and re-entry if the tenant failed to discharge his obligations; and that he could exact a "quarter-sale"—as much as one-third of the selling price if the tenant sold his improved farm to another. All these particulars carried overtones of feudalism: if only in the sense that they were agrarian, aristocratic, and showed how the past could be used not as a creative but as a paralyzing force. With such insecurity as his reward, why should a man become a tenant of Mr. Delius, or Colonel Schuyler, or Mr. Livingston? Obviously, the landlords did not use all their powers with all the rigor that their leases allowed them—some rents remained in arrears, some obligations were not punctually discharged. But until the Revolution itself, this question and its answer lie at the heart of New York's failure to expand.

The Manor of Livingston did not acquire a tenantry until Governor Hunter arrived in 1710, bringing with him some three thousand refugees from the Palatinate, whom the optimistic British Government hoped to employ in the production of naval stores. For this purpose, six thousand acres of pine barrens in the manor were reconveyed to the Crown, for £400, which exceeded the whole cost of the original purchase. Livingston, at the same time, received a contract to subsist the newcomers, treating them, according to the record, much as he had treated the "poor soldiers" in Lord Bellomont's complaint; he also lent them money; and for three years he was one of their salaried inspectors. In 1711, their conditions were already so wretched that they rebelled and were forced to work under military guard; in 1713, the money for maintaining them ran out, and they were permitted to flee into the Schoharie Valley. But there were some too deeply indebted to go; and from these enforced tenants, the manor received its first substantial body of settlers.[19]

Governor Hunter did not publicly lament the fate of the Palatines or deplore the treatment they had received from Livingston and from himself: he was in debt to Livingston for advances made on their behalf. It has been said that he offered to settle with his creditor, not in cash, but with a new manorial patent, reconfirming the Lord's title. Since a cash settlement was afterward made, this account of the new patent's origin is open to some doubt: the new patent itself is not. It was dated October 2, 1715, and it gave the manor its own seat in the Assembly; that is to say, it conferred upon Livingston the inestimable boon of a pocket borough.[20]

From then onward, the manor's tenantry increased year by year, in numbers if not in contentment. Around the manor house, the slave quarters grew larger, the storehouses bulged with produce, which the manor fleet bore down the river to New York or the West Indies. And from the Manor, the first Lord went down to the Assembly, as the member from his own borough, to do battle with the incumbent governor; not merely as the governor's creditor, but also as a leader in the Assembly's effort to gain and hold the initiative in provincial affairs.

IV

The granting of a new manorial patent in 1715 is, at first glance, a perplexing and contradictory event. The tendency of British colonial policy, after the fall of James II, was to encourage emigration: a land system like that of New York, which left (the description is Lord Bellomont's) three-quarters of the province in the hands of a dozen men, loomed like a giant in the path of this policy, blocking the way. In the first decade of the eighteenth century, both the Lords of Trade and the Privy Council had taken measures to shrink or destroy the system: but their efforts were feeble, they were too far off, they were not truly interested. The Lords of Trade ordered a thousand-acre limitation upon land grants, the forfeiture of lands not improved or settled within three years, the annulment of extravagant grants. In 1707, the Privy Council upheld an act of the Assembly of 1699, which had been repealed by the assembly of 1702, and which vacated certain of the more preposterous grants. But the influence of the great landlords extended to the Assembly, to the Council, to the closest of the royal governors—for, with a few luminous exceptions, the governors contrived to make money out of the very system they were supposed to control and correct. Even Cadwallader Colden, a lieutenant governor for many years, and a determined and forthright critic of the great New York landlords, was amassing a small fortune from fees he took for land grants in the Green Mountain region. The effect of land upon the early American conscience is famous and it is intelligible: if it was especially bad in the colony of New York, that is because New York inherited from the Dutch a land system which, in whatever form, Dutch or English or Anglo-Dutch, became too massive to overturn. The new manorial patent granted to Livingston in 1715 is perplexing and contradictory only in the dim light of the act of 1699, the policy of the English Government, and the edicts of the Lords of Trade and the Privy Council: in the harsher light of the land system itself, it is merely typical.[21]

There was a flood of European immigration in the eighteenth century. With the encouragement of the British Government and of the colonies themselves, despairing men fled out of Germany, France, Switzerland, and Ireland, from war, persecution, pestilence, and famine. Some of this flood seeped into the Manor of Livingston and other great New York estates. But it is most unlikely that the immigrants, where they had any choice or any knowledge to direct a choice, deliberately or knowingly chose the colony of New York. Fear of the Iroquois in the Mohawk Valley; the barriers of the Catskills and the Adirondacks; the story of the Palatines; the quasi-feudal conditions on the land—all these were formidable deterrents.[22] And the land system was the most formidable. Men did not wish to fall into the hands of the great New York proprietors, or, indeed, to be tenant farmers under any landlord. The system, said Governor William Tryon with approval in 1772, "created subordination."[23] And while subordination, a very harsh subordination, was the lot of most immigrants into the British New World in the eighteenth century, it was not, for many reasons, a permanent subordination. Where it was threatened with permanence, it would try to turn itself by force into something else.

Sooner or later, for example, the tenant farmers, extracting a wretched subsistence out of soil they could never hope to own, were bound to make unfavorable comparisons between their own small holdings and legal bondage and the immense estates and minute quitrents enjoyed by their overlords. With the exception of the Palatine rebellion, which was in every way exceptional, there was little overt trouble in Robert Livingston's day or in that of his son Philip, the second Lord of the Manor of Livingston: the experience of Robert Livingston, Jr., the third Lord of the Manor, was altogether different. In the 1750's, the smoldering, accumulated grievances of many years, blown upon by a boundary dispute between New York and Massachusetts, blazed up into a revolt against the Van Rensselaers and the Livingstons, whose eastern boundaries lay in the disputed area.

The dispute, which was an old one, inevitably touched upon a most sensitive spot—the unextinguished Indian titles that lay like an open nerve among the Livingston and Van Rensselaer estates. As the supply of cheap land dwindled in Massachusetts, settlers and speculators began to think of the disputed land west of the Connecticut River. Indian deeds and Massachusetts grants were offered to would-be farmers from New England; and in the ears of the discontented Livingston and Van Rensselaer tenants it was whispered that they could leave the house of bondage merely by applying to the Massachusetts Government. In the spring of 1751, the Massachusetts General Court awarded two hundred acres to Richard Treat, a squatter in the Taconic area claimed by Robert Livingston, Jr., who had made some settlements there.[24]

This was the beginning of an obscure and desperate struggle between Robert Livingston, Jr., and a minority of loyal retainers, on the one hand, and, on the other, a majority of discontented tenants from whom, if they were tenants at will, he threatened to withdraw their leases should they apply for a Massachusetts grant. The dispute was complicated by the agitations of colonial commissioners, the intrigues of New England speculators, the invasion of settlers by way of the Housatonic, and the dark promise of Indian reprisals. By 1755, what had begun as a landlord-tenant quarrel was threatening to turn into border warfare. In January of that year, a certain Robert Noble, leader of the dissident Van Rensselaer tenants, was given a commission in the Massachusetts militia. In April, the insulted Council of New York issued a proclamation for the arrest of Noble; and Robert Livingston, Jr., with his ally, Sheriff Abraham Yates, of Albany, led a foray into Noble's territory which resulted in the flight of Noble himself, the arrest of Josiah Loomis (one of the most disaffected of Livingston's tenants at will), and the death of another rebellious tenant, named William Rees. In May, there was a counterattack upon the Livingston ironworks at Ancram, then engaged in manufacturing war materials for use against the French, and eight workmen were carried off. Livingston's anguish at this reprisal—the Ancram ironworks had become one of his most cherished projects—was scarcely lessened by the fact that Lieutenant Governor James De Lancey, to whom he applied for help in his extremity, was one of his worst enemies and responded in a most lukewarm manner.[25]

The replacement of De Lancey by Governor Sir Charles Hardy in the fall of 1755, and the arrival in Massachusetts of Governor William Shirley, who cared little for speculators, brought some sense to the distracted border. In May, 1757, the Lords of Trade recommended to the King that a line twenty miles east of the Hudson should be the boundary between the two colonies.[26] Although no settlement was reached, the recommendation itself was positive and peaceful. Robert Livingston, Jr., it is true, alarmed by the threatening aspect of the Stockbridge Indians, who persisted in thinking themselves disinherited by the terms of his grandfather's patent, was at one time obliged to ask for the protection of fifty soldiers; and received, along with the soldiers, the additional bonus of a secret proclamation, which sanctioned the arrest of any rioters upon his manor. But as the Seven Years' War approached its *annus mirabilis* of 1759, the disturbances died down; the intercolonial dispute was almost as if it had never been; and only the formation of a Rioters' Club in 1762 reminded the third Lord of the Manor that what was at question upon his estates was not merely the terms of his conveyances, but also the purity of his title.[27]

Then, in 1766, a new and more complicated uprising vexed the East Hudson Valley from Westchester to Albany, threatened at one time to spill over into Connecticut, and promised a renewal of the boundary dispute with Massachusetts. In May, it was reported that "some hundreds" of tenants in Livingston Manor—the number was no doubt exaggerated—had "turned Levellers and are in arms to dispossess some and maintain others in their own, without rent or taxation." In June, a message came from the manor to New York to the effect that two hundred men were marching "to murther the Lord of the Manor and level his house unless he would sign leases for 'em agreeable to their form . . . and that they would neither pay Rent, taxes &c nor suffer other tenants."[28] Since the militia (made up of small farmers) was sympathetic to the rioters, and the Twenty-eighth Regiment was immobilized in Poughkeepsie by seventeen hundred armed "Levellers," the situation was exceedingly serious. But Walter Livingston, the third Lord's son, with an armed band, saved the manor for the time being. The rest was up to the Provincial Government, which turned its regular troops loose to suppress and plunder the rebellious farmers; and thus by September the worst of the rioting was at an end.

Historically, the uprising of 1766 is part of the chain of events that led to the antirent wars of the 1840's. As regards the Livingston fortunes, it had a more immediate and more ironical significance. The proximate cause of the uprising of 1766 was almost certainly the Stamp Act rioting, which, it should be remembered, took place in Albany as well as in New York.[29] And the Stamp Act rioting, strange to say, was popularly attributed to the influence of the great landlords. The connection is hard to trace; but one Dutch farmer from the Hudson Valley told the province's attorney general that a Livingston "had spoke treasonable words against king and parliament we must rase a rebellion against the damned stamp act and I wil shed blood against it and turn us sels to a free republic as Holland is this is the vue of the Livingstons the robbers and murders of common poor people."[30] The farmer did not say who this Livingston was, and it is more than possible that the treasonable words were never spoken: but the accusation itself is significant simply because it was made and because, in the light of the antirent rebellion, we are justified in presuming that the accuser did not speak for himself alone.

This is the irony, simple and innate, that reveals itself in the uprisings of 1766: in their own domains, the landlords were regarded as oppressors of the "common poor people"; in the larger world of the province, they were held or held themselves to be among the leaders against parliamentary oppression. The same irony exists in any comparison between the *furor Provincialis* of the government of New York when, as the agent of the landlords, it suppressed the antirent rebellion of 1766 and the mildness of the same government when, as the agent of Parliament, it attempted to suppress the Stamp Act riots. Perhaps this ironical comparison occurred to the farmers, so many of whom, when the Revolution came, turned against it wherever the landlords were for it. It is implicit in the uneasiness of those New York landowners who supported the patriot cause as, with honest compunction, they shrugged themselves into the unaccustomed costume of revolutionaries and subversives. It haunts any examination of the "popular" party, of which the Livingstons were the core until the Revolution made it meaningless.

V

Indeed, the existence of such a party in provincial politics accounts for much that might otherwise be inexplicable in the demeanor of the Chancellor long after the Revolution was over; long after the party was forgotten by all but the historian and the antiquary; for all his life. For he, certainly, did not forget it. He had been brought up with it; it lingered in his mind like an ancestral presence, giving him at once a contempt for common politics and a difficult identification of political ambition with personal and social pride. If the De Lanceys, the family who gave their name to the opposing party, had survived the Revolution, everything might have been different; the De Lancey–Livingston battles might have gone on until, like some moribund natural object, venerable and but faintly agitated, they were absorbed into a larger and more vivid landscape. But the De Lanceys went down with George III. The Livingstons remained, bearing the political name that, of all names, linked the history of the province with the history of the state. The Chancellor stood at their head; able, useful, wealthy, born for leadership, but unwilling to come to terms with his followers; at once the victim and the beneficiary of his own past.

The origins of the Livingston–De Lancey feud are naturally obscure; they are rooted in the depths of provincial history; but it is at least permissible to suggest that what was involved was essentially a clash between Land and Trade. The suggestion itself is full of difficulties, since the Livingstons, if they were primarily landlords and land speculators, were also merchants; and the De Lanceys, if they were primarily merchants, were also landlords and land speculators. One is almost tempted to think that the reason for this grouping was not historical but eschatological—that a family feud was first elevated into a party warfare because, at the very end of the story, the De Lanceys opposed the Revolution and the Livingstons joined it.

Almost, but not quite. There is a valid political story, which begins in the year 1720, in a relatively intelligible clash between the landed and the mercantile interests. In that year, Governor William Burnet made a grand proconsular attempt to destroy the illicit trade between Albany and Montreal, in which English woolens and other goods were sold to the French at a great profit, because the French found them less expensive than French goods imported directly from France. Governor Burnet's argument was not merely that the trade was illicit; he also maintained that the same English goods, sent directly to the Indians in exchange for furs, would undersell the French in a spectacular manner; and if his argument had been upheld, it is barely possible that English influence would have spread as far as the Mississippi. He first attempted to enforce his will by prohibiting all northern trade between Albany and Montreal: and when his prohibition was easily and universally evaded, substituted for it a double tax on the northern trade and a single tax on the more westerly traffic with the Indians. He was supported by Robert Livingston, partly for statesmanlike reasons, partly from a speculator's belief that a chain of military garrisons (the logical consequence of any anti-French policy) would have a stimulating effect upon the value of land in the north and west: and he was opposed by the New York wholesalers, whose backbone was supplied by the Philipse and De Lancey families, and whose leader was Stephen De Lancey. In the end, the merchants applied to their correspondents in England; their correspondents moved the Lords of

Trade; and the Lords of Trade persuaded the Crown to disallow Burnet's trade laws. As good imperial laws or as the seedbed for future Livingston–De Lancey disputes, they are no doubt questionable: but if they are questionable, they are also suggestive.[31]

The feud remained dormant until the 1740's, when James De Lancey, Stephen's son, fell out with Governor Sir Henry Clinton. The Livingstons claimed that their support of De Lancey in this crisis cost them many valuable offices, and that De Lancey had proved—what else could be expected from the head of such a family?—grossly ungrateful.[32] It has been suggested that by 1752 the Livingstons were already organizing the northern proprietors in opposition to De Lancey, who, in spite of his desertion of Clinton, was promoted to lieutenant governor in 1747, and who, after Clinton's retirement and the suicide of his successor, governed the province in that capacity from 1753 to 1755.[33] As the agent and representative of the Crown during these three years, and at the same time as the leader of a movement to reduce the Crown's representative to a mere creature of the Assembly, De Lancey's position was a delicate, not to say an anomalous, one: and its delicacy was hardly diminished when, in 1754, he led the movement for a royal charter for King's College, an institution admittedly dominated by Episcopalians. Everybody knew what an Episcopalian, armed with a royal charter, could do. A frightening vision of Erastian conspiracies spread itself before the dismayed eyes of those who were not sons of the Church of England, and of many who were. In the arguments that preceded and followed this event, the opposition was led by William Livingston, the third Lord's brother, a formidable and brilliant lawyer, shambling and slovenly in appearance, whose height and thinness, combined with the cutting quality of his writings, had earned him the nickname, the "Whipping Post." It is not surprising that in 1755, when the Livingston ironworks were overrun by the antirent insurgents, James De Lancey's offer of assistance should have been so feeble, so grudging, so late, and so much resented.

The controversy over King's College was not primarily a theological one; and it was only partly ecclesiastical. What was really at issue was the chartering powers of the Assembly and the Crown. But nonconformists followed Livingston in his opposition to this threat to Assembly rule, and the Livingston party came to be known as the Presbyterian party, since William himself was of that persuasion. In 1758, under the leadership of William Livingston and two fellow lawyers, William Smith, Jr., and John Morin Scott, this party gained a notable victory at the polls over the De Lancey—or Episcopalian—faction. It would seem that the liberals in the province had grouped themselves around Livingston in a battle involving freedom of conscience, on the one hand, and the prerogatives of the Crown, on the other.

And yet, it may be, this grouping was more apparent than real. The contestants in the 1758 election may have gone to battle under the flags of Church and Chapel; but the decisive blow was delivered in another cause and from another quarter. What defeated the De Lanceys in 1758 was William Livingston's accusation—uttered with all the painful accompaniments of his most mordant prose—that the DeLanceys and their adherents had been very lukewarm about driving the French from North America in the early stages of the French and Indian War.[34] This was, in effect, a revival of the old landlord-merchant dispute, in which the landlords were for a strong policy against the French regardless of expense, and the merchants were for a weak and frugal one. And it is certainly true that in later years, the Livingstons of the manor, the titular heads of the Presbyterian party, did not much care for the religious flavor that William Livingston had imparted to their struggle with the De Lanceys. When his father, the third Lord, scolded him for religious bigotry, Peter R. Livingston replied in genuine consternation: "Am Sorry to find that you think the present Parties are whether the Church or Meeting shall rule. But the De Lanceys are striving their utmost to make our famally rediculous and to keep them out of all Posts of Honour or Profit and . . . oppose everything and every body that they support."[35] And the third Lord himself, writing to his son-in-law James Duane, was much of the same mind. "It is forren to say," he wrote, "I, & my family, are persecuted on account of the Presbyterians, no these folks, or at least some of them, mean none else but me, & my family, they don't value Presbyterians, nor even their own Church, where it happens to be in opposition to their favorite scheme of ruling over all the familyes in the country."[36] "Am I, a presbyterian," he asked plaintively, "is the Judge one, no neither." The third Lord was a member of the Dutch Reformed Church. The "Judge"—Judge Robert R. Livingston, Sr., the Chancellor's father—was an Episcopalian. The Judge's father-in-law, Henry Beekman, though a member of the Dutch Reformed Church, had voted with the Episcopalians for the chartering of King's College, and so had the Judge's cousin, Philip Livingston, who was a Presbyterian. The religious issues were certainly confusing when expressed in terms of persons, although it was these issues that first gave the Livingston party its "popular" reputation and name.

They were not, to be sure, undeserved. While the Livingstons controlled the Assembly—a small, exclusive gathering of great landlords, merchant princes, and their spokesmen—from 1761 to 1768, they instituted a series of mild reforms, designed to ease the fiscal burden of poor men.[37] They were among the leaders in the early criticisms of Parliament, after the close of the French and Indian War. But as the Sugar Act of 1764 was succeeded by the Stamp Act of 1765, and the provincial leaders came face to face, not with the King and his governors any longer, but with the greater menace of a centralizing Parliament; as the power moved gradually from an aristocratic Assembly to less exclusive and less legal committees—the Livingston and the De Lancey parties ceased to be parties and became factions. The power and, with it, the prestige drifted down to the radicals, the Sons of Liberty, the populace. They awoke to find that if the power were to return to them, they must gain control of those to whom it was drifting; and here that troubled entity the conservative conscience became decisive. Should they gain control by obeying Parliament, or by opposing it? The De Lanceys went with Parliament and disappeared; the Livingstons, in honest distaste for despotism, sided with the Revolution and devoted their energies to rescuing it from what they conceived to be itself.

CHAPTER THREE

The founder of the Clermont branch of the Livingston family* was Robert Livingston, the Chancellor's grandfather, third son of Robert the first Lord of the Manor. In the first Lord's will, Robert Livingston, "merchant of New York," was given "all that tract of land part of ye Mannor of Livingston which lies on the south west side of the River commonly called Rodloft Johnsen's [Roeliff Jansen's] Kill . . . and so runs up into ye woods South East somewhat Easterly Eleven miles and three quarters. . . ." It was an exceptional inheritance, in the sense that it would ordinarily have gone to Philip, the second lord of the Manor: family tradition asserts that it was devised upon Robert because once, at great personal risk, he had rescued his father from a band of Indians who—possibly with some justification—had planned to murder that gentleman in his sleep. The whole estate comprised some thirteen thousand acres, and part of it was already settled when he entered into possession in 1728. In 1730, he built a mansion, a conventional Georgian brick residence, on the banks of the Hudson; the estate and the mansion he called Clermont or "Claremont"; and there he seems to have spent the rest of his long life.[1]

According to his granddaughter Janet Livingston Montgomery, Robert Livingston was, in his dress and his manners, conspicuously a gentleman of the old school. Even when he was lying speechless on his deathbed, he would attempt—such was his concern for the amenities—to raise his head and bow to those who entered his chamber. Angelica Schuyler Church, a demanding belle who met him in his old age, declared that no one flattered her so much to her taste as he did. He rose invariably at five in the morning, "read without ceasing," retained his mercantile connections with New

* A third branch of the Livingston family was descended from Robert Livingston, nephew of the first Lord of the Manor, who came to America at his uncle's request. One of his very numerous descendants was Maturin Livingston, the Chancellor's nephew by marriage; another was Peter R. Livingston, who married the Chancellor's sister Joanna. All three branches constituted, in colonial New York history, especially, a powerful political clan. At the beginning of the Revolution, the third Lord of the Manor, Robert Livingston, Jr., was still the head of this clan; the leadership then passed to the Clermont Livingstons, with whom this study is chiefly concerned.

York, and was an active and optimistic land speculator with large holdings in the Hardenburgh Patent across the river. The news of Lexington and Concord filled him with rapture—"Now, he exclaimed, "we have got the bull by the horns"—and the news of Bunker Hill was thought to have been the death of him.[2] His great ambition seems to have been to transmit to his descendants a property of such dimensions that they would have no urge to increase it; he would tell his only son that he had brought him up "to keep an estate not to get one"; and his son could only respond, rather wistfully, from time to time, by wondering how much of it there would be to keep. For Robert Livingston, like other men of a genial and sanguine disposition, was an inveterate "projector." He hoped to exploit his wild Catskill lands, for example, by entering into the lumber business in a grandiose manner; and anyone with a scheme, however impractical, found a way to his patronage and his purse. It was the story of the mousetrap in reverse. "You have a parcel of people about you," wrote his son, on one occasion, "who are endeavouring by the slyest & most cunning artifices, leading you from one barren Project to another, to fatten themselves on your Spoils. If the income of the Manner [Manor] would satisfy them I would forgive them. . . . He who had the consummate Impudence to tell you that you might make money by making Oars carried his abuse of the confidence you placed in him to the greatest height. He might as well have put you on making brooms." And so the indictment went on, from ash trees ("Ash trees my dear Father are not so singular a thing as you imagine") to cured maple ("£20 worth will be more than can be sold to any Locksmith") to improvident dreams of establishing an ironworks; until it reached the prudent conclusion—"Our country is too young for any large Business not managed with the utmost Oeconomy."[3]

Whether Robert Livingston did or did not profit by this filial advice is irrelevant, since he never actually ruined himself: what is more to the point is that, in those days, in that almost patriarchal society, such advice could be given and received without causing any breach in family relations. Robert Livingston and Robert R. Livingston, Sr., his only son and the Chancellor's father, were always on the best of terms.

II

Robert R. Livingston, Sr.—he was named Robert Robert to distinguish him from the other Roberts who were roosting or soon to roost on the rapidly multiplying branches of the family tree—was known for the exceptional sweetness of his temper. "God Almighty bless you, Robert,"

Councillor John Watts, one of the leaders of the anti-Livingston party, is supposed to have exclaimed at their last meeting, "I do not believe you have an enemy in the world."[4] These words may even, as to their scope, have extended beyond the world of the provincial upper classes: it seems that Livingston was far from unpopular with the mobs who enlivened New York City in the days of the Stamp and the Tea taxes. The compliment was not exactly returned: no Livingston, with a dissident tenantry always in his mind, approved of mobs. But his daughter Mrs. Catharine Garretson remembered in her old age the terror with which she gazed at a Stamp Tax crowd that—carrying in its midst the effigies of Lord Mansfield, the Devil, and Lieutenant Governor Colden, all dangling from a gallows—had paused outside her father's house to give him an ovation. Being only a little girl, she had somehow got it into her head that Lord Mansfield was her father in his judge's robes. During the Tea Tax crisis, she recalled, another crowd appeared before her grandfather Beekman's house, where her father was taking dinner, and cheered him until he appeared at the window with a cup in his hand. "No tea! Judge, no tea!!" "No tea," he responded, emptying his cup at the same time—he had been drinking coffee—"No tea."[5]

He had been bred to the law, and at some unspecified time in Governor George Clinton's administration (1743-1753) was offered, on the advice of Cadwallader Colden, a place on the Supreme Court bench, which, "thro' modesty and the apprehension of being thought to enlist in the Govrs party" (at that time unpopular), he felt obliged to decline. It was Chancellor Livingston's belief that Stephen De Lancey was always jealous of his father's abilities, and that he was kept out of politics until the De Lanceys lost control of the Assembly.[6] It is certainly true that he did not enter the Assembly—as a member from Dutchess County—until 1758: up to that time, he busied himself as a lawyer and as a merchant, two professions that were not necessarily incompatible in the middle of the eighteenth century. In 1759, he was made a judge of the Admiralty Court, and on March 14, 1763, he received his commission as puisne judge of the Supreme Court of the province.[7]

It is true that Supreme Court justices in 1763 were not as they had once been. Their tenure, after a bitter fight between the Livingston faction and the royal-minded Lieutenant Governor Colden, had become less secure; they were to serve during the King's pleasure and not during good behavior.[8] But Judge Livingston had a sound reason for feeling relatively immune, both to the unsound schemes of his father and to the insecurity of his judicial tenure: on December 8, 1742, he had married Margaret

Beekman, only surviving child of Colonel Henry Beekman, of Rhinebeck, a great landholder in Dutchess County.[9]

It was a marriage such as was dear to the engrossing heart of the provincial upper classes; it joined land to land, and great name to great name; Margaret Beekman was even a Livingston and a Schuyler on her mother's side.[10] Moreover, Colonel Beekman's fondness for his daughter was increased by the fact that, after the death of her mother, "a woman [so he wrote in his will] of the most amiable temper," he married, in 1726, Gertruyd Van Cortlandt, who had been brought up in the inverted court of Governor Lord Cornbury, and who was in every respect her predecessor's opposite. Colonel Beekman, therefore, left to his second wife only his New York real estate and the privilege of residing six months every year in his modest Rhinebeck house: all the rest of his properties he left to his daughter, as a testimony of the "great affection" he had for her and for her mother. At the time of her marriage, therefore, Margaret Beekman was a great heiress.[11]

The marriage may well have been one of convenience, the union of two adjacent estates; but, like many such marriages, it turned out to be a happy one. Moreover, it had certain obvious advantages, not always proven in marriages of convenience. The husband was not only a man of character, but also a man with a singularly winning personality. The wife, if one can judge by a portrait painted some ten years later, was a full-bodied Dutch beauty. A certain pietism, excessive by our standards, is to be discovered in her diaries when she was a young matron; but Livingston was pious, too; and their concern for things not of this world did not prevent them, as their surviving letters attest, from enjoying what would be considered, by any standards, a very earthy affection. And this continued until the Judge's sudden death in 1775.[12]

Since the Judge survived his father by only a few weeks, and Colonel Beekman did not die until 1776, they were not, during their married life, particularly rich: but their prospects were alluring. If things looked dark at Clermont, if his father had exhausted his personal estate in unprofitable schemes, the Judge could still write in 1762:

When I consider all things that have happened within these past twenty years I am ready to say Invenimus portum spes et fortuna valete, lusisti nos satis nunc ludite alios. We have certainly been very unfortunate but when I consider what is left of the wreck We have Reason to be abundantly satisfied & thankfull. . . . I am sure of an ample provision for my Children by the Division of Mr Beekmans Estate . . . & though I am not rich it is possible in a Course of years, & I think not improbable, that I may be absolutely [the] Richest man in the whole Government.[13]

As for what was left of the wreck, it amounted to "near eight hundred and fifty pounds from yearly Real Estate between us, besides your farm at the Manor & the house I live in [in New York City] besides this there is the profits I may make of my mill this I think so handsome a thing that I am satisfied." And, indeed, a family that could command £850 a year from real estate had little to complain of. The aristocracy of the province was aristocratic in the sense that it was privileged and that it was potentially very wealthy: it did not dispose of much immediate wealth. Clinging to the far edge of the mercantilist British Empire, it was stripped—as by some strong gravitational pull—of the obvious means of acquiring a fortune. Robert Livingston, Jr., the third Lord of the Manor and the Judge's cousin, said, in 1765, that his ironworks and his corn mills between them brought in "nearly one hundred pounds pr week, which is I believe more than any gentleman in America can this day say."[14] The claim was scarcely excessive. The northern New York landlords constituted a pastoral aristocracy: their coachmen and footmen, domestics, and laborers were slaves or indentured servants; their tables groaned, but chiefly with home-grown provisions; if their confectionaries were famously elegant, it was because sugar was a staple commodity in their exchanges with the West Indies. Their tenants were not usually either prosperous or punctual with their rents: they were more often illiterate and desperate men, the denizens of a cruel wilderness, apt to remove themselves from the rent-roll by the fearful expedient of wandering off into nowhere, leaving behind a ruinous hut and some fainting signs of cultivation. The landed aristocracy, in other words, had means ample enough for comfort and even for ostentation: but their chief resource was hope, or speculation. When the choice ultimately lay between Revolution or Empire, it was this resource that made their decision: from which had they more to hope, or less to fear?

They lived, according to Anne Grant, who wrote about Albany of the 1760's, in a style that was a curious and not inappropriate blend of simplicity, solidity, crudeness, pride, and pretension. In the Schuyler mansion on the Albany flats, the furniture was valuable but ill chosen; the family portraits, no doubt a forbidding congregation, presided over the sanctities of the best bedroom; the dining room—rarely used for dining—was enlivened with scriptural paintings; drawing room there was none. And the Schuylers were among the first families of the province—famous for their munificence, visited by every notable foreigner, and capable of projecting upon situations or persons they conceived to be beneath them—as General Philip Schuyler proved in the Revolution, and as John Barker Church experienced when he asked for the hand of Angelica Schuyler—a freezing pride of place.[15] It is not surprising, on the one hand, that the fine manners of Robert Livingston of Clermont should have been thought exceptional; or, on the other, that Colonel Beekman should have referred to himself, for all his great holdings in Dutchess County, as "an old Esopus farmer."[16]

It was thus in an atmosphere of simplicity, piety, and pride—the atmosphere of a new Protestant elite—that one must conceive the Judge and his wife to have lived and brought up their family. They were loving parents, as their letters show; they believed, and it was unusual for those days, in sparing the rod, indeed they never used it at all: and Clermont was always, in the Chancellor's day no less than in his father's and his grandfather's, a very happy place for children.[17] But to this there was added the peculiar political element—the bitter factional battles in a privileged Assembly which ranged themselves around their family and its enemies, the divided loyalties and unacknowledged guilt of quasi-feudal landlords who were also Whigs, the populace, the Parliament. However peaceful the family may have been at home, it was always surrounded by strife, uncertainty, and even danger.

III

For example, there was the controversy that arose around the case of *Forsey* vs. *Cunningham*. While subtle and complex in its legal aspects, it is, to a layman, comparatively clear; what is perhaps less clear is the Judge's relationship to it, not as a judge, but as a member and a representative of the colony's landed proprietors. The essential facts are these: Forsey was attacked and severely wounded by Cunningham in the streets of New York in the summer of 1763. In the fall term of 1764, he brought a civil action of trespass for assault and battery against Cunningham in the Supreme Court; the jury awarded him £1,500 damages; and the court denied Cunningham's plea to have the verdict set aside on the grounds that the damages were excessive. Cunningham then appealed for a review of his case before Lieutenant Governor Colden, Colden ordered the Supreme Court to send the case to him for appeal, and the Supreme Court unanimously refused to do so.

That Colden acted from an obstinate misinterpretation of the Governor's instructions of 1753, a massive ignorance of the law, a desire for personal power, and a sincere belief in the extension of royal authority seems beyond doubt. The Supreme Court contended that appeals might only be had on writs of error—that is, on errors of law noted in the court record or set forth in bills of exception—and that a jury's verdict, being a trial of fact, was altogether distinct from a judge's declaration of law upon the facts, and could not be re-examined. As the common law of England then stood, the Supreme Court was right: it was difficult to obtain an appeal against the verdict of a jury, unless the jury had been misdirected as to the law. And there was no question of misdirection in *Forsey* vs. *Cunningham*.[18]

In the correspondence that passed between New York and the English authorities, Judge Livingston was not behindhand. In a singularly clear and fearless letter to the absent Governor Robert Monckton, he declared that in the Province of New York the laws of England "are better known and more strictly adhered to than in any other, and therefore I can't imagine that any practice so unwarrantable, by any Law or Custom in England, as an Appeal from the Verdict of a Jury will be countenanced here. . . . I should be extremely glad that, as the Country has shewn that your appointing me to the Office of fourth Justice was not disagreeable to them by their doubling the salary, my conduct met also with your Approbation."[19] Wherever Monckton's approbation may have gone, that of the authorities, it seemed, was to be given to Colden. The Lieutenant Governor had advised Cunningham to go directly to the King in Council; Cunningham had done so; and in the fall of 1765, he received an order that no appeal to the King in Council could be had until he had first appealed to the Governor and Council of New York.

The whole controversy had been agitated by rumors that a Stamp Tax was pending, and then by the knowledge that a Stamp Act had actually been passed; and it was while he was sitting in the Stamp Act Congress in New York that Judge Livingston received the news that Cunningham had apparently won his claim. "The King & Council," Judge Livingston wrote to his father, "have determined the matter of appeal against us contrary to the highest assurances that we had from all hands that we should be successful in opposing it. We have in consequence been served with the order of King & Council & another writ to send up the proceedings but we remain firm to our principles & will not obey."[20]

And certainly they had need of firmness. Colden's triumph seemed to be complete. He was about to set on foot the preliminary move in his revenge—he was about to petition for the dismissal of Attorney General Kempe and the removal of Judge Livingston—when Sir Henry Moore, the new governor, arrived in New York with fresh instructions upholding the Supreme Court against the Lieutenant Governor. It seems that the agent of New York in London had long since been assured by the secretary of the Board of Trade that the judges would be upheld; that the Lords of Trade had in fact advised the King in Council to cancel his previous decision; and that their advice had been accepted as paramount. With the arrival of Sir Henry Moore, therefore, the controversy came to an end; Colden retired snarling into the background; and the judges emerged victoriously from their long ordeal.[21]

And yet, such is the intransigence of history, the completeness of their victory in a moral sense has often been questioned: the question, indeed, is still asked today. Cadwallader Colden was certainly deficient in his knowledge of the common law; but his knowledge of the land system of New York, though tainted with personal animosity, was formidable and extensive. He declared that the court's opposition to an appeal from the jury in *Forsey* vs. *Cunningham* was due to the influence of the great landed proprietors. "They know," said he, "what must be the consequence of suits depending between them and other the King's tenants . . . in case the merits of the Cause be brought before the King & Council."[22] As for the judges and the principal lawyers in the colony, they were, he said, either proprietors of extravagant grants of land, or allied with such proprietors through interest or marriage: and he professed to see in the combination of bench and bar an alliance dangerous to the Crown's prerogative, authority, and rights in the province.[23]

In other words, juries could be counted on to favor the landlords in any suit for ejectment against troublesome tenants or mere intruders, or in suits where tenants sought for justice against landowners, for jurors were usually required to be substantial freeholders: and if appeals were allowed from the verdict of juries, if case after case was brought up on appeal to the King in Council, who could tell what alarming discoveries might not be made concerning preposterous land grants and fraudulent titles?[24]

And Colden was also contending—as he had often contended before— that the judges and the principal lawyers, like the great landlords and the great merchants, constituted a privileged, an aristocratic class; and that this class was now in close and mischievous alliance with the landed interest.

The truth of this statement could be established statistically. The number of substantial landholders among the chief justices, the associate justices, the surrogates and registers, and the admiralty judges bore out Colden's contention. The great majority of licensed attorneys bore landed names or were connected with landed families.[25] Judge Livingston himself was not only his father's heir, but also his father's agent in New York.[26] In the midst of the *Forsey* vs. *Cunningham* crisis, when he and his colleagues were defending the common law and the landlords' interests against an imminent combination of the Lieutenant Governor and the King in Council, and when the Stamp Act was looming in the background, a truculent giant, the Judge had been disturbed by the rumor that a bill for a general New York land tax was soon to be introduced in Parliament. "If this project takes," he wrote his father on April 10, "then farewell to all the great Patents in the government, and for the purpose of breaking them I suppose it is proposed. . . . It will I fear be impossible to ward off all the Attacques that will be made by designing Fellows against the men of Estates in this Country and every Parliament I fear will bring some new imposition."[27]

It was under the dire influence of this rumor, no doubt, that he wrote his "Reasons Against a Land Tax," in which he attempts to prove that the great landowners are not "such mischievous animals" as their enemies make them out to be, since "to them our happy Constitution owes its preservation." If the early governors, the Judge argues, had granted lands only to those who settled them, and only so much to each settler as he was able to cultivate, their successors, by continuing such practices, would have been able to carry every farthing of specie out of the country; and if they had increased the quitrents as the land grew more valuable, they would have raised such a revenue to the Crown as would have rendered the Assembly —"our House of Representatives"—quite useless. Nor does he stop here. Where lands are granted in small parcels, he continues, the husbandmen consume the whole produce, "and a Habit of Idleness and Sloth is produced for want of Employment." But the proprietors of large tracts, by parceling them out in a proper manner, "enable, &, by the Rents they insist on, oblige their Tenants to raise more than they consume. . . ." In this way there will never be wanting a sufficient spur to industry; industry furnishes the materials for trade; and so the colony fulfills its colonial destiny.

To prove that there was some vital connection between large land grants with small quitrents, on the one hand, and the preservation of all men's liberties, on the other; or between quasi-feudal leaseholds and the unique production of a marketable surplus, was certainly no mean feat. Whether it would have satisfied the enemies of the great landowners cannot be determined, for the Judge's "Reasons" were never published: but the Judge himself, strange to say, seems in the end to have found them insufficient. If the system he is defending is at fault, he says, who is to blame? Not private persons, who generally think it right to improve their estates by such methods as the law permits, "even though it be somewhat injurious to their Country for this Vulgar & I think good reason, 'If one does not another will. . . .' Juvenal, you know, gives this excuse for writing, tho' he had better ones. Stulta est Clementia, cum tot ubique/ Vatibus occurras, periturae parcere Chartae."*[28]

But Juvenal, alas, was of little assistance to the Judge. It was not the many, it was the few, who could hope to be landowners in New York. Indeed, the paper is interesting, not for the quality of its reasoning, but for the light it throws into the mind of a landowner who was also a lawyer. If so truly upright a man as Robert R. Livingston, Sr., could resort to such fanciful arguments and so lame a conclusion, then there must have been some merit in the strictures of Cadwallader Colden.

IV

This, then, was the Judge's state of mind as he sat in the Stamp Act Congress—itself an extralegal entity. The economic recession that followed the French and Indian War, the system of taxation set up by Parliament in the Sugar Act of 1764 and the Stamp Act of 1765, the assault upon juries that arose from *Forsey* vs. *Cunningham* and was developed in the extended powers of British Admiralty Courts, the rumors of a general land tax— all these were, in their several ways, threats against a way of life that was at once too sacred and too equivocal for free discussion. At heart, he was more a landowner than a jurist. He asked for his way of life—it was a typically agrarian position—nothing more than that it should be left alone, to go on doing the same things for ever and ever. If you tax us, he said, we shall be forced into illegal manufacturing in order to find money for our taxes; we shall be obliged to become wealthy in spite of ourselves. "I hope the ministry will never think a trifling revenue raised in a poor country worth so great a risk. For poor the country must be while it continues to transmit to Britain all its acquirements & this is the state I heartily wish we may continue in for ages to come happy in their [*i.e.,* our] several frugal undebauched subordinate governments with just enough riches to supply the conveniences of life."[29]

It is not surprising that he should have been one of the delegates to the Congress (it contained delegations from eight colonies) who did not believe in too much opposition. The real battle in the Congress was not over the Stamp Act—everyone detested that; everyone agreed that stamp

* Roughly paraphrased, this means: If everyone is writing poetry, it is foolish not to write it too.

taxes were unacceptable. The real battle was over the far deeper and more delicate question of whether or not the Congress should *acknowledge* that Parliament had a right to regulate the trade of America. It was a cardinal belief with him—as it was, generally, of the Livingston party—that levies on trade were preferable to taxes on property; and he was willing to make "an explicit declaration . . . that we ought to obey all acts of trade and that they should regulate our Trade." What troubled the Congress, however, was not so much the Stamp Act of 1765 as the Sugar Act of 1764. For the Sugar Act of 1764 was not just an act to raise taxes or just an act to regulate trade. It was a startling and horrible innovation, a mixture of both, an act to raise revenue by regulating trade. To acknowledge that Parliament had a constitutional right to regulate trade, therefore, might be taken as an admission that the taxes levied under the Sugar Act were also constitutional.[30] The Judge had as good a mind as any other delegate: it was his bias as a landholder that made it impossible for him to accept this distinction. Indeed, he found the Congress tedious; there were too many men there, he thought, who were leaders in their own colonies and who would not submit to leadership. What was needed, he told his father, was "a dux gregis or two or three before our business can be done in a consistent manner." But of the necessity for such a congress, he entertained no doubts. "*See the three great points we have to contend for,*" he continued, "*& of what importance they are:* trials by Juries, a right to tax ourselves, the reducing of admiralty courts within their proper limits."[31]

And so, when the Congress decided on a compromise, when it agreed neither to acknowledge nor to disavow the regulating power of Parliament, but to declare in the first of its resolutions that "his Majesty's Subjects in these Colonies . . . owe *all due Subordination* to that August Body the Parliament of *Great Britain,*" Judge Livingston was ready to agree. The real meaning of the Congress's resolutions was far from clear, and is still debated. Did they say that Parliament had the right to make laws for the colonies within the limits of its authority, but had no right to levy taxes of any kind? Or did they distinguish between internal taxes, which Parliament had no right to levy, and external taxes, which came within the scope of its regulating power? The Judge evidently accepted the latter definition, and told his father so: and there were others, inside and outside the Congress, including, it seems, the redoubtable William Livingston, who held this milder view.[32]

The Congress adjourned on October 25. Of its twenty-seven members, General Thomas Gage had already remarked that "it's to be feared, in general, that the Spirit of Democracy, is strong amongst them."[33] By "democracy," the General meant no more than a dislike of the control of Parliament; and yet, in a roundabout way, there was a certain prescience in his words. It was not the spirit these delegates embodied, it was the spirit they evoked that mattered. The riots that envigorated and alarmed New York City in the early days of November were not the less vigorous because of the example of the Stamp Act Congress. The same could be said of the New York merchants who, meeting on October 31 at George Burns's Tavern, the property of James De Lancey, decided to import no more English goods, nor sell any on commission, after January 1, 1766.[34] Indeed, they may have gone farther than the setting of an example: they may have had some hand in inciting the riots themselves. The evidence is tenuous and usually far from impartial; the same accusation was made, in Parliament, against those British merchants who, more, even, than their American counterparts, were likely to suffer from the Stamp Tax, just as in New York it was also made against the lawyers.[35] But one thing, at any rate, is certain. If the evidence is to be believed, then the merchants, or the more conservative of them, got a great deal more than they had bargained for.

"Last night and the night before," Judge Livingston wrote on November 2, "we have had mobbing. There was such a one last night as was never seen before in the city." On October 31, there was nothing more than what he characterized, rather contemptuously, as the "mobbish" behavior of a crowd of boys and tailors. But on November 1, the day when the Stamp Act was to come into force, "a mob the most formidable imaginable" paraded the streets, with an effigy of the Lieutenant Governor and one of the Devil, which they had hung on a gallows and which they carried to within ten feet of the walls of the fort. After showering the garrison—whose patience and temper, said the Judge, were admirable—with bricks, stones, and objurgations, they carried their effigies to the Bowling Green and burned them; gutted the house of Major Thomas James, who had sworn that he would cram the stamps down the people's throats; and finished the night's "mischief" by sacking some bawdyhouses, whose connection with the Stamp Tax, like the location of the houses themselves, is veiled in mystery.[36]

On the following day, there were rumors that the fort itself was to be attacked. Judge Livingston, who was popular and fearless, moved around the city in an attempt to keep the peace. James Duane, conceiving the "prudent" notion that sailors were at the bottom of it all, enlisted the help of the sea captains. Lieutenant Governor Colden, forgetting his previous intransigence and remembering perhaps that effigy on the gallows, roundly declared that he would not meddle with the stamps at all. For three days there was an uneasy truce. And then, on November 5, there was renewed talk of an attack on the fort; and only when the Mayor and Common Council wrung from Colden an assent to their taking the offending stamps into their own custody was tranquillity of a sort restored. If the fort had been attacked, its commander told Parliament later on, and if he had been forced to fire, he would have killed or could have killed at least nine hundred of the assailants. General Gage was of the opinion that such a firing would have meant the beginning of civil war.[37] And Judge Livingston, writing to former Governor Monckton, used the same words of the Stamp Act—its enforcement, he said, would mean "the utmost danger" of civil war.[38]

Obviously—that is to say, superficially—the General placed himself on one side in such a war, the Judge on the other. If the Stamp Act were persisted in, said the Judge, the whole colony would be united in disaffection, and he certainly included himself among the disaffected, and continued to include himself until the day of his death. But there their differences ended. The Judge, no less than the General, regarded such disaffection with alarm and dismay. His greatest hope was that there would be no occasion for it. His mind perpetually revolved the necessity of rebellion if Parliament did not mend its ways, and the awful consequences of rebellion should it ever become necessary.[39] He, like the General, and like every other man of property, consequence, and conservative disposition, saw in the Stamp Act riots a threat to himself. With the possible exception of the sailors (who would be thrown out of employment if the Customs refused to allow ships to clear with unstamped papers), the new proletarians who menaced the fort on November 1 and 2 had little to suffer by the new tax.[40] Their motive was deeper and, except in riot, it was inexpressible. They were the ill-paid, the submerged, the unpropertied, the unenfranchised. The Judge declared that he knew nothing of "the secret party . . . known as Vox Populi" which managed the riots, except that it was dangerous; and while the leaders of his own faction in the Assembly—the "triumvirate" of William Livingston, John Morin Scott, and William Smith, Jr.—must have learned something about the composition of this secret party, no evidence has connected them directly with it. The rioters, in the end, appeared as the outcasts of an aristocratic society: quite as hostile as the Parliament in Westminster and perhaps more so, because more volatile, more impressionable, desperate, and near at hand.[41]

The Judge's mind was rendered uneasier, and his position was further complicated, by the fact that he was, primarily, a landowner. When the Stamp Act was repealed, when "the Tumults, Rage & Contempt of

Majesty & Government"[42] came to an end in the city, there were still other dangers to be considered.

Lately [he wrote on May 2, 1776], a parcel of Tenants imagining that mobs would continue to rule, gathered together & marched to this city to the number of five or six hundred to relieve two persons, who have been committed for riotously putting two out of possession, and of putting others in who had been dispossessed by their Landlords. They imagined they would have been joined by those who call themselves "Sons of Liberty" in this Town, but finding themselves disappointed, they marched back as they came, & the Government has issued a Proclamation for apprehending their leaders. I mention this trifling incident least it should be misrepresented by our enemies on your side of the water, as proceeding from another cause.[43]

To the correspondent in England, the incident might be described as "trifling"; it was hardly so to the writer in New York. The Stamp Act riots in New York and Albany had inflamed the tenant farmers of the Hudson Valley; and though there was no sympathy between the Sons of Liberty and their followers and the tenant farmers and their leaders, the mere coexistence of two sets of rioters—a proletariat and (to his mind) a *Jacquerie*—was, to say the least, deeply perplexing to the upright Judge. Everything he had done for the rights of juries, for the limitation of admiralty jurisdiction, and against parliamentary taxes was inextricably involved with a defense of the landowners' way of life: everything riotous in the city and the valley seemed to be undermining this defense. Parliament should have been his bulwark. "Whatever Jealousy," he wrote in the same letter, "may have obtained at our aiming at an Independence nothing is more foreign from the thoughts of every man of property amongst us, for the confusions and disorders which would arise if this were the case would render this country the most disagreeable of any in the universe. Our duty and our interest oblige us on all occasions to demonstrate a firm attachment to our mother country & obedience to her laws." These sentences, to be sure, might have been written by any moderate New Yorker, whether or not he belonged to the landed aristocracy. But when the repeal of the Stamp Act was followed by a Declaratory Act, which openly justified what had been repealed; when the Declaratory Act was followed by a Quartering Act, and the Quartering Act by the Townshend Acts; when, in short, a centralizing Parliament seemed determined to bend the colonial empire to its will or force it into rebellion—then, indeed, the Judge became more explicit. "I have nothing very agreeable to write," he told his father on September 18, 1767. "Madness seems to prevail on the other side of the Water, Melancholy and dejection on this. . . . Mr. Colden by writing a vindication of himself has thrown aspertions on every Station of man amongst us but his Enmity is most pointed at the Landed Interest. . . . This country appears to have seen its best days."[44]

V

It was certainly true that the Livingston party had seen its best days. By whatever name it went—"Popular," "Presbyterian," or "Whig"—it stood for moderation. It was moderate in its reforms, moderate in its resistance to Parliament, moderate in its notions of popularity. It was a loose cohesion of individuals—anywhere from Peter R. Livingston, eldest living son of the third Lord of the Manor, who was blankly conservative, to John Morin Scott, who was too radical for the moderates of his own party but not radical enough for the "warmer" Sons of Liberty. What held it together was a general distaste for taxes on property, fear of Parliament, an appetite for office and patronage, and a suspicion of the lower orders. "Some little time of calm seems necessary," Judge Livingston wrote in 1766, "before government can regain the authority & the lower sort can be reduced to a due submission."[45] Its strength lay in the fact that, while no less aristocratic than the De Lancey party, it was far less disposed to obey the authorities in England: its weakness lay, precisely, in its aristocracy. It had no more sympathy with the Stamp Act rioters than it had with its own dissident tenants. And there seems little question that out of the city riots of 1765 and the farmer rebellions of 1766 there had arisen something—something powerful and impalpable, a kind of exhalation—which infected the whole province. In the elections of 1768, on a cry of "No lawyers in the Assembly," the party went down to defeat; even the Judge was unseated in Dutchess County; and of its four candidates for New York City, only Philip Livingston was elected. William Livingston returned to the attack, when the Assembly was dissolved and new elections were called for 1769, with some violent language against the proposed creation of an Anglican episcopate for America. The battle was to be fought on the old Presbyterian-Anglican battlefield; and William, the giant of his party, was sure that the day could be won. His followers took heart, and prepared for a stern ordeal but a victorious issue. "Our canvass stands well," Peter R. Livingston wrote to Philip Schuyler from New York, "but there will be a vast deal of cross voting. The two they pitch on of our four are Philip [Livingston] and [John Morin] Scott which will putt them in, but there is a great deal in good management of the votes our people are in high spirits and if there is not fair play there will be blood shed as we have by far the best part of the Brusers on our side."[46] But the bruisers were assembled in vain; and even the threat of bishops, strange to say, failed to move the electorate. The Anglican De Lancey party refused to accept the religious issue, but raised the cry of "No lawyer"—"No Presbyterian," wrote John Jay, "has given place to no lawyer"[47]—and, after a bitter campaign and, it was supposed, a corrupt one, Philip Livingston, as well as John Morin Scott, lost his seat. The Judge, who tried again in Dutchess County and lost, had the mortification of finding that the Livingston and Beekman tenants had voted against him "notwithstanding all the pains was taking [taken] with them."[48] When the Assembly met on April 4, it was firmly in the control of the De Lanceys.

It was not that the De Lanceys were popular; it was, rather, that they had exploited the growing unpopularity of the Livingstons. They put it about in New York that merchants, not lawyers, should properly represent that city: but this could not have affected the Judge's campaign in Dutchess County. Campaigns in the Hudson Valley, even in the midst of a rebellious tenantry, went in favor of the landowner's nominee; for there was no secret ballot, and it would take a bold man to stand up and, viva voce, give his vote against his landlord, armed with his rights of distraint and re-entry, with the sheriff beside him, and the Provincial Government at his back.[49] Moreover, the Judge was personally liked; so that if the cry of "No lawyer" carried the day in Dutchess County, it must indeed have had some especial, some peculiar appeal.

It has been said that the lawyers had lost everybody's confidence; that the lawyers were accused, by the conservatives, of instigating the Stamp Act riots, by the radicals, of opposing the plan of doing business on un-stamped paper; by churchmen of supporting dissenters;[50] and perhaps even by dissenters of favoring the church. This is no more than to say that lawyers were apt to be unpopular, a condition to which they were used and which they sustained with equanimity. What seems altogether more probable is that they were now recognized as a privileged class, equal in power, or nearly so, to the great landlords and the rich merchants; a class which had risen to wealth through the practice of expensive, unin-telligible, and (who could tell?) unnecessary mysteries, and which was now in alliance with the landed interest, because the landed interest had more litigation to offer. Were not titles to land generally determined through an ejectment action, of all legal actions the most complicated; was it not through such actions that the landlords usually got rid of their "trouble-makers"; and were they not usually handled by the Supreme Court, whose judges went on circuit once a year in every county?[51] "I am so uneasy at the Disappointment of the Judges not coming up to hold the Circuit Court," Robert Livingston, Jr., the third Lord, wrote in 1768, "that I can hardly express it, as it is not only a loss & damage to me, but to a number of people in the County, tho' more grevious to me than any as I possess a Large Estate into which a Raskal has presumed to enter & now he finds I cannot bring him to tryal he will encourage other Villins to do the same by which I may be ruind."[52] Had not "Philanthropos" suggested in an admonishing pamphlet that the tenants had been driven to violence because the law "was absolutely barred against them . . . the lawyers generally refusing to take their cause in hand"?[53] Were not the Livingston partisans the instrument of this alliance between Land and Law, and their political moderation the expression of it? Thus the new self-consciousness of 1765-1766, which animated the urban and rural underworld of the province in those years, stirred the emotions—though it scarcely united the ideas—of the urban and the rural freeholders. The Judge and his cousin Philip were equally its victims, and the great loser by its workings was the Livingston party.

VI

The victory of the De Lanceys in 1768, and their emergence as a "popular" party, only serves to deepen the mystery of colonial politics in New York, unless we remember Professor Ross J. S. Hoffman's statement that both Livingstons and De Lanceys considered themselves Whigs. The Livingstons were, on the whole, reforming Whigs; the De Lanceys, on the whole, were not. But the objective of both parties was control of the Assembly—an exclusive gathering of twenty-six—because the Assembly was the disbursing and taxing power, and appointed its own provincial treasurer. All other appointments, with one or two minor exceptions, were made by the Crown or the royal governor: but many salaries, in whole or in part, were granted by the Assembly. The chief justice was appointed by the King, but three-quarters of his salary was disbursed by the Assembly; the puisne judges were appointed by the governor, but the whole of their salaries depended upon the Assembly. The governor's salary was paid by the Crown, but he, too, could not have existed without an annual grant from the Assembly. To parties whose intellectual existence was largely predicated upon their views on direct taxation, and whose physical existence depended upon office and patronage, control of this body was a matter of the first importance: and the De Lanceys were perfectly capable of taking over the role of the Livingstons, of becoming Whigs with radical connections, of leading the battle against the encroachment of Parliament, if this was the best way to exploit the unpopularity of the Livingstons and regain command of the Assembly.[54]

It was not a role, however, that they could sustain for long. In 1768 and 1769, they led the assault against the Townshend Revenue Acts (which threatened, among other things, to remove the control of salaries from the colonial legislatures) and against the Restraining Act of 1767, which sought to restrain the New York Assembly because it had supplied the royal troops in a more niggardly manner than was required by the Quartering Act of 1765. Then their opposition gently, but openly, collapsed. They refused to reaffirm the "constitutional resolves" that they helped to draw up; and they made a bargain with the governor by which a deficiency bill for provisioning the royal troops was conceded in return for the governor's promise to help obtain royal approval for a bill to emit £120,000 in bills of credit. By 1770, though they were still in control of the Assembly, their popularity had vanished.

And what contributed to this loss of popularity was their treatment of the Livingstons. A place had been found for Philip Livingston, when his nephew, Peter R. Livingston, who represented the manor, agreed to resign in his favor; but this forthright family maneuver was neatly countered in an Assembly dominated by the De Lancey faction. The Assembly ruled that Philip Livingston, whom it had just elected speaker, could not sit for the manor because he was not a resident. The Livingstons, never easily daunted, were more than usually resolute where their own pocket borough was concerned. They asked the Judge to take his cousin's place. No one could say that *he* was not a resident, since Clermont, by the terms of the first Lord's will, paid the manor an annual quitrent of eight shillings. The Judge was overworked—he complained that all his colleagues were infirm and that all the business of the Supreme Court fell on his shoulders—but he allowed himself to be persuaded. The manor freeholders, or the loyal and chiefly Dutch minority which alone cared to vote, obediently elected him. The Assembly at once passed a bill to the effect that no judge of the Supreme Court could be one of its members.

Year after year, the freeholders elected the Judge; year after year, he presented himself at the doors of the Assembly; year after year, he was turned away. When the Assembly appointed Edmund Burke to be their agent, the Judge thought that he had an excellent chance to regain his seat. For Governor Lord Dunmore was horrified at this appointment, which had been made behind his back. "Burk," wrote the Judge, "is the Kings personal Enemy & is the most detested of any Man in the

Opposition." To get the appointment altered, Dunmore believed he might need the help of the Livingston minority, "who will agree to it only on these two conditions that I be received & that they name the Agent."[55] But the Judge's hopes were dashed; Dunmore accepted Burke and went completely over to the De Lanceys, "a thing his Friends had particularly guarded him against." In his extremity, the Judge on one occasion even brought himself to accost Speaker John Cruger in the street: "whose answer was, with a most obsequious bow, that he owned politics had run too high, that he was sorry for it, that he had no manner of Objection to me, for I was a very good man, only I was not of his Party."[56] In such a warfare as this, the third Lord of the Manor was not behindhand. He conceived the idea of turning the Assembly into the likeness of an Athenian gathering by having the manor freeholders take their seats in person— "for represented we will be, as having a right by law." The "lovers of liberty," he said, would not object to putting them all up for a month or so. The scheme proved abortive, and in an idle and angry moment he even spoke of selling his estates and moving to another colony. This would hardly have annoyed the De Lanceys, or "The Tyrants" as he now preferred to call them.[57]

In the end, in 1774, the Judge grew weary of presenting himself to the freeholders of the manor, and Peter R. Livingston was elected in his place. The Judge was no Wilkes: yet the inhabitants of the colony could hardly help making a comparison between the way in which their Assembly treated the representative from the manor and the way in which the Westminster Parliament dealt with the member from Middlesex.

At the same time, however, how obvious it was that party politics such as this had little or nothing to do with popular issues. While the colonies revolved more and more shakily in their imperial orbit, under the decisive influence of the Tea Act, the power passed away from the New York Assembly into the hands of extralegal committees and congresses. It became more and more blatantly an aristocratic gathering, occupying itself with obscure political maneuvers and the delicious bickerings of personal intrigue, even while its leaders made up their minds on which side of the great imperial struggle they would take their stand. It was in this atmosphere, where questions of enormous consequence were mingled with all the momentous niceties of a "family" feud, that Chancellor Livingston spent his youth and early manhood.

CHAPTER FOUR

Catharine Livingston Garretson recalled that, once, when she was a little girl, she ran up to her father, the Judge, in the gardens at Clermont with some berries that she had picked for him and that she presented to him on a broad leaf. Mr. Justice Livingston was delighted with this artless gift: he exclaimed that he only wished he had twenty children. His wish was halved.* Of his ten surviving children, the second, and the eldest son, was Robert R. Livingston, the future Chancellor of New York. He was born in New York City on November 27, 1746, and was baptized into the Church of England.

Of his childhood, nothing is known except that he was raised in the city—so much can be deduced from occasional references to him in his father's letters—and spent his holidays at Clermont, where his younger sisters lived much of the time, and where he was remembered by them as a remote figure, "very fond of country life, of shooting and taking solitary walks with his gun."[1]

---

* The children of Judge Livingston and Margaret Beekman Livingston were:
1. Janet. Born August 27, 1743; married Richard Montgomery, July 24, 1773; died November 6, 1828.
2. Catharine. Born February 20, 1745; died April 29, 1752.
3. Robert R. Born November 27, 1746; married Mary Stevens, September 9, 1770; died February 26, 1813.
4. Margaret. Born January 5, 1749; married February 22, 1779 to Thomas T. Tillotson, Physician and Surgeon-General, Northern Department; died March 19, 1823.
5. Henry Beekman. Born November 9, 1750; married March 11, 1781, to Anne Hume Shippen; died November 5, 1831.
6. Catharine. Born October 14, 1752; married June 30, 1793 to the Reverend Freeborn Garretson; died July 14, 1849.
7. John R. Born February 13, 1755; married (1) Margaret Sheaffe, 1779, (2) Eliza McEvers, May 30, 1789; died September 1851.
8. Gertrude. Born April 16, 1757; married Morgan Lewis, May 11, 1779; died March 9, 1833.
9. Joanna. Born September 14, 1759; married Peter R. Livingston; died March 1, 1829.
10. Alida. Born December 24, 1761; married John Armstrong, January 19, 1789; died December 24, 1822.
11. Edward. Born May 28, 1764; married (1) Mary McEvers, April 10, 1788, (2) Marie Louisa Valentine D'Avezac Castra Moreau, June 3, 1805; died May 23, 1836.

But the Judge, as his son testified many times in later life, was nothing if not an affectionate and confiding father: and the boy grew up to accept ever around him, as part of his family atmosphere, the hum and stir of the legal and political world. When he was twelve years old, the Livingstons first gained control of the Assembly; when he was fifteen, his family's representatives were bitterly engaged in a judiciary fight with the Lieutenant Governor; when he was seventeen, his father, as a Justice of the Supreme Court, was deeply involved in the controversy over *Forsey* vs. *Cunningham*. His entry into professional life coincided with his father's exclusion from the Assembly; his only position under the Crown was due to an intrigue arising out of the endless Livingston–De Lancey battle. To him, as to all Livingstons, the politics of pre-Revolutionary New York were never entirely distinguishable from the intimacies of family life, or from family loyalties and family ambitions.

He entered King's College, the bane of William Livingston's politico-Presbyterian conscience, in 1761; and although an Anglican Livingston would scarcely have been refused admittance to that institution under any terms short of total ignorance, it is to be presumed that he satisfied the fairly simple requirements—"a rational account of the Latin and Greek grammars, a reading of the first three of Tully's *Select Orations* and the first three books of the *Aeneid*, and a translation of the first ten chapters of St. John's Gospel from Greek into Latin." An eighteenth-century boy, adequately tutored, could have picked his way through these tests without much trouble; and Livingston's intelligence was never questioned, only the uses to which it was sometimes put. As for arithmetic, he was asked merely to be "expert as far as the rules of Reduction."[2]

Livingston was a tall, slim, graceful youth, not handsome by any means, but high-spirited and self-assured: as heir to the Clermont estate and a good deal more, he was a considerable *parti* in provincial New York. The regimen and curriculum of King's College—the perpetual study of the Greek and Roman classics, of natural and moral philosophy, interspersed with meals of an invariable sameness—was enough to provoke, though not to permit, undue frivolity: the students were expected, on paper at least, to keep pretty strict hours; but when his friend Nathaniel Du Bois, Jr., describes him as "a very Proteus in Love," and as "devoted to all the gay amusements that the favor of the Ladies & an agreeable set of companions afford," it sounds as if he made some effort to combine the pursuit of higher learning with the life of a young man of fashion.[3] It could not, to be sure, have been a very fashionable life: the urban patriciate of New York had rather more to learn in that way than it had to teach; and, in any case, there existed within the walls of King's College for some of his stay there, a stern counteracting influence.

John Jay, the future chief justice of the United States, was a year senior to Livingston at college. Although, with a characteristic exactitude, Jay declared that their friendship was first "particularly professed" on March 29, 1765, it appears that they were on good terms long before that. "You are one of the few select ones," Du Bois wrote in 1763, "who visit Jay's room; which might very justly be called a receptacle of agreeable young fellows." The word "agreeable" has an odd sound, in connection with such a room and such a host. Jay came from a solid New York merchant family, of Huguenot origins. He was a solemn, dyspeptic young man, who—once he had conquered a slight impediment in his speech—was inclined to get his way by mingling sarcastic disputation with the daily and hourly profession of the loftiest moral principles. His influence upon what Livingston called "a spice of melancholy in my nature" may be discerned in their early correspondence; the two wrote only with the highest ends in view; and one is tempted to suppose that one is perusing the correspondence, not between two provincial youths, but between two pseudoclassical busts of a frigid but sentimental cast of feature.[4] "Agreeable to your advice," Jay writes in 1765, "I shall keep a Watchful Eye over my conduct; and hope with your Assistance to preserve it fair and unspotted." A few months later, the roles are reversed.

By your account of the matter [Jay writes], you have attained every qualification necessary to form a Buck and entitle you to the appelation of a man of pleasure. You are now in the country, separated from Temptation, your passions are reduced to their usual Calm, and your spirits like a silent stream whose woods defend it from the winds that rage on Shoars more exposed to storms again unruffled flow and glide with ease. Reflect for a moment what time has elapsed since we have been free from the Drudgery of business, that such an opportunity probably will not offer again [etc. etc.]

Such were the exchanges between the two friends.[5]

At another time, in an introspective mood, Jay gave a different version of their relationship. At the beginning, he said:

I took it into my head that our dispositions were in many respects similar. Afterwards I conceived a different opinion. It appeared to me that yours had more vivacity. Bashfulness and pride rendered me more staid. Both equally ambitious, but pursuing it in different roads. You flexible, I pertinaceous. Both equally sensible of indignities, you less prone to sudden resentments. Both possessed of warm passions, but you of more self-possession. You formed for a citizen of the world, I for a College or a Village. You fond of a large acquaintance, I careless of all but a few. You understood men *and women* early, I knew them not. You had talents and inclination for intrigue, I had neither. Your mind (and body) received pleasure from a variety of objects, mine from few. You were naturally easy of access, and in advances, I in neither.[6]

The evidence of their later years suggests that this description may not have been inaccurate for their earlier ones. Livingston respected Jay's abilities; Jay admired Livingston's manners. But it is not difficult to detect, amidst Jay's apparent self-abasement, something that is not abased at all. How pleasant it is for a young man of principle to confess that he is un-fitted for, that he is set apart from, that he is in a way superior to, the unprincipled ways of the ordinary world! In 1762, Jay's father presented him with a copy of *The Humorist,* possibly because he suspected a certain deficiency in his son. It is superfluous to inquire whether his suspicion was justified or whether it was not.

II

Livingston was graduated, one of a class of eight, in 1765. In the com-mencement exercises, held in Trinity Church on May 21, his English ora-tion "In Praise of Liberty" was greatly admired. The New York *Gazette* said that it surpassed in "sublimity" no less than in "graceful propriety" the efforts of the other seven young men, though all of them were praised and one of them was a Schuyler: and thus a gift for oratory, which Chancel-lor Kent in his old age remembered with peculiar vividness as being one of the ornaments of the New York bar, was first presented to the world.[7]

In the same year, he entered on his legal apprenticeship, first in the office of William Livingston and then in that of William Smith, Jr.—the offices, that is to say, of two of the triumvirs who had led the Livingston party to its victory in 1758. Their methods of dealing with an apprentice appear to have been quite different: for whereas William Livingston had denounced the system of uninstructed apprenticeship as early as 1745, the office of William Smith—according to Peter Van Shaak, who left it in 1770—still abandoned a young man, as far as his education was con-cerned, to the mercy of his own devices. And the life of a young man so abandoned was hard indeed. He had to be his own instructor, but only in such time as he could spare from the endless copying of interminable legal documents. And to dig out the law for oneself, when even the whole of Blackstone's *Commentaries* was not available; to pass, without guidance, from the mysteries of Sir Henry Finch to those of Sir Matthew Hale, from Wood's *Institute* to Bohun's *Institutio,* from the dictionary of Giles

Jacob to the darkness of Coke on Littleton—this was a task only for a hardy and determined mind. Yet it was expected and it was, somehow or other, accomplished. "For my part," said Van Schaak, "how many hours have I hunted, how many books turned up for what three minutes of explanation from any tolerable lawyer would have made evident to me!"[8] The nature of Livingston's experiences as a lawyer's clerk must be left in doubt: he himself has said nothing about them. But he had an exceptionally quick, a very able mind; he had the example and perhaps the instruction of a father whom he loved and who, in turn, declared that "Robert has the talents to be at the head of his profession"; and then he had something almost equally valuable—he had the benefit of his father's influence. He was admitted to the bar after serving the minimal apprenticeship of three years: this much is certain, for the biographer of John Jay has discovered that a Jay-Livingston partnership began in 1768, and that its first recorded case was in the September vacation of that year.[9] In 1770, he was a member of that exclusive legal society The Moot—only twenty attorneys out of a bar of more than seventy in New York were admitted to it—which met at various taverns and, after discussing a comfortable dinner, would debate certain abstruse cases and hand down decisions of genuine importance to the instructed of the province.[10] In 1772, he was doing business for his father; his partnership with Jay, never very active, was amicably dissolved; and he had proposed himself and Jay to Governor Tryon as candidates for an office of their own invention, that of chief justice (or presiding judge) of the Common Pleas and Sessions. Jay, "whose character and eminence in the profession is too well known to need any recommendation," was to serve in Westchester and Orange counties. Livingston would move around Albany, Ulster, and Dutchess counties, attending as many courts as he could, for the modest fee of three shillings on the list of every writ. The work, he said, was important because the judges of these inferior courts, while reputable enough, were usually farmers whose knowledge "is seldom equal to their integrity"; and it would not be inconvenient. Clermont, "where my inclination leads me to spend the greater part of my time," was central to all three counties.[11]

Governor Tryon, prompted (he said) by Justices Livingston and Ludlow, presented the scheme to his Council on December 11, 1772, as a sound "amendment of our policy in the Administration of Justice." But James De Lancey vehemently opposed it; and though the Governor brought the matter up again five days later, saying that Jay and Livingston had agreed to serve for nothing and would take their seats below the country judges, only Councillors Smith and Watts were ready to support it. "Jay's friends as well as Livingston's," wrote Smith, "are disgusted & consider Mr. Tryon as terrified or led by the DeLancey's."[12]

Nearly a year later, in an effort "to cross the De Lanceys," always too importunate for their own good, Tryon offered the Recordership of New York City to the younger Livingston, though he had previously promised it to Stephen De Lancey. Livingston was far from eager; but the Judge added his persuasions to those of the Governor; the patent was sent "in secret" by the cautious Tryon on September 30, 1773; and Livingston held the office until April 5, 1775.[13]

Governor Tryon was a man who liked to please everybody; and if the disposal of a recordership or the fate of a minor administrative reform depended upon his good will, it is clear that this good will was, in fact, merely a function of his varying relationship with the Livingston and De Lancey factions. This was not young Livingston's first public brush with the De Lanceys. In 1770, some letters signed "Americanus" appeared in the New York *Journal or The General Advertiser*; and one of them, dated May 3, attacked the Livingstons in general for lukewarm politics. "I do not wonder," he wrote in reply, "at the attack made on the character of Mr. L—— in a late paper signed —— or at the reflections thrown on the whole L—— family by Americanus as if their errors wd have justifyd the faults of Mr. D——y —" Did not the supporters of weak and ambitious governments always endeavor to reduce others to their own level? "Had the authors of those papers confined themselves to the facts they might have railled on unanswered & the Livingston family would have smild with as much contempt at their abuse of them as the world does on the panegyrick on the glorious and disinterested Assembly which met in 1768."[14] The Livingstons were not merely a family; they were a political entity; and so they remained.

In The Moot, however, the leaders of the opposing parties met in the most amicable fashion: they had previously agreed that no discussion of "the Party Politics of this Province" should be permitted.[15] Such politics were for the Council, the Assembly, the newspapers, the family conclave, and the depths of the unforgiving and unforgetting heart. In the dancing assemblies and the social clubs, the drawing rooms and the parlors, politics were forgotten. James Duane had married Maria (or Mary) Livingston, a daughter of the third Lord; but his best friends were among the De Lancey faction; and all he would do when the Judge was suffering his annual exclusion from the Assembly was to attempt to persuade them to take a more charitable course.[16] John Jay, in spite of his admiration for the Livingstons, courted both the daughters of Peter De Lancey before he married Sarah Livingston, the daughter of the great William. The De Lanceys constituted a "court" party and the Livingstons, if anything, an anticourt one; but this did not affect their social relations with the governors. Of Lord Dunmore, it is true, Janet Livingston Montgomery felt that the less said the better; but Sir Henry Moore was one of her father's best friends, though the Judge deplored his excessive passion for the theater, and the morals of Lady Moore and her beautiful daughter made it impossible for the Livingston ladies to visit them.[17] As for Governor William Tryon, he "was literally our affectionate father." His wife, Margaret Wake Tryon, was a strong-minded lady—"the many called her mad, she was certainly eccentric"—who had written and published a treatise on fortifications. Her social duties were "essential to the town," but they were hateful to her, and she made the lively Janet Livingston her substitute hostess, to amuse the circle or make up the card tables.[18] At such functions as these, until the Governor left "for his health" in 1774, young Livingston and his quiet wife expected to be present.[19]

Ever since his admission to the bar, he had been sufficiently established to marry, as became an eldest son and heir: and on September 9, 1770, accordingly, he did so. His bride was Mary Stevens, daughter of John Stevens, a great New Jersey landowner who resided in New York. It would be idle to inquire whether this was or was not a love match: such considerations were secondary where the families were equal in consequence, and the bride had a sizable reversionary interest in the paternal holdings in Hunterdon County and in the Ramapos. All that was required was that the young people should not be personally disagreeable to each other; and a long and equable marriage proves that they never were. Mary Livingston was not the kind of woman to attract or to court attention: the only description of her appears to be William Strickland's "a polite, sensible, well-bred woman." The references to "Polly" in the family letters are always affectionate, never critical. Her health was not good, she had little taste for adventure—she would never, for example, accompany her husband on his tours to England and Holland and Italy when he was minister to France—she preferred the *vita umbratilis* of the retiring wife of a distinguished, gregarious man. In later years, she was always "Mrs. Chancellor"; and when she died, a year after her husband, her death was taken for granted; it was a natural consequence of his, as if she was as much a part of him as the title that clung to him long after he had resigned the office.

Mr. Stevens furnished their house in town. In the country, Livingston began building a house within sight of the family mansion at some time in 1773. It was completed in May or June of 1774; he called it Belvedere. It had some three and one-half years of existence before the British burned it in 1777.[20]

PART TWO

REVOLUTION

CHAPTER ONE

On April 14, 1775, a handful of freeholders from Dutchess County—only four of its eleven precincts had cared to cast a vote—elected Robert R. Livingston as one of three delegates to the New York Provincial Convention. The Provincial Convention met in New York on April 20, and dissolved itself on April 22, a few hours in advance of the news of Lexington and Concord. On April 21, it elected twelve delegates to the Second Continental Congress, which was to meet in Philadelphia on May 10—"and my son Robert," wrote the Judge, "is made one of them."[1]

II

Chancellor Livingston's thoughts upon the dramatic breakdown of the machinery of empire, between the Tea Act of 1773 and his entrance into the recorded history of the Revolution, have not survived. But his father was, he said, "the warmest friend, the tenderest parent, the most instructive and agreeable companion";[2] and it is not improbable—it is indeed likely—that in 1775 he thought much as his father did on public matters. After he had left for Philadelphia, the Judge sent him a letter, which, for lack of any evidence to the contrary, could be taken to represent their joint thinking at this critical moment. The Judge wrote:

Every good man wishes that America may remain free: in this I join heartily; at the same time I do not desire, she should be wholly independent of the mother country. How to reconcile their jarring principles, I profess I am altogether at a loss. The benefits we receive of protection, seems to require we should contribute to the support of the navy, if not to the armies of Britain. I would have you consider, whether it would not be proper to lay hold of Lord North's overture, to open a negotiation & prevent a suspension of hostilities. . . . This seems to be the thought of our Council here, as Mr. Jay & Mr. [Philip] Livingston will inform you. I should think, if you offered Britain all the duties usually paid here, by our merchants[,] even those paid since the disturbances began, that on Tea excepted, which is too odious, and that all other duties they may think convenient for the regulation of trade shall be lodged in the Treasury of each colony to be disposed of by their respective assemblies & legislatures on an engagement on their side that no other taxes shall be imposed on them but by their own representatives, we ought to be contented. Some specious offer should be made to increase our friends in England. This or something of that kind, if Lord North meant anything by his motion but to deceive the people of England, ought to put a stop to his proceedings for the present, otherwise the odium he lies under must increase. The Boston charter ought by all means to be restored, & even the tea paid for, as a douceur, by the whole continent, it would be no matter. But this you will not insist on except you are well supported. These are my present thoughts, however judge for yourself, and unite by all means, for on this all depends.[3]

The dilemma of the conservatives in early 1775—a dilemma that haunts every sentence of this curious letter—was how to remain within the empire on terms that would somehow satisfy both the British and the radicals: it must be admitted that the Judge had failed to offer even a plausible solution. He was, to be sure, a benign and moderate man, who recoiled from violence: it is none the less exceedingly odd that he should still, on the face of it, cling to the same doctrine that he had uttered in the days of the Stamp Act Congress. It was well known by this time that duties for the regulation of trade were—as the Tea Act proved and the Sugar Act had proved before it—duties for revenue as well; so that the Judge, in effect, still distinguished between internal and external taxation; he still agreed that revenue could be raised through duties on foreign trade. (The three pence a pound on tea was exceptional, or "odious," because it created a monopoly, not because it raised a revenue.) The further distinction between parliamentary taxation, which was inadmissible, and parliamentary legislation, which was not, was still clear to him, although to many American eyes it was becoming invisible. The Coercive Acts ("the Boston charter ought by all means to be restored") must be repealed, because they were a fatal impairment of civil liberties: yet even here he was ready to proffer, by way of compensation, something as intolerable to the Massachusetts conscience as a continental payment for the tea destroyed at the Boston Tea Party. Never had the old Livingston party program of toleration toward duties on trade and resistance toward taxes on property been more dutifully advanced: it was somewhat less reassuring in its imperial disguise than it had been in its provincial one.

And yet it would be doing the Judge the gravest injustice to take his words literally, and suppose that they represented a mere surrender to Parliament. What they represented was the extreme reluctance with which the landowning mind relinquished its utopian dream—its desire, not merely that things should be as they had been before 1763, but that they should never change. And the last sentence in the letter shows to what extent this dream itself had faded: "unite by all means" is neither particularly conciliatory nor very conservative advice. Indeed, the Judge's actions had already shown that his letter was merely the last cannonade of a lost battle. In April, when the Dutchess County elections were pending, it was obvious that the small freeholders of that county were so opposed to anti-British measures that no elections would be held at all: whereupon the Judge had gone down from Clermont to Rhinebeck and had been so successfully persuasive that Rhinebeck and its three adjacent precincts had recognized the Provincial Convention by sending delegates to it. These four precincts were afterward known as the "radical" precincts. For an officer of the Crown, and a justice of the Supreme Court at that, to meddle in such matters scarcely argues a conciliatory disposition. And when the New York Association of April 29—a pledge to support the Provincial Congress and the Continental Congress—was sent around for signing in June, the Judge made a point of putting his name to it, though officers of the Crown were expressly excused from doing so.[4] While he was performing this public act at Rhinebeck, his cousin, the third Lord, went even further: he "put ye Mannor people under arms" for the meeting of June 14, with the result that two-thirds of those present prudently signed the Association: the rest hung back.[5] In July, the younger Livingston told his friend Jay that "many of our tenants refused to sign the association, & resolved to stand by the King as they called it in the hopes that if they succeeded they should have their lands"; some had even gone so far as to send a petition to the New York Provincial Congress complaining about the Clermont rents, although these were not equal "to one per Cent on the value of the lands."[6] As the landlords became less conciliatory toward Parliament, the tenants became more Loyalist: it almost seemed as if the latter were pushing the former into rebellion. When troops were being raised in the province for the Canadian venture, many Clermont tenants said they would take no part in the controversy, for what would happen to their families if they were killed? The Judge and his father then offered new leases "with peculiar privi-leges" to the family "of every every man killed in the service." But the offer had no effect.[7]

It would be easy to see in this sullen, remote controversy on the Hudson, as the tenants became more hostile to the landlords, and the landlords strove, usually in vain, to convert the tenants, a situation emerging in which a Livingston had little choice but to plunge deeper and deeper into the revolutionary movement. The city radicals, as allies, were more amenable to control than the tenant farmers, as enemies. And Parliament—who could say what Parliament would do next, as it sought to impose order and efficiency upon its American empire? The Quebec Act of 1774* did not affect the Hudson River proprietors except in one vital, if intangible, particular—it was a land act, vast and comprehensive, and one land act could lead to another. What if Parliament tried, successfully, to rationalize the New York land system? to inquire into the legality of patents? to extinguish preposterous grants or reorganize the schedule of quitrents?

One cannot assert that all or any of these considerations presented themselves to Judge Livingston: one can, however, presume to say that, if they did, they were not decisive. The little evidence he has left behind him supports the theory that it was not the centralizing but the coercive aspect of Parliament that seemed odious to him, that his deepest reason for moving more and more openly into opposition was not economic and was only partly social, that it was the product of an emotion that is scarcely susceptible of analysis—the aristocrat's moral contempt for any despotism but his own.

He never could rid himself of the belief that armed resistance would prove fatal to both sides. As his cousin Robert Livingston, Jr., put it: "I pray the Almighty to interpose and preserve both them [Parliament] and us in peace & reconciliation . . . least we be both Ruind & become a pray to any daring aspiring Prince in Europe."[8] Many other Americans in those days were convinced that they would remove themselves from the empire only to fall to the French or the Spanish Bourbons. But if the Judge believed that a fighting America would die like Samson, he also came more and more to believe that America might have no choice but to fight. Like his father, Robert of Clermont, he was exhilarated by the news of Lexington and Concord: but exhilaration, for so peaceful a man, was an alien feeling. He soon reverted to his earlier conviction that the fight against English despotism was more important, in a moral sense, than its presumably fatal consequences would be, in a political one. "It is said and generally believed," he wrote, "that the King is determined to subdue us by force[.] he may be convinced that it will [be] far from an easy matter, that if America falls, it will fall like a strong man, and that the

---

* The Quebec Act of May 20, 1774, provided a highly centralized administration for Canada, and was regarded in the Colonies as a move to promote Catholic autocracy; but its most hated feature was that it extended Canada's boundaries to the Ohio, into an area where Connecticut, Virginia, and Massachusetts had claims.

power of Britain will fall with it."[9] This was written on November 15, 1775. He had already been left out of the Commission of Oyer and Terminer—that is to say, suspended from the performance of duties as a judge. Within a month, he was dead.

III

Writing from Belvedere, his Clermont farm, in March, Robert R. Livingston said that he was "sick of politics";[10] and he had been made a delegate to the Provincial Convention in April chiefly through his father's efforts in promoting an election at Rhinebeck. Father and son were together in New York when the Convention met; no doubt the paternal influence was exerted again: but the younger Livingston was qualified to reach the Second Continental Congress on his own. Forensic eloquence, a quick mind, a facile pen, a personality far from self-effacing, a family name famous in earlier Whig politics—these qualities and attributes in the curious ferment of New York, where radicals acquiesced in conservative infiltration, and conservatives strove to adjust themselves to the exuberance of radicals, were quite appropriate. Livingston had already resigned from his Recordership, the only office he had held under the Crown: he now, as a necessary preliminary to taking his seat in the Second Congress, signed the Articles of Association which the First Congress had drawn up. The Articles constituted a set of nonimportation, nonexportation, and nonconsumption agreements, which, with a punitive clause against those who refused to abide by them, were nothing if not revolutionary. Yet among the signers there were many—John Jay is a conspicuous example—who signed for the sake of unity: in other words, because they wished to maintain their franchise in an effort to achieve, not revolution, but reconciliation.

Livingston himself, writing in 1788, gave it as his opinion that there was no thought of independence in the spring of 1775. If he held this opinion at the time, he must have been somewhat disabused when he took his seat in the Congress on May 10: there was a small but active group there which thought of nothing else. The atmosphere was immediately so disturbed and perplexing that he wrote to his father for fresh instructions. The Judge replied that "it is impossible for me to give you directions in the midst of so many sensible and disinterested men."[11] Sensible and disinterested they were, and much more than that; but the majority of them still could not quite bring itself to believe that the revolution had evolved from a long series of antecedent circumstances; that if it had begun, it was irrevocable; that it had already begun. The British Tea Act and Coercive Acts, which were gross threats to American trade and American liberties; the American Articles of Association, which struck such a heavy blow at British industry; Lexington, Concord, the siege of Boston—all these events proved that the ponderous machinery of the mercantilist empire was grinding dryly to a halt, that it lacked the essential lubricants of wisdom, on the one side, and consent, on the other. In July, the Congress voted an Olive-Branch Petition—a curious document which begged the King on the throne to protect America against the King in Parliament. A few days later, however, it publicly announced that Americans had been offered a choice between "unconditional submission to the tyranny of irritated ministers or resistance by force," and that they had chosen the latter.[12] The ties that bound America to the empire were now purely verbal and illusory: resistance was not yet independence, force was not yet revolution. The colonists were at this moment nearly, if not quite, in a state of nature: it has never been a comfortable condition for the sons of men.

By the middle of July, Livingston was at his country farm, Belvedere, complaining to Jay that he detested the thought of returning to a hot room in Philadelphia; nor would he do so, he said, until he found out how long Jay intended to stay there himself. The spirit of Toryism, he continued, was very strong in the Province; a certain Leister was active in Dutchess County and had got several signers to a counter-Association; and to apprehend him might produce a "division among ourselves"—a Whig-Tory battle or civil war—which Livingston confessed he dreaded more than all the power of Great Britain. The thought that weighed much with him, in short, "is one that we cannot mention: the necessity of a serious regard to the affairs of our own province."[13] And, indeed, the condition of the province under its own enfeebled Provincial Congress, with economic conditions pushing the city conservatives toward submission and the city radicals into more and more open revolution, with Loyalism infecting every rural county, was such as might well discourage a moderate landholding Whig. The whole letter breathed discontent and dejection: and its ultimate suggestion, that it would be better to repeal the prohibition against selling tea than ruin some "true friends to Liberty" or bring the laws of the Continental Congress into contempt, was very nearly, if not quite, despair itself. He would not have confided it to any other.

When it was written, moreover, the Livingstons of Clermont were already involved in a series of events that made it impossible for them— emotionally if not rationally—to indulge too immoderately in provincial despair or political moderation. The head of the family, Robert Livingston of Clermont, had always maintained a belligerent attitude toward Parliament. "God grant," he told the Judge in the days of the Stamp Act, "the Parliament will maturely consider Mr. Hampden's case which was only for 20/-[.] what a deluge of blood was spilled in the bowels of the Kingdom. . . . God grant us peace & tranquillity."[14] The prayer for peace imperfectly conceals a taste for war. In the Tea Act crisis, he declared over and over again that it was intolerable that a continent like America should be governed by a small island. "America *must* and *will* be independent," his granddaughter remembers him as saying; although he predicted that neither he nor his son, the Judge, would live to see that day. With the news of Lexington and Concord, "he was in raptures. . . . He seemed to begin life again. His eye had all the fire of youth." But when the story of Bunker Hill, magnified into a tale of irremediable disaster, found its way to Clermont, "he took to his bed immediately: lay a week without pain & died. The last words he uttered were 'What news from Boston?' "[15] Even allowing for the pieties of memory, and of patriotism, one can deduce from these stories that the old gentleman, in death as in life, must have exercised a disturbing influence upon the political moderation of his son and his grandson. Judge Livingston—it was a faintly incongruous occupation for such a man—even started a powder factory before his death.

But what bound the Livingstons to a course altogether at variance with the family reputation for conservatism in 1775 was the fact that the Judge's son-in-law Richard Montgomery was a leader in the Canadian invasion of that year. In the fall of 1774, the First Continental Congress urged the Canadians to join the cause of their fellow colonials; in the winter of 1775, the Boston Committee of Correspondence sent an emissary as far as Montreal; and in May of that year, some New Englanders, under Ethan Allen and Benedict Arnold, seized Crown Point and Ticonderoga and opened an invasion route from the south. After many hesitations, the Second Continental Congress ordered Major General Philip Schuyler to advance toward Montreal: his second in command was Brigadier General Richard Montgomery.

Mongomery was an Irish-born soldier, who had served with the British army at the siege of Louisbourg, in the Lake Champlain campaign, and at the captures of Martinique and Havana. At the close of the Seven Years' War, he was a captain in the 17th Foot; and when his offer to purchase a majority was overlooked and another officer was promoted over his head, he resigned in disgust. He returned to America in 1772, purchased a farm at King's Bridge, New York, and renewed an acquaintance with the Livingstons which he had first made when he was stationed in New York in 1762. On July 24, 1773, he married Janet Livingston, the Judge's eldest daughter, and moved to Rhinebeck, where his wife had a small estate, and where he built a mill and laid the foundations for a house. He came of a family of Anglo-Irish landowners. His elder brother was a member of the Irish House of Commons. His sister was married to an impoverished nobleman named Viscount Ranelagh. He expected to spend the rest of his life as a gentleman farmer, a profession for which he had conceived a more than Virgilian passion.[16]

He was very modest, most attractive, much beloved by his American relatives, and a great friend to the colonial cause. His election to the New York Provincial Congress in April, 1775, was probably gratifying: his appointment by the Second Continental Congress, in June, as one of its eight brigadier generals most certainly was not. The army was then an anomalous entity, the adopted child of anarchy and of perplexity. In whose name was it to act? To what civil authority was it to be subordinated? Moreover, though he was a bold and imaginative soldier, with a rare gift for leadership, he had lost all taste for military command. But he was not the man to refuse a responsibility.

The news of Bunker Hill, which terrified the Whig ladies of New York City and filled the Montgomery lodgings "with a crowd of mournful faces," was quite satisfactory to the new brigadier general. "The experiment has succeeded," he said, in one of his more prescient and less tactful moments. "The Americans will fight."[17] Though a friend to colonial civilians, he never entirely freed himself from the regular officer's prejudice against colonial soldiers: a prejudice that he had some reason to cherish.

The campaign did not open in an auspicious manner for him. He was not sure of Philip Schuyler, in the first place. "His consequence in the Province," he told his brother-in-law, "makes him a fit subject for an important trust—but has he strong *nerves?*"[18] The troops under his command, in the second place, wanted "dexterity in handling arms": he could only hope that they would make up for this in resolution and vigor. This was in August.[19] In October, he complained that they suffered from lack of discipline "and to my sorrow I say it want of spirit. . . . New Englanders, I am now convinced are the worst stuff imaginable for soldiers. . . . I don't see among them that zealous attachment to the cause I flattered myself with—but indeed they are homesick. The first regts of Yorkers is the sweepings of the York streets—and they have not more spirit than the New Englanders—their morals are infamous, and several of them has deserted." Nothing, he was determined, would induce him ever again "to hazard my reputation at the head of such ragamuffins. . . . Would I were at my plough again."[20] The New Yorkers, said Gouverneur Morris, who had found his way to St. John's, "are officered by the vulgar for the most part the soldiers . . . not the cream of the earth but the scum."[21]

The campaign called for an attack by Schuyler and Montgomery upon St. John's and Montreal: after the capture of these places, they would meet with Benedict Arnold, who had been dispatched by a separate route, under the walls of Quebec. The nicest timing, the most resolute and fortunate advance, might have achieved these objectives before winter set in: but Schuyler, growing daily more nervous and despondent, lingered on until September 16 before returning to his headquarters and leaving the command to Montgomery; while Arnold, after a march of extraordinary hardship by way of Maine, reached the Plains of Abraham just too late to make an assault upon Quebec before its garrison was reinforced. He withdrew down the St. Lawrence to wait for Montgomery, who, after capturing St. John's on November 2 and marching unopposed into Montreal on November 13, eventually joined him on December 2.

Both Montgomery and Arnold were dashing and fearless officers; and Montgomery had a way of inspiring affection, even among those who thought it the better part of valor not to stay with him. "Not a sick soldier, officer or deserter," wrote the Judge in November, "that passed through the country these several months but has agreed to praise you wherever they stopped."[22] The letter reached Montgomery as he lay under the walls of Quebec. He was highly pleased with the compliment, he wrote on December 16, but feared he could not return it. "The unhappy passion for going home" had left him and Arnold (he calculated) with only eight hundred effective troops; indeed, it was only by offering a month's pay for re-enlistment that he had been able *"to prevail on a few* to go with me to Mr. Arnold's assistance."[23] The troops that remained were, to be sure, hardened, vigorous, and willing to go wherever they were led, though they had no idea of discipline and Montgomery had small means of enforcing it: but no man would stay once his term of enlistment had expired; Montgomery's light artillery made little impression on the city, whose defenders answered and silenced it with heavier metal; provisions were scanty; it was the dead of winter. Under these circumstances, Quebec would have to be stormed; but under these circumstances, too, the storming of Quebec was almost certainly doomed to failure. Moreover, Montgomery had made the mistake of underestimating his opponent. He was convinced that General Guy Carleton was desperate, and attributed his despair to "wretched politicks and still more despicable military conduct"; whereas Carleton was actually a cool, brave, and tenacious officer, who was determined never to yield and who had inspired what Montgomery described as the "ragamuffins" in his garrison—an unpromising miscellany of sailors, civilians, and a few regular troops—with a resolution equal to his own.[24] But Montgomery was always high-spirited and hopeful in the hour of battle; Arnold, in those days, was of a like mind: and they attacked the city on the river side in the wind and snow of the night of December 30. Arnold, storming the eastward defenses, was immediately and gravely wounded and had to be carried out of the fight: Montgomery, gallantly advancing at the head of his troops against the westward wall, was trapped in a narrow defile and killed.

The last Americans did not leave Canada until June, 1776; but the issue of the campaign had been decided on that fatal night of December 30. It was, however, by no means a fruitless campaign. "If nothing else, Montgomery, Arnold and the northern American army had won time, and a British offensive from the north which might have succeeded at the start of the conflict was doomed to disaster when launched at a later day."[25] In the last letter he is known to have written, Montgomery asked his brother-in-law: "When, my dear Robert shall we meet in peace and ride our favorite Hobby Horse. O rus quando te aspiciam! I most fervently pronounce." He still hoped that the British ministry would not reduce the Americans to the "melancholy necessity" of fixing a date beyond which no reconciliation could occur: he still believed, and believed to his last day, that success in Canada would produce a total change of mind in London. He died, not for independence, but for home rule.[26]

IV

The two brothers-in-law had always been on the best of terms. Their "favorite Hobby Horse" was natural science—the lawyer and the soldier both foresaw for themselves a gentlemanly future of enlightened farming—and Montgomery, in the will that he wrote at Crown Point in the middle of his last campaign, had made Livingston one of his executors. Livingston's letters followed him into Canada: to Livingston, he confided his modest unfounded suspicion that he was not equal to his command. A younger Clermont son, Henry Beekman Livingston, had joined the expedition as a captain, and was present at the fall of St. John's and of Montreal. Brave as a lion, but arrogant, rough, and almost pathologically quarrelsome, Henry Livingston could not bear to serve under men whom he believed to be his inferiors. He wrote to his father to that effect from Montreal, and the Judge appealed to Montgomery. "I would rather advise him," Montgomery replied, "to quit his present corps, and get into a genteeler regiment, should such a one be established"; and he sent him home with dispatches, a tactful dismission, if not exactly a happy one.[27] None the less, his presence in Canada until the middle of November identified the Clermont Livingstons—in their own minds, emotionally, and as a family—with attack and not with reconciliation. It was an identification that the eldest son, when he returned to Philadelphia in September, refrained from carrying into public life. In the October debates, he was still taking the conservative position that the colonial ports should be opened to commerce: for the consequence of too strict a compliance with the Association would be the decay of business, disunion, the belief on all sides that Congress was more oppressive than Parliament. Such at least was the recollection of John Adams.[28] Livingston's own brief notes have him arguing for a strict nonimportation, but for exportation to Ireland and England, as a means of draining specie from the latter. The proposal was, he noted, coolly received: and well it might have been.[29] It was a purely provincial, indeed, a local, solution—an effort to save New York City from drifting into submission to Parliament, on the one hand, and anarchy, on the other, because of economic strangulation.

With the news of the fall of St. John's, he was appointed to a committee of three—the other two members were Robert Treat Paine, of Massachusetts, and John Langdon, of New Hampshire—whose mission it was to confer with General Schuyler at Ticonderoga as to the best methods of supporting the expedition to Canada. It was then to proceed, if possible, into Canada, and persuade its inhabitants to "accede to the association of the United Colonies." Since the inhabitants of Canada were composed of "old subjects," the handful of Englishmen who had gone there after the peace of 1763, and "new subjects," or the original French settlers; since the "new subjects" were divided into a small but powerful group of landlords and churchmen, who were confirmed in their privileges by the Quebec Act, and a large majority of *habitants,* or humble Frenchmen, who had few privileges to confirm; and since the *habitants* were equally suspicious of the Quebec Act and of the invading colonials—the task of bringing them all into the American fold certainly presented some difficulties.[30]

On November 27, the committee of three was huddled around a fire on the icy shores of Lake George, with a single blanket apiece.[31] On November 29, it reached Ticonderoga; and from Ticonderoga, Livingston wrote to Montgomery in a curiously mixed strain—condoling with the General for being in a situation "such as can hardly be borne by a man of any sensibility or feeling—" and inveighing against the rascality of the New York Tories.[32] On November 30, he drew up in his own handwriting the committee's thoughts in an appeal to the Canadians, in which he refers to the British in revolutionary language as "the enemies of the natural rights of man."[33] Whether this argument would have persuaded the Canadians was never discovered, for the committee did not proceed into Canada. "General Schuyler and yourself," Livingston told Montgomery, "have in great measure anticipated our business . . . which we rather decline on account of the advanced season of the year and the improbability of your being able to render us any assistance."[34] On December 6, he was at Albany, where he repeated these arguments in a letter to Jay, adding as a chief and certainly a characteristic reason that "your Committee I am persuaded would not greatly raise the reputation of Congress, nor answer any good purpose among the polished people."[35]

V

On December 15, while the son still lingered at Albany, Judge Livingston died at Clermont. He had been suffering for some time from a low fever, but the symptoms were not alarming, and his wife was away at Rhinebeck, at the bedside of her father, Colonel Beekman, who was slowly and patiently dying of a mortified foot. The Judge used to say that he could never bring himself to utter those words in the Episcopalian litany which ask for God's deliverance from the affliction of sudden death: no other kind, he declared, was more to be wished for. He had his wish: he passed away quietly, unexpectedly, without pain, and "with a pious ejaculation uttered with his usual serenity." He had been suspended from his judicial office at some time toward the end of November, an event that caused him the greatest satisfaction. He left behind him an unfinished essay in which (said his son) he expressed "his warm attachment to his country & the great cause in which we are engaged."[36]

Within nineteen days, Colonel Beekman, too, was dead. Before the end of January, it was known that General Montgomery had perished before Quebec. "A more lasting monument [of him]," wrote Livingston to Lord Ranelagh, "may be found in the breast of every free American and of every friend to the rights of mankind—I ask pardon of your Lordship— the different mediums thro' which the same actions are seen may make that appear criminal on your side of the water which we esteem the highest glory."[37] Thus the household at Clermont was plunged into grief.

VI

Livingston stayed at home for many weeks. He was now the head of the family: "the sudden deaths of three parents and Montgomery," he told James Duane in February, "have made my attention to [their] affairs so necessary that I know not how to quit them for any long time."[38] Besides, he was ill. A low fever, "which has been lurking in my veins for some time," very similar to the one that carried off his father, had convinced his physicians that he should stay at Clermont. The truth seems to have been that he was prostrated by grief; and he later confessed that he was haunted by the thought of not having reached Clermont in time to say good-by to his father. "We may, we must grieve," he said, "when we are not permitted to take leave. It is, I am sensible, a weakness."[39] He endeavored to conceal this weakness from his mother and sisters, who had been thrown into despair by all their losses; and he told Jay that his illness was physical and not nervous. But Jay, who had been convinced in January, on political grounds, that his friend should return to Philadelphia, was now sure, on personal ones, that he must do nothing of the sort. "The state of your health for some time past has given me much anxiety," he wrote in March. "Notwithstanding your letter, I shall expect that your disorder is to be ascribed more to your solicitude than [your] constitution. I well remember that though to appearance not robust, you could endure great fatigue. . . . Don't permit anybody to say a word about your causes, your rents, your farm—nay, for the present avoid even politics, defer joining the Congress, the Assembly, or any other body of men whose object is business."[40] Livingston had been elected to the New York Assembly in February, as the member from Dutchess; but he had been too ill to attend the election, the Assembly was visibly declining into Loyalism, and his friends did not think it would meet, or that his attendance would be necessary.[41] Such was his farewell to a body through which, ten years before, in all the pride of family politics, the Livingstons had aspired to rule the province. It was not until May that he returned to Philadelphia.

CHAPTER TWO

In retrospect, the Revolution appeared to John Adams to have been "complete, in the minds of the people, and the Union of the colonies, before the war commenced in the skirmishes of Concord and Lexington on the 19th of April, 1775." In other words, the Revolution in essence is not to be discovered in any single pronouncement or overt act on the part of the colonials, but, rather (as a modern authority puts it), "in the gradual evolution of their constitutional ideas and program." Until the work of the First Continental Congress was completed in 1774, independence was desired by dreamers and thinkers of a rare and peculiar intensity, such as Samuel Adams: most American patriots asked only for autonomy within the empire, but more and more the autonomy they asked for was one that would give them perfect freedom in all internal and most external matters. When the British ministry made it clear that proposals of this kind were inadmissible, the patriots then took the "logical step" of declaring their independence of the Crown, as they had already (in the First and Second Congresses) virtually declared their independence of Parliament.[1] Such is the retrospective view, not easily disputed.

II

Yet the retrospective view, clear and ever so faintly inhuman in its clarity, may impose order and seemliness upon much that was puzzling, or unpredictable, or merely chaotic to the contemporary one. The politics of New York, for example, at any time between November, 1775, and May, 1776—between the time when Livingston left the Congress in Philadelphia and the time when he returned to it—had, to those who observed them or had to live with them, some of the senseless agitation of a nightmare. While the Loyalists withdrew more and more into silence and conspiracy, or open resistance, the radicals and the conservatives also drew apart from one another, and the patriotic, the iron grasp of the Continental Association seemed to be the means by which this division was being effected.

The second Provincial Congress, like the first, was a self-constituted government in the peculiarly trying position of having to maintain its prestige by carrying through a policy of economic decay. With nonimportation rigidly enforced, and nonexportation becoming effective in September, business came to a halt, and the people were destitute. The Loyalists were sure that this state of affairs would bring with it submission to the Crown; the radicals were no less certain that it was the prelude to revolution and reform; the conservatives were apprehensive, melancholy, and bewildered. And the conservatives, as so often before, had edged themselves into the government, and were, after a fashion, in control of it. No sooner had the second Provincial Congress organized itself, with difficulty, in December than it handed over almost all its powers to a Committee of Public Safety: after which it adjourned on December 22, met again for a month in February and March, and again handed over its powers to a Committee of Public Safety, which sat until the organization of a third Provincial Congress in May.[2]

It is possible now to discern behind these spasmodic movements the controlling force of a steady drift toward independence: it was not so possible to discern it then. The first Committee of Public Safety could not raise a quorum of seven until January 3, 1776: one member protested that his feet were swollen and that he could not wear his shoes, another was afflicted with a "scorbutic complaint," a third (it was Peter R. Livingston, the eldest son of the manor) excused himself because his wife was unwell. And when the Committee did at length produce a quorum, it refrained as far as possible from exercising its powers. Governor Tryon, who had returned in July and removed himself to a warship in the harbor in October, received a steady stream of open sympathizers and, which was worse, of secret information: the royal ships in the harbor were dutifully provisioned, by order of the Provincial Congress. Neither Congress nor Committee could bring itself to utter the dreadful word "rebellion." They labored, therefore, "succeeding, one must admit, wonderfully well, to carry the principle of accommodation to the verge of absurdity."[3]

In mid-January, moreover, the news of Montgomery's disaster and death before Quebec was followed by a report that a British squadron was headed for New York. There was something like a panic in the city, nor was the panic allayed by the news that General Charles Lee was approaching with a Continental army composed, apparently, of twelve hundred Connecticut soldiers. The presence of New Englanders was bad enough in itself: but suppose it provoked the British ships in the harbor

into a bombardment of the city? In its agitation, the Committee of Safety
sent a letter to General Lee, asking him to halt in western Connecticut.
Lee, who had received no authorization from the Continental Congress
for what he was doing, wrote to that body to explain the necessity for an
advance to New York, sent a polite letter to the New York Committee announcing that he would "in deference to their request" enter their city with
a force just strong enough to secure it against any designs of the enemy,
and then became incapacitated with a convenient attack of gout. It was not
until he received a qualified approval from Philadelphia that his health
was restored and he resumed his march. His arrival on February 4 had
a galvanic effect on the ordinary people, who actually began to do something about defense; while the Committee and the Congress—or "that
accursed provincial congress," as Lee called it—could only wring their
hands in agony. Lee cut off communications with Governor Tryon, obtained the support of the militant radicals, and might even have stopped
the flow of supplies to the royal ships if he had not made the mistake of
attempting, at gun's point, to administer loyalty oaths to suspected Tories.
The radicals at once deserted him, protesting—it was the beginning of anti-
Federalism—that this was a rank usurpation of civil and local powers;
the Continental Congress agreed; and Lee was removed from his command
and ordered to Canada. In March, his place was taken by the Earl of Sterling, a gentleman whose title of nobility was a good deal more doubtful than
his patriotism, but whose conservative tendencies no man questioned.
Under Sterling, some effort was made at disarming the Tories on Long
Island, which was the center of danger; a rational plan for supplying
the royal ships—if any such plan, at such a time, could be called rational
—was put into effect; the defenses were strengthened; tensions were
eased: but it was evident that the cautious policy of the Provincial Congress
and its Committee still prevailed.[4]

Two events, one economic and one military, now brought this unhappy
state of affairs to an end. On April 6, the Continental Congress opened
the ports of America to all the non-British world: no longer would the
colonies strangle themselves in the double noose of nonimportation and
nonexportation. This was to nullify the British Navigation Acts, which
bound the mercantilist empire together. This was independence, though
nobody, to be sure, exactly saw it that way in New York. And on April
13, George Washington arrived in the city.

The appearance of this extraordinary man, whom no one could accuse
of an extravagant taste for democracy, but whose stern belief in independence would have satisfied the most demanding radical, was altogether

too much for the Provincial Congress and too much for the Committee of Safety. On April 17, Washington wrote the Committee one of those scathing letters, couched in the politest language, which were among the most potent weapons in his armory of persuasion. The traffic in provisions with the enemy's ships must cease: and the General hoped, indeed he was sure, that the Committee would joyfully assist him in putting it down, "for while such correspondence exists, the reputation of the whole colony will suffer in the eyes of their American brethren." The Committee hastened to thank the General for "your most delicate attention to the civil government of this colony," and by a resolution of April 18 prohibited all inhabitants of the province from having any intercourse whatsoever with the British ships.[5] It had already, on April 17, prevented the Council from visiting Tryon on the *Duchess of Gordon;* Tryon was therefore unable to prorogue the Provincial Assembly; and the Assembly, which had been living a furtive, shadowy existence since the April elections, thereupon vanished from provincial history. Thus all useless formalities, and all efforts at accommodation and compromise with the royal Governor, ceased at the same time: and General Washington's was the magic which had accomplished all this.

But even General Washington's magic, persuasive though it was, could not transform the Provincial Government, all at once, into a revolutionary body. The process was slow, painful, indirect. The elections of April, from which the Loyalists had absented themselves, produced a third Provincial Congress, which not only contained a few inactive Loyalists, but which also—in so far as its active members were concerned—was locked in the old battle between radicals and conservatives. Independence was now, surely, as certain as any future event could be. Yet when should it be declared and by whom? By the Provincial Congress, whenever it thought fit? by the people? by the delegates to the Continental Congress? These questions were still just beginning to be canvassed when Robert R. Livingston at length left his Clermont retreat. He reached Philadelphia in the first week of May.[6]

III

He, too, during his period of mourning and of sickness, had found some difficulty in determining both the course and the speed of events. The Royal Proclamation of August 25, 1775, and the King's Speech of October 26, 1775, had denounced the patriots as rebels and declared that they would be suppressed by force; both the proclamation and the speech were well known in America in January; and yet, with their strident anathemas ringing in his ears, Livingston could still, on February 16, 1776, assure a correspondent in Philadelphia that late advice from England indicated that the ministry had undergone a change of heart. He believed that ministers were preparing to give up the right of taxation, and that they would not consider "our external government of sufficient consequence to make it the subject of a war." This was credulous to the point of oddity; but his conclusion was odder still. "This I know," he said, "that another year of war and devastation will confirm me a republican."[7]

The idea that it would take another year of fighting before one could be brought to admit that one was no longer a subject of the Crown was certainly eccentric: but it is more eccentric to the retrospective mind than it ever was to the contemporary one. Many Americans, even while they admitted that they were virtually independent of Parliament, required direct action from Parliament before they could take the further step of declaring themselves independent of the Crown. A proclamation was only a proclamation; a royal speech only a speech. Parliament was still, for England, the supreme legal authority; and Parliament, though it had legislated directly against single colonies or groups of colonies, had yet to declare the whole thirteen to be outside the pale of British law. It was not until February 27, 1776, that it was known in Philadelphia that Parliament had at length performed this Draconic deed. On that day, the terms of the Prohibitory Bill, which had become an act on December 22, were read and discussed. It interdicted all trade with the American colonies and denounced as rebels and traitors all Americans who did not make a humble and unconditional submission.[8] The Crown was empowered by this act to send commissioners who could enquire into grievances and receive submissions; and there were some who still believed that these dubious Mercuries would carry with them the terms of an accommodation; and who awaited their arrival with unconcealed patience. James Duane, for example, confessed in March that he was "unwilling while Commissioners are daily looked for, we should by any irrevocable measure tie up our hands." But to Livingston, as to almost everyone, the Prohibitory Act was decisive—he remarked sardonically that the only commissioners they could expect were the "34,000 commissioners" of the British and mercenary armies. His retreat at Clermont had to some degree isolated him from the contagion of New York politics. As John Adams said, the Prohibitory Act was "a complete dismemberment of the British Empire"; and so it seemed to the watcher at Clermont. To patriots like John Adams, however, this dismemberment was a triumph, as indeed it was in the history of mankind: but to some it was also a tribulation.[9]

When Livingston arrived in Philadelphia, and was looking about for lodgings and preparing himself (for he was still unwell) to play a valetudinarian role as a delegate to Congress, he already regarded independence as inevitable—an unfortunate and melancholy necessity which justice and common sense alike required him to accept. His reactions in this respect were typical: as a member of one of the great landed families of his province, his reason was still the captive of his provincial past. He was a Livingston first and a revolutionary second; radicals and Tories were equally distasteful to him; and his hesitations were due to the fact that New York was a vulnerable colony, seething with Loyalism, and at the mercy of any really vigorous British attack. To rush precipitately into independence, therefore, while it might be exhilarating for a man with few possessions or none, was dangerous and irrational for a man of wealth. This state of mind was scarcely exciting or subtle or profound: but it existed, it was human, and it is intelligible: and like anything human and intelligible, it is worth examination.

It was complicated by the peculiar position that the Livingstons, as creatures of the past, occupied in the present state of New York affairs. The De Lancey party, the party of rich merchants who dealt directly with England as importers or agents, had foundered on the rock of fair trade; its leaders had scrambled for safety into Loyalism; it had ceased to exist. The Livingston party was only a memory, too; but the memory was charged with echoes of early Whig battles against Parliament and church; and the Livingstons, having chosen the patriot cause, might well be expected to be its leaders. They were, after all, the first political family in the colony.[10] They were not the less suspect for that.

The social relations of the Judge and his family with Governor Tryon, for example, had always been good up to the day that gentleman departed for England in 1774. On his return in June, 1775, the Governor apparently expected that they would continue to be good. He had let it be known that his friend Judge Livingston would never give up his position on the Supreme Court for the sake of his principles, if principles he had. When the Judge, by word and action, informed him that he was totally wrong, the Governor had then, with many opprobrious words, suspended him from his office. But the suspension failed to persuade everyone, and even the family involvement in the Canada expedition was, in some quarters, disregarded as evidence of patriotism. It was well known that Governor Tryon, in his refuge aboard the *Duchess of Gordon,* had received a good

deal of information concerning the plans of the revolutionists and the debates of Congress: who had brought him this information was not so
well known, indeed was not known at all. Many persons were hinted at,
and as late as February, 1776, it was even rumored in New York that
Robert R. Livingston was the man. When this story reached him in Clermont, Livingston dismissed it with contempt. The accusation, he wrote
to Jay, gave him no pain, since it was so palpably absurd. "The little contemptible resentments which Mr. Tryon discovered in suspending my
father from his office, shews that he did not think he had many friends in
this family."[11]

But the absurdity of the accusation only gives additional emphasis to
the ferment which was its source—the deep and excitable suspicion in
which men like Livingston, Jay, and Duane, men who had been born or
had married into the landed gentry, were held by such radical spokesmen
as the leaders of the Mechanics' Committee. They were called oligarchs.
"They will speak fair," said one writer, "they will join the country's cause
so far as will be best, not to go too fast and run into danger. . . . They
will soon . . . subject you to a British tyranny or to a tyranny of oppression
among themselves not much better."[12] It is unlikely that the objects of
these suspicions would be tempted to advance the views of the men
who held them: particularly since the suspicions, like a distorting mirror,
gave back to the moderates an image of themselves that was barely but
frantically recognizable. Talk about British tyranny was nonsense; but
the words "a tyranny of oppression among themselves" still, to the reader
of today, reverberate faintly among the clauses of the New York Constitution which the moderates were soon to write.

Livingston, to be sure, was soon as far removed from the thinking of
James Duane as he was from that of the Mechanics' Committee. There
was another side to the Livingstons' predicament. In New York City, their
social prominence combined with the relative moderation of their views
might make their position an uneasy one; that was by no means the case
in Philadelphia. In Philadelphia, a Livingston would be a desirable ally
to men of moderate views; while to men of militant ones, anxious to stir
New York out of its apathy, he would be no less desirable as a convert.
Within the ranks of Livingston's kinsmen, in and out of Philadelphia,
there were few rivals to dispute his position with him. The great William
Livingston, a member of the Continental Congress until June, was now
identified with New Jersey; William's brother Philip, also a member
of the Congress and eventually a signer of the Declaration of Independence, was often absent in order to attend the New York Congress. In

New York, Peter Van Brugh Livingston, once the hope of the city radicals, had retired from the scene because of ill-health. All these men were brothers of the third Lord of the Manor. The third Lord's eldest son, Peter R. Livingston, a member of the Provincial Congress and heir to the titular headship of the whole clan, was plunged deep in conservatism and deeper still into debt.[13] Moreover, the deaths of his grandfather and father had made Robert R. Livingston the head of a family which, with the acquisition of all the late Colonel Beekman's estates in Dutchess County, was now greatly increased in consequence. And so the leadership of the New York Livingstons, in Philadelphia no less than in New York, passed to the Livingstons of Clermont; and there it remained.

Livingston himself, having acquired for his use and his wife's a set of commodious rooms in Bristol, where he waited in vain for the arrival of Mr. and Mrs. Jay, was inclined at first to take an easy view of his duties in the Congress. His health, he contended, did not allow too much riding to and fro.[14] But the Congress itself had different ideas. The New York delegation was small, and that was all the more reason why so suddenly prominent a member should be put to use. The Continental Congress was on the verge of great events. On May 15, it resolved that colonies with insufficient governments should adopt such forms as they saw fit, since it was "necessary that the exercise of every kind of authority under the ... Crown should be totally suppressed." "This resolution," John Adams wrote long afterward, "I considered as an epocha, a decisive event"; and so it was. "It has occasioned great alarm [in Philadelphia]," Livingston told Jay, "& the cautious folk are very fearful of its being attended with many ill consequences next week when the [Pennsylvania] Assembly are to meet." He approved of it and hoped that New York would form a new government; as, indeed, did Jay, and every man who did not wish to place himself out of the patriotic movement entirely. Or almost every man. On May 18, James Duane could still tell Jay that he hoped New York would not be too precipitate. It was the presence of supremely cautious men like Duane in the New York delegation—men who regarded any kind of movement as precipitate—that made it necessary for Livingston to be pushed forward.[15]

On May 24 and 25, he was appointed to two committees to confer with General Washington, General Horatio Gates, and General Thomas Mifflin. The second committee, of fourteen members, submitted its report on May 29. The report recommended that "an animated address be published, to impress the minds of the people with the necessity of their now stepping forward to save their country, their freedom, and property." Congress liked this proposal, which, in effect, called for a declaration of independence, and appointed a committee of four, with Thomas Jefferson and Samuel Adams as its leading members, to draw one up. But the time was not yet ripe.

From the surviving fragments of Livingston's correspondence at this time, from the *Journals* of the Congress, and from the notes of Thomas Jefferson, it is possible to discern, though with difficulty, the state of mind of the New York delegation. Livingston was now its leader. He had supported the resolutions of May 15, but the *Journals* of the Congress record that he "endorsed," in his own hand, a decision to postpone for three weeks the far more portentous resolutions of June 7; those resolutions in which Richard Henry Lee swept aside, like an old cobweb, all that remained of the great imperial complex: "That these United Colonies are and ought to be, free and independent states, that they are absolved from all allegiance to the British Crown, and that all political connection between them and the State of Great Britain is, and ought to be, totally dissolved."[16]

These words were dynamic, but to a minority of the Congress, they were also deafening. On June 8, Livingston wrote a letter in the name of the whole delegation to the New York Congress, asking for new instructions; nobody, he said, knew how to vote on the resolutions, and some believed they had no right to vote at all. And on June 8 and June 10, when Congress debated the Lee resolutions, Livingston sided with Edward Rutledge, of South Carolina, and James Wilson and John Dickinson, of Pennsylvania, in speaking for caution and delay. According to Jefferson's notes, they argued "That tho' they were friends to the measures themselves, and saw the impossibility that we should ever again be united with Gr. Britain, yet they were against the adopting them at this time." In the elaboration that follows, Jefferson does not tell us which speaker was responsible for any particular argument: but the tenor of the opposition speeches was that the people of the middle colonies were not yet, though very nearly, ripe for independence; that "if the delegates of any particular colony had no power to declare such colony independent, certain they were others could not declare it for them"; and that the colonies would get better terms of alliance with France and Spain "by waiting the event of the present campaign, which we all hoped would be successful" before declaring independence. However vigorous these speeches may have sounded in point of eloquence, they were certainly not forceful; the arguments urged in rebuttal by "J. Adams, [R. H.] Lee, [George] Wythe and others" were cogent, if not unanswerable, and calculated to leave a barb in all but the thickest skin: but in the end it was thought best to postpone a final decision until July 1.[17]

Livingston's appearance among the leaders for postponement offers his memory the solitary consolation that he was now important enough to be a leader: it was not the happiest moment of his career. But one cannot tell what exactly he said; whether he spoke for himself or merely gave the sense of a majority of his small delegation; or to what extent he was bound to wait for the decisions, or, rather, the indecisions, of the New York Congress. On June 13, that body replied to his letter of June 8. It said that it could give its delegates no authority to vote on the question of independence; nor could it request the people of New York to give their sentiments on this enormous subject, because such a request would create divisions and have an unhappy influence on the forthcoming elections. On June 17, writing over his own signature, Livingston replied that the delegates were happy to assure the New York Congress that "we have hitherto taken no steps inconsistent with their intention."[18]

If Livingston had divined the intention of the New York Congress, he was more fortunate in this respect than subsequent historians have ever been. For the past three weeks, the Congress had been lost in what might best be described as an agitated trance, in which decisions and men changed sides with a futile rapidity. On May 24, for example, the aristocratic Gouverneur Morris made himself the spokesman of the Mechanics' Committee and called for a new convention in order to create a new provincial government: this popular motion was opposed by John Morin Scott, who usually aspired to be a popular leader. Morris had his way, a committee was appointed to report on his motion, and on May 27 its report gave the Mechanics everything they wished for. On May 31, this report was amended, so that, while the county committees were given detailed recommendations concerning the time of the elections, there was a certain ambiguity on the vital question of whether or not the electors could issue instructions to the men whom they elected. On June 10, fortified by the return of George Washington, by the news that Virginia had resolved for independence, and by the plan of the Continental Congress to employ nineteen thousand militiamen in Canada and New York, the New York Congress began to debate Livingston's letter of June 8, which had been sent by express. In the course of this debate, John Jay actually introduced a resolution requesting the electors to invest their deputies with the right to declare New York independent. This resolution was adopted. It was then immediately "agreed" not to publish the resolution until after the election. Thus the electorate was not permitted to express itself in a manner that would have been binding both on their own deputies and on the delegation at Philadelphia; and the destinies of the colony were not committed to the emotional seas of Continental debate. If New York had a Continental intention, it was an intention to wait and see: an intention to have no intention. Such was the burden of the letter of June 13.[19]

This Fabian thinking was sufficient, for the New York delegates in Philadelphia did indeed succumb to the wonderful spell. On July 1, when the debate on independence was renewed, they roundly declared that "they were for it themselves & were assured that their constituents were for it." Only their instructions held them back. On July 2, after the close of the first great debate, they sent another urgent message to New York, pleading for positive commands. They never did receive them. The third New York Congress lingered on through June, waiting for the results of the election, and itself slowly yielding to the grip of Washington, of the army, and of history. On June 30, it pronounced New York to be a state; but did so with a subtle nuance which showed that its own independence was somehow unrelated to events in Philadelphia. On June 31, in the absence of Jay, who would have deplored such a move, and at the prompting of Gouverneur Morris, whose mercurial nature had yielded to a fit of discretion, if not of panic, it suddenly adjourned. The reason for this was visible and might soon be palpable. On June 29, in the morning, forty-five British transports and warships—"those murderous queens walking in summer sleep"—had glided into the outer harbor; by nightfall, the number had increased to one hundred and ten; "and more were to be seen about dusk in the offing."[20]

The third New York Congress announced, on adjournment, that it would meet again in White Plains on July 2, there to await the organization of the fourth Congress, planned for July 8. The third Congress never met again. On July 4, as on July 2, its delegates in Philadelphia were left without a vote.

IV

One curious circumstance arose from the abortive debates of June 8 and June 10. On June 11, Robert R. Livingston was appointed to the committee of five that was to draw up a declaration of independence: the committee whose other four members were Thomas Jefferson, John Adams, Benjamin Franklin, and Roger Sherman.

"I think he had one more vote than any other," John Adams wrote concerning Thomas Jefferson, "and that placed him at the head of the

committee. I had the next highest number, and that placed me second."
Jefferson's reputation for "literature, science, and a happy talent for
composition" had preceded him to Congress, where, though a silent
member on the floor, he was prompt, frank, explicit, and decisive in his
committees. "Not even Samuel Adams was more so." He was thirty-three,
"so young a man"; so inspired a choice.[21] Adams, says Benjamin Rush, was
the first man in Congress: the most learned, the most eloquent; he "spoke
like an angel let down into the convention to illumine the assembly."[22]
As with Adams, so with Franklin, the choice was not so much inspired as
foreordained. Sherman was a Connecticut puritan "as firm in the cause of
American Independence as Mount Atlas." If there was an Atlas in Livingston's composition at this time, it had been submerged by the instructions
of his own Congress. It may have shown itself—it is quite likely that
it did—in his private conversations: but he was appointed to the committee, presumably, to represent a minority or to commit New York.
He himself never made in his later writings, nor did the recorded
memories of any other man, any allusion to his labors in the Congress or
his experiences in this committee; the subject vanished forever, like a stone
thrown into the waters. Whether the committee first discussed the subject, and then appointed a subcommittee, composed of Jefferson and
Adams, or whether it "unanimously," and without discussion, "pressed
on [Jefferson] alone to undertake the draught"—these are questions upon
which Adams and Jefferson disagreed in their old age, and the correct
answer has never been found. What is certain is that Adams and Franklin alone emended Jefferson's draft: when it was reported to the full committee, no further alterations were made. "We were all in haste." Thus
fame evaded Livingston on this unique occasion, as it did Sherman. To have
sat in silence among the immortals is a memory from which few men—
and those unduly gifted with modesty or serenity—would extract any
gratification: and Livingston certainly was not the man to do so. His later
reticence speaks for itself.[23]

V

He had been elected to the fourth New York Congress, or Convention,
as it soon called itself, as a member from Dutchess County.[24] The Convention was to meet on July 8; a copy of the Declaration of Independence
was accordingly dispatched in its direction; and its first object—it could
have no other—was to approve the Declaration and thus bring the colony
of New York into line with all the rest. On July 6, Livingston was still

in Philadelphia. "The Congress," he wrote John Jay on this day, "have done me the honour to refuse to let me go—I will however apply again today—I thank God I have been the happy means of falling on a[n] expedient which will call out the whole militia of this country [*i.e.,* Pennsylvania] in a few days—tho' the Congress had lost hope of it from [an] unhappy dispute & other causes with which I will acquaint you in a few days." He had just received Jay's letter, telling him of the Congress's undignified removal to White Plains: he was extremely mortified. "I think as you do on the subject," he wrote. "If my fears on account of your health would permit I shd request you never to leave that volatile politician [Gouverneur Morris] a moment."[25]

On the next day, he set out for White Plains to take his seat in the Convention; but the Convention, meeting on July 9, while he was still on the road, passed a unanimous resolution approving the Declaration of Independence. As at Philadelphia, so at White Plains, he had no chance to record his vote. When the Declaration of Independence was signed at Philadelphia on August 2, he was deeply immersed in the business of local defense.[26] Philip Livingston signed for the family.

CHAPTER THREE

Robert R. Livingston's mother, Margaret Beekman Livingston, wrote
him a letter from Clermont on July 6, 1776, and addressed it to
Philadelphia.

Whether this will ever meet your Eye [she wrote], I can't tell, I hope
it may—God only knows what will be the End of these troubles, I fear
much for your safety—I Beg and Entreat you for my, and my Childrens
sake, that you do not cross at Powlas [Paulus] Hook Ferry—the Enemy
may have you before you are aware, & we shall be miserable. . . . We are
here I fear in some danger from the Tories.

And she went on to describe the activities of "four thousand" Tories
or Loyalists, who had been hiding in the woods at Staatsburg and roving
through the Little Nine Partners in Dutchess County, intimidating and
disarming patriots, and who were now pursued by "1200" armed men.
Thus pursued, they had vanished, spiriting away with them "a Congress
member," whose name was unknown but who was said to live near
Poughkeepsie.[1]

II

In the light or twilight of such a letter as this, so full of improbable
statistics and untraceable rumors, with the kidnaped congressman as a final
touch, a letter written, moreover, by a lady who was rarely intimidated by
anything, the almost wanton prudence of the conservative patriots in
the New York Congress becomes intelligible. The whole colony was disaffected, from the patriots' point of view no less than from that of the
Loyalists or the British. The disaffection of the Loyalists was obvious,
in the sense that it was the disaffection of men who called themselves
loyal to Crown and Empire; but in rural areas, such as Dutchess County,
where Crown and Empire counted for little, did not this disaffection take
the form of an antirent movement, a fearful threat to property? And then,
from the conservative point of view, there was another kind of disaffection, which the conservatives themselves could not acknowledge with

propriety, and which was much more insidious—the disaffection of the radicals, who considered themselves revolutionaries, and who hoped to bring into the aristocratic composition of the colony the vital and transforming leaven of democracy.

The conservatives employed, with conviction and sincerity, the word "revolution" to describe the situation that had arisen from their disagreements with Parliament and had ended with their repudiation of the Crown: but it was revolution reduced *ad absurdum*, revolution standing on its head. In 1800, the Reverend Samuel Miller, of New York City, was rebuked by John Jay because, in the course of a sermon on the death of George Washington, he had referred to "our glorious emancipation from Britain." What intemperate language! If he would but consult the statements of the Continental Congresses of 1774 and 1775, said Jay severely, Mr. Miller would discover that the Congresses had "regarded the People of this Country as being *Free*," and had decided to fight only when Britain "recurred to arms to put a Yoke upon us."[2] This was the conservatives' position: the position of John Jay, of Judge Livingston, before his death, of the Judge's eldest son, of scores of prominent and patriotic New Yorkers. They had gone into the Revolution in defense of old liberties, not in search of new ones; they were determined to win their independence because it had been forced upon them; the British, and not they, were the revolutionaries.

Of all the different pressures that forced them over the brink in June —the radicals, the grave Roman conscience of George Washington, the presence of the Continental army, the hostile Loyalists, the approaching British—the British constituted the most compelling one. They had attempted to maintain the empire *vi et armis*, which was tantamount to dissolving it; and in the course of dissolving it, they had aroused the fury of the Loyalists and the hopes of the radicals. Next to independence lost, what the conservatives most feared, it has been hinted, was independence gained. But this is not so: what they most feared was independence running amok. They hoped, but they could not be sure, that in the New York Convention they could tame the dangerous creature.

III

Robert R. Livingston reached White Plains on July 15, 1776, and took his oath of secrecy and his seat in the Convention.[3] It had already endorsed the Declaration of Independence, in four resolutions which had been written by John Jay: but the influence of John Jay was by no means so strong in this body as in the previous one. It is generally agreed that the Convention was, as to the majority of its members, a more radical entity than the third New York Congress. A Livingston of Clermont might, therefore, be expected to approach it, and to be received by it, with a certain uneasiness.[4]

But the speedy reconciliation of opposing views in the Convention was made possible, was in fact determined, by the fearful circumstances in which the Convention met. General William Howe's troops lay in their cantonments on Staten Island; Admiral Richard Howe's navy sailed in on July 12; the City of New York was indefensible and was guarded by a deficient army; the forts on the Hudson were too weak to prevent the enemy's sailing up the river; a thrust toward Albany by General Howe would be met by a thrust down from Canada by General Carleton, before whom Schuyler and Gates were slowly retreating; the overrunning of New York—by routes that led through rich communities and fruitful cultivated lands, all deeply infected with Loyalism—would be the inevitable result. All this, to be sure, was contingent upon one essential and, as it turned out, nonexistent factor—British resolution: but nobody knew this at the time.[5]

Under these circumstances, unity, or the semblance of unity, was imperative. Moreover, the presence of aristocrats as leaders or would-be leaders in the Convention was testimony—if anyone cared to see it that way—to the depths of colonial history out of which the Convention had, after so many changes, finally evolved; in the distant New York past was it not the aristocratic assemblies that had fought with and wrested power from the royal governors? And men like Livingston, Jay, and even young Gouverneur Morris were able lawyers and passed for a highly educated elite, at a time when the thinking of the Convention as a whole was more likely to be energetic than coherent. One of the purposes of the fourth New York Congress was to form a new government for New York—that is why it changed its name from congress to convention; and when a committee was appointed to draft a constitution, it was only common sense that Jay, Livingston, and Morris should be placed upon it, and only rational caution that they should be surrounded by a radical majority, which chose its own chairman in Abraham Yates. Thus conservative talents could be employed for radical ends; or so it appeared at the time, though not in the outcome.

The committee was appointed on August 1, 1776, but its members were too busy to get to work at once.[6] As Gilbert Livingston and Christopher Tappen put it (they were building vessels for the Convention at

Poughkeepsie), "it would be well to secure a State to govern, before they discussed a form to govern it by."[7] Soon after his arrival, Robert R. Livingston had been set to work on a secret committee, whose object was to supervise the fortifications of the Hudson—a task for which he was peculiarly unfitted but which, in that civilian atmosphere, he performed with small misgiving. On August 12, the Convention wrote a letter to him and to Jay, requesting their immediate return, since the draft of a plan of government must be ready by August 26; but August 26 passed, October 12 (the next date set) passed, months passed, and still the report had not been prepared. Committee work of all kinds, by which the Convention carried out its duties as a temporary government, absorbed every man's attention and energy. On August 27, when Livingston at last became free of his fortifications, he was supposed to form, with John Sloss Hobart, a committee of two to wait upon General Washington "on Nassau [Long] Island," to confer with that great man on measures to distress the enemy and defend the inhabitants of the island. Precisely what advice two gentlemen totally unversed in military affairs could have given the Commander in Chief at a very critical moment was never revealed for the instruction of posterity; for by August 28, the Battle of Long Island had begun, and the General had something else to think about.[8]

On August 28, Livingston moved that the Convention retreat to Fishkill, since it was manifestly in danger of being captured if it remained in White Plains a day longer than was necessary, and this prudent motion was adopted. Washington, meanwhile, having withdrawn his defeated army to New York, reluctantly abandoned the city on September 12, and General Howe moved in. On September 15, there took place the "disgraceful and dastardly" retreat—the words are George Washington's—to Harlem Heights; on September 16, after some gallant and redeeming resistance on the part of the Americans, this position was secured; on September 17, the Convention appointed a Committee of Correspondence, of which Livingston and William Duer were the active members, with instructions to establish post riders between Fishkill and headquarters, write letters, and obtain intelligence. Thus it maintained a connection with the flux of military events.[9]

IV

The temptation to interfere in military events is, for most amateurs, difficult to resist: when they have been instructed to interfere, when the temptation becomes a duty, one can hardly blame them if they succumb to it.

Livingston, undeterred by a familiarity with military science that probably extended no farther than the campaigns of Julius Caesar and the events of the Peloponnesian War, found, as did other civilians, no difficulty in writing "pretty freely" to General Washington. The necessity of sinking blocks in the Hudson, which he thought would have secured the river against the whole British navy, struck him forcibly; indeed, he believed that the General was inclined to it; but it was overruled at headquarters. He then became eloquent on the subject of magazines and stores to be laid up "on this side of the [Hudson River] Highlands" unless head-quarters intended to gamble everything on the event of a single battle.[10] George Washington received this advice just as he was preparing to retreat from Harlem Heights to White Plains; and he was obliged to wait, he said, until he had executed this dangerous and necessary maneuver before replying. The reply, though evasive, was certainly flattering. "I thank you for any hints you may be pleased to communicate as I have great reliance upon your judgment and knowledge of the country (which I wish to God I was as much master of.)" Washington's dependence upon civilian aid and good will extracted from his character, outwardly so cold and unbending, every ounce of that tact and modesty which formed so unexpected a part of its extraordinary composition: no civilian could be blamed for taking the General at his word. In return, he begged Livingston to use his influence to send provisions to White Plains: he wanted flour, he wanted beef, he needed a number of teams to aid in removing the army should it be necessary. "In short, Sir, our situation is really distressing."[11] In truth, it was desperate. The army was sick, ill-fed, ill-clothed, homesick, discouraged, and on the verge of dissolution: the roads were busy with soldiers returning home; there could be no recruiting because no commis-sioners had come from the states to nominate officers for that purpose.[12] Washington's faithful aide and friend Tench Tilghman told Livingston on November 6 that they had done well to "stop the career of Monsr. Howe with the finest army that ever appeared opposed to as bad a one as ever appeared in any part of the Globe." Meanwhile, Howe had van-ished, said Tilghman, perhaps into winter quarters, perhaps up the North River road. On the next day, he wrote that Howe was probably moving into New Jersey; but that three thousand troops had been dispatched toward the strategic Highlands, the gateway to Albany, in case he should be taking the northern route. Livingston replied on November 9 with the suggestion that Forts Washington and Lee might not prove to be very useful—a prediction that turned out to be correct—and that their stores and cannon could be employed to advantage in the Highlands.[13] And so the

Committee of Correspondence continued to correspond until Washington's army, withdrawing to New Jersey and to fame in that fateful winter, passed beyond its reach.

The stream of military advice and strategical comment flowing between the civilian and the military headquarters has an almost frivolous appearance until one remembers that every man, or almost every man, civilian or soldier, was a desperate amateur engaged in upholding a cause that he believed to be cardinal—one of the great hinges of his time—"the cause of Liberty," no matter what interpretation he put upon the word "liberty." In the fall and winter of 1776, the cause was in terrible straits: it was held together by the ineptitude of the British and by the ability of the Americans, somehow or other, to maintain the semblance of armies and governments. It was as much Livingston's duty to pepper soldiers like Washington with advice as it was Washington's duty to maintain contact with civilians like Livingston. All together, in their several ways, heroic or administrative, as soldiers or as managers, they held off the British and saved New York for the Revolution.

But while he pursued the problems of defense—now conferring with Generals Charles Lee and William Heath at Peekskill and at North Castle, now joining a committee at Albany that was to co-operate with General Schuyler in measures to repel invasion on the northern frontier, now reporting to the Committee of Safety his views as to the enemy's intentions, or discussing the obstruction of the Hudson at Popolopen Kill with General George Clinton, or simply "riding about the country counteracting the schemes of the Tories," it was not in such activities as these, absorbing though they were, that Livingston's inner nature expressed itself.[14] He did his duty as he saw it: but this is not a record of military events.

As so often in Livingston's career, it is a record of withdrawal—not indeed from duty, but from the distressing environment of duty: from having to work with people whom he considered unfitted for the work to be done. Time and time again, this disposition, which, whatever else it may have been, was certainly not calculated to ease his way in the political world, came into conflict with a laudable ambition for service and for fame. On September 23, his friend Edward Rutledge, of South Carolina, wrote him a letter from the Congress in Philadelphia, requesting that he or Jay return there immediately. Nothing less than the salvation of the country, said Rutledge, a temperamental young man of extremely conservative views, depended upon their presence.[15] Livingston told Schuyler that he could guess the reasons for Rutledge's alarm—though he did not, unfortunately, commit his guess to paper: and on October 10, after due consideration, he sat down to write a reply.

You little know, my dear Edward [he began], the state of this colony when you press Jay and me so warmly to quit it and take our seats in Congress. . . . Every thing is at stake here—*two thirds of our gentlemen fell off early in this controversy,* the stagnation of our trade, and the large openings to wealth in the Eastern States have taken from us the few merchants who have been hitherto supports to the cause of Liberty.

Even Gouverneur Morris, from some cause or other, had deserted them in this critical hour and "retired to some obscure corner of the Jerseys, where he enjoys his jest and his ease while his friends are struggling with every difficulty and danger." Livingston's wife, mother, and sisters at Clermont were in an "exposed situation," exposed, that is, to an uprising in Dutchess County, which was daily expected. A plot had been formed—"it was headed by a relation"—to carry Livingston off, and it was defeated only by a discovery on the very night it was to have been executed. Bullets had been shot at night into the beds of some of the more active patriots; other men had been fired at and wounded on the public roads around Fishkill.

The letter to Rutledge was despondent, but its despondency was due, not only to the immediate state of New York's affairs, which was perilous, but also to their tendency, which was democratic. A government was to be formed, Livingston continued, under which New Yorkers were to spend the rest of their lives "without that influence that is derived from respect to old families wealth age etc," a government that would have to contend with the envy or the love of power of people, who showed

that mixture of jealousy and cunning into which Genius long occupied in trifles generally degenerates when unimproved by education and unrefined by honor. . . . Believe me there is a greater mixture of intrigue, artifice and address in the [Convention] of N.Y. than in a conclave of cardinals.

He was "sick of politics and power"; longed for "more refined pleasures, conversation and friendship"; was weary of crowds; "nor would in my present humor give one scene of Shakespeare for a 1000 Harringtons, Lockes, Sidneys, and Adams to boot." (From this it would seem that the work of drafting a constitution for New York had begun, and that John Adams's *Thoughts on Government* was already part of the required reading.)[16]

"My present humor," although it was rather more than a humor, passed; the pose, and it was partly a pose, was abandoned: only to return again and again through the many phases of a long, active, and distinguished career. At this stage, it is clear that the presence of fellow delegates, whose lack of polish seems to us somehow exhilarating, did not have precisely that effect upon Livingston; that he was, to say the least, uneasy in political circles "unimproved by education and unrefined by honor." But on a predicament such as this, the commonplaces of the retrospective judgment are best left unuttered. One has simply to remark how difficult it was for a man brought up in the politics of privilege to adjust himself all at once to the politics of opportunity.

V

The report on the Constitution was ready on March 12; debate was begun on March 13; but the pressure of business postponed discussion until March 20. There are two drafts among the papers of the Convention; neither is in Jay's handwriting; and the incomplete draft in the Yates Papers is in the handwriting of Yates and of Livingston. Handwriting is, needless to say, inconclusive as to authorship in a case like this: it is generally agreed that Jay played a leading role in the writing of the New York Constitution and that Livingston and Morris were his chief advisers.[17]

In this way—and it was surely an ironical comment on earlier colonial battles—the draft was committed to the tender mercies of King's College. The radical Yale College, in the person of that forceful graduate John Morin Scott, seems to have left no mark upon it: Scott was presumably too busy, and possibly too unwelcome. But Jay, Livingston, and Morris were all reputed to be brilliant and learned men. They were all familiar with Pufendorf and Grotius, to the extent, at least, that Pufendorf and Grotius were studied in the final year at King's.[18] They knew their Blackstone, from whom (though a Tory) American Whigs extracted much comforting political theory. We may assume, without doing violence to probability, that they had read and studied Montesquieu and Locke.[19] And they had Adams's *Thoughts on Government* to guide them: its orderly features, somewhat disguised and occasionally disfigured, can be observed among the articles of the New York Constitution.[20] A Convention distracted by other business—"the suppression of the Tories, the equipping and mustering of the militia, the withdrawal of the patriots from the southern counties as the British advanced"—in short, by the necessity of being not only a convention but also a government—naturally, one might say inevitably, resigned the business of drafting a constitution into the ablest and most willing hands.

The Convention had removed from Fishkill in February. At Kingston, beyond the Highlands, in radical Ulster County, it settled down in circumstances of some discomfort. Its chamber was situated above a jail, whose "disagreeable effluvia" the members attempted to dispel with clouds of tobacco smoke.[21] Here, from March 20 to April 20, they debated the draft which had been submitted to them.

Not many changes or additions were made. The members were busy, quorums were sometimes hard to find, and the laconic character of the entries in the *Journals of the Provincial Congress* gives the impression—possibly a false one—that the debates were desultory at best. Since the votes were recorded by counties and not individually, it is difficult to guess, and wrong to try to guess, what each member thought on any given question. Under these circumstances, it would be more judicious to inquire how far the New York Constitution, as it emerged from deliberations at Kingston, fulfilled or disappointed what one might call the normal expectations of constitutional theory at that time.

These expectations were: that the legislature should be representative, that the legislature should be qualified in its power by the doctrines of separation of powers and of checks and balances, that the suffrage should be exercised by males of full age who held property or paid taxes, and that a written constitution should contain a bill of rights.

Within these expectations, there was, it must be admitted, a good deal of freedom for maneuver and compromise: it was a freedom of which the New York Constitution took every advantage. It offered a government in which the legislature was one of three separate powers in a government of checks and balances. But the legislature was composed of two chambers—a popularly elected Assembly, and a far less popularly elected Senate. Although the whole Declaration of Independence was made a part of the Constitution, the principle of natural equality was given no undue prominence in its provisions. Few men, it is true, would have championed universal male suffrage in those days: almost everyone agreed that the voter must have some stake in society. In this respect, the Assembly of New York was a democratic entity. All £20 freeholders or renters of tenements worth forty shillings a year could vote for assemblymen, as could also—and this took care of the merchants, tradesmen, and independent artisans—all freemen of New York and Albany. Since tenant farmers who were not merely tenants at will usually came within the term "freeholder," and since they usually paid their rents in kind, their right to vote depended upon the price of wheat: it is fair to assert that, if wheat were not abnormally low, most tenant farmers could vote. For the Senate, on the other hand, only £100 freeholders, whose freeholds were clear of all encumbrances, could vote:

this was a very strict interpretation of the "stake in society" principle; and, since the twenty-four senators were also required to be £100 freeholders, the Senate was transformed into a stronghold of the landed interest. On the other hand, an amendment (moved, strange to relate, by John Jay, and vigorously and vainly protested by Gouverneur Morris) substituted ballot voting for viva voce voting; and it was through viva voce voting that landlords in colonial days had maintained their ascendency over their tenants.

The executive branch of the government retained the governor and the lieutenant governor from colonial days, but subjected them to the ordeal of election. The governor and his lieutenant, however, had to be £100 freeholders, and only £100 freeholders could vote for them. The governor was to serve for three years, which gave him an unusual strength; but his strength was modified by two ingenious and, on the whole, mischievous provisions. His appointing powers were to be exercised by a Council of Appointment, in which he held the casting vote, and his veto powers were undertaken by a Council of Revision, of which he was merely a member.

The Council of Appointment was composed of the governor and four senators, one from each of the four districts, and these senators, in turn, were elected by the Assembly. In this way, if the governor commanded a majority of supporters in the Assembly, he was sure of getting the Council he wanted, and would be in control of an immense patronage. But if there was a majority in the Assembly hostile to him, his Council would become a focus for intrigue and dissension.

The Council of Revision was no less ingenious and perhaps it was more mischievous than the Council of Appointment. It was composed of the governor, the chancellor, who presided over a court of equity, and the justices of the Supreme Court. It had the right to veto bills within ten days of getting possession of them; its right could be exercised by a quorum; and its veto could be overruled only by a two-thirds majority in both houses. It was proposed by Livingston on April 1, as an amendment that would improve upon the governor's power of veto: and all through his life he contended that this had been his great contribution to the new government. The Council could veto bills that were simply inexpedient as well as bills that were or seemed to be unconstitutional; this gave the chancellor and the judges a right to interfere in legislation; and what then became of the doctrine of separation of powers? The doctrine of checks and balances, needless to say, did a little too well out of the Council of Appointment.

The judiciary maintained, in its glory, the old colonial "hierarchy" of courts—Supreme Court, Chancery Court, Admiralty, County and Probate courts. One new court, the Court for the Trial of Impeachments and Correction of Errors, was created: it was composed of the president of the Senate, the chancellor, the Supreme Court justices, and all the senators. The Assembly had the impeaching power. The judiciary, traditionally a friend to the landed interest, was made independent by permission to hold office during good behavior and up to the age of sixty.

Between conservatism and originality there exists, in politics if not in art or manners, an inverse ratio: the more of the former, the less of the latter. The New York Government of 1777 was far from original. The common and statute law of England and the acts of the colonial Legislature in force on April 19, 1775, were to be the law of the new state. More could not have been expected from judicious minds working in a hurry: more, indeed, might have been dangerous. Between conservative purpose and originality, however, the ratio is not only inverse but blatantly so. Thus, the Constitution provided that nothing in it was to be construed as affecting grants of lands made by the King before October 14, 1775, and that no charters granted by him were to be voided because of nonuser or misuser since April 19, 1775. The old land system had emerged intact; even primogeniture and quitrents were left for future legislation; and the worst fears of the New York aristocrats were at once dispelled. With a strong Senate, a strong judiciary, an unregenerate land system, it was not likely that the Revolution would get entirely out of their control.

Bill of rights there was none: only the traces, here and there, of what might one day become a bill of rights. The Declaration of Independence, incorporated in full, uttered its majestic promises and denunciations; the thirteenth article hinted at "due process of law"; provision was made for trial by jury; court procedure was based on common law; freedom of conscience was upheld, though ministers of religion might not be elected to office. Freedom of conscience was, indeed, attacked by John Jay, whose Huguenot imagination readily discerned an equation between Catholicism and conspiracy: he proposed an amendment that would deny civil rights to the church of Rome unless its representatives swore in the Supreme Court that no priest, pope, or foreign authority had the right to absolve the subjects of New York from their allegiance. This might not have troubled the church's representatives so much as his second suggestion—that they should also renounce the dogma that priests had the power to absolve men of sins—"a false, wicked, dangerous and damnable doctrine," said Jay. He was supported in this singular diatribe by Ulster, Orange, and Tryon counties: but Albany, New York, and Dutchess, led by Gouverneur Morris, easily defeated him. Morris was addicted to deism ("Foolish Deism," wrote the Reverend John Henry Livingston to his kinsman, "is perhaps now as characteristic as Bigotry once was"[22]), and was not disturbed by sectarian differences: the leveling tendencies of the ballot, particularly in the election of senators, seemed to him a more dangerous engine of disorder than the church of Rome. In the end, Morris had his way.

If one places this Constitution, or attempts to place it, in the contexts of conservative and of liberal preference, in which of the two does it seem more at home? The conservatives did not want a strong governor—they had been draining the strength from governors throughout their colonial past; they did not want a strong legislature if there was to be found anywhere in its formation the influence of the small freeholder; they were disposed toward a strong judiciary, since the law, in their experience, was always on the side of property; they liked their government to be complex and slow to act. The radicals feared a strong governor, and wanted, above all things, a strong popular legislature: for this reason, they favored annual elections, male taxpayer suffrage, and no property qualifications for officeholders, as well as a simple government. On the whole, the New York Constitution fits snugly into a conservative context: it should have given little comfort to the radicals.

And yet it was accepted, with little debate, by an ultrademocratic convention, and in the midst of a revolution. How can this have come about? The preoccupations of the delegates and the extremely perilous situation in which they found themselves may have had something to do with it: better any government than none. But this could not have been the decisive factor. Against the background of revolution, the document has an odd look. It remains only to ask into what kind of revolution it best fitted: or, rather, with what interpretation of the American Revolution was it most compatible. With the Revolution considered as something violently engineered by a small but vigorous minority? with the Revolution seen as the outcome of a general consensus, in which the differences were political rather than theoretical? with the Revolution as a method of exploiting the people, by making a few concessions to them; the Thermidor of a cunning bourgeoisie and a clever aristocracy? The New York Constitution fits in with the theory of consensus and the theory of exploitation. The New York conservatives had managed the radical Revolution so that, while it rid them of Parliament, it did not deprive them of privilege. But why did the revolutionaries allow themselves to be managed? Aristocracy can persuade as well as exploit. If the New York colonial landlords had robbed their tenants, they had also resisted Parliament: if they had lived by privilege, they had fought prerogative. They carried their past into the Convention like some spell—suspect, dangerous, but potent. The New York democracy was reluctantly captivated by the magic of a history which it only in part detested; and accepted, in constitutional form, a way of life it proposed to change politically. Moreover, the Constitution was compact, well-written, fertile in compromise, and apparently not in conflict with accepted theory— or in conflict only to the point where it dissatisfied but did not actually outrage radical opinion. In short, a long history of aristocratic rule can paralyze as well as provoke opposition, if the representatives of the aristocrats are still to be found on the side of the revolution.

The Constitution was accepted on April 20, with only one dissenting vote—that of Peter R. Livingston, heir to the Manor of Livingston, who found it dangerously radical. The manner of its acceptance contains the final paradox: though it expressly stated that its authority was derived from the people, it was not submitted to the people's vote. On the same day, a committee was appointed for the organization of the new government. Its members were Livingston, Jay, Hobart, Morris, John Morin Scott, and Abraham Yates—a conservative majority of three to two. It issued a report that the Convention itself should proceed to appoint the judges, the chancellor, the attorney general, the sheriffs, and the county clerks; the report was approved on April 29; and on May 3, the Convention elected John Jay chief justice of the Supreme Court over John Morin Scott by a vote of 19 to 15. On the same day, it made Robert R. Livingston chancellor of the State of New York by a vote of 21 to 15 over the same antagonist.[23] He was now an integral part of a highly conservative government—so conservative that young Alexander Hamilton, although he thought it "the best that we have yet seen," complained to Livingston that "Your Senate . . . will be liable to degenerate into a body purely aristocratical."[24] The cornerstone had, however, still to be hoisted into its place: it was necessary to elect a governor. But first, since the election was not to be held until the middle of June, and the new government was not expected to meet until September, it was thought best to appoint a Council of Safety, composed of leading men of all shades of opinion: of this body of fifteen, which was to perform the functions of a temporary government, Chancellor Livingston was made a member.[25]

He was certainly now in a position to influence the choice of candidates; but it was not until June that he realized that his influence might not count for much. Early in May, the conservatives were so sure of themselves that Jay had modestly (and, to be sure, quite genuinely) told the radical Abraham Yates that he had no wish to be governor. The conservatives then turned to Philip Livingston, the old "rough rapid mortal" of John Adams's memory, who still sat in the Continental Congress, despite his ill health and the protests of his immediate family, and who was anxious for higher office. But "politicks have taken a strange turn here," Chancellor Livingston wrote to William Duer on June 12; it seemed that objections were being made to "the impropriety of having two brother Governors"—William Livingston, Philip's brother, was soon to be governor of New Jersey—and this "made it absolutely necessary to change our battery or see our Government drowned in a sea of grog." In other words, if they persisted in the support of Philip Livingston, they would lose the election to Brigadier General John Morin Scott, or "General Shoulders," as the Chancellor preferred to call him, whose drinking habits were notorious.[26]

"Schuyler has consented to take it upon him," the Chancellor continued, "and I am in great hopes that he will be elected. I am fearful that our friend Mr. Livingston will find himself hurt at this, but were he here he would acknowledge the propriety of swimming with a stream, which it is impossible to stem. I saw when at Philadelphia what has since happened; & Wilson will remember that I long ago advised that they should yield to the torrent if they hoped to direct its course."

It was, perhaps, a little optimistic to hope that the torrent would sweep such a personage as Philip Schuyler into the governorship. No man was so quick to resent a slight or a familiarity; no man more rigidly preserved, except in his own set, which was a very narrow one, the appearance of unbending pride. His manners provoked the wildest suspicions; in 1776, for example, when he was major general in command of the Northern Department, it was rumored that he held a commission in the British army.[27] His recall in March at the hands of an Eastern clique and his return in May had to some extent restored his prestige and popularity; but even the £100 freeholders might have hesitated before they elected such a man.

The details of the remote contest are beyond recovery: there were no formal nominations and no stump speeches, no campaign and no parties; men wrote letters to the press or corresponded vaguely among themselves. In the end, by one means or another, the choice was confined to three candidates: Philip Schuyler, George Clinton, and the indefatigable John Morin Scott. Scott was an able and well-to-do lawyer, with a taste for elegance which had once astonished John Adams, a leaning toward radicalism which often threatened to become extreme, a ready tongue, and an undignified manner. His patriotism was far less exceptionable than his deportment: he had served as a brigadier general of militia in 1776 and the early months of 1777; and in the course of his military duties had contracted the rheumatism that afterward killed him.[28] He yearned for office:

to be chief justice, to be chancellor, to be governor. In the June elections, as usual, he was outvoted; and the governorship went to George Clinton, after a fairly close race with Philip Schuyler.[29]

The choice of George Clinton came as a shock to the Chancellor and his friends: the torrent had, after all, refused to be directed. There is a charming family tradition that relates how the Livingstons and their allies gathered at Clermont, before the election, to discuss their choice of a candidate, and how Margaret Beekman Livingston resolved their indecisions by suggesting that Clinton should be their man. As the Chancellor's letter to Duer shows, however, the first choice of the family was Philip Livingston, the next Philip Schuyler: but even if this had not been the case, and even if Mrs. Livingston, determined and attractive matriarch though she was, had been permitted to raise her voice in a masculine gathering, it is most unlikely that she would have raised it for George Clinton.

Clinton embodied the hopes of the wilderness yeomanry and of the city tradesmen and artisans. His radical Whig politics, politically tempered by a mild indulgence in land speculation, his firm friendships and implacable enmities, his passion for economy, even the ineffectiveness of his public oratory and the flatness of his prose—all these, surely, bespoke a man about whom there was no nonsense. His outer appearance was all of a piece with the rest of him: a short powerful body, a countenance all plainness and determination, a rugged dignity, a frank manner, no taste for finery. If he had his faults—hunger for power, parsimony, a provincial intolerance in the face of opposition—they were not incompatible with his belief in the future of plain republican institutions.[30]

Like Schuyler, he was in the field against the British when the election took place; like Scott, he was a lawyer who had risen to the rank of brigadier general of militia. He had even once had some military experience, as an ensign in the French and Indian War. His military attainments were far from brilliant; but he was an energetic, courageous, and hopeful soldier: and there have been few times in American history when these qualities were more needed; or when brilliance, and even success itself, played so relatively minor a role in deciding the course of events. Indeed, he was just the man to be a great wartime governor: but this was still to be proved in 1777. What was certain then was that, in spite of a marriage that gave him some consequence among the landholders of Ulster County, he was quite outside the world of the landed oligarchy; that they had not supported him for governor; that his election had not been welcome to them.

The radical torrent, naturally, having carried Clinton to the heights, also filled the lower levels of the government with his supporters. When a sufficient number of members had met on September 10 at Kingston, they elected Walter Livingston, a younger son of the manor and scarcely less conservative than his brother Peter, their speaker: but their choice of a Council of Appointment was nothing if not radical. The conservative victory in the Constitution had, temporarily, run its course: it was not until the late 1780's that Clinton lost his grip on the state.[31]

The arisocrats did not welcome Clinton; but the times were such that they were soon glad to make the best of him. "His family connections," said Schuyler, "do not entitle him to so distinguished a predominance"— never did pride utter itself with so naïve a voice—"yet he is virtuous and loves his country, has abilities and is brave." *"We are all hellishly frightened,"* Morris wrote Chancellor Livingston on October 8, *"but don't say a word of that* for we shall get our spirits again. . . . We fought gloriously below. . . . We shall beat them soon. We should soon do so if we had as good officers as our Governor."[32]

VI

Fear, indeed, had been the portion of New York throughout the summer and fall of 1777. The circumstances are nowadays too familiar for detailed narration: while Sir William Howe lingered on in New York—"He is such an unintelligible gentleman [Alexander Hamilton told the Chancellor in July] that no rule of interpretation can possibly be found to unravel his designs"—General John Burgoyne captured Ticonderoga and advanced toward Albany. Could this be the beginning of the end—the capture of New York through the juncture of the northern and the southern British armies? Nobody could have guessed in July that Howe's final plan precluded any assistance to Burgoyne; or that Burgoyne, encumbered by artillery, baggage, an idle optimism, a pretty mistress, would dawdle on his way until the patriots engulfed him; or that Colonel Barry St. Leger and his Indian allies would fail to capture Fort Stanwix. When Howe at length embarked for Philadelphia on July 23, it still seemed that Albany might be doomed. General Arnold, stopping in that city that day as he hurried north to fight Burgoyne, informed the inhabitants that they could expect no reinforcements from General Washington.[33]

The news of the capture of Ticonderoga, which reached Albany on July 7, and Burgoyne's subsequent advance, produced from one gentleman residing there a series of letters which preserve, in their faint way, some of the gloom and suspicion that hung over the frontier and was only dispelled by the triumph of Saratoga. This gentleman was John Barker Church, an English entrepreneur and duellist who had found a last refuge in American patriotism, had taken the temporary name of "John Carter," and was now engaged in a flutter in rum. His partners in this venture were Walter and Henry Livingston of the manor, and John R. Livingston, of Clermont, the Chancellor's brother.

"I think it probable," Carter wrote to Walter Livingston on July 7, "that Howe may push up the North River on hearing of Burgoyne's success." "What could be the motives of the General officers for this precipitate Retreat," he wrote two days later, "I cannot conceive. . . . I think Byng's fate should attend some of them . . . remove what rum there is at the Manor away." On July 14, John R. Livingston went off to Fort Edward as a volunteer, and Carter advised Walter Livingston with admirable *sang-froid* that "if any accident happen . . . you must have an Eye to the Rum at his place [Clermont]." On July 23, however, he was thrown into something like panic by Arnold's news. "I find we have been deceived in the account of Genl. Washington's army. Arnold says it is not near so strong." On August 10, when Nicholas Herkimer had already fought the Battle of Oriskany and American resistance was stiffening all along the line, he informed Walter Livingston that Burgoyne's army was greatly superior and that the patriots were "out of Order, in want of Discipline and dispirited by continuous retreats." "Nothing can save your State," he then continued, "but a vigorous exertion of its inhabitants. Men of Family and Consequence must now turn out and lead the way, their Inferiors will follow. . . . It pains me to hear people censure the Conduct of your family, in the free manner they do, they declare that not one of you takes a single step to assist to save your Country and add that you mean to make your Peace."[34]

Walter Livingston's reply to this distressful missive was in keeping, not with its accusations, which were senseless, but with an attitude that might conceivably have provoked them. He replied:

I plainly see the leveling principle of which our Constitution savors too much has already taken root. You say the cry is the Livingstons intend making their peace [with the British]. The truth is they are envied and jealousy is endeavoring to divide them from the Country. They would be happy if we did attempt to make our peace, they don't want to see a gentleman have influence in the Country. In forming the Constitution, they deprived us [the Livingstons] of sending a Representative to the house of Assembly which right unalienable right we held by law, usage & Pattent. The antient & inestimable Priviledges to be plucked from a family without more ceremony than a Crab from a Tree? While I was serving them faithfully [as a deputy commissary], I was placed in such a predicament as would have reflected disgrace had I continued to serve. As soon as I quitted the service I was ordered up with the militia. You know I was ordered to return. I retir'd to my farm, as I was laid aside by the Public. The country took me up [and] elected me one of their Representatives. I am now waiting to attend on that duty and am censured for my conduct. An Angel cannot please the populace long. . . . I fear the little aristocracy which we formerly enjoyed in this State is torn up by the root.[35]

Walter Livingston's elevation to the speakership of the New York Assembly was, in its way, a far more succinct reply to Carter's letter: his own words merely proved that he was incorrigible. Only a patrician palate could have detected in the New York Constitution the savor of leveling principle: only a mind more than usually impervious to the course of events could have expected a family pocket borough to survive the collapse of British government in New York.

The Chancellor also heard that the Livingstons were being accused, not, indeed, of intending to make peace, but of doing too well out of the war. His brother Lieutenant Colonel Henry Beekman Livingston, of the 4th New York Regiment, was an officer wholly admirable in combat, but proud and quarrelsome in camp. After the Peekskill retreat of March 23, he had seen fit to make unflattering remarks on the conduct of his commanding officer, General Alexander McDougall, one of the more famous of the Liberty Boys and a soldier just as fiery as himself. For this—and for other evidences of intractable behavior—Livingston had been court-martialed and reprimanded. He remained unconvinced. He told his brother on June 30 that McDougall was spreading sedition in the army by traducing the character of his superior officers and that he was endeavoring to make a party against the Livingston family. "You and Mr. Jay have been particularly mentioned," he wrote, "vizt. that you are Grasping at all Offices Both here and in Jersey and that the Livingstons or their connections possess every place of Proffit." His only consolation was that McDougall's behavior would soon "reduce him to that Rank which will make it excusable in me to Cain him."[36]

General McDougall's reputation, then and thereafter, was high; the Colonel was, to say the least, prejudiced: so that whether he was repeating McDougall's words or merely the gossip of the camp must remain in some doubt. But as in John Carter's letter, so here, the accusations show how inevitable it was, in a revolutionary situation and a time of great doubt and danger, for the old political aristocracy to be under attack. If the Revolution had been, qua revolution, less mild and enlightened, enlightened in the sense that the principles of the Enlightenment—such as constitutionalism, individual liberty, equality before the law—were applied to *all* classes, the attack might have been carried a good deal farther.

VII

The Chancellor was never slow to resent slurs on his family or himself: but this summer he seems to have been too busy on the Council of Safety to pay much attention to them. He probably added to them by suggesting, in his usual offhand but peremptory manner, that the Continental Congress should be given direct taxing powers: no suggestion could have been more unpopular. His notions on economy—"we have been shamefully profuse of honours & money, the rank given to everybody on every occasions degrades the officers of your regiments, the number of supernumerary officers is an immense tax"—were scarcely less so.[37] But his main preoccupations were, on the one hand, the disaffection of the tenant farmers—he reported in May that almost every tenant in the "upper manor" (*i.e.*, Livingston Manor as distinct from Clermont) was secretly engaged to the enemy— and, on the other, an intense desire to make them realize, in Congress and at Washington's headquarters, that New York might not survive the year.[38]

In June, he told John Hancock that the state could do no more about the defenses of the Hudson, that they had become a continental concern: the fact that his lands and his heart lay just beyond the Highlands and directly in the path of any junction of the British armies added special urgency to these representations.[39] In July, he was convinced that General Howe intended a "coup de main" in the Highlands: he did not quite realize that General Washington had the same conviction and was sure that a junction of Howe and Burgoyne would be attended by "the most fatal consequences."[40]

With the news of Ticonderoga, Washington moved into Orange County, New York, and made his headquarters at Smith's Clove; and there he received a letter from Chancellor Livingston urging him to request the New England militia to exert themselves against Burgoyne. In the midst of his distress of mind, for he did not know whether Howe intended to move up the Hudson or toward Philadelphia, Washington found time for a courteous reply. "Agreeable to the idea you have so obligingly hinted to me," he told the agitated Chancellor on July 18, "I have written to the Brigrs. in the western parts of Massachusetts & New Hampshire States, urging them by every motive of prudence and a regard to their own security to step forth at this critical and interesting conjuncture."[41]

Three days later, on orders from the Council of Safety, the Chancellor set out for Washington's headquarters: the condition of the remoter western frontier, prostrate before the Indians and the Loyalists, was now his concern. He returned on July 25, to report that General John Glover had been sent into Tryon County. The news that General Howe had set sail, for Philadelphia or New England, but, in any case, not up the Hudson, relieved the pressure a little. In August, the Chancellor was at Clermont, complaining to Gouverneur Morris that the New York Legislature, when it met in September, would do much that was contrary to the best interests of the state "in spite of my best endeavors to set them right." Clearly, the debates in the Council of Safety had not been agreeable. "I am at present equally unwilling to go abroad [*i.e.*, be sent to Philadelphia] or to stay at home," he wrote. "I want to do my duty & yet be clear of censure. This I fear cannot be done except in a private station to which I most earnestly wish to be reduced." On August 13, he was back in Kingston, reading the Council a letter from his brother John in Clermont to the effect that the militia there refused to go to Stillwater, claiming that their oath to the state was not binding on them. Thus, in much agitation and some despondency, the Chancellor spent his summer.[42]

VIII

General Burgoyne's military gifts, more suited to staff duties than to independent command, were in any event quite modest. One thinks of him, with his literary tastes, his handsome appearance, his convivial habits, as imprisoned in the polite antitheses of the heroic couplet—he was an Addisonian general, a little belated with his appearance in history. But Burgoyne was also vain, reckless, and ambitious: an Addisonian general in search of a Shakespearean role. He was not likely to find it in the American forest. There, although his mere presence was dangerous and depressing, he was somewhat more of a puzzle to himself than to his opponents. He was a brave man, however, and if he had not behaved too discreetly toward the murderous propensities of his Indian allies, or if the New England militia had conformed to what Alexander Hamilton called (in a letter to the Chancellor) "the unpardonable backwardness of your eastern neighbors," he might perhaps have reached Albany.[43] As it happened, his toleration of his Indians' worst habits made him more hateful than feared, and his foraging expedition under Colonel Baum was roundly defeated by the New Hampshire militia under General John Stark: these events, together with the collapse of St. Leger before Fort Stanwix, put him, before the end of August, in grave danger.

While he dallied with his mistress (like Howe, he favored the wives of his commissaries) or, what was worse, with need for a swift advance, the rural calm of that slow-moving world in a measure reasserted itself. The Chancellor traveled to and fro between Kingston and Clermont: he was occupied, almost preoccupied, with the question of taxes, paper money, and price controls. Gouverneur Morris wrote that there was strength enough to recapture New York City, where Howe had left Sir Henry Clinton to conduct (so Clinton thought) "a d——d starv'd deffencive." At Clermont, John R. Livingston, having returned from his volunteering and disposed of his rum, was thinking of the possibilities of a profitable business venture in New England. From such fragments as these one can deduce that manorial life on the middle Hudson, so long as Burgoyne and Sir Henry Clinton were inactive, and in spite of the disaffected militia and tenantry, was not entirely given over to panic, or sunk altogether in pessimism. "We purpose remaining," Walter Livingston wrote his mother-in-law, "until danger approaches much nearer."[44]

At length, on September 14, General Burgoyne crossed to the west bank of the Hudson, which now became his Rubicon: he was prepared to wager everything on a single victory. General Horatio Gates, who had again been substituted for the unfortunate Schuyler, moved up to meet him on September 19; the two armies clashed at Freeman's Farm; the battle was inconclusive, and Burgoyne was doomed. Too vain and too brave to retreat, if retreat was indeed possible, he was hoping as late as September 27 that he could still break through to Albany and that Sir Henry Clinton would relieve the pressure on him by sending a force up the Hudson toward him. His best chance, and a slight one at most, was that General Gates's army would dissolve.

Henry Beekman Livingston, who had passed under Gates's command and had fought with his usual gallantry at Freeman's Farm, wrote a letter to his brother on October 1 which suggested this dire possibility. The want of bread, he told the Chancellor, was about to create "mutinous dissentions that can only end in the ruin of this Army. We have for the body of them at this Post only two days Bread or Flower. Harry Livingston has been sent down to forward what is at his Fathers mills, if Mama has any do get it sent as soon as possible. I am desired by General Gates to assure you in the most pressing manner that any price will be given. Pray exert yourself at Esopus [Kingston] and the Mills adjacent. . . . Our want is kept as secret as possible and known to very few Officers in this Army. . . ." Three days later, he was more concerned with the dispute between General Gates and General Arnold, between the policy of containment and the policy of attack, than with the need for bread: possibly it had been supplied. "Since the Battle [of Freeman's Farm] we have been fortifying and suffering the enemy to do the same Very few in the army but sees the absurdity of it. ... General Arnold was the adviser of the late Battle & the Honour his Division obtained on that day created a jealousy that prevented our taking advantage of the Enemy the next."

In the decisive battle of Bemis Heights on October 7, Colonel Livingston and his 4th New Yorkers were the first to follow the raging Arnold when he finally, and without orders or command, broke into the British entrenchments. As between Arnold and Gates, the glory was Arnold's, but the strategy that ruined Burgoyne must be ascribed to Gates.[45]

The feelings of the Livingstons of Clermont would have been satisfied with Colonel Livingston's part in this battle, and with his presence at the surrender at Saratoga: but the Saratoga campaign touched them more nearly. Sir Henry Clinton had written to General Burgoyne in the middle of September that he would make a push up the Hudson; he received reinforcements from England on September 4; and on October 3 and 4 an expedition of four thousand men, in flatboats and bateaux, with an escort of frigates, moved up the river. Its objectives were Forts Clinton and Montgomery, about forty miles above New York, beneath their rocky eminences in the midst of the Highlands, guarding the narrow half-mile of river that led to the upper Hudson. Governor George Clinton, with his brother Brigadier General James Clinton, was in command of these forts: when he heard of his namesake's approach, he hurried away from Kingston, where he had been attending the Legislature. Sir Henry's attack by land was well conceived and well executed; the forts were vigorously defended, but they were undermanned and stood no chance; on the evening of the 6th, the two Clintons escaped with little more than half of their troops. On the 7th, Sir Henry broke the boom and chain across the Hudson at Fort Montgomery; on the 8th, he sent a cheerful message in the direction of Burgoyne, who was by then beyond help; but he never intended to do any more. He garrisoned the two forts; dispatched General John Vaughan with a small expedition up the river to Kingston; and then returned to New York.

The news of the loss of the forts reached Kingston on October 7, and on the 8th the Legislature adjourned, having first resolved itself into a Convention, which chose a Committee of Safety: on the evening of the 12th, Captain Sir James Wallace, R.N., with "2 gallies one schooner & one little brig," appeared in the river. Gouverneur Morris wrote the Chancellor, whom he believed to be at Clermont:

The alarm in the town exhibited more of the Drolerie than the Pathos of Distress. The good Dominie and his Yefrow by the Help of the pale and astonished Antoine and the gallant Mr. Brush blowing between Resolution & palid Fear laded about half a Ton upon my waggon and then eight of them Children included were dragged only slowly—before they went Willy squealed Sally bawled Adam played tricks and the Yefrow like Hecuba at the taking of Troy [cried] Mou Mou Mou. The eldest daughter of Low at all times sufficiently affecting to the sight but now bedewed with pearly Drops stood a second Medusa. . . . I believe the enemy will destroy Fort Montgomery &c. make an alarm along the shores of the River with their Gun Boats &c attempt to march a little way into Dutchess and then retire to New York.[46]

On October 13, when this letter was written, Morris could afford to be facetious: it was not until the evening of the 15th, according to General Vaughan's report, that the enemy landed troops, silenced the shore battery, and moved on into the town. Vaughan was already embittered by the news that Burgoyne had asked for an armistice. "Esopus [Kingston] being a nursery for almost every villain in the Country," he wrote, "I judged it necessary to proceed to the town. On our approach they were drawn up with cannon, which we took and drove them out of the place." Firing continued from the houses, and so "I reduced the place to ashes . . . not leaving a House."[47]

This dispatch was written on October 17. On October 19, he wrote his second dispatch, which he dated from "Livingston's Manor." "We are about 45 miles from Albany," he wrote, "the Pilots not chusing to be accountable any farther, I therefore must remain here." He himself had not chosen to report—he never *did* report—that he had also landed some troops and burned some undefended houses.[48]

IX

In Livingston Manor itself, on October 8, Walter Livingston loaded two carts and one wagon "with my most valuable effects"; he would not actually leave his house, Teviotdale, he said in a covering letter to Mr. Dibble Sharon, until the danger came nearer. Neither the letter nor the furniture was sent, for it was not at the manor proper, but at the "lower manor," Clermont, that Vaughan had landed. According to the *Journal of the Provincial Congress*, a British officer named Captain Montgomery, a relative of the late General Montgomery, had been, with his surgeon, a prisoner at Clermont since July 21; and a family tradition insists that the Chancellor (who in fact was not there) refused to allow this gentleman's presence to be used as a plea for mercy from General Vaughan. The Captain and his surgeon were removed from the scene; the family departed with whatever they could seize in their haste; the servants buried the silver; and the mansion of Clermont and the Chancellor's farm, "being at the waters edge and [under] cover of the british shiping," were left to the mercies of General Vaughan. Vaughan burned everything, mansion, farm, barns, outhouses: only the stone walls of the mansion and the farm were left standing.[49] The family fled to Rhinebeck; the British General remained. "We shall want arms for the inhabitants," he wrote, "who come in very well and we expect more. . . . We shall want a spare ship to receive the inhabitants."[50] He lingered for two days more; but the presence of General Israel Putnam, he reported, placed him in a "very uncomfortable position." On the 23rd, he was lying off Kingston again; and on the 26th, back in the Highlands, he made a final report to the effect that he had burned Kingston because of "its being a Town notorious for harboring the most rebellious people in that part of the Country." He was not easy in his mind about his destruction, which was certainly extensive: "Taken [he wrote] 14 pieces of cannon 150 stands of arms 12 barrels of Flints 6 sloops loaded with provisions of all kinds. Destroyed 1150 stands of arms 44 barrels of gunpowder 80 small vessels 400 Houses, Barns, Mills etc."[51]

These reports were very late in reaching Sir Henry Clinton. His first news of Vaughan's exploits came in the form of a letter from "Colonel Henry B. Livingston from the Honble Major General Gates Commanding in Chief the Forces of the United States of America in the Northern Department to His Excellency Lieutenant General Clinton." It was dated October 31, and its language was certainly forcible.

Sir [it began], Destroying defenceless Houses and Villages cannot in the least contribute [to] the Conquest of the Country nor to Increase the Revenue of your King. You have reduced to ashes the Beautiful Village of Kingston and many buildings the Proprietors of which could never have injured you Helpless Widows and Children are left exposed to all the Inclemencies of an approaching Winter. This conduct sufficiently evinces your Despair. . . . Should your Further Conduct be delineated by such Horrid Barbarity our utmost efforts may prove ineffectual to preserve you from the resentment of a Justly Incensed People.

Lt General Sir Henry Clinton [was the reply] has recd. a paper without signature from a Mr. H. B. Livingston supposed to be intended as a message from Genl. Gates—This paper is couched in terms so reprehensible that Lt. General Clinton cannot suppose it comes from General Gates. Whenever the General shall address Genl. Clinton in a proper manner, he will be ready to give him every satisfaction upon this or any other subject.

Privately, Clinton was not too sure that he had had the better of the exchanges: he did not understand Vaughan's behavior. "Sir H. C.'s orders," he noted on the back of Livingston's missive, "were to proceed d[i]rect for Burgoyne cooperate with him nay join him if necessary He stopt at Kingston burned it & Esopus fr what reason I am yet to learn this letter is the only information I have." When he finally received Vaughan's reports, his notes on the back of them hint at the same displeasure: he did not approve the burning of Kingston.[52]

The Chancellor was too proud to complain about the destruction of his home: he seems to have told his friends that he thought he would keep his farm, at any rate, just as it was as a memento of General Vaughan.* "I hear you intend to keep your burned home as a monumental ruin," Gouverneur Morris wrote in December. "An inscription—

> When the King of Great Britain attempted to establish
> Tyranny over the extensive regions of America
>   The Roof of Hospitality
> Sacred to Friendship to Science & to Love
>   Was violated by the Hand of War
> To perpetuate the Pleasure he received from British
> Barbarity this Pillar is erected by
>   Robert R. Livingston
> Who would have blushed to be exempted
>   From the calamities of his country."[53]

* Livingston soon decided that a more fitting memento would be a gift of five thousand acres of land to the inhabitants of Kingston, in any part of the Hardenburgh Patent "that falls to my share," provided it was not located near Woodstock or Shandaken or any other place already settled. RRL to the Trustees of Kingston, Poughkeepsie, March 1, 1778. RRLP. This offer was accepted, and the Trustees chose five thousand acres in Great Lots 39 and 40, at a place called Plattekill, near Pakataken: *i.e.*, near the present Margaretville in Delaware County. Marius Schoonmaker, *History of Kingston, N. Y.* (New York, 1888), 323-24.

CHAPTER FOUR

When the Legislature fled from Kingston in October, 1777, devolving the duties of government upon a Committee or Council of Safety, Livingston and his family were also homeless. His mother and sisters made their way to Connecticut and to Rhinebeck. Having seen them safely to their destinations, he found a refuge for himself and his wife, first in the manor, and then at the parson's house at Staatsburg. There he took stock of his melancholy situation. He was landpoor, he wanted hard cash or its equivalent; indeed, he was so severely straitened at this time that he offered his farm, Belvedere, in payment of a debt he had contracted before the Revolution with the neutralist merchant John Alsop.

I have a farm upon Hudsons River [he wrote] at which I lived till burned out. Before the war I valued it at [£]3000 which indeed I would not have taken for it as lands pleasantly situated upon the river were daily rising. I had buildings upon it to the amount of £1000 these the enemy have burned down but as the walls of the house were stone & still are in pretty good repair it might be rebuilt for a much less sum than a new house would cost. The farm contains about 140 acres & has beside a right to cut wood in my commons so that the whole farm may be cultivated. . . . I therefore now as my best offer tender you this farm all except two acres adjoining my mothers garden.[1]

Fortunately for the Chancellor, Alsop did not accept this offer: whether he closed with the alternative—six thousand acres in the Hardenburgh Patent—or settled for depreciated paper, or whether the debt went by default, is not a matter of record. For the head of the Clermont family to offer any part of his original estate for sale, however, was a sign of the changing times. Another sign was the fact that the head of the manor family—Robert Livingston, Jr., the third Lord—was being accused of extortion by the Rhinebeck Committee. It seems that he was selling his iron for £17 a hundredweight. "I wish you would go to the old Gentn.," Egbert Benson wrote to the Chancellor, "and give him your best advice —People are exceedingly clamorous and he is rendering both himself and

Family very odious, *and you must be convinced many (and of no small influence either) will seize the opportunity and cherish the Odium.*"[2]

This was the reason for the Chancellor's melancholy—the old landed families were suffering, not merely from the effects of war, which could have been borne, but from a loss of prestige. He had been confirmed in his office of Chancellor by the Governor and the Council of Appointment, at the hamlet of Marble Town, on October 17, while General Vaughan was still on the loose: this confirmation was all he had to console him.[3] He thought the Council of Safety, the temporary government, unconstitutional: and he had as little to do with it as possible. But when the Legislature at length collected a quorum, at Poughkeepsie, on January 14, 1778, he found it altogether distasteful. More than a year later, he poured out his feelings in a letter to John Jay. "Our legislature," he wrote, on February 2, 1779,

have been three weeks called but did not assemble until two or three days ago—I shall atend regularly & endeavor to render them all the little service in my power—not with a view to increase my own interest or popularity which I learn every day more and more to despise—From habit & passion I love and pity my fellow creatures would to God I could esteem them —My spirits never flagged while our necessity called for great exertions— or while I was compelled by love for my country to contribute to the establishment of a government which was to be the basis of its future happiness —But I feel myself unequal to the little scale of party politicks—I can't combat a knave with calumny—And to manage fools to which I have sometimes submitted disgusts me when it is no longer justified by some important end —I cannot enjoy the tranquil pleasures of a rural life—I converse with men I can't esteem and I am engaged in a round of little politicks to which I feel myself superior—A happier hour may come. . . .[4]

It was not merely the legislation that was at fault; it was the character of the legislators. Having helped to write a constitution that was calculated to protect the state from the dangers of popular government, the Chancellor now discovered that the popular party of small farmers and tradesmen was running the state. "The ignorance of some, & the wickedness of others," he wrote in 1778, when the Legislature had been in session for only a fortnight, "are hourly perverting the constitution." He told General Schuyler in March that the Legislature was "daily committing the most flagrant acts of injustice." At the opening of the June session, he complained of the ignorance and the weakness of the local politicians and of "the violence of the faction here." And so it went.[5]

As for the legislation that this agrarian body produced, the chief reasons for the Chancellor's disgust with it were laid down in a letter to Gouverneur Morris, who had written to say that he hoped New York would never tax bonds. "It is needless to tell you," the Chancellor answered on April 6, 1778,

how far I agree with you in sentiment when I inform you of the measures our wise Legislature has taken to banish both money & monied men from the State—The first is effectively done by an embargo on flour which deprives us of every remittance but money—The second not only by a tax on money, but by a most unprecedented tax of £5 per cent on all Traders & Manufacturers who have made more than £1000.[6]

Both these measures were vetoed by the Council of Revision, both vetoes were overruled. The embargo on meal, flour, and grain was a great favorite with Governor Clinton—he believed that when these commodities were exported from the state, they passed by way of Connecticut into Long Island and so into the maw of the British army. The Chancellor, on the other hand, held that, without such exportations, the state could not obtain even such a necessity as salt, unless it wished to be drained of all its specie. The "tax on money" was an act to raise three pence on the pound on real estate, one and a half pence on the pound on personal estate, and £50 per thousand on money gained by trade since September 12, 1776. It was a mild agrarian measure, aimed at the large landowners, the hoarders of hard money, and the war profiteers, and the only mischievous feature in it was the almost unlimited power it seemed to give to the assessors. The Chancellor, however, saw it as an attack on the foundations of society. When he heard the news of the French treaties of alliance and commerce, he hoped, he said, that the British would now be fully occupied with fighting the French: this would give them no time to spare for America, and independence would be agreed upon without any more ado. "Let them go at it, & God send them a good deliverance for I do not find that this [war] has produced the effect I expected from it upon the manners of the people, or rendered them more worthy, by making them more virtuous, of the blessings of a free government."[7]

When this was the Chancellor's frame of mind, all details of the Revolution seemed depressing, especially since he himself was an able administrator, and revolutions are never well administered. He complained about anything and everything. The quartermasters and forage masters were inefficient, redundant, ignorant of the country's needs, and the certificates with which they paid were worthless.[8] If General Putnam, no longer trusted, was left in command of the fortifications of the Hudson, the inhabitants within many miles of that river would move away and the lands remain unsown "lest the enemy reap."[9] The Chancellor's brother, the

Colonel, had not been promoted as he deserved.[10] All available men in the upper part of the state should have been drawn down to the Highlands, instead of being kept on to make an expedition into Canada "in which [General Washington wrote] I was never consulted, but which I saw from the beginning could never succeed."[11] The act to fix prices in terms of depreciated paper was abominable, and it was only to avoid the jealousy of the New Englanders, who alone would profit by it, that the Chancellor had brought himself to recommend it.[12] The custom of calling out a quarter of the militia in rotation, after having furnished every fifteenth man to the Continental regiments, was having a dreadful effect upon agriculture. Such crops as there were would be badly harvested, and all the wheat that could be found by the forage masters was being used to feed the horses they were buying up in such quantities—"which not only hazards the existence of [the] army," but also that of the horses, who usually died of such a diet.[13] The Congress itself was paying no interest on its paper, but giving orders for the principal just as fast as it came in—"if this does not look like public bankruptcy I know not what name to call it."[14] In the Legislature, efforts had been made by some assemblymen to pass a bill facilitating the impeachment of the Council of Revision.[15] In short, "what can you expect of me unaided and without support—In a dirty village [Poughkeepsie] where no society can be maintained?"

His friends' response to such *cris de coeur* was not displeasing. If they rallied him for spending too much time at Clermont, where he and his mother were rebuilding their houses,[16] if they accused him of indolence, of listlessness, of hiding his light under a bushel, they did so in terms that were certainly flattering. "Suppose yourself young ambitious sensible versed in mankind a good lawyer," Gouverneur Morris wrote, "and (but for Easiness) a good politician. . . . You cannot be *mediocre*, you must be brilliant."[17] Even John Jay, whom the Chancellor had thought incommunicable and dogmatic, began to rally him in the same complimentary tone: "I admire your sensibility, nor would I see less milk in your veins, you would be less amiable"; and with jests that were certainly uncharacteristic: "Morris is busy and useful, more busy indeed than others—for besides the affairs of Congress, he is daily employed in making oblations to Venus and Aesculapius. Remember this is to be translated in the best sense, and not so construed as to mean Vice or P-x."[18] This was written in February, 1779, when Jay was president of the Continental Congress: it was not the burden of Jay's discourse—nothing pleased the Chancellor more than to be called a mass of sensibilities—it was the eminence from which it came that hurt. He felt that he was being left behind.

Nobody accused him, then or thereafter, of not supporting the Revolution. "Nothing could be more hurtful to us at home & abroad," he wrote to William Duer in July, 1778, when Duer seemed to hint that the British commissioners, with their offer of home rule, might be worth listening to, "than the idea of reconciliation on any terms short of independence. Our situation is extremely delicate, deliberation would be as dangerous to our honour & safety as to a woman's chastity which your own experience will probably tell you seldom survives five minutes' hesitation."[19] And yet, when Jay suggested in January, 1779, that he might be sent abroad on a mission to France, he replied that he would do so only if he were not to bankrupt himself as a result—only if the salary were equal to the position, "so that I do not go abroad a great man to be a little one all my life after at home."[20] He was still an unreconstructed aristocrat, to whom any change in status was unthinkable, and who accepted everything about the Revolution except the fact that it was revolutionary.

In these veering moods and unwelcome activities—now meditating in some country retreat upon the pleasures of retirement, the wastefulness of government, the crudity of legislators, the absence of friends, now striving at Poughkeepsie to keep the Legislature on what he conceived to be an even keel—the Chancellor spent his time until the fall of 1779.

II

If the Revolution is construed in revolutionary terms—as the first application on a grand scale of the principle that governments are created by the people—then the Chancellor's attitude becomes difficult to accept. It is, of course, always easier to pass judgments upon what is gone than to attempt to understand it. Livingston spoke, indeed, of "the blessings of free government"; and by this he meant a representative, republican government dedicated to the preservation of those liberties that the British Parliament had attempted to subvert: he did not mean an emerging democracy. When he found himself dancing attendance upon local politicians whom he did not like and could not manage, he became disgusted and tried to escape.

In the same way, though to a far greater degree, his brother Colonel Henry Beekman Livingston never could bring himself to see that war implied anything more than the expulsion of the British, whom, to be sure, he was glad to expel. That it could be conducted only with the good will and the assistance of very humble people was a hard fact that he was quite unable to assimilate. He himself, in spite of his faults, indeed because of them, was no ordinary man. He carried his notion of class distinctions a good deal farther than they could be made to go: he chafed at the ill breeding of many of his fellow officers, and it was because that warrior was of humble origins that he chiefly resented General McDougall. If his own abilities were questioned, it was for opposite reasons: because he had pretensions to aristocracy, not because he was a poor soldier. He had served with great distinction as a raider on Long Island, where he had done as much damage as he could to his old family enemy, Oliver De Lancey.[21] He had fought with courage and skill at Freeman's Farm and at Bemis Heights. Under General John Sullivan, on Rhode Island, his behavior in combat had been exemplary. Once the battle was over, he resorted to his usual expedients: he became haughty, rough, jealous; he was convinced that his services were underestimated.[22] There was one great exception to this behavior: throughout the terrible winter at Valley Forge, though he complained (as did everyone else) of the frightful conditions, he remained on the best of terms with his fellow sufferers: it was not the rigors of war to which he objected, it was the lack of social amenities. When the worst was over, he declared that he would stay only long enough to learn Baron von Steuben's New Discipline, "more agreeable to the dictates of Reason & Common Sense than any mode I have before seen"; he would then retire to his farm.[23] After the retreat from Rhode Island, he was sure that General Sullivan had not done him justice. But what rankled with him was the fact, relatively remote, that he had not received the command of James Clinton's regiment when that gentleman had been promoted to brigadier general late in 1776.[24] When he resigned his commission on November 19, 1778, he was, he told the President of Congress, "not yet so callous to the Impressions of Insult as to be insensible of the repeated Indignities offered me in the Promotion of Officers my inferiors."[25] His resignation was accepted by Congress, said Gouverneur Morris, "with tokens of regard equally flattering and uncommon." He had, after all, displayed rare gifts in the field. "Indulge me," Morris wrote to the Chancellor, "while I wish that he will make the proper use of Congress's praise which certainly is not the raising of Ill Will and Envy among those who were his brother officers."[26]

Colonel Livingston suffered from the assumption—unfortunately by no means an uncommon one—that the War of the American Revolution ought to have been a gentleman's war. When he left Sullivan's army—he had gone there on furlough and had fought in Rhode Island as a volunteer—he went first to Boston, where he was "treated with the greatest Hospitality and politeness by every Body of note in town."[27] There he lingered for a while, before going to Philadelphia to resign his commission, to contract a disastrous marriage, and to disappear from public life: and there he found his brother John R. Livingston. John R. Livingston used not to think well of the young ladies of Boston—"they are very hansome [he once wrote] but very auckward and ignorant, so that I am in little danger of getting married among them"[28]—but he was about to succumb to the charms of a Miss Sheaffe, daughter of a late collector. This was certainly romantic of him—the young lady had no dowry, and her mother (though moving in the first circles) had been reduced to keeping a shop:[29] moreover, he was frankly a businessman to whom, as to his former partner, the censorious John Barker Church, the Revolution was simply a means of making money. Early in 1780, he thought of going to Holland, to drive a trade between that country and Saint Eustatius, "a plan that cannot fail to make a fortune," and he wrote to William Duer and to Robert Morris in the hopes that they would help him raise the necessary capital.[30] Morris replied that a residence in Holland might involve some trading with the enemy; and although there has been some debate of recent years as to the lowness or otherwise of Morris's business ethics, it can scarcely be denied that if Robert Morris said that a venture was morally unsound, morally unsound it must indeed have been.[31] These considerations did not trouble John R. Livingston. He continued to think about going abroad; he even meditated a brief trip to London, and when the Chancellor mildly but firmly remonstrated with him, replied that he would give it up, although he was certain there was no "danger" in it. "Poverty is a curse I can't bear," he wrote, "with it a man had better not exist—and you must know that the family are too much distressed to give me any assistance." This was in November, 1780.[32]

It was not that Colonel Henry Beekman Livingston and Mr. John R. Livingston were particularly exceptional in their behavior. Many officers resigned their commissions if they had reason to believe that they had been passed over for promotion; it was what was expected from a gentleman; and it was rarely condemned. Most businessmen looked upon the Revolutionary War as a profitable enterprise—in this respect, the Revolutionary War was no different from other wars—and if John R. Livingston was somewhat frank in his expressions of self-interest, that was because he had always considered himself a privileged person. In the same mood, John Barker Church, who never lifted a finger for any interest but his own, could blandly lecture Walter Livingston for not being more active in the patriot cause. In a way, the Revolution has a resemblance to that Odyssean island where night and day were so close together that the herdsman driving his flocks out in the morning met the herdsman driving his flocks back into the twilight. As the army and the Congress sank from one desperate expedient to another in the gathering darkness of 1779 and 1780, there were businessmen, there were neutralist farmers, there were enterprisers of all sorts, who went whistling out to meet the dawn.

It is not, therefore, surprising that when the Chancellor became a delegate to the Continental Congress, his brother John should have suggested that he ought to aim at the presidency of that body. "It will be," he said, "productive of great advantages to your friends."[33]

III

The Chancellor himself never thought of the Revolution in these terms. If he sometimes professed a taste for retirement, that was in part an affectation, and in part the effect of the extreme difficulty he found in adjusting the commands of the past to the realities of the present. He was proud of his role in helping to write the New York Constitution. He felt that he had performed that duty with great spirit and energy: and he had. The New York Constitution was not simply an effort to rescue from the colonial experience whatever was institutionally valuable. It was also an attempt to suit the mechanical materialism of the eighteenth century to the need for individual freedom, subjective expression, and spiritual no less than physical opportunity: to the concept that government arose from the people and did not descend upon them. As a written instrument, it was more lucid, more brief, and better organized than most state constitutions: with its checks and balances, and its novel if useless armature in the form of the Councils of Revision and Appointment, it was a good example of mechanistic thinking; but would it satisfy the £20 freeholder? The Chancellor and his colleagues thought that by admitting this personage, they had gone quite as far as they needed to go: having been admitted, he was expected to behave. The £20 freeholder, strange to say, thought otherwise. The majority of the New York Legislature was distinctly agrarian—dedicated, that is to say, to the interests of an ideal community of small farmers and artisans: as such, it was frequently eccentric in its behavior, and sometimes absurd. As long as his patriotic duty required him to dance attendance upon this essential body, which lay in the heart of the Revolution and contributed both strength and irregularity to its heartbeat, the Chancellor was not very active in the performance of his patriotic duty. He subscribed to the old fallacy that reasoning was in itself rational, and that logic was more powerful than sympathy: he was not, in brief, by temperament or training or background, equipped to play Mentor to rural lawmakers.

In the fall of 1779, he was made a delegate to the Continental Congress, in the place of John Jay, who was being sent to Spain.[34] He set out on November 4, with his wife and his youngest brother, Edward, on a slow wintry journey: it was not until November 20 that he presented his credentials to Congress.[35] It was then sitting in a lofty chamber on the second floor of the State House, at the eastern end of Philadelphia, that orderly city, with "its broad straight streets, its regular rows of uniform brick houses," its frankly profligate and fashionable air, its taint of Loyalism. Like every wartime capital, it was a city of extremes: the severest patriot and the most unregenerate profiteer, the modest Whig matron and the flaunting Tory belle, the pious and the dissipated, the prude and the dandy, jostled one another in its decent purlieus. The center of its social life was the great Dickinson house, at the western end, where the Chevalier de la Luzerne, the French Minister, had set up his legation. Luzerne was amiable, polite, myopic, and far abler than he appeared to be: few men were better versed in the arts of cajolery, few men could offer a bribe with such a delicate air of receiving a favor. His weekly dinners and fortnightly balls were held in high esteem, as were the attentions of his Secretary of Legation, Barbé-Marbois—a man *"bien fait à son métier,"* said his chief, *"mais chercheur de conversations, de bavardages même."* Luzerne himself disliked music and detested dancing, and behind his agreeable mask he looked out at the scenes of his own creating—"such a swarm of French beaux," wrote Martha Dangerfield Bland, "marquises, counts, viscounts, barons"—with a certain distaste. "A rich commercial city," he wrote in one of his reports, "offering the most frequent opportunities for pleasure and dissipation is not suitable to the representatives of an infant republic which can sustain itself only by economy, activity, and application to work."[36]

Economy, in one form or another, was the theme of that disastrous winter of 1779-1780: economy of money, economy of force. "Let me tell you," John Sloss Hobart wrote the Chancellor on November 19, "it will take all your virtues and abilities, great as they are, to oppose the torrent and prevent the ruin of your country." Judge Hobart was thinking of the price-fixing system, which, whatever else it may have been, was scarcely torrential: the torrent could be measured in another way, in the decline of Continental bills of credit from a specie ratio of four to one in January to one of fifty to one, or lower, in November. Hobart was not a merchant, but he took the extreme mercantile view—the view of the importer and the profiteer—that a depreciation was, on the whole, desirable. Its effect upon the army, however, languishing between campaigns, was nothing less than deplorable.

The General [Washington] has confidentially communicated to me [Philip Schuyler wrote from headquarters on December 7] his apprehension from the distressed state of our affairs. . . . The public officers are without money and Incredibly in Debt. . . . [Distresses will soon increase] to such an extent as to bring on a separation of the Army, or the necessity of living on free quarters. . . . For Gods sake urge that something be done with the Money, that is to establish it at some rate of depreciation, that alone can and will save us.[37]

Nor was the news from New York any more reassuring.

I have not felt equal Distress at the Situation of our Affairs at any Period since the commencement of the War [wrote Governor Clinton on January 7, 1780]. It is with the utmost difficulty that we feed the Troops stationed at & in the vicinity of the Posts in the Highlands—They have been frequently Days together without Bread, and now subsist on a precarious supply daily brought in to them; and I am informed the Army at Morris Town are in the same disagreeable situation—Our Public Magazines are entirely exhausted, and, owing to an extraordinary Drought [last year], it is with difficulty the Commissaries can get the Wheat, which has been collected from the Farmers in consequence of our Laws, manufactured.[38]

The monetary crisis has often been blamed on the weakness of the Continental Congress and its faith in the emission of bills of credit—the credit, in this instance, being derived from the people's belief in the outcome of their revolution. Certainly it had no other. It was devoid of taxing powers, and depended upon the states for the maintenance of an army and a treasury through requisitions in money or in kind. Under these circumstances, it is difficult to see what answer there was but the printing press; or to imagine how the country could have struggled through four years of war without Continental paper money, however dubious. But now the time was approaching when paper money could do no more, except subside under its own weight.

The states were probably more to blame than the Congress. They had been willing enough to receive their proportion of the "Continentals," but, instead of providing for their redemption through taxes, they had blandly made emissions of their own. They dreaded taxation, or, where they did not dread it, had no strength to enforce it. New York, for example, changed from a specific levy on individuals to a system of county quotas late in 1779; if the quotas were inequitable, adjustments would be made after the war.[39] What faith could anyone have in so fanciful a remedy as postwar adjustments? In the meantime, the county supervisors, collectors, and assessors could do very much as they pleased.

Poor Harry [Colonel H. B. Livingston] has been used very ill [the Chancellor's mother wrote on December 30, 1779], the assessors have Taxed his farm £1500. . . . John Dewitt is as Arbitriary as a Bassha—Radley is taxed £900 while Bogardus who is Clerk to the Assessors is Txd £100—The most shameful Impossisions are practised. Mr. Benson says they the Supervisors are the last resort & that the Legeslature designed that there should be as much confusion as possible—I was going to see him [Egbert Benson, the Attorney General] in my suit against the Collector but he owned that he had advised him to seize My wheat and that he was Imployed on the other side—I am assessed £1500 in Rhinebeck precinct & Dewitt told Tillotson that I was to be assessed in pawlding & Beekmans [Precincts]. I am taxed in the Manor £2000 & you £3000, Cozen Robert [Robert Livingston, Jr.] £16000—Benson says in 2 months the same sum is to be Taxed on each individual. . . . By the time you will have received this we will have entered on another year—May the Almighty pour out his best Blessings upon you & polly, give you Wisdom Grace and Health, and as much fortitude as the times require—May he give us Peace and Independence and deliverance from the persecution of the Lower Class.[40]

It was, no doubt, inevitable that the "lower class"—small farmers such as John Dewitt—would take their revenge upon the great landowners, now that they could do so through assessments and taxes; but one cannot tell, since Mrs. Livingston was writing in terms of depreciated money, just how great the revenge was. Yet the landowner's plight was nothing compared to the miseries to which the small tenant farmers were being subjected by this confused system. "Van Ness has already collected half the rents," Mrs. Livingston wrote in February, 1780, "which will be very small this year, especially yr. part of the Mannor. The people having scarce there Bread and many not that. . . . The people at large complain that they cannot pay goods & cattle are distrained & many put to great hardships I am apprehensive of a famine before ye new crop can be used."[41]

The truth seemed to be that the state authority was breaking down. The Legislature was willing to tax, but could not—and perhaps would not—actually enforce its will. The theory behind the embargo on exportation of wheat could be disproved on practical grounds—not only did it drain the state of negotiable paper, but the state commissaries, empowered to seize wheat at fixed prices, sold what they had seized across the state lines at highly inflated ones. The tenant farmer, isolated and helpless, was forcibly taxed in kind at an unfair valuation, or lost his cattle if he could not pay, or was visited by the army forage masters, who rewarded him with worthless certificates. The only answer, a natural one for a man whose patriotism was usually far from fervent, was to conceal what he had, or sell it in the black market should one be accessible. The states were prosperous: what threatened their prosperity was that most fearful of calamities, the ultimate calamity of administrative collapse.

Or, rather, one should say the penultimate calamity: for in a very simple economy, a barter economy to a large extent, all sorts of administrative blunders may be perpetrated which would be quite lethal in a more complex one. The ultimate calamity would have been the surrender or the modification of independence, and that never came.

IV

When the Chancellor went to Philadelphia in November, 1779, he left behind him a system of state finances which was rapidly deteriorating, which grew worse with each succeeding month, and which, from a landowner's point of view, was inequitable and malicious. In April, 1780, his horses were sold in order to pay his taxes: otherwise, his cattle would have been distrained, and disposed of at a nominal price. In May, he felt obliged to write to Governor Clinton to ask for relief. His last assessment, he told the Governor, had been for a rating of £3,000; he had again been rated, but this time at £9,000, and his total income, in spite of his agent's best endeavors to collect it, did not amount to six hundred bushels of wheat. "I have no personal property," he added,

& occupy a small farm which does not half pay the expence of cultivating it. The profits of a valuable profession & my whole time I have devoted to the publick for a very triffling compensation which I have seldom recd. but to give to others who I thought more distressed than myself together with considerable additions out of my private fortune. I have already since I have been at this place expended upwards of sixty thousand dollars in order to maintain the character with which I am invested a small proportion of which will be repaid by the State—I need not add to this the unremitting endeavors I have exercised to promote the freedom & happiness of my country or the heavy losses I have sustained by the ravages of the enemy.[42]

The inflation that rendered these taxes so formidable in appearance made it possible also for the Chancellor to discharge them and more than discharge them out of an income of under six hundred bushels of wheat: but they were undoubtedly burdensome and arbitrary; and the Governor did not exactly mend matters when he replied, some two months later, that the temper of both Senate and Assembly was such that an application for relief "at this time would at least have been fruitless if not injurious."[43]

The point of all this was, not that a wealthy New York landowner ever found it impossible to get along during the Revolution, even if his rents were largely unpaid and he had used up his reserves of hard money, but that he learned during the Revolution to distrust the state, and began to fear that, if left to its own devices, it would end by taxing him out of existence. The State Government was manifestly unable to control its own fiscal agents—it would have been little less than super-human if it had been able to do so at such a time and little less than angelic if it had wished to spare its wealthier citizens. This did not diminish his fear and distrust.

The Chancellor, in short, came to Philadelphia ready to increase the powers of Congress, if that were possible, at the expense of those of the states: his tax burden as a landowner, no less than his predilections as an aristocrat, urged him toward this decision. But, needless to say, it was not for this purpose that he was being sent to Philadelphia. His legal standing was high, he was held to be one of the most learned men in the state; and so, since the state did not permit him to hold two offices except in a specific emergency, it was primarily in order to settle the problem of New York's eastern and western boundaries that he had been made a delegate.[44] And certainly the jungle presented by this problem, a jungle of crouching historical contradictions, of intertwisted land titles, of prejudices grown gnarled and rigid with age, of half-buried boundary disputes, was enough to baffle the keenest legal mind.

Here, from the beginning, his attitude was clear and statesmanlike. On the eastern boundary, in the region of the New Hampshire Grants, the future State of Vermont, the inhabitants were calling for independence from New York—were threatening, that is to say, a revolution within a revolution. In strict law, their position was dubious; in equity, it was not unsound: complicated and incomplete as the evidence was, it seemed to point to these conclusions. The Chancellor, whose thinking was not distracted by the ownership of any land in the disputed region, held that it was wrong to attempt to govern people against their will: and he strove for an equitable solution along these lines. His fellow delegates, James Duane and John Morin Scott, were absent from Philadelphia—were, in fact, plodding diligently up and down between Albany and Pough-keepsie—in search of evidence that would support the sovereignty of New York.[45] But Duane was certainly, and Scott possibly, a considerable landowner in the New Hampshire Grants: the Chancellor's position was not the less independent and courageous for that.

As to the western boundary of New York, the difficulties there presented no insuperable problem if—as was the Chancellor's case—one had no interest in any of the great land companies. New York possessed certain claims, founded on shadowy colonial "protectorates" over the Six Nations, to immense stretches of territory between Lake Erie and the Mississippi. She was one of the "landed" states; and the question was: Should she yield to the demands of the "landless" states and cede her claimed possessions to Congress? The question gave rise to two considerations: on the one hand, a cession was obviously patriotic and sensible; on the other, it would play into the hands of the land companies, who, in many cases long before the Revolution, and usually by questionable methods, had bought up vast quantities of the lands claimed by various states. Moreover, the leading figures in the land companies were also, strange to relate, the most prominent politicians in the "landless" states. The Chancellor cut this somewhat Gordian knot by suggesting that New York had a good deal more to gain from holding intact what she had east of Lake Erie than by fighting over what she might or might not possess to the west of it. He wrote a letter to Governor Clinton to this effect, suggesting a western boundary that was roughly the boundary as it is today; the Governor accepted this suggestion; the Legislature was of a like mind; and the cession was offered, much to New York's advantage, on March 1, 1788.[46]

The Chancellor's action, in this case as in that of Vermont, was conscientious and statesmanlike: it was also, which is equally to the point, nationalistic.

V

The winter of 1779–1780, in the annals of the northern army, was perhaps even more fearful than the one that had seen it freezing and sickening at Valley Forge. Everything was lacking—pay, provisions, and clothing; weapons; medicines; transportation. Only the presence of George Washington held together the shivering, hungry, sick, and despairing host; and even George Washington, at times, gave way to despair. Without proper support from Congress and the states, the army could not minister to its own wants. As Philip Schuyler had written in November, it almost seemed as if the soldiers would have either to "separate" or "go upon free quarters"; either disband entirely or become a mob of marauders, an object of terror and hatred to the countryside. The situation was rendered even more tragic by the curious status of the Continental soldier during the Revolutionary War. It was the status of a mercenary eighteenth-century soldier, not that of a civilian who had enlisted or been drafted in order to perform a high, essential duty. The common Continental soldier occupied the lowest place in the hierarchy of popular values. The idea of a nation in arms came with a later revolution; it was not present in this one. Even a Congress that, with all its weaknesses, labored faithfully and diligently at its enormous task was able to bear with fortitude the extreme misery of the Continental line; the states, each with its own militia, were, or seemed to be, indifferent; and the ladies and gentlemen who danced through the night at Luzerne's balls in Philadelphia, the duelers, the gamblers, the speculators in public funds and scarce commodities gave no thought at all to the starving wretched in Morristown, only a few leagues away. "Poor fellows," said General Nathanael Greene, "they exhibit a picture truly distressing—more than half naked and two thirds starved. A country overflowing with plenty are now suffering an Army, employed for the defence of everything that is dear and valuable, to perish for want of food."[47] "If you were on the spot," Washington wrote Joseph Reed, "if you could see what difficulties surround us on every side, how unable we are to administer the most ordinary calls of the service, you would be convinced . . . that we have everything to dread. Indeed, I have almost ceased to hope."[48] "Certain I am," he told Joseph Jones, "unless Congress speaks in a more decisive tone; unless they are vested with powers by the several States competent to the great purposes of the war, or assume them as a matter of right; and they, and the States respectively, act with more energy than they have hitherto done, that our cause is lost."[49] This was on May 31, 1780; it might as easily have been written the previous November.

Had not Congress tried everything? It had called upon the states for requisitions in money and in kind; it had established loan offices; it had fixed prices; it had issued money and even borrowed it back; it had denounced the emission of state paper and stopped the printing press on its own: all was in vain. Only the power to tax—in other words, power—could have rescued it from this predicament; but there the states might well ask themselves if they dared bestow such power upon their "Common Council"; if they could reasonably agree, having broken the grip of one Parliament, to put themselves in the grasp of yet another. It was not taxation without representation that was at issue; it was the taxing power in all its majesty: and a majority in Congress agreed with the states. Was not the dubious Continental paper, sinking in value from one depth to another, in itself a kind of tax?

It is unnecessary to explore in detail this famous and most human crisis: what is relevant to this study is the influence it exerted upon a single mind. Although he was regarded in his own state as a financial expert, and liked to dabble in fiscal expedients of one kind or another, the Chancellor, in his attitude toward congressional measures, was simplicity itself. On March 18, after months of wrangling, Congress decided to forgo regulation of prices in favor of regulation of money. It devalued its bills of credit so that they now stood at forty Continentals for one specie dollar; made arrangements that the old bills should be destroyed as soon as they came in; and empowered the states to issue one new dollar for every twenty they returned, the new dollars to be redeemed through state taxes specifically levied, and to bear an interest of 5 per cent, which the United States would pay through bills of exchange on Europe. It is easy to see from this that the public debt would be reduced from $200,-000,000 to $5,000,000 and that the new money could never exceed $10,000,000. A draft of a message from the New York delegates to the Governor, in the Chancellor's handwriting, no doubt expresses his views on this optimistic and (as it turned out) futile measure. The New York delegates, the Chancellor said, had unanimously concurred in the resolutions of Congress. No money could be raised in aid of taxes because "the moneyed interest refused to lend, tho' we offered them near fifty pr. Cent advance in sterling bills. . . . The continuation of the tax to the amount required, tho' desirable to be complied with must however be limited by the situation of every State. Perhaps with us it may be advisable after the establishment of funds to take in part of the old exchange for the new emissions in order to lighten the tax"—this does not seem to be quite what Congress had in mind—"perhaps too it might be advantageously funded upon our confiscated estates & back Lands. The resolution to receive specie & the new bills at 40 times the value of the bills of credit now in circulation was founded on the belief that it is about the average value at which it was recd. by the present possessors." The draft ends with the statement that the new bills would not depreciate because of the reduction of the national debt to a moderate size, and because of "the funds on which they [the new bills] are to be issued, which it is expected will be sufficient to convince the publick that this money rests on a firm basis."[50]

This statement was, if anything, circular. The firm basis on which the new money rested was to be the conviction of the public that it rested on a firm basis. Needless to say, the public entertained no such thoughts.

The only basis it could see was the spongy basis of repudiation. The new money, though so much less voluminous than the old, began immediately to sink; very soon it vanished altogether; and the sad drama of the Continental bills of credit was thus played out.

The Chancellor's attitude toward the Continental finances was simple, and his thinking on them was perfunctory to say the least: he was already meditating more characteristic and more dangerous solutions. On January 8, 1780, he offered a series of resolutions for reducing the size of the army, by dismissing all the troops whose enlistments were to expire on April 1, and bringing the number of battalions down from eighty-eight to sixty. Since Congress was still, after a fashion, considering a measure for the promotion of enlistments, these resolutions might seem paradoxical: but they led directly to the appointment of a commission of three (one from Congress, two from outside it), which was to proceed to army headquarters and endeavor to regulate the staff departments of the army. Philip Schuyler was named the member from Congress on this commission; but he suspected the other two—Timothy Pickering and Thomas Mifflin—of hostility to Washington, and he declined to serve.[51]

The Chancellor had seen the commission as a preliminary move in the restoration of Schuyler to his former rank in the army; the post of quartermaster general was to follow, and after that some office equivalent to that of secretary of War;[52] in the same spirit, his resolutions of January 8 were intended rather to stimulate than to check the promotion of enlistments. George Washington's letter of January 23, demanding a more strenuous enlistment program, was a vivid response to these resolutions; the letter was referred to the Board of War, and in February the Board of War recommended the appointment of a committee, armed with ample powers, which should repair to headquarters to co-operate with General Washington.

The recommendations of the Board were not taken up: but amidst these cloudy moves and countermoves, of resolutions that meant the opposite of what they said and of commissions designed to advance the fortunes of a single commissioner, the figure of the Chancellor can be discerned, among many others, scouring the waters of debate in search of national power.

At length, on April 6, taking advantage of a favorable situation, he moved that a committee be appointed to proceed to headquarters. This committee, Schuyler told Alexander Hamilton with approval, was to have "a kind of dictatorial power, in order to afford satisfaction to the army, and to arrange the great departments thereof." The device of sending a committee was old: the contemplated power was new. After six days of debate, the motion was passed.[53] On April 13, Philip Schuyler, of New York, John Mathews, of South Carolina, and Nathaniel Peabody, of New Hampshire, were appointed. They were empowered, in consultation with General Washington, "to carry out various reforms, to institute regulations in a number of departments, and to supervise the execution of plans adopted; and their action in every case to be reported to Congress." The last clause was the fatal one. The powers were large, but they were temporary, they were limited, and they did not conform to General Washington's wishes.

It appears to me of the greatest importance [he wrote to Joseph Jones on May 14], that a *small* Committee should be immediately appointed to reside near head Quarters vested with all the powers which Congress have so far as respects the purpose of a full cooperation with the French fleet and Army on the *Continent*. The Authority should be Plenipotentiary to draw out men and supplies of every kind and give their sanction to any operations which the Commander in chief may not think himself at liberty to undertake without it as well beyond, as within, the limits of these States.[54]

And to James Duane he wrote on the same day: "I wish the Chancellor or yourself could be in the appointment. A well composed committee is of primary importance." The day before, Schuyler had written to Duane from headquarters to say that dictatorial powers should be lodged in the Commander in Chief, either alone or conjointly with a committee of Congress. He, too, wished that Duane or the Chancellor could be one of its members.

Washington's phrase "as well beyond, as within, the limits of these States," suggested, it has been well said, the equivalent of giving a modern president wartime powers.[55] Nothing that is known about Washington authorizes the belief that he even contemplated a sole dictatorship: but he was attracted to centralized authority, he was a soldier at bay, and he may well have looked for the solution to his troubles in a committee of Congress that would exercise dictatorial powers through him. That was the farthest extent, also, of the Chancellor's plans. On June 9, he wrote to Schuyler about the possibility that General Washington's powers might be limited by act of Congress to the boundaries of the United States. "I consider this a thing of no consequence," he wrote, "except as it may remove the blind behind which it would have been possible to mask our designs."[56] The weakness of the Articles of Confederation, should they be ratified, made these designs imperative: "greater power must lodge somewhere," he told Duane. Otherwise, the people would take matters into their own hands and "will vest elsewhere what Congress are unwilling to trust themselves with—Or some daring Genious, with necessity for his plea, shall seize what they dare not give."[57]

In 1780, the nationalist group in Congress was not strong enough to impose its will, and, if the Articles had been ratified in that year, could have imposed it only by revolution. Dictatorial powers, in any event, whether exercised by Congress or by a committee of Congress, were extraordinarily dangerous. They meant that Congress could use the army to extract money or provisions or soldiers from recalcitrant states; or the navy, if navy there was, to enforce its decisions by seizing their vessels and prohibiting their trade. Nathaniel Peabody might complain that he had heard of people being led through the wilderness by a cloud, but not in a fog: yet if Congress had been less foggy and more forcible, would even the "nominal union" of the states have survived?[58]

Such considerations did not at first trouble the Chancellor or his fellow nationalists. Here was the crisis: there the solution; only one step was needed in order to bring them together. The Chancellor had already, as chairman of a committee for increasing the powers of Congress, thrown out the bold suggestion that Congress should immediately and "by the authority which the nature of the trust reposed in them vests them with" assume the necessary powers. The report which contained this suggestion—or "the grand design" as he called it—was hastily tabled.[59]

Since nationalism ended by conferring dictatorial powers, not on a committee or a general, but on a financier, one may assume that its motives were chiefly economic. The financier, elected in February, 1781, was Robert Morris, an international merchant who took up his duties with great reluctance in September, performed them ably, but never hesitated to mingle private interest with public office. He had always made money out of the war; he proposed to continue to do so: no man was in less danger of confusing patriotism with self-restraint. His dictatorship, however, was more dictatorial in scope than in practice: it never succeeded in obtaining permanent revenues for Congress. None the less, since the connection between nationalism and the public debt and between nationalism and the dominant land companies is sufficiently obvious to be a truism, this was no doubt the kind of dictatorship that the nationalists preferred. When, as a result of the Boston Convention in August, the New York Legislature—of all bodies—proposed on October 10 that the right method for dealing with a deficient state was for Congress to direct the Commander in Chief to "march the Army, or such part of the Army as may be requisite, into such State; and by a Military force, compel it to furnish its deficiency," James Duane shrank from proposing such a measure. It would, he said, be "not perhaps proper for publick Inspection."[60] When John Mathews, of the Committee at Headquarters, actually moved on the floor of Congress that Washington be given sole dictatorial powers, his reception was enough to convince anyone that Congress was in no mood for such proposals. Indeed, when he made them, the committee itself had already been dismissed.[61]

It is difficult to see the militancy that men like the Chancellor professed in 1780 as other than the clamor of a minority group. When the nationalists became more powerful in 1781, they were more disposed to look upon Congress as a respectable body, capable of exerting its own powers without calling upon the army. The Chancellor's own motives were, in any case, sufficiently mixed: he was not a speculator in land or in the public debt; he was a great landholder, who did not wish to increase his holdings but simply to preserve them from the state tax gatherer. But his motives were not only fiscal: he also had an unfortunate contempt for state legislators. It was not the strength, but the weakness of the state, which he deplored; not its selfishness, but its democracy.

VI

After he had moved for a committee at headquarters in April, and sustained the subsequent debate, the Chancellor left Philadelphia for a while. His wife was very near her time, and she had chosen one of her father's houses in Lebanon, New Jersey, for her accouchement. He went to Lebanon with her, and there, on May 5, a daughter was born and christened Elizabeth Stevens Livingston. His intention, it seems, was to move on to Clermont as soon as his wife was fit to travel again: a letter from Philip Schuyler, written on April 23, begged him to return to Philadelphia. "I should deem myself Inexcusable and failing in duty to my country," Schuyler wrote, "if I did not urge you to lay aside every thought of leaving us in the present Critical not to say extremely distressing conjuncture. . . . I need not tell you that our affairs are running rapidly to some violent crisis, that the present distresses do not seem to admit of remedy in the Ordinary Course of things."[62]

But the Chancellor, as usual, was undergoing one of his fits of revulsion at politics; the debates of April 6 to 12 were said to have been very severe, because the antinationalists moved in on their opponents. Having helped to appoint his committee and done his best—but in vain—

to give them adequate instructions, he seems to have felt that he had done enough. John Mathews wrote on April 24, begging him at least to ride to headquarters. "Can you at such a time find it in your heart to leave us?" Mathews wrote. "For heavens sake, deprive us not of your assistance at such a time. Let me repeat my earnest request, my worthy friend."[63] His worthy friend, however, lingered on in Lebanon, maintaining a desultory correspondence with his friends in Philadelphia.

Not the least of these was François de Barbé-Marbois, the self-styled Marquis and Secretary of the French Legation. With the legation, the Chancellor had always striven to be on good terms. "I am happy to hear that you stand so well with the Minister," his mother had written in February: and, indeed, the connection between the nationalists and the French was always close. The French may not have entertained any sympathy for a strong American republic; but a strong government pro tempore very much suited their desires. There were, also, the attractions of good society. Luzerne pleased the Chancellor because he was a nobleman, and Marbois because he had charming manners: and the Chancellor, with his genial and fashionable airs, his habit of command, his sensibilities and revulsions, his manorial wealth, was at any rate intelligible to men like Luzerne and Marbois. He was sympathetic as a man and useful as a politician; he was quite above bribery, but might he not offer for nothing a friendship that other men sometimes extended only for cash? *"Nous regrettons tous les jours,"* Marbois wrote on April 9, in a letter which hinted (and rather more than hinted) at a possible mission to France, *"que les circonstances vous aient éloigné de nous, et que nous ayions du être privés des avantages de votre amitié et de vos lumières, au moment même où une connaissance plus intime pouvoit vous inspirer plus de confiance pour nous."*[64]

More confidence. They believed that the Chancellor was accessible to flattery: they did not think him a fool. He was independent and would think for himself; and French demands for strong congressional action ought, in his opinion, to be accompanied by some military action on the part of the French. After receiving Marbois's letter, he set out for Kingston, where the New York Legislature had convened: but, stopping off at headquarters to consult with Mathews and Schuyler, he heard the great news that six French ships of the line and six thousand troops were to have left France in April "and should call at Rhode Island early in June." On May 18, he was in Philadelphia, writing to Governor Clinton to say that, in spite of his determination not to return to that city, he had been stopped on his way home by important intelligence "too delicate to dwell upon in a letter." He was determined to stay as long as he could, but "as my money and credit are exhausted and my affairs are not in the most promising situation at home," he had some doubts on this point.[65]

He settled down in the lodging house kept by Mrs. Mary House and her daughter, the gentle and motherly Mrs. Eliza Trist, at the corner of Fifth and Market Streets. It was the home of nationalists—James Madison, John Mathews, when he was not at headquarters, Joseph Jones, James Duane. Six specie dollars per diem, or $2520 a week in the new money, which was already quoted at sixty to one, would cover—he told the Governor—his essential expenses: for board alone "according to a late demand for a gentleman and his servant [cost] £270 cont[inenta]l per week, exclusive even of table beer." He only wished that the Legislature, which might well question the economy of its delegates, since New York had not yet "reached the summit of extravagance which prevails in this city," would provide a house and table under the direction of a steward.[66]

In the meantime, he plunged once again into the politics of nationalism. He was chairman of the committee which, at Luzerne's request, consulted with that gentleman on the proper reception for the French fleet and army, and which, on May 24, produced a powerful report. He endeavored, once again, and once again without success, to strengthen the powers of the Committee at Headquarters. He worked on the report of the committee for strengthening the powers of Congress. He wrote a circular letter to the states, calling on them for greater exertions, and using language so energetic and indeed so intemperate that two passages were struck out. His labors reached their culmination in a series of resolutions of August 22, two of which—a proposal for a state tax of 2½ per cent on exports, to be collected for congressional purposes by congressional officers, and the proposal for a state levy of 5 per cent on captured vessels and cargoes, to be used for the maintenance of the navy—were certainly striking. They were aiming, tangentially but distinctly, at a congressional impost on imports and exports: but the Committee of Ways and Means laid them aside. By this time, the Committee at Headquarters, whose language had grown more and more forcible, as its membership grew numerically more and more feeble, shrinking by the sickness of Peabody and the absence of Schuyler to the solitary but obstreperous Mathews, had been recalled by Congress. With its recall, the militancy of nationalism departed from Philadelphia, and flared up in Boston, in Hartford, in the New York Legislature. In September, the Chancellor, also, prepared to depart: like John Mathews, he had experienced the rough side of the antinationalists' tongue: but, unlike Mathews, he had not developed that carapace which is so necessary to the evolution of political men.[67]

His stay in the city that summer led to one curious and melancholy incident. The Livingstons of Clermont had always kept a soft spot in their hearts for General Benedict Arnold. He had been Montgomery's companion at Quebec and had been wounded in the same assault that had killed Montgomery; he had befriended Henry Beekman Livingston during the Saratoga campaign, and had testified to the Colonel's courage in the Battle of Bemis Heights. Arnold, who was now military commander of Philadelphia, had two predominant passions—money and social recognition. He was attracted to the Livingstons on both counts. John R. Livingston, in July, 1778, had entered into one of his many dubious financial ventures—something to do with the purchase of Loyalist goods in New York, in advance of the capture of that city.[68] The Chancellor was the last man to be tempted by such offers; but he was very susceptible to other advances. Female companionship was always a necessity to him. No man displayed a more agreeable *empressement* in the presence of attractive ladies; like his grandfather Robert of Clermont, he delighted in fashioning compliments; and in sets of verses and series of notes would lay himself at the feet of any enchantress—of any enchantress, that is to say, who moved in tolerable society. His conquests were purely metaphorical; he was a loyal husband, who carried his gallantries toward others up to but not beyond the point where they would be acceptable to any woman of spirit; and his wife herself became in time one of the most equable and amused of confidantes. But his egotism, which was certainly not small, was warmed by female attentions: and in the summer of 1780, when he was living by himself in Philadelphia, no woman was more attentive to his cajoleries than Margaret Shippen Arnold. Mrs. Arnold was a bewitching young blond, whom a disastrous fate had endowed with a wanton temperament, a warm heart, and a vain, cold purpose: in the summer of 1780, she was deeply involved in treachery. What she and her husband needed was his appointment to the command at West Point: and in the Chancellor she found just the assistance she required.

He fell quite innocently into her trap. West Point was in danger; its commander, General Robert Howe, was not very active; and, like Schuyler, Livingston believed that General Arnold would be an admirable substitute. The Livingstons thought of West Point almost, if not quite, as if it were a family fortress: if it fell, their lands would be ravaged; its proper defense was a matter, to them, of profound personal concern. The Chancellor would not have written to George Washington, as he did, suggesting that General Arnold should be given the post, simply because Peggy Arnold was a charming young woman.

The letter to Washington was written on June 22, and the General replied that "when a general arrangement is gone into—& a disposition is made for the Campaign, I can with propriety—and shall most certainly—bring G. H. [Major General Robert Howe] into the line of the Army, & place the Gentleman you have named at that Post: if the operations of the campaign are such as to render it expedient to leave an officer of that rank in that command." And he told Joseph Reed that the appointment had been "hinted to me by a very respectable character, a member of Congress (not Schuyler)" as "not unacceptable to the state most immediately interested in the welfare and safety of the post."[69]

And so the appointment was made, and the fatal Arnold left for West Point in the middle of July.

As you have neither purling streams nor sighing swains at West Point, 'tis no place for me; nor do I think Mrs. Arnold will be long pleased with it [his sister Hannah wrote to him]. Though I expect it may be rendered dear to her for a few hours by the presence of a certain chancellor; who, by the by, is a dangerous companion for a particular lady in the absence of her husband. . . . I could say more than prudence will permit. I could tell you of frequent private assignations and of numberless *billets doux,* if I had an inclination to make mischief.[70]

Hannah Arnold never betrayed an inclination more clearly: and since nobody else ever mentioned this incident, we must assume that she mistook, and purposely mistook, one of the Chancellor's customary flirtations for an infidelity he was careful to avoid.

When the news of Arnold's treachery reached him, he was as stunned as the next man: everybody who knew Arnold suspected him of everything but an unwillingness to fight for his country. It was because he was a fighting man that the Livingstons wanted him at West Point. "I have felt much for Mrs. Arnold," the Chancellor wrote, however, for he was never disloyal to a pretty face. "If as is supposed she is ignorant of her husband's crime she is really to be pitied—if she is still at Philadelphia either by yourself or her sister make any comps. to her & her sisters in whose distress I most cordially participate."[71] His mother's comment from Clermont was a good deal more to the point. "Had Arnold's treachery taken effect," she wrote, "what must have been my situation!"[72]

CHAPTER FIVE

When the Chancellor left Philadelphia toward the end of September, 1780, he did so with a determination never to be a delegate again. Fate, he was convinced, had not cut him out to be a politician. In his confidential intercourse with Luzerne and Marbois, however, he had tasted blood: it was unlikely that he would be satisfied for long with a vegetable diet—with settling down, that is to say, with his wife and child in his rebuilt farm at Clermont; attending the Legislature, when his attendance was required; holding a Chancery Court, should one be necessary; cultivating leisure, with the country at war.

The condition of the state, to one who returned to it after an absence of many months, did not encourage such ideas. It was reaching the melancholy climax of a long series of accumulated disasters. The five lower counties, which had borne three-fifths of its colonial burdens, had long been lost; in the year of Burgoyne's expedition, it had been ravaged from end to end, except for a thirty-mile radius around Albany; in 1778, the Indians had laid waste, with all the hideous accompaniments of savage warfare, the whole of Tryon County south of the Mohawk; in 1779, the crops had been blighted and the harvest poor; in 1780, the enemy had again devastated Tryon County and captured all the northern forts except Fort Edward. Such had been its mournful history—a history, moreover, that required it to keep, at its own expense, a larger number of militia in the field than any other state.[1] Had the British and the Indians been halted on the north and the west? Had the disclosure of Arnold's treachery ended all threats to the Highlands from the south? These were old questions: but the public mood that now projected them had become almost counter-revolutionary.

The immediate cause seems to have been that Colonel Udny Hay, the state purchasing agent, had forbidden all private dealings between the farmers and the contractors for the French army: he and his agents alone had the right to supply them. The farmers, without exactly impugning Colonel Hay's motives, came back with the argument that he was favoring the French army at the expense of the Continental one—an early example of the nativist thinking that so often accompanies a state of agrarian distress.[2]

The distress went much deeper than anything for which Colonel Hay and his cohorts could be made accountable. Colonel Hay was a faithful public servant; and if things went wrong under his control, they were only superficial symptoms of some greater malady. A more disturbing, a far more enervating symptom was the lack of money of any kind: the state embargo on exports, the hoarding of specie gained through trade with the enemy, the fact that quartermaster's certificates, received in exchange for army supplies, were not legal tender and did not circulate rapidly—all these were part of the ulcer that drained away the state's financial energy. As for the origin of the ulcer—what else could it be than a distrust of civil authority at any level, continental or state, county or district?

In January, 1781, the Chancellor told George Washington that if all the money in New York State could be collected, it would not amount to more than "£20,000 in specie or an equivalent in continental money even at 40 for one. Wheat is at present the only currency in the country." His own account books certainly bear out this contention. But the price of wheat, contradictory as it might seem, was very low because of the "apprehentions which any possessor of wheat is under that it will be forceably taken from him & exchanged for certificates which are of no value to him."[3]

We have taken effectual means to prevent the admission of any [money] [he told Gouverneur Morris in the same month] by refusing to let our staple commodities go out or the french agent to purchase except through Coll Hay—In the mean while taxes are called for & supplies impressed for the use of the army—The powers of government overstretched are ready to burst—The people are clamorous the whole county of Dutchess have chosen precinct & County committees to instruct their members &c.—Some districts in Albany have gone further & chosen members for a State convention— You have seen the Manor resolves. . . .[4]

It was only too true. The people of Livingston Manor, for example, met on January 5, in order to formulate their grievances and appoint a committee. This committee was to consort, ten days later, with other and similar committees at Albany. The upshot of it all was to be the summoning of a convention of delegates from the counties, which would lay before the State Legislature their intentions "to get certain laws repealed and if the Legislature will not ease the People of their fears and lighten their Burdens to throw the Burdens off their shoulders even if they should fall on some other People's necks." The Livingston Manor tenants were notoriously lukewarm in their patriotism; but they had not initiated the meeting of January 5. It had been carefully advertised in such language as would whet their curiosity; the resolutions they were to vote upon were "first read to them in English and then explained in Dutch"; they had then voted in favor of each one, in a spirited but decorous manner.[5]

The resolutions railed at everything—exorbitant taxes, plural office-holders, state commissaries and French army contractors, delegates to the Continental Congress who had lost touch with their constituents, arbitrary state laws. The tenth resolution, calling for the repeal of a law which assessed a fine upon persons whose sons had gone over to the enemy, without exemption for parents who were good Whigs, was held by some to be a Tory scheme to bring about a reconciliation with England. But the real intention of the committee, to which the Livingston Manor tenants would certainly have objected had they known of it, was compressed into a secret instruction to make every effort to increase the state's quota of Continental troops to prevent the expense and inconvenience of calling out the militia to protect the frontiers. "If these are not Whig sentiments," wrote Walter Livingston, "I do not know what are."[6]

The Chancellor was profoundly distressed, not merely at a movement which, he thought, could only "encourage the enemy and shock the Govt. at least if not the Constitution,"[7] but also at the thought that his own kinsmen, Walter and John Livingston of the manor, were deeply involved in it. Indeed, only an agitated letter of his, which reached Walter Livingston just as he was alighting from his horse at the place of meeting, prevented that gentleman from taking the chair. He yielded it, with difficulty, to Captain Jacob Shaver. The union of landlord and tenant in Hudson River politics was certainly unnatural; and it resembled other unnatural events in seeming distinctly ill-omened.

George Washington's response to the Chancellor's distressing news is full of interest.

Dear Sir [he wrote from New Windsor on January 31], the disagreeable events which have taken place in the Pennsyla. and Jersey lines—the general discontent of the army for want of pay, cloathing & provisions—added to the usual course of business (which increases with our perplexities) will, I am persuaded, be admitted as a sufficient apology for my not acknowledging the receipt of your confidential and obliging letter of the 8th., till now.

To learn from so good authority as you, that the distresses of the Citizens of this State are maturing into complaints which are likely to produce serious consequences, is a circumstance as necessary to be known, as it is unpleasant to hear—and I thank you for the communication.—The Committees now forming, are at this crisis, disagreeable things; & if they cannot be counteracted, or diverted from their original purposes, may outrun the views of the well meaning members of them, and plunge this country into deeper distress and confusion than it has hitherto experienced; though I have no doubt, but that the same bountiful Providence which has relieved us in a variety of difficulties heretofore will enable us to emerge from them ultimately—and crown our struggles with success.

To trace these evils to their source is by no means difficult—and errors once discovered are more than half corrected—This I hope is our case at present—But there can be no radical cure, till Congress is vested by the several States with full and ample Powers to enact Laws for general purposes—and till the Executive business is placed in the hands of able men & responsible characters—Requisitions then, will be supported by Law—Jealousies, and these ruinous delays, and illtimed compliances—arising from distrust, & the fear of doing more than a Sister state, will cease—System and order will take place—and oeconomy must follow—but not till we have corrected the fundamental errors, enumerated above.—

It would be difficult not to prove that less than half the present expenditures (including certificates) is more than sufficient if we had money, and these alterations were adopted—to answer all our purposes—Taxes of course would be lessened—the burthen would be equalled & light—and men sharing a common Lot, would neither murmur nor despair.

The picture you have drawn of the distresses of the People of this State I am persuaded is true; and I have taken the liberty in a late letter, and in as delicate terms as I could express my sentiments to hint to Congress the propriety of leaving the resources of this State, and Jersey, as a kind of reserve—further than this might bring on me the charge of an intermeddler—till I could speak decisively of my own knowledge.

At all times—and under all circumstances—you will please & honor me by a free communication of your sentiments, as I can with much truth assure you that with the greatest esteem and affection, I am—Dr. Sir. yr. most obedt., and obliged servant, Gọ Washington. The Honble Mr. Chancelr. Livingston.[8]

This was certainly a gallant letter on any terms; and one that must have gratified its recipient, both as a nationalist and as a local magnate. What it could offer by way of remedy for a situation in which it was soon to be clear that the new Continental money would never be exchanged for the old, since there was not enough of the old to effect an exchange—where, in the course of time, what was left of the old money was idly and sluggishly to circulate at the rate of a thousand for one, where deflation seemed to have settled in the heart of inflation—is perhaps doubtful. But then, it was not in order to suggest specific remedies that General Washington had written his letter. As for the committees and the convention, they fortunately never passed from the ominous to the numinous: the committees disbanded, the convention came to nothing. The manor Livingstons, prompted by the Chancellor, soon defected from this alliance with the tenantry; but the counterrevolutionary mood was more difficult to dispel.[9]

II

"You wish to know how I employ myself here abstracted from politicks—Like our own first parents—I dig plant prune walk talk &c and am even guilty of one sin which so far as I can learn the seductions of the devil could never bring them to—I write bad verses."[10] Such was the Chancellor's description of himself in April, 1781: as usual, it was partly an affectation. He was a patriotic and an ambitious man; and although his fondness for country life was genuine, his idleness at this juncture was a pose which he sustained with difficulty. Beyond the boundaries of Clermont, there was nothing to gratify a man who found—or professed to find—that he had no influence with the Legislature, and who watched its doings with a show of detachment which was manifestly irritable and insincere.[11] In Continental politics, he had shown none of the brilliance of James Madison, his fellow lodger in Philadelphia, whom he had learned to admire and perhaps to envy; and none of the sly persistence of his colleague James Duane. He did not abandon hope. After the world of politics, from which he had fled to bury himself in "the small sphere of my State where I believe I can be of some use," there might be—who could tell?—the world of statecraft.

On s'occupe du choix d'un Secrétaire du départment des affairs étrangères [Marbois had written on January 2]. *Si ce choix tomboit sur vous, je ne doute pas de l'avantage que tous les ministres accrédités auprès du Congrès trouveroient à négocier avec quelqu'un qui réunit les lumières à l'attachment le plus pur à Son pays. Mais vous êtes trop philosophique solliciter les distinctions et les emplois. . . .*[12]

One can but admire the deftness with which Marbois touched the two chords—natural ability, philosophical detachment—most likely to charm his correspondent into a good opinion of himself. The Chancellor replied that he was "extremely flattered by the opinion you are pleased to entertain of my capacity to serve the publick at this interesting period. . . . I deem it an honor to have been named to the place [the Department of Foreign Affairs] you mention tho' . . . I have no reason to expect the appointment about which indeed I am little solicitous."[13]

Ever since the fall of 1779, when he had been considered for the mission that was ultimately bestowed upon John Adams, he had been a possible candidate for some diplomatic post. In February, 1780, and again in

May, there was some talk of sending him to France. In this, much more was at stake than a mission: it was part of the endless maneuvers between the radical Adams-Lee group in Congress, determined to weaken George Washington and Benjamin Franklin, and the nationalists and the French Legation, determined to uphold them. The sending of young John Laurens to France in December put an end to the Chancellor's hopes, if he had ever entertained them.[14] But he was not simply a shuttlecock in this game; he would not have been considered at all, and certainly not by Luzerne and Marbois, if he had not been one of the abler and more personable of the nationalists.

Marbois's letters, as 1781 wore on, grew more numerous and more pressing. He urged the exile at Clermont to return, if not as a candidate for the Department of Foreign Affairs, then as a delegate: but at all events to return. The Chancellor, on his side, began to show signs of relenting: what ambitious man, conscious of his abilities, anxious to employ them, could have resisted such flattering pressure?

He appeared in Philadelphia, merely as a visitor, in summer, having stopped on the way to visit General Washington. "I see nothing within my reach worth grasping," he wrote to Gouverneur Morris in June, "peace & ease are my present objects but I feel I would sacrifice both if I saw any means of rendering more useful services to the community at Philadelphia than in my present situation."[15] At Philadelphia, he found that among the names most frequently mentioned for the Foreign Department, his own and Arthur Lee's led all the rest. On August 10, 1781, he was elected secretary for Foreign Affairs.

III

The executive departments, which emerged in 1781 out of a cloud of committees, represented a modest triumph for the nationalist or constructionist group in Congress, for the entrepreneurs of the middle states who supported them, and for their allies in the French Legation. Their radical opponents had an honest instinctive dread of centralized power: as Burke had put it, before he lost interest in the Americans, the Americans were accustomed "to snuff the approach of tyranny in every tainted breeze." To Samuel Adams, for example, the Continental Congress presented itself in all the simple majesty of an enlarged New England town meeting: were it to assume a more powerful aspect, it would, to his mind, be defeating the very ends for which it had been called into being. The radicals' system of conducting congressional business through a multitude of small special committees seemed providentially designed to prevent such a defeat.

But power, as we know, or think we know, tends to corrupt: and behind their feeble decentralizing system of small committees, the radicals were gradually gathering power into their own hands. They became remarkably efficient in the manipulation of inefficiency. They were, after all, only human: and their motives had more of the pure revolutionary fervor than could be discerned in those of their opponents.

Whether the change in congressional personnel was responsible, or the distressful winter of 1779-1780, or the erosion of plots and counterplots, it is certain that the New England–Virginia alliance, which was the backbone of the radical group, was seriously weakened in 1780. At the same time, the system of management through small committees began to harden into a system of management through boards and through standing committees: thus the power that the radicals had gathered into their hands was, to some exent, dispersed and reordered. When the military nationalism of 1780, visibly represented by the congressional Committee at Headquarters, was replaced by the respectable nationalism of a businesslike majority, the idea of executive departments could be realized.

Ironically enough, such an idea could have succeeded, at such a time, only under a dictatorship. The Articles of Confederation, finally ratified in 1781, were founded, it would seem, on the charming assumption that men could be like angels, and should be given every chance to prove it, whereas the Constitution of 1787 was based, after a brief experience of government under the Articles, on the belief that mankind was essentially depraved and must be restrained from depravity. The Articles provided, no doubt, as strong a government as could be hoped for in 1781; and in some instances, notably in its handling of the western territory, government under the Articles did very well. Yet the Confederation depended upon the good will of the several states; there was, at its very heart, an innocence which made it one of the least effective and most amiable of experiments.

The Department of Foreign Affairs, during the first year of the Confederation, was only in little better shape than its otiose predecessor, the Committee for Foreign Affairs. Congress as a whole was still the executive; the committee system was still in existence, ready, like a wounded but not moribund hydra, at any moment to bring forth some special head which could usurp, temporarily but completely, the functions of the secretary.

The Department was first heard of in May, 1780, when a committee was appointed to report a plan; the report was made in June; but it was not until December that consideration of the report was again recorded in the *Journals* of Congress. In January, 1781, it was resolved to create a Department of Foreign Affairs; and the "Remarks & Resolutions" of the committee, in James Duane's handwriting, and dated January 10, duly found their way to the Chancellor in Clermont. He had, from the beginning, been a leading contender for the office of secretary: his leading opponent, from the beginning, had been Arthur Lee.[16]

Whatever considerations may have prompted the consideration of Lee, it is safe to say that the efficiency of the new Department was not among them. He was quarrelsome and unstable; but the New England–Virginia alliance (the so-called [Samuel] Adams-[R. H.] Lee faction) was still united enough to push him forward. As one of the three commissioners for negotiating a treaty with France, he had, at any rate, conceived a hatred for France and for Benjamin Franklin: and detachment from the French monarchy, together with the ruin of Benjamin Franklin, seemed the leading feature of the radicals' foreign policy. The Chancellor, on the other hand, was known to be very intimate with the French in Philadelphia, from whom he never bothered to conceal (for example) his distaste for John Adams, who, in turn, was distrusted by the French Foreign Minister, M. de Vergennes. It was assumed that the Chancellor would be the mouthpiece for M. de la Luzerne. Thus the radical and anti-Gallican forces were arrayed behind Lee, and the nationalist and Gallican forces behind Livingston.

There were several attempts at voting—probably one between March 21 and April 6, another on May 18, and others toward the end of July.[17] What remains of the Chancellor's correspondence at this time does not help one to confirm or deny these probabilities. It does show that he believed that James Madison—for whom he had the greatest esteem—would be nominated along with himself and Arthur Lee; and that in the first week of May his friends had given up hope of making him secretary, but wished him to come to Philadelphia for other reasons. "You will be made President of Congress," Gouverneur Morris wrote on May 7. "There is not a moment to be lost." And he added, by way of inducement, "Should I tell you the pretty or rather soft Things which many Ladies here say of you your Modesty might doubt my Veracity. I think I perceive some Sparks of Jealousy among them with relation to each other on the score of your Honor—You are a sad wicked Fellow." The Chancellor was proof against these charming insinuations: he remained at Clermont. He had not himself given up hope of obtaining the Department of Foreign Affairs, did not wish to do so at the expense of James Madison (who never wanted it), and was, on the whole, disposed to follow the direction of Marbois. The contest was, after all, one between those who mistrusted and those who trusted the French.[18]

Marbois said that the French Legation did not care to state its preference openly, *"car avec certaines personnes ce seroit un motif d'exclusion"*:[19] but from March until July, in a stream of letters, he besought his friend to come back to Philadelphia. It appears that the secretaryship, while important in its way, was a secondary consideration with him: what he needed most was friends in Congress. In this respect, his letter of June 29 is particularly suggestive: "more than ever" the French Legation needed the Chancellor. (*"Je vous ai invité à venir dans le Congrès mon cher Chancellier, et je presse plus que jamais d'y venir."*) He went on to say that certain features in the news from France concerning the peace negotiations there might well be disturbing to a New Yorker; and that it would take enlightened men in Congress to approve the disinterested conduct of the King of France.[20] On June 15, the French party had gained a notable triumph, when John Jay, Benjamin Franklin, Henry Laurens, and Thomas Jefferson were united to John Adams as peace commissioners, with instructions that put them unequivocally in the hands of France.[21] Yet even after this triumph, Marbois was more pressing than ever.

The truth was that the military and financial situation of France had become so ominous in the winter of 1780-1781, and the condition of the United States apparently so desperate, that the Comte de Vergennes was almost ready to abandon the cause of American independence. In a confidential memorandum, dated February, 1781, he declared himself ready— if the worst came to the worst—to close the war "as far as the United States and Great Britain were concerned, by means of a long time truce *uti possidetis* between Colonies and mother country." This truce would accept the actual war map as it was at the beginning of 1781, with the British in control of the ports of New York, Charleston, and Savannah, most of Maine, the Great Lakes country, and the far Northwest. The French King could hardly make this proposal himself: but he could persuade the United States to attend an Austro-Russian mediation congress at Vienna, and the mediators could then propose it themselves. It is perhaps needless to add that such a truce would have been fatal to the American cause.[22]

Vergennes composed a set of instructions to Luzerne, dated March 9, 1781, which were designed, in the words of one authority, "to prepare the Americans to be led, if necessary in the last extremity, to the abbatoir at Vienna." In other words, Congress should declare itself willing to accept a mediation; and, what was infinitely worse, resign itself to the possibility that, in a crisis such as might arise at any time, "His Majesty will accept conditionally for himself and for the United States."[23] The French would manage American affairs for them, even though the Americans already had a minister plenipotentiary in Europe.

But this minister was John Adams; and John Adams was growing suspicious of Vergennes and was soon to penetrate into the heart of his schemes. When Vergennes's dispatch of March 9 reached Luzerne in Philadelphia, the Minister communicated portions of it to a committee of his own choice, and among these were "several observations respecting the conduct of Mr. Adams." Upon the sturdy independence of Mr. Adams, at this juncture, much depended: but Luzerne warned the committee that he expected Congress to order its minister "to take no steps without the approbation of his majesty; and . . . to receive his directions from the Count de Vergennes, or from the person who might be charged with the negotiation in the name of the King." The French Minister had already (on May 25) communicated to Congress the offer of a new subsidy of six million livres turnois; he now concluded his conference of May 28 by observing "that a great object was to secure the United States from the proposition of *uti possidetis*; that the surest way to obtain that end was to induce the English to confess that they are not able to conquer them." In short, if the Americans could obtain some outstanding military victory, they might save themselves from the dreadful truce the King of France proposed to wish upon them: this suggestion was thrown out at the moment when Cornwallis seemed headed for an inevitable victory.[24]

There is no doubt at all that Vergennes and Luzerne hoped that the United States would, by some miraculous exertion, obtain the upper hand: they were not unfriendly men; they were not even false according to their own lights. Was the same true of Marbois? Even more than Luzerne, who boasted to Vergennes of his success with bribes,[25] he had a poor opinion of American politicians. In his letter of June 29 to the Chancellor, he was writing to a man who was altogether above bribery; and yet in this letter he suggested, in very guarded language, that even an eminent New Yorker might—through some peculiar insight into the disinterested character of the King of France—bring himself to accept a truce which would leave vast portions of his state in the enemy's hands. Or, rather, since nobody in America at the time was in a position to fathom Vergennes's designs, this was what Marbois expected the Chancellor to do when at length these designs were made known to him. No misunderstanding could have been more complete.

As it happened, the mediation came to nothing, owing to the obstinacy of George III, who never failed in his own way to further the cause of American independence: and then the victory of Yorktown provided just the sort of miracle that should efface, for the time being, these wandering traces of a scheme for some shameful truce. The French party never learned of the duplicity of Vergennes and Luzerne. They continued to believe in the good faith of their allies. Upon this uncertain foundation, the Chancellor commenced his career as secretary for Foreign Affairs.

Luzerne, having shown his mastery of Congress in the matter of the instructions of June 15, was thereafter free to meddle in the secondary problem of the Foreign Department. He told Vergennes that he alone was responsible for the election of Chancellor Livingston.[26] He was certainly exaggerating: but his purse was always ready, and his influence was useful even where he dared not use his purse. On August 8, 1781, the final election began. On that day, Arthur Lee received the votes of Massachusetts, Connecticut, New Jersey, Delaware, and Virginia—two short of the necessary majority of seven. On the second day, so Lee told Samuel Adams, "Virginia was prevaild on to throw away its vote, and the Chancellor had Hamps'e, R. Island, N. York, Jersey, S. Carolina and Georgia. Dr. Witherspoon [of New Jersey, who was in some eccentric way both pro-Lee and pro-French, and who was amenable to Luzerne's cajoleries though not to his bribes] stayd away, and his Colleagues changed sides. On the third day [August 10] Mr. [Thomas] Smith of this State [Pennsylvania], with his senses hardly recovered from a fall that took them away entirely, was brought in and with Mr. [George] Clymer [of Pennsylvania] carried the Election."[27] The Chancellor had been elected by eight votes to four, with Virginia giving her vote to James McClurg. "This morning," the New York delegates wrote to Governor Clinton, "Mr. Chancellor Livingston was Elected Minister for Foreign Afairs—an appointment which will be very agreeable to the foreign courts in our Friendship on account of his Rank, Connections, and abilities."[28] Just how much value the foreign courts placed upon the rank of a Hudson River magnate must remain in some doubt: but the appointment was certainly agreeable to the Chevalier de la Luzerne and his industrious apprentice, M. de Barbé-Marbois.

IV

It should not be too difficult to guess, it would be impossible to state with precision, what Luzerne and Marbois expected of Chancellor Livingston. It is not to be supposed that their expectations were, morally, on a high plane. Had they been intellectuals, which they demonstrably were not, their ideas of American society would have leaned more toward those of DePauw and Linguet than those of Brezard, or Mandrillon, or, later, Raynal—more toward the belief that Americans were degenerate than toward the hope that they would soon inaugurate a new golden age.[29] Luzerne and Marbois had lived too long at Philadelphia; and if Luzerne had any belief in an American golden age, it would have been in the meager and transient one that trickled from his own purse. He was tolerant, friendly, and skeptical. He was far too wise to suppose that he could bribe the Chancellor: but if he treated him with deference, with attention, would that not produce the same result? What Luzerne needed was a secretary for Foreign Affairs who would be his mouthpiece in his communications to Congress, and in Livingston, he thought, mistakenly as it turned out, that he had found just such a man.

It is well to remember what France hoped to gain out of the American Revolution, and the sacrifices that she expected the Americans to make in return for her manifold assistance. The American Revolution was, from a French point of view, merely a logical extension, one might almost say a renewal, of the Seven Years' War. It was because the fear of French Canada had been removed by that war that the American colonies had felt secure enough to argue with the mother country; and when that argument eventually grew strident and became an exchange of shots at Lexington and Concord, the French saw in that exchange their chance for the revenge they had been seeking for the Treaty of Paris. Revenge is not a word a Frenchman utters lightly. The Comte de Vergennes used to say that he could never think of the Treaty of Paris without a shudder. When France entered the war against Great Britain after Saratoga, his dreams embraced a world-wide variety of objectives: a share in the Newfoundland fisheries, both for the profit to be derived from them and because they would be a nursery for French sailors; a strong position in the West Indies; control of the gum trade of West Africa; and, above all, a sphere of influence in India. These dreams were almost Napoleonic, nothing less than mastery of the trade routes between America and India—a renovation of the empire that had been ruined by the Seven Years' War. American independence entered into them only peripherally: it was something to be abandoned if the war went against France, and something to be tolerated if it did not. In return, the Americans were expected not to press their demands for a right to the inshore Newfoundland fisheries, and not to oppose the Spanish command that they should keep away from the east bank of the Mississippi.

Spain had, fatally enough, thrust herself into the French dream: she was demanding Gibraltar and Minorca and the integrity of her South American empire: the British were to be driven from Honduras and the Gulf of Mexico, the Americans were to be pent up inside the Alleghenies. The latter consideration was never, to be sure, a *sine qua non* with Vergennes, but he did not altogether disagree with it; for he perceived in the American Revolution, dimly, instinctively, and correctly, the eventual downfall of his own order. Although the radicals in the Continental Congress scarcely guessed at the sweeping nature of France's ambitions, their instinct warned them to be suspicious of the French: what had monarchists to do with republics, or autocrats with rebels? Would not France sacrifice American objectives to European ones? We are not authorized to say that these suspicions were unfounded.

Livingston was supposed to be on far too good terms with the Chevalier de la Luzerne; he was one of the leaders of the French party, in and out of Congress. But of the American representatives abroad when he was elected secretary, only Benjamin Franklin in Paris was well-disposed toward the French. His venerable figure, in its sober garments, passing and repassing between Passy and the capital, moved easily between two conflicting worlds —the world of the Encyclopedists, who considered him a child of Nature and of Reason, the prototype of a new race, and the world of Versailles, which believed that he was a subtle but a manageable cosmopolitan. Both were mistaken; but the court was more in error than the *salon*. Franklin only appeared to be manageable. As for Jay, he had been obliged to wander from Madrid to the Prado, from the Prado to Aranjuez, from Aranjuez to St. Ildefonso, in the dull orbit of a dusty court which refused to recognize him, but found him useful as a cat's-paw. It had at length dawned upon Jay that the French were no more amicable than the Spanish. In Holland, where he was an unrecognized minister in place of Henry Laurens, whom the British had captured and consigned to the Tower, John Adams had long since reached the same conclusion; as had Francis Dana in Saint Petersburg.

It was not a position from which a secretary of Foreign Affairs who believed that France was to be trusted could hope to extract much comfort. Moreover, his hands were tied. Franklin, Adams, and Jay, when in due time they took up their duties as peace commissioners in Paris, were expected to abide by the instructions of June 15, 1781, and make no move without first consulting with the French. What happened in America would profoundly affect the history of Europe; but to affect and to manipulate are two very different things; and neither Congress nor its Foreign

Secretary had any conviction that either was in touch with events across the Atlantic.

None the less, the pretense of contact had to be maintained. The drama had to be composed, message by message, scene by scene, even though the actors—the diplomatic representatives abroad—were either unable to speak the lines assigned to them or else refused to take direction. And what a sublime and simple drama it might have been! Ideally, and in spite of all the subtleties and refinements that arose from juridical or historical or geographical or military considerations, the successful independence of the United States turned upon two poles: a right to share in the inshore Newfoundland fisheries, and a right to a western boundary on the Mississippi north of the line of 31° North latitude, together with free navigation and commerce along the whole river. But if the American Revolution relied for its success upon the quarrels and jealousies of Europe, the quarrels and jealousies of Europe reacted in turn upon the American Revolution. The right to the fisheries had been abandoned, as a *sine qua non*, as early as 1779; free navigation of the lower Mississippi went the same way in February, 1781; and the instructions of June 15, 1781, left the western boundary at the mercy of the French. And if the French were, to say the least, cool toward American claims to the fisheries, the Spanish were even cooler toward an American boundary on the Mississippi: and the Spanish were allies of the French, but not of the Americans. The Congress and the Secretary, it seemed, had been left without a policy.

The official news of the election reached Clermont on August 24; and it is not surprising that Chancellor Livingston should have experienced, at the last moment, some qualms of doubt. "I feel myself unequal to it," he wrote Marbois, in response to his letter of congratulation. "The subject [is] new to me, & foreign to the line in which my studies have lain." He told the President of Congress, Thomas McKean, that he could not commit himself until he knew how far he was to be consulted in the choice of a secretary, an interpreter, and the necessary clerks. He was unable to tell what provision had been made for defraying the expenses of the office. He was deeply perturbed by the fact that Congress had made his salary lower than that of the other secretaries. McKean wrote a soothing answer, and the Chancellor accepted his new office on September 23; rented a house at the corner of Sixth and Chestnut Streets, with a coach house and stable nearby; and was able to wind up his affairs and bring his family to Philadelphia in time for him to take the oath of office on October 20. The anomalies he had mentioned in his letter to McKean were, eventually, disposed of: the anomaly of the secretaryship itself—could that be overcome?[30]

Congress, it seemed, required not a secretary for Foreign Affairs but an amanuensis; someone who would diligently attend its debates, take down its instructions, and, having put them into shape, bring them back to be corrected. On one occasion, Congress requested Livingston to arrange with the tavern-keeper for a dinner to be given in honor of the Minister of France. He scanned the list of guests and found that a great many prominent personages had been omitted; and then he made an even more alarming discovery. His own name was not there! It took two letters, written in his most seignorial style, to correct this error: but the error shows in what light Congress was disposed to see its foreign secretary. "It is hard to convince several Members," wrote James Duane, "that it [the secretaryship] will be a Trust of Toil and Difficulty." It was all too true.[31]

Livingston himself expected to behave rather more like a foreign secretary. "I am not to consider myself a mere executive officer," he wrote in an early letter to the President, which on second thoughts he decided not to send, "thro' whom despatches are to be forwarded. But . . . I am to digest such plans with respect to foreign negotiations as I conceive the United States interested in promoting, to submit them to the examination of Congress, to attend to their debates, to collect their sentiments & make them the ultimate rule of my conduct." But even this was asking for a degree of freedom which Congress was not disposed to grant. As for the attendance of the secretary at congressional debates, which McKean had thought a special inducement, it was merely a source of frustration: he might sit through a whole debate (so Livingston reported in January, 1782) and yet come away ignorant on the one point upon which he needed information; or he might have information of his own which, if only he were allowed to give it, would have shortened or obviated some tedious dispute. But could he ask questions, could he offer unsolicited knowledge, on the floor of Congress? Obviously, this was never intended and never allowed. And if he did succeed in obtaining a clear idea of the wishes of Congress, he could not feel safe in communicating it to a foreign minister: Congress had a way of changing its mind overnight. But then, again, under certain circumstances, it might almost have been said to have no mind to change. When a legislative body is also an executive one, confusion is inevitable; but here the confusion was confounded further by the "chaos" in the Articles of Confederation, by which the affirmative vote of nine states was required for important decisions, and the affirmative vote of seven states for any decision. Unrepresented states were held to have

cast a negative vote, and this was also the case with states whose delegations could not agree. A thinly attended Congress, therefore, might
never be able to express its wishes at all. Surely no secretary for Foreign
Affairs began his task upon such inauspicious terms.[32]

An office was rented, a narrow three-storied house on Sixth Street.
Here the sadly deficient files of the old Committee on Foreign Affairs were
lodged; and here came two clerks—Mr. Lewis R. Morris, a nephew of
Gouverneur Morris, and M. Pierre-Étienne Du Ponceau, a brilliant
young French philologist who had been on the staff of Baron von Steuben
until the threat of consumption forced him to resign. Du Ponceau in his
old age said that James Lovell and John Peters recommended him to
Livingston.[33] At the time, it was supposed, and the supposition seems to
have been correct, that Luzerne had made the recommendation. Livingston
could only hope that the privilege of lodging in his house, eating at his
table, and meeting whatever there was in the way of good society would
be a sufficient recompense to these two young men for the meager emoluments and title of clerks.

After Livingston had made an urgent representation to Congress in
January, 1782, the Department of Foreign Affairs was given a more
precise form in February and March. The committee sent to confer with
the Secretary—Nicholas Everleigh, of South Carolina, Edmund Randolph,
of Virginia, and William Ellery, of Rhode Island—had not, to be sure,
yielded on one point. They could not recommend that the secretary for
Foreign Affairs should be permitted that freedom of correspondence with
the ministers of the United States or the ministers of foreign powers
which alone could make him an effective secretary: all letters having a
direct or indirect reference to foreign policy must still be submitted to
Congress. The Chancellor managed, now and again, to circumvent this
recommendation; but it remained to mortify him throughout his tenure
of office. His salary, however, was raised to $4,000 a year, which at any
rate put him on a level with the Secretary at War, if status is to be
judged by salary; and in a resolution of March 1, he was allowed to
appoint two under secretaries at $800 and $700 a year, instead of a
secretary and a clerk. Thus Du Ponceau was transformed into Under
Secretary for Foreign Affairs at $800 and Lewis Morris into Under Sec-
retary for Domestic Affairs at $700. In the course of time, a clerk, Walter
Stone, was added to the staff, and an interpreter appeared, a Monsieur
Jean P. Têtard, who lived and worked on the top floor. Têtard was a
French divine, of some Protestant persuasion, who had been with General
Montgomery in his Canadian campaign and had fled from New York

with the patriots, leaving all his possessions in British hands. In 1781, he was given a home at Clermont, where he instructed the Chancellor (as long as he was there), his younger brother Edward, and his sister Joanna in the mysteries of the French tongue. *"Savés vous,"* we find him writing Livingston from Clermont on December 10, *"que Mr. Edward vous devance dans le français, que Mlle Annah* [Joanna] & *Mr. Tillotson* [Thomas T. Tillotson, Livingston's brother-in-law] *ont passé leur conjugaisons il y a quelque tems, et que vous nous faites un grand ban de ne nous avoir envoié ni Perrin ni Chambaud. . . . En un mot Clermont est pour nous un vrai* séminaire." In 1782, he was taken from this pleasant retreat and put to work in Sixth Street, somewhat against his will, and much to the dissatisfaction of those members of Congress who believed that Du Ponceau was already one Frenchman too many.[34]

Samuel Osgood complained to John Adams that the system was "unaccountable," and grumbled that Livingston was all too accessible to the wrong visitors, and all too "misterious and secret" to the right ones, such as himself; and Arthur Lee warned Francis Dana that "whatever you receive from him [Livingston] you may consider as dictated by the French Minister. He made him what he is. . . ."[35] But most men, even a majority of the anti-Gallicans, agreed that Livingston was a first-class administrator. Order, regularity, and system had been brought into the office on Sixth Street, all radiating out from the room on the first floor where the Secretary composed his dispatches and received his visitors. A fault-finding committee, appointed in July to examine into his proceedings, reported in September that he had shown the greatest ability, and that whatever errors had been discovered were too trivial to be reported to Congress. The files had been brought up to date, the correspondence at home and abroad had been copious and regular.[36] The great question still remained—though the committee refrained from suggesting it: To what purpose did the Under Secretaries and the clerk drive their pens, or the interpreter interpret, or the Secretary compose his admirable dispatches and conduct his interviews?

In a purely technical sense, one almost insuperable barrier interposed itself between him and the wartime world of foreign affairs; and that was the problem of transmittal. A dispatch, if it evaded capture (and in order to evade capture, an original and three copies of each dispatch were sent by different routes), would take six weeks to pass from Philadelphia to Paris under the best sailing conditions: under the worst, it might take as many months. It was often opened, by the enemy who captured it or by the friend through whose hands it passed. The ciphered passages were hardly so difficult as to defy skilled analysis, and although they usually dealt with the impoverished state of America—which could not have been a very deep secret—the suspicion that their contents were known tended to diminish their authority. And, in any case, the amount of time consumed in the passage between Europe and America not only obliged the diplomatic representatives abroad to act on their own initiative, but also gave a certain unreality to each transaction.

Livingston eventually compressed, into one letter, written on September 5, 1782, to Benjamin Franklin, the substance of all his complaints.

Having written to you lately, I should not again trouble you so soon were it not necessary to remind you that your latest is dated in March, since which there have been frequent arrivals from France, and since which, too, we have reason to believe the most interesting events have taken place in Europe.

We learn from private letters and common fame that Mr. Adams was received by the united provinces in his public character on the 19th. of April. We have yet no account of this interesting event, nor of the measures he has pursued to accomplish our other objects in Holland. Mr. Laurens, it is said, has been liberated, has travelled to Holland and to France, has entered upon the execution of his trust, but has left us to gather events so interesting to him and to us from private letters and the public prints. Mr. Jay tells us on the 24th of May that he is about to set out for Paris and that he presumes Dr. Franklin has assigned the reason for this step. Dr. Franklin has told us nothing.

As to Mr. Dana, if it were not for the necessity of drawing bills in his favor, we should hardly be acquainted with his existence. . . . I can hardly express to you what I feel on this question. I blush when I meet a member of Congress who inquires what is passing in Europe. When the General [Washington] applies to me for advice on the same subject, which must regulate his movements, I am compelled to inform him that we have no intelligence but what he has seen in the papers. The following is an extract from his last letter to me: "But how does it happen that all our information of what is transacting in Europe should come from indirect channels or through the enemy? or does this question proceed from my unacquaintedness with the facts?"

But let me dismiss a subject which gives me so much pain. . . .[37]

"The ignorance in which we are kept of every interesting event renders it impossible," was his conclusion, "for the sovereign to instruct their servant, and of course forms them [Franklin, Adams, and the rest] into an independent privy council for the direction of their [Congress's] affairs, without their advice or concurrence." But Livingston, when he wrote these words, had no idea how much of "an independent privy council" the commissioners in Paris had already become.

Franklin's answer gives, as clearly as it has ever been given, the *formal* reply to such a complaint as Livingston's—that is to say, a picture of the technical difficulties that beset a diplomat whose sovereign happened to be in America.

I am honored by your several letters [he wrote on December 5, 1782], dated September 5th, 13th, 15th, and 18th. I believe the complaints you make in them of my not writing may now have appeared less necessary, as many of my letters written before these complaints must since have come to hand. I will nevertheless mention some of the difficulties your ministers meet with in keeping up a regular and punctual correspondence. We are far from seaports and not well informed, and often misinformed, about the sailing of vessels. Frequently we are told they are to sail in a week or two, and often they lie in the ports for months after, with our letters on board, either waiting for convoy or other reasons. The post-office here is an unsafe conveyance; many of the letters we received by it have evidently been opened, and doubtless the same happens to those that we send. . . . Again, the observation that you make that the Congress ministers in Europe seem to form themselves into a privy council . . . may be in some respects just, but it should be considered that if they do not write as frequently as other ministers here do to their respective courts, or if when they write their letters are not regularly received, the greater distance of the seat of war, and the extreme irregularity of the conveyances may be the causes, and not a desire of acting without the knowledge or order of their constituents. There is no European court to which an express cannot be sent from Paris in ten or fifteen days, and from most of them answers may be obtained in that time. There is, I imagine, no minister who would not think it safer to act by orders than from his own discretion; and yet, unless you leave more to the discretion of your ministers in Europe than courts usually do, your affairs may sometimes suffer extremely from the distance, which in the time of war especially, may make it five or six months before the answer to a letter may be received.[38]

Even if there had been a perfect unity of sentiment between Congress and its commissioners in Paris, the latter would have been forced, by the mere urgency of events, into acting on their own. In such a case as theirs, time's wingèd chariot itself rolled, like a car of Juggernaut, over the agonized niceties of diplomatic procedure. But suppose there should be no unity of sentiment—what then?

V

On October 20, 1781, when Livingston took his oath of office, the news that Cornwallis had surrendered at Yorktown was daily, indeed hourly, expected in Philadelphia. When the news came, it was not given quite that finality which we are disposed to grant it today: the British were on the defensive, but they were still in possession of rich seaports, of valuable lands, and dangerous fortresses; their navy had reasserted its accustomed authority. The aftermath of Yorktown was swift as to its arrival, and morose and protracted as to its character. It could be written only in terms of apathy, poverty, disunion, and discontent. But late October of 1781 was still an auspicious time in which to begin, with whatever limitations and on terms however unreal, the conduct of foreign affairs. All the concessions that had been made with regard to fisheries and boundaries had been squeezed out of Congress by the pressure of military stalemate or of military defeat: after Yorktown, there could surely be no chance of some disgraceful truce on the terms of *uti possidetis*. And could not foreign policy itself be adjusted to meet this new situation?

It is characteristic of Livingston, however, that even in the first flush of victory what preoccupied his mind was a question of procedure not of policy. It could have been argued that, if the surrender at Yorktown had materially changed the fortunes of the United States, a corresponding if immaterial alteration had become visible in the public character of the American representatives abroad. On their brows, as emissaries, there now glittered the laurels of a military victory over a major power. It might be to the advantage of Europe to limit their consequence and that of their country, but consequence they now had. Such considerations, evidently, did not appeal to Livingston. He was convinced, from his study of international law no less than from his own ideas of correct behavior, that it was both undignified and impractical for an emissary to proclaim himself a minister plenipotentiary—to proclaim himself, that is, if the court to which he was accredited was unwilling to receive him in that character. To men like John Adams and Francis Dana, this kind of reasoning was altogether foreign. They believed, as did the radicals in Congress, that the representatives of a new republic should dispense with the ordinary punctilios of diplomatic life; that they should endeavor rather to force themselves upon the attention of their hosts than efface themselves until they were called for; that they should act upon impulse; that they should not wait for the still voices of prudence, calculation, and good breeding. Theirs was the way of "militia diplomacy," and between their way and that prescribed by Livingston the mind might oscillate forever without being sure which of the two was the more correct. The diplomatic world of the eighteenth century was decidedly brutal in its methods, but very meticulous in its rituals. Because he had disregarded its rituals, John Adams had, hitherto, not been successful in France: but, conversely, he was soon to enjoy a great triumph in Holland. A revolution, one might well think, ought to behave in a revolutionary way, in its diplomacy no less than in its politics; yet history is full of incidents that seem to disprove this theory. Livingston, of course, in this stage of his career never could quite reconcile himself to the fact that revolutions may have to be revolutionary.

He began—it was the first letter he wrote after taking the oath of office—with an aside to John Jay. "Holland claims your particular attention," he wrote. "Our minister there is zealous & laborious but [what follows was in cipher] I will not answer for his prudence. His memorial, his ridiculous display of his public character when everything was against it cannot be accounted for on principles that will do him honor."[39] Mr. Adams had written a memorial on April 19, 1781, which was published in three languages in the Dutch newspapers, and in which he demanded that he should be recognized as minister plenipotentiary of the United States of America. Since Holland had been dragged into the war against Great Britain, the stadtholder's court remained pro-British; but M. de Vergennes's influence was paramount with the States-General; and M. de Vergennes disliked Mr. Adams, both on personal grounds and as a possible competitor for loans in the Dutch money market.

The character of John Adams as a diplomatist has, to be sure, improved with time: historians can now discern upon it the signs, not only of success, but also even of ripeness. In his own day, however, these were not so evident. Franklin admired him, but confessed that he seemed at times absolutely out of his senses; while to such an observer as the Comte de Vergennes, he was the epitome of ignorance, inexperience, and ill breeding. He blustered, he lost his temper, he ventured to question the importance of M. de Vergennes. His standing at the French Legation in Philadelphia was very low; and the prejudices of the French Legation, no less than his own predilections, urged Livingston into a correspondence that threatened at times to descend into a lecture.

We have learned from Mr. Dumas [he wrote on November 20] that you have presented your credentials to the States-General. We are astonished that you have not written on so important a subject and developed the principles that induced you to declare your political character before the States were disposed to acknowledge it. There is no doubt from your known prudence & knowledge of the world that some peculiarity in your situation or that of the politicks & parties in the United Provinces furnished you with the reasons that overballanced the objections to the measures which arise from the humiliating light in which it places us. Congress wd. I believe wish to have them explained & particularly your reason for printing yr. memorial. . . . Your business . . . I think lies in a very narrow compass. . . . I would recommend it to you to be, both in your language & conduct, a private Gent & this will give you many advantages in making connections that will be lost on your insisting upon the assumption of a publick character. And the rather as this sentiment prevails generally with respect to you among the members of Congress tho for reasons of delicacy I have not chose to ask the sense of Congress to whom it is my sincere wish as well as my leading object in the free Letters I write you to enable you to render yr. measures acceptable. . . .[40]

And in a passage which he subsequently deleted, he begged Mr. Adams to caution his "zealous friends" (*i.e.*, Mr. Adams) against all such imprudences "as serve to throw an air of ridicule on your mission."

This is certainly not the kind of advice that one gentleman cares to receive from another, even if that other is a secretary of Foreign Affairs, and Mr. Adams's feelings and language when he received the Chancellor's missive may safely be left to the imagination. His responses were certainly vigorous. "I stand now in an honorable light," he had written on February 14, in reply to an earlier and milder admonition, "openly and candidly demanding an answer in my public character. But it is the republic [of the United Provinces] that stands in a less respectable character."[41]

And on February 21, 1782, having at length received Livingston's letter of November 20, he broke out into an impassioned defense of his memorial.

The period since May 4, 1781 [he wrote] has been thick sown with great events, all springing out of the American Revolution and connected with the matter contained in my memorial. The memorial of M. Van Bercke; the proposition of the burgomasters of Amsterdam; their attack upon the Duke of Brunswick, and the battle of Doggersbank; the appointment of Senor Del Campo to treat with Mr. Jay; the success of Colonel Laurens in obtaining orders for the French fleet to go upon the coast of America; their victory over Graves, and the capture of Cornwallis . . . these traits are all subsequent to that memorial, and they are too sublime and decisive proofs of the prosperity and glory of the American cause to admit the belief that the memorial had done it any material hurt. By comparing facts and events and dates it is impossible not to believe that the memorial had some influence in producing some of them.[42]

By this time, the misunderstanding was complete. Adams could no more be made to agree that "militia diplomacy" was hurtful than Livingston could be expected to perceive a connection between the Adams memorial and the surrender at Yorktown. The appalling slowness of communication, in any event, while it confirmed their differences of intellect and temperament, made their political disputes almost, if not quite, unreal.

The imagination, none the less, and Livingston was certainly an imaginative man, is by no means abashed by unreality. Never was he more lucid than in his correspondence with Francis Dana in Saint Petersburg, where every letter took between three and nine months to reach its destination. Dana always believed that he should make himself known as a minister plenipotentiary, even though it was a settled policy of the Russian Empress never to recognize the American Republic. But Dana had been sent to Saint Petersburg in order to wring from this formidable sovereign an invitation to the United States to accede "as principals and as an independent nation" to the Armed Neutrality. Since the Armed Neutrality was, as its name implied, a league of neutrals, it is difficult to see how the United States could accede to it. But this was of small consequence. Dana felt that he should attempt to get himself recognized even if no Russian official cared to admit that he or his country had any existence. Livingston, on the other hand, contended that it was by discreet behavior, by acting in every instance as a private gentleman, by tact, conciliation, watchfulness, and a strict attention to the advice of the French Minister there that Dana would best serve his country at Saint Petersburg. He explained, too, in one of his most serene passages, that in a northern court it would do no good to indulge in violent diatribes against the British. Since Dana could speak neither Russian nor French, since the French Minister had not a word of English, since the few English in Saint Petersburg cut the American dead and there were no other Americans there, the possible audience for Mr. Dana's diatribes was limited to the few Russians who could understand him and his secretary, young John Quincy Adams, who certainly profited by them in later life if (which is uncertain) they were ever uttered. It was indeed a hypothetical correspondence: for, with no assurance that any letter would ever be received, or that any answer would come back, the two correspondents were dealing in guesses and assumptions. Here the Secretary, whose letters were models of tact, had perhaps the best of the exchanges.[43]

In the meantime, Livingston found some consolation in the thought that his friend John Jay was carrying out his duties at Madrid with forbearance and dignity, and under the most difficult circumstances. "You can hardly experience more pleasure than I do," he wrote on April 20, 1782, "in knowing the satisfaction which Congress express at your conduct. Your character [here he had recourse to cipher] stands extremely well with them while Adams & Dana are proportionately low [and] daily losing ground tho they have a party who still support them. Every step that the first has taken has only served to disgrace the United States." "They suppose," he added, but crossed the addition out of his draft, "the dignity of the United States to consist in differing with the Minister of France."[44]

VI

"The Minister of France!" It was a cardinal principle with the Chancellor that Adams at The Hague should be guided by the advice of the Duc de Vauguyon and Dana at Saint Petersburg by that of the Marquis de Verac: yet his deletion of the phrase from his letter to Jay seems to indicate a certain uneasiness with this principle. It is true that from the beginning of his relations with Luzerne, and long before he himself became secretary, Livingston had been infected with the French distrust of Mr. Adams. It has, indeed, always been assumed that Livingston was persuaded into doing very much what Luzerne and Marbois wanted him to do: and certainly he was flattered by their attentions and far from unamenable to their cajoleries. But he not the man to go the whole way: there was a vein of independence in his composition, which resisted dictation and resented influence. He believed in the good faith of France with a genuine fervor that nothing could extinguish; yet neither Luzerne nor Marbois, nor their united voices, could have persuaded him to such a conclusion if he had not already reached it on his own. No doubt, their dislike for Mr. Adams was easily communicated; but the Chancellor already distrusted New England radicals, as Livingstons had distrusted them for generations. He was independently convinced that "militia diplomacy" was harmful and—it was much the same thing to him—ill-bred. No Frenchman, however charming or well born, could teach a Hudson River magnate the meaning of good manners. The Chancellor's ideas on this prickly subject were his own.

Moreover, it is apparent that the French Legation, although it had worked so hard for Livingston's appointment, and although it had no reason to suppose that his adherence to the French party was anything if not adhesive, became early a little uncertain about their protégé. What could the matter be? "*Il paraît,*" Luzerne reported on November 1, 1781, "*jusqu'ici se tenir à l'abri de toute observation à laquelle des liaisons particulières avec moi pourroient donner lieu.*"[45] He took good care not to excite any comments that might arise from too marked a relationship with Luzerne: or, to put it less circumspectly, he was no longer quite so friendly with the French Minister.

It was not until January 7, 1782, that he set forth in a letter to Benjamin Franklin what must be taken for an acceptable interpretation of the foreign policy of Congress at this time. Official, or not, it is a highly personal interpretation—one of the most powerful and curious of the Chancellor's papers. To the late Henri Doniol, the great historian of Franco-American relations at this time, Livingston's words seemed to embody a reversal, one might almost say a betrayal, of his obligations to the Minister who had helped elect him. He spread before Franklin, writes M. Doniol, as if they represented the future policy of Congress, all the excessive pretensions of a former day; on everything relating to boundaries or fisheries or the confiscation of Loyalist estates, he repeated the very sophistries that had been used with far too much insistence on far too many occasions in the past.[46] M. Doniol's judgments are always weighty; yet there is some reason to believe that this particular one was founded upon a partial reading of the Livingston letter. The letter is not so much sophistical as prophetic; it offers a strong course of American foreign policy and plants in the middle of it the seeds of doubt and of contradiction. It was written before the triumph of Yorktown had lost its emotional force; and its author became, for the occasion, an instrument upon which contemporary history, playing with confidence its *io triumphe*, struck here and there, also, a jangling and incongruous note.

Livingston began by asserting that "our extension to the Mississippi" was founded in justice, not merely from the evidence of charters and grants, not merely from the fact that the Proclamation of 1763 did not remove but evidently restrained an existing right to extend westward, but also from a resort to general principles, by "asking whence Great Britain derived her right to the waste lands in America." Obviously, he argued, the right was derived from the false principle that a subject carries his allegiance with him wherever he goes; and that the oppressed subjects of Great Britain, seeking their freedom in the wilds of America, extended to these wilds the sovereignty of the kingdom from which they had fled. Upon this false principle, therefore, the rights of the King of Great Britain to America were incident to his right of sovereignty over those of his subjects who settled it or explored the wastelands that he still claimed: "for the idea of right derived from mere discovery, and the vain ceremony of taking possession without planting and continuing that possession is now fully exploded. If the principle is false; if we further admit what is necessary to our independence, that the right of sovereignty over the people of America is forfeited, it must follow that all rights founded upon that sovereignty are forfeited with it; and that upon our setting up a new sovereign in America, the rights which the first claimed as such devolve upon the second."

It would be vain to argue that George III held the vast back lands by a cession from other powers, "since those cessions were grounded upon a prior claim derived through the people of America, and only served to confirm the right which they gave the King of Great Britain while he was their sovereign, and which he loses with his sovereignty over them." Moreover, Great Britain invariably dealt with the Indians through their American governors, who sometimes extended the royal protection to the nations inhabiting the wastelands now in question; the expense of maintaining a friendship with them almost always devolved upon the respective states; and it therefore follows "that if the King of Great Britain has any right over the back lands in America it must be as king of the people of America; ceasing to be the king of those people, his right also ceases." Nor can he claim the back lands as protector of the Indians, since the Indians evidently claimed that protection from him as king of the colonies, not as king of a country several thousand miles away. "This country [America] having chosen a new sovereign, they may rightfully claim its protection."

Livingston's ideas on the origins of colonial history are somewhat fanciful, and his reasoning itself is scarcely flawless: for if the King's sovereignty were based on a false principle, would not this false principle taint the new American sovereignty upon which it had devolved? These considerations may perhaps have wrung from M. Doniol the word "*sophistique*"; they certainly did not disturb Mr. Franklin, who replied on March 9 that the Chancellor's opinions exactly coincided with his own. Nor was it flawless reasoning, but forceful argument, that the Chancellor wished to display: and his argument was certainly forceful. Never had nationalism been clothed in more glowing, indeed more positive, terms. The sovereignty derived from the American people as a whole was held to be paramount everywhere over the states.

On the question of the American claim "to fish on the banks of Newfoundland," he was, if anything, even more downright. He based this fishing right, partly on the fact that the Americans, having once been tenants in common with the British, must continue tenants in common unless they relinquished those rights by their own act; and partly on the law of Nature, "the right which nature gives to all mankind to use its common benefit so far as not to exclude others."

The sea cannot in its nature be appropriated [his argument ran]; no nation can put its mark upon it. Though attempts have sometimes been made to set up an empire over it, they have been considered as unjust usurpations, and resisted as such in turn, by every maritime nation in Europe. The idea of such empire is now fully exploded by the best writers. The whale fishery in every sea, and even upon the coasts of princes who do not exercise it, is considered as a common right, and is enjoyed by those nations that choose to pursue it. The cod fishery upon the Dogger bank, and other parts of the European seas is claimed exclusively by no nation. The herring fishery is carried on daily by the Dutch on the coast of England; and if the banks of Newfoundland are not equally common, it is because some nations have relinquished their rights and others find it impossible to exercise them for want of harbors to receive their vessels or to dry their fish on.

When we say we are willing to exercise it under these inconveniences there can certainly be no further dispute about our right, and the only remaining questions will be the distance that we ought to keep from the shores possessed by the enemy; though, strictly speaking, from our first principle we have a common right in them.

This subject is treated so much at large by Grotius and Vattel, that I do not think it necessary to detail arguments, which, though urged by people here from their feelings, you will find much better stated there. . . .

This was patently *not* French policy: every line must have been an offense to Luzerne. On the question of confiscated property, too, Livingston, who invariably in private adopted a moderate view, now came out in as vengeful a light as any radical might have done. Those who had been banished, he said, could never return, for they would be a perpetual menace to the republic; nor could their confiscated estates be restored without doing infinite damage to its economy. And he suggested to Franklin a counter-argument which Franklin afterward used with great effect: a list of the damages done by the British to American property might, if presented in all its length and costliness, silence any demands for compensation.

Such were the arguments derived "from the humiliation and misfortunes of Great Britain"; such were the demands that, said the Chancellor, America might reasonably make on the close of a successful war. And yet—it is astonishing, but it is true—in the very midst of these arguments, so obviously based upon the assurance of victory, he sounded a dissonant note.

There is some reason to believe [he wrote] that Great Britain considered their rights in many instances as extending no further than their rights of pre-emption and protection, as may be inferred from many passages in negociations for a peace with France in the year 1761. . . .

This suggests a new idea, which, however, I am not warranted by any act of Congress in mentioning, and therefore you will only consider it as the sentiment of an individual. If the mediators should not incline to admit our claim, but determine on restricting our limits, either by the extent of our grants, the course of the mountains, the source of the rivers, or any other of those arbitrary rules that must be sought for when solid principles are relinquished, perhaps it would not be difficult to bring them to agree that the country beyond those limits belongs to the nations which inhabit it;

that it should enjoy its independence under the guarantee of France, Spain, Great Britain, and America, and be open to the trade of those whose lands border upon them.

The new Secretary might be excused for not realizing that "the mediators" had no longer the slightest chance of mediating between Great Britain and her former colonies, at Vienna or anywhere else; but what made him suggest "the course of the mountains, the source of the rivers" as a possible boundary? If this meant anything, it meant that the United States, so far from extending to the Mississippi, was to confine itself within the Appalachians. Indeed, Professor Samuel Flagg Bemis has suggested that in this paragraph one can observe the open influence of the French Minister, to whose court the independence of the United States was acceptable but not its imperial extension to the Mississippi; who knew how greatly the Spanish feared the march of republican principles along the road to Mexico; who was, after all, no lover of republican principles himself. And certainly the Chancellor's paragraph might have been written under the direction of Luzerne. But there are other considerations. It is possible that the paragraph, inserted into the midst of so many resounding arguments, all disagreeable to France, was merely a sop to Luzerne; and that the Chancellor, by making a clear distinction between "arbitrary rules" and "solid principles," let Franklin know that his suggestion was not to be taken seriously. And Franklin himself, if his answer has any meaning, certainly did not do so.[47]

But an examination of the Chancellor's papers shows that early in 1781 he was ready to state openly that any claim to navigation of the Mississippi was inadmissible. "I lost some friends by speaking my sentiments freely on it—Never was a claim worse founded nor more repugnant to every principle of Justice & policy." It has been suggested by James Madison's latest, most diligent, and, indeed, most distinguished biographer, that Livingston's letter was merely a paraphrase of the lengthy report that Madison presented to Congress on January 8 and that was printed in the *Journals* for August 20.[48] But Livingston's nationalism was far more pronounced in his letter to Franklin than Madison's in his report to Congress: so that the letter and the report may possibly have been drawn up in consultation— the two gentlemen were on the best of terms—but the former can hardly have been a paraphrase of the latter. Indeed, it could be suggested that Livingston, always an impulsive man and apt to be more impulsive as he grew older, was giving public utterance to some private and personal debate. Was he a continentalist or was he not? Did his nationalism extend to the Mississippi, or was he really interested in a smaller more centralized republic? He was a great landowner, the proprietor of vast stretches of wild country; and American sovereignty over uncounted acres in the fertile Mississippi Valley, even while he contended for it, may have aroused some ancestral warning. Who would settle for a leasehold in the Hardenburgh Patent, among the stony and savage Catskills, if the empire of the Mississippi lay open in fee simple? And the fear of westward expansion, as of something that would certainly be democratic and might be uncontrollable, troubled American history for many years. It is indeed possible that Livingston's paragraph displayed an influence less Francophile than atavistic: possible but not probable.

VII

In any event, Livingston never again so much as mentioned a boundary at the eastern watersheds. And in other respects, as the triumph of Yorktown faded and its discouraging aftermath set in, he asserted his independence of Luzerne and Marbois. As M. Doniol put it, "he relied upon the strange ideas thrown out by the Arthur Lees and the Izards that 'France had never undertaken a war which had cost her less.' "[49] Whether the Chancellor ever relied upon the thinking of Arthur Lee or of Ralph Izard—whether, indeed, there was at this time much agreement between Izard and Lee—must be held in some doubt: but it is certain that he could not bring himself to realize the appalling condition of the French Treasury. In his circular letter of February 19 to the state governors, he urged, it is true, the total inability of France to give or lend another penny: but this was to stir up the conscience of the state governors and their constituents. In private, to Benjamin Franklin, on February 13, he told a very different story.

That France can aid us is not to be doubted, for it is certain she never carried on a war that distressed her finances less. She has no expensive subsidies to pay; her money is either expended at home or in a country from which it returns. Her army is not greatly increased, and her commerce, under the protection of her fleets, enjoys a security that it seldom experienced before. I would not, however, have you suppose that this is the language I hold here. I know too well the necessity of making every exertion which in our present impoverished situation we are capable of; and I neglect no means which my present situation puts in my power to call forth.[50]

What was the situation after Yorktown? The government of Lord North did not fall until March, 1782; and the war—in so far as it was a general or world war reaching out to Africa, Asia, and the East Indies—

still revolved around Spanish ambitions for the recovery of Gibraltar and French hopes to diminish the power of Great Britain in Africa and India. In the eighteenth century, one did not look for the total annihilation of one's enemy: what was desired, for international politics had its mechanistic side, was a territorial adjustment of that delicate abstraction known as the balance of power. No European statesman supposed, for example, that Great Britain had to be driven from Canada, or that Spanish claims to territory east of the Mississippi ought to be surrendered to the needs of republican America. In Spain, John Jay now despaired of obtaining either a loan or an alliance from a set of noblemen who wished the Americans to stay at war just long enough for Spain to recover Gibraltar, who then hoped to coop them up east of the Alleghenies, and from whom he had borrowed almost nothing except, perhaps, their habit of prolixity in the writing of dispatches. In the Netherlands, John Adams could not be sure that he would ever obtain a loan, although the news of Yorktown, which he received in February, at once precipitated a movement for acknowledging the independence of the United States. From the Armed Neutrality, one could expect only such consolation as could be derived from the Neutrality's denial of British maritime pretensions—a somewhat empty consolation so long as Russia was even more hostile to American independence than she was to Britain's salty misconstruction of the term "freedom of the seas." Only France remained.

In the Office of Finance, once a week, there was a grave meeting of the Financier, the Secretary for Foreign Affairs, the Secretary at War, and (whenever he was available) the Commander in Chief himself: and here, as if in some shadow cabinet, all questions of policy were discussed. The Prince de Broglie, in the summer of 1782, came into this office just as one of these meetings broke up, while Morris, General Benjamin Lincoln, and Livingston were still together. He found himself amused by the contrast between the rotundity of the Financier and the General and the extreme leanness of the Foreign Secretary: but Livingston's face, he noted, was "very fine, and it is generally conceded that he is a man of talent." Such portraits were nothing if not political—the Chancellor was still in favor, even if his demands for money were inconvenient and his ideas as to fisheries and boundaries seemed to be drifting out of the French orbit. The point was that he still believed that an absolute monarchy was capable of keeping faith, in spite of the most pressing temptations to do otherwise, with a nation which its statesmen, unlike its intellectuals, were apt to regard as a useful but dubious nest of rebels.

The victory at Yorktown did not remove the taint of rebellion or the disadvantage of poverty. When the news of that event was ridden post-haste to Philadelphia, the messenger, it was said, demanded his fee in hard money: but the Continental Treasury was empty and the money had to be raised, dollar by dollar, from individual members of Congress.[51] The story is possibly apocryphal: it is certainly charming. How well it suited itself to a pastoral America such as the *philosophe* had conjured out of the pages of Rousseau or the prophecies of the Physiocrats! How little comfort it would give to the mind of a Luzerne or the calculations of a Vergennes! Indeed, as the tide of military success turned toward the flood, that of economic prosperity no less visibly ebbed away. In 1782, the good harvests of 1781 were offset, and more than offset, by a decline in commercial vigor.[52] Even privateering—a doubtful source of wealth at best—ceased to attract much capital after French Admiral de Grasse removed his fleet to the West Indies in March, and the British navy tightened its blockade.

The activities of Robert Morris had at least brought to the Continental line, through his system of contracting, a promise of better food and better clothes. His "Morris Notes," issued on his own credit in anticipation of taxes, were acceptable, his Bank of North America was about to do business, his dreams for a federal impost shimmered with optimism. But it was all delusive. Morris circulated a letter to the states on February 15, which, like his previous letters, was a mixture of despair and exhortation: he submitted it, according to his Official Diary for February 8, to Washington and Livingston, who gave it their approval.[53] No one supposed that it would persuade the states to lay taxes sufficient to fulfill their quotas. In a letter to Franklin, which was submitted to Livingston on March 8, with a request that he should observe a "profound secrecy" with regard to its contents, Morris admitted that of the $8,000,000 demanded from the states for 1782, prudence would forbid him to rely upon more than $4,000,000. It would seem that even this estimate was imprudent. Every state in the Confederation, Livingston told Schuyler in February, seemed to plume itself on the late success and "fold its arms as if . . . never determined to be successful again."[54]

He, too, exhorted the governors of the states, and in his letters abroad called for foreign loans in the virtual certainty that these domestic exhortations would come to nothing. "The want of money my dear Sir," he wrote to Lafayette in cipher, "is and will continue a radical evil till it is removed by foreign aid. The sums necessary for the ensuing campaign can not be got at all in time to be of use. Let this be ever in your mind. Never cease to persuade the Ministry that this money can nowhere be put to better use than in America." But in a letter to a Frenchman, even so pro-American a Frenchman, the Chancellor was careful not to criticize the states or the people. "If I could envy you anything," he continued in plain text, "it would be in the satisfaction you must feel in greatly contributing to the happiness of a people whose rising glory will in the course of a few ages eclipse that of Europe. Should this letter by some singular chance be preserved it may 500 years hence be considered as a prophecy & while you are recorded as the adopted hero of America, I may be considered as one of its druids."[55] This posthumous consolation seemed all he was likely to receive.

With the resignation of Lord North, it was clear that some effort at peacemaking, more definite than the offers of North in 1778, would be in keeping with the mood of Parliament. The King, who had manfully resisted his own offer to abdicate, may have persuaded himself that much could still be salvaged. If the government that succeeded North's was nominally under Lord Rockingham (who had repealed the Stamp Act), it was actually more responsive to Lord Shelburne, who still seems to have hoped for some "Colonial" adjustment. But it was a divided government, and Shelburne, as Secretary of State for the Southern Department, was confronted by the brilliance, the wit, and the liberal ideas of Charles James Fox, in the Northern Department, the man most responsible for the overthrow of North. Shelburne hoped that something might be done in America through General Carleton and Admiral Robert Digby. Perhaps, in Philadelphia, or in the state legislatures, a separate peace might seem desirable—a curious peace, indeed. Carleton and Digby were instructed as follows:

You must lose no time to avail yourself of the change of measures which has lately taken place, for the purpose of reconciling the minds and affections of His Majesty's subjects, by such open and generous conduct, which may captivate their hearts, and remove every suspicion of insincerity. . . .[56]

One need waste no time with these tactics, designed to separate America and France, but based upon some saurian reluctance to come to terms with the plain facts of history. Carleton's advances were coldly refused by Washington; Livingston addressed a circular letter to the states calling, among other things, for such spirited resolutions from each legislature as would "prevent the attempt I apprehend"; Congress itself resolved that it would adhere rigidly to the French alliance. As Luzerne said, "it is impossible the seat of negociation should be in America."[57]

A more practical effort at detaching America from France was made in Paris, whither Shelburne (as secretary responsible for the colonies) and

Fox (as secretary for foreign affairs) dispatched each his own emissary. Fox believed that America should be given her independence immediately, without any conditions, whereas Shelburne wished to make American independence one of the conditions of the general peace. It had occurred to him that France's demands would be so exorbitant that she and not England would seem to be the enemy of America's hopes. Shelburne may have been more subtle than Fox and Fox more simple than Shelburne; but, in a case like this, it could be argued that the simple approach was really the subtler of the two. In any event, both statesmen hoped to persuade the Americans to desert their ally and come to terms on their own.

The Shelburne representative was Richard Oswald, an elderly, benevolent Scots merchant, whose benevolence was somewhat dimmed by too close a connection with the slave trade. Oswald was so sympathetic to the American cause that he was ready to concede almost anything; but then, he was, at best, a decoy. Fox's agent was Thomas Grenville, an upright young man of the official caste. Both were, from the beginning, quite helpless in Franklin's hands. The wily old gentleman liked to give the impression that for the Americans to desert their ally was by no means an impossibility; and then, when Oswald was flushed with confidence and the Cabinet in London with hope, he would blandly lecture Grenville on the morality of keeping one's word. In this way, he whetted British appetites without exactly tainting his own integrity. When the British had disclosed everything they had to offer, the comedy was abruptly ended. And what brought it to an end was an announcement by Vergennes that the United States and Great Britain might proceed with their own negotiations, which should march at an equal pace with those of France and Great Britain, "provided that the final efficacy of each depended upon the signature of the other." Whether this formula originated with Franklin or with Vergennes is still a matter of scholarly debate; what is certain is that it put an end to the schemes of Fox and Shelburne. The United States would negotiate separately but they would not desert their French ally.[58]

And all these maneuvers were performed on the understanding that the less one consulted with Philadelphia, the better for all concerned: upon Franklin and his fellow commissioners, and the degree to which they proposed to be guided by Vergennes, depended the character of the peace. When the formula of simultaneous negotiation was once pronounced, all power passed from Philadelphia. Mr. Franklin summoned Mr. Jay to Paris, and on June 14, after a journey which "excepting some bad Roads, Fleas, and Bugs, was not unpleasant," Mr. and Mrs. Jay were at Bordeaux.[59] They had not only passed from Spain to France, but, considering what Jay was soon to accomplish as a negotiator, they were also moving from the eighteenth to the nineteenth century. For once, Mr. Jay was to be ahead of his times. Helpless in Philadelphia, and stubbornly convinced of the good faith of his allies, Livingston remained where Mr. Jay had left him.

CHAPTER SIX

Jay's feelings when he crossed from Spain to France are easy enough to understand. He had become deeply suspicious of both Bourbon courts. He perceived that they would—willingly or regretfully, with a smile or a sigh—sacrifice the patriot cause to their own interests. As a Huguenot by descent, he had no love for Catholic France, and as a moralist from New York, he was repelled by it. He faced his task, therefore, in the dual role of statesman and provincial; looked out over the world with a sweeping but darkened gaze, through the spectacles of a Low Church Episcopalian. He saw far; you could never be sure that he saw fairly. Happily for America, it was not fairness that was needed at this juncture; what was needed was anger, suspicion, and resolve. When John Adams arrived toward the end of October, the union of conscious virtue with deliberate deception was complete; whether Franklin, who had the wisdom of the serpent and the charm of the dove, might or might not have achieved the same results in apparent co-operation with Vergennes, instead of behind his back, can never be known. He bowed to the majority, and so the trustfulness of Livingston and the Gallicans in Congress was—perhaps fortunately for their reputation—never put to the test.

Since this is a study of Livingston, a secretary *enchaîné*, the great achievements of Jay, Adams, and Franklin in Paris require only a summary relation: for Livingston never learned about them until they were all over; never influenced them; never ceased to lament them, as a man of honor, without (it would seem) precisely understanding them as a man of the world. To let the facts speak for themselves, as we all know, often results in an unseemly clamor; but the clamor, unseemly or not, has rendered Livingston's arguments inaudible.

Four stages may be discerned in these famous peace negotiations after Jay's arrival in Paris on June 23, 1781. At the end of the first, Jay having been stricken with influenza which confined him to his bedroom for three weeks, Franklin had conducted certain significant interviews with Oswald. Lord Rockingham had died on July 1, Lord Shelburne was now the first minister of the Crown, and Mr. Fox had resigned. Shelburne had abandoned all hopes of a colonial adjustment, and was now prepared to apply to the American problem a nostrum composed in equal parts of resignation, charity, and the principles of Adam Smith. During his talks with Oswald, Franklin displayed, as a keen observer has noted, a disposition to neglect his instructions regarding close co-operation with Vergennes; and the terms that he laid before Oswald as "necessary" included the cession of Canada, a project as dear to him as it was odious to the French.

At the end of the second stage, Jay had emerged from his sickroom, and had learned from a series of conversations with the Spanish Ambassador, the Conde de Aranda, and with Gérard de Rayneval, Vergennes's private secretary, that France and Spain would prefer to keep America away from the Mississippi south of the Ohio, and that France was not indisposed to see all territory north of the Ohio recognized as British. Jay then heard, on September 9, that Rayneval had departed on a secret trip to London. On September 10, the British gave him a translated copy of a message from Marbois to Vergennes, which had been intercepted and deciphered, and in which—much to Jay's horror—Marbois stated that the United States had no right to the Newfoundland fisheries and that, by claiming such a right, "they set forth . . . pretensions without paying regard to the king's [the King of France's] rights."[1] M. Marbois, though sociably inclined toward Americans, even to the extent of marrying one of them, never forgot that he was wedded to France.

At the end of the third stage, Jay had decided to act independently of Franklin, who had taken to his bed with an attack of gout and gravel. As we now know, Rayneval did suggest in his discussions with Shelburne that France would not support America in her claims to the fisheries and to territory beyond the Ohio. ("The point of Independence once settled," Shelburne told George III, "he [Rayneval] appears rather Jealous than partial to America on other points, as well as that of the fishery."[2]) Jay now sent an Englishman named Benjamin Vaughan, who had been hanging about Paris on some ill-defined mission from Shelburne, and had become more American than the Americans in his sympathies, back to England with certain suggestions. Among them was the suggestion—one might call it a threat—that no peace could be concluded unless Oswald received a commission empowering him to treat with the commissioners of the United States—in other words, that the preliminary step to peace must be the recognition of American independence. This was not quite the same as requiring that Parliament be asked to recognize American independence *whether or not there were any further negotiations*; and the Cabinet eventually accepted Jay's formula.

Vaughan was also to make it known that America could not give up the fisheries, and that Great Britain—by asking for and obtaining free navigation of the Mississippi—might have a great market open to her in the American back lands.

At the end of the fourth stage, Vaughan had returned to Paris, September 27, with Oswald's commission, made out with a certain ambiguity of language, which did not alarm the Americans to the point of putting off the negotiation; and Great Britain had received, on September 30, the news that the great attack on Gibraltar had failed. She had, therefore, managed to bring the Americans to a separate discussion of the preliminaries of peace, and at a time when she herself felt more than usually confident. On October 5, Jay had completed, and Franklin had approved, a set of preliminary articles which should take effect when, and only when, preliminary articles had been signed between Great Britain and France.

And what had Jay and Franklin escaped, if Franklin could be persuaded to negotiate with Oswald and *not* to consult Vergennes? "The French line of reasoning," writes Professor Vincent T. Harlow, "was obvious enough. Let England first strike a bargain with France and Spain, and all three would benefit. England herself would have Bourbon support (which would be decisive) in retaining the Ohio-Mississippi region: Spanish control over the lower Mississippi basin would be confirmed: and France would have no American competitor when presenting extended demands for fishing privileges in Newfoundland. Very possibly Vergennes also calculated that British territorial retentions in North America would serve as a useful compensation for the loss of Gibraltar, which Spain was bent on acquiring, and for substantial concessions to France in India."[3] The list is appalling. Yet have we any reason to assume that Franklin, if he had continued to co-operate with Vergennes, would not have persuaded that gentleman—always open to reason—into taking a more rational course? Or that Britain, once the attack on Gibraltar had failed, would not in any case have seen a paramount advantage to her trade of friendly American markets in the West? Only one thing is certain: We are simply not authorized to disagree with Jay in his suspicions of France and of Spain; or with Adams when, arriving in Paris on October 26, he helped persuade Franklin to complete the preliminaries of peace without consulting the Comte de Vergennes.

II

Thus Jay and Franklin sat down to discuss terms of peace which included a boundary upon the Mississippi and the right to share in the inshore fisheries of Newfoundland. Undoubtedly, the turning point in all the arrangements that had brought them to this posture was the British Cabinet's resolution—not made without some striking scenes in the royal closet—that Oswald should be given a new commission which recognized (however ambiguously) the independence of the United States. This took place on September 19. And on September 19, Washington was writing to Livingston: "Why we have nothing from our own Ministers is, as you observe, truly unaccountable."[4] A total silence hung between Congress and their commissioners at Paris. Nothing had been received from Paris that was dated later than June. Nor was it distance alone, or the difficulties of transmittal, that accounted for this singular reticence. Even if their subsequent letters had been received in September, Jay's and Franklin's information would have been totally noncommittal. It was not until September 18 that Jay, once eloquent enough on that topic, ventured to write to Livingston concerning his suspicions of France, and to hint at his intention to proceed on his own. "Let us be honest and grateful to France," he wrote, "but let us think for ourselves."[5] He knew that any answer he could receive to this message could not possibly arrive in time to interfere with his peacemaking.

One might search all history for precedents and never discover so strange a relationship between a sovereign body and its diplomatic agents. What Jay, Adams, and (it must be assumed) Franklin feared was the paramount influence of Luzerne and Marbois in Philadelphia. They dared not write freely to Congress, or its Secretary for Foreign Affairs, because they believed that Luzerne and Marbois would be privy to all their communications, and would pounce upon any hint that the American commissioners be obliged to think for themselves. It has been suggested that that was not all that the commissioners had to fear. "The issue was fundamental," writes Professor Harlow. "Were the United States to be deprived of the fruits of the British-American victory of 1763, which had appeared to open the gates of the West, and to become an unimportant Power on the Atlantic seaboard, cramped and dominated by a huge Spanish North America as well as a British North America extending down to the Ohio? Jay was aware that the American Secretary for Foreign Affairs, R. R. Livingston (and probably a majority of Congress too) would be prepared to accept such a boundary; and he began to realize that if he and Franklin continued to accept French guidance in accordance with their instructions they would have no option in the matter."[6]

This was not the case. After that one baleful paragraph in his letter to Franklin of January 7, 1782, Livingston never again suggested a boundary short of the Mississippi. Early in April, a dispatch was received from John Jay in which that gentleman explained that, in accordance with his instructions of February 15, 1781, he had offered to exchange America's right to navigate the lower Mississippi for an alliance with Spain; but also that he had done so with a masterly qualification. He had said that America would "forbear to use the navigation of the Mississippi," and that this offer would be withdrawn if Spain expected (as she did) to postpone any discussion of an alliance until a general peace had been reached.[7] In a letter written on April 27, and in accordance with the directions of Congress, Livingston concurred in Jay's arrangements; and a resolution of Congress, on April 30, gave them its formal approval.[8] But among Livingston's private papers there is evidence that he went a great deal further. In the draft of a letter written to Jay on April 28, there is a passage that is marked as having been reported to Congress and subsequently enciphered. It runs as follows:

They [the Spaniards] appear to me to extend their views to the country on this side of the Mississippi beyond the bounds of the Floridas, & to entertain hopes of holding it in virtue of their conquests—They must presume [sic] that the acceptance of a cession [of West Florida] from us would militate against their further claim, & be considered as a tacit acknowledgement [of] our right to all we do not cede. It is not impossible that they are acquainted with the powers which the court of Versailles will have over the negotiations for peace. They may build much upon their friendship & expect to obtain more thro' it than we are willing to cede.
Should you believe these apprehentions well founded you will doubtless endeavor to counteract these designs by shewing on every occasion the right of these States to all the country on this side of the Mississippi not included in the bounds of the Floridas. You will urge too the rights which may be derived from Willing's expedition. I shall send you a copy of his letter & the capitulation of the inhabitants. It may well be, when it can be done without the appearance of design, to take occasion to mention this as included in the ultimata of Congress as part of the United States. . . .[9]

The man who wrote these words was certainly not prepared to accept an Appalachian boundary; and the reference to Major James Willing's abortive expedition down the lower Mississippi in 1778 and to the "capitulation of the inhabitants" can have only one meaning. Livingston wanted the United States to claim the British settlements which Willing had briefly captured, and which lay on the left bank of the Mississippi in West Florida itself. This would have made Spain's possession of West Florida, not to mention her claim to the exclusive navigation of the Mississippi below the line of 31°, a somewhat hollow affair. And on August 9, for example, in a letter to Franklin, and in a ciphered passage which remained hidden for many years, Livingston said:

The claims of Spain are the dreams of one who sighs for what he has no title to or which if attained would only add to the misery he has already hoarded. The degree of estimation in which she stands with us you will judge from the resolutions transmitted to Mr. Jay—I wrote to him in your cipher.

And in the ciphered letter to Jay of August 8, apparently a private letter which was never reported to Congress, he said that nothing but trading privileges in the Spanish Empire—which Spain notoriously would never grant—could compensate the United States for concessions on the Mississippi.[10] It can only be repeated that Livingston was a man who liked to think for himself. He may have retained until the end of his secretary-ship a deluded belief in the good faith of France: he did not try to reason like a Frenchman.

Congress, on the other hand, if we can rely upon the debates of August 8, still contained a *minority* of men who believed, with the Franco-phile John Witherspoon, of New Jersey, that "some of the States had their boundaries fixed and determined; that the State he had the honor to represent was one of them; that it had not entered the war nor would it, he believe, be willing to continue in it for the sake of boundless claims of wild uncultivated country, more especially as it was a matter of dispute. . . ."[11] This sort of reasoning, to be sure, must be considered less in terms of foreign policy than of the internal politics of the national domain: but one can understand that a commissioner in Paris might hesitate before he disclosed his thoughts to such a divided body. None the less, if a minority in Congress might have consented to a limited boundary, it is safe to assert, from the debates of Congress and the correspondence of Livingston, that a majority of Congress and its Secretary would *never* have agreed, in the fall or winter of 1782, to anything short of the Mississippi. That a majority of Congress and the Secretary would not, had they known of it, have permitted the commissioners to negotiate behind the back of M. de Vergennes is undoubtedly true: but that is not quite the same thing.

In any case, the commissioners did keep their own counsel, and the effect on the foreign policy of Philadelphia was to make it an abstraction, an exercise of reason and imagination, offered into the void. Livingston himself, for example, was most eloquent on the subject of unrestricted trade to the West Indies, a subject dear to the heart of every Hudson River magnate: he believed that Great Britain could be persuaded into conceding it if only she could be made to understand that, without such a concession, the United States would be forced to become a manufacturing nation. Nationalists can be agrarians; and Livingston at this time was firmly convinced, as his father had been before him, that Americans would be happiest if they contented themselves with an exchange of raw materials for foreign manufactures. What effect these letters, or any of his letters, had upon the commissioners will never be known. From the beginning of July to the beginning of December, they acted on their own.

On October 26, John Adams arrived in Paris. He was fresh from triumphs of no uncertain nature—recognition, a treaty of commerce and amity, a loan. He sided at once with Jay, and on November 1, Franklin yielded to their arguments and agreed to negotiate without consulting Vergennes. Oswald had now been joined by Henry Strachey, an Under Secretary of State. The discussions proceeded with remarkable smoothness; the preliminary articles were signed at Oswald's lodgings on November 30, 1782; then, and only then, were they communicated to the French. They contained, to be sure, the stipulation that they were preliminary only, and that no final treaty should be concluded until Britain and France had agreed on terms of peace. The commissioners had disobeyed their instructions: but had they broken the terms of the alliance with France?

Philadelphia was now completely cut off, not merely from news of its commissioners' activities, but from any precise idea of their sentiments. Back in April, John Jay had written quite freely about his distrust of the French;[12] thereafter he had been silent until September. It was not until October 31, after his arrival in Paris, that John Adams ventured to remark that the instructions of June, 1781, were intolerable and that he would resign if he was asked to abide by them.[13] On November 6, he went a great deal further, attacking not only Vergennes ("his knowledge is insufficient and his judgment too often erroneous") but Livingston himself.

If it were in my power [he wrote] to do anything for the Department or Minister of Foreign Affairs, I would cheerfully do it, because I am a friend to both; and to this end you will, I am sure, not take it amiss if I say that it is indispensably necessary for the service of Congress and the honor of the office [*i.e.*, Livingston's office of Foreign Affairs] that it be kept impenetrably secret from the French minister [Luzerne] in many things. The office will be an engine for the ruin of the reputation of your ministers abroad, and for injuring our cause in material points, the fishery, the western lands, and the Mississippi, etc., if it is not.[14]

Never had a commissioner stated more bluntly his reasons for not communicating with Philadelphia. They were bold and honest words, written by an enemy to an enemy; but their valor was somewhat diminished by the fact that they could not possibly arrive in time to affect the negotiation in Paris.

Toward the end of December, 1782, while Congress hesitated between hope and gloom, but inclined more and more toward the latter, it was heard that George III had consented to a negotiation with the thirteen states of America. Was this a virtual acknowledgment of independence or was it not? Would it be accepted by the British nation? Was it truth? Was it illusion? For ten more weeks, men waited in an uncertainty "with never a word from the commissioners, but with many and contradictory rumors drifting in by side winds," the air-borne debris of those mildly explosive events that had occurred during October and early November. In mid-January, for example, one vessel came in with news that the negotiations had been broken off, and another with information that they were almost within reach of their goal. In the beginning of February, the contents of a letter from Colonial Secretary Thomas Townshend to the Bank of England, bearing the date of November 22, came ashore: they seemed to indicate that peace was at hand; the King's speech to Parliament, in which it was plainly said that provisional terms had been made with the Americans, was known on February 13; and Townshend's letter to the Lord Mayor of London, dated December 3, and announcing that preliminary articles had been signed on November 30, arrived soon after. But this was anxiety, not certainty, for not a word had come from Franklin, Jay, or Adams. Indeed, Townshend's letter to the Lord Mayor was pursued into port by word from someone in France that the negotiations were about to end in "an obstinate continuation of the war." In Philadelphia, it has been said, they read the newspapers from New York City, hoping for news; in New York City, the British headquarters searched the papers from Philadelphia: patriots, Loyalists, enemy all were in the dark. "Here," wrote one member of Congress, "we wait with anxiety the stage from Elizabethtown and at New York the shores are crowded, the evening they are to hear from Philadelphia."[15]

It was not until March 12 that the *Washington* packet, Captain Joshua

Barney, arrived in Philadelphia with dispatches from the commissioners and the terms of a provisional treaty signed November 30, 1782.

When the terms of the treaty were examined in Congress, they appeared, said Madison, to be "on the whole, extremely liberal."[16] They offered the United States all that could reasonably have been expected. Canada was not ceded, it is true, which was perhaps just as well; and the right to the inshore fisheries had descended to a "liberty"—a word that was to trouble those waters for many years. The British garrisons were to leave America "with all convenient speed," another disturbing phrase in American history. But the boundaries, "the familiar, present-day, river-and-lake boundary," were respectable on the north; on the west they were the Mississippi down to 31° North latitude; and the free navigation of the river was conceded to both nations, which effectually excluded Spain from the Mississippi basin. Only a total commercial reciprocity, which would have satisfied and more than satisfied Livingston's West Indies policy, was omitted: it was to have been an equivalent for Britain's demand for free navigation of the Mississippi; it would have been a singular triumph for the trading instincts of Jay and for the doctrines of Adam Smith, which had found such an unlikely lodgment in the mind of Lord Shelburne. It was, however, postponed until a commercial treaty could be written; and the postponement went on and on, until, through his insistence upon it at any awkward moment, it contributed its mite to the inevitable downfall of President John Quincy Adams. On the whole, however, could anyone find anything but praise for the work of Jay, Adams, and Franklin?[17]

When it was all over, did they sit down at their writing tables to explain, in their letters to Livingston, their reasons for behaving as they had: for violating their instructions; for acting as a "privy council"; for not advising with Vergennes or informing Congress? On the contrary, they followed the sensible principle of *qui s'excuse s'accuse*, offered only the most laconic explanations, and waited until the expected praise and the inevitable criticism should come from Philadelphia.[18]

Criticism was inevitable. What had alarmed "many of the most judicious members of Congress," above everything else, was the addition to the provisions of a secret article which stated that the boundary of West Florida, should the British conquer it or be put in possession of it, should be along the latitude of the mouth of the Yazoo—that is to say, about 32° 28' instead of 31°. Jay's aversion to Spain, where he had been treated with implacable neglect or condescending effrontery; his belief that she would continue to make trouble on the east bank of the Mississippi;

and his notion that Britain would make easier terms if she were given this vestibule to the trade of the West—all these had contributed to the admission of this secret article, which would certainly have had rather fatal consequences if Congress had agreed to it. But this, Congress could not bring itself to do. The question was: Should the existence of such an article be revealed at once to the French Minister? If it were revealed, would it not destroy the confidence that France reposed in the United States? If it were not, and France learned of it elsewhere, would not that produce exactly the same result? Many members believed that the commissioners "had joined with the enemy in taking advantage of the delicate situation [of France] between Spain and the United States . . . and that they had made the safety of their country depend on the sincerity of Lord Shelburne, which was suspected by all the world besides, and even by most of themselves."[19] To this ferment, the Chevalier de la Luzerne—it was only to be expected—gave such added inducements as lay in his power. He told Livingston that according to his dispatches, the American ministers had practiced the grossest deceptions upon Vergennes. Had they not told him that an agreement between them and the British was very distant, when actually it was only a few days away? The result was (said Luzerne) that when Vergennes took the preliminary articles into council, "the King expressed great indignation and asked if the Americans served him thus before peace was made and whilst they were begging for aids, what was to be expected after peace &c." To several members of Congress, he declared that the King had said that he did not think he had such allies to deal with; and when one of them asked whether France meant to complain to Congress, he replied, in menacing tones, that great powers never *complained*, but that they *felt* and *remembered*.[20] And all this when he had not yet heard of the secret article.

The truth was, as Vergennes also intimated to Luzerne, that Franklin had managed to win him round. When Vergennes seemed disposed to complain that the commissioners had gone behind his back, in defiance of their instructions, Franklin's reply was so persuasive and so charming that Vergennes not only forgave him, but also made no objection to a new French loan of six million livres. He may have been, secretly, not displeased. The preliminary treaty between America and Britain scarcely permitted Spain to go on with a war, which France could not afford, merely for the sake of Gibraltar.[21] And, in any case, he was a most singular man. He would have been content to condemn his ally, the United States, to some dismal future as a weak littoral republic. Confronted with a *fait accompli*, he accepted their expansion to the Mississippi with a courteous and kindly smile, in which there was no trace of insincerity. He simply murmured that the war was not yet over.

As for Livingston, he wrote at once to George Washington to say that the preliminary articles were entirely satisfactory except for the fifth and the sixth—the articles concerning leniency for the estates and the persons of Loyalists. But he was profoundly upset, not only by the complaints of Luzerne, but also, and perhaps even more so, by the secret article. In a letter to the President of Congress he urged that the following resolutions should be submitted to Congress:

That the Secretary for Foreign Affairs be directed to communicate the separate article in the provisional preliminary treaty with Great Britain to the minister of his most Christian majesty, in such a manner as will best tend to remove any unfavorable impression it may make on the court of France of the sincerity of these States or their ministers.
That the ministers for negociating be informed of this communication, and of the reasons which influenced Congress to make it. That they be instructed to agree that, in whatever hands West Florida may remain at the conclusion of the war, the United States will be satisfied that the line of northern boundary be as described in the said separate articles.
That it is the sense of the United States in Congress that the articles agreed upon between the ministers of those States and those of his Britannic majesty are not to take place until a peace shall have been actually signed between their most Christian and Britannic majesties.

"Congress will easily believe," he added, "that I offer these sentiments with the utmost diffidence; that I see many and powerful arguments that militate against them; that I feel extreme pain in advising a measure which may hurt the feelings of ministers to whom we are indebted for their continued zeal and assiduity, all of whom I respect, and with one of whom I have had the closest and most intimate friendship from our earliest youth."[22]

As for the deception that the commissioners had practiced upon Vergennes, he could not bring himself to agree that it might, perhaps, have been necessary. It was, so far as he could see, nothing more or less than an inexcusable combination of bad faith and bad manners. He was haunted by one paragraph in a letter from Vergennes which Luzerne had shown him.

I accuse no person [said M. de Vergennes]; I blame no one, not even Dr. Franklin. He has yielded too easily to the bias of his colleagues, who do not pretend to recognize the rules of courtesy in regard to us. All their attentions have been taken up by the English whom they have met in Paris. If we may judge the future from what has passed here under our eyes, we shall be but poorly paid for all we have done for the United States and for securing to them a national existence.[23]

This was the most extreme language that Vergennes permitted himself, and it was more than enough for Livingston. On March 25, without consulting Congress, he sat down to give the commissioners what amounted to a tremendous wigging. He admitted that the articles had met with the "warmest approbation," that the commissioners' steadfastness in refusing to proceed without an acknowledgment of American independence was highly approved, that the boundaries were as extensive as anyone had a right to expect, and that there was "nothing to complain of with respect to the fisheries."

But, gentlemen [he continued], though the issue of your treaty has been successful, though I am satisfied that we are much indebted to your firmness and perseverence, to your accurate knowledge of our situation and of our wants for this success, yet I feel no little pain at the distrust manifested in the management of it; particularly in the signing the treaty without communicating it to the court of Versailles till after the signature, and in concealing the separate article from it even when signed. I have examined, with the most minute attention, all the reasons assigned in your several letters to justify these suspicions. I confess they do not appear to strike me so forcibly as they have done you; and it gives me pain that the character for candor and fidelity to its engagements which should always characterize a great people should have been impeached thereby. The concealment was, in my opinion, absolutely unnecessary. . . .

The secret article is no otherwise important than as it carries in it the seeds of enmity to the court of Spain, and shows a marked preference for an open enemy. It would, in my opinion, have been much better to have fixed on the same boundaries for West Florida, into whatever hands it fell, without showing any preference, or rendering concealment necessary. . . . The separate article is not, I suppose, by this time a secret in Europe; it can hardly be considered as such in America. The treaty was sent out to the General, with this article annexed, by Sir Guy Carleton, without the smallest injunction of secrecy. . . . Congress still conceal it here. I feel for the embarrassment explanations on this subject must subject you to, when this secret is known to your allies. [He enclosed his letter to the President of Congress with his proposed resolutions.] I make no apology for the part I have taken in this business [he concluded], I am satisfied you will readily acquit me for having discharged what I conceived to be my duty. In declaring my sentiments freely, I invite you to treat me with equal candor in your letters. . . . Upon the whole, I have the pleasure of assuring you that the services you have rendered your country in bringing this business to a happy issue, are very gratefully received by them, however we may differ in sentiments about the mode of doing it.[24]

The letter had, in one great respect, already lost its sting. Two days before it was written, a French cutter out of Cadiz had brought word that the preliminaries for a general peace between France, Spain, and Great Britain had been signed on January 20. When Livingston's strictures reached them, the commissioners received them with the good humor of men who were conscious that their reputations were quite secure. John Adams, who was very unwell, grumbled that "your late dispatches, sir, are not well adapted to give spirits to a melancholy man or to cure one sick of the fever"; but he defended his actions with calmness and dignity. The commissioners were not afraid of communicating the terms of their provisional articles to Vergennes. The French had already done their worst. But they *were* afraid of communicating them before they were signed; for then Vergennes would have insisted that "You must not sign till we sign"; and, as the Duc de Vauguyon himself told Adams, the inevitable consequence would have been that "d'Estaing would have sailed from Cadiz, and in that case nobody would have signed to this day." "We are none of us," said Adams, "men of principles or dispositions to take pleasure in going against your sentiments, sir, much less those of Congress. But, in this case, if we had not done it, our country would have lost advantages beyond computation."[25] As for Jay, he showed no disposition to be angry with his old friend. He began his letter "Dear Robt," and continued, in a gentle and friendly manner, to show that the commissioners had been most unwilling to communicate the terms of their provisional treaty to Vergennes because, on every important British concession as to independence, boundaries, fisheries, and the reinstatement of the Tories, the French held views which were "far from being such as America would have preferred." Here he disagreed with Adams; he believed that the French had *not* done their worst, and that they could and would have spoiled the negotiation if they had been consulted during the course of it. On the question of communicating the provisional articles after they had been made but before they had been signed, he and Adams thought alike. Such a course would have been fatal. Vergennes would have insisted that they could not be signed until the French had come to terms; George III would then have disavowed Oswald; the negotiation would "all be to do again"; and Vergennes, backing the British in every objection they made, would have advised the Americans "to recede from demands which in his opinion were immoderate, and too inconsistent with the claims of Spain to meet with his Concurrence."[26]

The tone of this private letter was mild; this was not true of its indictment of the French. It could have given no comfort to a Gallican

Secretary for Foreign Affairs. When he received it, however, Livingston was no longer secretary; he had given the office up and was safe at home at Clermont.

III

Livingston actually resigned on December 2, 1782, when the prospect of preliminary articles, still less of a general pacification, seemed very far away.[27] His reason for resigning, he told the President of Congress and James Madison, was that Chancery business in the State of New York had become so pressing that it had begun to interfere with his duties as secretary. And, indeed, it was common knowledge that a cabal in New York, headed by Judge John Sloss Hobart, James Duane, and John Morin Scott had for months been trying to remove him as chancellor, on the grounds that he could not hold two offices and that his absence from the Council of Revision put an undue burden upon its remaining members. Judge Hobart's motive was obvious—he wanted to be chancellor himself. James Duane's were mischievous: he had married a daughter of Robert Livingston of the manor, with whom the Chancellor was in dispute over the milling rights on Roeliff Jansen Kill; and he wished to make what trouble he could. Scott's motives are clouded in obscurity.[28] To George Clinton, however, the Chancellor had explained many months before that he might have to resign because of the expenses of the office and the limitations which Congress imposed upon it; and this was the view of Luzerne. Livingston was a man of talents, said Luzerne when he reported on his resignation, but he had been given few opportunities to exercise them, and his self-esteem would not permit him to remain in a position where he could make no important move without the consent of Congress.[29]

Congress had sent a committee in December to beg him to reconsider his resignation, and, after some hesitation, he had agreed to remain until May, 1783; all he asked in return was a short leave of absence in order to attend to his Chancery business. There is no doubt that the chancellorship was important to him. James Madison was shocked that a man could put a state office above a national one: he had thought better of Mr. Livingston, a nationalist like himself. But then, he had not quite understood his man as Luzerne, for example, understood him. *"Sa vanité,"* Luzerne had written, *"ne lui à point permis de vivre ici sans éclat."*[30] The Chancellor enjoyed life, he liked to cut a dash in the world: he expected to entertain and be entertained in a manner becoming a foreign secretary;

and he had played a conspicuous part in Philadelphia society, much to his mother's regret and to the mortification of the sisters whom he had left behind to languish at Clermont, and to enjoy (when they could) the meager amenities of wartime Albany. No doubt he did things expensively, but not lavishly. He was too prudent a man to attempt to live in the style of a Robert Morris or to rival the entertainments of the French Legation. But he would not have objected to the expense, even if his rents were in arrears and he was hard put to it for ready money. What he objected to was the thought that these expenses were all to no purpose. Congress would not permit its foreign secretary to act like a foreign secretary: both socially and politically, the office was not as important as it should have been. In the State of New York, the chancellor was a chancellor: in Philadelphia, the secretary for Foreign Affairs was—what? If his thoughts on this or that feature of foreign or domestic policy received the approbation of Congress, then they could go out to the world just as he had written them—but the approbation of Congress they had to receive. Sometimes, surreptitiously, he sent them off in private; but that is not the way in which a man who is fond of power and of the attributes of power likes to behave. Nor could he be sure that what he wrote would be received with the proper attention: for were not the American ministers abroad a "privy council"? Caught between the interference of Congress and the inattention of its diplomats, could the office of secretary for Foreign Affairs conceivably have satisfied a man of ability and spirit?

No doubt, when Luzerne used the word *"vanité,"* he meant what he said. There was a streak of vanity in Livingston, which implies, in turn, a certain frivolity: when circumstances did not suit him, he was tempted not to take them seriously. None the less, in spite of this temptation, he had done a great deal of work and he had done it well. The Department of Foreign Affairs was efficient and happy: the two Under Secretaries were devoted to their chief. The chief himself, when tact was called for, had usually been extremely tactful in his handling of men— the prickly radicals, the high-handed Spanish, the sensitive French. Nothing could have been more admirable than the way in which he kept Francisco Rendon (Spain's unofficial observer) at arm's length, without exactly hurting his feelings, or his management of Luzerne's complaint that the King of France was not to be mentioned before the American Republic on the Yorktown column.[31] His circular letters to the state governors were, in their way, models of strength and sense. And in large things, no less than in small, he had displayed both vision and independence. Although he was accused in his own time, and is still accused today, of being merely a creature of Luzerne's, it must be repeated that, month by month, he developed a foreign policy that was not French at all.

As for procedural matters, he may have possessed (as one student has put it) "an uncanny divination of the type of advice most needed by a Minister."[32] One can hardly believe that John Adams, for example, would have endorsed this verdict. But his dispatches are certainly notable for brevity, clarity, and good sense; and he had developed, before he left Philadelphia, very definite ideas about the character and scope of American diplomacy.[33] The ideas he put down in a report to Congress. The "divination," the clarity, the good sense—all these were spread before state governors, who could not act upon them even if they had wished to do so, or before diplomats who believed that they were in a position to know better and who, in the event, went on to a resounding success upon their own terms. If one adds the persistent and galling interference from Congress and its committees, the pressure from New York to return and save the chancellorship, the expense involved in maintaining appearances, the humiliating thought that the appearances thus maintained were not equal to the expense, can one be surprised that he refused to continue in his office? "I frankly confess," he wrote when it was all over, "that I have found the culture of Laurels the most expensive husbandry I ever engaged in."[34] The operative word is "Laurels." He always found it difficult—and surely the difficulty is not uncommon—to make a distinction between duty and prestige. The laurels had been costly, but that was not really the point; the point was that they had been insufficient.

His departure was hailed with relief by a group of men who believed—quite wrongly—that he was in far too close relations with Robert Morris, the Financier.[35] Livingston approved of Morris's concepts of strong central government, he had supported him in his financial expedients, but he had never endorsed the Financier's rather loose ideas as to the location of the boundary between public administration and private advantage. In any case, Congress as a whole was genuinely sorry to lose so able a servant; and Livingston received the rare and flattering tribute of a resolution which expressed its "high sense of the abilities, zeal and fidelity" with which he had discharged his trust.[36] He was duly gratified, but not unduly so. It was not that he thought of himself as a failure or of Congress as insincere; he was perfectly well aware that he had been zealous and capable, and that he had nothing whatever with which to reproach himself. The empire, the conspiracy, of circumstance had been too much for him. What gentleman of an independent mind could run an executive department under the Articles of Confederation as they then were? He took refuge in a point of view which, whatever else it may have been, was decidedly aristocratic. The whole thing had become disagreeable and unnecessary and a bore, and he was best off at home. But then, suddenly, there was a revulsion. For two or three weeks, in July and August, he thought of returning as secretary pro tempore, so that his signature could appear on the definitive peace treaty which was rumored to be on its way. He wrote to Marbois, and to Alexander Hamilton. Hamilton consulted with James Madison. "We need not assure you," he wrote, "how happy we should both be to promote your wish." But Congress was too thinly populated for anything "which has something of novelty in it" to receive the necessary votes; and "we fear the Strictness of the ideas of many Gentlemen will be a bar." Livingston took the hint in good part: it was his last effort to do something with a position that had never given him the satisfactions he craved. "I consider it," he wrote, "as a feather that would have graced my cap but do not feel much pain at going as plain as my neighbors."[37] He could not help admitting that he was finding it difficult to philosophize himself into "that tranquil indifference which is perhaps necessary to rural happiness"—to the shades of Clermont and the honorable duties of a chancellor. A second daughter had been born to him in Philadelphia in April: there was still a chance that a son would follow. The landlord was back where he should have been most at ease, the statesman was home: but somehow—it was ungrateful but it was true—in the shades of Clermont he was restless and uneasy. But then another thought asserted itself. Would he not be more useful at home? Was it not his duty to lead his state into "moderation"? If the Revolution were successful, should he not save it from the consequences of success?[38]

PART THREE

FEDERALISM

CHAPTER ONE

In 1783, when he started once more to make his way in New York, Chancellor Livingston was thirty-six years old. He was already growing deaf, and his affliction was not helped by the eminent Dr. John Bard, who issued the truly dreadful ukase that an electric current should be passed through both ears. How this was done, one cannot exactly tell; but it *was* done; and the Chancellor grew deafer than before.[1] In every other respect, now, in the prime of his life, he presented a vigorous and confident front to the world. James Kent, the future and great chancellor, remembered that his first glimpse of the full resources of the New York bar had been when he attended an ejectment suit, "brought by Chancellor Livingston against Hoffman, the cause [being] tried at the bar of the Supreme Court at Albany, in October term, 1784." This was the case against Zachariah Hoffman, an old family dispute about certain lands on the southern boundaries of Clermont which had been pending since at least 1744. Aaron Ogden, of New Jersey, Egbert Benson, and Alexander Hamilton were counsel for Hoffman: the Chancellor appeared at the bar as advocate in his own case.

He won his suit; Alexander Hamilton then moved for a new trial; and in arguing this motion, he and Livingston, said Kent, were "the brilliant and master spirits." Hamilton was new to the bar, and had never before met so distinguished an opponent: but he was scarcely the man to be daunted by opposition; and his motion, a criticism of uncontrolled jury trial in property matters, was able, eloquent, and courageous. The Chancellor in his reply made great play with the decisions of Lord Mansfield, whom Hamilton had cited extensively, and whom Livingston described as a power-hungry Scotsman, always ready to destroy the old Saxon liberties. What would the Genius of Liberty say, he inquired, if she were present, and saw some gentlemen, who had wielded the sword in her defense—it was a graceful tribute to Colonel Hamilton—now brandishing the arbitrary decrees of Lord Mansfield?

The motion was lost, Hamilton issued a writ of error, and the case was eventually settled by compromise. Everybody had done very well:

but "it was the tall and graceful person of Chancellor Livingston, his polished wit and classical taste . . . the ingenuity of his argument, the vivacity of his imagination, and the dignity of his station" which most impressed James Kent. His concluding address to the jury contained, wrote Kent,

a boldness of illustration and a burst of eloquence never before (it was said) witnessed at our bar. He rebuked severely the opposing counsel for their attacks upon the character of one of his ancestors, relative to the early Grants of the Manor, and for "raking over the ashes of the dead in the presence of a great-grandson." He brought his ancestor up from the grave and led him into the court to speak for himself by a daring metaphor which surpassed and confounded the audience as well as the jury. He carried his cause, as it were, by a *coup de main* and obtained a verdict, rather by the weight of his character and the charm and power of his eloquence, than by the force of evidence, or the merits of the case.[2]

The details of this case have been lost: but if they involved the First Lord's patents, then it must be admitted that the Chancellor had need of all his eloquence.

II

Livingston was always under the spell of contemporary history, on the one hand, and of family history, on the other: indeed, he spent much of his time trying to turn the one into the other. A landowner and a jurist, he united in his single person those two classes that Cadwallader Colden had once denounced as the backbone of a conniving colonial aristocracy—the sort of aristocracy which, purged of the denunciations of Colden and equipped with certain modifications suited to that purpose, he still expected to adapt itself to the republican environment of New York. For if he was caught in the past, he was not a worshiper of the past, condemned, like his friend Gouverneur Morris, to live out the paradox of a vigorous and active obsolescence. Far from it. He looked into the future with confidence; accepted change as a leading principle of political, no less than of physical, life; and was often accused of being too visionary for his own or his country's good. He returned to New York in 1783 determined to introduce a certain "moderation" into state affairs and a certain vigor and pre-eminence into national government; he was a staunch Federalist by 1788; and by the middle of the 1790's he was an equally staunch Jeffersonian, whom his enemies did not hesitate to call a Jacobin. Surely no change, no conversion, could have been more violent, even if we grant that Federalism meant one thing in 1788 and quite another in the 1790's. Yet this conversion was due to no sudden and total reversal of the convictions and habits of a lifetime; nor was it, as has often been claimed with a little too much facility, merely the result of political pique. It was due, rather, to an innate conservatism. Livingston was by no means lacking in the more acute business instincts, and could have been, had he wished, a practicing Federalist in the more pejorative sense of the term: but he was under some evident necessity to keep faith with the pieties of the past, with family history, while at the same time endeavoring to modify his environment with all the éclat which America's destiny seemed to require. It was not difficult for Livingston, as a Hudson River aristocrat, to see himself as a Jeffersonian: whether he could be a good Jeffersonian or (which was much the same thing) a happy one—that was the question.

III

His career during the coming years might be described as obscure because much of his time was absorbed in the business of the Chancery Court; and because here the student of his life is faced with one insurmountable difficulty. While the records of the court, from 1785 onward, are in one sense plentiful, while we know when the court sat and where, what its rules were, what kinds of cases were tried there, and by what lawyers: yet, in another and more important sense, they do not exist at all.[3] In Livingston's day, no decisions were handed down in writing and preserved in print. Since a Chancery Court is a court of equity, affording relief in realms where the common law is inoperative, a chancellor's decisions can give an unusual insight into his concepts, not merely of what is legal, but of what is fit. Of the Chancellor's philosophy in this respect the only remaining traces are in his rulings in the Council of Revision, which are too few and a little too political to be of much service, and in the one or two recorded decisions against him in the Court of Errors.[4] In his own court, Livingston has become voiceless.

The court, as handed down to him from colonial days, had a poor reputation: it was expensive, it was dilatory, and (since the royal governor himself was *ex officio* the chancellor) it was sometimes amateurish and almost always corrupt. As with the Department of Foreign Affairs, so with the Court of Chancery, Livingston had to build from the ground up. The fact that no complaints—as distinct from appeals—have survived as to his methods of conducting the court seems to indicate, in so far as negative evidence can indicate anything, that he was both efficient and just.

It may well be that this absence of a record would not have seemed inappropriate to him. From his allusions to it, it would certainly appear that he preferred to think of the chancellorship in terms of status—in precedence, it made him second only to the governor and it placed him at the head of the bar. Mingled as it always was with politics, through the Council of Revision, it was none the less not a political office. The chancellor was chancellor *quamdiu se bene gesserit,* during good behavior, and until the age of retirement. It was as a potent figure in society, not as a learned judge, that he evidently preferred to see himself. He had a reputation for legal and classical scholarship; yet, in all the mass of his surviving letters and papers, there is as little trace of the one as of the other.

What interested him was natural philosophy, as he called it: he aspired to be a practical scientist. The two hundred acres that he reserved for his own use on the Clermont estate were to be devoted to experimental agriculture, to studying the effects of gypsum upon buckwheat, maize, lucerne, and clover; to improving his breeds of cattle and of sheep. His tenants, no less than himself, were expected to profit from these experiments, for as a landowner he was distinctly paternal. If his leases were quasi-feudal in nature, he did not bear hard upon tenants who tried to improve their holdings: it was from their improvements, not their rents, that the land increased in value; and in his own remote world, for practical as well as for sentimental reasons, he played the role of benevolent autocrat. He was capricious, jealous of his rights, a hard man to cross: in that small leasehold empire, it was difficult to be otherwise; but he tried to be just, and he was essentially kindhearted. The tenant riots, which were to disturb the manor in the 1790's, never spread to Clermont.

Nor did he limit himself to agriculture and stockbreeding. He was interested in anything and everything—from manufacturing paper out of river weed to rebuilding all of his eight mills on some novel principle designed to prevent friction between the upper and nether millstones. His family, he told Thomas Jefferson, took this sort of thing very hard. "I must tell you that they are all in arms against me & that without your assistance [in obtaining a patent] I do not know when I shall compose them. They alledge that my politics have half ruined my fortune . . . & occasioned the loss of all my houses by *fire* [i.e., in the Revolution], & that now my mechanicks will render water equally injurious to me & them & occasion the destruction of my mills."[5] This tone of rueful amusement hardly disguised the fact that his family—his brothers at any rate—

thought of him as some inveterate "projector," like his grandfather Robert of Clermont, who could never resist an impracticable scheme. "This is the worst of Bob's follies," said his brother John R., years later, when the newfangled *Steamboat* lay at its New York wharf, an unlikely object, ready to start on its triumphant maiden voyage to Albany and the future. And, of course, they were wrong.

Chancellor Livingston was by no means lost in the clouds. He was an imaginative man, but his imagination was that of the eighteenth-century amateur scientist—certainly no contemptible or useless personage—who believed that the physical universe might at any moment yield any one of its innumerable, its extraordinary secrets to some fortuitous experiment or sudden flash of insight. Immersed in a multitude of occupations, he had no leisure for prolonged and exhaustive experiment: but—who could tell?— if one gave what time one could to the development of some new idea, something might turn up, as, in the end, something did. Nor was he the man to pour good money after bad: he would spend up to, but never beyond, the limits prescribed by prudence. His friends were apt to accuse him of indolence, of burying himself in the country to dabble in this scheme or that, when he should have been occupied with public affairs; nor were they entirely unjustified. There was a touch of frivolity in the Chancellor; he found it extremely difficult to be serious about things that threatened to upset his comfort or disturb his peace of mind; and he was too proud and too intransigent to make a good party man. But there was a vein of iron in him as well. He was a born improver, deter- mined to alleviate the lot of his fellow man while at the same time—he was, after all, of Scottish and Dutch descent—materially advancing his own fortunes. Yet it is possible, it is even probable, that his inner nature was most truly expressing itself on those many occasions when he held his Chancery Court at Clermont and could visibly unite the two personae of judge and of landlord. In his library, the law books rose to the ceil- ing; outside, was the peculiar, the fascinating world in which one incul- cated the principles of scientific farming in a tenantry which paid its rent in wheat and personal services and which had not yet learned to read. Cler- mont was already a monument to the colonial way of life, with a special character—pastoral, simple, patrician; harsh and beautiful; stern and drowsy; possessive.

When he was asked to go abroad as a diplomat, he found himself, as usual, torn between the spectacular and the typical choice; between the hope of aiding his country by some dramatic coup, which his common sense told him was a slim one, and the certainty of leading a useful life at home;

and, as usual at such times, he tried to maintain an indifference he did not exactly feel. When the Chevalier de la Luzerne wrote from Paris to suggest that Thomas Jefferson's health was so bad that "every hope to see you Minister in France is not vanished," he replied that no man alive was so well qualified as Jefferson, and that he himself had no thoughts of going abroad. Against his own consent, he said, he had been put up in opposition to John Adams for England, but "happily Mr. Adams's interest prevailed & saved me the pain of refusing an honor which I knew to be above my merit. I have already been nominated for Spain & at my particular request withdrawn." And he had since had an offer to replace Adams at The Hague, "which I have peremtorily refused tho I might I believe have been unanimously appointed."[6] Charles Pinckney, to be sure, was convinced that he had expressed a wish to go to The Hague; and he replied that he had refused that appointment chiefly because he did not wish to interfere with the chances of Edward Rutledge, his old friend. Then he added, a little lamely, that he was perfectly indifferent to the post itself.[7] But it was not indifference he had felt, it was indecision: and in the end, yielding to the stronger pull, he decided for Clermont, with whatever it carried in the way of judicial and political duties.

He was, in other words, sufficiently contented with his ancestral position. He invariably acknowledged, in every word that he ever wrote on the subject, the influence of his father, the Judge, whom he had loved unconditionally, and who would surely be proud of him as he was now—a prosperous, attentive landowner who was also the acknowledged head of the bar. Nobody who has studied the Chancellor's life would deny the strength of this benign influence, which, in fact, pervaded the whole Clermont family, and made it, in spite of its temperamental differences, a singularly corporate body.

He was now the father of two daughters—his second, Margaret Maria, had been born in Philadelphia in April, 1783—and still very likely to have a son. He was the head of the Clermont family in every respect except one—the *tone* of life at Clermont was set by his father. With the Judge's death, Margaret Beekman Livingston became tenant for life of the Clermont mansion and its demesne, and with her tenancy she assumed—they were by no means unsuitable—the airs and the sway of a benevolent tyranny. She was very much on the side of simplicity and of piety—of the standards, that is to say, that prevailed when the Judge was alive. She had no doubts as to the standing she possessed in her own county or in New York: the Beekman heiress, the mistress of Clermont, she was already an institution, and she knew it. But she did not care for society in its more frivolous aspects, and she had lectured her eldest son when she heard that, as Foreign Secretary, he was cutting quite a figure in Philadelphia. "I have heard of the gay life yr family lead," she wrote. "It was perhaps necessary, at first setting out, to give in to the customs of the people with whom you converse—But is it not equally necessary my dearest Son that people in your rank of life should stem the torrent of Luxery and dissapation which must end in the ruin of these infant states. . . . You have been invited out —I suppose you have returned it—there stop, at least by degrees."[8] The Chancellor did not, of course, stop: Philadelphia was a long way from Clermont, and he had his own ideas as to the right behavior for a foreign secretary. But when Mrs. Livingston referred to rank, she was not thinking of the secretaryship; she was thinking of what was to be expected of a Livingston of Clermont. She did not suppose that this included ostentation. Indeed, she was so sure of her family's rank and fortune that she was able to dispense with such considerations when it came to the marriage of her younger children. Four of them had married during the Revolution. One daughter, Gertrude, became the wife of Morgan Lewis, a deputy quartermaster general and the son of a respectable patriotic New York merchant: another, Margaret, married Thomas T. Tillotson, of Maryland, a surgeon in the Northern Department, whose birth and talents (said Gouverneur Morris) were nothing extraordinary. If her sons-in-law were respectable and considerate, Mrs. Livingston did not care too much about birth or talents. "I believe I told you in my last," she wrote to her daughter Catharine, "that Gitty was become Mrs. Lewis. . . . The young Couple both Looked Charming." But what especially charmed her was the tender and considerate behavior of Morgan Lewis to "my apprehensive Girl." "Spare my girl this evening," he had said, when somebody made a broad jest at supper. As for Tillotson, "Tillotson I find I did not know. Oh my caty whenever you marry Let yr man, yr choice, be what he is & you can't fail of being happy."[9] When John R. Livingston became engaged to a dowerless Boston beauty, whose mother had been reduced to keeping a shop, he wrote in some trepidation to his eldest brother, asking him—not so much to approve the marriage himself—as to "solicit Mama's approbation," which perhaps might not be given to such a match.[10] He need not have been alarmed. No doubt it was an ordeal for any young lady, however well qualified, to make her first entry into that woodland stronghold, with Livingstons for miles around: but at Clermont, a bride was sure to be welcomed, so long as she displayed a suitable *empressement*, a willingness to be absorbed into the family. Henry Beekman Livingston's unhappy bride, Anne Home Shippen, had reason to complain of everything except her treatment there. "My house is peace & love," Mrs. Livingston told one of her daughters-in-law. "Never did three estimable brothers and six sisters love each other better than they do."[11] She excluded the fourth brother, Henry Beekman Livingston, nursing an ungovernable temper at Rhinebeck: but it was true of the others. Moreover, the feeling that prompted her words was genuinely simple.

No one cared less for appearances as such. When Clermont was burned by the British, she had a hut built for herself near the ruins; and there she proposed to live, working in her ruined garden, waiting until the mansion was rebuilt. "I have done all I can to wean Mama from this object," the Chancellor wrote in April, 1778, "but in vain—She has no pleasure any were else . . . nor can I wonder at it."[12] He, too, often felt that he had no pleasure anywhere else. Although he built a second mansion in 1794, in a style considerably more grand than that of the older Clermont, it was built within sight of his mother's gardens; and as long as his mother reigned in the older Clermont, some of her spirit dominated the new one. The air of mingled formality and carelessness, of profusion and simplicity, which puzzled the unimpressionable Strickland on his visit in 1795, was due to the standards of an earlier day, which the Chancellor had not outgrown.

He was, indeed, never entirely to outgrow them; even in his later days, on his return from France, when he lived in some splendor. He was a prototype of the Hudson River squires, an individual who did not believe that there could be a better way of life than his own, and who borrowed from other ways of life only what happened to suit his fancy.

As the years went on, he began to take more and more money rents from his Clermont tenants, but the majority of them still paid in kind. The average Clermont farm was seventy acres, of which as much as one-third might be under cultivation; the average rent was twenty-five bushels of merchantable winter wheat a year, four fat hens, and one day's "riding." The usual lease was for three lives. The Chancellor retained milling and mining rights, and the hated "quarter-sale"—the fine exacted from a tenant who sold his lease to another farmer—still prevailed on his estates. On the Clermont estate, the Chancellor demanded one-fifth the selling price; in the Hardenburgh Patent, he asked only one-tenth.[13]

He had inherited the Clermont estate, which was entailed upon the heirs male of his grandfather, the first Robert of Clermont, under the old laws; but he had not claimed the family holdings in the Hardenburgh Patent, as he might have done, since his father's will, written during the grandfather's lifetime, made no mention of these lands. He retained his grandfather's pet project, the Woodstock settlement across the Hudson; but in 1779, when there was no compulsion on him to do so, he began to divide the rest, some three hundred thousand acres, equally among himself and his brothers and sisters. These lands lay between the forks of the Delaware and spread eastward below the east branch of that river: that is to say, in northwest Ulster County and in what would now be Delaware and Sullivan counties. There had been little or no effort to settle them before the Revolution: remote, precipitous, and stony, they were valuable only beside the river branches and along the kills. When settlement began in the middle and late 1780's, rents were not demanded for the first five years, and thereafter they varied between sixteen and twenty bushels of wheat per hundred acres, to be delivered at one or another of the Hudson River landings. The customary tribute of fowls and "riding" was sometimes omitted, and leases were sometimes "for ever." "For ever" was a hollow term. A desperate, a tragic mobility, prevailed in the Great Patent. The pioneers who ventured into that stormy wilderness, with its fearful winters, often disappeared, leaving no trace: if they stayed, they were usually in arrears. The words "forgiven by the Chancellor" appear again and again in the Great Patent accounts: he was not disposed to be harsh with men whose rents counted less than did their labors in bringing the land under cultivation and opening it up for settlement. But settlement was slow; turnpikes were begun and wandered vaguely off into nowhere; the rivers and streams were scarcely navigable and never along all their length. Only a system of freehold might have tempted a large movement of settlers; but outright sales were not encouraged, at least to small farmers. The dearest wish of the American, to own his land, was rarely gratified on the Livingston estates.[14]

Mr. Strickland, the Chancellor's English guest of the 1790's, was surprised at the candor with which his host discoursed upon the feudal nature of his rents and privileges. How odd, he thought, that a man who was reputed to hold almost Jacobin views in politics should be so very baronial on his own lands! And even odder that he should admit it with such impenitent pride; Strickland had, of course, stumbled on that simple political dualism which permits a man to be one thing at home and quite another abroad. Every impulse of family piety, every motive of comfort and convenience, prompted the Chancellor to be satisfied with his way of life at Clermont. If he observed—what, as a keen student of farming conditions, he was bound to observe—that leasehold farms were almost always more slovenly and less productive than their freehold counterparts, he could soothe his conscience with the thought that he himself was spreading around him the principles of progressive farming. And then there was always the belief that as the lands filled up, as values increased, as conditions improved, one could begin to sell: this, as he told Joseph Bonaparte in 1803, was the hope of the New York landowner. In the meantime, he was living half in a world whose conditions were much as they had been when Cadwallader Colden was denouncing them to the Lords of Trade, and half in a world from which the Lords of Trade had vanished and where their place had been taken by public opinion. Public opinion, to be sure, was not yet very vocal; but it existed. It murmured around the Chancellor whenever he plunged into public affairs and political battles; it made him unduly sensitive to criticism and unduly eager to combat it; and it made him somewhat capricious and undependable where politics were concerned. He was a valuable, a powerful ally and a formidable enemy; yet his friends could never be sure that he might not be dawdling at home, lost in some impractical invention or attending to his farm, when he should have been putting forth his best efforts in some political cause; and his enemies could be fairly certain that, although the most genial of men when he was not crossed, he would become touchy and assertive when he was. He was very conscious of his position as a Livingston of Clermont, as *the* Livingston of Clermont—to uphold it was a duty that he owed to himself, to his immediate family, and to the Livingston tradition, of which he was becoming more and more both guardian and exemplar.

The truth was that the Manor of Livingston, the senior branch of the family and its natural leaders, had not done too well out of the Revolution. Three sons of Philip, the second Lord of the Manor, had once upheld their position before the world: but when the great William Livingston moved into New Jersey, when Peter Van Brugh Livingston sank under the weight of his infirmities, when Philip Livingston, who had signed the Declaration of Independence, died in 1778, it seemed as if their ancestral spirit—that *"daimonion ti"* which had once animated their politics —had dwindled away into pride and petulance. The old third Lord of the Manor, Colonel Robert Livingston, Jr., regarded the whole revolutionary business as an unpleasant necessity thrust upon him by the intransigence of the British Parliament. It was not that he and his sons were not anti-British: on the contrary, they were extremely angry with the British for not leaving them alone, and would have surrendered to George III only with their dying breath. But they observed with distress the rise of a popular party under the new state Constitution; they disapproved of the Constitution itself, in that it had deprived them of their family seat in the Assembly; and they were convinced that the taxes they were called upon to pay were evidence of nothing more than a vindictive and leveling spirit. Their pride was affronted when Colonel Udney Hay, for example, marched his soldiers across their lands, seizing wheat which should have been paid in rent and (which was worse) sending it to be ground at non-manorial mills.

Indeed, they had nothing to gain from a popular revolution. The law of 1782, the first of several laws that struck at entail and primogeniture, although primogeniture had never been strictly observed in colonial New York, struck also at the very heart of the manor: thereafter, it became, not a single entity, but the property of a group of individuals held together by ties of blood—and blood, in such cases, has by no means the fixative powers of fee tail. They could hardly have been blamed for not displaying an enthusiasm for this new turn of events. The old third Lord was first accused of selling his iron too dear, and then obliged to let his Ancram ironworks fall into disuse for lack of money to pay his workmen. By 1781, his two eldest sons, Peter R. and Walter, had ceased to sit in the State Assembly. Peter remained at home, the colonel of a manor militia that never left the manor, made himself responsible for raising the quotas for the Continental line, and was assisted in these duties by his two younger brothers John and Henry; while Walter drifted into the commissary business, as a partner of Comfort Sands. It was not an impressive record: but then it had never occurred to these particular Livingstons that it was either necessary or desirable to make an impression. They were represented in the Continental Congress by their brother-in-law James Duane; in the Continental army (during his lifetime) by their uncle Lord Stirling: for the rest, they did their duty as they saw fit, and cared little if people said that they were doing as little of it as they decently could.[15]

And so the political leadership of the family passed, almost by default, to the Livingstons of Clermont, and specifically to the Chancellor. If, during the Revolution, he had indulged from time to time in what might have been called (had he been born two generations later) a faintly Byronic detachment, he had emerged with his prestige enhanced and his position assured. His brother Colonel Henry Beekman Livingston, so long as he found it compatible with his feelings as a gentleman, had fought valiantly—at Saratoga, at Monmouth, on Rhode Island, and had received the thanks of Congress: and those excessive sensibilities, which made him so quarrelsome and caused his retirement, were, if the story of his marriage is any evidence, undoubtedly due in part to some deep-seated maladjustment. The youngest brother, Edward, who was destined to a career of singular charm, storminess, and brilliance, was too young to play a part in the great convulsion. The second brother, John R., had devoted his energies to making what he called "something clever" out of the Revolution in the way of business; but he was, after all, only following a tradition which decreed that in any circumstances at least one younger son should be engaged in that manner.

The Chancellor himself, in 1783, if not exactly trusted or admired by the radical New Englanders and Virginians in Congress, was on the best of terms with the conservative nationalists in and out of that body. He had been one of the self-constituted shadow cabinet, which Washington always attended when he came to Philadelphia, and the General, in 1782, when he was on his way from Newburgh to Albany, had made a point of leaving Mrs. Washington at Clermont, to stay for a week with Margaret Beekman Livingston. Mrs. Livingston dutifully took her guest to the manor to dine with Peter R. Livingston and to spend the night at Walter Livingston's house; and on the next day they all went to Red Hook church, where a large crowd assembled to see the General's lady, and where Dr. John Henry Livingston preached the sermon. The rest of the week was spent at Clermont. The General also passed the night there on his way back from Albany, and took particular care, the next day, to call on Colonel Henry Beekman Livingston before he left for Newburgh. Mrs. Livingston would have been less than human if she had not experienced a modest triumph over the way in which the Clermont family had been distinguished above the manor one.[16]

It was, of course, due to the fact that Chancellor Livingston had been on excellent terms with the General, both as a nationalist member of Congress, and as Secretary for Foreign Affairs. Washington, whose military perplexities had been rendered even more perplexing by the hostility of a section of Congress, was not unmindful of his supporters: and if one of these supporters happened to be a substantial landowner, whose prejudices might be presumed to be similar to his own, he would unburden himself in a manner not the less startling for being outwardly cool and reserved. What he and Livingston feared, as nationalists, was any sign of deficiency in the national character. "Such an avidity appears among our people to make money," the General wrote on one occasion, just after it was known that preliminary articles of peace had been signed, "and so feeble the reins of Government (where there is an attempt to exercise them) to restrain the illicit & pernicious intercourse of Trade with the enemy that the fence between them and us is entirely broken down. . . . In truth, I am quite discouraged and have nothing left but to lament the want of virtue & depravity of my countrymen." Livingston replied that the country's prospects were indeed obscured by "the general depravity you so justly lament." It pervaded "the mass of the people" in every state, brought faction and injustice to every legislature, and made nothing of such considerations as national faith and national honor. "And I must fear that in some States even so little integrity will be found as to lead them openly to refuse to pay debts contracted with England before the war."[17]

Sentiments like these, to be sure, are not exactly private: they represent an effort to outline the sort of character the writer wishes to assume as he makes his way through the world. In the Chancellor's case, it was for the time being the character of a man who has turned his back upon popularity and the thoughts that make for popularity. "It is a sad misfortune," he told Alexander Hamilton, in the flat language of self-regard, "that the more we know of our fellow creatures the less reason we have to esteem them."[18]

CHAPTER TWO

New York City became, at first, and for a while, the center of interest for the whole state in these so-called "critical" years from 1783 to 1789. It was evidently destined to be the entrepôt for the trade, not only of New York, but of New Jersey and Connecticut: large revenues could be anticipated from the duties on its imports. The disposition of these future revenues, therefore, became one of the great issues between the proponents of a strong national government and the champions of state rights. Nor was this all. The British army did not leave the city until the end of November, 1783; and in the meantime it had become an ark of refuge for all those Loyalists who had not yet fled the state. What was to be done with them? This problem, which loomed very large before the British evacuation, actually settled itself. Those Loyalists who took to their heels were not, usually, permitted to return; those who remained were not, usually, either driven off at once or persecuted beyond endurance. It was, in fact, a question of what kind of society *might* have emerged if the Loyalists had been treated with more forbearance than was actually the case—a purely academic question.

It did not seem so at the time: on the contrary, it became a focus for political discussion. No sooner had the first rumors of a preliminary peace been circulated, than the patriots of New York began to flock to New York City. Although Governor Clinton refused to issue permits (Margaret Beekman Livingston wrote), "the sloops go down, and such numbers of people flock to them yt. they are fighting for their passage—farmers are selling their farms, to go and settle in Town, in short to go down is all the rage." What intrigued the wealthy at first was the state of their town houses: thus, Mrs. Livingston, for example, learned to her relief that her house in Queen Street had been occupied by a Colonel Crosbie, the British Barrack Quartermaster General, and was therefore in good repair; while James Duane, although he could find out nothing about his houses in Fly Market and King Street, was delighted to hear that his villa and farm (in what is now Gramercy Park) had been occupied by Rear Admiral Robert Digby, who had added two rooms and a piazza, and had built a summerhouse of latticework on the hill behind. Such was the news sent back by Robert Cambridge Livingston, of the manor, who went down in May, but could not get near his father's property.[1]

But other considerations soon supervened. These property-owning visitors reported to a man that the Loyalists in the city were in a dismal state of alarm. Alexander Hamilton, passing through the city in August on some business for his mother-in-law, Mrs. Schuyler, found that a considerable detachment of Hessians was embarking, and that this movement, combined with the appearance of several violent broadsheets, had started a large Loyalist migration. "Many merchants of the second class, characters of no political consequence, each of whom may carry away eight or ten thousand guineas, have I am told lately applied for shipping to carry them away. Our State will feel for twenty years, at least, the effects of the popular phrenzy." And Henry Livingston, after busying himself in the manor store, "measuring Ells of Muslin and calico to the Country People," went down in July and again in September, and found the people in great dejection, selling off their goods and preparing to depart. "All is confusion, Horror, and fear," he wrote. "In short they are a poor, abject cringing sett as ever lived." Nobody knew whether or not a definitive treaty of peace had been signed: but when the news of its signature arrived, when the British departed—what then? "I do hate that Nation more and more," wrote the old third Lord to James Duane, "for the barbaritys & crueltys parpitrated among us. It would please me to have no connection with them, was it not for the individuals among them who have always been our friends Especially these of the Cityes of London & Bristol, together with all Ireland, God bless them." But what was the use of persecuting Loyalists? And were not the persecutors "restless macannicks, who wish to see all their craft out of it [the city] that they might engross all to themselves without any regard to treaties or the Vertues of Brotherly affection? O what a pity it is that we do not after so long & dangerous a Struggle live in Peace. . . ." He, like every propertied man, feared the effects of too harsh a treatment of the Tories—on trade, on world opinion, on social stability.[2]

The Chancellor was of a like mind. "I seriously lament with you," he told Alexander Hamilton, "the violent spirit of persecution which prevails here and dread its consequences upon the wealth commerce & future tranquillity of the State—I am the more hurt as it appears to me almost unmixed with pure & patriotic motives—In some few it is a blind spirit of revenge & resentment but in more it is the most sordid interest." "Has our decline been as rapid," he wrote to Elias Boudinot, "as our advances from

Childhood and have we already in the words of Shakespeare got into the last stage of this strange eventful History—Second childishness & mere oblivion?" And he told Barbé-Marbois that "the Government of New York suffers in its reputation by too cruel a triumph over a vanquished foe."[3]

There was an element of genuine humanity in these thoughts; but what chiefly prompted them was the fear that a respectable and propertied section of society was being lost forever by the expulsion of the Loyalists. "The Government of New York"—that is to say, Governor Clinton and his "radical" following—were, needless to say, of a very different opinion. Nor is it an otiose speculation to ask ourselves what might have happened, what change might have occurred in the history of America, if the exiled Loyalists—like the French *émigrés* after the French Revolution—had been permitted to return. Certainly the history of the Federalist party would have been very different and vastly more respectable or, at any rate, enduring: and perhaps we have some reason to be gratified that the views of men like Chancellor Livingston and Alexander Hamilton did not prevail. It is doubtful if the fortunes of the United States would have been advanced by the addition to its early political forces of a strong counterrevolution. The Chancellor, of course, was not thinking of counterrevolution; he was looking for some counterbalance to the radicals who, he said, "have acquired influence in turbulent times which they are unwilling to lose in more tranquil seasons"; and that was not quite the same thing. He was also, as a jurist, worried lest a persecution of the Loyalists should violate the preliminary or the definitive treaty of peace with Britain. And, as usual, he was concerned with appearances. How could the new nation gain any credit in the world if it behaved with savagery toward the Loyalists? As John Jay put it, in a letter from Passy: "Europe hears much, and wishes to hear more of Divisions, seditions, violences and confusions among us. The Tories are generally and greatly pitied—more indeed than they deserve—The indiscriminate Expulsion and Ruin of that whole Class & Description would not do Honor to our Magnanimity or Humanity."[4] In one way or another, for one reason or another, all nationalist opinion was on the side of leniency.

This letter reached Livingston before he left for New York. He had been appointed a member of the Temporary Council which was to run the city until a mayor could be selected; but he did not leave Clermont until he heard from General Washington of Sir Guy Carleton's intention to "relinquish the posts he holds on York Island as far as McGovern's pass inclusive, on the 21st. inst., Herricks and Hampstead with all to the Eastward on Long Island on the same day, and if possible to give up the City, with Brooklyn on the day following. . . ." He was apparently present when Washington made his entrance, at last, on November 25; he was inexpressibly moved at returning to his native city after seven years, horrified at its dismal appearance, and surprised, as was everyone else, by the tranquillity which prevailed in it—"which is certainly as much to be admired at [he told Marbois] as any other part of this singular war."[5]

Grim and shabby, the city displayed on every hand either the effects of the two great fires which had ravaged it since its occupation, or some slovenly or filthy memento of the occupying army, as always the worst of housekeepers. Although a majority of the Tories had left, for England or, in most cases, for Nova Scotia, a considerable minority remained "to brave the fury of the democrats." The leading patriots, as a matter of fact, whether conservative or radical, had no use for physical violence; and once, when an angry crowd seized two men, whom they mistook for Americans in the British service, and were carting them off "to shew them Cunninghams gallows & then as they say to turn them out of the State," Governor Clinton and Chancellor Livingston came up together, "in time to rescue them and to seize the principal offenders whom we committed to gaol."[6] It is even possible that the Loyalists who remained, although treated as enemies and as aliens, felt themselves strong enough to repel a concerted proscription. In one instance, certainly, they acted with a most provoking boldness. The British-appointed vestry of Trinity Church (whose burned steeple on Broadway uplifted a black, reminding finger) had the hardihood to appoint the Reverend Benjamin Moore to the vacant rectorship—"a man," said the shocked Chancellor, "who had preached and prayed against us during the war." Was it possible, he asked a correspondent, that the "extreme lenity" shown them since the departure of the British would still lead the Tories on to their ruin? For the moment, it seemed as if an ecclesiastical civil war was about to break out, as if the Whigs would be obliged to seize the churches by force: but in the end the nine trustees (of whom Livingston was one) appointed by the Temporary Council to supervise the affairs of Trinity parish permitted Mr. Moore to preach, on the understanding that he would never be rector. "I begin to believe," Livingston wrote, "(contrary to my former sentiments) that it is next to impossible that a man who has been an advocate for arbitrary power for ten years can be a good subject in a free republic."[7]

It is quite likely that the New York Loyalists suffered far more from the legislation enacted against them during the war than from the violent measures passed after it was over. The Confiscation Act of 1779, for example, with its various supplementary acts, had placed some $3,600,000 in specie at the disposal of the state, not always in the most legal manner. Livingston, like all conservative Whigs, was opposed to it at the time. "Never," he told John Jay, "was there a greater compound of folly, avarice & injustice than our confiscation bill"; and Jay, later, in Spain, wrote Clinton a letter inveighing against "injustice too palpable to admit of palliation." Clinton was unmoved. What concerned him was the fact, also all too palpable, that New York was in danger of being overrun by Loyalists, for perhaps half the population was disaffected during the early years of the war.[8]

In any case, a closer acquaintance with the Loyalists of New York City evidently modified Livingston's humane sentiments. He believed that they formed one of the three parties in the city and that they actually hoped to regain their old power. Of the other two parties, one was composed of "warm and hotheaded Whigs," who wished to expel all Tories; the other was made up of moderate Whigs, who did not wish to injure the Tories in person or property, or banish them from all social intercourse, but simply to make a distinction between them and "the virtuous Citizen who has done his duty."[9] No doubt he would have preferred a policy of amnesty; the restoration to the community of such families as De Lancey, Robinson, Bayard, Rapalje, would not have revived old enmities but would certainly have strengthened the old aristocracy. But his earlier opposition to confiscation bills did not prevent him now from investing in confiscated property. "The number of people who from fear and dislike have quitted the State," he told the Dutch Minister, P. J. Van Berckel, "the quantity of forfeited property & the little command that any persons have of money, has opened a large field for the employment of money in the purchase of real property; so as to make immediately an interest of 8 to ten pr. C.t" He himself had invested £2,800 in "good, substantial brick houses"; but he needed £6,000 sterling for further ventures. "For which," he continued, "(tho' I believe my simple bond would be considered as sufficient for ten times the sum) I am willing, as the loan must be obtained from abroad, to mortgage improved lands of twice or three times the value, and to allow an interest of six per C.t, the principal payable in six years. As I am not nor ever was engaged in trade, as my property consists altogether in Lands & houses, as I live within my income & the very money I wish to borrow is to be vested in real property, it is impossible for any person to offer better securities than I do." And he asked John Jay to establish a credit for him of £6,000 or £8,000 upon some good house: perhaps the business could be done in England, perhaps in Holland.[10]

Thus compassion for the Loyalists, from whatever source it arose, was modified by experience and by circumstance. Livingston befriended the notorious Tory printer James Rivington, and continued to buy his books from him: but that was partly because Rivington had the best collection of books, and partly in order to express an opposition to the politics of John Lamb, Issac Sears, Marinus Willett, and the other radical leaders in the city. But the fugitive landowners—had they not put themselves beyond the pale? One might as well invest in what had once been their property. One might as well collect, at the same time, any small but agreeable trophies. It was not without satisfaction that Mr. Tillotson rented, for the use of the Chancellor's family, a large square pew near the pulpit in St. Paul's Church, where Oliver De Lancey had once sat.[11]

II

The interesting feature in Livingston's dealings in confiscated property is his belief, which was central to every transaction, that in his improved lands he owned an enormous source of credit. His willingness to go into debt to the extent of £12,000 sterling, at a time when money was hard to come by, shows how high he placed himself among the credit-commanding class: but only as a proprietor of land. In 1784, indeed, he carried his proprietary (one would almost say agrarian) predilections so far as to join in a movement to obtain a charter for a land bank, to be called the Bank of the State of New York. Its original prospectus seemed to indicate that its capital would be composed two-thirds of pledges of land, one-third of cash. In a paper, written anonymously after the publication of this prospectus, which had cheerfully neglected the dangers inherent in so much nonliquid capital, the Chancellor proposed that the land pledged should be cultivated land, and that houses insured either by the bank or the proprietors should be included. He contended, too, that the bank's circulation should be proportioned, not to the security, but to the cash in the bank, and that means should be devised to obtain the subscriptions of moneyed persons without forcing them to draw too much of their capital from trade in order to vest it in lands. He therefore proposed that the Legislature should declare that no land bank could circulate more than its capital, and that its capital should consist of at least one-third in money and the rest in houses or improved lands. The Legislature should also provide that a certain proportion of the stock, not exceeding one-third, should be divided into enumerated shares. The proprietors of these shares were not to mortgage land, but the bank, upon receiving the money proportion or third part of a share in money, should undertake to procure the land, and the subscriber, being rid of the risk and inconvenience of mortgaging his own land, would pay out of his dividend at the rate of 4 per cent on the whole share. "This I am well informed will be sufficient to obtain mortgages from people who have not money to engage in the bank." Thus each share would (exclusive of the charges of the bank) bring in 18 per cent on their money to the persons mortgaging their lands and 14 per cent to those who only deposit their proportion of money. But moneyed men should be permitted to assign mortgages taken for money lent to individuals, and should be granted the privilege of receiving not only their dividend, or 18 per cent on the money deposited, but also the lawful interest on their securities.

The central structure of such a bank seems clear enough—no doubt the Chancellor had in mind something on the order of the old colonial land offices. How it could have been made to work is rather more obscure. Two things, at any rate, are certain: one, that Livingston put an inordinate faith in the liquidity of improved lands and of houses; the other, that his proposal was strenuously and successfully resisted by Alexander Hamilton. Hamilton had a scheme of his own, which, combined with another plan hatched by the ingenious John Barker Church, his brother-in-law, and by Jeremiah Wadsworth, was to produce a commercial institution called the Bank of New York. The rival Bank of the State of New York he regarded with supreme contempt not unmixed with fear—Chancellor Livingston, Hamilton said, had convinced "the country members . . . [that] the land bank would be the philosopher's stone that was to turn all their rocks and trees into gold." And the "country members," the representatives of the small freehold farmers, were no contemptible opposition: they saw to it that the Legislature did not bestow a charter upon Hamilton's bank. Hamilton, on the other hand, was able to muster enough commercial votes to deprive the Chancellor's land bank of its charter.[12]

Hamilton's opposition may have produced at the time a certain awkwardness, but it did not prevent him and the Chancellor from working together as Federalists. When Hamilton's Bank of New York went into business, without obtaining a charter, and William Seton, a reformed Loyalist, was made its cashier, there was a momentary consternation. *"Le choix qu'il a fait de M. Seton,"* Marbois wrote from Philadelphia, *"nous a paru extraordinaire . . . mais nous pouvons que garder le silence depuis qu'il a été choisi par vos concitoyens pour Caissier de la Banque."* Livingston replied that Seton was a deserving man, and that his appointment was injudicious only because it might seem unfriendly to France. "What you say of the Bank, however, has little weight in this question as would appear if you knew the subscribers and the state of parties here."[13]

And it is certainly true that no political sense could be extracted from the maneuvers that had accompanied the introduction and the destruction of the land-bank scheme. Isaac Sears, for example, whose politics the Chancellor detested, was the chief proponent of his land bank in the Assembly; but Isaac Sears's name was also found upon the list of those who subsequently appealed (in 1785) for the chartering of Hamilton's bank. If Seton's choice as cashier suggested that the Hamilton bank was the creature of a pro-British party, the election to its presidency of Alexander McDougall, one of the old Liberty Boys, might—with at least as much justification—be made to lead to quite opposite conclusions. As is manifest in the later story of the founding of the Manhattan Company, it is most unwise to look for strict political alignments in the early banking history of New York. Nor did the Chancellor lose any affection for John Barker Church, whose wife was one of his great favorites, because of their banking disagreements.[14]

What is, in fact, interesting about the land-bank controversy is that the Chancellor betrayed in the course of it a certain distaste for commercial banks. He admitted that they could be wisely and virtuously managed, but he feared that some "adventitious spirit" might take control of their policies: he disliked, in other words, the new moneyed men who were rising in the city.[15] It might seem odd that he should have betrayed this fear when he was a Federalist, but have shown no trace of it later on when, as a Jeffersonian, he became one of the leading promoters of the Manhattan Company. But in the history of Federalism, as in the history of banking, one must not look for uniformity. In banking, the Chancellor, as a great landowner, sought and obtained the political support of the upstate agrarians: in Federalism, as a great landowner, he found that the upstate agrarians were among the most determined and intractable of his opponents.

III

In the great battle of the "critical period," the struggle between Federalist and Anti-Federalist, between the supporters and the haters of strong central government, the Chancellor simply extended into state affairs the nationalism that he had once professed in the Continental Congress. At first, it seems, the battle was in abeyance. In the spring elections of 1783, which amounted (in all but a technical sense) to the first postwar elections, the

Clermont Livingstons supported George Clinton for governor,[16] even though Philip Schuyler was one of his opponents; for Clinton had been very tactful in parrying their demands for workmen when Clermont was being rebuilt or in soothing them down when they complained of exorbitant taxes, and in the matter of the chancellorship he had consistently given them his support. As a wartime governor, he could not afford to make powerful enemies; and the Livingstons, sensibly enough, admired him for his fighting qualities. Moreover, in the fall of 1781, he might almost have been called a nationalist himself. But with the coming of a definitive peace, he began to move toward that obstinate particularist position around which the great state conflicts were to swirl for the next few years. He was a radical, the natural leader of the small upstate farmers: but, as his record attests, he was no violent radical. With all his honest and salutary fear of centralized government, he was also deeply imbued with the notion that it was better to be the ruler of an independent state in a weak confederation than to have his claws pared and his vigor abated by some strong national entity. He was a lion who roared with great effect, a rough impressive creature, but one who, left to himself, would not have preyed too severely upon the vested interests. His great battle against the federal impost merely hastened the death of the Confederation, which it was his earnest wish to preserve. But this his opponents could not have known as they prepared to fight him on the Federalist issue.

The first difference between the Federalists and the Anti-Federalists could have been discerned, a little dimly, in the question of tolerance or intolerance toward the Loyalists. By the middle of 1784, their differences had come out into the open. In 1784, the Legislature ignored the request of Congress for the right to collect a national impost through officials responsible to Congress: instead, the state established its own system of tariffs. At the same time, in the Assembly, as if to emphasize the Chancellor's nationalism, it was proposed to reduce his salary from £400 to £200; while in the Senate, it was suggested that it should be stricken off the civil list altogether. But what could one expect, said Mr. Tillotson, who reported these measures to his brother-in-law, from men who were doing their best to dissolve the Union through "contracted and unconfoederal measures"?[17]

None the less, when commissioners were chosen to settle the old boundary dispute between Massachusetts and New York, all of them—Chancellor Livingston, James Duane, John Jay, Egbert Benson, and Walter Livingston, of the manor—were politically opposed to Governor Clinton. This has been taken to prove the importance of the boundary dispute—the best men were chosen, regardless of politics; but one cannot help observing that, as the original commissioners fell out for one reason or another, they were replaced by Clintonians. Thus, while the dispute remained as important as ever, political differences seem to have become more acute. The Chancellor himself served from the beginning until the end; and even consented to spend a brief time in the Continental Congress, presenting his credentials on December 7, 1784; for, at least in the beginning, it was expected that the question would be settled in a federal court, in accordance with Article IX of the Articles of Confederation.

The problem, to state it as simply as possible, was that Massachusetts had yielded all claims to territory to the west of a meridian running north and south through the westernmost point of Lake Ontario, but still maintained that she owned all the land that lay beween that meridian and the New York settlements farther to the east. Some millions of acres of fertile land were involved, and it was obvious that, if Massachusetts were to have her way, there would be little comfort for expansionist sentiment in New York. The Chancellor maintained that the controversy would prove "of the last importance to our State," since Massachusetts was claiming the greater part of it; but there were few signs of excitement or anxiety in the newspapers, and probably everyone expected that the matter would be settled by a compromise.

Massachusetts, at any rate, appealed to Congress to determine where the New York boundary lay; Congress called on both disputants to send agents or commissioners; and these commissioners were then supposed, in accordance with the provisions of Article IX, "to appoint by joint consent . . . judges to constitute a court for hearing and determining the matter in question"; but this they were quite unable to accomplish. Either the two sides could not agree upon judges satisfactory to them both, or, when they did agree, the judges fled like patridges before such a formidable task. Never had the weakness of the Confederation, juridically, been more evident; Livingston's reference to the dispute soon became laconic; and it is in the papers of James Duane that we must trace the wandering steps of the commissioners or observe the changes in their ranks. John Lowell, James Sullivan, and Theophilus Parsons remained for Massachusetts, but by September, 1786, Rufus King had fallen out; on the New York side, John Jay (now Secretary for Foreign Affairs), Walter Livingston (who had been appointed one of three commissioners of the Continental Treasury), and Egbert Benson were replaced by Robert Benson, John Haring, Robert Yates, Melancton Smith, and John Lansing, Jr. The two legislatures decided in April to dispense with the services of Congress, and it was in the old style—as between two embassies from two independent governments—that proceedings were brought to a close at Hartford on December 16, 1786.[18]

The result is certainly interesting. New York made two concessions to Massachusetts. She granted Massachusetts full pre-emption rights to 230,400 acres to be located north of certain specified grants between the Oswego and Chanango rivers. She granted full pre-emption rights in six million acres lying to the west of a line drawn from Lake Ontario through Seneca Lake to the Pennsylvania boundary. New York retained full sovereignty over this immense territory, but the Massachusetts grants were to be exempted from quitrents for fifteen years, Massachusetts could negotiate any necessary treaties with the Indians, and Massachusetts could delegate the negotiations to private individuals, provided that a state commissioner was present and that the state ratified within six months any treaty so made. In other words, while a certain statesmanlike impetus was given to the settlement of western New York, it seems that Massachusetts got the better of the bargain and that the great land speculators in both states would reap the profits.[19]

When Governor Clinton announced this result to the New York Legislature on January 13, 1787, he stated, with evident delight, that the settlement had been made "otherwise than by a Foederal court"; the Anti-Federalist in him was profoundly gratified.[20] But what he approved as an Anti-Federalist, he was later to frown upon as a governor. In August, 1787, he felt obliged to warn Governor John Hancock that a syndicate headed by John Livingston, of the manor, had conceived a scheme for dealing directly with the Iroquois beyond the line of Seneca Lake. Unauthorized purchases were, it is true, forbidden by the Constitution of New York; but John Livingston and his friends believed that they could surmount this obstacle by obtaining leases from the Iroquois which would run for one thousand years and carry only a nominal rent. They had even been forced to absorb into their Genessee Company, no doubt with patriotic reluctance, a group of former Tories operating out of Canada upon the same ingenious plan; and, despite the denunciations of the Legislature and a stern proclamation from the Governor, they proceeded with their negotiations in the hope that the law courts would uphold them. In Massachusetts, meanwhile, Oliver Phelps and Nathaniel Gorham, representing a syndicate which may have contained Robert Morris, the former Financier, proposed to buy *all* the Massachusetts rights for about $1,000,000 in Massachusetts scrip, then worth about $175,000; in other words, for some five cents an acre.[21]

It is unnecessary to follow these schemes any further: the point is that they arose, one might say inevitably, from the nature of the agreement between New York and Massachusetts. What were the New York commissioners about when they made this agreement? James Duane, John Livingston's brother-in-law and himself a confirmed speculator, may possibly have been laying plans in which he was to figure as an agent for making wholesale purchases from Massachusetts: but Chancellor Livingston was never interested in remote western lands, was not on good terms with James Duane and John Livingston, and would not have done them or any other man a *specific* favor of this kind under any terms. As for Melancton Smith, John Haring, and John Lansing, Jr., they were confirmed Clintonians, so that one can rule any political bias out of these odd proceedings. Was it possible that New York's commissioners had been simply outwitted by the superior bargaining powers of their Massachusetts opponents? Or could it be that they were unable to resist the appeal of a boundary compromise that bore the mysteriously mingled features of a statesmanlike settlement and a gigantic land grab? In those days, when land exercised such a powerful influence upon history, such a scheme might have captivated even the most upright and prudent of men; and Chancellor Livingston and his fellow commissioners were all from rural districts, where land was held to be almost divine as a source of energy. Only when speculation was carried to extremes, when a John Livingston tried to get around the Constitution with his thousand-year leases, or Messrs. Phelps and Gorham proposed to purchase six million acres for about one-twentieth their value, only then, and not always then, did assemblies and governors denounce and proclaim.

IV

Thus it seems that in the "critical period" Livingston was governed on the whole by his instincts as a landowner, as in the Massachusetts dispute, or by his desire to consolidate and preserve his own landed position, as in the land-bank scheme. His nationalism, now stronger than ever, was not without a relationship to his holdings: for it was prompted in part by fear of what an agrarian state could do to landed aristocrats. It seemed to him that a man who supported the Confederation had become almost, if not quite, degenerate in his politics. When Elias Boudinot told him in November, 1783, that Congress had "hastily passed a Vote for two places of residence & fixed the other at George Town on the Potowmack, and their temporary residence alternately year about at Annapolis & Trenton," he was so disgusted that he was obliged to resort to Buffon for a proper rejoinder.

I begin to think with some speculative writers [he answered] that the air soil & climate influence the principles of every government—This system is strongly supported by the example of our [government] when compared with [that of] the natives who have undoubtedly acted under that influence—first their governments are for the most part federal unions [*i.e.*, confederations]—Next the nation is governed by a set of select men that may very well represent the Congress—These have a right like Congress to advise while the people have a right like those of the United States to follow that advice or let it alone—Neither have distinguished dignity, neither have a halfpenny in their Treasury & the only thing in which the resemblance failed was that we did not like them hold vagabond councils.

Buffon, perhaps, would not have been disturbed by these arguments: but when a New York landowner is reduced to citing the *Histoire Naturelle* against his own environment, one can but remark upon the strange ferment that nationalism could work in a rational mind.[22]

For a while, Livingston kept such thoughts to himself or to his private correspondence: he was content to oppose the Clintonians from behind the modest entrenchment of the Council of Revision. He was present, and presumably approving, when the Council vetoed a bill for incorporating the mechanics of New York City: he tried, but in vain, to prevent the emission of paper money, even so cautious an emission as the £200,000 put forth in 1786. When the Clintonian majority in the Legislature in 1784 and 1786 resisted the introduction of a federal impost of 5 per cent ad valorem on all imports, when the Governor in 1786 refused to consider the recommendation of Congress that he should call a special session to reconsider such measures, Livingston resisted in the Council rather than outside it. He told Luzerne in 1785 that if "the general system [*i.e.*, the federal impost] had been established it would have rendered it easy to fund our debt which is all that ought to be wished on the present occasion." And he assured Charles De Witt that "from the time that this regulation [the federal impost] takes place, I shall believe that we have a confederation."[23] But, on the whole, he seems to have cultivated, politically, a relaxed and optimistic state of mind. When he was appointed a delegate to the Annapolis Convention of 1786, he did not even bother to put in an appearance: he preferred to preside over his court in New York. And he informed Marbois that the grave depression of that year was healthy, that it was a necessary factor in the restoration of industry and economy, in other words, that it had been caused by overtrading. He insisted that nothing

more was necessary than for Europe to forbear from exporting "the necessaries to life to America," and to open her ports to American lumber,
potash, flour, rice, and tobacco. Did the Europeans not realize that the
price of their manufactures must rise or fall with the expense of living?
Could they not see that they had only to establish an exchange of American
raw materials for European manufactures to bring back a healthy economy?
And that otherwise they would force Americans "to live independent of
Europe & manufacture for ourselves"? What Marbois thought of these
propositions is not known; but the propositions show that the Chancellor's
Federalism, whatever else it may have been, was scarcely Hamiltonian.
If he wanted a strong federal government, it was in order to force
Great Britain to abandon her mercantilist ways and allow a complete
freedom of intercourse with the United States in every part of her empire
("the territories of the East India and the Hudson Bay companies only
excepted"). This, he thought, would produce the same healthy exchange
of American staples for British manufactures: for to his mind, as to his
father's before him, a healthy America was an agrarian America.[24]

In 1787, he was perfectly willing to assure Luzerne that the depression
was over and prosperity had returned. Any stories of a different nature
came from the English papers or from discontented Americans. "I have
known this country before the revolution, complaints of decay of trade
&c have always prevailed among the merchants in peace when fortunes
were only to be made by patient industry. That we have suffered abroad
cannot be doubted—That we are happy at home is equally true. . . . Our
present taxes do not amount to more than ½ a dollar a head upon the
people of the state exclusive of duties which are not felt so that upon the
whole I may venture to say that we are among the happiest people in the
world." For this reason, he feared that the Articles of Confederation,
"which render us contemptible abroad," would survive even the Constitutional Convention soon to meet in Philadelphia. As far as he knew at the
time, the object of this Convention was simply to revise the Articles. "I do
not expect much from their endeavours," he told Luzerne, "& for this
obvious reason that the people, finding themselves happy, will not wish
for a change, tho those who think public reputation & public credit of importance may."[25]

V

The rather painful dichotomy—the people, on the one hand, and those
who care for public reputation and credit, on the other—which lay at

the center of his nationalist reasoning at this time, was bound to reveal itself in public sooner or later. Who were "the people"? Obviously, those who supported and worked for such agrarian governments as that of George Clinton. For Livingston, at this period in his life, was in the odd position of wishing for an agrarian America which should, somehow or another, not be run by agrarians. At length, perhaps because this position was untenable, perhaps because his equable pose was no longer able to sustain the pressure of his nationalism, perhaps because he was by nature a most impulsive man, he gave vent to his feelings in public and before a somewhat embarrassing audience.

On July 6, 1784, he had been elected an honorary member of the Society of the Cincinnati, which had just become respectable by shedding its hereditary character, but which was still, as a society of former officers, highly and justly suspect among democrats.[26] The New York branch, to be sure, found room for men whose political differences were acute—men like the Federalist Samuel Webb and the Clintonian Marinus Willett; but George Clinton, a charter member, found it advisable as time went on to have less and less to do with it. As for the Chancellor, when he was requested to deliver an oration before the New York State Society on July 4, 1787, he at first declined. Though the composition of orations came easily to him, and their delivery was a delight, he declared that he had not sufficient leisure. The Society was insistent; he changed his mind; and then, almost at the last minute, changed it again. Baron von Steuben wrote, in his odd and agitated French, to beg him to reconsider. All the preparations were made, he said, and he did not see how the Chancellor could break his engagement without incurring the displeasure of his brother Cincinnati. And then he added, as a final inducement, that Governor Clinton had left New York in order to avoid the occasion. (*"Le départ de notre Gouverneur pour Eviter cette occasion est selon moi un motif de plus pour Vous montrer Votre Attachment à la Société. Le contraste serat bien in Votre faveur."*)[27] Whether this final argument satisfied Livingston or not, he changed his mind again, and, after meeting with his fellow members at the City Hall at 9:00 A.M. on July 4, proceeded with them to St. Paul's Church, and there delivered a most inflammatory address.

"Can it be believed," he asked the Society, "that an enlightened people think the science of government level to the meanest capacity—That education, experience, application, & genious [are] unnecessary in those who are to frame laws for the government of a State? Is it [not] well known that in some states the competence which affords leisure to attend to the affairs of government even in the hands of men who have risked their all for the establishment of freedom is urged by some as sufficient cause for their not sharing in the administration of their country? Are not abilities & education proscribed by those who want them & supply their place by that cunning which renders them suspected in others? Have you yourselves escaped the general obloquy, are you not calumniated by those you deem unworthy of your society, are you not shunned by some [*i.e.*, Governor Clinton] who should wear with pride & pleasure this badge of former services? Brests glowing like yours with patriot ardor will ever be dreaded by the tools of faction—You have learned in the school of adversity to appreciate character—You are not formed to follow the lead of those you despise— Men used equally to command & to obey are sensible of the value of government & will not easily consent to its debasement. Your services entitle you to the respect & confidence of a grateful people. Envy & the ambitions of the unworthy concur to rob you of the rank you merit—To these causes we owe the cloud that obscures our internal governments."

Nor did he hesitate to join these exclusive sentiments to the cause of Federalism itself. When he turned his eyes, he continued, to "the other great object of a patriot's attention, our federal government, I confess to you, my friends, I sicken at the sight. Nothing presents itself to my view but a nerveless Council, united by imaginary [bonds] brooding over Ideal decrees which caprice or fancy use at pleasure to annul or execute—I see trade languish, public credit expire & that glory which is not less necessary to the prosperity of a nation than reputation to individuals a victim to opprobrium & disgrace."

The Confederation, he said, was weak in itself, weaker because some states forgot to send a delegation or sent an unworthy one, and weakest of all from another cause "which operates with peculiar force in some states— the love of power, of which the least worthy are the most tenacious," and which they do not want to share with Congress. As a result, the Confederation had become so debilitated that it could do nothing to prevent Great Britain from imposing her mercantilist rule upon American trade. "Who but owns that we are at this moment colonies for every purpose but that of internal taxation of the nation from whom we vainly hoped our swords had freed us." It was one of the Chancellor's fondest agrarian beliefs that an exchange of raw materials for manufactured goods was "colonial" if it was restricted by the British Navigation Acts and not "colonial" if it was free.

It was only at the end of his speech that prudence came to the rescue. He was, after all, one of the writers of the New York Constitution. "Our internal constitutions," so ran his peroration, "may make us happy at home, but nothing short of a national one can render us safe or respectable abroad.

Let us not however in our eagerness to attain this forget to preserve our internal constitutions safe & inviolate, for better is distress abroad, than tyranny or anarchy at home." With these unexceptionable sentiments, the speech came to a close; the "Eulogium" was pronounced; and the New York Society of the Cincinnati, on the whole well satisfied with its entertainment, strolled down to the Battery, where a substantial collation had been spread in the shade of several tents. No one could doubt that Chancellor Livingston had uttered extreme Federalist doctrine, in the heart of a Federalist city, and in the most provoking terms: but what such radical members of the Society as Marinus Willett said upon this occasion has not been recorded, and perhaps could not be.[28]

CHAPTER THREE

While Chancellor Robert R. Livingston was delivering his Federalist philippic before the New York Society of the Cincinnati, the Constitutional Convention at Philadelphia was about to lose two of its three New York members. John Lansing, Jr., and Robert Yates were already meditating withdrawal, because the Convention was headed, not toward a revision of the Articles of Confederation, but toward the creation of a new general government. In their letter to Governor Clinton, explaining their withdrawal (which took place on July 10), they said that they had not been appointed to write a new constitution, that the consolidation of the United States into one national state would subvert the Constitution of New York, and that a national state would be wrong because a central government could not be controlled nor could it enforce the law. It would also be too expensive. In short, they expressed the rather disingenuous position of the Clintonians up to this point—their pretense that they were opposed to a general government because it would be too weak—but had injected into their argument the notion that a central government might be uncontrollable or (which was the real Clintonian belief) that it would be altogether too strong.[1]

The third New York delegate, Alexander Hamilton, left Philadelphia on June 29, and on July 3 was in New York City, writing to George Washington that he feared the Philadelphia Convention would "let slip the golden opportunity of rescuing the American empire from disunion anarchy and misery." According to Baron von Steuben, a somewhat impeachable witness, to be sure, Hamilton had come to the city expressly to attend the meeting of the New York Society of the Cincinnati. "*Je suis persuades*," Steuben wrote on June 29, shedding his accents in his excitement, "*que Hammilton fera L'impossible pour etre ici.*"[2]

It was certainly true that Governor George Clinton was becoming one of the foremost enemies and New York State one of the centers of resistance to any significant constitutional change. In the elections of 1786, no one could be found to oppose Clinton as governor; from that time onward, he had become less cautious. The ambiguous attitude of Congress toward the dissident Vermonters; its inability to urge the British out of their western posts, five of which were in the State of New York, where they interfered with the western fur trade; the shining economic future of New York itself—all these were elements in his decision to become if not exactly a secessionist, at least no friend to the Confederation, not to mention some stronger union. Moreover, it is arguable—as the Chancellor told Luzerne in 1788—that the state was making a rapid recovery from the depression of 1786, and that it was, on the whole, content with such government as it had.

The chief focus of opposition to the Governor lay in New York City itself. Even the mechanics, who would naturally have supported Clinton, had been seduced by the argument that a stronger central government would have some mysteriously healthy effect upon trade and employment; while the various merchant groups, for a variety of reasons, were also turning against him. A meeting held in New York, at which the chief speaker might be expected to utter strong Federalist doctrine, had its importance. Hamilton, at any rate, would not have considered the meeting inopportune or the Chancellor's language intemperate. According to the rule of secrecy, he could not confide in the Chancellor as to what was actually taking place in Philadelphia: but any reasonable man might have guessed that the divisions in the Convention were likely to be acute and perhaps irremediable; and any well-read man would have had some idea of the sort of plans that were being discussed, even though the details were necessarily hidden from him. It is unlikely that the Chancellor, when he made his speech on July 4, was altogether in the dark.

II

Since the absence of Lansing and Yates deprived New York of its quorum, Hamilton's appearances at Philadelphia were brief and sporadic; but he remained the chief exponent of extreme nationalism; and he was present to sign his name to the Constitution. Compared to his role in Federalist politics, that of Livingston had been simply parochial; and so it remained. Where state rights were concerned, no Livingston could have taken Hamilton's position; for Hamilton really had no state loyalties, and the Livingstons, by every ancestral and material tie, were bound to New York: even if they did not approve of its government; even if they feared the consequences should it become too independent. The Chancellor must have read the letters of "Publius" (the *Federalist* Papers) as they appeared in the press; he is not on record as having said anything about them. While the great battle over the ratification of the Constitution was pending, he was to some extent preoccupied with the manifold and obscure details of a family dispute which was, in its way, not without an influence upon the later politics of New York.

In 1779, he had written to his kinsman Robert Livingston, Jr., the third Lord, a long and quite extraordinary letter in which he claimed, by the terms of the first Lord's will, the right to erect a gristmill on Roeliff Jansen Kill, the powerful stream that divided the manor from Clermont; the exclusive right to two falls upon that stream; and the exclusive right to the stream itself wherever it flowed through lands which (as occasionally happened) belonged to him on both sides of it. And in 1780, he built a gristmill without his kinsman's consent. The question was in abeyance during the war, although it probably accounted for James Duane's attempt to remove Livingston from the chancellorship: for James Duane had married a daughter of the third Lord, and was considered a son of the manor. But as soon as peace came within sight, Robert Livingston, Jr., began to consult the law. He asked John Morin Scott and his nephew Brockholst Livingston (the son of the great William) for their opinions, and both were agreed that he could either bring an action of trespass against the Chancellor or else "abate" (*i.e.*, pull down) the mill and dam, and make himself a defendant. Brockholst Livingston suggested that Alexander Hamilton should be called in: and Hamilton's opinion was a miracle of tact.[3]

In strict law, said Hamilton, the manor had the best of it; but in equity much might be said for the Chancellor. He had searched carefully for authorities to endeavor to settle the legal ground on which this question ought to be decided; "but I find few ajudications in any degree applicable, and it is my duty to acknowledge that the decision I have seen most in point rather countenances the claims of the other side in this article; though it is far from authorizing sanguine expectations." No doubt an action for trespass *quare clausum fregit* would lie; it would be better than abating the Chancellor's mill and dam; but surely the whole thing could be settled by a compromise.[4]

A compromise, however, was the last thing that either side had in mind at this point. The old third Lord, on the one hand, was very tenacious of what he conceived to be his rights, while the Chancellor, on the other, was already dreaming of that novel invention which would revolutionize the working of mills by eliminating friction between the millstones. A mill had already become a sacred object to him.

Nothing, obviously, is more apt to embitter relations in landed families than a dispute about land; and if the Chancellor had had any strong political ambitions in 1783, when the dispute was reawakened, he would have been wiser not to have estranged his kinsmen by an absolute defiance, for the manor Livingstons, even if their influence had diminished as a result of the Revolution, were still a power in the state.*

Livingston, however, as so often in his life, seems in this instance to have decided that his rights as a landowner were altogether more important than his prospects as a politician. And so, when the Livingston clan needed most to be united as Federalists, a division had been created over the grand question of a dam and a mill; and the manor and the Clermont families began to oscillate between alliance and hostility, between political necessity and family recrimination. The necessity emerged with each election, for each election—as Henry Livingston saw it in 1785—was becoming more and more openly a "hard trial . . . between Demo & Aristo." In the crucial election of 1787, Henry Livingston wrote from the manor to the Chancellor concerning the delegation from the newly created Columbia County, which had been made to include the Clermont estate. "John Bay, Mr. [William] Powers & Mr. John Livingston," he said, "will be the best representation we can get . . . if we are unanimous in the above persons I have no doubt of our success. I wish your opinion on this matter . . . before you leave home for New York." Thus there were consultations on these important matters at the very time when the old third Lord "was going furiously to the attack," mustering his battery of lawyers, and remarking to anyone who would listen that he did not know "whether my honored Parents left me anything but what I may enjoy by the Courtesy of the Great Chancellor, which [I] abominate."[5]

* One of the political consequences of this dispute was that, when Columbia County was to be formed out of part of Albany County in 1786, Livingston's manor relatives refused to heed his advice and petition against it. Livingston warned them that, in the projected new county, one of two things would happen. If the Livingstons and Van Rensselaers joined forces politically, the three members of the Assembly for the new county might well be opposed to such a union of landlords: if the Livingstons and the Van Rensselaers disagreed, the Van Rensselaer influence would be preponderant. RRL to Henry Livingston, undated, but probably 1788 or 1789, in which RRL gives a retrospective view of the family dispute, particularly as regards Columbia County. RRLP. The act that erected Columbia County out of the southeast portion of Albany County was passed April 4, 1786. 2 *Laws of the State of New York* (Albany, 1886), 234-36. Livingston's prediction was fulfilled. When the Livingstons, as a whole, broke with the Van Rensselaers in the 1790's and became Anti-Federalists, the Van Rensselaer influence did prove to be predominant in Columbia County. After 1800, the county was run by the Federalist junto of Jacob Rutson Van Rensselaer, Elisha Williams, and William W. Van Ness. See Dixon Ryan Fox, *The Decline of Aristocracy in the Politics of New York* (New York, 1919), 40-44, for a good description of the so-called "Columbia Junto."

The Chancellor, on his side, refrained from any verbal attacks on his venerable kinsman, who had been, after all, one of his father's best friends: he expressed himself in oblique assaults upon the more vulnerable members of the manor family. Upon James Duane in particular—although the two remained ostensibly upon speaking terms—he performed some of his more telling attacks. James Duane was the first mayor of liberated New York, when Livingston was just beginning to acquire property in that city; and it was a source of pleasure, while suggesting the many ways in which the Corporation might really do better if it tried, to know that one was also irritating the mayor. "I do not mean Sir to censure your conduct or that of the other Gent. of the corporation . . ." Such was the opening of one letter, with its almost inevitable sequel: ". . . yet these facts are so evident & depend upon such obvious principles that I am astonished that they should thus long have escaped your attention." A man not usually backward in prophecy, the Chancellor now contented himself with the very modest assumption that "the Island of New York contains a sufficient quantity of ground for a much larger city than New York will ever be." This being the case, would it not be as well to keep the water front along the North River free from any further building?

Put a stop to your improvements (as they are falsely called) upon the north river—No rem. offers for the houses that are already on its warves. Improve them as much as possible but discourage the erection of others[.] Lay out no new streets & let Greenwich street terminate at trinity church[.] The lots to the southard of these are in the hands of opulent persons[.] Prevail on them to shut up the street, to extend their gardens to the river . . . & instead of the noxious odor of warves & dram shops they will in the midst of a town enjoy the pure air of the country—Few among them are so tasteless or so interested as to permit the sight of wretched houses smokey chimneys & dirty streets to shut off their prospect of one of [the] finest rivers in the world & the beautiful shores that limmit its extent—Be cautious how you exercise the power with which the Legislature have perhaps imprudently invested you by *compelling* every citizen to cast his bread upon the waters. . . .[6]

"Perhaps imprudently" was a master stroke; nor could Mayor Duane have been rendered much happier when the Chancellor renewed his assault with an "Essay" on the fruity subject of the Corporation's courage.

The fire which consumed a part of the town [he wrote] left open a door for improvement[.] The Corporation had the example of the City of London upon a similar occasion. They show an ardor to follow, they apply to the Legislature, their wishes are complyed with, three streets heretofore the abode of dirt & disease are to be widened & thrown into one, a measure which would have contributed to the health & imbellishment of the town—half a dozen old women scold, they exclaim against the profanity of permitting the dark recesses of Stone Street to be exposed to the public view or suffering the garish sun to look upon the hallowed mysteries of Petticoat Lane—The scheme is relinquished with the same speed that it was embraced—It gives place to another[—]the most beautiful street in this town wanted to be cut down & regulated[—]an order was given for the purpose[—It] was revoked & re-adopted[—]at length some citizen objected and it was determined to leave broadway as it was with one side of the street several yards higher than the other & a pavement equally calculated to discourage riding or walking.[7].

It is almost needless to add that the Chancellor at this time possessed not only a house on Bowling Green but also other properties, such as a water lot on Greenwich Street; that the Corporation had rather followed than deviated from the example of London after the Great Fire; and that the city which would have emerged from the concepts in the letter and the "Essay" would have displayed upon its North River side, not a great harbor, but the lawns and mansions of an elite. Possibly this would have been an improvement upon the course of Nature, which seemed to announce that a great harbor must come into being; it was certainly an attempted reversal of the course of history, already evident. But it is a human, a universal failing not to recognize the course of history when it reveals itself: and for this the Chancellor may (like the rest of us) be forgiven. Whether or not Mayor Duane forgave him is another matter.

One cannot, of course, from mere fragments of evidence, construct with any confidence the skeleton of a family quarrel. It seems that a kind of peace was maintained until 1787, and that in 1788 this was becoming very shaky. In the elections of 1788, when the Livingstons needed every ounce of concerted energy to carry Columbia County, the third Lord was describing the Chancellor, from whom he prayed deliverance, as "this covetous troublesome man";[8] the manor and Clermont families were clearly finding it more and more difficult to work together; and the Columbia County Federalists as a whole, perhaps in response to this situation, were at odds for all sorts of obscure if not frivolous reasons. Thus Mr. Jacob Goes, though still calling himself a "foederalist," was offended with the Van Rensselaers for not inviting him to an interesting March meeting at Claverack; the citizens of little Hudson, while friendly to the Chancellor, could not abide the manor Livingstons; John Livingston, who had been placed on the Assembly list along with Thomas Jenkins, of Hudson, and William H. Ludlow, said that he would oppose the election of Mr. Jenkins and of every person unfriendly to his (the manor) family; while Henry Livingston, in spite of the most tactful hints by Philip Schuyler, would not yield his place on the convention list to the more popular Edward Livingston, the Chancellor's youngest brother. As for the meeting at Claverack, from which Mr. Goes had been so unwisely omitted, it seemed, said the Chancellor's bailiff, to be "as much a meeting of the Associates in the Indian purchase as anything else." John Livingston was using it to drum up political support for his projected Genessee Company, which the Governor was determined to bring to nothing.[9]

Thus the election of 1788 was, from a Federalist point of view, sadly ill managed in Columbia County: and surely, from any point of view, no election called for a more serious struggle. In spite of the best efforts of official New York in the Continental Congress, and of the Clintonian majority in the Legislature, a convention was to be summoned for the purpose of ratifying or rejecting the Philadelphia Constitution; and according to a reluctant resolution of February 1, 1788, elections for delegates to this convention were to be held on the third Tuesday in April and for a maximum of five days until the voting should be completed. It was small wonder that there should have been, in the manor, "a number of emissaries daily going about to poison the Tenants"; for the resolution had one provision that, to this day, contains an element of mystery. Delegates to the ratifying Convention were to be chosen by the ballots of all free male citizens of the age of twenty-one or upward: in other words, the unpropertied artisan and the poorest tenant at will could now, for the first time and for this occasion only, cast his vote.[10]

Who could have been responsible for such a provision? Since no record exists of any objection to it in Senate or Assembly, or, indeed, of any call for votes, could it have been passed unanimously? The Federalist city merchants may have been sure of the artisans; but it seems difficult to believe that the great Federalist landlords could have been so infatuated as to depend upon the support of their poorer tenants. A more probable conclusion is that the Clintonians, who controlled the Legislature, presented these tenants with the ballot in the certainty that they would vote for Anti-Federalist delegates: but this hardly explains such a general silence on such a controversial measure. Since the vote was a light one, it is possible that both sides depended upon the traditional inertia among the voters. Whatever the reason, the result was a great victory for the Anti-Federalist cause: Albany, Columbia, Dutchess, Montgomery, Orange, Queens, Suffolk, Ulster, Washington, and Clinton—all these counties sent Anti-Federalist delegations. Only Kings, New York, Richmond, and Westchester were prepared to support the Constitution. If figures meant anything in advance, ratification would be defeated by 46 votes to 19.[11]

Livingston, who may have agreed with Philip Schuyler that little good could be expected from his own and the manor's tenants, in Columbia County, had taken the precaution to get himself elected as a delegate from New York County; and thus it was from a mercantile stronghold that the leader of the Hudson River landowners came to the Convention in Poughkeepsie.[12]

III

It would be only just to Livingston to say that his Federalism, at this stage, remained distinctly pastoral. It was concerned, that is to say, with the establishment of a free trade with Great Britain, the essence of which was to be an exchange of raw materials for manufactured goods; with the social dignity of the United States; and with the status of the landowning class within the State of New York. It was not concerned with public securities, where the Chancellor's holdings were minimal; nor did it arise from any belief that the economy was foundering and could be rescued only by a stronger central government. Livingston, it is true, had revealed a certain mixture of motives when he had objected to the state's emission of £200,000 in 1786. For while, on the one hand, he was opposed to state emissions on principle, as being financially unsound, on the other hand, this particular emission was to be devoted in part to a thoroughly sound expedient of the extinction of a certain amount of the national debt. And Livingston, like every other Federalist, believed that the assumption of the national debt by the national government was a cardinal feature in a strong United States; and that for the state to take over any part of it was a declaration of independence from national government. As for the primacy of the landowning class within the state—and his insistence on this made him a pastoral rather than an agrarian thinker—Livingston certainly feared at this time that the state, if left to its own devices, might contrive to tax this class out of power if not out of existence.

In a letter to Governor Clinton, written in 1787, he complained that he was being taxed just as if he had no tenants at all. For it was one of the disagreeable features of leases among the former manors and the great patents of New York that tenants were required to pay taxes: or, as he put it in his letter, "the whole of this estate [Clermont] is possessed by persons who pay taxes by express stipulation for the Lands they hold, excepting so much thereof as is appropriated for commons, & about two hundred acres of Land which I retain in my possession." Yet the county assessors had rated him in September, 1786, at the "enormous" sum of £475 instead of the £187/10/0 to which he was liable according to the rate charged in the old tax lists. And even this £187/10/0 was an "exemplary" tax for one year on an estate "that has never yet averaged me £300 a year." He submitted to this imposition, believing that it would be rectified in future assessments: when, lo and behold, he found himself charged with £53 in specie as part of his proportion for building a new courthouse. The proportion of the whole of Livingston Manor was £600, "and I have," he wrote, "a *reversionary interest* in no more than one 12th of it. So that I am charged at *more* than my proportion would be if I actually occupied, not only all the Land with the improvements thereon, but all the personal property of about 80 able farmers that possess it, whose improvements alone are equal in value to the right of soil. . . . [The majority of the assessors are chosen] from the north side of the Roeloff Jansens River or what is erroneously called the upper manor. The farmers on my land pay 1/3 more if I am rightly informed than others in much better circumstances on the other side of the River." It was only with great difficulty, he said, that he had rooted out the purpose of the £475 tax: it was designed to discharge the arrears on three taxes imposed for sinking the Continental bills of credit by a law passed in June, 1780. The assessors did not know this: and how should they—"not indeed being able to write or read."[13]

This letter is remarkable, not only because it throws an odd light upon the landlord's idea of the nature of leasehold, but also because it shows that there was little faith, among propertied persons, in the state's ability to control its own agents. The tax was high, but the tax assessors—as regards the odor in which Livingston held them—were higher still: they were illiterate, they were prejudiced; they had even imported into the business of assessing taxes some of the quarrel between the manor and Clermont. It was a fear not only of taxes, but also of an unjust or ignorant interpretation of the state tax laws, which helped to drive the big landlords into Federalism.

In the manor itself, Colonel Robert Livingston, Jr., supported the Federalist cause because a trade "in our staple commodities in our own vessels" to the British West Indies was, he believed, essential. Otherwise—this was in 1784—"our wheat and our flower must lay on our hands and sell for 4/- a bush. and 12/- a cwt. & under. . . . Much, nay even our well-being, depends upon it, altho' some people talk light of this matter, its of great consequence to the Landed Estates in this, and all other countryes." A year later, he felt that everything depended upon Congress's being empowered by the states to regulate trade: the alternative seemed to be the extinction of "all our ship carpenters, salemakers, salors, fraights of shiping &c. &c. &c." Indeed, all trade with Great Britain should be stopped until "they give us leave to trade to their West Ind$ Islands on the same footing we did formerly, to enable us to make remittances & supply ourselves with Salt Rum Sugar Molasses &c. in our own bottoms, & not lay at the mercy of Forroners for these articles & save the fraight & saylors wages spent among us." He did not, to be sure, altogether disapprove of state tariffs. When Massachusetts laid a duty of £5 a ton on foreign iron, he felt obliged to applaud as the owner of the Ancram ironworks; he rather hoped that New York would also lay a duty on "bar iron and holloware"; and he was sure that "Beef, Pork, butter, Candles, Sope from Ireland ought to have a high duty laid on it, it's a Shame this country should import any of these staple commodities. Our country must be encouraged our Lands must be settled & we must have all manner of remittances for things we have & can make in the county. . . . All I mean is to Encourage our young Impire & save all the money we can from being sent abroad from which it never returns again." By "country," the third Lord meant New York and by "Impire" the United States: he was by no means a fanatical nationalist. And, unlike the Chancellor, who was all for free trade, and the use of economic sanctions to the attainment of this end, he was distinctly a mercantilist in his thinking. None the less, at the heart of his Federalism lay the conviction that only a strong national government could make any impression upon the British Navigation Acts in the West Indies. There he asked for the simplest exchanges: and what he asked, of congressional powers to regulate trade in the West Indies, was only a little more than what the radical majority in the Legislature had been willing to grant in 1784. The majority of the merchants of New York City, on the other hand, never favored strong measures against the British, who offered better credit terms than those of any other nation; nor did they scruple to avoid the Navigation Acts, or submit to them, by trading in British ships. One cannot say that the Federalists who went to the Poughkeepsie Convention, or were represented there, thought exactly alike on any given issue, except one—they were all agreed that the propertied classes should be given the control of the affairs of the state and the affairs of the nation.[14]

The ratifying Convention assembled at the Court House in Poughkeepsie on June 17, 1788. By this time, eight states had ratified; two more, New Hampshire and Virginia, were now debating the question; and should either one of these ratify before the New York Convention made up its mind, the issue before that Convention would become one of ratification or quasi-secession. The more optimistic among the Anti-Federalists were sure that neither New Hampshire nor Virginia would approve the Constitution, and that New York, therefore, if she declined to ratify it, would not be in the odious position of refusing to join an American Union.

The Anti-Federalists were more remarkable for numbers than for gifts: among their debaters, only Melancton Smith and John Lansing, Jr., were outstanding. The remainder followed the example of George Clinton, a man of few words, and proposed to resist the arguments of their adversaries with silence and with votes. But they were not all optimistic, either about the attitude of New Hampshire and Virginia or about the consequences to themselves of a refusal to ratify. Within their ranks, so loquacious on petty issues, so mute on important ones, there were divisions which no amount of stolidity could altogether conceal.

The yeomanry who formed the backbone of Clinton's party were, indeed, afraid that if the state surrendered its impost to the general government, the deficit would be made up by heavy taxes upon yeoman farmers. Actually, the reverse was the case; as a result of the financial plan of 1786, and the subsequent funding and assumption of debts by the United States, New York was soon in the happy position of laying no direct taxes for a decade. But the farmers could hardly have foreseen this. None the less, as the single economic issue of any importance to them, a threat of taxation was by no means strong enough to hold their delegates together in the Poughkeepsie Convention.[15]

What really united these delegates was their honorable and traditional fear of strong central government, and their belief that their own political consequence would be diminished, would perhaps disappear, if the state were to yield some of its powers under a new federal Constitution. It is hard to discover, in their *economic* arguments before they came together at Poughkeepsie, anything more precise than young De Witt Clinton's litany: "From the insolence of great men, from the tyranny of the rich—from the unfeeling rapacity of the excise-man and the Tax-gatherer—from the misery of despotism—from the expense of supporting standing armies, navies, placemen, sinecures, federal cities, Senators, Presidents, and a long train of etceteras Good Lord deliver us." With returning prosperity, they believed they could manage on their own; and they perceived a connection between Federalism and aristocracy which Federalists like Chancellor Livingston, in his speech to the Cincinnati, had made a little too clear—or, at any rate, a little too resonant.[16]

But philosophical and political reasoning—could this hold the Clintonians together? For the economic argument that really counted seemed to call for an adherence to the Constitution, not a rejection of it. What would happen if New York, by refusing to ratify, found herself isolated among her neighbors? If they then discriminated against her commercially, would not the City of New York and all the southern counties secede from the state; and how then would what remained of the state raise its taxes, or dispose of its surpluses, or, indeed, survive at all? As for the restoration of a free trade with the West Indies, or a reopening of the port of Havana to American wheat, or any similar feat which could be accomplished only by a strong Congress—would not the farmer profit from these events along with everyone else? If we accept the assumption that the small independent farmer was the most energetic element in the Anti-Federalist party, it seems clear that he drew his energy from sources other than economic ones; that his vote for Anti-Federalist delegates to the Convention was largely an expression of distaste for the Federalist landlords who surrounded him; and that this distaste, while strong, was not strong enough to hold the ground at Poughkeepsie, where so many of the Anti-Federalist delegates were themselves landlords in a modest way, and one or two in a large one.

At any rate, the Clintonians in the Convention were evidently divided into at least two wings—those who believed in nonratification at all costs, and those who were prepared to ratify with severe conditional amendments. Upon the latter wing, influence could be brought to bear: and so it came about that what was said upon the floor of the Convention was of far less consequence than what was proposed or threatened behind the scenes. If the Federalist minority was small, it was united and somewhat shameless: for it did not always bother to vanish discreetly behind the scenes before exercising its cajoleries. "All the arts of a Hamilton &c will have no effect," Charles Tillinghast wrote to John Lamb on June 21, "although he, the Chancellor & Mr. Jay are continually singling out the Members in opposition (when out of convention) and conversing with them on the subject. . . ."[17]

Hamilton himself admitted that the Federalists' arguments "confound but do not convince" the opposition: that is to say, their arguments from the floor. To the most eloquent burst of oratory or the closest reasoning, the most elegant tropes or the nicest syllogisms, the Anti-Federalists opposed their silence. What effect their private conversations had was another matter. But because of the unreality of the debate itself, it does not, in whatever versions or fragments of a version it has survived, strike the reader today as being as urgent as it should have been.

Among the delegates from New York County—if one looks no farther —the Federalists had some of the first men in the state. There was Alexander Hamilton, small, handsome, and fiery, whose fate as a speaker it was to compel every emotion but assent. There was John Jay, thin, pale, and as wierdly impressive as a walking statue, over whose irritable nature, unquenchable vanity, and iron contempt there lay a quite persuasive veneer of gentle and conciliatory manners. And there was Chancellor Livingston, tall and elegant, with his musical voice, his flow of vivid imagery, and the oddly puzzled and puzzling expression upon his face, which Gilbert Stuart and John Vanderlyn caught in their portraits, and which seems to be composed in equal parts of kindness and derision. Such men were impressive; but would they not express, by their very bearing, precisely what the Anti-Federalists most suspected in Federalism—its tendency to identify itself with "the Well Born Few" as against "the common people"?[18]

And, indeed, the speeches on the Federalist side threatened to subside into an ill-advised defense of the habits and prerogatives of rich men: one assumes that the speakers, confronted with something stolid and bucolic in the ranks of their opponents, had begun to lose their tempers. Even in the beginning, when they spoke by the book, rarely advanced arguments which had not been set forth in the letters of "Publius," and endeavored in every case—as Charles Tillinghast said of Hamilton—to give the appearance of "an *amazing Republican*" ("*but he is known*," added Tillinghast darkly), they could not altogether conceal this prejudice.[19]

The Chancellor, perhaps, to whom the opening speech was committed, was able to found his case upon such considerations as might occur to "simple citizens assembled to consult on measures that are to promote the happiness of our fellow citizens." He addressed himself chiefly to the chilling thought of what would happen to New York, so rich, so prosperous, and so vulnerable, if she were left to defend herself. As for the present Confederation, he said, had it repelled invaders, maintained domestic peace, supported their credit, or extended their commerce? Obviously, it had not. But he made the mistake of appealing to the example of the "illustrious Henry IV of France," who had dreamed (to be sure, in vain) of a universal peace on the basis of "a general union of the nations." Lansing's retort to this, on the next day, was that Henry IV intended to set himself at the head of it. And Livingston got himself a little deeper into trouble by incautiously holding up to the opposition what was, when all was said and done, a mirror in which they could observe, too clearly reflected, an image of themselves at their weakest. "Many of us, Sir," he said, addressing himself to George Clinton in the chair, "are officers of government, many of us have seats in the Senate and Assembly—let us on this solemn occasion forget the pride of office. . . . As magistrates we may be unwilling to sacrifice any portion of the power of the State—as citizens we have no interest in advancing the powers of the State at the expense of the Union."

He had been given the responsibility of opening the debate for the Federalists because he was considered the first orator in the state and because of his standing as Chancellor and as a Livingston. It was probably well-enough known by then that Hamilton was a more impressive theorist; but Hamilton was, in many respects, still an upstart and a stranger. Livingston's proposal that the entire Constitution be considered clause by clause before any general vote be taken was passed without difficulty, and was agreeable to both sides: ostensibly because the Federalists trembled at the thought that the Constitution could be rejected by a single vote, and because the Anti-Federalists wished to delay such a vote until they knew how matters had gone in New Hampshire and Virginia. But it is clear that Livingston had rather irritated than moved his opponents; for no man, when his back was to the wall—and that was the apparent posture of all Federalists in the Poughkeepsie Convention—was less calculated to be modest or conciliatory.[20]

The Convention, at any rate, had now the soothing prospect of several weeks' delay before it need bring matters to a general vote. For first the Chancellor's argument had to be answered: his insinuation, that is to say, that the opponents of ratification were men who wished to preserve their political consequence, and were willing to sacrifice the Union to it. Once that was done, was there anything in the debate that must justly be described as original? The argument that Hamilton, who was certainly the Federalist field general during the next six weeks, offered no more than what had already appeared in the letters of "Publius" is, of course, true: on the Federalist side, "Publius" had said all that there was to say. What is more significant is that the debate began with, and rarely departed from, some underlying sentiment that what was at issue was the question of rich against poor, aristocrat against "common men."[21]

It was in vain that Hamilton protested on June 21 that "for my part, I hardly know the meaning of the word ["aristocracy"] as it is applied. The arguments of the gentlemen only go to prove that there are men who are rich, men who are poor, men who are wise, and others who are not. . . ." Yet he felt himself obliged to admit that "as riches increase and accumulate in a few hands; —as luxury prevails in society; virtue will be in a greater degree considered only as a graceful appendage of wealth. And the tendency of things will be to depart from the republican standard. This is the real disposition of human nature: it is what neither the honorable member nor myself can correct. . . ."[22] This observation did not satisfy Melancton

Smith, to whom it was addressed and who thought it irrelevant; and Mr. Smith ventured to change his ground and remark that, while he did not consider aristocrats to be destitute of morality or of virtue, he must insist that they could not have a sympathetic feeling toward the wants of the people.[23]

When the debate was resumed on June 23, the Chancellor accused Smith of describing the rich as vicious and intemperate people. "Is there less intemperance in feeding on beef than on turtle; or in drinking rum than wine?" Nor were the rich more unfeeling than the poor. "I believe they are less so. . . . For it seems to me probable that those who are most occupied by their cares and distresses have the least sympathy with the distresses of others." As for the argument that the rich will always "enjoy the suffrages of the people," he did not believe this to be the case. On the contrary, "the rich are always the objects of envy."[24]

If one stresses these arguments, rather than the clash between nationalists and particularists, it is because they lay at the very heart of the debate, and gave it—or give it to the modern reader—its peculiar air of being at once irritable and otiose. It was in vain that the Chancellor declared: "We are all equally aristocrats. Offices, emoluments, honors are open to us all." He knew that the term "aristocrat" in New York carried with it no idea of merit or of excellence: an aristocrat, rather, meant a man whose wealth purchased for him certain political privileges, including the privilege of education. This arose directly from the colonial history of New York, and was therefore within the experience of many of the delegates at Poughkeepsie. Whereas Alexander Hamilton, when he said "I hardly know the meaning of the word as it is applied" meant precisely that he had not shared this experience.

And from this it becomes evident—as the modern reader *feels* from the beginning—that the debate itself was predetermined. No matter that the Clintonians were divided between those who declared they would never ratify and those who believed they might ratify conditionally, or that the Federalists put all their efforts into separating one of these wings from the other, or that there were dramatic or despairing moments when the Federalist cause tried to think of itself as lost—the fact remained that New York was obliged to ratify the Constitution and to ratify it unconditionally. This was apparent from the moment that Governor Clinton, however unwillingly, agreed to call a ratifying convention; or, to bring it a little nearer in time, from the moment when a motion to consider the Constitution clause by clause was passed in Convention without difficulty. The Anti-Federalists did not pass this motion merely out of a formal regard for the decencies of debate. As Clinton himself put it, "I am open to conviction."[25] He might describe his party as "the friends of the Rights of Man," and his opponents as "the Advocates of Despotism," or growl that the Federalists might yet push them all into "convulsions and a civil war"; but still he was open to conviction. So were all the Clintonians.[26] They might think the new Constitution radically defective, they might be well content with the government of New York as it was: but the isolation of New York would have been unbearable.

And so the debate really turned, not around ratification of the Constitution, but around the nature of opportunity in the world that would emerge after the Constitution had been ratified. Both sides were agreed upon the fundamental proposition, the truly revolutionary proposition, that government arose from the people. The question then remained: What access would the people have to the government they had created? Whenever the Anti-Federalists spoke of representation, or the exclusive character of the Senate, or of rotation in office, or even of the absence of a bill of rights, it was this that they had in mind. Or, to put it in another and perhaps more accurate way, what they feared was a resurgence in state and national form of that privileged government which New York had experienced as a colony. The Federalists, on the other hand, were sure that the people should be satisfied with creating government: the administration of it should be left to those who were equipped for the task. Nobody was so crass as to declare openly that poor men would make poor administrators: but in the taunts that were flung at the Anti-Federalists, this was always implied. Of the three leaders of the Federalist cause—Hamilton, Jay, and Chancellor Livingston—Jay was always polite, and Hamilton often outrageous; but it was the Chancellor who succeeded in arousing the keenest hostility.

There he stood, from his head to his toes radiant with privilege, the visible embodiment of aristocracy: and there, on July 1, he uttered what— to every man present—was a sarcastic equation of Anti-Federalism with stupidity. He addressed himself to the argument that the powers of Congress, as granted in the new Constitution, would be both dangerous *and* impracticable; and specifically to the imagery of "a gentleman from Washington" (John Williams) who had contrived to say that taxation would shut out the light of Heaven in order to pick the taxpayer's pocket. "With these melancholy ideas, no wonder he mourns for the fair damsel of American liberty, harassed with oppressive laws, shut up in a dismal dungeon, robbed of the light of Heaven, and, by a beautiful anticlimax, robbed of the money in her pocket. Yet, says the gentleman, tho' Congress will do all this, they cannot do it. .... This is fine reasoning. To what shall I compare it? Shall I liken it to children in the market place, or shall I liken it to children making bubbles with a pipe? ... But let us see if we cannot, from all this rubbish, pick out something which may look like reasoning."

This was certainly no way to conciliate or to persuade. But then it was not with conciliation or with persuasion that the Chancellor was concerned. His object was to expose, by pillorying their representatives, the political incapacity of the New York agrarians. Men who cannot reason cannot govern. It was in the same mood, a mingling of sarcasm and irreverence, that he lashed out at Gilbert Livingston, a delegate from Dutchess. It was Gilbert Livingston's contention that under the new Constitution, the general government and the state governments would be a consolidation—or, as Chancellor Livingston preferred to put it, would form one government. "Let us see how this matter stands. The State of Pennsylvania and New-York form two distinct governments; But New-York, Pennsylvania and the general government together form one government; The United States and New-York make another government; The United States and Connecticut another, and so on. To the gentleman's optics, these things may be clear; but to me they are utter darkness. We have thirteen distinct governments, and yet they are not thirteen governments, but one government. It requires the ingenuity of St. Athanasius to understand this political mystery. Were the gentleman a minister of the gospel, I might have faith; but I confess, my reason is much too weak for it."[27]

Gilbert Livingston was a grandson of the manor and the family's sole representative on the Anti-Federalist side. He was not unmindful of the quarrel between Clermont and the manor: and he imported into his reply, which was delivered on July 2, an unusual degree of vehemence. He accused his kinsman of mocking the cap of liberty in his speech, that very cap of liberty which in 1775 had been the target of "the Tory wit of Verdill, or some of his associates about King's college, (as was supposed.) The member who now exactly follows their track (if they were the authors of it) at that time found it not to his purpose, openly to avow the sentiment." To accuse the Chancellor of having been a crypto-Loyalist was bad, indeed inexcusable: yet the height of Gilbert Livingston's invective was not reached until he condemned his relative for making a "fashionable" attempt to ridicule not only the sacred Gospel itself, but also the faith necessary for a sinner if he is to partake of the benefits contained in it. Certainly the Chancellor had wandered rather far from the recognized paths of good taste when he decided to sport with the Athanasian creed: but the real sting lay in the word "fashionable." He was now made to appear as a heartless malignant dandy, who would not even resent such an image of himself. "I cannot suppose . . . that it is disagreeable to the gentleman . . . as he appears to delight to dabble in dirty water."[28]

As for Mr. Williams, he said that he would not condescend to fight the Chancellor with his own weapons. Would that not be "as ridiculous as it was for Don Quixote to fight a windmill upon the mad supposition that it was a giant."[29] And Melancton Smith supposed that it was for the purpose of diverting the Convention that the Chancellor "was induced to make so handsome a display of his comic talents, to the no small entertainment of the ladies and gentlemen without the bar."[30] Then he, too, according to De Witt Clinton (who thought it all very apropos) went just a little too far. On the old and tried political metaphor of the purse and the sword, he remarked that "the Honorable Gentleman [Livingston] very well knew that some people who had no great inclination to handle the sword, were notwithstanding very fond of thrusting their hand into the purse." This was almost as nasty an accusation as Gilbert Livingston's: but the Chancellor, De Witt Clinton admitted, "answered and acquitted himself with great address."[31] Why, he exclaimed, should he not expose false reasoning? He appealed to the committee to decide whether or not gentlemen had declared that the powers of Congress would be dangerous and yet impracticable. As for the sword and the purse, he could not reconcile to his reason the argument (it was Melancton Smith's) that Congress should keep the sword and the states use it, or that Congress should use the purse and the state keep it. If such an argument, on such a subject, struck him as ridiculous, he could not conceal his emotions; he had to attack it boldly, "without any apprehensions from those elegant attacks which have been aimed at me from every quarter."[32]

This July 1 to July 2 debate contains, in its singular bitterness no less than in its apparent irrelevance, the very essence of the division between the two parties in the Convention. In the Chancellor's case, it seems to represent the survival of some old habit rather than the beginning of a new one—the culmination of a long distrust of popular legislators, because they were uneducated, because they were not elegant, because they were of the people. But he, at least, had contented himself with sarcasm; his opponents had carried the argument *ad hominem* farther than it could decently be made to go in any responsible debate. It is for this reason that one feels, beneath the constitutional arguments, so close, so formal, and so familiar, the presence of some older quarrel between the representatives of New York aristocracy and the representatives of those who had suffered under its rule, and who did not wish this rule to be perpetuated under the new, national Constitution, by now inevitable.

IV

The climax of the political drama took place between July 19 and July 25. Up till then, everything had been tried. Even the news that New Hampshire had ratified, followed in due time by the far more exciting word that Virginia was in, failed to make any *apparent* impression upon the Anti-Federalists.[33] The Federalists even went to the length of persuading Hamilton to write a letter to James Madison, asking if a ratification carrying with it the right of New York to withdraw from the Union if its amendments were not enacted within a given period would be acceptable. Madison replied, of course, that it would be no ratification at all. "The Constitution," he said, "requires an adoption *in toto* and *for ever.*"[34] At length, on July 19, Lansing moved to ratify the Constitution with two qualifications: one, "an express condition" that a long bill of rights should be accepted; the other, an expression of "confidence" that a formidable list of amendments should be submitted to some future convention.[35] If this motion had been carried, New York would have rejected the Constitution. But, oddly enough, the Anti-Federalists, with the game at last in their hands, took no such step. On July 21, they confined their debate to Lansing's amendments, not to his motion. On July 23, Melancton Smith moved for a ratification, "in confidence" that the bill of rights and the list of amendments would receive an early consideration: which brought him nearly, if not quite, over to the Federalist side. He was still convinced, he said, that the Constitution was laden with defects of the most perilous kind; but the alternative to ratification was even more perilous—"convulsions in the Southern part [of the state], factions and discord in the rest." The vote was 40 to 19 in favor of his motion; and Clinton, Lansing, and Robert Yates were among the majority.[36] A more explicit motion by Samuel Jones, of Queens, was passed by 31 to 29. On this occasion, Gilbert Livingston and Zephaniah Platt of Dutchess explained that they would feel obliged to vote against their convictions, while Clinton, Yates, and Lansing returned to their fold and did not again desert it.[37] On July 24, Lansing again moved for a conditional adoption; on July 25, his motion was turned down by a vote of 31 to 28.[38] The committee then resolved itself back into a convention, and the Constitution was welcomed as it was, "in full confidence," so ran the ratifying report, that the bill of rights and the amendments would be accepted at some later date. This report was adopted by a vote of 30 to 25, and on July 26 the Constitution was ratified by a vote of 30 to 27.[39]

Among all these votes and oscillations, only one thing is clear: the Anti-Federalists, when it came to the point, were unwilling to reject the Constitution. What kept them from this fatal step was not any argument they heard from the floor: it was the constant reiteration, off the floor, of the theme that New York City and all the southern counties would secede from the state if it condemned itself to isolation. This threat was known from the beginning; it had been uttered before the Convention met; and it was the burden of Melancton Smith's speech of July 23. After that there was nothing more to be done but for the Anti-Federalists to meet in caucus on July 24, and there decide who should change their votes on the following day.[40]

No one would suggest that the Convention, from the Anti-Federalist point of view, was a solemn farce, staged only for the purpose of losing everything but honor. But it seems obvious to the inquirer of today that the Anti-Federalists substituted obstinacy and stolidity for resolution and purpose. It also seems clear that the forcefulness of the Federalists—particularly Hamilton, Jay, and Livingston—not only kept their opponents irresolute, but also offered them sound reasons for being so: to such an extent, indeed, that we should call the Federalists the victors, and not merely the survivors, in a predetermined debate. As so often in the colonial past, the radicals of New York carried their urgencies up to, but never beyond, the point where they might have been expected to win: and thus, in the Convention of 1788, a conservative minority was at length permitted to transform itself into a majority of 30 to 27.

V

It was a startling transformation. But it was only the superficial symptom of some deeper change, invisible then, but quite apparent now to the historian, or narrator, of these events. From now on, as he looks back upon the Convention and ponders its meaning, he may find that the words "radical" and "conservative" have changed their roles. Surely the "radicals"—the Anti-Federalists or Clintonians—had been, ostensibly at least, eager to conserve everything for which the Revolution had been set in motion. What had the Revolution demanded? Local government, arising from the people. This demand found its apotheosis in the Articles of Confederation of 1781, whose second article proclaimed that "each state retains its sovereignty, freedom and independence." What had the Constitution brought? Surely the consummation of a plan that George Grenville had introduced in 1765; the difference, the very happy difference, being that the plan was to be administered by Americans and not by Englishmen.[41] The new government, whether it resided in New York or in some savage spot near "George Town on the Potowmack," was spiritually as remote and as menacing as Parliament had been. It was a national government, acting directly upon individual Americans, and abridging, in every conceivable manner, the old powers of the states. Nothing so radical had ever been contemplated by Americans in all their colonial history.

It is one of the traits—one might almost say the functions—of revolution to change itself as the price of survival. It begins by overthrowing one power and ends by setting up another. In one sense, the American Revolution was not complete until the government set up by the Constitution of 1787 established its credit abroad through Hamilton's assumption plan in 1791. In its way, Hamilton's assumption must be considered the most radical of events. But at this point, Chancellor Livingston declined to go along with Hamilton, and, by joining his own and the Livingston fortunes to those of Jefferson and Clinton, returned to that conservatism which he had fought with such sarcasm, effrontery, and success in the Convention of 1788.

PART FOUR

ANTI-FEDERALISM

CHAPTER ONE

When John Jay returned from Europe in July, 1784, he received a letter of warm welcome from Robert R. Livingston. Only the sickness of his elder daughter, which called him back to Clermont, had prevented the Chancellor from greeting his old friend as he stepped off the boat in New York. In his letter, Livingston ventured to suggest to his "dear John" that "if you are not cured of your ambition, you have everything to hope for both in the State and Continental line." Jay replied in the familiar style of "Dear Robt."; he said that he would come to Clermont as soon as possible; but somehow he found himself unwilling to renew the intimacies of former days. "How far either of us have been, or may be, under the influence of ambition," he answered, "are questions which, however clear to ourselves, must necessarily be less so to others." He lingered for weeks in New York, where he was presented with the freedom of the city and an address from Mayor Duane, suitably enclosed in a gold box; he was elected a delegate to the Continental Congress; he went to Trenton; he called at Philadelphia; but he does not seem to have found time to pay that visit to Clermont.[1]

The old friendship between him and Livingston had been founded upon the roles they had elected to play while they were students at King's College and, afterward, when they first entered upon the world. Livingston was cast as the pleasure-loving fashionable young man, with a strain of sensitivity and refinement which shrank from the coarse exchanges of political life; while Jay chose to muffle his astringent vanity, his private conviction of intellectual and moral superiority, in the humble cloak of one fit only "for a village or a college." Somehow or other, subjected though they were to the grinding business of the Revolution, these disguises had not been worn completely threadbare: when Jay left for Spain in 1779, Livingston railed at state politics as contemptible and execrable "for detaining me here [in Kingston] when I so ardently wish to receive your last adieu"; and Jay replied from Martinique and from Madrid in the cordial but melancholy tone of a receding mentor.[2] It is not to be supposed that in these somewhat high-flown expressions of friendship they were insincere. They had a genuine respect for each other's attitudes, a genuine enjoyment of each other's company: but respect and enjoyment alike depended upon a relative stability in their positions—Livingston representing social accomplishment, Jay moral worth.

When Jay came back from Europe, he was quite a different man in his own estimation and a far larger one in the eyes of his compatriots. He had gone out into the formal but savage colosseum of eighteenth-century diplomacy, and he had bested the ministers or agents of three great kingdoms. Now, surely, he was a man of the world. A Vergennes or an Oswald might observe that his personality was uncomfortable and his manners not all that they might be: but Jay, who strove to conceal his asperities behind a plausible façade of moderation and modesty, and to impart to his usual coldness at least a reasonable degree of warmth, would no longer have agreed with them. As a puritan, no doubt he suspected worldly ambition in himself no less than in others, but he was now assured enough to stifle these misgivings and to enter upon the new American stage with the confident step of an experienced, important, and successful man.

Livingston, remaining in America, had performed his duties creditably; but the Department of Foreign Affairs was not designed, in wartime at any rate, to produce a successful secretary. No laurels glistened on his brow. Moreover, he had felt himself obliged, while secretary, to read Jay a stern lecture on the morality of keeping one's word; and Jay had replied with what amounted to a good-humored defense of expediency and opportunism. For a moment, their roles had been reversed, and it is possible that their friendship never entirely recovered from this reversal. And then there was the inscrutable process of change itself. No two men who had lived through the Revolution in a public capacity, one at home, one abroad, and who had been separated for nearly three years could expect to find themselves as they had been before the separation. It would have taken a high degree of mutual forbearance for these two in their maturity to have resumed their youthful friendship: we are not authorized to suppose that they possessed this quality.

It was not that their friendship cooled at once: it was, rather, that it ceased to occupy a central position in their lives. In December, 1784, Livingston could still write with evident sincerity to Luzerne that "our friend Jay will to my great satisfaction"—an emotion that Luzerne could scarcely have shared—"accept the place I have quitted so that order and system will I hope again be restored to our foreign department."[3] Thereafter, the name of Jay vanishes from his surviving correspondence during the "critical period." This is negative evidence: it does not mean that they ceased to correspond, but only that they corresponded with far less regularity. They worked together on the Massachusetts boundary commission; they fought shoulder to shoulder through the *stürm und drang* of the ratifying Convention: but their relationship was becoming conventional. The two men were going their separate ways; while Gouverneur Morris, the third member of this oddly assorted trio, who for all his brilliance and ability had occupied the position of jester and go-between, had now far less time to spend upon the other two.

The Continental Congress moved to New York City in 1785, and with it came John Jay, who had raised the position of secretary for Foreign Affairs almost, if not quite, to that of secretary of State. And with him came Mrs. Jay—handsome, high-spirited, opinionated, ambitious—the daughter of that William Livingston who had left New York to become in time the Revolutionary governor of New Jersey and who was himself a son of the manor. The Jays soon became among the smartest people in the city: Mrs. Jay saw to that, and Jay was willing enough to follow her lead. Night after night, the doors of their house on lower Broadway were opened to admit all that was best or most agreeable in New York society—the members of the *corps diplomatique;* Alexander Hamilton; the enigmatic Aaron Burr; James Madison; General and Mrs. Henry Knox, looming beside each other like wedded mountains; the learned Dr. Witherspoon; the congenial Bishop Provoost. From Philadelphia came the Robert Morrises, or William Bingham and his ravishing wife—people who had decidedly extravagant ideas as to the kind of entertainment they expected. And the old New York families, whom nothing surprised or excited, Beekmans and Schuylers, Van Rensselaers and Van Hornes and Van Cortlandts, met and mingled in Mr. Jay's rooms with the foreigners, the politicians, and the professional men.[4]

The Chancellor and Mrs. Livingston were, of course, on Mrs. Jay's "visiting lists." They lived close by on the Bowling Green, from which the Chancellor hoped one day to expel the hogs which rooted and squealed there, and to remove the pedestal which had once carried an equestrian statue of George III.[5] Mrs. Livingston, equable as always but decidedly an invalid since the birth of her second daughter, never seems to have entertained the social ambitions of Mrs. Jay. The Chancellor was festive and hospitable; but he took his social position for granted, and may have been rather astonished at the seriousness with which Mr. Jay accepted his own transformation into a leader of what passed for the *beau monde.* It did not show itself in Jay's appearance—New York gentlemen at the time left brilliance in dress to their ladies—but in his assiduousness. The lean, marmoreal personage had now undergone an astonishing metamorphosis: he had been changed into "a most pleasing man," wrote one of his female guests, "plain in his dress and manners, but kind, affectionate and attentive; benevolence is portrayed in every feature."[6] As he gazed at his old friend across the little dividing seas of assemblies and balls and dinner tables, what could have been the Chancellor's emotions? Only one thing is certain: even before Jay's return, Livingston hoped to interest him as a friend, no less than as a lawyer, in the great family dispute over the gristmill[7]: but it was a vain hope. Jay had married a manor Livingston; and his sympathies, if any, were on the other side.

For the family dispute increased in intensity once the Livingstons had experienced a brief period of political unity at the ratifying Convention. The Chancellor was now returning to a position that he had held in 1787. Not only was the manor unreasonable in the matter of the gristmill: it had also failed to consult him on the important matter of the boundaries of Columbia County; and in other respects, it had shown an open hostility. "I have no political views," he told Henry Livingston, "with respect to myself but I can no longer submit to be considered as an inferior[.] My birth fortune & education place me upon the same ground with your brothers who still assume superiority."[8] In 1790, Chief Justice William Smith, of Quebec, a former Loyalist, could refer to the great dispute half humorously as "the waters of contention & Bitterness." He, too, had been asked for an opinion on the gristmill and had been obliged to declare the Chancellor in the wrong. The *medium filium aquae* was, he said, an unnatural boundary; and, in any case, the first Lord's will had confined the Chancellor's grandfather to the use of sawmills as opposed to gristmills, precisely because sawmills become useless once the lumber has been all cut, and therefore constitute no permanent support of a house and an estate.[9] This sort of verdict served to increase the determination of the old third Lord; but as the third Lord's determination increased, the Chancellor's claims no less steadily grew with it. He was now asking for control of the kill in its whole extent, a proportion of the profits of the manor mines and ironworks, and the right to all land (which would have included Walter Livingston's farm) on his side of the stream. He was willing to make an accommodation: he would have given up his claim to profits and lands, he told Peter Van Schaack (a friend to both houses) and would have made substantial concessions in the region of the lower and middle falls. But what was the use? Every concession only brought fresh demands from the manor. "The ties of friendship are now broken between us, (except as relates to the old Gent.)," he said, "[and] I am perfectly indifferent about their renewal."[10]

II

The growing coolness with Jay, and the increasing warmth of the family quarrel, have, each in its way, a place in the political transformation that the Chancellor experienced in the year 1791. The transformation was neither as sudden nor as opportunistic as has sometimes been claimed.* Nor, indeed, was it entirely altruistic—such transformations rarely are. It was due in part to a rational disappointment; the Chancellor had expected and deserved to receive some recognition from George Washington. But it was also due to certain deep-seated agrarian prejudices; prejudices not the less agrarian for being lodged in the mind of a landed aristocrat.

Once the Constitution was ratified, the Chancellor settled down—as did every leading Federalist—to view, with a certain complacence, the prospect before him. He wrote to George Washington in October, 1788, taking for granted that Washington would accept "the station to which you will shortly be called," and discerning in his "health and popularity the same providential attention to the happyness of this country which was displayed by heaven in the preservation of your life amidst the dangers of the late war." "I cannot but hope," he concluded, "that your civil administration will be equally blessed with your late military command."[11] In April, 1799, he wrote Marbois, in some glee, that "nothing is thought of or talked of but the new Congress for whose reception we are making every preparation—We have under the direction of L'Enfant laid out £20,000 in a State house whose elegance & beauty exceeds anything of the kind in America."[12] In the spring elections, the Clermont Livingstons fought Clinton with all their power, though their tenants—it was most unobliging of them—voted against their wishes. The Chancellor himself, his mother noted with some distress, had not on this occasion bothered to appear at Clermont; if he had done so, he might have turned the scales against Clinton.[13] But the Chancellor's mind was already, it may be, preoccupied with other matters.

On April 16, George Washington set out from Mount Vernon for New York, "with a mind oppressed with more anxious and painful sensa-

* As, for example, De Alva Stanwood Alexander, *A Political History of the State of New York*, 3 vols., New York, 1906, I, 48; Henry Adams, *History of the United States . . .*, I, 109; *DAB* (1946 ed.), Livingston, Robert R., XI, 323.

tions than I have words to express . . . [but] with the best disposition to render service to my country in obedience to its calls." He arrived in the city on April 23. "The claps—the Shouts, the Huzzas from the surrounding thousands—exceeded all description," wrote David Gelston. "He landed at the Coffee House—(a pair of stairs being made on purpose) was recd by the Govr—Conducted to his Quarters (the old Presidents House in Cherry Street) about 2 o'clock—& then returned without parade in the Govrs. coach & dined at the Governor's—a lucky circumstance—I declared to you I never felt such strong emotions on any public occasion." David Gelston was a stern Anti-Federalist: but party considerations, at this moment in Washington's career, gave way to a veneration such as few men have received. On May 2, the Chancellor was writing to Washington—the subject of his letter was presidential etiquette—that "as my heart tells me that if the highest esteem & the most perfect undeviating attachment afford a title to that honourable disinction I may, however unworthy, rank myself among the number of your Excellency's friends. . . ." On second thoughts, he did not send this letter: but the sentiment was typical—everyone courted Washington.[14]

Moreover, Livingston had crowned his labors at the Convention by playing a conspicuous role at the inauguration of April 30, 1789. As Chancellor of the state, it was his duty to deliver the oath of office: and a story exists that no Bible had been provided and that the Chancellor, who had been the state's Grand Master since 1784, was obliged to send for one from a nearby Masonic lodge. Of that famous ceremony, Livingston himself has left no word. It is known that he accompanied the President-elect as, preceded by Vice-President and senators, and followed by the representatives, he moved through the Senate Chamber in Federal Hall toward the window and the gallery which looked out over Wall Street. On the gallery, as Washington stood between two pillars, he was flanked by John Adams, the Vice-President, and by Chancellor Livingston, dressed for the occasion in "a full suit of black cloth." Between Washington and Livingston stood the diminutive Secretary of the Senate, James Otis, scarcely visible above the Bible which he upheld on a large crimson cushion. The Chancellor read the words of the oath, the Bible was raised, the President bowed to kiss it, murmured audibly, "I swear," and added, "So help me God!" "It is done," intoned the Chancellor, and turning toward the crowd, he waved his hand, and in his loudest voice exclaimed, "Long Live George Washington, President of the United States!" But an eyewitness states that, having proclaimed George Washington President, the Chancellor could do no more than wave his hat with the rest, being too choked with tears to join in the repeated acclamations.[15]

In the evening, the city was illuminated, among the most resplendent efforts being those of Don Diego Gardoqui, the Spanish Minister, and the Comte de Moustier, the French Minister; a lamp-lit painting on the De Moustiers' house, which contrived to represent not only the past and the present but also the future of American history, was particularly admired. And when the fireworks began, the President viewed them, first from the Chancellor's house and then from General Knox's. At the Inaugural Ball a week later, among the conspicuous guests were the former triumvirs of the Convention—Colonel Alexander Hamilton, John Jay, and Robert R. Livingston.[16]

III

It was the last time in recorded history that the three were to appear together as political allies. On May 15, Chancellor Livingston wrote a letter to George Washington which has vanished altogether: but which, as one can tell from the President's answer, still preserved among the Chancellor's papers, was an application for office in the new government. Washington felt obliged to say that he had uniformly declined giving any decisive answer to such requests, "being resolved whenever I am called upon to nominate persons for those offices which may be created, that I will do it with a sole view to the public good. . . . The delicacy with which your letter was written, and your wishes insinuated, did not require me to be thus explicit on this head with you; but the desire which I have that those persons whose good opinion I value shd. know the principles on which I mean to act in this business has led me to this full declaration."[17] Applications for office, or expressions of a willingness to serve, were rather the rule than the exception; and certainly the President's answer was not altogether a rebuff: but Chancellor Livingston must have been pretty sure of his ground before he wrote such a letter, and proportionately disturbed when he received such a reply. What the office was that he had in mind is not known: at the time, it was assumed that he aimed at the Treasury, but this he later denied; nowadays, one supposes that he would most have preferred to become chief justice.

In July, Janet Montgomery, the Chancellor's eldest sister, was in New York, preparing to sail for Ireland to visit her sister-in-law, Lady Ranelagh. "I have been often at the President," she wrote, "who each time is more pleased to see me. Mrs. Washington has asked me to visit with her this evening and is to introduce me to Mrs. Adams. . . ."[18] It was natural that the President should pay rather particular attention to the widow of General Montgomery, especially since the widow was quite a personage in her own right. But in a letter, undated but clearly written just before she sailed, Mrs. Montgomery revealed that her object in visiting the Washingtons had not been a mere exchange of civilities:

I have not been unmindful of your interest [she wrote] even to the last moment of my stay here and altho it has been some fatigue to me I have continued to see those people from whence I conceived I might get intelligence—Armstrong [John Armstrong, who had married the Chancellor's sister Alida] by this time has informed you that Morris has convinced the P—— of the independence of W—— and that in consequence he will have the appointment he wishes—but a long conversation with Lear [Tobias Lear, Washington's secretary]—which gave me an opportunity of carelessly throwing out this report convinced me no thing of this kind could take place—as he said Wil.— was not within six of that place—Mrs. K. I have seen only once her Child has been ill and is still very ill with her Husband I had a long and interesting conversation in which I was mostly the listener. He began with the friendship he had for you with the wish the P—— had to serve you and have you in place— that nothing could prevent this but the fear of making so many appointments from this State—this gave me the opportunity of supposing H——[Hamilton] in the Treasury—he answer'd immediately or the Chancellor—which he said was the present Idea—this confirmed me in the notion that he had advised this measure to the P—— rather than to take up H—— whome he fears— However it is he seems to have much friendship for you and of yours to him I assured him—he told me he did not doubt it as he had proofs of it from several confidential conversations he had with him on the whole it appeared to me that he had much of the confidence of the P—— at least as much as any man—tell John [John R. Livingston] that he has also mentioned him to the P in a very hansom Manner—he told him [the President] that if he took him into his family he would take a Gentleman who would do honour to his choice. . . . Thus my friend you have my last services may all your wishes be answerd and when they are so may you be completely happy. . . . I am constantly at General Washington and am each time very kindly received—I had one moment of conversation with him in which I mentioned to him having heard from you and that you had requested your compliments—he thanked me & suddenly asked if you were not soon to be in town—At this important moment I should think you should be here— . . . Jay and his wife very formal— I have been to see her—and met with him at the Presidents when I dined there —he was closetted more than 2 houres—[19]

From this letter, it appears that James Wilson, of Pennsylvania, had some hopes of becoming chief justice, and that "K," who can only be General Knox, was—or pretended to be—at the moment a decided enemy of Hamilton. Mrs. Montgomery evidently believed that her brother wished to be promoted to the Treasury, and, failing that, to become chief justice.

However this may be, the letter is certainly a curious one. At the end of May, Washington had administered a mild rebuff to the Chancellor, who preferred thereafter to remain at Clermont, and to leave the political pressure to his sister. The President by this time must have become accustomed to resisting political pressure, but when it was exerted by the white hand of a lady, it became a matter of some delicacy and also (one ventures to think) of some irritation. And all the while, Mr. and Mrs. Jay observed these sisterly maneuvers not with friendship and concern, but with constraint and formality.

But the Chancellor did not have long to wait in suspense. On September 11, Alexander Hamilton was named secretary of the Treasury; on September 26, John Jay became chief justice of the United States. On the last day of December, 1789, the Chancellor and Mrs. Livingston dined at the President's house with the Vice-President and Mrs. Adams, Baron von Steuben, and four members of the House of Representatives: it was Livingston's last appearance in the President's diary, and, presumably, at the President's dinner table.[20]

IV

If these events are recited in some detail, it is only to show that a good case could of course be made for the argument that the Chancellor had reason to seek for a political revenge upon the government of George Washington. After his loyal support of Washington in the dark years of the Revolutionary War, after his recent labors at Poughkeepsie, with his known abilities and his prominence in the State of New York, he had been left in the cold; and left in the cold after having placed himself in the mortifying position of asking for office, both in his own name and through his sister. Meanwhile, Alexander Hamilton and John Jay, his former allies, and one of them his former boon companion, if one may apply such a term to so austere a personality, were reveling at the feast from which he had been excluded.

The veil has never been lifted entirely from these proceedings, but conjecture has always named Alexander Hamilton as the man responsible for the omission, not only of the Chancellor, but of all the Chancellor's family, from any share of national or state patronage in this first year of George Washington's administration. With the President's friendship, with the backing of Philip Schuyler, his father-in-law, and of Schuyler's influence among the Federalist landlords, Hamilton may well have thought that he could be master of the State of New York without any assistance from the Livingstons. No one knew better than he the extent of the quarrel between the manor and Clermont; while it was common knowledge that the manor was also ill at ease with itself, and that Peter R. Livingston, the eldest son, who scarcely dared leave his house for fear of his creditors, was on bad terms with his other brothers. Thus the Livingstons' great political asset, family solidarity, was visibly disintegrating, and John Jay, who was connected by marriage with the manor, could assist in this process by his unfriendly detachment from Clermont. Some overtures may have been made from the manor toward Hamilton: Walter Livingston certainly hoped for advancement through his influence, and received in reply only the emptiest professions.[21] By the end of 1789, the break was complete as regards Clermont; and only a fondness for Jay and a distaste for the Chancellor kept the manor on the Federalist side.

But the Chancellor, whom Hamilton had most to fear, did not immediately ally himself with the Anti-Federalists. First he had to find reasons for his defection; and reasons, as it happened, honest and compelling reasons, were not far to seek. He began with a mild complaint against the rumored assumption of state debts; speculators were investing so much money in that kind of paper that the price of Continental paper was unduly depressed. It had also occurred to him, even before the President had decided to bestow the chief justiceship upon John Jay, that it was next to impossible for a landowner to sell his land "even if you should offer it at 1/5 of its value & for this obvious reason, the farmers who are the purchasers of land have no money[,] the speculators in certificates have it & it may be commanded at a moment's warning." He did not dare assume his father-in-law's debts, even for a consideration, because he himself had no certificates which could be turned into money, and the creditors would immediately attack his Clermont estates and sell them at vendue for a quarter of their value.[22] This kind of thinking was not new with him; it can be traced back to the days when he had tried to establish a land bank: as a landowner he was afraid of the rise of a consolidated moneyed interest.

The speculators were not necessarily, as he was sometimes disposed to fear, "new" men. In his own family, John R. Livingston had plunged heavily in 1783. His kinsman Walter Livingston was engaged in a scheme that involved the purchase of Continental securities in order to sell them and invest the proceeds in North Carolina debt, if that could be bought at any price under "four shillings specie in the pound": his guide in this venture was William Duer, Assistant Secretary of the Treasury, who had married one of the Sterling girls, and was therefore connected with the manor.[23] Duer's schemes involved some of the great Dutch banking houses, which gave the whole plan a dubious international aspect. Indeed, the most characteristic speculators at this time were men of substance and standing; but the Chancellor, as it happened, was not one of them. What he really feared was not new men, but new ways of making money: the deep conservatism, which underlay his somewhat volatile manners, prompted him to suspect that the paper speculation could have only a bad effect upon the liquidity, if not the value, of land. "The only evill here," he wrote in January, 1790, "is that money continues as scarce as ever & that no property or credit can raise a shilling. This is principally owing to the rise of our funds & the spirit of stock Jobing which has invaded all ranks of people."[24] Nothing remained but to connect this speculative mania with the general government: and in Hamilton's assumption plan of 1790, which funded the foreign and Continental debt at par, and assumed state debts to the value of over $25,000,000, he found, as did everyone else, the obvious connection. He continued to believe that funding the Continental debt was necessary, in order to keep one set of creditors attached to the general government; but he was convinced that the states should take up their own debts, in order to divide and disperse the moneyed interest. The "precipitate assumption" of both categories of debt had united the moneyed interest, taught it to look up to the federal government, and created in effect a moneyed aristocracy. Moreover, Hamilton's proposal for a national bank seemed to him, even before the bank was chartered, a deliberate sacrifice of New York's commercial interests to some fanciful "public good." He was still suspicious of commercial banks; but if they had to be established, let the center be New York and not Philadelphia.[25]

Nobody would call these ideas of the Chancellor's original. The question is: Had they been nurtured by political pique, or could not one truly say that there was present at their cradle some other and perhaps more characteristic influence?

V

Late in January, 1791, Livingston received an agitated letter from his brother-in-law Morgan Lewis.

The affair of Burr's election in the place of Schuyler [wrote Lewis], with your Activity on the Occasion, has been detailed here [Philadelphia] for some Days past, accompanied by the Report of a Coalition between you and the Governor. I confess to you the thing was both unwished for, and unexpected by me—Unwished for because I am persuaded nothing beneficial either to the public or yourself will result from the Change; unexpected, because the very last Time I heard you speak on the Subject you declared for Schuyler, and in a former letter, where you requested your Comps. to your friends, you particularized Hamilton.[26]

The accusation was true. Governor Clinton's masterly appointment of the neutral Aaron Burr to the state attorney-generalship had borne fruit; Burr had allowed himself to be put forward as Schuyler's opponent for United States senator; the Legislature, by a small majority in both houses, had elected Burr; and the Chancellor, suddenly and openly deserting his old Federalist allies, had played a conspicous part on this occasion. In his reply to Lewis, he admitted that his conversion could be ascribed to a mixture of motives.

What you say is reported of a coalition between me and the Govr. [Clinton] is so far true as related to a union of interests in opposing Schuyler's election [he wrote], and unfounded if carried beyond that object. . . . I shd. be sorry to have it believed that I had not the sincerest esteem for Coll Hamilton. I respect his talents & integrity & so far was I from opposing in any sort his appointment [as Secretary of the Treasury] or coming in competition with him that I repeatedly declared that I would not accept the appointment were if offered me[.] I have disapproved his political measures & the event will show whether he or I was right[.] It is already operating those effects which I at first predicted & given birth to the dissension I apprehended.

As a reason for joining hands with Clinton, whom Livingston had opposed with all his strength since 1784, this might be deemed sufficient: but this was not all. Impulsive as ever, the Chancellor went on to admit that

pains have been taken to prejudice me in the presidents opinion by men whom I have never injured & who professed a friendship for me. The best proof of this is what you just now tell me that the President would have appointed me *Agent* to borrow money if he had not been embarrassed by numerous applicants. I shd. have hoped (had you not informed me otherwise) that he would have thought the offer of such an appointment affrontive to a man of my standing in life & who has not been deemed unworthy of the highest offices in this & the United States.

Having dealt with the President, Livingston went on to admit that it was only natural for him to help turn Schuyler out of the Senate, in order to convince him, if nothing else, that "I knew how to make adequate return in kind for political injuries though offered by private friends." But caution at length intervened; deleting this passage, he substituted a more respectable one.

I ever believed as you say that his [Hamilton's] opposition to me & my friends was founded upon political motives & no personal resentment as I have never *even politically* injured him—he will therefore the more readily conceive that I can esteem both him and Schuyler while I disapprove their politics. I make no comparisons between Burr and Schuyler they are both men of understanding [but] there is one view in which the State will certainly be the gainer by the change. Schuyler in the public estimation leads the [New York] delegation & is supposed to be led by the Treasury[.] This Idea has not been very honourable to the State and they begin to think that it has not been very promotive of their interest.[27]

Any man not endowed with the temper of an angel would have resented such an administrative snub as Livingston had received in 1789; and it is not surprising that his letter to Morgan Lewis should have been filled with personal bitterness. But this does not mean that his opposition to Hamilton's policies was insincere; far from it. Nor did his manifest wish to join the national government in 1789 imply that he was ready to approve, in advance, every measure that government might undertake in the years to come. Meanwhile, as Janet Montgomery wrote from Ireland, "now is not the reign of your friends."[28]

It has sometimes been supposed that he called a meeting of the Livingstons, before his attack on Schuyler, and roundly informed them that they must no longer support the administration of Washington. If this were the case, Morgan Lewis, his brother-in-law, knew nothing about it; while the manor Livingstons would never, under any circumstances, have attended such a meeting or listened to such commands. Their head, Robert Livingston, Jr., the old third Lord, had died suddenly on November 28, 1790: it was believed that the sons were all the more determined to pursue the quarrel with the Chancellor. Attending the funeral, Margaret Beekman Livingston found that only Peter R. Livingston was prepared to confide in her. He used to visit her at Clermont occasionally and now confessed that he and his wife often wanted to call on the Chancellor and his lady as well, "but the moment they came to see me every thing was in an uproar in the old house &c."

As for Peter R. Livingston, he had now every reason to feel alienated from his brothers. Under his father's will, he was, as a punishment for running into debt, made nothing more than tenant for life to fifty farms, the old manor house and its mills; and "to have all the manor on the East of the road with the iron works tools oxen &c &c and 9 houses in the city of N.Y. with that vast tract on the Susquehanna bough with all his certificates given to his 4 brothers & he not a particle of the above leads him to accuse the P. [his father] of partiality & Injustice."[29]

Such were the consequences of improvidence. Primogeniture and entail had, it is true, been abolished by law: so that Peter R. Livingston, as an eldest son, could legally expect no more than his brothers. Primo-

geniture, in any case, had only come into operation when a man died in-
testate, and partible inheritance—the great example is the Clermont
estate—had certainly been practiced by the Livingstons. But primogeniture
and entail had been the spirit if not the letter of manorial existence. Now
they had departed, and the result was to set the eldest brother against
the others, and to reduce the political consequence of the family as a
whole. "I hope heaven has preserved my children," was Mrs. Livingston's
conclusion, "from the hatred I see in them".[30]

They were certainly not yet prepared to come to terms with the
Chancellor, and the more he moved toward Anti-Federalism, the more at
first were they inclined to proceed in the other direction. And "I doubt not,"
said the Chancellor, "great pains will be taken to keep up these family
divisions." In 1791, there was no coalition between Governor Clinton and
the Livingstons as a whole: the alliance was solely between Clermont and
Clinton.[31]

But even now events were moving slowly toward a different settlement of the family dispute. Early in January, 1792, John Jay made a
momentous decision to run for the governorship against George Clinton.
As Chief Justice, he had been, as it were, above the controversy between
Hamilton and the Chancellor: but the Chancellor could never forget that
Jay had not been his friend in the days when Washington was forming
his government; that he had stood coldly aloof; that he had identified
himself, at least by his silence and possibly in some more positive way,
with the exclusion of the Livingstons from all share in the state and
national patronage. Now he had descended into the arena.

Before the terms of the election had grown as clear as this, Clinton
himself took a hand in the effort to unite the Livingston interest on his
side. He appeared at John Livingston's house in the manor on November
13, and "did me the *honor* to stop & breakfast and on his return staid
& supped." The conversation turned to a "strip of land," about one mile
wide and forty to fifty miles long, on the east side of the strait between
lakes Erie and Ontario. John Livingston wished to purchase it, and the
Governor said that he believed the state was forbidden to sell it; but he
advised his host to look at the law and to make proposals if the sale was
legal; and, in short, he "promised to keep it to himself & we must succeed
or be rejected before the Election comes on." Thus the Niagara River,
"exclusive of the Fort at Niagara," hovered for a moment within the
reach of John Livingston and his associates: it was no wonder that he told
his brother Walter, in March, 1792, that "I am clearly in his [Clinton's]
interest. Was not the Chancellor in his favor, I should be very warm for
Clinton."[32]

Nor was it land alone that brought John Livingston into, or almost into, the Anti-Federalist lines. John Jay's running mate was to be Stephen Van Rensselaer, the young patroon, who was Schuyler's son-in-law and therefore a brother-in-law of Alexander Hamilton. The manor Livingstons now began to remember that Van Rensselaer had been opposing them of late in various local matters. Worse still, North Duane, the son of James Duane and Mary Livingston, was allied with Van Rensselaer and was writing the most condescending letters to his uncle John, saying that if John Livingston would only vote for Jay, Van Rensselaer would get him elected as state senator from the Eastern District. A vision of social distinctions among the Hudson River landlords hung before the angry eyes of John Livingston: he was determined to resist.

Now if *Clinton* will take you up for Lt. G[overnor] [he told his brother Walter] and will do as he ought to do, I have no objection to support him to the utmost. As to the [state] Senatorship Peter Van Ness [who had been one of the Anti-Federalists at the ratifying Convention] ought to have it. . . . I do not wish to oppose him[,] at any rate I am determined not to swallow *Toads* nor *Skiblepots* for any of the party [the Federalists] as none of them wish us well farther than we can be of service to their promotion. I wish you and Harry to keep aloof. I would rather have nothing to do in the Elections than promote these Elections [of Jay and Van Rensselaer].[33]

Poor Walter Livingston! He had little choice but to keep aloof from the elections of 1792. He had allowed himself to become involved in the mysterious speculations of William Duer and had not only over-extended himself in the purchase of Vermont lands, but had also entered into an agreement to give notes and endorsements to Duer for a sum not to exceed $800,000. Duer in turn, it is true, was to deposit an adequate collateral in national and New York bank stock and in various kinds of public debt before requesting such notes: but Walter Livingston had already endorsed more of Duer's paper than was healthy. Duer's ventures collapsed, and on March 23, 1792, he was taken to prison. "I am now secure from my Enemies," he wrote to Walter Livingston, "and feeling the Purity of my heart I defy the world—Be firm my dear Walter; and avoid Weak, or false Friends." Walter Livingston, no doubt, wished that he had avoided William Duer; for a financial panic followed Duer's imprisonment, such collateral as had been deposited with him could not be turned into cash, and a horde of Duer's creditors was about to descend upon him with a pressing and unanimous wish for payment of the notes he had endorsed. In the Bank of New York alone, these amounted to $79,000. An angry crowd gathered each night around Duer's prison, calling out for his blood, or—as the prisoner himself somewhat euphemistically put it—"still Contemplating to effect a rescue of me from this Jail." Walter Livingston began to wonder if he, too, might not be in danger; in the first week of April, he decided that he was; and by April 10, he had gone into hiding at his house in the manor. "There existed in the minds of the Citizens," he told his son-in-law, "great apprehensions of a riot and it was generally supposed, that the Victims would be the unfortunate characters, who by their own failure, or the failure of others, were themselves ruined." On the whole, it was not probable that in the coming elections the manor Livingstons would be able to exert an influence proportionate to their wealth and history.[34]

VI

The Chancellor himself has left among his papers the draft of a curious article,[35] evidently written during this election, and after the list had been drawn to show that Jay and Stephen Van Rensselaer were to be pitted for governor and lieutenant governor against George Clinton and Pierre Van Cortlandt. Hitherto, he began, he had paid no attention to the idea of an aristocracy "so often preached by Mr. Clinton & his friends," because he had conceived that there were forces at work in a republic— not least education—which would prevent its being realized. But now "I own that the peculiar situation of the State has subverted all my former reasonings & given me reason to fear that its freedom hangs in some sort on the ensuing election."

Was not General Schuyler, argued the Chancellor, the head of an aristocratic party in New York? He owned a great deal of real and personal property; he was talented, industrious, and ambitious; and his residence at Albany allowed him to maintain a close and intimate connection with an extensive back country principally settled by strangers who would be flattered by his attentions and ready to adopt his politics. Moreover, he united in his person a great landed and a great moneyed interest. His son-in-law was head of the Treasury, with an enormous patronage at his disposal; and he was also regarded as "the Magnus Apollo of the speculators of every denomination."

Mr. Van Rensselaer was also a son-in-law of General Schuyler, and Mr. Van Rensselaer owned a landed estate of twenty-four miles by forty-eight, already thickly settled; so that he could command 1,600 votes, not to mention the influence which his tenants might exert upon their connections. Add to this the concurrence of Mr. Duane, who, through sympathy or fear or because he was a federal district judge, would join the supporters of the administration, and bring about two hundred votes into the fold of Mr. Van Rensselaer. Did not this form the basis of a party in some measure independent of the will of the people?

As for Mr. Jay, he would be served by his family connections—the Chancellor at this point revealed his want of faith in the manor Livingstons—and he would be supported by the New York bar, because his election would open a general line of promotion: and Jay would in all probability be elected because the people were not alarmed.

What was there to prevent his election? Only the "close union of the L[ivingston] family with the democratic interest of the State." The Livingstons, said the Chancellor, would be tempted into such a union because in every change of government—here he fell back into colonial history—they had always adhered to the popular party; because the aristocrats were determined to keep political power in as few hands as possible; because "the C[hancellor] who may now be considered as the head of the family has openly declared against these measures of the federal government which tend to introduce a moneyed aristocracy & to annihilate the State governments"; and because they were, after all, a numerous family, many of whose members, not being rich, could hope to find consequence only in a popular government where "virtue & talents independent of wealth have some degree of consideration." Would not the leaders of the aristocracy always crush them? Had not Mr. Van Rensselaer worked against Morgan Lewis and Edward Livingston, "both his friends & relations," in their endeavors to be appointed attorney general?

Whatever merit these arguments possessed at the time, they certainly have an odd appearance today, coming as they do from one of the most solid and aristocratic of the landed proprietors in the state. But the oddness arises, not from anything inconstant or insincere in the Chancellor, but from a quite opposite source: from constancy and from piety. He seems to be trying to turn the Schuyler party into something resembling the old De Lancey interest; and to be giving the Livingstons that "popular" look which they had once worn when they were the leaders of the colonial Whigs. At the same time, in order to adjust Schuyler-De Lancey to the circumstances of 1792, he had to prove that the General had betrayed his own caste to a moneyed aristocracy—or, as he described it in another and more furibund paper, "the new made monied men that it [the administration] has created."[36] In any crisis, the Chancellor had a tendency to turn contemporary history into family history; and, in defense of his own inherited aristocracy, to find some other set of aristocrats who were out to crush his family. From this point of view, his fear of the moneyed interest was anything but insincere.

Yet there was much danger in such a defense. Could he leave the Livingstons afloat on a sea of indigence and popularity? He therefore felt obliged to state that the wives of General Schuyler, of Mr. Jay, of Mr. Duane, and of Mr. Van Rensselaer were all children of Livingstons— which was another and indirect way of saying that his family was related to all the great families in New York; and he also admitted that the Livingstons were involved in "directorial disputes"—the old quarrels about the gristmill and about family precedence—which were nothing if not the offspring of wealth and of status. Nor could he refrain from suggesting that the popular leaders were afraid, or affected to be afraid, of the Livingston influence; had wounded the Livingstons' feelings by their jealousy; and were so sure that the Schuyler-Jay-Hamilton forces—or "the Anglocrats" as he called them—would win the election that they dared not put up a serious battle, for fear of reprisals.

He was still distrustful of Clinton and his followers. As a conservative, he approved of Clinton's administration to the extent that it had, in spite of his fears, reduced taxation almost to nothing. And was it not, after all, opposed in principle to the "new made monied men"? But he could not forget that Clinton had once been a "radical," the leader and spokesman of the agrarian masses. At this point in his career, it should be repeated, he was looking for an agrarian world, but not an agrarian leadership: an agrarian world, moreover, in which Anglo-American exchanges would be such as to lead inevitably to English dominance. This latter consideration, to be sure, never occurred to him. To him, "Anglocrat" meant a friend of monarchy, or an enemy of France: and to France, in spite of its looming revolution, and thereafter through all its scenes of regicide and bloodshed, he remained firmly attached. One might almost say that he was becoming an orthodox Whig.

Whether his article was ever published cannot be ascertained; if it was, it was published anonymously. One would suspect, however, that it was too revealing to be allowed to see the light of day. In any event, it disproves the usual theory that the Livingstons passed easily over into the alliance with Clinton. On the contrary: the movement was disunited, slow, sporadic, and halfhearted.

VII

In other respects, in the light of its insistence on popularity, the article is full of suggestion. Could Livingston already have received some potent laying on of hands? It is well known that James Madison spent many weeks in New York during the spring and summer of 1791, and that Thomas Jefferson joined him for a botanical jaunt which insufficiently disguised a political foray. Since Livingston held his court in New York at the end of April and through the first two weeks of May, it is quite impossible that he should not have met and conversed with Madison, an old and admired friend of the days of the Continental Congress. Jefferson himself arrived in New York just before the Chancellor left for Clermont, and "there was every appearance of a passionate courtship between the Chancellor, Burr, Jefferson and Madison," Robert Troup wrote on June 15, "when the two latter were in town." On May 23, Livingston held a court at Clermont; and on May 23, Jefferson and Madison arrived at Poughkeepsie and took three full days to drive from thence to Albany. It is arguable, it is even likely, that they lingered at Clermont.[37]

With no evidence to support this hypothesis but Troup's letter, one would certainly not venture upon the further "creation of the Clinton-Burr-Livingston axis, with an agreement among the quintet to support Clinton for Vice-President against Adams." Indeed, so far was this from being the case, that Livingston, late in 1792, declared that Clinton would betray his party by leaving the governorship for the vice-presidency, and that, rather than support him, "the little weight I have shall be thrown into the scale" of Adams.[38] But a meeting between the Chancellor and the two great Virginians is, if only as a speculation, singularly suggestive. Two great Virginians, two fellow landowners, who, when they pleased, could throw over every conversation an indescribable charm—what effect would they not have had upon an impressionable and imaginative man?

CHAPTER TWO

The conversion from Federalism was now complete, but the election of 1792 marked the beginning of the end of Livingston's commitment to a political career in New York. Just as in the days of the Revolutionary New York Legislature, he found himself unable to play a fully active role because of a private distaste for rustic lawmakers, so now he imported into the campaign against John Jay a private virulence which was quite out of keeping with the principles involved. His weakness as a politician was that he could never achieve a necessary and convenient marriage between private taste and public principle; the two were always at odds. Now, when his alliance with Clinton and his allegiance to Jefferson called for a dignified and reasoned attack on Federalist economics, he found himself engaged in a personal campaign against John Jay.

II

It was customary in those days and for a long time thereafter for a man's political writings to the press to be anonymous: it would therefore be wrong to suppose that an anonymous attack upon a former friend represented a stab in the dark. But anonymity had, then as now, its irresponsible as well as its preposterous side: for if it allowed a writer, on the one hand, to say things about himself which would be vainglorious and absurd above his own signature, it encouraged, on the other, certain freedoms with the truth which an informed and worldly man could not openly perpetrate.

Thus the Chancellor, on February 27, wrote an anonymous letter to the New York *Daily Advertiser* in which he actually said that "surely it would be the grossest flattery to Mr. Jay to attribute the treaty with Britain to him alone, when we consider that the immortal Franklin, *the philosophic & amiable Jefferson,* & the learned Dr. Adams were his associates in this work. . . ." The philosophic and amiable Jefferson had been at the time some three thousand miles away. As for Jay's reputed leadership in writing the New York Constitution, "the points that particularly distinguish it from that of other States in the Union are the Council of Revision & the stability it possesses from a senate elected by the substantial yeomanry of the county—for both of these it is indebted as I have heard to Chancellor Livingston. . . ."[1]

It was only under an exceptional strain that Livingston would have resorted to such expedients: and it is not difficult to understand why he was so bitter against Jay. The office of chief justice had little of the power it was to assume under John Marshall; but one would not doubt that it conferred a status upon its incumbent jurist which was considerably higher than that of a state chancellor; while the governorship of New York had, in Livingston's eyes, always some of the characteristics of a social reward. He saw it, less as an opportunity for the display of political power or administrative ability, than as the highest pinnacle in the state. In 1792, he did not particularly want this office for himself: but that Jay, who had forestalled him on the supreme bench, should now propose to ascend this pinnacle, seemed to him the grossest kind of social climbing. The old friend, so cold and even hostile in 1789 when he could have been of service, was now actually proposing to become the first gentleman in New York. Only when one considers what a reversal this was of the terms of their earlier friendship can one quite understand the intensity of Livingston's bitterness. Where status was concerned, he was never reasonable. It was not exactly jealousy but, rather, an outraged sense of proportion which led him on against Jay; and led him on to words which, in turn, were quite disproportionate to the events that had inspired them.

Possibly he had no particular objection when—in a campaign notable even in New York for the peculiar fury of the press—he was assailed in the *Daily Advertiser* in these terms: "My dear friend, I know that thou art a wag and readest merry books—thou rememberest it is written in *Rabelais*, that when Pantagruel f——ted, he shook the earth three leagues around. Dost thou seriously believe that the C*****'s influence, will extend over as many acres in any county? And yet he is a gentleman of eminent genius and abilities."[2] Livingson had a robust eighteenth-century sense of humor, and could perhaps appreciate this sort of joke against himself. It was a very different matter, however, when he was taken to task by a correspondent whom the New York *Journal* admitted to its pages, on March 31, under the *nom de guerre* of "Timothy Tickler."

"Timothy Tickler," in a tone of elaborate irony, affected to be a friend of the Chancellor's. "From a friend of the M[ano]r of L[ivingsto]n to RRL——n Esq. C—r"—such was the heading of his letter. He began by saying that Livingston's several packages—his various letters to the newspapers—would be made "as serviceable as possible to our common purposes."

The secret, however ["Timothy Tickler" continued], that you are the author of most of them, particularly Aristogiton and Oldcastle [two anonymous anti-Jay warriors, one or both of whom may have been Brockholst Livingston] had unfortunately got abroad, and will, I fear, defeat much of their usefulness. The friends of C[linto]n (I mean the staunch ones) seem to relish the praises you have lavished upon *yourself* almost as little as if they had been bestowed upon J[a]y. It was but this morning that one of them (who is pretty much distinguished for laughing in his sleeve) could not help regretting that "the C——r's modesty should be so often obliged to violate itself." . . . While a third, of graver cast, thought that he could discover something more at bottom than a pure and unmixed vanity. . . . "I am the more induced (said he) to think myself right in this opinion, when I hear that the important quarrel of the *straw mill* [*i.e.*, the gristmill controversy] which, like the siege of Troy has lasted these ten years, was the other day sacrificed on the altar of politics and that the whole clan . . . [has] entered a solemn league and covenant . . . that in good time they should proceed to the distribution of the loaves and fishes. Now though this can not be called an *aristocracy* (composed as it is of many of the worst and weakest men in the state) yet it is such a combination as every genuine republican will, in his heart, either despise or abhor. . . ."

Having thus disposed of the Livingstons in general, "Timothy Tickler" turned his guns upon the Chancellor in particular.

On the subject of your talents, which you and I have never once doubted, many affect to talk as M[elancto]n S[mit]h and the G[overno]r etc. did at the time of the [ratifying] convention, viz. That you had some imagination but no judgment; that of course you are always to be found on the surface of things, never at the bottom; and, in general, that there are some coins that are current for more than they are worth. Others are ill natured enough to deny that you ever gave evidence of anything like genius; and when I mentioned your eloquence in the Hoffman cause, they wickedly remarked that even an ass spoke at the sight of an *angel,* and that on you interest could always work some miracle. "But look," they said, "at his Chef d'Oeuvre, his Cincinnati oration, devoted to the *rights of man,* and the memory of heroes. How grand and animating the subject in the hands of genius! But Alas! how mean and despicable they become in his. The finest gold is converted into dross; the purest incense into ordure."

It was not in Livingston's nature to refrain, under provocation, from leaping before he looked. This letter, which was viciously wounding, was bound to provoke and was intended to provoke some imprudent rejoinder. But what followed was somewhat more to the point.

Their spokesman continued [said "Timothy Tickler"]: "This admitted let us proceed to his doctrines: —— Who now talks loudly against aristocracy? The C——r. Who in 1788 declared it the phantom and bugbear of party, the creature of a distempered mind? The C——r. Who now contends for the feelings of the people? The C——r. Who in '88 represented them as a set of creatures, unable to see or judge their own interests. . . ? The C——r. Who now talks of corruption in the general government? The C——r. Who, not long since, contributed his efforts to turn Gen. S[chuyle]r out of the Senate, for no better reason than because he was the father-in-law of Col. H[amilto]n? The C——r. Who in '88 expressed so much fear least the state governments, subject to irregular passions, should listen to some factious demagogue who should misrepresent, distort, recall and disgrace their absent and faithful senator? The C——r. . . . Such a bundle of inconsistencies rarely fall to the lot of one man. . . . The new government had many high offices and snug places to bestow. The C——r's vanity would not permit his ambition to sleep. He tendered his services. The President knew how to appreciate merit, and passed him by. This was the enchanted sword which awoke him from his dream, and showed him in the same view, the beauty order, energy, wisdom and virtue of the state governments; and the deformity, weakness and wickedness of the national."[3]

The charge of inconsistency was admittedly the hardest to fight. But made, as it was here, with so many wounding irrelevancies, extending, as it did, far back to the Hoffman case, which the Chancellor had fought in a spirit of family piety—how could it be borne? Characteristically, Livingston first asked himself who "Timothy Tickler" could be. And, without troubling to separate what was probable from what was not, he decided that John Jay himself was the man. Jay, it is true, had not been well treated by his brother-in-law Brockholst Livingston when Brockholst Livingston was his secretary in Spain; and now Brockholst Livingston had gone over to the Clintonians; but Jay was the very last man, no matter what the provocation, to say even an anonymous word in public against his wife's own family. If nothing else, his sense of what was due to his own consequence would have restrained him. The "Timothy Tickler" letter, in its postscript, made a vigorous attack upon John Armstrong, the Chancellor's newest brother-in-law, and author of the Newburgh Letters. Could the attack have been a little too vigorous, a little too obvious? Could "Timothy Tickler" have been, sad to relate, none other than John Armstrong, an unreconstructed Federalist with a certain gift for fanged and venemous prose? Had the family been nurturing a serpent in its bosom? The Chancellor, to be sure, had some suspicion that this might be the case; but he selected, with a wild surmise, quite the wrong personage for the role of serpent.

There are two drafts in his papers on the subject of "Timothy Tickler." The first, "To the Printer," is on the whole a very reasonable reply to the charge of inconsistency. The assumption of the national and state debts, Livingston said, had been in its turn the parent of "a *general excise*" (the Whisky Tax of March 3, 1791), which had never been contemplated except as a resource in the greatest emergency. With it came a host of officers who, if the state debts and the state excise had been left to the state governments, would be employed by the states and not now be "marshalled under the banners of Administration." No man who had agreed to the federal Constitution had ever thought of this; still less had he foreseen "a *national bank* & an attempt to consolidate the whole monied interest of the continent in a few hands." Such events, "so repugnant to the genious of the people," were in fact unforeseeable "since the constitution itself has been violated to bring them about."[4]

If Livingston had contented himself with this rejoinder, all would have been well: but it was not in his nature to stop short. A second letter, signed "Aristides," was now prepared. It was addressed: "To the Honble Timothy Tickler, C——f J—st—ce of the U.S."; and its tone can best be conveyed by reciting the suggestion in its first paragraph that Jay was friendless, and especially friendless among his relatives by marriage and by blood, because "your cold heart, gradated like a thermometer, finds the freezing point nearest the bulb." The simile was certainly ingenious; but it betrayed, as did almost every word that followed, the fact that it had been composed in a fit of rage. "Come forth, Sir," said "Aristides," "& show us a single act of yours even in politics . . . that betrays the smallest mark of genious." Did he or his friends dare make any reference to the New York Constitution? What could they oppose to the Chancellor's own invention, the "qualified negative" of the Council of Revision, which, "tho' a perfect novelty in government has been imitated by the most enlightened of the United States. . . . What sir will you oppose to this? that wretched blot in our constitution the Council of Appointment, a Council calculated to destroy all responsibility in the Executive." Here, at least as regards the Council of Appointment, "Aristides" was just: but he went on to call the Chief Justice a monarchist in everything but the drab and frugal circumstances of his private life; and he ended with the accusation that he had sacrificed "the earliest friendship of your youth to the cause of avarice & ambition."[5]

Under these circumstances, it was most improbable that "Aristides" could conceal his identity from anyone, let alone the earliest friend of his youth: and Jay, immediately guessing the source of this attack, proceeded to write a temperate reply. He declared upon his honor that he had written no political paper that year; he said he did not know the authors of the writings which supported him; and he maintained that he had neither advised nor desired their publication. With the administration at his back, and with no talent for political invective, he sat down to await the outcome in a dignified and, no doubt, a galling silence.

III

It would surely be very mistaken to assume that if a proud and intelligent man writes a foolish letter in a fit of rage, and if that letter is published, he does not hurt himself deeply in his own estimation. The contrary is certain to be the case. The evidence of the Chancellor's papers, the withdrawal from the urgencies of state politics which they show from this point onward, makes it clear that the "Aristides" letter was a decisive event in his career. Never again, try as he would, could he get much satisfaction from the maneuvers or the war cries of local factions. The state, as the proper scene for a dignified and useful life, began to preoccupy his imagination: he left the search for its ephemeral rewards more and more to his relatives and friends; and, for himself, began to look to the general principles and the high abstractions of statesmanship for a fitting expression of his friendships and enmities. If his letter, as a political effusion, was simply scurrilous, as an act of political *felo-de-se*, it was distinctly honorable. "Aristides" had aimed his dagger at the bosom of John Jay, but had plunged it unerringly into his own.

The outcome of the 1792 election merely completed the destruction of "Aristides"; it placed, as it were, a visible tombstone upon his grave. It became clear as the campaign drew to its close that the race would be exceedingly even. The ballots from each county were slow in arriving: they were received at the office of the Secretary of State, and there counted by a board of twelve canvassers, one of whom was Livingston's brother-in-law Thomas T. Tillotson. On June 3, Tillotson wrote an agitated letter to say that Clinton had been carried into Dutchess with a majority of only 609, less than his friends or even his enemies had imagined. In Dutchess, it looked as if there would be a Jay majority of from 150 to 180. "The Jay party is in great spirits," said Tillotson, "in consequence of the present state of the votes": for it seemed that Columbia County would not be able to counterbalance the increase of strength that Jay had received in the Western District. All seemed to depend on certain legal niceties. The Clinton and Tioga votes, for example, had been delivered at the Secretary of

State's office, not by the sheriff, as the law required, but by a deputy. The Tioga votes had even been delivered by the deputy of a deputy. But the Otsego votes were in a far stranger situation: the sheriff who received them was no longer a sheriff, his commission having expired some days before. "How can the canvassers," wrote Tillotson, "(who are under oath to canvas the votes delivered by the Sheriffs according to Law) go by [avoid] rejecting these votes? The case is a singular and a hard one that the County [of Tioga] should be deprived of their suffrages in the choice of a Chief Magistrate by an accident not in the power of man to rectify. . . . From the present view of the thing I should not hesitate to decide against receiving any votes delivered in by a deputy were it not sanctioned by the conduct of our predecessors in canvassing." Fortunately, a solution suggested itself—that "the Otsego votes should be destroyed and the Tioga ones preserved": a solution all the more fortunate in that it would give the election to Governor Clinton.[6]

The final outcome, if no less outrageous, was more tactful. By a strictly party vote, the canvassers rejected the Otsego ballots, which gave a large majority to Jay, and the Tioga and Clinton ballots, which gave a smaller majority to Clinton. Jay had been robbed of his victory just as surely as the voters of Otsego, Tioga, and Clinton had been robbed of their suffrages.

Robert Troup, Hamilton's lieutenant, whose language was just as political as was the majority vote of the canvassers, declared that his own opinion was asked for by Edward Livingston; that it was against the rejection of the Otsego ballots; and that it

threw the party into consternation. A Cabinet Council of the Governor, the Chancellor, Ned, Brockholst, etc., was immediately called. Soon afterwards Brockholst went about almost like a madman vociferating against the legality of the return of the Otsego votes.[7]

If such a cabinet council was called, there is no evidence of it other than the words of Troup. "Oh, how is the name of Livingston to be disgraced," said Sarah Livingston Jay. "Brockholst, Edward, William S., Maturin. These shameless men . . ." It is to be observed that, even in her rage, she did not mention the Chancellor. For, indeed, the Chancellor was very unhappy about the Otsego ballots. His respect for the common law did not permit him to forget that precedents existed which should have guided the canvassers into an opposite decision, and he believed, as a sensible man, that no good could come from a martyrdom of John Jay. Moreover, he entertained the private belief that Clinton had run too often, and was as much responsible as anyone for the vote against him. "I find the determination of the canvassers," he wrote to his brother Edward, "occasions much uneasiness. I confess I could have wished that all the votes had been counted whatever might have been the event." His conscience as a jurist had been profoundly disturbed by this illegal and inequitable action. As a Clintonian, he tried once or twice to compose a paper in favor of the canvassers' decision; but the language was mild and faltering. He had always been too independent to make a good party man: and now his heart was not in it.[8]

IV

The defeated party at first believed that it should apply to the Legislature for a new constitutional convention, which would, among other things, declare the recent election illegal. It would also, according to Morgan Lewis, who said that he had received this news from General Schuyler himself, amend the Constitution "by destroying the Council of Appointment and making some few other Alterations." "At Kinderhook," Morgan Lewis wrote, "the Partisans, who, I suppose, speak the sentiments of Van S[c]haa[c]k, are loud for Monarchy, and say we shall never be happy till we adopt the British Constitution."[9] Such were the rumors now afloat. Indeed, it was believed that Schuyler and Van Rensselaer would carry their resentment so far as to make a separation between the northern and the southern parts of the state; and that it was the duty of "the Republicans" (as the Anti-Federalists now called themselves) to defeat this plot by vociferous meetings and sternly worded resolutions. The Chancellor himself was not perturbed by these rumors.

Whether the canvassers were right or wrong [he said] is no longer a question of any moment. Their determination is conclusive, nor do I know of any constitutional mode of reversing the question. . . . Nor can I conceive that Schuyler & Renselaer when they come to reflect can seriously think of an experiment which may terminate in a separation of the southern from northern part of the State. . . . Shd. the controversy be determined by arms he [Schuyler] has everything to fear from a union of his own ten[ant]s with the southern interest. Their view is merely to keep up a party to have the appearance with the other states of governing this. . . .[10]

In the end, it was not through "destroying the Council of Appointment" that General Schuyler hoped to reverse the course of events. On the contrary: it was in the Council of Appointment that he and his friends found, ready to hand, precisely the engine of mischief they needed. The Federalists, who controlled the Assembly, led by Josiah Ogden Hoffman, a brilliant New York lawyer, now proposed to choose a new Council of Appointment, although the term of the old Council had not expired. They forced the election of this Council, composed of three Federalists and one Republican, with General Schuyler at its head: and the Council claimed that it had a concurrent right of nomination; that it could increase at will the number of officials not otherwise limited by law; and that it could replace any officer, whose commission must be renewed annually, at the expiration of his commission. Thus every officer in city, county, and state, civil and military, except the governor, the lieutenant governor, the members of the Legislature, and the aldermen, seemed to depend for his survival upon the will of the Council, quite regardless of that of the governor. "This arbitrary proceeding," wrote a historian of New York State, "led to twenty years of corrupt methods and political scandals."[11]

It led to something else. One need not ascribe to Chancellor Livingston an astuteness or clairvoyance not possessed by his contemporaries: yet his instinct was certainly a sound one when it directed him, in 1792, toward a disengagement from the intrigues and scurrilities of state politics. The division of the landed gentry into Federalists and Republicans; the uneasy union between Clermont and Clinton; the assault upon the state Constitution, through the Council of Appointment, by a Schuyler, a gentleman whose survival depended upon doing it as little harm as possible—did not all these events form part of that political decline of the state aristocracy which had begun with the Revolution and was proceeding gradually on its course? There were times when the Chancellor hoped for the governorship in the years to come: but he never again imported into his own hopes for himself the passion, the virulence, the extreme concern which he had shown in the cause of Clinton against Jay in the elections of 1792.

V

The world had already encroached upon these parochial events and decisions. The French Revolution, more than any other complex of events, returned the American Revolution to world history as a central and not a peripheral movement. That this was clear to Americans at the time, that they realized the causal connection between their own upheaval and that of the French, may be doubted: to some men the existence of such a connection would have been odious. Jay, for example, to his dying day, protested that the American Revolution was nothing more than a respectable defense of established rights. The supposition that it had been founded upon a new concept of government filled him with the greatest uneasiness. He approved of the French Revolution as long as it appeared to be a movement that "limited the power of the king and restored liberty to the people"; but with the appearance of a national convention, he became seriously alarmed; and the execution of the King, with all its consequences, terrified and disgusted him.[12] Nor in this was he singular. Livingston, on the other hand, though the revolutionary nature of the American Revolution had made him very uncomfortable, though he had tried to cage the dangerous beast in a state Constitution of which he was on the whole extremely proud, though he was not exactly an ardent friend to popular government, usually gave his approval to the French Revolution. Nor was this all. He praised *The Rights of Man* as "a manly & spirited publication," talked of the civilized world as "a great national republic," and was disgusted by the frantic behavior of the French Minister, Genêt, because "the true republicans" suffered most from it, their interest being connected with that of France.[13] "The favorable accounts from France," he told his youngest brother in 1794, "are received very ungraciously by a great proportion of the [Federalist] party who can hardly bring themselves to speak on the subject & when they do cannot conceal their mortification. For in fact there is no event that can be more injurious to them if they really entertain sentiments subversive of freedom."[14] Thus, as the world went to war, the philosophies of the Federalists and the Republicans were charged with an English or a French sympathy; and the fortunes of the French nation in arms became a subject for the frenzies of partisan debate.

The fact that the United States was England's best single customer somewhat forcibly implied to *official* England—which infrequently, where America was concerned, realized the implications of anything—that the United States themselves might have some national future. It was not until after the War of 1812 that official England could bring itself to swallow this unappetizing concept: but by 1791, it had, at least, realized that there might be some other policy than tampering with the Indians, imposing commercial restrictions, and dreaming of the control of the trans-Allegheny West. When revolutionary France at length, in February, 1793, declared war on Great Britain, the British, with their hands full in Europe, saw that it might be unwise to arouse too bitter an enmity in the United States.

The news that France had decided to add George III to her list of enemies was received with consternation in Philadelphia. The name of

George III would arouse every latent anti-British sentiment in favor of the French, who had, after all, nourished the American Revolution with their own blood. And did not the old treaty of 1778 with France require that the United States should come to her aid if she were attacked in the West Indies? Might this not be taken to extend to Europe? And how, in any case, could one avoid some quarrel with England if England interfered, as inevitably she would and in the most highhanded manner, with the flow of neutral commerce on the high seas?

The perplexities and subtleties of this problem are not relevant to these pages except in so far as they concern one observer in New York. Livingston, from the beginning, took the position that it was of little use to make friendly gestures toward England. She still, in defiance of her treaty obligations of 1783, held on to her western posts within the boundaries of the United States: let her be driven out of them by force. Her commercial restrictions should be answered by strong countervailing measures, among them a moratorium on the payment of all debts to English creditors. If she became too highhanded on the ocean, letters of marque producing a cloud of American privateers would soon bring her to her senses.

He even went so far as to say that America should "connive" at the outfitting of French privateers in her ports. All this would have the effect, on the one hand, of preparing for war with Great Britain, and, on the other, of giving a fresh impulse to the British desire for peace with America. Such concepts of neutrality, it is needless to say, are more easily entertained by men in opposition than by men in office. But the Chancellor went even further. When James Madison once again brought forward his famous resolutions, designed to impose economic sanctions upon Great Britain, Livingston not only applauded them; he also believed that he himself had suggested them, in a letter delivered to Madison by Dr. James Adair. Moreover, both applause and belief arose from his hope that the resolutions might be the beginning of some permanent system.[15] To such a degree had he modified his agrarian ideas that he was now ready to abandon free trade in favor of something that might well lead to a system of protection. It is true that he pursued this line of thinking because he was persuaded that Great Britain would never otherwise consent to free trade in the West Indies: it is true that it did not last. But that he should have pursued it at all shows how violent are the processes of conversion. In order to become a good agrarian Republican, he was now prepared to abandon the pacific, the simple, the aristocratic agrarianism of his colonial and Federalist days.

His policies no doubt influenced only his immediate circle; but his Francophile and warlike sentiments were those of any New York Republican; and, uttered as they were by one of the leading men in that state, could not have added to the administration's peace of mind. The whole structure of George Washington's government rested, by now precariously, upon two supports: friendly relations with England; no entanglement in the thorny and encroaching quarrels of Europe. It was not that Washington's spirit was not affronted by the arbitrary behavior of the British Government, codified (as usual) in a series of sweeping Orders in Council:[16] but there was a singular and delicate balance wheel in his system, which regulated his thinking in spite of some truly seismatic disturbances within his own Cabinet. Moreover, Alexander Hamilton was his chief adviser; if his government had any meaning, it would be found in Hamilton's financial measures; and Hamilton's financial measures depended upon the good will of the London money market. He was also, by predilection and because of his experiences with the states as commander in chief in the late war, by no means well disposed toward popular governments, still less toward such a popular government as that of France. The effect of all this was to lead him to the conclusion—surely a just one under the circumstances—that neutrality was the first condition of American existence as a nation: that it could, for the time being, be equated with freedom. It was for this reason that he agreed to send John Jay to England in 1794, in order to reach some settlement that would avoid an open break.

Jay had retired from the governor's election of 1792 bathed in a gentle glow of approbation: for a man intellectually not popular, it might well be described as a blaze of popularity. He now faced a prospect that was certainly bleak and that might prove disastrous. His only hope was that the British Government would prefer not to come to an open break with the United States: the question was—how far would they go to avoid one? Their views on the rights of neutral trade on the high seas were no different from what they had been when the Armed Neutrality had proposed a countervailing system: but now the chief members of the Armed Neutrality were in coalition against France. The coalition was possibly beginning to look askance at British maritime practices: but no entity in the world could be more stubborn than a British Government confronted with some proposal to modify, in any essential particular, its peculiar concept of the freedom of the seas; and Jay had little to comfort him but the belief that he was, on the whole, well liked in England because of the part he had played in the treaty of 1783.

His mission produced the last recorded exchange in the clashing lives of himself and Robert R. Livingston. On the eve of his departure for London, he received this note from his old friend:

The Chancellor presents his compliments to the Chief Justice of the U.S:— Tho' political differences have excited a coolness between them perhaps inconsistent to the liberality of both—The Chancellor is not so unmindful of past friendships as not to be sincere in wishing the Chief Justice a safe passage, a happy return to his friends & a successful issue to his mission—"

That night Jay replied:

The Chief Jutice of the U.S. presents his compliments to the Chancellor of the State. It is now late at night, and want of Time imposes Brevity. He assures the Chancellor that while he regrets what is, he will always remember with pleasure what has been their relative situation to each other. Time here or hereafter will correct Errors. He thanks him for the kind wishes expressed in his note; and without Hesitation reciprocates them.[17]

The wheel had turned full circle. If their youthful correspondence resembled a discourse between two somewhat sentimental busts, in this final communication there was not even the softness of the first person singular. All was marble. Yet who knows what unacknowledged grief, what unrecognized mourning, might not have been imprisoned there?

VI

The sincerity of the Chancellor's wishes for a successful issue to the Chief Justice's mission depended upon the amount of meaning that the term "successful" could be made to bear. To Livingston, the only successful mission would have been one that exacted a complete surrender from Great Britain on every important issue. In a confidential correspondence he was conducting with James Monroe, he had already said that if the public were ever to be aware of the injuries America had received from Great Britain, it would turn against the Federalists; and that "the p——— [George Washington] was too cautious & too fond of popularity" to support his own advisers under such circumstances. And he told Sir John Temple, the British Consul at New York, that "the causes for the oppression of our trade [are] to be found in Mr. Pitt's conviction that we are governed by the President & that the people in power have an aversion for the French & are willing to be plundered by the British rather than that republicanism shd. prevail. I can easily conceive what Mr. Hammond [the British Minister, and a confidant of Hamilton's] has written on this subject & as easily foresee that his error will be fatal to the British interest in this country—For be persuaded that notwithstanding all the efforts of our deluded ministers *the people* will govern."[18] If Jay's mission was not successful, then the Republicans would come into power: some such thought was also in the Chancellor's mind when he wished the Chief Justice that statuesque farewell.

Even before Jay left for London, George Washington, perhaps in order to placate the New York Republicans, had written to offer Livingston the post of minister to France. He was to replace Gouverneur Morris, who had become, for numerous reasons, obnoxious to the Republic. The whole Clermont connection urged the Chancellor to accept—the appointment, declared Morgan Lewis, with pardonable hyperbole, had been forced upon the administration by "the nation itself"—and to these entreaties were added those of the French Minister. "*Je joins ma prière,*" wrote Georges-Pierre LeBlanc, Secretary of Legation, "*à celle que le Ministre de la République vous fais d'accéder au veu [voeu] essentiel de l'humanité.*" This was certainly flattering: but although the President renewed his request, the Chancellor persisted in declining. His private reasons, he told James Monroe, were two: on the one hand, if he resigned the chancellorship to go abroad, the Council of Appointment would certainly bestow it upon a person "of very different political sentiments"; on the other hand, "differing so much in sentiment as I do from some of the administration, I am satisfied that I shd either be compelled to violate my own principles by yielding to theirs, or risk my reputation by incurring their resentment."[19] The latter consideration, in the light of what happened to Monroe when he accepted the post, was certainly prudent; the former was possibly the compelling one. He did not wish to abandon the safety and the dignity of the Chancery Court.

Thus, when the Federalists selected the absent Jay as their candidate for governor in 1795, Livingston betrayed very little excitement. For a brief while, after Clinton had announced that he would not run again, he thought that he might be a candidate himself: so much one learns from his correspondence with his bailiff, Dr. William Wilson. But when it became clear that the Republican assemblymen would fix upon Robert Yates, he acquiesced with hardly a sigh. This was in February, 1795; and already his thoughts were straying elsewhere. The terms of Jay's treaty with Great Britain, he told Dr. Wilson, were, "if we may depend upon our private accounts," just as bad as they well could be.[20]

The treaty did not arrive until the end of February, and its terms were not exactly known until they were printed in the Philadelphia *Aurora* on June 29, 1795. In the meantime, Jay had landed in New York on May 28, while the votes of a dull and verbally almost harmless election were being canvassed. On June 5, it was known that he had, without saying a word or lifting a finger in his own cause, obtained an honorable majority of 1,589 in a total vote of 23,373. On June 29, he resigned his chief justice-ship, and on July 1, he was inaugurated governor.[21]

"The Governor," wrote Edward Livingston on July 6, "entered upon his office very inauspiciously. The Treaty was just published & the indignation it excited was then universal, tho' it is now by unremitting exertions a little softened—I waited on him the fourth of July & was very politely Recd. with a great many enquiries about your health & that of your Family &c—"[22] He certainly had need of friends; for, with the publication of the treaty in the *Aurora*, a storm of unparalleled violence had broken about his ears. The Senate had debated it in secret, ratified it in secret, with the suspension of one odious article, and then refused to publish it: only the energy of Senator Thomas Steven Mason, of Virginia, who defiantly took a copy to the office of the *Aurora*, made it available for inspection and for execration.

Whether Jay deserved the abuse that was heaped upon him, and the number of times his effigy—occasionally a most speaking likeness—was burned or blown up or hanged, is a more difficult question. His original draft of September 30, 1794, which, fortunately for his reputation, the public never saw, vigorously denied the position he finally assumed in the treaty signed on November 19. He certainly was not constrained by exact instructions, he knew that his mission was at least as much concerned with peace as with the forcible expression of American rights, and then, at a highly critical moment, when he might have obtained much that he was expected to obtain, no less a personage than Alexander Hamilton ruined his chances. Hamilton told the British Minister, Hammond, that the Cabinet had decided it would have nothing to do with the new Armed Neutrality which Sweden and Denmark had concerted in 1794. Hammond relayed this gratifying news to Lord Grenville, and Lord Grenville, who had been afraid that the United States would join Sweden and Denmark in resisting the maritime pretensions of Great Britain, immediately stiffened his attitude. It is possible that the blandishments of London society may, at the same time, have softened that of Jay. The treaty, at any rate, bore upon its front all the signs of a humiliating surrender to Great Britain.

It provided for the abandonment of the western posts after June 1, 1796; but there was to be no remuneration for stolen negro slaves and no provision for ending the impressment of American seamen. The principle that "free ships make free goods" was surrendered and the contraband list was extended.

British claimants could appeal to the Mixed Debts Commission without first exhausting their resources in American courts, while the American claimants had to exhaust the resources of the British courts before appealing to the Commission. The Mississippi was to be opened to British trade; and the West Indian trade, which Jay was specifically instructed to secure, was granted to American ships of seventy tons burden only [this was the odious Article XII which the Senate rejected] and then on condition that the West Indian trade should be wholly free to British vessels and that American vessels should not carry molasses, sugar, coffee, cocoa, and cotton to any ports but their own. The East Indian trade was opened to Americans provided no further restrictions should be laid on British commerce. And Jay agreed to provisions—despite specific instructions to enter into no obligations incompatible with our treaty obligations to France—which amounted to an alliance with England against America's ally in the Revolution.[23]

This is a partisan account, written in the 1920's, and corresponding, with some accuracy, to the sentiments uttered against the treaty in 1795. There was, as it happened, another side to the treaty, which, like the dark side of the moon, was quite inaccessible to American scrutiny. "There was also," says one of the first of modern authorities, "the great achievement of redeeming the territorial integrity of the United States throughout the Northwest, which coincided with General Anthony Wayne's decisive victory over the hostile Indians at the battle of Fallen Timbers (August 20, 1794)."[24] But the Northwest was then insufficiently mapped. It represented mystery and speculation, not that shrinkage of the Earth which follows upon exact measurements and which leads to exact historical judgments. The concert of action suggested in Article IV of the treaty was not concerted until 1818.

Any Republican would have been justified, and more than justified, in condemning the treaty; and among the innumerable voices raised against it, that of Chancellor Livingston was not the least resonant. He wrote to George Washington, asserting, among other things, that the treaty's implicit alliance with Great Britain against France might lead to civil war. He urged Samuel Adams to do the same: the President surely "will pay some respect to the voice of the Whigs of 75"; but the President did not reply until after he had signed the treaty. Livingston also corresponded with James Monroe in Paris—the treaty, he wrote, was a "fatal instrument, hostile in every respect to our Liberties. . . . Such is the force of the stock jobbers & the British party that their [the people's] voice is unattended to." Jay's good wishes, extended through Edward Livingston to the whole family on July 4, found no echo in Clermont. Then and thereafter, the Chancellor was implacable.[25]

He reserved his most serious efforts, however, for a series of sixteen articles, signed "Cato," which appeared in the New York *Argus* between July and September, 1795. In the drafts of these articles there is evidence, here and there, that "Aristides" was attempting to struggle out of his tomb: but from the articles themselves, in their final shape, all personal abuse of Jay was carefully banished. "Cato" represented a new Chancellor; and the words of "Cato," where they addressed themselves to such questions as impressment, contraband, "free ships, free goods," and the countervailing duties which the British Government was now permitted to lay against American tariff and tonnage laws, were able and persuasive. But the articles suffered, as was often the case with Livingston and so many others, from an undue prolixity; and the printer set them up, as often as not, in very small print, which concealed from all but the most pertinacious reader both his own errors and the arguments of "Cato." Two other Romans, "Decius" and "Cinna," also appeared in the *Argus* and in arms against the treaty; they represented, so the Chancellor told Monroe, the efforts of Brockholst Livingston, Jay's brother-in-law and a man somewhat given to duplicity. On the other side, the publisher of the *Argus* occasionally condescended to produce an article by "Camillus," or Alexander Hamilton, who defended Jay with a skill that Jefferson himself was compelled to admire, but who, by admitting that the object of the treaty was rather to conciliate Great Britain than to negotiate with her, certainly did not destroy the position of "Cato."[26]

One need not linger over this controversy. "Cato" was most uncertain on the statistics and geography of the boundary question, and most bizarre when he declared that a treaty might well depend, not upon the advice and consent of the Senate, or even upon the concurrence of the whole Congress, but upon the agreement also of individual states: but the series as a whole did him great credit for acuteness of perception and fertility in argument. Thereafter, he left the battle to his brother Edward, who had been elected to the House of Representatives in 1794, and who was, with Madison and Gallatin, one of the Republican leaders in the great and brilliant debates which raged around the treaty in 1796.

The extraordinary anger which, in town after town in almost all the states, had testified to the unpopularity of Jay's diplomacy, eventually burned and shouted itself into embers and silence: but not before there had been a small but symbolic encounter between the Livingstons and Alexander Hamilton.

Nothing can equal the vexation of the tory party [Edward Livingston wrote to his mother on July 20, 1795] on discovering that their favorite leader

[Hamilton] had lost his influence except the indecency with which that leader testified his mortification—in the afternoon of Saturday a number of gentlemen of [both] parties accidentally stopped at my Door. [When in New York he lived on Wall Street.] We entered into conversation on the politics of the Day, at first cooly and afterwards with some warmth between Peter [Peter R. Livingston, a distant kinsman and descendant of Robert Livingston "the Nephew"] & Jo [Josiah Ogden] Hoffman. It at last grew personal and Mr. [Rufus] King, myself and others interposed begging that if there were any personal disputes they might be settled elsewhere—Hamilton then stepped forward declaring that if the parties were to contend in a personal way, he was ready, that he would fight the whole party one by one. I was just beginning to speak to him on the subject [of] this imprudent declaration when he turned from me threw up his arm & Declared that he was ready to fight the whole *"Detestable faction"* one by one—Maturin [Livingston] at this moment arrived, he stepped up to him told him very cooly that he was one of the party that he accepted the challenge & would fight him in half an hour where he pleased. Hamilton said he had an affair on his Hands already with one of the party (meaning a quarrel with Commodore Nicholson) & when that was settled he would call on him—Neither Nicholson nor Maturin have as yet heard from him—I mention this Circumstance that you may Judge how much he must be mortified at his loss of Influence before he would descend [to] language that would have become a street Bully.[27]

No man was less apologetic than Alexander Hamilton for the numerous congregation of sharks and stockjobbers which attended and disgraced his financial measures. No man was more sure, and rightly so, of the grandeur of his success in building the credit of the United States. He had, indeed, crowned the work of the Revolution by the radical solution of making it financially respectable. He was a genius, a genius of a kind, and he knew it; but he had little taste for democracy and no real affinity for politics; so that, when the two combined against him, as they did in the aftermath of the Jay Treaty, everything that was peremptory and male in his nature was aroused to do battle. He had already endured the mortifying experience of being stoned from the platform when he attempted to defend a treaty which he may have secretly despised:[28] and it was not likely that he would forgive the Livingstons, either for refusing to retire from politics at his bidding, or for taking the popular side, against all his calamitous notions of what was becoming in the wealthy and the well-born. One can well believe that their posing as tribunes of the people against Jay and the administration, even though he had now resigned from it, was peculiarly galling: and it is entirely possible that Edward Livingston was not exaggerating when he said that Hamilton, confronted with some of the more lively members of the clan, had descended to language that would have become a street bully.

The Chancellor at this time never held a Chancery Court in New York between June and October. Secluded at Clermont, he left the personalities of the conflict to younger men. "Aristides" had been a politician; but "Cato" aspired to be a statesman.

VII

Victrix causa diis placuit, sed victa Catoni. What ironical spirit had presided over the Chancellor's choice of this stern cognomen? For certainly "Cato" fought upon the losing side. The treaty was ratified; it survived, with all its deplorable weaknesses, the most brilliant and vivid debates in the early history of the House of Representatives; and Jay remained to govern the State of New York for yet another term. When the election of 1798 drew near, the Chancellor received at last a compliment which he had long thought to be his due; but which, when it came, he accepted only as an empty one. He was nominated by the Republicans in the Legislature as Jay's opponent for the governorship. The manor-Clermont feud had, it is true, at last been settled; the Livingston-Clinton alliance, therefore, was probably as symmetrical as it could ever hope to be: but Livingston himself was a determined and outspoken friend to France, and Francophile sentiment, even among Republicans, was beginning to wear thin. France had chosen or been forced—as she was so often in the future to choose or be forced—to counteract British piracies on the high seas with certain measures that were no less piratical, at least as far as American shipping was concerned. Moreover, she had broken off diplomatic relations with the United States. It required no very skillful reading of the omens to predict a victory for Governor Jay.

None the less, it has been stated that Livingston's candidacy was a dash for the presidency; that "he reasoned, as every ambitious New York statesman has reasoned from that day to this, that if he could carry the State in an off year, he would be needed in a presidential year."[29] This was written long before the mass of the Chancellor's papers came to light; and the evidence in his papers, collated with other documents only recently accessible, seems to point, if anywhere, to an opposite conclusion.

It is true that he was not indifferent to the governorship—no Livingston could have been: but when he was interested in anything very close to his ambitions, he was the last man to refrain, sooner or later, from betraying his interest in some vehement and impulsive way. His name was mentioned, as it had been in every election: but it was not until February 19, 1798, that he wrote to De Witt Clinton to enquire what steps were being taken with regard to the election in May. "If any determination is to take place," he said, "it shd. certainly not be delayed to so distant a period as to prevent all exertion—I do not say this because of any personal anxiety on a matter of the most perfect indifference, but I find a very general wish to know the intentions of the politicians at head quarters." In the "old," or southern, counties, there had been, he believed, a great change in sentiment; but whether these counties "could ballance the new ones I know not."[30] The settlers from New England, streaming into the north and west of the state, were all Federalist. One need not be unduly suspicious to detect, in this profession of indifference, a certain anxiety; and he asked his bailiff, Dr. Wilson, to sound out the feelings of the people in his own neighborhood.[31] The answer was hardly reassuring: but the anxiety had been mild.

De Witt Clinton replied on March 2, that, after several conferences, the Republicans in the Legislature had that evening nominated Livingston for governor, and had chosen as lieutenant governor none other than Stephen Van Rensselaer, who had been Jay's running mate in 1792 and 1795, who was again on the Federalist ticket, and whom the Chancellor regarded as an enemy. This nomination had been made, said Clinton rather lamely, "to lull the exertions of himself & his friends." He could only hope, he added, that Livingston would consent to accept the nomination for himself; and could only trust, considering the Federalism that was rampant in the north and west, that "the attempt is not a *forlorn hope*. My invariable maxim has hitherto been *nil desperandum*."[32]

From all this, it seems obvious that the Chancellor scarcely lifted a finger to advance his cause in Albany; and that only the thought that he could hardly turn his back upon a fight with John Jay had permitted him to accept a nomination that carried with it the name of Stephen Van Rensselaer. He replied on March 7, in the most laconic manner. "As far as I can learn," he said, "great animosity will prevail." And he added that nothing could be "more gloomy than the prospect of our affairs with France."[33] Thereafter, except for a certain natural concern about the vote among his tenants and neighbors, he did not betray, or, at any rate, has left no evidence of betraying, the faintest interest in what was going on.[34] With the middle of April came the story of the XYZ scandal, which intensified feeling against France, and ruined whatever chance Livingston might have had; but by the middle of April, he was, as in fact he always had been, only a nominal candidate. Anyone who has studied the Chancellor's character could say, with some measure of certainty, that if he had had presidential ambitions in 1798, he would have behaved in a very different manner.

The campaign itself was listless; the press was almost silent. The issues, such as they were, were confined to accusing Jay of extravagance and the Chancellor of Jacobinism. The former was a monarchist; the latter was numbered among the *sans-culottes* and the revolutionaries. When all the votes had been counted, around the middle of June, it was found that Jay had won by a majority of 2,380—the greatest majority ever polled up to that time in the history of the state.

VIII

It requires only a cursory reading of Livingston's two extant letters of this year to De Witt Clinton to see why he was not personally engaged in the election of 1798. Both letters show an intense anxiety, not over the governorship, but over a bill which was presented to the New York Assembly by Samuel Latham Mitchill, and which was designed to repeal an act of 1787 giving John Fitch sole rights to use steamboats on the Hudson. Instead, Chancellor Livingston was to be given the privilege for twenty years, provided he could within a year build a boat of twenty tons and propel it by steam at the rate of four miles an hour. Mitchill was a professor at Columbia, a philosopher, scientist, teacher, and critic, "the friend of Joseph Priestley, the author of scientific essays, and the first in America to make mineralogical explorations." He was an ardent supporter of Thomas Jefferson, because Jefferson was a philosopher: "for the same reason he became the personal friend of Chancellor Livingston, with whom, among other things, he founded the Society for the Promotion of Agriculture, Manufactures, and the Useful Arts [*sic*]. It was said of Mitchill that he was equally at home in studying the geology of Niagara, or the anatomy of an egg; in offering suggestions as to the angle of a windmill, or the shape of a gridiron: in deciphering a Babylonian brick, or in advising how to apply steam to navigation."[35]

Only such a man could have presented such a bill, which invariably, like Hephaestus among the Gods, excited the deathless laughter of the members of the Assembly. Never had the Chancellor appeared more shallow or more visionary to his contemporaries; never had he been more serious. The fact that the steamboat was infinitely more important to him than the governorship in 1798, when the steamboat was held to be a chimaera and the governorship was at least an intelligible objective, shows in what direction he had developed since the days when he had called himself "Aristides." That direction was not political: but it may perhaps be called typical.

CHAPTER THREE

Anyone who studies the *Minutes* of the Chancellor's court will make the discovery that, year by year, certain changes were taking place which might be described as antipolitical. Originally, the terms of the court were held on the third Tuesday in October, the last Tuesday in December, and the last Tuesday in March in New York; and on the third Tuesday in July in Albany. Sittings in Albany were few—in twenty-three years, the court sat there only fifty-three times: the bulk of the court's business was done in New York. On December 28, 1797, it was ordered in the Chancellor's "Rules and Orders" that the stated terms of the court should be held on the first Tuesday in May, the first Tuesday in December, and the third Tuesday in February in New York, and on the first Tuesday in July in Albany. The effect of this change in the rules was to sanction what had already been going on—namely, that the Chancellor held his court (which he had a perfect right to do out of term) more and more frequently at Clermont.[1]

Whatever changes in the nature of Chancery business were reflected in this alteration of the rules, or whatever relation it had, if indeed it had any, to the prevalence of yellow fever in New York City during the hot weather, it certainly answered to Livingston's own predilections and to his idea of himself as a chancellor. Jabez D. Hammond was a contemporary of Livingston's who consulted those who knew him before committing himself in his *History of Political Parties in the State of New-York*. He says that Livingston was "perhaps defective in that intense, persevering application to study absolutely necessary in order to sustain and retain a high standing among the legal profession as a jurist"; and adds that he was said to be one of the most eloquent, agreeable, and fascinating men of his day. The portrait is distinctly social and successful.[2] Nor does one need much insight, after a study of the Chancellor's papers, to see that, while he was a conscientious jurist, he was apt to think of the Chancellorship in social terms. And nothing, one has a right to believe, could have satisfied him more than to hold his court in his own mansion, built in 1793, and in the middle of his own estates.

In 1797, when there were twenty-three hearings at Clermont between July 23 and November 27, Nathan Pendleton remarked on the difficulty and expense of employing counsel to attend a single motion at such a distance, and in 1799, Aaron Burr ventured "to take the liberty to suggest the propriety of requiring an eight day *notice date* for all motions to be made at Clermont." One supposes that there were other complaints. In summer, the traveler went from New York to Clermont by public or private stage over abominable roads, or else by sloop. It was at least a two days' bruising journey by land: by water, if the weather were bad or the wind unfavorable, it could take as long as four days, and even longer. In winter, unless and until there was a good fall of snow for sledding, one could not get there at all: the great river was frozen over, the roads had ceased to exist. There were fifty-three hearings at Clermont between July 5 and November 29, 1799: and in 1800, there were twenty between December 26 and February 20, and sixty between June 2 and December 23.[3]

In 1799, there was some grumbling because the Chancellor refused to attend the Legislature at Albany for more than a week.[4] No doubt it was not too pleasant for him to linger there, or work in the Council of Revision, so long as John Jay was governor, since the two were not properly on speaking terms: but the real significance of these grumblings was that they were aimed at a man who was politically in retreat. At Clermont especially, presiding over his own court in his private fastness, the Chancellor might have embodied that *political* union of landlord and jurist which Cadwallader Colden had so feared in the colonial days: might have, but did not.

He had already begun to delegate his political ambitions to his youngest brother Edward. Since Edward was so much the younger of the two, and since the Chancellor's whole family consisted of two daughters, the relationship between them was at first very much that of father and son. The Chancellor criticized and scolded his youngest brother with a freedom he would never have ventured to use toward the other two; and not the less freely because he perceived that Edward had some of his own traits, which now presented themselves as shortcomings. The boy "has genious enough," he said, "to make a great figure," but suffered from a "habitual indolence."[5] Moreover, no sooner had he set foot in the post-Revolutionary world than he became one of the most fashionable young men there, as the Chancellor had been in the colonial world, but displaying—much to the distress of the elder brother, who was meticulous in such matters—remarkably little aptitude for managing his financial affairs.

In appearance, Edward Livingston might be described as a *beau laid*. His high-domed head, his long concave nose, his wide mouth, his expression of quizzical amusement, gave him a most engaging ugliness; and he was, by all accounts, one of the truly fascinating men of his time. A brilliant mind, an eloquent tongue, an agreeable fondness for female companionship, a delight in dazzling clothes: these qualities and tastes were summed up in his nickname, "Beau Ned." He stalked through the last years of the eighteenth century like some tall, comical, gorgeous male bird; but the appearance was deceptive. He had been trained for the bar, and had grasped all the minutiae of a legal education with such ease that on April 24, 1786, he was accorded the rare privilege of being admitted, after examination, to practice in the Chancery Court both as solicitor and as counsel. This was not due to nepotism; the Chancellor admitted James Kent without an examination at all: it was a tribute to his gifts. And as the years went on, it became more and more clear that under the agreeable surface lay something fine and formidable: for the dandy imperfectly concealed a serious personage who was to become one of the great legal minds of his day and who was to advance in the Jacksonian world to secretary of State.[6]

In 1794, Edward Livingston was elected to the House of Representatives; he was re-elected in 1796; and again in 1798; and his dashing assaults on the Jay Treaty and the Alien and Sedition Acts marked him out as one of the leaders of the Republicans. That a Livingston should have political *flair* was not yet surprising: what *was* surprising was the lengths to which this particular Livingston was prepared to go. Nobody displayed with more success such extremes of behavior: he lived, said one of his fellow legislators, "like a nabob"; he talked like a Jacobin. He had swallowed without difficulty the most exciting tenets of agrarian democracy; he had inwardly digested (unlike many democrats) even the more indigestible doctrines of the French Revolution; and among "the mechanicks and cartmen" of New York, he was exceedingly popular. Nor was his easy conversion to the Republican church due, as was the Chancellor's, to an innate conservatism. Edward Livingston was a temperamental radical, a born Romantic—a younger son of good family and high fine manners, who seemed to dedicate himself to the undoing of his own order, and who bodied forth, therefore, in his own brilliant way, one aspect of the decline of aristocracy in New York. Was not that decline to be observed (except by the aristocrats) everywhere: in the uneasy political alliance of the Livingstons with the Clintonians, in their uneasy political quarrel with Schuyler and Van Rensselaer, in the increase in the number of yeoman farmers, in the flood of immigrants into the fee simple north and west, in the rent wars already renewed along the borders of the manor? Even in the political faineance of the Chancellor?[7]

To Edward, the Chancellor sent a request that he must be sure to write punctually from Congress, "as it is a kind of reflection to one of my standing in the political world not to have the earliest & the best intelligence." This was in 1795. Politics were already becoming, for him, not a matter of power, but a matter of status.[8]

II

He had now made up the old quarrel with the manor family. This was due partly to the death of Robert Livingston, Jr., the third and last Lord of the Manor, which left the manor sons without a leader; and partly to the financial embarrassments of Walter Livingston, the ablest of the sons. Walter Livingston's relations with William Duer, already recorded, had been both optimistic and complex, as would have to be the case where Duer was concerned. When the whole extent of his involvement was calculated, he admitted that he had endorsed Duer's notes to the extent of $375,000: and Duer had left with him, as partial security for this immense sum, certain lands which he held under judgment in Tioga and Herkimer counties.[9]

When the crash came, Duer's creditors pressed hard on Walter Livingston, and it seemed for a while as if the worst would happen: as if he would either have to join Duer in a debtor's gaol or lose his portion of the manor estates. With an adroitness which his creditors did not relish and which the manor tenants, when they heard of it, celebrated with lawsuits and riots, he managed to convey these estates to his brother Henry Livingston and his son-in-law Philip Henry Livingston; he then tried to disentangle himself by selling the Tioga and Herkimer lands. The Herkimer lands were the more immediately salable, but the sheriff there, with Walter Livingston's execution in his hands, was prevented from selling by injunctions unfairly obtained by Duer's friends from one of the clerks in Chancery, without the Chancellor's knowledge. Indeed, up to 1794, the Chancery Court had offered no relief to Walter Livingston.[10]

Then, in the summer of 1794, an action for dissolving the latest Herkimer injunction was heard by the Chancellor at Clermont. This led to the first friendly exchange in many a day between Walter Livingston and his kinsman.

Dear Sir [wrote Walter], The enclosed notice of trial I recd. this day from my council, Mr. B. Livingston, who desires me to send it to you for information. Should it not be convenient for you to attend to business on that day any other time that you may appoint will be equally agreeable to me, and I will notify my Council accordingly—If it is consistent with the rules of your Court to postpone the trial until Saturday next it will be more satisfactory to me, as I daily expect the death of my brother R.C.L. [Robert Cambridge Livingston] every hour, his fever continues unremitting—Feeling myself interested in the welfare of your children and hearing that your youngest daughter has been very ill, I would be glad to know if the fever is broke.

Dear Sir [was the reply], The hearing will suit me as well on Wednesday as at any other time out of term nor can it conveniently be postponed without giving a new notice as the Council [Counsel] will have to attend here—I am extremely sorry to learn of your brother's situation & obliged by your inquiries about my daughters health. Her fever remitted all day yesterday but has returned this morning & continues yet—I am Sir, with regard, your most obd. hum: Svt.[11]

Thus the ice was broken. On Wednesday, August 27, 1794, the hearing was held. Walter Livingston's counsel was the Anti-Federalist John Bay, instructed by Brockholst Livingston, the future justice of the United States Supreme Court, who had once been distrusted by the whole manor family but who was now coming into his own. The trial had a distinctly family appearance, being held in the heart of the Livingston country, with a Livingston as appellant and a Livingston on the bench: but if the Chancellor had disqualified himself every time one of his name was involved in Chancery proceedings, he might just as well have ceased to be Chancellor. In this instance, he "readily" dissolved the injunction, but on terms which made it impossible for Walter Livingston to attend the Herkimer sale and bid up the price: nothing would have induced him to grant his kinsman an extralegal favor. None the less, any dissolution was better than none, and Walter was duly grateful.[12]

In 1795, after setting forth his rights in an immense letter, the Chancellor offered to settle the gristmill dispute on terms so reasonable that they could not be refused; and so the last barrier was broken down, and the Clermont and manor families were on visiting terms again.[13] That this reconciliation should be sealed by marriage was quite in accordance with the Livingston tradition: and so, on November 17, 1799, the Chancellor's elder daughter, Elizabeth, was married to Edward Philip Livingston, a grandson of the signer of the Declaration of Independence, and great-grandson of the second Lord of the Manor. She had been preceded to the altar on July 8, 1798, by her younger sister, Margaret Maria. Margaret

Maria, the family beauty, married Robert L. Livingston, son of Walter Livingston, who had died in 1797 with his estate almost free from embarrassments. On this occasion, the bridegroom's uncle Henry, who had been one of the most determined of the Chancellor's detractors in the days of their family dispute, wrote to say that only "a Damn Black Eye which will not suffer me to go into genteel Company" would prevent his being present. "I would have lossed an Eye, if I could only make this one decent now," he wrote, "that I might attend your Nuptials." Nothing makes it clearer that the standing of the Clermont family was now as high with its manor relatives as even the Chancellor could have wished. If the quarrel had been settled, at some earlier date, if it had been settled as early as 1791, what a change it might have made in the Chancellor's political fortunes! He might then have led a united family into the Clintonian camp. But now he made up in prestige for what he had lost in politics: it had become a fair exchange.[14]

III

In 1793, the Chancellor's new mansion at Clermont was finished; and in the summer of 1794, a few months before Mr. Strickland's visit, water was brought into its cellar "in pipes of a proper bore and dimensions Laid at least two feet under the ground." The pipe-layer, Ebenezer White, received $10 and a tract of one hundred and sixty acres near the east branch of the Delaware. It was in this way that great landlords settled their accounts.[15] From this new mansion, whose library served as a Chancery Court, the Chancellor traveled in the autumn down the Hudson to New York and his handsome residence on the Bowling Green; and from this new mansion in the summer, he drove out, when the roads permitted, in his chariot with four matched white horses, postilions, and outriders, to visit his neighbors.

The world of Clermont was, and remained, relatively pastoral, with the anomaly of slaveholding in its midst, and a certain harshness always present in its leases.[16] The Chancellor was now beginning to import into it a sort of personal splendor which his father would have thought unnecessary, and which seemed to increase in proportion as he became more and more alienated from the political world. He emphasized it in other ways. When the New York Society for the Promotion of Agriculture, Arts and Manufactures, organized in 1791, was incorporated by an act of March 12, 1793, he became its first president. Its original membership was seventy-two; no one could be a member unless elected by a majority of all the members; and no one but a gentleman farmer or a solid professional man ever was elected.[17] The Society's *Transactions*, mainly agricultural, did not, perhaps, enjoy a wide circulation among the small independent and tenant farmers, most of whom could not read, and who, when they could read, entertained a decided aversion for "book" farming. But the popularity of lucerne and of gypsum was said to be due to the Society's efforts: and upon these two subjects the Chancellor was always eloquent.[18]

To be president of such a society had, in fact, a peculiar appeal for him as a landowner, a scientist, and a gentleman. The Society was useful, there was no doubt of that: the agricultural world of New York had an increasing market in New York City; and the Albany and Hudson sloops, loaded with produce, often went directly to the West Indies or even farther. One could not observe the depletion of New York soils with equanimity, even though wastefulness was held to be one of the conditions of American farming; and the Society was one of the early champions of soil conservation.[19] The Chancellor, moreover, knew enough about chemistry to be able to read and understand every book on the subject that came his way; and the results appeared on his experimental farm and in his speeches and writings for the Society. But there was more to this than mere usefulness. He was not simply a benevolent local magnate, anxious to improve his own lands and those of his neighbors; experimental farming was becoming, had already become, one of the vocations of a more intelligent section of English aristocracy; and English aristocracy, even among Anglophobes like the Chancellor, had a strange but perhaps, in agricultural matters, a deserved prestige. To be a practical farmer of progressive views—surely this was one of the duties of an enlightened landed gentleman.

While Livingston was its president, the Society flourished; it was only after he had left for France that its numbers dwindled and its meetings and *Transactions* languished. He had brought to it not only his administrative gifts, which were considerable, not only his enthusiasm, which was contagious, but also the compelling presence of a self-image.

IV

It was not a delusive image. Natural philosophy had always fascinated him. Perhaps he was never happier than when, for example, he was discoursing to Arthur Young on some possible relationship between the sulphuric acid in powdered gypsum and certain alkaline vapors or gases afloat in the atmosphere. It had occurred to him that between them they might form salts which pass into the composition of plants and that "these salts in their solution seize upon a certain portion of the caloric in the air, destroy its elasticity, compel it to deposit the infinite variety of matters that are borne upon it or dissolved in it and perhaps decompound the air itself, and render it, or part of it, food for plants."[20] The high wild note of enthusiasm sounds faintly but clearly in this restrained passage.

Eighteenth-century gentlemen did not waste much time upon the physical beauty of the visible world: or, rather, they responded to it most keenly when it seemed to float before them like some divine laboratory; and, unless they were poets, and not always then, never came closer to poetry than when they were behaving like chemists or engineers or archaeologists. Everything that the Chancellor's opponents called "visionary" (that is, impulsive, inconsistent, and absurd in his political behavior) seemed to justify itself when it was not being given a political expression. He was certainly not visionary to the extent of forgetting that theories ought to be verified by experiments and that experiments could be profitable. "After all," he wrote, at the end of his letter to Young, "I consider this as a mere System, like all other Systems to be viewed as the sport of imagination unless so far as it shall appear to be confirmed by experiments." And of what use was an experiment if it did not increase the yield of wheat or raise the height of clover?

Yet the sport of imagination was there. Once, on a shooting party on the Hudson flats, the Chancellor noticed a river weed called conserva, which was locally known as "frog's spit" and which looked like paper. It not only looked like paper but, except for an unfortunate brittleness, it acted like paper. Suppose it were properly triturated, would it not then produce a material that would have all the useful properties of paper but that could be manufactured at one-tenth the cost? Visions of considerable profits danced before the Chancellor's eyes: but what really moved him was the thought that he might have extracted from a common river weed values that no man had perceived there before.[21]

It so happened that he had a protégé, a gentleman who was prepared to combine the functions of courtier, apprentice, and familiar spirit, and who, as so often happens in such cases, acted as an extension of the fantastic side of his patron. This gentleman was a certain Pierre Delabigarre, a French *émigré*, who had settled near Clermont with the idea of building on the banks of the Hudson an ideal colony, to be called Tivoli. The site he had chosen was unusually steep; but plazas that should spill down a hillside or streets with a gradient of one in two did not deter M. Delabigarre, who seemed to think them an incentive to high living.[22] In the meantime, he had come to the attention of his powerful neighbor, whom he called his Maecenas, and to whom he offered the meed of a high-flown but respectful applause. *"Cher Moecene,"* one finds him writing from New York in 1794, *"Vous êtes bien heureux au Sein de la paix et de l'étude de la nature, le monde savant a été singulièrement frappé de vos nouvelles observations sur les effets de la Lumière relative aux plantes. . . . Continuez, cher Moecene, de vous immortaliser par vos Découvertes et vos Recherches."** This was consoling to a man who had only recently buried "Aristides"; and what country gentleman, who had read his *Eclogues* and his *Georgics,* or perused his Horace, would object to being called Maecenas?[23]

All in all, Delabigarre was an innocent and artless enthusiast: but here he struck, as deftly as Marbois had once touched it in the days of the Continental Congress, precisely the chord which Livingston most wanted to hear. The Chancellor had long been interested in the baleful effects of the shade of some trees "upon the vegetation of corn." He had consequently planted some maize on the west side of a young wood consisting of oaks, poplars, a few chestnuts, and a large mulberry; and, after careful observation, he had communicated his findings to that universal savant Dr. Samuel L. Mitchill. The shade, made by the rising sun, extended at its fullest nearly across the field, and did not vanish until 10:00 A.M. As far as the shade of the chestnuts reached, the corn was extremely injured; that of the black oaks was less injurious; the poplar shade did very little harm; and the corn under the mulberry shade was small but healthy. This could not be due to mere absence of light and heat, or the trees would have been equally harmful; nor could it be traced to the droppings from trees, since the corn grew under none but the mulberry's. As for effluvia, said the Chancellor, these would either be "smelled in circles," or wafted irregularly by the wind. Could it be that the damage was due, not to the shade at all, but to those rays of light which passed through the trees and which either perforated the leaves or were brought into contact with them? Could it be that the light served both as an agent for dissolving "certain parts" of the tree noxious to corn, and also as a vehicle to convey them in the direction of the rays, which must necessarily be that of the shade? What important discoveries did not this idea, if just, open before the philosophical eye! What medical purposes might not be served! Physicians might once again claim Apollo for their patron, and instead of "pills &

* "Dear Maecenas, You are very happy in the bosom of peace and of the study of nature, the learned world has been singularly struck with your new observations on the effects of light upon plants. . . . Continue, dear Maecenas, to earn immortality by your discoveries and researches."

boluses they shall prescribe Zephyrs & sunbeams." Such experiments and meditations as these occupied the Chancellor's leisure hours.[24]

Delabigarre was, of course, a visitor to Clermont, and sometimes Livingston would condescend to dine with his protégé in his "thatched retreat," which lay just beyond the Clermont demesne: and there he would confide to him even his most unlikely schemes. To the projector of Tivoli, however, no project could seem unlikely. And so, having triturated his conserva with a mortar and sieve and produced a substance not unlike paper, the Chancellor left the rest of the experiment up to Delabigarre. Armed with eighty pounds of river weed, the Frenchman set out for Major Pitkin's paper mill at Catskill. The workmen there would at first have nothing to do with him, but yielded at last to his persuasions "& a few gallons of brandy." Because their vessels were too large for his quantity of material, "& indeed as he wished at all events to save himself from ridicule (a number of Gents. attending to see the experiment) by making paper of some sort," he was obliged to make the trial with ten pounds of rags of the worst kind added to his eighty pounds of conserva. Whatever the workmen and the gentlemen may have thought, the result exceeded, at any rate, both his expectations and those of the Chancellor. "I am not without hope," wrote the latter, "that the conserva (for such I believe it to be) which I apply to this use is peculiar to our country. If so we may undersell the world in paper."[25]

A patent was prepared. "Various attempts, as you well know," Livingston wrote to Timothy Pickering, "have been made by the philosophers of Europe to find some cheap substitute for rags but hitherto without success—I believe that I have been more fortunate." And the patent was duly signed, on October 28, 1799, by John Adams, Timothy Pickering, and Charles Lee. Some fragments of this plausible material have been preserved among the Chancellor's papers. His brother-in-law John Stevens, who had an inventive genius and an independent mind, thought that it might possibly become a substitute for wrapping paper but could not, on the whole, hold out much hope for it; and John Stevens seems to have been right. In 1800, even Delabigarre, whose numerous embarrassments had at length confined him to the debtors' gaol at Poughkeepsie (whence the Chancellor rescued him in the course of time), was obliged to confess that nothing would come of it. "We meet," he said, "with unbelievers & prejudiced minds, notwithstanding everyone affects in your presence or before me to think that this conserva will do well enough." And so no more was heard of conserva.[26]

This adventure is worth narrating if only because it shows that there was apt to be an element of the fantastic in the Chancellor's schemes. Yet what is fantasy today may be fact tomorrow; and what charms the student of Livingston's career is his willingness to surrender to fantasy in his experiments. It was in 1797 that he first began to think seriously about the steamboat. In this he was abetted by his brother-in-law John Stevens, who had long been an enthusiast, and who had observed the brilliant experiments of John Fitch and of Rumsey with all the impatience and anxiety of a born inventor. At this time, the steamboat was almost universally considered a nonsensical project.

A lack of ready money had deterred John Fitch and James Rumsey, and had also deterred John Stevens. He had inherited a great deal of property in New Jersey from his father, as had his sister, the Chancellor's wife, Mary Stevens Livingston. But the property, neglected during the Revolution, was still sadly underdeveloped and encumbered with debts; returns were relatively small; and the land-poor Stevens was usually in the condition, not in itself unusual, of floating through the world on a cloud of his own promissory notes.[27] The Chancellor, therefore, whose estate was both larger and far better managed, was expected to provide the more solid financing. His cash reserves were often small, but his credit was excellent: as, indeed, it would have to be where such a venture as the steamboat was concerned.

He was not content to be merely a financier: far from it. As he told Dr. Joseph Priestley, "mechanicks is my hobby horse"; he had found time, in the midst of his other pursuits, to read every available book on the subject; and it was as a pioneer inventor that he proposed, in 1797, to enter into a partnership with John Stevens and with Nicholas J. Roosevelt, who had a foundry in New Jersey at what was then Soho, on the Second River, and what is now Belleville, on the Passaic.[28]

The history of steamboat invention was by no means new, and, if the genius of John Fitch had not been totally deficient in the exacting art of calculating costs and cajoling entrepreneurs, it might have already passed or been passing out of the peculiar Nephelococcygia, the realm of clouds and cuckoos, to which eighteenth-century common sense had hitherto consigned it. Innumerable problems vexed the would-be designer: but chief among them was the question of building, on the one hand, a boat not too heavy to be propelled by available machinery and, on the other, of creating a machine light enough not to sink the boat. No doubt, everything would have been simplified if it had been possible to obtain a Boulton & Watt engine from England: but here the mercantilism of the British Government interposed its dour visage. No valuable inventions could be exported.

It says much for the Chancellor and his associates that they refused to be daunted either by these considerations or by the ridicule of their contemporaries. Livingston, indeed, was never more himself than under circumstances such as these; his vaulting imagination and his fertile mind were equally challenged; and even before his steamboat bill had been passed through a jocose Legislature in March, 1798, he had expected to have a working boat on the Hudson. The problem of propulsion had no difficulties for him. A horizontal wheel, hung below the keel, and driven from the engine by a vertical spindle, would, he was convinced, do the work: while his boat, contrived originally (he told Roosevelt in December, 1797) for a horse machine, was built "on perfectly new principles which both in the model & one on a large scale has exceeded my expectations."[29]

Roosevelt had in his employment two English mechanics, named Smallman and Standinger, who had some knowledge of the Boulton & Watt engine and who might—though the difficulties of production were immense—produce something like it at the Second River foundry. Neither was impressed by the Chancellor, who was happier with theories than with tools, and who was perhaps unduly irritated by a cautious reception of his ideas. "Everyone," said Standinger, "has a certain portion of philauty, and rich people particularly, they are not used to hear the truth."[30] Roosevelt was of a like mind: his stubborn Dutch nature did not take kindly to the Chancellor's rather offhand and peremptory approach to problems of great complexity.

None the less, if it had not been for Livingston's enthusiasm and the torrent of his ideas, not to mention his credit and his capital, it is doubtful if Roosevelt and Stevens would have gone into steamboat construction, though Stevens had been thinking about it for many years. At any rate, an agreement was reached in April, 1798; and all that remained was to put a boat on the river within the term specified by law. Here, as was only natural, there were disagreements: Roosevelt was attracted to the idea of propulsion by means of "two wheels of wood over the sides fashioned to the axes of the flys with 8 arms or paddles," Stevens favored elliptical paddle wheels, while Livingston clung stubbornly to his belief in a horizontal wheel beneath the keel.[31]

As to the construction of the engine, their differences were acute, but in the end this was left to Roosevelt and his workmen, while Livingston was permitted to retain his horizontal wheel. The boat was built, the machinery installed, the great day—after many postponements—was set for early August, and M. Delabigarre had prepared a small battery of guns at Red Hook which would salute the new invention with a *feu de joie* as she moved up the river toward the Clermont landing. But, alas, it was discovered that the ship was quite incapable of movement of any kind. Could it be that the engine was too weak to turn the Chancellor's wheel? Or was the Chancellor's wheel so geared for speed that three-quarters of the power was lost? Roosevelt was convinced that the wheel was to blame; Livingston assailed the engine, and in language so intemperate that for a while it seemed as if the association must come to an end.[32] An apology was offered and received; further experiments were made; and in October, with the Spanish Minister on board, and with the Chancellor's wheel beneath, the ship proceeded out of Soho at a rate of one mile an hour against wind and tide, or three miles an hour in still water.[33] Whether she could ever steam *up* the Hudson at the rate of four miles an hour was now an academic question: but the Chancellor was undaunted. He wanted her "instantly" fitted up for passengers, with a back cabin for the ship's company. "We have got one month to use," he wrote on October 28, "and a pretty important one because the roads will soon be bad, and tho' we should only go 3 miles an hour we shall still be able to pick up something beside our expences and acquire some experience of what further is necessary. I have provided a Captain at £5 a month—you say you have a steward and fire engine hand. . . ."[34]

In the end, Roosevelt, after agreeing to bring the ship to Clermont, declined to move her at all: the month was November, and one can but applaud his prudence. "You designed . . . a compliment to my patience & philosophy," said the Chancellor.[35] He was determined to get a new law passed in his favor the next year.

V

Early the next year, he became involved in something which might uncharitably be called an escapade but which must charitably be ascribed to his inventive passions. The story of the Manhattan Company is one of the strangest passages in New York financial history; and although it has recently been given a brilliant and detailed reconstruction, much of it is still conjectural.[36] Aaron Burr was deeply involved in it, and Aaron Burr was pursued by conjecture, as by his own shadow.

The Manhattan Company, one of the progenitors of what is now the Chase-Manhattan Bank, was originally and ostensibly designed to supply New York City with "pure and wholesome" water. Upon this understanding, a committee of six prominent New Yorkers, among them Alexander Hamilton, was persuaded by Burr to go before the Common Council and plead its cause; a directorate of twelve persons, including three leading Federalists and six Republican merchants in excellent standing, was chosen to manage its affairs; and a number of gentlemen, both Federalist and Republican, agreed to subscribe for shares in advance. The cause was a worthy one, or, if not worthy, then laudable; or at least apparently laudable toward the end of March, 1799, when Aaron Burr left New York for Albany, where he was to guide the incorporating bill through the Legislature. In Albany, he made one change in the company's charter, which he may or may not have confided to his associates before he left New York: upon this question the evidence is obscure to the point of nonexistence. He added an eighth section, which read as follows:

It may be and shall be lawful for the said company to employ all such surplus capital as may accrue to the said company in the purchase of public or other stock or in any other monied transactions or operations not inconsistent with the constitution and laws of this state or of the United States, for the sole benefit of the said company.[37]

This was a sweeping, indeed, an unprecedented grant of powers. Ever since the English Bubble Act of 1720, incorporation had been strictly limited, not in a positive, but in a negative way. What a corporation might do was unclear, what it might not do was set forth in severe detail. In the latter respect, Section VIII of the new charter was, to say the least, unusual: what the company might do, what it might not do—each aspect of its activities melted into a limitless haze.

Burr steered the bill through the Legislature with his customary skill. To the Federalists, one must suppose, for all is supposition, he pointed out that the bill had solid Federalist backing: or, conversely, that if it was a Republican bill, then it could not be directed toward serious banking, for the Republicans hitherto had not been very friendly toward banks. As for the Republicans, he was himself still a leading Republican, and that in itself might have been enough. Whatever his maneuvers were, they sufficed: and on April 2, 1799, "an Act for supplying the city of New York with pure and wholesome water" was presented to the Council of Revision.

Here the controlling Section VIII was attacked in the most vigorous terms by Chief Justice Lansing, both as a democrat who suspected all banking procedures and as an eighteenth-century jurist to whom banking was a quasi-public enterprise to be hedged about with the thorniest safeguards. The water company to be incorporated, he said, would have a capital of $2,000,000, the surplus of which might be applied "to trade or any other purpose which the very comprehensive terms in which this clause is conceived may warrant." This was a most speculative venture. It demanded "the application of the policy which has heretofore uniformly obtained; that the powers of corporations relative to their money operations, should be of limited instead of perpetual duration." The proposed company's powers were to be perpetual.[38]

Livingston, whose appearances at the Council had been infrequent, made a point of attending on April 2; and, with the help of Justice Benson, was able to overrule the objections of the Chief Justice. Governor Jay was also present but did not say a word. He was supposed to have supported Lansing, but it was claimed that "he had no vote," although, according to the constitution of 1777, a vote was what he had. Thus, with the help of the Republican Chancellor, the Federalist Benson, and the silent Jay, the bill became law, except for the formality of the Governor's signature, which he could not refuse: and a water company had become, to all intents and purposes, a banking institution.[39]

Some two weeks later, on April 17, writing in a genial vein to Nicholas Roosevelt, the Chancellor said that "the Water Work charter has . . . passed & is the most liberal granted by the State since it is for ever[,] & gives them the right to use their capital as they please *in any monied operation whatever*. I would advise you and your friends to get as large a share of it as you can."[40] On April 22, the stock of the Manhattan Company was to be offered for public sale.[41]

On May 16, a writer who called himself "Socrates" published in the New York *Commercial Advertiser* a series of "Interrogatories to be administered to the Lord High Chancellor of the State of Manhattan," in which he asked the Chancellor if it was true that he had subscribed $100,000 to the Manhattan Company, and if he had reserved the right not to take up his shares until their price on the market had been established. "Socrates" certainly betrayed in his letter an insufficient knowledge of the scope and functions of a Chancery Court, and he had refrained from mentioning that the right not to take up shares belonged to every one of the original subscribers. But the attack was a deadly one, and, what was worse, it was substantially true.[42] When he cast his vote for the company in the Council of Revision, the Chancellor had already put himself down for two thousand shares and was, along with John Swartwout, Burr's lieutenant, its leading stockholder.[43]

The Federalist Benson was severely criticized for his vote in the Council of Revision, but, except for the accusations of "Socrates," not a voice was raised in public against Livingston. No contemporary pamphleteer, no early historian, ever mentioned his name in connection with the Manhattan Company, although the company itself was freely and somewhat scandalously treated. The student of the Chancellor's career today can hardly keep silent; but, equally, he cannot help asking himself if this was not one of those hopeless inconsistencies which plague the student of any man's life, and which can best be left among the mysteries of human nature. For inconsistent it was. Livingston was extremely jealous of the good name of his court and of his own reputation as its chancellor; he had never used the Council to advance his personal interests, as distinct from the interests of his party or class; he was known to be unfriendly to the "new" moneyed interests of New York City; he had never before indulged in a paper speculation of this kind; and for the rest of his life, even in his fevered dealings with the American claimants in the days of the Louisiana Purchase, he never descended to personal jobbery.[44]

Yet one cannot escape from the fact that those gentlemen, Federalist and Republican, who were permitted to subscribe to the Manhattan Company in advance, were in a very enviable position. When its shares came on the market, it had already received its formidable charter; business in New York was booming because of the war between England and France; and those who had already subscribed could dispose of their holdings at very considerable advance. Moreover, although two thousand shares at par would have cost $100,000, the preliminary payment on April 22 was only to be $2.50 a share.[45]

One cannot say for certain that Livingston did not follow this course and dispose of his holdings at profit. There was a great demand for shares, and Burr, for example, was certainly offered a 26¼-per-cent advance if he would sell his holdings. On the other hand, one has no right to say that Livingston did anything of the kind. The record of his two thousand shares has vanished. It is known that in 1801 he owned two hundred and forty Manhattan shares; the same number of shares appear in the schedule of his personal estate which was compiled after his death; and it is entirely possible that these were all that he ever bothered to take up, and that what he lent the Manhattan Company was less his capital than his name.[46]

And for this there was a motive at least as obvious as a simple greed for profits. The Republicans contended from the beginning that the Manhattan Company was designed to break a Federalist monopoly; for the only two banks in New York City were the Bank of New York and the branch Bank of the United States, and both were managed by Federalists. In the strictest sense of the term, the Manhattan Company was not wholly Republican. The three Federalist directors remained upon its board, and Federalists were among its leading stockholders. But in a looser sense, it was Republican all the way, and when Alexander Hamilton called it, in 1801, "a perfect monster in its principles but a very convenient instrument of *profit* and *influence*," he meant, not only that he had been tricked in 1799, but also that the Manhattan Company had begun to fulfill its purpose.[47]

It is true that it would have been difficult to prove that the Federalist bankers exerted a strong political influence; in other words, that it had "become impossible for men engaged in trade to advocate republican principles, without sustaining material injury." The Federalist bankers, it has been well said, were "so exclusive, socially and commercially, that even the bulk of Federalist voters would not have qualified for bank services."[48] None the less, and perhaps because of this exclusiveness, a Republican bank could not have failed to attract votes to the Republican cause with a promise of less exclusive services.

The Chancellor, who was the best of risks both socially and commercially, kept a balance at the Bank of New York, and the Bank of New York faithfully discounted his notes: but this is not to suppose that, where so bad a risk as the steamboat was concerned, these discounts would ever have been very liberal.[49] In 1799, with the prospect of great experiments still before him, this consideration may well have been paramount. If it is difficult to suppose that in this instance he would have given his vote in Council for the sake of personal gain or political advantage, it is all too easy to believe that he would have done so for the sake of an invention. Just as he had once sacrificed the family unity to a gristmill, so now he offered the chancellorship to a steamboat, which had, in its turn, become a sacred object. Fortunately for him, the full sacrifice was not required—his reputation was not blown upon.[50]

VI

The Legislature, in the same session, also granted him a renewal of his exclusive privilege for another twenty-year term, if he could get his boat to perform within a specified number of months.[51] And now he and Stevens, through a positive blizzard of argument and counterargument, at length struggled to a union of ideas. The horizontal wheel gave way to paddles; the engine was designed to meet the Chancellor's concepts of a rotatory engine, which had derived from the experiments of a seventeenth-century savant named Dr. Barker: and they had agreed on a system of preventing friction by the introduction of mercury.[52] Mr. Roosevelt, in spite of the Chancellor's mistrust, remained at their service. In October, 1799, Livingston was able to tell Benjamin De Witt that "I have made the most important improvements [in the steam engine] & by the application of a common phisical principle . . . to mechanicks, I have remedied all the defects in Watt's engine & obtained with the same fewel & quantity of steam at least 5lb more power upon an inch that Dr. Watt has—& have not only simplified the construction of the engine but have prevented any wear of the parts. . . ." James Watt, strange to say, did not agree with this. A correspondence of a kind had been set on foot between the two men; and at long last, after more than a year of delays and misunderstandings, Watt told a friend (in a letter that was eventually forwarded to Livingston) that "I have been able to digest my thoughts on Chancellor Livingston's memorial so as to give him satisfactory reasons against the adoption of *any* of his schemes which though ingenious & founded on good principles are in my opinion not eligible & the best of them not new to me. I mean that which is similar to Sir Samuel Morland's quicksilver pump, which I attentively considered as applicable to a steam engine more than 30 years ago but abandoned it for several reasons especially the enormous expense of the mercury."[53] But the Chancellor's enthusiasm was unquenchable and his vision undimmed; and when he went to France in 1801, he was still a believer.

From France there came, in due time, a curious sequel to the distressing story of the Manhattan Company. Discussing the character of Burr with his brother-in-law John Armstrong, the Chancellor boasted that it was he and not Burr who had first conceived the idea of a water company that was also a bank.[54] How far the boast was justified, or if it was justified at all, will never be known: but the cheerfulness with which Livingston made this final connection between the chancellorship and a company-promotion scheme is certainly surprising. When he wrote, he was once again, and this time in the stimulating company of Robert Fulton, dreaming of a successful steamboat, and had already put an experimental craft upon the Seine. The historian who makes inferences from what might or might not have lain in the subconscious of any given personage is certainly far out of his depth: but one may perhaps remark on the coincidence between the boast to John Armstrong and the steamboat on the Seine.

VII

Livingston had learned some mechanical theory at the feet of Dr. Robert Harpur at King's College; the rest of his stock of information was the fruit of long hours of uninstructed reading; and it is not surprising that his ideas, although their ingenuity did him the greatest credit, should have proved to be impracticable. But if his theory was defective, his vision was not. He foresaw that the steamboat would revolutionize the river traffic of

America, and trusted to his foresight at a time when only a few choice spirits ever thought of such a vessel as anything but a monstrous and unseemly jest. The hope of personal gain entered, of course, into his schemes; but it was not at this time—if indeed it ever was—their strongest component. His inner ear was attuned to the far faery horn-call of unprofessional "philosophy." He had some of the hardness of an entrepreneur, and all the innocence of an eighteenth-century amateur; and would express his thoughts, now like a company promoter, now like a White Knight. Science, patriotism, profit were so inextricably intermingled in his thinking that it would be impossible to determine which was the uppermost as he traced his rough plans for an engine that would excel James Watt's, or, mashing his American river weed, dreamed that his country would one day undersell the world in paper. One thing, however, seems probable to the point of certainty: side by side with his chemical speculations and his more conventional experiments in agriculture, his mechanical inventions were just another feature in that magnetic image of himself which drew him farther and farther away from the world of popular politics. "I fear I tire you with my projects," he wrote to Roosevelt in 1799, "but this is no place for news and, as for the politics of the day, they are too unpleasant to be thought of. It is well we can find sources of amusement while the winter excludes us from the pleasures of gardening and agriculture."[55]

"Sources of amusement"—the phrase could have come only as a rare surprise to Mr. Roosevelt, to whom Livingston usually presented himself in his letters as a man who was importunate, arrogant, and in deadly earnest. But to other and more distinguished correspondents, he would often adopt a more modest and, no doubt, in its way, just as sincere a posture. "There is a certain degree of partiality in both heat & cold," he writes to the eminent Dr. Joseph Priestley, "which I think cannot be accounted for by the mere presence or absence of the sun or the accidental intervention of clouds or winds as the medium of heat or cold—But which I have long thought might be resolved into some chemical mixture in the great laboratory of the sky. The rapid formation or solution of salts wd. certainly produce these effects—but I must not [he adds with proper humility] treat of war before Han[n]ibal."[56] Here he is the gentleman scientist with his head in the clouds, wandering with his gun and his dog along the Via Sacra of some field at Clermont, *nescio quid meditans nugarum, totus in illis,** absorbed in trifles, but what momentous trifles!

One could never tell what might come of such exchanges. Thomas Jef-

---

* *"Ibam forte Via Sacra, sicut meus est mos Nescio quid meditans nugarum, totus in illis."* Horace, Satires I.ix. 1, 2. (I was strolling by chance along the Via Sacra, meditating after my fashion on some trifle or other, and wholly absorbed in it.)

ferson, for example, after commenting in a letter upon "the superior simplicity" of Livingston's plans for a steam engine, went on to ask if it might
not be adapted to filling a large reservoir at the tops of houses, not only
for use by pipes in the apartments, but also as a protection against fire.

> Every family has such an agent [wrote Jefferson], it's kitchen fire. it's
> small indeed, but if it's constant action could be accumulated so as to give
> a stroke from time to time which might throw ever so small a quantity of
> water from the bottom of a well to the top of the house (say 100 feet) it
> would furnish more than would waste by evaporation or be used by the
> family. I know nobody who must better know the value of such a machine
> than yourself, nor more equal to the invention of it. . . . I have imagined
> that the iron back of the chimney might be a cistern for holding the water
> which should supply steam & would be constantly kept in a boiling state
> by the ordinary fire.[57]

A month or so later, in a long letter to Sir John Sinclair, Livingston could
not help ending his remarks upon the use of mercury with these words: "I
shd. Sir perhaps apologize for having intruded so long upon your time
but I find so much pleasure in communicating my ideas that I think may
be useful to a man of science that I give myself great credit for stopping
where I do & not communicating to you another scheme by which at the
most trifling expense & the simplest machinery reservoirs of water (as a
security against fires) on the top of a house may be supplied & kept perpetually full—" The temptation to pass off one of Jefferson's ideas as his
own hung for a moment before his eyes, but it was manfully resisted.[58]

This kind of correspondence was a delight to the Chancellor. Moreover,
in America itself, where political differences were becoming dangerous, it
served as the best, or at any rate as the most dignified, social currency. To
be interested in agriculture, to promote invention—it was in such ways that
one preserved one's franchise as a patriot. Thus Livingston, after he had
declared undying warfare on Washington's administration, sent the President a copy of the New York Society's *Transactions*, together with a polite
letter as from one farming enthusiast to another; and Washington, not to
be outdone, replied with some cordial sentences and a pamphlet on potatoes.[59] With political sympathisers, one ventured upon far less solemn
and far more serious exchanges; and it is a tribute to the times that Livingston, less than a fortnight after Jefferson's inauguration, could write to the
President a long letter entirely devoted to the speculations that arose from
three teeth, "evidently the dentes incisores of some enormous carnivorous
animal," which had lately come into his possession and which had been discovered in western New York. The teeth, argued the Chancellor, prove

that the prehistoric creature which had once owned them was carnivorous but had no trunk. He must have had some substitute—his claws? his fore-feet? "A vivid imagination," said the Chancellor, who was not lacking in this respect, "may conclude from these discoveries that the animal was shaped either like a Baboon or a bear."

That the animal is extinct [he continued], we have reason to believe and certainly to wish. . . . Why Sir since the earth itself is undergoing perpetual change should we find a difficulty in believing that Nature may form animals fitted for those different situations in which they are placed by those changes or without going quite so far why may we not admit the extinction of one animal to be necessary to the increase of another better adapted to the present circumstances of the earth—Many animals if not extinct have been so altered by the labour of man that the original state cannot be traced by the most industrious naturalist—Where for instance is the dunghill fowl to be found except among the habitations of man? . . . In all parts of the globe providence has provided some means to prevent the degeneracy and per-haps the destruction of graminivorous animals that would be the consequence on their multiplication beyond their regular means of subsistence. This useful purpose was probably effected in America by the mammoth and the megalonix. . . . When a race of savage men were transplanted into our forests they were no longer necessary. . . . And we learn from you that the Indians assign as the reason for the destruction of the mammoth the havock that he made among the Bison & the deer that the great man above designed for the support of his red children.[60]

It is hardly necessary to say that Livingston had a Buffon among the works in his library; or to add that, at this period in American natural his-tory, to throw out the suggestion that a species could ever become extinct was to be daring to the point of impiety. As for the glimpses of evolution vouchsafed in this letter, they may have been remote and fantastic, but they were more daring still. They were not the less agreeable on that account to the man who read and the man who wrote them: to the President of the United States and the gentleman whom he had just appointed minister to France.

CHAPTER FOUR

W hen the Chancellor was offered and accepted the position of minister to France, the Livingstons, at long last, seemed to be swimming into power on some high tide of factional success in the politics of New York. Whether they were really swimmers, in a measure self-propelled, or whether they were merely an elegant flotsam, the victims of some predetermined scheme—such questions lead one down by easy steps into the depths of New York's character at that time: and the study of New York's character at that time resembles Virgil's *Avernus*, in the sense that it is easier to get into it than it is to get back.

II

Henry Adams, for example, declares that the moral and intellectual character of New York, although well defined in 1800, was not susceptible to definition. Low motives and gifted men; "a society, in spite of its aristocratic mixture, democratic by instinct"; an alliance with Virginia in order to promote the fortunes of Thomas Jefferson, but yet no principles of any kind—this congeries of faults and paradoxes represents less a character than a conundrum.[1] A description of the Republican elements in this society seemed to leave the conundrum darker, more puzzling than ever. "The New York Republicans," Adams writes, "were divided into three factions, represented by the Clinton, Livingston and Burr interests; and among them was so little difference in principle or morals that a politician as honest and an observer as keen as Albert Gallatin inclined to Burr as the least selfish of the three."[2]

Nobody doubts the honesty of Gallatin's politics or the keenness, in general, of his observation: but how he reached this conclusion, it would be difficult to say. The elder Clinton, for example, though he was, to be sure, only the titular head of his faction, had retained throughout his long career some of the admirable simplicities of the Revolutionary radical: one would hesitate before condemning to total perdition either his principles or his morals. Whereas Aaron Burr was an adventurer and nothing more: he came of a good Calvinist family, his manners were unexceptionable, he had a great deal of charm, and he was a most dangerous associate—a human upas tree, under whose shade all reputations, not the least his own, were apt to sicken. No man was more sincerely anxious to write dishonesty into the Decalogue. The Chancellor, for example, looks none the better in history for having allowed his inventive passions to draw him into a conspiracy with Burr in the matter of chartering the Manhattan Company.

One disagrees with Henry Adams (or, for that matter, with Albert Gallatin) only with the utmost diffidence: yet to lump all three factions together is almost to miss the point. Along with the question of principle and morals, there is the problem of aptness. The Livingstons, at any rate, though never backward in their demand for offices, had but a slight and decreasing aptitude for popular politics. Even Edward Livingston, the most popular of them all, was, in politics, a brilliant dilettante; even Brockholst Livingston, the toughest and the most persistent, was a mere weathercock compared to De Witt Clinton. De Witt Clinton had deserted the law in order to assist his uncle; he was a new phenomenon, a politician who had no other profession than politics. He was not an ordinary man, far from it; he loved learning for its own sake; and, in the field of natural philosophy, had gathered and disseminated a wide store of curious and useful knowledge. His biography tells us that he discovered a native American wheat and a species of salmon, and that he wrote with authority on a variety of subjects from the habits of pigeons to the cultivation of rice. His *Introductory Discourse* (1814) has been called the most effective summary for its time of the state of American scientific knowledge.[3] In the matter of public education and public improvements, too, he seems to the modern observer a progressive and original thinker. But nobody could suppose, or ever did suppose, that he would allow anything to deflect him from his lifelong business—the heavy, charmless, unremitting pursuit of political advantage.

To compare De Witt Clinton with Robert R. Livingston—a hypertypical member of his family and its faction—is to perceive that there is some essential flaw in the reasoning that lumps the Clintonians, the Burrites, and the Livingstons all together. Clinton never once lost sight of his main objective. But Livingston was an eclectic: he devoted his life to what he called the culture of laurels. But were they to be the laurels of a statesman, an agronomist, a naturalist, or an inventor? Was he to be a politician or—the very question spelled doom for anyone who asked it of himself in New York—a landed gentleman? From 1792 onward, he was leaning, on the whole, toward the latter alternative—which meant that, as a leader of the Livingston interest, he was leading it into the past.

It was not that he was unwilling to grasp whatever presented itself in the way of political benefit for himself or his family: he was, after all, a child of his colonial history. But his political disengagement, his gradual withdrawal from the melee of party warfare, gave him a more eccentric, if not a more disinterested, appearance than his rivals for the leadership of the Republican party. Certainly he was not popular; the Livingston interest as a whole was not popular: and here, perhaps, we can discern, however faintly, one clue to the conundrum of New York society in 1800, as presented to us by Henry Adams: obscure as it may have been as an intellectual or moral entity, its political effort was always toward purging itself of its aristocratic mixture.

III

Jefferson never much trusted Burr, and he did not care for the Clintons: the Livingstons, on the other hand, constituted the ablest single group in the state and, properly encouraged—who could tell?—might still reveal a hitherto buried ability for popular politics. For a while, his influence upheld the Livingstons. Perhaps it was natural, even inevitable: but could it endure?

Chancellor Livingston himself, genial, hospitable, well-read, endlessly curious about the mysteries of the physical world, reigning among his domestic slaves and his quasi-feudal leases, and upholding with all the conviction of a convert the more general principles of revolutionary politics— here was an anomaly which Jefferson could, if not exactly approve, at any rate appreciate. Moreover, throughout the puzzling and perplexed administration of John Adams, the Chancellor had not wavered in his opposition. He condemned the President, whom he usually and unfairly described as "the ministerialists", for his attempt to unite the jarring philosophies within the Federalist party; and as regards Adams's valiant efforts to lead that party to the final bourne of peace with France, he supposed that any rational president would have done as much. At the height of the Directory's intransigence toward America, after the XYZ scandal, during the undeclared naval war, he refused to express belligerence; and in the sad depths of Adams's domestic administration, in the days of the Alien and Sedition Acts, he carried his opposition to these measures so far as to try to get the Virginia Resolutions adopted by the New York Legislature.[4] If anything further was needed to stiffen his resolution, it was the administration's proposal of a land tax—the bugbear of all landed Livingstons at all times—as a means of sustaining its military and naval establishments. Thus, in national affairs throughout the presidency of John Adams, he maintained his franchise as a man of "revolutionary name and principles."

IV

"It is essential," Jefferson wrote to him on December 14, 1800, "to assemble at the outset persons to compose our administration, whose talents integrity and revolutionary name and principles may inspire the nation at once, with unbounded confidence."[5] When he wrote these words, he believed that he had been elected president; and he was offering Livingston the secretaryship of the Navy. The invitation was more inviting than the office: a secretary of the Navy, under Jefferson, had little more to look forward to than the superintendence of some gunboats and sloops of war and the laying up of all the larger ships. Livingston was not expected to accept it, nor did he: but the overture, as an overture, was friendliness itself.

Since the choice of a president to succeed Adams lay between Jefferson and Burr and was thrown, owing to a tie vote, into the House of Representatives, this offer of the Navy Department to Robert R. Livingston was once held to be a device for keeping Edward Livingston and his followers loyal to Jefferson in the House. The notion of such a bribe between three such men is preposterous in itself, although it has been advanced by historians as sturdy as John Bach McMaster: and it is rendered meaningless by the fact that when Jefferson made his offer, he believed, having received a false account of the South Carolina vote, that he was already president-elect.[6] A few days before this, Aaron Burr was himself convinced that South Carolina would give eight electoral votes to Jefferson and eight to the Federalist Charles Cotesworth Pinckney: on December 9, he said that Jefferson would be president and Adams or Pinckney vice-president.[7] On December 15, however, one day after Jefferson had sent his offer to Livingston, it was known in Washington that South Carolina had not cast any Federalist votes, nor had she, as was hoped, given eight votes to Jefferson and withheld one from Burr.[8] The South Carolina vote stood eight for Jefferson and eight for Burr: a tie vote in the electoral college would be the inevitable consequence. "There is the highest probability," Edward Livingston wrote to his brother from Washington on December 16, "that they will both have 73 votes—Congress must decide if this is the case & there is not much doubt in whose favor." As a leading Republican, he took it for granted that Jefferson's election would express the will of the people.[9]

Both Edward and Robert R. Livingston were personally on good terms with Burr; each drew a line between personal and political friendship. Burr's career had been a curious one since his too-successful management of the Manhattan Company campaign. Driven from the Legislature in the election of 1799, he had arisen, a dubious but charming phoenix, from the ashes of this defeat and of his own reputation: in the election of April, 1800, he had managed a Clinton-Livingston-Burr slate to victory in New York City. This had given the Republicans a narrow margin of control in the state Legislature; and Burr had emerged from it all as New York's Republican candidate for the vice-presidency and the choice, also, of the Republican caucus in Philadelphia.

After this election, Chancellor Livingston wrote to Jefferson to congratulate him on "the returning good sense of our countrymen." He took it for certain that his great correspondent would become president when the electoral votes were cast on December 4. "You will I dare say my dear Sir," he said, after expressing his faith that the Constitution under Jefferson would be strictly construed, "consider it a singular felicity if after having drawn the instrument that guarded us against foreign usurpations you should give a fiat to that which is to secure us against domestic tyranny."[10]

He did not, however, take any pleasure in the Clinton-Livingston-Burr alliance, in which his kinsman Brockholst Livingston had represented the family. "The same jealousy of our family," he warned his brother Edward, "that governed Clinton's politics formerly will now prevail, nor will Burr be less anxious to keep us down." Edward Livingston must expect no help from either: yet "perhaps a more favorable opportunity than the present never offered itself to put an end to the perpetual fluctuations of little interested factions if it is boldly & earnestly embraced." In other words, the family would prosper if it supported Jefferson and not otherwise. This was written on December 1, when everyone was wondering whether a tie vote between Jefferson and Burr might not be possible.[11]

And certainly the family did support Jefferson. On January 1, 1801, the Chancellor wrote to Burr, blandly complimenting him on his accession to the vice-presidency.[12] By January 4, it was known in Washington that Burr had by no means disclaimed his constitutional right to try for the presidency; and the House, already deep in strategem, became a scene of the most indecent intrigue. But Burr's disclaimers—it was altogether in character—continued: he continued to talk of any attempt to defeat Jefferson as nothing less than "usurpation." This virtuous side of him would, he hoped, be represented by Edward Livingston: the other side, which proposed to be president by any means, could be left to more dubious managers, while he himself remained in Albany. On January 29, the whole affair had grown so dangerous and disreputable that, years later, in 1825, people trembled at the thought of having to repeat it. Edward Livingston wrote to his brother on that day to say that he took it for certain that Jefferson would be elected "in spite of intrigue & . . . wicked and mischievous design." The Chancellor, on February 7, wrote to Gouverneur Morris excoriating "the profligacy of some who profess in their private letters to see in one of the candidates [Burr] (tho I trust without reason) all the vices of a Cataline yet assign these very vices as a reason for placing him at the head of the government. . . . Such moral turpitude! such a disregard for public opinion!" But public opinion was disregarded for thirty-five ballots, beginning on February 11; it was not until February 17, on the thirty-sixth ballot, that Federalist abstentions gave Jefferson the office that had always been intended for him. The Chancellor was in New York when the great news arrived: he wrote at once to his brother to congratulate him on this "happy issue" and to beg him to present his compliments to the President-elect.[13]

V

From the Chancellor's point of view, the election had one side issue, which was rather quaint than otherwise, but which does throw a certain light upon his attitude toward public office at this time. Gouverneur Morris, when he returned from France at the end of the century, had been welcomed by his old friend with open arms. The Chancellor, much to his youngest brother's surprise, had even approved of Morris's appointment to the United States Senate in 1800. "Can you believe," said Edward, "in his conversion? or do you think his [Federalist] principles will make converts to republicans by their violence?"[14] The Chancellor was presumably of the opinion that the state Legislature, as then constituted, would only send a Federalist to the Senate; and that, if so, he might as well be a friend. On January 23, 1801, Morris wrote to him in these terms: "Had you run with Mr. Jefferson you would beyond all question under the present Circumstances have been chosen by the Representatives to fill the first office of the Union. How much I lament that this is not the Case I need not say, but I feel equal and trust that you will feel greater Regret that you should still be bound in the Chains of Opposition to your oldest and best friends."[15]

One of the historians of New York declares that Livingston had been mentioned in Congress as a candidate for the vice-presidency after the spring elections of 1800: but that his increasing deafness had told against him.[16] Deafness was no doubt a good excuse; but one is tempted to suggest that, for such an office, it could hardly have been urged as a disadvantage. In any event, the Chancellor told Morris that if the Federalists were his oldest friends, he ventured to remark that they were not his best ones; and that they would be made no better by his joining them on such treacherous terms. As for the presidency, it clearly belonged to Jefferson, and, for himself, "I have too much faith in the vox populi vox dei to run counter to the wishes of the people and fill a seat which they evidently intended for another. He [*i.e.*, Livingston: or, for that matter, Burr] must certainly feel himself very uneasy under his blushing honors who reflects that not one out of the sixteen States intended them for him."[17] At this time, he had no doubts whatsoever about his lack of popularity. Indeed, he had only recently heard from Albany that a Republican caucus, meeting to decide the candidate for governor in the coming election of 1801, had passed him over in rather insulting terms in favor of George Clinton; and that the gentleman behind all this was Ambrose Spencer.[18] Spencer was arrogant and intelligent, and until recently had been a Federalist. As a Federalist, he had earned the distrust of the manor Livingstons by giving legal advice to their rebellious tenants;[19] he was now on the best of terms with De Witt Clinton; and it cannot be supposed that the Livingston-Clinton alliance had been rendered any more substantial by the addition of this energetic convert. The rumors, totally unfounded, that the Chancellor was looking for Federalist support, in a campaign for the governorship against the elder Clinton, did not make for easier relations. In the year of Republican triumph in New York, the Clinton-Livingston alliance was, as usual, a grudging and shaky affair.

VI

Jefferson had accepted, with suitable regret—"men possessing minds of the first order . . . do not abound"—Livingston's refusal of the Navy Department: six days later, and seven days after his election in the House, he proposed to nominate him as minister plenipotentiary to France. "I cannot suppress the desire," he said, "to add it [your talent] to the mass to be employed on the broader scale of the nation at large."[20] On such a scale, the appointment was a good one. The Chancellor had experienced a certain *frisson* of revulsion during the Terror: otherwise, in every change, from monarchy to Directory, he had been conspicuous for his friendship to

France. "*Personne*," wrote the French chargé d'affaires, "*ne pouvait re-cevoir cette mission avec des qualités plus propres à maintenir et à ac-croître la bonne intelligence qui vient si heureusement d'être rétablie entre les deux États.*"*[21] It was a great honor, and the Chancellor's family and friends received the news with joy; but, at the time, it promised to be an empty one. When he left, it was with vague offers that he was to return in time to run for governor in the next election: but the promotion, from any but a friendly point of view, was a promotion into exile.

The rest of the Livingston-Clinton alliance seemed, it is true, heavily weighted in favor of the Livingstons when the rewards were distributed after the victories of 1800 and 1801. In November, 1800, John Armstrong, the Chancellor's brother-in-law, a stubborn and acidulous Federalist who had been converted to Republicanism by the Alien and Sedition Acts, was elected to the United States Senate by an almost unanimous vote of the retiring Legislature. It was the beginning of a landslide. John Jay, whose uprightness no man questioned, refused to summon the Council of Ap-pointment after his exclusive right to nominate had been taken away from him: when the Council was reconvened in August, 1801, under the new Governor, George Clinton, the Livingstons were, it has been said, "gorged" with honors. Thomas T. Tillotson, another of the Chancellor's brothers-in-law, resigned from the House of Representatives, to which he had been elected in 1800, and became secretary of state in New York. Morgan Lewis, yet another brother-in-law, was elevated to chief justice of the state. Smith Thompson, who had married a daughter of Gilbert Living-ston, of Poughkeepsie, became Supreme Court justice. Edward Livingston was appointed mayor of New York, which was worth at least $10,000 a year and probably more: President Jefferson had already made him federal district attorney. Brockholst Livingston was promised the next promotion to the State Supreme Court. The Chancellor had been approved as minis-ter to France.

The treatment meted out to Burr was scandalous, even for so scandal-ous a man: no fragment of patronage, not so much as a tidewaitership, came his way. If the Livingstons and the Clintonians had conspired to ruin him, the conspiracy was outrageous: but the conspiracy was not a united one. Chancellor Livingston, for example, thoroughly disapproved of it; he called it "slashing work" and said that he feared the Council had gone altogether too far.[22] But then, from a political point of view, the Chancel-lor was already, as it were, in Paris. And the old Governor, George Clinton,

* "No one could receive this mission with qualities more apt to maintain and increase the good understanding which has just been re-established so happily between the two States."

is also believed to have opposed so wholesale a slaughter: but the Governor had lost his exclusive right to nominate and at the Council he had only one vote in five. The power belonged to Ambrose Spencer and to De Witt Clinton; and the conspiracy, which had seemed to be the monstrous offspring of the Livingston-Clinton alliance, can now be seen as threatening to devour the Livingstons, too. They were securely near the top, where, as the children of privilege, they expected to be: but underneath them, the spoils had gone elsewhere. The comptroller, the district attorney of New York City, the clerk of the Circuit Court, the assistant attorney general, and so on through sheriffs and surrogates, county clerks and justices of the peace, mayors of cities and county judges—all these posts were held by the relatives and supporters of the younger Clinton and Ambrose Spencer.[23] This was the politics of opportunity in all its surreptitious glory. The Livingstons were not aware of it, but their success had been built upon sand. Such was the ominous domestic background out of which the Chancellor sailed on his way to France.

PART FIVE

THE LOUISIANA PURCHASE

CHAPTER ONE

After lingering for many weeks in America, waiting in vain for word of a French confirmation of the amended Convention of 1800, Livingston at length went aboard the *Boston* frigate, under Captain McNeill, in New York Harbor, and on October 15, 1801, dropped down the Upper Bay.[1] He had with him his wife, his two daughters and their husbands, their personal servants, Mr. Thomas Sumter, who had been appointed his secretary of Legation, the beautiful little Mlle. Delarge (a protégée of Aaron Burr), and several French gentlemen—one of them an unfortunate M. de la Colombe, who expired during the voyage of a diet of spoiled halibut. "I don't know where the devil they'll store themselves," Richard Somers wrote of the latter contingent, "for every apartment that is decent is filled with stores & servants." Livingstons for generations had been accustomed to moving their households from New York to the manor and back by water; and this had taught them habits, not of economy, but of profusion. The Chancellor had fortified himself against the rigors of an autumnal voyage by bringing with him, not only the usual mountain of luggage, but also a quantity of livestock ("poultry, hogs, sheep, & a cow and a calf, and they say that's not half"), while his carriage was lashed to the quarterdeck, where it was to serve as a parlor for the four ladies.[2]

One member of the Clermont family might have ventured a qualified disapproval of this new phase in the Chancellor's career. Margaret Beekman Livingston had always been a great lady in Columbia and Dutchess counties, and also in New York City, when she took up her winter quarters in Pearl Street: but she had never aspired to be a fashionable one. She remained one of the sturdiest of the old, unreconstructed colonial aristocracy. When she found that she was expected to be patroness of a "Grand Belvidera Ball" in 1793, "how awful," she expostulated, "to be called to meet our judge out of a play house or assembly Room!"[3] She had once rebuked her eldest son for being too fond of amusement in Philadelphia: what dangers might he not fall into in Paris, the home of frivolity, of republicanism, of immorality, nay, of atheism itself! But Mrs. Livingston was no longer present to voice her misgivings: she had died, at Clermont, in 1800.[4] She had already, as her father's will permitted her to do, divided the greater part of her lands—in Dutchess County and in the Hardenburgh and Saratoga Patents—equally among her children: but her death, which everyone mourned and none more genuinely than her eldest son, made the Chancellor master of the old Clermont mansion and its demesne: so that he was now, in point of possessions, one of the solidest, and, in point of family status, one of the first landowners in New York State.[5] This in itself became a factor in the singular train of adventures that lay ahead of him.

Although the Livingstons and their party did not reach Paris until December 3, the sea voyage itself took less than a month. It was not exactly uneventful: transatlantic voyages rarely were. The Minister's family was seasick whenever the sea was rough—at any time, that is to say, after the second day out. On the eleventh day, the captain had the decks cleared for action, believing that he was being pursued by "an Algarene or a British ship of war"; much to his mortification, the pursuer turned out to be "an unarmed poor devil, who in the storm had lost her reckoning." On the sixteenth day, they were twenty miles south of Belle Isle when a ferocious onshore wind seemed about to drive them onto the rocks: every gentleman took off his coat and prepared to swim, every hand was at work wearing the ship round, the seas ran mountain high, the ladies were brought on deck to take their chances in the lifeboat ("rather to die together than with any hope of saving them"), the officers gallantly and suddenly refrained from swearing in deference to the ladies, when the wind as suddenly shifted from southwest to north, "& by a most extraordinary providence we were saved from certain destruction." It was not until the sixth day after this that the weary *Boston* felt her way into Belle Isle.[6]

The travelers were in L'Orient on November 13, and after a day or two spent in receiving visits and compliments from a horde of civil and military officers, all uniformed like peacocks, set out for Nantes with an escort of dragoons. "We travelled in two coaches with six horses each & two of our servants mounted on horseback. . . . The horses were small[,] the Jack boots large[,] the drivers dirty & noisy[,] & no intreaty will prevent their setting off full gallop while they are on the pavement & can bring the inhabitants of the town or village through which they pass to the window by the continued infernal smack of their wips." It was a matter of indifference to them whether or not the carriages were damaged, "as you find your own voitures." Apart from this circumstance and the terrifying din of sabots on the cobbled streets of Nantes, the travelers were delighted with everything they saw and heard.[7]

In Paris they were greeted by Lafayette, an old visitor to Clermont during the Revolutionary War and an official friend to all Americans: and by another old friend, Barbé-Marbois, who was now Minister of Finance. On December 5, Livingston had his first meeting with Talleyrand, the Minister for Foreign Affairs, and on December 6, he was formally presented to Bonaparte.

It was all somewhat unexpected. M. de Lafayette had procured a room at the Tuileries for Livingston and his suite, and from there, at noon, they had gone to the apartments of M. Hugues-Bernand Maret, the Secretary of State, from the windows of which they watched the First Consul, mounted on a beautiful white horse and gorgeous in a red coat embroidered with gold, as he reviewed his Consular Guard. They were then told that Bonaparte expected the Minister to be introduced at 2:00 P.M. They hastened to their lodgings: the Minister changed into his plain republican version of a court dress, the two sons-in-law got themselves into the uniforms of aides-de-camp to the governor of the State of New York. Mr. Sumter, the Secretary of Legation, was nowhere to be found. They returned to the Hall of Ministers, which was crowded with public personages far more gloriously dressed than they: they waited an hour, all standing, while coffee, chocolate, and liqueurs were handed round; and then, passing through a suite of apartments lined with Guards, entered the Audience Room, where the victor of Marengo stood between the Second and Third Consuls, Jean Jacques Cambacérès and Charles François Lebrun. The First Consul passed around the circle, moving with his usual catlike grace, and when at length he came to the American Minister, he was understood by that gentleman to ask if he had ever been in Europe before. Livingston replied that he had not. *"Vous êtes venus,"* said Bonaparte, *"à un monde bien corrumpu"* ("You have come to a very corrupt world"). Such was the conversation as Livingston and his son-in-law Robert remembered it.[8] Madame de Staël, however, had a somewhat different version.

The United States [she writes, in her *Dix Années d'Exil*] also made peace with France, and, apparently ignoring the fact that the most perfect understanding of the language scarcely sufficed to unravel the truth in a government which knew so well how to conceal it, sent as plenipotentiary a man who did not know a word of French. The First Consul, at Mr. Livingston's presentation, paid him, through an interpreter, a number of compliments on the purity of morals in America, and added: "The old world is very corrupt." Then, turning to M. de Talleyrand he repeated twice: "Explain to him that the old world is very corrupt. You know something about that, don't you?" [*Expliquez-lui donc que l'ancien monde est bien corrumpu; vous en savez quelque chose, n'est ce pas?*][9]

II

It was not true that Livingston, who read the language with ease, did not know a word of French: but, since his command of spoken French was far from a courtly one, and he had the added disadvantage of deafness, he probably did talk to the First Consul through an interpreter. However, any exchange between Madame de Staël and M. de Talleyrand must be taken with some caution. When she wrote her *Dix Années d'Exil,* they were old and tried enemies. (It was in 1802 that he had made the asplike comment on her somewhat masculine style of beauty when, hearing that she had introduced him into her novel *Delphine* as Madame de Vernon— Madame de Vernon, who loved nothing and believed in nothing—he said: "I'm told that Madame de Staël has put the two of us into her novel, both disguised as women [*elle et moi déguisés en femmes*].")[10]

But whether Madame de Staël's story is apocryphal or not, and it probably is, none the less it is very much to the point. Charles Maurice de Talleyrand-Périgord was corruption itself. He is often called "the ex-Bishop of Autun," as if this phrase alone would encompass the obliquity of his character. But he had been forced into the priesthood as a youth, had always predicted that nothing good would come of it, and might have defected from the church even if there had been no revolution. It would be somewhat more exact to say that he was a man, by birth an aristocrat and by preference a legitimist, who had seen fit to glide adroitly to the front rank by serving certain forms of government which he despised and detested. He used to say that no one who had not lived before the Revolution had any idea how pleasant life could be: and he endeavored to preserve in his manners and his surroundings all that was exquisite and profuse in that vanished world. The profusion he maintained in part by blandly and coldly exacting enormous bribes as the price of his official services: the manners came easily and without expense.

He was a short man, with a pronounced limp, a body menaced with stoutness, and a bloodless impassive face—the face of a dead angel, and a fallen one at that.[11] He had an exquisite amenity of address, when he chose to use it, and a mastery of the *sous-entendu,* which was the very salt and essence of good conversation in his own circles:[12] in short, he was a fine gentleman toward those who were his friends and, in his indifference no less than in his enmity, a deadly human being toward those who were not. His official family, toward whom he displayed that gentleness and sweetness which was also a part of his somewhat monstrous character, was devoted to him: in return, he exacted from it an undue proportion of work. He was so indolent that the shortest note seemed as far beyond his powers as the longest memorandum: in either case, he would throw a few ideas onto paper in his almost illegible handwriting: the composition was performed by someone else, usually M. Durant de Mereuil, head of the First Division of the Ministry of Foreign Affairs.[13]

What he offered the First Consul was not unremitting diligence, but a fine brain and a certain relentless and peculiar gift. His genius, says M. Lacour-Gayet, *"fut fait . . . d'une sorte de prescience . . . barométrique."*[14] He was so prescient and so faithless that he resembled a delicate political barometer. His fidelity to any regime was an assurance of its stability: when he showed a disposition to betray it, that was the sign that its existence was in danger. When he fell from power in the days of the Directory, as a result of the XYZ scandal—an effort to extract a bribe from George Washington's peace commissioners as the price of their formal presentation—it is not to be supposed that he was dismissed simply because he was detected in a bribery scandal too scandalous even for a bribe-ridden government. He had, in fact, already perceived that the Directory was tottering to its fall; he had gambled an outrageous bribe against his downfall, at the most unfavorable odds; and the downfall no doubt came as a relief from an intolerable situation. Shame he had none: but to be on the losing side was more than he could bear.

No political astronomer, on the other hand, had charted with more accuracy the ascending path of the star of Bonaparte. *"Notre Bona Parte,"* he had written to a compatriot in New York in 1797, *"il a tout."* He has everything.[15]

Bonaparte, on his side, had no special respect for faithfulness; it was one instrument like another: whereas in the faithless Talleyrand he perceived at once a rare, a unique servitor. Talleyrand would devote himself to Bonaparte so long as Bonaparte's star continued to ascend; and Bonaparte never asked for more than that. After all, he believed in nobody but himself. At the end of his sulphurous career, in Saint Helena, he used to say that betrayal was Talleyrand's character (*"[il] était toujours en état de trahison"*):[16] no doubt he knew this as well at the beginning as he did at the end.

Talleyrand, of course, disliked the Americans because of their role of outspoken victims and critics of the XYZ affair: but then, he had never cared for them. Fleeing from the Terror, he had once spent many months in the United States. It was as if an officer in the British Brigade of Guards had been condemned for his sins to spend some time in a line regiment:

everything in his surroundings aroused boredom, disgust, and contempt. In all America, he seems to have found only one man to please him, and that man was Alexander Hamilton. *"Il a dévina l'Europe,"* he said of Hamilton: coming from such a source, it was a compliment most Americans could have dispensed with. It was now Livingston's fate to have to deal with this quite fascinating, rather horrible, and somewhat hostile personage.

III

Livingston's mission was complicated by the fact that, if it had any meaning at all, it was dedicated to undoing the work of Talleyrand and the dreams of Bonaparte. The two were not necessarily compatible, far from it: for Talleyrand had made, for him, the extraordinary mistake of assuming that the First Consul's career depended upon the maintenance of peace, whereas Bonaparte never conceived of any other eventuality, near or remote, than one of war. Nevertheless, to both of them, the possession of Louisiana had become a matter of the first importance: and Livingston's instructions required him, first, to ask whether Louisiana had in fact been retroceded by Spain to France, and, secondly, to suggest that such a retrocession could not be to France's best interests. If the retrocession proved to be irrevocable, "it will deserve to be tried," he was then told, "whether France cannot be induced to make over to the United States the Floridas, if included in the cession to her from Spain, or at least West Florida." Such a proof of good will would go far to reconcile the United States to the presence of the uprooted revolutionary sons of France upon her most vital borders; and Livingston might suggest that, in return for West Florida, his government would assume certain outstanding claims of American citizens against France. If, on the other hand, the Floridas had not been included in the retrocession, might not France persuade Spain to cede them to the United States?[17]

The grand question of the retrocession of Louisiana, with which Livingston was thus entangled from the start and in such cloudy terms, was—and remains—one of incalculable magnitude: it involved, on the one hand, the commerce of the Mississippi and the peace and union of the United States and, on the other, the various destinies of the French, British, and Spanish empires. To make this gigantic problem even more problematical, neither France nor Spain would admit that a retrocession had taken place. It is no wonder that James Madison's instructions were drowsy with hypothesis and speculation; or that Livingston, armed with no more pointed an argument than a distant threat of Anglo-American accord, and with nothing more attractive to offer than the assumption of some American claims, was tempted almost from the beginning—a temptation which he fortunately resisted—to ask for his recall.

There had been a time when France seemed about to realize her majestic project of an empire that would control the trade routes between America and India. The American terminus was conceived of as a chain of forts linking Canada and the Great Lakes with the huge province of Louisiana—a domain that would stretch from Quebec to New Orleans and squeeze the British colonies against the Atlantic seacoast. The India terminus, before the eruption of the genius of Clive, was already a formidable affair. All this came to an end with the end of the Seven Years' War. In 1763, the British owned Canada and the Floridas, Louisiana had gone to Spain, and in India the work of Dupleix and his colleagues had almost vanished—from sight, though not from mind.

When France entered the Revolutionary War in 1778, her American intention was to restore the old empire in terms of the Newfoundland fisheries and of a paramount holding in the West Indies. As regards India, if one follows the complex discussions that preceded her peace with England, and that surrounded and to some extent interpenetrated those of Jay and Adams, one can see that she hoped to regain there the favorable position she had held before 1754. But this was not to be. The British Empire, it is true, had experienced a humiliating defeat and dismemberment in North America: the Floridas had been returned to Spain, the new United States came down the eastern bank of the Mississippi as far as the line of 31°. The empire, also, had lost Tobago and Santa Lucia, Senegal and Gorée, and, in India, Pondichéry, Karikal, and Chandernagore. But the loss was more apparent than actual. One is sometimes disposed to forget that the empire's position, even in India, and certainly in the Indian Ocean, the western Mediterranean, the North Atlantic, and the Caribbean, was actually better than it had been when the war was at its height.[18] Nor would any realistic economist have objected to the territorial loss of the thirteen colonies, so long as their markets remained unimpaired.

In many respects, therefore (though of course not in all), the career of Napoleon Bonaparte must be seen as a grandiose effort to renew and to win the old Anglo-French contest for America and India and for the trade routes between them. His oriental designs had already received a setback when he was obliged to abandon his army in Egypt in 1799, but he never gave them up until, reeling back from Moscow in 1812, he deserted the dying Grande Armée at Smogornie and, wrapped in furs and dreams, took to the westward roads in his red sleigh. As regards America, his hopes in 1801, though just as delusive as his dreams for India, were even more compelling and far closer to realization. On October 1, 1800, he concluded a long series of negotiations with Spain which had begun in the days of the Directory, and by the secret Treaty of St. Ildefonso, in return for an illusory Italian kingdom for the King of Spain's nephew and son-in-law, the Hereditary Prince of Parma, had obtained the retrocession of Louisiana. When the secret leaked out, as it was bound to do, it seemed not unlikely that Spain had given France the Floridas as well.

But what was Louisiana with the Floridas? In American eyes, it comprised an almost lunar extent of territory and of influence. When the King of Spain possessed it "as an American ruler," says one of the most eloquent of historians

his empire dwarfed that of the United States. From the mouth of the St. Mary's, southward and westward, the shores of Florida, Louisiana and Texas were Spanish; Pensacola, Mobile and New Orleans closed all the rivers by which the United States could reach the gulf. The valley of the Ohio itself, as far as Pittsburg, was at the mercy of the King of Spain; the flour and tobacco that floated down the Mississippi, or any of the rivers that fell into the Gulf, passed under the Spanish flag, and could reach a market only by permission of Don Carlos IV. Along an imaginary line from Fernandina to Natchez, some six hundred miles, and thence northward on the westward bank of the Mississippi River to the Lake of the Woods, some fourteen hundred miles farther, Spanish authority barred the path of American ambition. Of all the foreign Powers Spain alone stood in such a position as to make violence sooner or later inevitable even to the pacific Jefferson. . . . To sum the story up in a single word, Spain had immense influence over the United States; but it was the influence of the whale over its captors—the charm of a huge, helpless, and profitable victim.[19]

By Thomas Pinckney's Treaty of 1795, which defined the boundary between New Orleans and Natchez, agreed to the principle of "free ships, free goods" and to a liberal interpretation of the vexatious "contraband," and won for Americans the right to deposit their merchandise at New Orleans without paying duty, Spain had put off the day of reckoning. The right of deposit, it is true, was granted for three years only, but the Spanish King agreed to renew it at the end of this period or else grant some other place of deposit. At almost the same time, humiliated by the Directory at the Peace of Basel, Spain ceded the Spanish portion of Santo Domingo to the French. The moribund character of its empire can be discerned in these concessions.

To venture to suggest what was in Bonaparte's mind at any given time has long been known as a vain enterprise, and his empire in America and India never came into being: yet the reconstruction of its American terminus, as it must have presented itself to him after the signing of the Treaty of St. Ildefonso, is hardly a matter of speculation. Santo Domingo was already French in name, though not in fact. If Bonaparte could occupy and tame Santo Domingo, then, with the Floridas and Louisiana in his grip, he could wed Louisiana to the Sugar Islands. He would be master of four hundred miles of Atlantic coast, master of the Caribbean, the Gulf of Mexico, the commerce of the Mississippi, the Eldorado of its valley, in short, of an American empire richer and more dangerous than anything ever ruled by the Bourbon monarchs.[20] There was only one flaw so far in his scheme, but that was a grave one: he could not persuade the Spanish Court—he never was able to persuade the Spanish Court—to give him the Floridas. From 1801 to 1803, negotiations for this vital territory continued; they became part of a battle for the mind and conscience of Carlos IV, fought between Bonaparte and Manuel de Godoy, Prince of the Peace. Two less evenly matched contestants for a more unprepossessing prize may never have fought before in all the annals of diplomacy; yet the feeble and worthless Godoy was, in the end, the stronger of the two.

The retrocession of Louisiana was known to Jefferson and Madison, at least as a well-substantiated rumor, by June, 1801; by November, Rufus King, the American Minister in London, had some of the facts and transmitted them to Washington. The only question that remained, and it was a cardinal one, was whether or not the Floridas had been included.

In any event, with or without the Floridas, the retrocession of Louisiana loomed as a fearful event in early American history. The Spaniard was hateful, but he was not dangerous: his rule was held to be, sooner or later, a doomed one. The militant and expansionist Frenchman, stepchild of revolution, sitting athwart the Mississippi at New Orleans, and claiming the western bank of the great river, was quite another matter. What influence might such a neighbor not have upon the high, volatile, and notably irritable spirits of the West? Whether the influence was one of attraction or repulsion, the result was likely to be crisis, calamity, and disunion. Only by the utmost tact and forbearance could France have kept the peace: and Consular France was Bonapartist France; it was by nature not peaceful.

This is evident enough in the coarse irony which made the Treaty of St. Ildefonso, retroceding Louisiana, follow by exactly one day the Convention of 1800—the so-called Treaty of Morfontaine—which ended the undeclared war between France and the United States. The convention was the fine flower of John Adams's diplomacy: it was a liberal, a rational answer to the Anglomania of a dominant section of his party; and only one major disagreement had appeared before it was concluded. The French negotiators insisted that American claims of indemnity for spoliations by French warships should not be admitted into the treaty. The American commissioners, on the other hand, demanded that the treaty should abrogate certain guarantees and obligations imposed upon the United States by the Franco-American treaties of 1778. Article II of the convention, as first written, reserved these two subjects for future negotiation. On February 3, 1801, the United States Senate consented to and advised the ratification of the convention if Article II were expunged. The French Government agreed to this, but added that Article II should be omitted only with the provision that "by this retrenchment the two States renounced the respective pretensions which are the object of the said article." The language was masterly. The treaties of 1778 had been abrogated; but, by way of exchange, the claims of indemnity had been nullified.[21] It was in hopes of news of this event that Livingston had been held in America; but the news arrived after his departure. When it arrived, the Senate approved the French reservation, and the convention was proclaimed in Washington on December 21, 1801: Livingston himself had heard of the French ratification when the *Boston* was hailed by an inbound ship some twelve days out of New York.[22]

The ironical note, none the less, still sounded as coarsely as ever. By the Treaty of St. Ildefonso, France had virtually undone those good relations with the United States which she had established just twenty-four hours earlier in the Treaty of Morfontaine. Talleyrand, it is true, would not admit that such an instrument as the Treaty of St. Ildefonso had been signed at all; and, in the face of this bland denial, one of the oddest tasks imposed upon Livingston was to persuade the Consulate that it was to France's best interests not to accept the results of the treaty. He was then to offer for West Florida, which had not been ceded to France, an American assumption of such private claims against France as had not been annulled by Article II of the Convention of 1800. Since the French were still negotiating for the Floridas, so vital to Bonaparte's project of an American terminus to his empire, and since Bonaparte's attitude toward debts of any kind was that one did not pay them, Livingston's chances for a successful mission were, to say the least, slim. When he arrived in Paris, he was little more than a small, amusing, discordant detail in a grand imperial design.

CHAPTER TWO

To extract concessions from the hostility of Talleyrand and the imperial dreams of the Consul would have been difficult enough if Livingston had been given adequate powers: if he had had, that is to say, something definite and valuable to offer. As it was—with his deafness, his inadequate French, his lack of advisers—he could not have seemed a very significant personage. Talleyrand, beneath his exquisite amenity of address, brought to his dealings with Livingston a painful armory of almost imperceptible snubs and frail but deadly sarcasms. Behind the American Minister, after all, there loomed neither armies, nor navies, nor wealth; neither the power to browbeat nor the means to bribe: he had only that indefinable something, that vague but vast threat, the *future* United States.

II

Livingston was, indeed, a lonely figure. In the first place, there was the problem of communication. Earlier, as Secretary for Foreign Affairs, he had experienced the greatest trouble in maintaining any sort of contact with the Congress's diplomatic agents in Europe. Now the situation was reversed: advices from Washington were infrequent; nor could he be certain that his own dispatches would cross the Atlantic in the right order, or arrive in time to influence the decisions of his superiors. And, in the second place, these decisions, when communicated to him, were apt to be ambiguous or obscure. Transatlantic diplomacy was, of necessity, a slow affair; and to its inherent slowness, Jefferson and Madison now added a delicate, delaying motion of their own. They were men of peace: and, as such, they were playing for time. The shadow of France hung over the Mississippi basin, over the Floridas, over Santo Domingo: it had not yet materialized in armies of occupation; all was still as it had been.

In Europe, meanwhile, the flood of events seemed to be raging and crashing toward a peace. In June and December of 1800, the bloody engagements of Marengo and Hohenlinden had brought to an end the second coalition against France. In March, 1801, the League of Armed Neutrality, which had threatened to complete the work of Bonaparte and General Moreau by closing a whole continent to British goods, was shaken to its heart when the demented Czar Paul was strangled in a palace revolution; and it was shattered in April when Nelson destroyed the Danish fleet in Copenhagen. One might be tempted to suspect a peace, the preliminaries of which were so barbaric; but England and France were almost ready to end their war; and Bonaparte was emerging, not as the most distinguished and insatiable child of the Revolution, but as the hope of the peaceful profiteering bourgeoisie: not as Satan, but as Saturn. It was thus that Talleyrand endeavored to construe him: and to Jefferson's amicable, as to Madison's cautious, mind, much might be gained from temporizing with this construction. If they neglected their Minister in Paris, during the winter of 1801-1802, it was because they had nothing definite for him to do: it was not because they thought him negligible.

He had not been sent to France simply in part payment of a debt which Jefferson owed to the Livingstons for their support. He was one of the most prominent Francophiles in America, and the race of Francophiles had been steadily diminishing; he was also held to be one of the ablest men in New York. In that state, to be sure, he had a reputation for political eclecticism: he was "unpopular," he was "visionary," his passage through life was beset with *ignes fatui*. A steamboat, a millstone theory, a family quarrel could lead him from the narrow path of political regularity. But in New York, from the beginning to the end of his career, his abilities were held to be of the first order.

He was, moreover, a man of the world. Until he left for France, his travels of a lifetime had been confined to New York, Pennsylvania, New Jersey, Connecticut, and Delaware: yet within that narrow compass, how much experience a man could acquire! Could acquire, that is, if he had played any kind of a statesman's role in the days of the Revolution and the Confederation. Disputes between states over backlands or borders had a diplomatic as well as political aspect; and the secretaryship for Foreign Affairs, although it had brought no fame, had been in itself a valuable education. The colonies before the Revolution and the states before the Constitution were a most effective school in statecraft for those who tried to manage their business. An American might be abashed or exasperated by the subtleties of Europe; but he had his native subtleties, too. And Livingston had another, a somewhat peculiar, advantage, when it came to dealing with the impassive and polished disdain of a *grand seigneur* like Talleyrand: he simply did not conceive that any man was a finer social specimen than himself. A Hudson River squire could be fascinated by an alien world and flattered by its attentions: he was incapable of supposing it to be more desirable than his own. Livingston stared at the gaudy splendors of Bonaparte's court like any provincial: but he was amazed, not envious, and he was never subdued. He took it for granted that he, personally, as an individual no less than as a minister, would always be listened to. And so he hammered away at the subject of claims and concessions, day in and day out, bringing to it, now the solid reasoning of a statesman, now the aery schemes of an incorrigible "projector"; persistently, unaffectedly, with everything he had. And to the supercilious or the amused point of view that he was merely an untutored American, a point of view that was equally untutored in its own way, he opposed that peculiar historical composition, the tough epidermis of a New York aristocrat who had not yet lost touch with his colonial past. Fretful and suspicious he may have been: but he never ceased to behave like a privileged person.

Moreover, he perceived almost at once that the great dream of a Utopian America, the grand but simple nurse of philosophy and of liberty, had lost its usefulness for France: or, which was much the same thing, found no favor with Bonaparte. He complained at first that he was too "republican" to be at ease in Paris, dancing attendance upon the First Consul's gorgeous, self-conscious, stiff military court. The morals of this court might be easy; it made no distinction (as far as he could see) between wives and mistresses: but its rituals were not. When one attended an official dinner, the guests were all bedecked like minor German princes.[1] And the expense was killing. But even while he complained, a curious change was taking place in his thinking—a change or a reversal. As a Francophile, he was almost obliged to be pleased with what he saw in France: and this, to be sure, was not difficult. The French, he said, were the happiest people he had ever encountered: "and I believe because women form the rosy links of their society."[2] And what women! "Whatever beauties the rouge may hide the spectator has not much reason to complain of any loss of them by their cloathing. . . . Those who want the evidence of their senses rather than of their imaginations need only walk the streets where every woman shows as high as her knees."[3] Yet how good humored, how well mannered they were: and, even though they were dedicated, men and women alike, to folly and dissipation, it was a delight to walk the streets in such lighthearted company. Even in the midst of a carnival, "when the streets are filled with masks on foot[,] in coaches[,] in chairs[,] on horses & on asses—[when] here you meet a coach driven by a bear[,] a brace of harlequins on the top[,] a bleeding nun[,] a magdalen & half a dozen painted Jezebels within & a devil & cuckold disputing about the length of their horns behind"—even then there were no quarrels, no woman was insulted, all was good humor and conviviality.[4] Others might find a certain ill-concealed ferocity in these people, who had outfought Europe, as they sauntered in the tree-lined boulevards outside their city, or minced and flaunted their way through its filthy medieval streets: Livingston could never encounter them without a lift at the heart.

And so he began to ask himself whether, since the people were so happy under a regime that was already nothing more nor less than a dictatorship, a dictatorship was not the best regime for them.

I am well satisfied from what I have seen [he wrote] that it is idle to think there is one form of government adapted to all the world. Manners[,] habits & wants are as much to be consulted in forming a government as the elevation of the pole is in setting a sun dial—The patriots here grumble but the people are satisfied[,] they have run through all the changes & they see something like the ancient pageantry—while Liberty & equality & 'le palais du peuple' written upon every public building [are] sufficient to assure them that they combine the energy of the old government with the freedom of Roman citizens.[5]

In other words, he perceived that the Consular regime was one that retained the Revolution in terms of Equality, but denied it in terms of Liberty. It was an adequate description of the tendency of Bonaparte's rule, which was to give opportunities to anyone, from any walk of life, who proved equal to them: but to abridge in the most drastic manner such elementary rights as the right of free speech.

This kind of thinking, he admitted to Gouverneur Morris, would make him an aristocrat by "example"—that is, a vicarious aristocrat, who believed that mankind might, in certain instances, profit by *not* following the American example. The Americans, he thought, should be thankful "for having seized perhaps the only moment in which our habits & manners qualified us for freedom."[6] The American Government was not, after all, the world's best hope: but it was merely the best hope for Americans. As for the French, "their fetters though sufficiently strong are entwined with roses. I own that it [is] a gratifying sight to me in spite of my democracy to see a whole nation combining to find happiness in social pleasures."[7]

There was a certain strain of frivolity in all this, quite genuine and probably intentional: but underneath it all, there lay a point of view that was anything but Jeffersonian. If one denied the political perfectability of man, and limited true freedom only to America, how long would it survive there? And in any case, was not the exclusive principle, even if one applied it to the enjoyment of a democracy, apt to reveal itself as an aristocratic principle? It is certain that Livingston never communicated these heretical thoughts to his superiors at Washington: what he told them was, in effect, that American democracy was very unpopular in Consular circles; that the President's inaugural speech had been severely commented upon by Bonaparte; and that when the National Institute wished to nominate Mr. Jefferson a member, the First Consul had forbidden it. The refusal to renew the Treaty of 1778 had aroused many absurd suspicions; and it was said that France could not have asked for Louisiana from Spain if the treaty had been renewed. Livingston therefore decided, and duly reported his decision to the Secretary of State, that if republicanism were unpopular, one could get nowhere by flaunting it: having been thought "too much attatched to democratic principles" on his arrival, he had been careful not to give the impression of wishing to interfere in domestic politics and he had avoided "any associations that might give umbrage."[8] This did not deprive him of the right to tough and even "harsh"[9] *argument* in his dealings with Talleyrand: it was a matter of social posture only, and as such it suited itself well to his naturally genial disposition and his innately conservative mind. He had never believed in "militia diplomacy"; whether that is to his credit or not, he did not resort to it now.

III

The American claims, which were involved in the negotiations from the beginning, were for embargoes, seizures of cargoes in French ports, arbitrary purchases, and so forth, which had accumulated between 1793 and 1800, and had not been annulled by the Convention of 1800. In all, the legitimate claims may have amounted to $5,000,000. American citizens who had gone into partnership with French citizens were considered, of course, to have denationalized themselves so far as such claims were concerned: and many of the claimants in Paris were of this order. Chief among them was James Swan, a speculating gentleman of insinuating manners, who was Swan & Cie du Nord, James Swan & Schweizer Jr., Swan & Cie d'Amerique, and also Brown & Francis, Henry Jackson, John C. Jones, and so forth—aliases that inadequately concealed his dealings with French entrepreneurs.[10] Livingston was indiscreet enough to patronize him—an indiscretion, incidentally, upon which far too much emphasis has been placed.

Among the legitimate claimants were Livingston's brother John R., the New York merchant, and his kinsman and future brother-in-law Peter R. Livingston: his son-in-law and unofficial secretary, Robert L. Livingston, was acting as agent for the former. Another leading claimant was Stephen Girard, of Philadelphia, whose cause was discreetly supported by the Secretary of State himself.[11] In short, the claims problem from the start was a highly delicate one, in which it behooved the Minister to walk like Agag, with a fair chance, even then, of meeting Agag's fate. That it should have been mingled, as it was, with the great solutions of the Louisiana Purchase and their aftermath was a thoroughly unfortunate business, for which Livingston was not to blame.

At first, since the Consulate officially refused to admit that Louisiana had been retroceded, Livingston tried to get the claims settled on the assumption (in which, to be sure, he had not the slightest faith) that the French really intended to make a settlement. He had tried out the suggestion that the American Government might assume the claims in return for certain territorial concessions, and was told by one of the ministers that "no one but spendthrifts satisfied their debts by selling their lands."[12] He also pointed out that a delay in settlement would have a poor effect upon French credit, and that this in turn would harm their manufactures and interfere with the subsistence of their expeditions to the West Indies: but Talleyrand, to whom he confided these sensible criticisms, airily replied that the matter was not within his department. This did not deter Livingston from returning to the subject over and over again: but the melancholy experience of Denmark, Sweden, and the Hansa towns—"all importunate creditors"—seemed to indicate that he would never extract a sou from the Consulate by arguments or appeals. The French system, certainly a masterful one, was to admit the justice of the claims and then do nothing whatsoever about them. Whether one ascribed this sort of behavior to want of cash in the Treasury or want of conscience in the First Consul, the result was the same.[13] Livingston continued to show a singular fertility in arguments and schemes for settling the claims: but, as time went on, he regarded them more and more as a form of pressure, a way of making himself felt when he addressed himself to the far greater problem presented by the retrocession of Louisiana.

Here Livingston, as has been shown, was expected either to prove to the Consulate that Louisiana was not worth its while; or, failing that, to obtain assurances that, out of a sense of justice and good will, the French would not abridge American rights of navigation and deposit. The business of getting men like Talleyrand and Bonaparte to behave with justice or good will had a touch of the lost cause in it: nothing was more calculated to concentrate Livingston's energies. It had its affinities, in the moral order, with problems like steamboats in the physical one: that is to say, there was something in it that appealed rather more to the "projector" than it did to the diplomat.

In the meantime, in Washington, one of the subtlest intellectual combinations in American history was meditating the same problem, day in and day out. For lack of adequate communication, there was no exact agreement as to method between Jefferson and Madison, in Washington, and the Minister, in Paris. It is, perhaps, permissible to suggest that even if communication had been more adequate, agreement would have been hard to reach. In Washington, the tendency was to behave as if everything could be settled in time, but always to brandish, as it were, behind one's back, some half-concealed thunderbolt: in Paris, the Minister's peremptory character compelled him to act as if there was almost no time left. In the end, these tendencies were united in a mutual triumph: but the misunderstandings engendered by them were acute and lasting.

Livingston was soon able to communicate the fact of the retrocession to Washington, as Rufus King had already done: and with King he established a useful correspondence. The Minister to Great Britain was a solid, dignified, and courteous figure, with whom no one took any liberties, and who got on well with the British. His information was always valuable. Livingston believed, for example, that the expedition which sailed from Brest at the end of November was headed in part for Louisiana: but, although the rumor was as strong in London as in Paris, King gave him the correct state of affairs. The whole expedition was headed for Santo Domingo; and not a soldier would be sent to New Orleans, until after a definitive peace had been concluded with England, whose government "will see with much concern," he wrote, "the accomplishment of this cession [*i.e.*, of Louisiana to France]."[14]

Was it conceivable that the expedition under General Charles Leclerc, Bonaparte's implacable brother-in-law, would *not* be able to subdue Santo Domingo? The island was under the control of the revolted Negro chieftain Toussaint L'Ouverture and his half-million former slaves; and Bonaparte, as a preliminary step to destroying Toussaint, had sent him a friendly letter before Leclerc sailed. "We have conceived esteem for you," wrote the First Consul, "and we take pleasure in recognizing and proclaiming the great services you have rendered to the French people. . . . What can you desire?—the liberty of the blacks? You know that in all the countries where we have been, we have given it to the peoples who had it not."[15] To the British Government, at the same time, with whom he was discussing the preliminaries of a peace, he explained that his intention was to annihilate the Negro leadership at Santo Domingo. Leclerc arrived in sight of Santo Domingo toward the end of January, 1802; made friendly overtures to General Henri Christophe in Cap-Français: and when these were rebuffed, began to attack. The campaign that followed was disastrous to France; but after Christophe treacherously yielded his posts and troops to Leclerc in April, Toussaint decided to trust the word of Bonaparte. On May 1, he surrendered to Leclerc. On June 10, he was suddenly arrested, hustled on board ship, and despatched to France.

Some weeks later he was landed at Brest; then he disappeared. Except a few men who were in the secret, no one ever saw him again. Plunged into a damp dungeon in the fortress of Joux, high in the Jura mountains on the Swiss frontier, the cold and solitude of a single winter closed this tropical existence. April 7, 1803, he died forgotten. . . .[16]

This lamentable fate was also designed for Christophe, Jean Jacques Dessalines, and the other leaders whom Bonaparte called those "gilded Africans." In June, hearing that Toussaint had surrendered, the First Consul cheerfully ordered the restoration of slavery at Guadeloupe and, with due caution, at Santo Domingo. Not a qualm disturbed Bonaparte's conscience, presumably because that organ had been wholly atrophied, or had been omitted altogether from his singular composition. Such was the faith he kept: such was the liberty that France was to give to "the peoples who had it not." The man who decimated France and Europe in order to serve his private vision had no understanding of such terms: in the blaze of his ego, both the niceties and the commonplaces of the moral judgment became totally invisible to him and are best left unspoken by us. The point is that as late as June 15, 1802, he was absolutely convinced that he had crushed all resistance in Santo Domingo.

Santo Domingo was the key to Louisiana. The next step was to obtain the Floridas. Bonaparte was still negotiating for them in 1802, and thus, when Livingston asked his questions about the retrocession of Louisiana, an event known to all Europe, he was first blandly informed that no such transaction had taken place, and then, when this statement became too absurd to be repeated, was put off with one evasion after another. At one stage in these negotiations, Talleyrand wrote a furibund reply to a very able note of Livingston's, in which he (Talleyrand) protested that it was inexcusable for a minister to attempt to discuss the terms of a treaty that had not yet been communicated to his government.[17] The reply was not sent, presumably at the First Consul's request, and obviously because it laid itself open to the retort: Why had a treaty so vital to American interests *not* been communicated to the American Government? The reason why was not far to seek, but it was one that Talleyrand certainly could not communicate—in spite of every pressure, it was not until October, 1802, that Carlos IV at length made a formal conveyance of Louisiana to the French. And in December, it was known in Paris that a fearful disaster had been meted out to the forces of Leclerc in Santo Domingo. The heroic resistance of the Negroes had done a great deal: and the work they had left undone had been completed by an even more terrible horde of warriors, the yellow-fever-bearing Aëdes aegypti mosquitoes. In November, Leclerc himself succumbed. The news of a restoration of slavery in Guadeloupe, the consequent insurrection, the defection of the Negro generals, the yellow fever—such had been the steps in Leclerc's downfall and the destruction of his troops. No more precise or appalling an answer to Bonaparte's treachery could possibly have been devised.

Bonaparte, to be sure, did not quite see it in that light. In the face of disaster, he was nothing if not resilient. He seems to have thought that, if one expedition and one Leclerc had failed, then a second expedition and a second Leclerc would do the work: he continued to think, or *pretend* to think, in these infatuated terms until March, 1803. But the fact remains that all Livingston's later negotiations were conducted, although he did not fully realize it, against a great dissolving background—nothing less than the gradual disintegration of Bonaparte's dreams of an American empire.

IV

Did anyone, aside from Bonaparte, realize the extent of these dreams? The British, who made a definite peace with France (the Peace of Amiens) in March, 1802, must have had some idea. Commercial empire was their business; they suspected the Peace of Amiens because it contained no commercial pact; and, although they had little more sympathy with revolted slaves than had the Americans (or anyone else), Rufus King observed on April 1 that they wished for a long resistance from Toussaint on Santo Domingo because it would help to make the peace more durable.[18] The connection between Santo Domingo–Florida–Louisiana, on the one hand, and the East Indies, on the other, was not lost upon them: and if they had said nothing about the retrocession of Louisiana during the discussions that preceded the Peace of Amiens, they had been deeply disturbed by it. Since they retained Trinidad and Ceylon in the terms of the peace, and since their naval strength remained unimpaired, they could afford to wait and see: but they were required to surrender Malta, something they would never do if Bonaparte showed any interest in the Near East; so that the Peace of Amiens was never much more than a truce. The British were as reluctant to make a formal surrender of Malta to France as Carlos IV (who did not sign an order to that effect until October 15, 1802) was unwilling to deliver Louisiana or to yield the Floridas.

In Washington, the Virginia administration was not in sympathy with the rebels of Santo Domingo; the South hated and feared them; and the North was uncertain. With the North, it was a question of trade. From a diplomatic point of view, therefore, the first American object was Louisiana: and the first duty of the Minister was to see that France maintained for America the rights of navigation and deposit which the Americans had won from Spain in Pinckney's Treaty of 1795.

Livingston made his final effort at performing this duty on February 20, when he wrote a note to Talleyrand, which was certainly intended to provoke rather than placate, and to which he received no reply. Apart from the fact that France was not actually in possession of Louisiana, what restrained the French from officially disclosing the Treaty of St. Ildefonso was their state of belligerence with England. Until the Peace of Amiens, they were in the semantic difficulty of not being able to admit what was known to everyone: if they admitted that Louisiana was theirs, the English might still attack it. And on top of all this, there was Talleyrand's habitual desire to make things as difficult for the United States as he could.

Livingston suffered at the time from the misapprehension that the Floridas had been ceded to France: if Natchez could be made into a free port, he told Madison, and if Santo Domingo would only hold out against Leclerc, something might be done if one was willing to pay.[19] He was, in other words, suggesting that a larger disbursement was necessary for West Florida than a mere assumption of American claims against France: France needed money for Santo Domingo.

A few days after he had written this letter, he heard from Rufus King in London. King had been told by Lord Hawkesbury, the British Foreign Secretary, that private advices from Paris were insisting that Leclerc was in great difficulties: and Hawkesbury had further given it as his opinion that if Leclerc's army were destroyed—which he thought very likely— the one that succeeded it would meet the same fate.[20] Livingston had, therefore, the less compunction about offering money which would certainly go toward the outfitting and subsistence of a new and probably doomed expedition to Santo Domingo.

He had almost lost hope of achieving anything with the impassive and contemptuous Talleyrand. Would the First Consul himself prove more amenable? To approach the First Consul directly was scarcely in accordance with accepted diplomatic procedure; and that dire personage was, in any event, "impenetrable." But he believed that he stood rather high in Bonaparte's esteem. In April, he had written to Talleyrand to suggest that, considering the uncertain state of affairs in Santo Domingo and the approach of the sickly season there, Madame Leclerc might perhaps like to retire to New York. His brother, the Mayor, would lend her his town house "in the best and the healthiest situation in that city"; or, if she preferred the country, she was only too welcome to make use of Clermont.[21] Madame Leclerc was Bonaparte's beautiful sister, Pauline, whose formidable list of lovers included (that gentleman was not above hinting) Bonaparte himself. One can with no difficulty imagine what Livingston's sisters, Mrs. Freeborn Garretson, Mrs. Morgan Lewis, Mrs. Thomas Tillotson, and Mrs. John Armstrong, would have said to this: and one dare only suppose that his most formidable sister, Mrs. Janet Montgomery, would have asked, in the manner of Lady Catharine, how the shades of Clermont came to be thus polluted. Fortunately, the invitation (which was not the most tactful of the Minister's ventures) was either not relayed or not accepted: but he was convinced that the First Consul was touched by it, and perhaps he was.

At any rate, the time had come for a more direct attack. He had still received no fresh instructions from Washington:[22] but by June 2, he had at length come to realize that France had not, after all, obtained the Floridas along with Louisiana. He had already written unofficially to the Spanish Ambassador to France, the Chevalier D'Azara, giving reasons out of Pinckney's treaty which should operate against the cession of the Floridas; and D'Azara had replied, unofficially, that the Floridas had not been ceded.[23] These revelations were, no doubt, one of the effects of the Peace of Amiens. And on July 3, he had extracted from Talleyrand a hint— it was scarcely more—that West Florida was not yet French.[24]

To Livingston, the possession of the Floridas by France suggested only one thing: the West, with France thus upon its borders, might secede from the United States. Rufus King was perhaps of the same opinion. He wrote on July 12 to say that America must neither explicitly sanction a transfer of the Floridas from Spain to France nor explicitly guarantee their possession by Spain: for if Spain continued to hold them (said King), both they and New Orleans would become eventually American, either by revolution or by the simple force of political gravity.[25] This advice was scarcely calculated to diminish Livingston's perplexities. And on July 20, Charles Pinckney, whose experiences with the arid and stubborn pride of Madrid were not dissimilar to those of John Jay, wrote in despair to say that the whole negotiation regarding Louisiana and the Floridas "rests principally with you."[26]

Livingston had already received two missives from Washington which, while certainly not in the nature of fresh instructions, could hardly have failed to stiffen his resolution. The first was from President Jefferson, and has since become one of the most famous of his state papers. There was one spot on the globe, wrote Jefferson,

whose possessor is our natural and habitual enemy. It is New Orleans, through which the produce of three-eighths of our territory must pass to market, and from its fertility, it will ere long yield more than half our whole produce, and contain more than half of our inhabitants. France, placing herself in that door, assumes to us the attitude of defiance. Spain might have retained it quietly for years.

Spain, after all, was pacific and feeble; and doubtless an occasion would eventually arise which would make the transfer of New Orleans the price of something more valuable to her. But France was impetuous, energetic, restless; and the United States, though quiet and dedicated to peace and the pursuit of wealth, was too high-minded to consider wealth when it came to suffering insult or injury: the two nations could not remain friends when they met in so "irritable" a position.

They, as well as we [continued the President], must be blind if we do not begin to make arrangements on that hypothesis. The day that France takes possession of New Orleans, fixes the sentence which is to restrain her for ever within her low-water mark. It seals the union of two nations, who, in conjunction, can maintain exclusive possession of the ocean. From that moment, we must marry ourselves to the British fleet and nation. We must turn all our attention to a maritime force, for which our resources place us on a very high ground; and having formed and connected together a power which may render reinforcement of her settlements here impossible to France, make the first cannon fired in Europe the signal for the tearing up any settlement she may have made, and for holding of the two continents of America in sequestration for the common purposes of the United British and American nations. This is not a state of things we seek or desire.[27]

It was certainly not anything that Livingston, whose Anglophobia was more pronounced than ever, could have sought or desired: what he wanted from England was not an alliance, but free trade; and although he was unable to see that free trade with England meant, in effect, an alliance upon unfavorable terms, he could certainly discern, among Jefferson's eloquent and, indeed, splendid periods, the features of a junior partnership with Great Britain. As Jefferson put it, France would hold New Orleans only during the interval of peace. And "will not the amalgamation of a young thriving nation continue to that enemy [Great Britain] the health and force which are at present so evidently on the decline?" All these considerations, said the President, might, in some proper form, be brought to the attention of France—not to give offense, not as a menace, but as uncontrollable consequences which Americans did not desire, but deprecated, and which they besought France as a friend to prevent. Thus the thunderbolt was brandished, but it was brandished by a peaceful arm.

James Madison, on May 1, wrote—as was quite in keeping with his nature—a less forceful but, in some respects, a more menacing letter. Nothing was said about Great Britain. He simply pointed out that, while the *"mere neighborhood"* of France would be harmful to Franco-American friendship, from the possession of the mouth of the Mississippi by France "the worst is to be apprehended." He asked the Minister, who had been sparing none, to spare no efforts to bring about an abandonment of this purpose: and he suggested that Livingston, having "prudently" tried to discover the extent of the cession, should, if it included the Floridas as well as New Orleans, ask at what price these may be had. But he gave Livingston no powers to offer a price.[28]

A minister, having digested the contents of these two notes, could reach only one conclusion: he had been abandoned to his own devices, and these devices could only be, officially, of an argumentative nature. If he suggested a price for Florida, or went further and made an offer for New Orleans, he would have exceeded his instructions. And so, while privately he entertained one scheme after another for purchasing the Floridas, from Spain or from France, he wrote in his official capacity one of the ablest and most forceful of his public papers.

V

This paper—"Is it advantageous to France to take possession of Louisiana?"[29]—examined the problem from two points of view. The first, as regarded French commerce and manufactures; the second, as it affected the positive or relative strength of France.

No wise nation, Livingston wrote, becomes a colonizer unless it has a surplus population which cannot be usefully employed at home; or unless it has superfluous capital which cannot otherwise be rendered productive.

Neither of these conditions prevailed in France. There was certainly not a surplus population; and, while soil and climate gave her great advantages as a commercial and as a manufacturing nation, France lacked capital. For this reason, her manufactures languished, and foreign merchants preferred to make their exchanges in terms of wines and brandies. In England, on the other hand, any species of goods can be obtained from a manufacturer at an hour's notice. This can be remedied only by an increase of capital in the hands of French manufacturers.

Moreover, capital is needed to open new markets for foreign merchants who are content to be the agents of those who furnish goods on credit—as the British do in America, thus losing no market because of American independence. That is to say, Great Britain has substituted for her formal political supremacy an American moneyed dependence. The United States, to be sure, is now increasing its capital and becoming just free enough of its dependence on Great Britain to be able to afford capital to other nations.

Lacking a superfluity of men or of capital, how can France justify her new adventure in Louisiana? "Transmarine colonies . . . are guarded at great expense of men & money, more particularly when they are placed in warm & unhealthy climates." In this respect, the West Indies must necessarily absorb French energies for years to come. To make Santo Domingo productive would require an immense capital in slaves, buildings, and improvements, to say nothing of the other French islands: and where is France to obtain the capital, unless she realizes the futility of attempting to raise a revenue upon foreign commerce—the futility, for example, of a duty of 20 per cent on articles introduced by foreigners? Unless the ports of Santo Domingo are thrown open to all vessels bringing *necessaries,* unless the inhabitants are permitted to buy cheap and sell dear by encouraging competition among buyers and sellers, unless every possible assurance is given that foreign capital introduced into the island will be secure, "ages will elapse before St. Domingo will cease to drain the wealth & strength of France without an equivalent return." And, in any case, is it not obvious that in the West Indies France will find room to place all the capital she can spare now and will probably be able to spare for years? If one adds her "immense territory in the brazils" (French Guiana), and those establishments in the East Indies which are necessary to provide French ports with that variety of commodities which invites exchanges and gives activity to commerce, it must be clear that a century at least will elapse before France needs to seek new establishments.

How then could the possession of Louisiana be useful? The first problem would be one of return of profit, after slaves arrive and are employed in unproductive clearing to which they are not accustomed. In the northern and middle states, when land is put out to lease, the usual terms are ten years free of rent, and, after that, twelve bushels of wheat per hundred acres forever. In slave-cultivated countries, it would take longer to bring the land into a rent-producing condition: so that few French citizens would be tempted to invest capital in so precarious a property with the hope of so distant a return. And, as an additional disadvantage, Louisiana is surrounded by an immense wilderness into which slaves will disappear to live a life of indolence with the natives.

And even supposing that Louisiana could be put into a thriving condition, what would be the commercial gain? Would not its products, in so far as they are similar to those of the islands, merely serve to reduce the price of island commodities? Would not France then find herself compelled, in order to rescue those who had invested their capital in the colonies, to imitate the Dutch, who destroy their spices and teas when they find that the quantity debases the value?

As regards commodities *not* produced in the West Indies, Louisiana has only lumber and rice, and these are expensive. In the United States, lumber for the islands comes from the free north, not from the slave-laboring South. If France supplied her islands with her own lumber from Louisiana, this would destroy the lumber-for-molasses exchange now prevailing between the northern states and the French islands—an exchange in which the islands may be said to get their lumber for nothing, since molasses is worthless to them. Louisiana, however, would not consume either molasses or rum, and the French island planter would be obliged to pay for his lumber with money.

From a commercial point of view, then, the possession of Louisiana would be injurious to France. How would it be as a market for French manufactures? In the first place, if the free population is to be supplied by emigration from France, that would deplete the present labor force, and, in the second place, some ten years must elapse before the emigrants would have much to give in exchange for manufactures.

It was, of course, argued that French commodities would find their way into the western United States by means of the Mississippi. But this shows "a perfect ignorance" of the navigation of the river and the needs of the inhabitants. The wines of France do not travel well through warm climates; nor, once they have reached the inhabitants of the American West, are they suited to their purses or palates. Glass and earthenware they make for themselves; china they scarcely use, and, in any case, French china is too expensive to compete with that of the East Indies. And the passage upriver is so slow and expensive: how could it hold its own against the large capitals of American and British merchants in Philadelphia and the great improvements in canals and roads, both of which will always see to it that goods are carried by land to the Ohio and other rivers, down which they can be transported "to every other settlement on cheap & easy terms." Even England, with her right to navigate the Mississippi and with the preference that Americans show for her fabrics, never uses that river, but prefers Baltimore and Philadelphia.

From the political point of view, the Minister continued, Americans have done homage to the wisdom of those French statesmen who, at the end of a successful war, thought it more to the advantage of France to obtain a lasting friendship with the United States than to excite their jealousy by acquiring territory adjacent to them. *This could only have the effect of turning them back to the very nation from whom France had helped to liberate them.*

Surely it was due to the "happy mutuality" of French and American interests that they should join in resisting the maritime pretensions of Great Britain: something that could be done only by a union of powers who agree on a liberal maritime code, and by a diminution of British resources through a transfer of part of her commerce to more moderate nations.

The situation of France, if she possessed Louisiana, would endanger and perhaps destroy this mutuality of interests, because, where one nation is bordered by the colony of another great and powerful nation, there is always danger of war. This is especially the case where the colony is as distant from the sovereign as Louisiana would be from France: for then the governor may be guilty of acts of hostility which cannot be immediately settled by the home government, and the wound would fester before the physician could be called in. And how true this would be of a military governor and his troops, "justly elated with the glory of their nation!" How they would look down upon the surrounding people! How arrogantly they would behave toward commerce and those engaged in it! And how impossible it would be to prevent the ardent spirits of the American settlers from taking revenge!

One should not attempt to find an analogy in Great Britain's possession of Canada. Great Britain had prudently separated her territory from that of the United States by a natural boundary which kept the inhabitants of the respective nations from coming into contact; the natural route for the exports of the United States is by her rivers, so that there is no communication between the Americans and the Canadians; and, in any case, the inhabitants of upper Canada are mostly emigrants from the United States.

None the less, the cession of Louisiana could be very important to France, in spite of all these disadvantages—("I speak of Louisiana proper, in which I do not include the Floridas"). When French manufactures had attained their perfection and French trade had been placed upon a proper footing, France would present a much greater variety of subjects for the support of a commerce with the United States than would Great Britain. Was not the United States, an agricultural country which did not manufacture for itself, the most important market for the Old World? And would not France afford a better market than Great Britain for many of the products of the United States? This could happen only upon one condition: namely, if France would immediately consent to cede the island of New Orleans to the United States. She could reserve for herself a right of entry at all times, free of any duties other than those exacted from the vessels and goods of the United States. This would give her ships the advantage over those of every other nation, would retain and increase the capital of New Orleans, from which the supplies for her islands will be purchased on the easiest terms, and will carry the fabrics of France into all the western territory, for the United States would have no motive to check such a trade. Thus France would have all the advantage of New Orleans without the expense of maintaining it, and she would keep on the best terms with the United States, whose friendship was, more than that of any other nation, important to her commerce and to the preservation of her West Indian islands.

Such were the arguments of the American Minister.

Livingston had his memorial translated into French and printed: and twenty copies—so he told James Madison, in a letter which enclosed a copy—had been placed in such hands as would be of most service to America. He went on to say that he did not know how much he could offer for the Floridas, with or without New Orleans. Perhaps he put them too high, but he thought that they would be cheap at $20,000,000. It seems that he had been conferring with Daniel Parker, the Boston speculator; and that between them they had reached this figure. (When Spain at length, in 1819, renounced all claims to West Florida and agreed to cede East Florida, she did so in return for an American assumption of $5,000,000 in debts: but by then her empire was altogether shakier than it had been in 1802.)[30]

Whatever James Madison may have thought of the Livingston mem-

orial, the reader today is apt to be struck by the fact that the first part of
it was a good deal stronger than the second. The discussion of the use-
lessness of Louisiana in a commercial sense was admirably managed: it
aimed a dagger at the heart of the Bonapartist empire. That empire,
it is true, is only dimly perceived in Livingston's pages: to Livingston, it
is Guiana, Louisiana, Santo Domingo, and certain trading establishments
in the East Indies. But he had made it clear that the wedding between
Louisiana and the Sugar Islands would, if it took place at all, have to
be a shotgun affair. Bonaparte, however, like any military dictator, was
a mercantilist: he always assumed that he could impose Louisiana on the
French West Indies planter by decree; and, if he had subdued Santo
Domingo, perhaps he might have done so. If Livingston's arguments are
unanswerable, it is only to the peaceful mind that they are so: to Bonaparte,
when he perused them, they would have been meaningless. This, in turn,
does not imply that they were without force: they had been carefully distributed among Bonaparte's advisers; and Bonaparte, even if he rarely
took his advisers' advice, was sensitive to atmosphere. As a form of
pressure, the memorial had its uses and eventually served its purposes:
not least because it had pointed out, in line with Jefferson's letter, that
an occupation of New Orleans must throw the United States into the arms
of Great Britain, and if there was one contingency Bonaparte dreaded,
it was an increase of British power in America.

The second part, however, which suggests that France might take
Britain's place in American exchanges if only she would cede the island
of New Orleans, suffers from the fact that Livingston had already proved
that climate, tastes, and geography were all against an upriver commerce.
His panacea was still free trade; and he blandly assumed that, granted
a free trade and the right to navigate the Mississippi, France would in
time be able to sell to the people of the western states the very commodities which he had been at some trouble to prove they did not want. On the
other hand, he had pointed out the importance of the commerce of the
United States in the business life of New Orleans. "I find," he wrote,
"that one third of the mercantile houses now employed in New Orleans
belongs to citizens of the United States." What would the value of New
Orleans be to France if this capital were driven away by a military occupation? On the whole, the memorial was a heroic thrust in Livingston's
still somewhat solitary combat with the emerging American empire of
Napoleon Bonaparte.

CHAPTER THREE

In August, 1802, a feeble plebiscite made Napoleon Bonaparte consul for life with the right to name his successor: he was now only one move away from an imperial throne. He was still deluding himself as to the American terminus of this emerging empire. He believed that Santo Domingo was firmly under the control of the doomed Leclerc: he supposed (the Duke of Parma having conveniently died) that the Floridas could now be obtained in return for the addition of Parma and Piacenza to the shadow Kingdom of Etruria. He had, in fact—it was a fault against which he always warned his generals—been "making pictures": he was predicating his future upon a set of facts that did not exist. In such a state of mind, was he likely to be moved by Livingston's memorial on the disadvantages of Louisiana to France? The memorial, though it soon assumed its rightful place in the diplomatic canon, was at the moment just another piece of printed matter, circulating languidly among Bonaparte's advisers, those advisers from whom he rarely condescended to take advice.

"There never was a government," Livingston wrote to Madison in September, "in which less could be done by negotiation than here—There is no people, no legislature, no councillors—One man is everything. He seldom asks advice and never hears it unasked—his ministers are mere clerks & his legislature & councillors parade officers. Tho the sense of every reflecting man is against this wild expedition, no one dares to tell him so."[1]

The expedition here referred to was that which General Victor was to lead to Louisiana as soon as the Spanish Government should deliver the royal order authorizing France to receive that province. It was supposed to sail from Dunkirk in the first week of October: actually, it was held up by inadequate transport, by the delay of the Spanish Government in delivering the order, and by a total lack of information concerning the military situation in Louisiana.[2] Livingston added that, in his belief, the end would be the same, expedition or no expedition: as soon as a state of war existed—"and the extreme hauteur of this government to all around them will not suffer peace to be of long continuance"—Louisiana (that is to say, Louisiana east of the Mississippi) and its capital of New Orleans would be transferred to the United States.[3] This was not the language of prophecy, but the utterance of personal bitterness and frustration. In this mood, he disappeared for two weeks into Belgium and Holland; whence he returned also with a revolutionary theory, derived from observing the peasants in Flanders, of the fructifying effects of sulphuric acid. He never forgot to be a farmer.

II

He began, almost directly following his return to Paris, what must have been a most satisfying quarrel with Talleyrand, from whom he had suffered, in silence and semicomprehension, so many wounding *sous-entendus.*

Sir [he wrote on October 19], I did myself the honor yesterday, to wait upon you with a view to obtain an audience . . . particularly on the subject of the enclosed note, which being peculiarly delicate, I hoped to make such arrangements with you as would satisfy the United States and the Captains Rodgers & Davidson without injuring the feelings of the high officer to whom it relates—but which cannot however be formally proposed. * It is with regret, Sir, that I find myself reduced to the necessity of transacting this business, and all other in future with your office, by note only—till I shall receive specific instructions from the United States, on the subject of the indignity offered them in my person yesterday—When, in violation of the established rules of your office, four different gentlemen who arrived, after me, were admitted to audience while I remained in waiting.[4]

The misunderstanding was adjusted, through the good offices of Marbois: but the point was that Livingston was now ready to do business through other channels than the official one. He realized that Talleyrand was hostile, evasive, and contemptuous; that he was too subtle to be met upon his own ground; that if he were first quarreled with and then circumvented, he might be persuaded to behave more openly. As it happened, the means of circumvention lay ready to hand, and a most dubious means it turned out to be, though far better than none at all: it was the First Consul's elder brother, Joseph, a lazy and somewhat hypocritical personage, who had, none the less, the ear of his brother, and who was ready to intermeddle in affairs of state.

On October 26, Livingston had a most interesting conversation with

* General Leclerc had imprisoned the two American sea captains without trial.

the elder Bonaparte, who professed himself willing to receive any unsigned and informal communication. "My brother is his own counsellor," Joseph was reported by Livingston as saying on this occasion, "[but] we are good brothers and he hears me with pleasure and . . . I have access to him at all times." Livingston then tried to find out what Joseph knew about the Floridas, by asking him whether all difficulties might not be removed if France returned Louisiana to Spain, but retained New Orleans, which she would then add to the Floridas, and transfer it to the United States in return for an assumption of American claims against France. Joseph did not reply directly to this complicated proposal: he asked if the United States really preferred the Floridas to Louisiana. Livingston said that his government most certainly did—"that we had no wish to extend our boundary across the Mississippi or give color to the doubts that had been entertained of the moderation of our views. That all we sought was security and not an extension of Territory." This was the official view at the time, which Livingston candidly revealed to Joseph Bonaparte, just as Joseph Bonaparte, in turn, had covertly admitted that France did not as yet possess the Floridas. But it was Joseph who first suggested that France might cede Louisiana to the United States—a suggestion totally at variance with his brother's ideas and one which, in the course of time and under the influence of British gold, he himself angrily rejected.[5]

Livingston's mind was always a fertile seedbed for the reception of unlikely schemes; the hint that Joseph Bonaparte had thrown out, in such a casual manner, was not thrown upon stony ground. It began to stir, it prepared to germinate. In the meantime, Livingston *"se refugia,"* says M. Renaut, *"à son tour vers la fin de l'année 1802 dans le silence et l'inaction"*: he in turn took refuge in silence and inaction.[6] There was, in fact, little more to do in November and December than observe the course of events: to watch, through a correspondence with Rufus King, the fluctuations between a peaceful and a warlike sentiment in the mind of the British Government. Every ambassador and minister near the Consul's court wondered how long the Peace of Amiens could possibly last: to tabulate their various fears would be to offer an emotional conspectus of the troubled dawn of the nineteenth century. If the British Government under Henry Addington was something of an old hen, yet every feather bristled at the thought of a foreign power which held Belgium garrisoned and controlled the Swiss and Cisalpine republics; which had sent an occupying army to Santo Domingo; and which was about to possess itself of Louisiana.

As if to take advantage of a final lull, Englishmen crowded into

Paris during the summer and autumn of 1802; "among the most pleasing of whom," Livingston told his brother Edward, "I find Mr. [Charles James] Fox with whom I am upon very friendly terms. He is one of the most open and candid men I ever met with." The private secretary of this most fascinating of all Whigs remembered Livingston at a levee in the Tuileries as "plain and simple in manners and dress,—representing his republic with propriety & dignity."[7] But these pleasant exchanges did not represent the usual currency of diplomatic life in Paris. Livingston believed, it is true, that he stood on the best footing at Court: had not his wife, on December 6, dined at the Consul's table, "& did so at the preceding public dinner, an honor that is very unusual twice running to the same ladies"?[8] And his younger daughter, Margaret, was "generally admitted both by the french & British to be one of the finest women in France. She certainly is hansomer than any I have met with out of my own country, since she has added the french air to her native grace."[9] Yet neither these consolations nor those of private dinners and parties were sufficient to make up for the awful tedium where each week "is nearly a picture of the last," in which official society could see, as in a mirror, its reflected reflection, dumbly revolving in a series of receding images. Monday evening at Madame de Forza's; Tuesday, receptions at the Second and the Third Consuls'; Wednesday, a reception at M. de Talleyrand's; Thursday, a "grand circle" at the First or the Second Consul's; Friday, a reception at Livingston's own Legation in the Rue Trudon; Saturday, a party at either the Minister of War's *hôtel* or that of the Minister of the Interior. Add to this at least two days a month when every diplomat was expected to attend a parade at the Tuileries at noon, then a levee at 2:00 P.M. which lasted till 5:00, then a dinner at 5:30, and then a reception which no one could leave until the Consul disappeared at eleven o'clock. "On such days we may be literally on our feet for at least 9 hours, except about three quarters of an hour at dinner, for no meal is so short as a court dinner."[10] Every time he was compelled to tie on his bag and his sword, he told John Armstrong, "I cry with Wolsey *Pomps & Pleasures of this world I hate ye.*" Yet what a curious world it was! "I play chess with a german in a french circle, an Italian looks over my shoulder & an Englishman & a Pole over his; while a Greek and a Tunisian dispute the propriety of our moves"; this happened the last time he played chess at General Berthier's.[11] Possibly, if he had been more certain that something definite would come of his endeavors, he might have taken it all a little more lightly. He was now convinced, however, that if France could obtain the Floridas in exchange for Parma and Piacenza she would never give them up: the First Consul, he had learned, was *"entêté"* (intoxicated) with the project. This was on December 20, almost the year's midnight, and the darkest moment of his career in France.

III

Oddly enough, it was at this period that he first put forward the most fruitful and decisive of his many suggestions. The dates cannot be ascertained with confidence: but a study of his drafts would suggest that he began a new series of negotiations—if negotiations they could be called—at some time between December 1 and December 24, 1802. The first move was, characteristically, a mixture of fantasy and statesmanship: it opened in the former mood and closed, by means of a postscript, in the latter. It was addressed to Joseph Bonaparte.

Louisiana, it begins, will be ruinously expensive to France; yet there is a way of obviating this difficulty and, at the same time, performing a service to the Bonaparte family. There is every reason to believe that Napoleon Bonaparte is soon to be raised to a higher rank; and that his new (imperial) title will be vested after his death in his family. But nations are notoriously ungrateful. If, after the death of "the hero and statesman," new convulsions should lead "either to a despotism or Democracy," who would be the first victim? Surely, the Bonaparte family, which is "alike the dread of Tyrants and the envy of popular Demoagogues."

Why not prepare some permanent establishment for the First Consul's nearest connections—an establishment that would contribute to their present ease and secure them against future hazards? This deserves Joseph Bonaparte's attention, "& *that of the head of your family*." Money placed in foreign funds might in some sort answer, but, for many reasons, including the uncertainty of all European funds, it might be hard to raise an adequate sum. Louisiana, however, "inclusive of the Floridas . . . a useless excrescence upon the body politic of France & which the bulk of the nation would see lopped off with pleasure . . . happily presents itself as the means of effecting this desirable object." By "Louisiana," Livingston meant only New Orleans and that strip of the great province which lay to the east of the Mississippi, to which he now added the Floridas.

Is there any solid objection to the First Consul's transferring the *territory* to his family and the *jurisdiction* to the United States? In return, the United States might offer certain commercial advantages which would place the trade of France upon the same footing as that of the United

States at New Orleans. The First Consul would then transfer to the United States one-half the land to be held in common with his family, this moiety to be sold on their joint account in such proportion and at such prices as shall be mutually agreed upon. If all this is acceptable to the First Consul, "I am ready on the part of the United States to pay ten millions of livres [roughly $2,000,000] either in money or in stock of the United States producing 6 per ct as shall be most acceptable." While the interest on this money will contribute to "the present splendour of your family," the rise in the price of land owing to the immigration of American citizens "will secure to your posterity a property which nothing attainable in France would in any degree equal."[12]

Such was the first part of Livingston's proposal. Founded as it was upon the happy assumption that the First Consul, when he became emperor, might easily be assassinated and his family driven into exile, it was not the most tactful of Livingston's *démarches*. Moreover, he had no powers to offer so much as a single livre to the French Government. Indeed, where it was not tactless, it was quite untenable: it was, one might assert with some confidence, the innocent offspring of an incorrigibly inventive mind. Joseph Bonaparte, it seems, when this note was read to him by the enthusiastic Minister, would not listen to the family part of it; but he consented to hear and to lay before his brother Mr. Livingston's postscript, which was neither innocent, incorrigible, nor inventive, but which was certainly statesmanlike.

If the First Consul could not agree to the first proposal, so the postscript ran, then let him cede to the United States New Orleans and West Florida as far as the Perdido. He could then build a port at Leon, directly opposite New Orleans, participate equally with the United States in the navigation of the river, but cede to the United States all that part of Louisiana (here he means the province itself) which lies west of the Mississippi and above the mouth of the Arkansas. This would calm the anxiety of the United States and prevent any union with Great Britain.[13]

Thus the seed which Joseph Bonaparte had planted threw up its shoot: Livingston was the first American to suggest that the United States would be interested in extending its borders across the Mississippi. Once having made the suggestion, he was the last man to stop short. But first one finds him writing to Joseph Bonaparte to say how much he regretted that "a too scrupulous delicacy" prevented Joseph from listening to the first part of his note. "There are duties," he wrote, "which a man owes to himself and his family [and] which ought not to be overlooked when they can be performed without the smallest injury to the public." But he was extremely obliged to the elder Bonaparte for having submitted his observations to the First Consul. If the First Consul also objected to helping his family in the way that Livingston had outlined, then there were certain modifications to be suggested which would enable him "to repay the services of those among his friends who have just claims upon the republic." This could only be done if the United States were to obtain the jurisdiction, since it was American jurisdiction that would raise the price of the lands. He also supposed that certain modifications of the payments of the American debts, which would redound to the advantage of Joseph Bonaparte, might also not be out of place. He was apparently convinced that the Consul and his brother could be bribed with the promise of a slice of the profits arising from a complicated and dubious conversion of the American debt into French public stock.[14]

This latter scheme was never formally presented to the Bonapartes, Livingston the "projector" having gradually but fortunately retired in favor of a more statesmanlike side of himself: and in the next note to Joseph Bonaparte, he again proposed that France should cede the territory above the Arkansas, New Orleans, and West Florida—"that narrow strip of land which lies between the 31st degree of latitude and the sea as far as the River Perdido." New Orleans itself was of little advantage to the French: "it is placed on the naked bank[,] it has no port[,] bason or quay for shipping, has no fortification of any strength, & the houses are only of wood subject to continual accidents." Moreover, in the event of a war, Great Britain would seize Louisiana and West Florida; add these new acquisitions to Canada, Nova Scotia, and Newfoundland; and then, with her powerful navy, would "annihilate the external trade of every other nation in Europe."

Whereas, if France made the proposed cessions to the United States, and fortified Pensacola and "the Bay of St. Esprit [Tampa]," or left them in the hands of Spain, none of this would occur. Indeed, "the wisest measure would be not only to make the cession I have asked but to hypothecate the whole of East Florida for a term of years, for such part of the American debt as may remain unsatisfied. . . ."

On the other hand, if France continued in her present ways: if she remained silent concerning the navigation of the Mississippi and the rights of entrepôt at New Orleans; if she made no effort to settle the American debt—was it not obvious that she would be in danger of driving the United States into an alliance with Great Britain?[15]

In a note dated December 24, he returned to the same theme. Time, he said, is pressing; Talleyrand has never given him a conclusive answer to any inquiry in the last twelve months; and Congress, now in session, is bound to feel that the French Government is determined to offer the Americans no comfort. Its designs for Louisiana are still obscure; its creditors are ruined and clamorous; it has treated American citizens in Santo Domingo with the utmost severity. In the meantime, Great Britain appears to be anxious to settle her southwestern boundary so as to secure a navigable portion of the Mississippi; and what can this mean but an ambition eventually to control the mouth of the river? Nor can any nation prevent this but the United States; and the United States will hardly be anxious to protect the interests of France, so long as France speaks a language so painful to the feelings of the Government of the United States (*"Un language si peu flatteur au Gouvernement américain"*).

Again, he pressed for the same cessions of territory; or, if Spain had not ceded the Floridas to France, at least for New Orleans and for all of Louisiana above the Arkansas. Such a treaty could also form the basis of a discharge of the American debt, in the course of which the price of French funds could be considerably raised, provided that such secrecy was observed as would prevent the debt being made the object of speculation, *"excepte celles que le Premier Consul pourrait autoriser"* (except such as the First Consul shall authorize).[16]

The end was scarcely worthy of the beginning: but since the scheme for a flutter in French funds was never presented, one should give Livingston the benefit of the doubt and assume that he himself reached the conclusion that it was not fit to present. Second thoughts are not less respectable because they are second.

His last surviving note to Joseph Bonaparte was written on January 7, 1803; and here Livingston's prose had been thrown into a veritable storm of agitation by the rumor, not officially confirmed, that the Spanish Intendant at New Orleans, on October 20, had forbidden American merchants to deposit their goods there. The United States, said Livingston, would hazard their very existence rather than allow the Mississippi to be closed against them. If Spain did not reopen New Orleans, the Americans would be driven into a close and intimate connection with Great Britain and perhaps into an open rupture with Spain. And what would be the use of sending General Bernadotte as French Minister to Washington, if he did not bear a treaty with him, but merely carried vague and disingenuous proposals that one should be made? Would it not seem that France, at the very time that she was sending large armies to Santo Domingo and seizing Louisiana and the Floridas, was actually trying "to paralyze such measure of security as prudence would suggest to the

United States"? Nay, was she not obviously trying to prevent any treaty from being made between America and Great Britain regarding their northwestern boundaries?[17]

The arguments were agitated, but they were certainly forcible. The story of the refusal of the right of deposit at New Orleans would, of course, have thrown any American into a frenzy. As to the possibility of General Bernadotte's going to Washington without any definite powers of negotiation, Livingston was, equally of course, in the right. It could have done nothing but harm.

Joseph Bonaparte was indeed an inconstant intermediary: able but vain; passing with ease from a pliant friendliness to a pompous obstinacy; easily shocked by any laxity but his own. He replied verbally to the communication of January 7, and repeated what he had to say by letter on January 11, to the effect that Livingston must in the future address himself to Talleyrand, *"le Ministre des Relations Extérieures qui seul porra vous faire connaître les intentions du gouvernement"* (who alone could inform you of the intentions of the government).[18] One is obliged to assume that Talleyrand, who could hardly have been unaware of these private communications, had decided to intervene.

But Joseph Bonaparte had, at any rate, served his purpose. He had brought Livingston's proposals under the eye of the First Consul, and, by doing so, he had forced Talleyrand into the open. Livingston was quick to seize on his advantage. On January 10, he wrote to the Minister of Foreign Affairs an extremely able note, in which he remarked that he would predicate what he had to say on the assumption that France possessed the Floridas; for otherwise Louisiana would be worthless to her.[19] This was going further, but in the right direction, than any argument he had ventured to suggest to the First Consul. Louisiana, without the Floridas, was certainly useless to imperial France. At the time, the negotiation between Spain and France for the Floridas had become a matter of general discussion in Paris; and Lord Whitworth, the English Ambassador, wrote to Lord Hawkesbury on January 4:

In a conversation I had with him [Mr. Livingston] two days ago he gave it as his decided opinion that should the measure be attempted it would have the immediate effect of uniting every individual in America, of every party, and none more sincerely than himself, in the cause of Great Britain. Should such be the event, we may, from the gentleman's known political bias, expect to have few enemies remaining in that country. I can perceive that the little intercourse which has arisen between him and myself gives a considerable degree of jealousy to Mr. Talleyrand.[20]

This was the diplomatic background against which the note of January 10 was written. It was made all the more uncertain by the fact that, on January 7, Napoleon Bonaparte had been obliged to publish in the *Moniteur* the fearful story of the death of Leclerc in Santo Domingo and the virtual destruction of his army. As for the expedition under General Victor, it had never set sail; it was now ice-bound in Helvoet Sluys, an object of alarm and disgust to the British Government. Bonaparte was pressing for the Floridas, as if to salvage something from all these calamities: whether to appease his vanity or to create, in the face of everything, something like an American empire can only be a matter of speculation.

In his note of January 10, Livingston repeated his demand for all of Louisiana above the Arkansas, since this would place a protective American barrier between British Canada and a colony of France; while France, by retaining the country lying west of the Mississippi but below the Arkansas (a country, he thought, capable of sustaining fifteen million inhabitants) would herself place a barrier between the United States and Mexico, "if (which I hope will never be the case) they should have the wild idea of carrying their arms into that country."

Let France own East Florida as far as the River Perdido, he said, but, along with the western territory above the Arkansas, cede New Orleans and West Florida to the Americans, which would give them the mouth of the Mobile River and of the other small rivers which penetrated their territory. As for the closing of New Orleans to American deposits, he exonerated France from any knowledge of the Spanish suspension; and added, in a sentence he was wise enough to delete, that Spain could only have done the deed in order to provoke the Americans into seizing New Orleans before the French could get there.

He then went on to say that, under any other plan but his, Great Britain could block up the seaports with her ships and easily attack New Orleans from Canada with fifteen or twenty thousand men "& a host of savages." Whether the British could do anything of the sort was, to say the least, arguable: but Livingston added that France, "by grasping at a desert & an insignificant town," would throw the United States into the arms of Great Britain and make the latter "mistress of the New World." And then "the precious metals of Mexico combined with the treasures of Indostan will enable her to purchase Nations whose aid she may require in confirming her power." The United States would buy these territories at a price suited to their value and to American circumstances, in the hope that France, at least, would reciprocate by satisfying her distressed American creditors.[21]

This note, the culmination of a whole series of reiterated demands for the territory above the Arkansas, was remarkable, not merely for the originality and daring of these demands in themselves—for Livingston had no instructions to support him—but also for the curious prescience which marked its final passages. The specie of the Americas had indeed been disappearing for centuries into the treasuries of the East; and, by looting India, the British had provided the capital for that industrial revolution which was to bring about the downfall of Napoleon I. The British Empire, as the First Consul most feared it in 1803, haunted Livingston's paragraphs, and just at the time when Bonaparte had heard that a fearful disaster had befallen Leclerc in Santo Domingo. A Great Britain firmly emplanted in America and in India—that is what he dreaded: that, and an Anglo-American alliance of any kind. The strength or weakness of the United States was a secondary consideration.

Livingston, while he continued to disturb the susceptibilities of Talleyrand by making marked advances to Lord Whitworth,[22] repeated this theme in his next report to James Madison. He said that he had dwelt in all his recent notes on the probable capture of the Floridas by Great Britain, if the Floridas had been ceded to France, and upon its subsequent effect—the conquest of the French West Indian islands, and a British monopoly of the trade between the West and the East Indies. That is why he had proposed a cession of the territory lying north of the Arkansas; with West Florida and New Orleans, it would be a barrier between British Canada and the French. He had not been able to speak of East Florida, "because I found they consider the suggestion of the Gulph as very important." He had proposed an indefinite sum, "not knowing what to offer," and had suggested as a condition of the treaty that the American debt should be "inscribed on their 5 pr. Ct. stock. I know it would be vain to render them our creditors by deducting this out of our payment," because money alone would have any effect in carrying out the purchase plan and even that must be managed in such a way as to afford "very heavy pots du vin or no plan will succeed. . . . Be persuaded that no treaty has been made for some time past that did not bring considerable business into the coffers of —[Talleyrand], nor will any be advantageously made if this means be neglected."[23]

Livingston was merely realistic; but he could hardly have supposed that this harping upon the theme of bribery would find any favor with his superiors in Washington. For years, American ministers abroad were to protest that without a resort to bribes no business could be done; and for years, the business was, somehow or other, done without a resort to bribes.

The realistic approach was not necessarily the most effective one. What worried and hampered Livingston more, as a matter of fact, was his lack of adequate instructions. "Indeed," he wrote in this same dispatch, "I am not satisfied from examining my instructions and commissions that I am empowerd to do anything but the common routine of business." It was all too true.

None the less, after the first rumor of a suspension at New Orleans, it was impossible for an active and intelligent man to sit in idleness, transacting nothing but the common routine of business. Livingston had to conceal his lack of instructions, and proceed as best he could upon his own. Nine days after writing to Madison, he took the extreme step of sending a note directly to the First Consul.

He began by remarking that the American claims against France were founded chiefly upon contracts for articles of the first necessity, furnished at great risk, and by men who were actuated by a keen "enthusiasm in the cause of France." If they had not been, would they not have carried their commodities to Britain or to neutral ports? This was a kindly description of men whose enthusiasm, while keen enough, was directed solely toward their own concerns: but it was also a mere formality. Livingston had learned by now that such considerations meant nothing to the First Consul. What mattered was the possible advantage to be gained from a funding of the American debt, which he computed at 20,000,000 livres.

Having expatiated upon this, Livingston then turned to the question of the withdrawal of the right of deposit at New Orleans. If the Spanish Minister had not interposed, and if the American Government had not shown an extreme solicitude to keep the peace, what fearful consequences might not have followed upon this act! As it was, if nothing were done to calm their anxiety before the season for bringing down produce occurred, he feared that the American Government "will be compelled to follow the impulse of the people," and seize New Orleans by force of arms. He felt that it could not be improper for him to press for a treaty, a treaty explaining the terms on which France had received Louisiana from Spain, and recognizing the rights of Americans as secured to them by Pinckney's treaty.

The whole note, which ended with the now familiar plea for a cession of territory to the United States, was studiously polite toward the First Consul, but scarcely so toward the Minister of Foreign Affairs. If the preamble in its English form—"Though I am satisfied that my notes to the Minister of Exterior Relations have been truly represented to you"—was far from tactful, its French translation—"*Quoique je suis persuadé que mes notes au Ministre de Relations Extérieures ayent été fidèlement mises sous vos yeux"*—seemed deliberately designed to provoke.[24]

Talleyrand waited eleven days before sending an answer, which the faithful Durant had composed in a vein of the most wounding sarcasm. As regards Livingston's effort to combine in one note an arrangement for settling the American claims and a demand for an explanatory treaty, it was altogether against the maxims of the French Government, said M. de Talleyrand, to mingle *"les rapports importans et delicats de la Politique avec des calculs de Solde et des Intérêts d'argent."* This mingling of diplomacy and finance was, as he well knew, Livingston's only way of getting anything done; Talleyrand himself always formalized it in its lowest form; but the cut was a stinging one, and it was smartly administered. The Consul, he went on, could appreciate Livingston's motives in insisting on an explanatory treaty and commanded him to say that, in view of the interest, "premature no doubt but natural and plausible," which the United States seemed to have in this discussion, he was sending a minister to Washington whose reports would help to enlighten him before he actually made up his mind. Never had a snub been administered more carefully: but, strange to say, in the middle of Talleyrand's insults there appeared a singular and shining concession. If Livingston would produce an exact statement of the American debt, he could be assured that every claim would be promptly and exactly settled (*"après un tel état tout sera promptement et exactement Soldé"*).[25]

Livingston was not in the least disturbed by Talleyrand's efforts to teach him manners: it simply would not have occurred to him that, in this respect, he had anything to learn. What *did* occur to him was that he had at last undermined Talleyrand's defenses and that he had extracted from the French Government, for the first time, a firm promise to honor its debts. He wrote an immediate report to Madison to say that he had told the claimants in Paris the hopeful news, in order to prevent them from selling their claims at some insignificant price, and that he had also written of it to a friend in America, telling him to speak of it publicly, so as to keep the creditors there out of the hands of speculators.[26]

Madison's present biographer, to whom one always listens with attention, says that Livingston's motives in giving such publicity to Bonaparte's promise were frankly political: that he was, in fact, "planning to run for the Vice President, with the American creditors as his expected backers and James Swan his Paris campaign manager."[27] A study of his letters at this time, however, shows that the vice-presidency never entered into his calculations except as a remote possibility; but that he had recently received a letter from Ambrose Spencer, his former enemy, saying that the governorship of New York was his if he wanted to run in the elections of 1804. ("In my opinion the government of the State will be at your service—I speak sincerely and confidentially.") He replied, on January 13, 1803, that "I shall leave France in one year from next Spring & if it shd. be absolutely necessary in the opinion of my friends at an earlier period."[28]

Political motives are always the easiest to ascribe to any human action: but it is well to remember that Livingston, while an impulsive and erratic politician, was anything but a simpleton. To publicize a Consular promise before it had been performed would have been, politically, a foolish gamble: how much better to wait until the debts were settled, or in such a train that the settlement had become irrevocable, and then give the whole correspondence to the world! Moreover, James Swan was not a popular or trusted figure with the merchants of New York; Livingston's brother John had written to warn the Minister against him;[29] and as a campaign manager in Paris, he would have been worse than useless with the Republican voters of that state. It is sometimes the part of wisdom to take a man at his word, and to assume that Livingston, knowing that the news was bound to leak out, had taken such steps as he could to rescue the claimants from speculation. And there is one further consideration: in spite of Talleyrand's finesse, government under Bonaparte was a coarse affair; if it did not respond to appeals to its honor, it was highly amenable to less chivalrous forms of pressure. Livingston, who had been trying for weeks to obtain certain vital cessions of territory, knew all too well that a settlement of American debts would almost certainly play a part in any cession he obtained. To publicize the Consul's promise was to apply diplomatic pressure in the most obvious but effective form.

IV

Talleyrand's letter had stated that General Bernadotte was to go to Washington as minister, supplanting the capable Louis André Pichon, who was only chargé d'affaires; and that Bernadotte was to make a report. Bernadotte's mission came as no surprise to Livingston. He had known of it as early as January 7; he thought it (considering the fact that Bernadotte was second in consequence only to the First Consul) "an honorable banishment"; he told Joseph Bonaparte that it could do no good. And in any case, he had already learned that President Jefferson had appointed James Monroe to a special mission to France, in order to convey to the First Consul the government's views on New Orleans and the Floridas.[30] Thus, while Bonaparte threatened to transfer the whole matter temporarily to Washington, Washington had decided to strengthen its minister's hands in Paris. Livingston, naturally, did not believe that his hands needed strengthening: but at least he knew that Paris, not Washington, was to be the center of the negotiation; and he continued to urge upon Talleyrand the necessity of making some guarantee of American rights at New Orleans, before Monroe arrived. After that, he said, they would have to discuss the whole question of the "inutility" of French acquisitions of territory on the American border. Talleyrand replied, in effect, that he would wait and see.

At this point, Livingston had told the French Government that the United States should be given Louisiana above the Arkansas, New Orleans, and, at least, West Florida, if the Floridas were ceded to France. In return, they would pay a price suitable to the value of the territory and to their financial circumstances, and would expect to come to some arrangement about the settlement of the American debts. And of these suggestions, the most fruitful, creative, and daring was the suggestion that the Americans might now be willing to extend their borders west of the Mississippi.

CHAPTER FOUR

The policy of Jefferson and Madison, until news reached them in November, 1802, of the closing of the port of New Orleans, is neatly summed up in a message from Rufus King to Robert R. Livingston.

The letter to which I have alluded from Washington [he wrote on April 25, 1802] is one from Thornton [Edward Thornton, English Chargé] to Lord Hawkesbury, and dated 4 Mar[ch]—it reports a conversation between *him and the President* concerning *the cession of Louisiana, the Floridas* and the settlement of our northwestern boundary—concerning the former *the President is* made to say that it will inevitably produce jealousies, irritation, *and hostilities* and with regard to the latter, instead of a commission which will be both dilatory and expensive *the President* suggested the expediency of a diplomatic settlement by its being agreed to run a line from the western bay of lake superior to such part of the Mississippi as is nearest to lake superior, or in other words making the shortest line between them the boundary. . . . It seems I confess a little extraordinary that we shd. [word illegible] this sort of information thro' this channel—but as it was recd. so it is given, in the most perfect confidence. [The italicized words between asterisks were in cipher.][1]

It was by attentions to Mr. Thornton, and by impressing upon Pichon, the French Chargé, the inadvisability of a retrocession that Jefferson and Madison made their feelings known to France. They did not confide in their ministers abroad. Even Jefferson's most eloquent and ominous statements were surrounded by careful qualifications.

We shall so take our distance between the two rival nations [France and England] [he wrote to Livingston, for example, on October 10, 1802] as, remaining disengaged till necessity compels us, we may haul finally to the enemy of that which shall make it necessary. . . . No matter at present existing between them [France] and us is important enough to risk a breach of the peace; peace being indeed the most important of all things to us, except the preserving an erect & independent attitude. Although I know your own judgment leads you to pursue this line identically, yet I thought it just to strengthen it by the concurrence of my own. . . . *My* letters to you being merely private, I leave all details of business to their official channel.[2]

Jefferson's great letter of April 18, 1802, may have stiffened Livingston's resolution, even though it deprecated resolute behavior; from *this* communication, however, he could have derived nothing but perplexity. Until the news of New Orleans changed the whole aspect of affairs, it was by delicacy and mystery that Jefferson and Madison proposed to make themselves felt in Europe. The dispatches of Pichon, a most able observer who was by no means in sympathy with the dictatorship of Bonaparte, testify that this course had had its effect. He always urged upon his government the suggestion that unfriendly behavior toward the United States —and the retrocession of Louisiana was nothing in essence if not unfriendly —could only produce a friendliness toward England. He would calculate the degrees of warmth in the President's and the Secretary's behavior toward Mr. Thornton, and then report to his superiors the same ominous conclusion: French coldness was alienating the Republicans. A *rapprochement* with England, sooner or later, must be the fateful consequence. This was the burden of a dispatch from him received in Paris on December 22: it was one of the most persuasive he ever wrote.

II

The reason for the Spanish Intendant's action remained, for one hundred and thirty years, buried in the almost bottomless archives of the Spanish Government. It was once believed that Carlos IV's orders to Don Juan Ventura Morales, dated July 14, 1802, were due to the intervention of Bonaparte, who wanted to take over New Orleans without the right of deposit, which he could then use as a bargaining point or a blackmailing one.[3] And certainly the fact that the order to Morales was followed, in one day, by an order providing for the delivery of Louisiana to France, seemed to support this conclusion. "A bundle of documents," however, discovered some twenty-five years ago in the Archivo Historico Nacional, shows that the order to Morales was nothing more or less than a Spanish reprisal against American smuggling (particularly of gold and silver) through New Orleans, and against lack of consideration shown to Spanish sailors in American ports. The French were so little in the secret that they heard the story of the closing of the port only through Pichon in Washington.[4]

In Washington itself, the news was received with consternation, tempered by the hope that both the Spanish Minister and the French Chargé would help to reverse the Intendant's ruling. And, indeed, the young and high-spirited Spanish Minister, convinced that Morales had acted without orders, wrote that unhappy gentleman a letter so extremely sharp that the new French prefect at New Orleans described it as a "veritable diatribe."[5] The President's language was less severe; as a matter of fact, in his annual message of December 15, he contrived not to mention New Orleans at all. He was, as he afterward explained, trying to gain time. No one knew better than he what a violent effect the closing of the port and the denial of the right of deposit would have upon the feelings of the West. Congress he could manage for a time; and the resolutions of Congress of January 7, 1803, were mildness itself. The West was another affair. Legislature after legislature expressed the most violent resolves: they were, he thought, honest and natural, as compared to the agitation in the seaports, which "proceeds from a desire for war which increases the mercantile lottery," while "in the federalists generally and especially those of Congress the object is to force us into war if possible, in order to derange our finances, or if this cannot be done, to attach the western country to them, as their best friends, and thus get again into power."[6]

The measure that he took to quiet the West and thwart the Federalists was to appoint a minister extraordinary to go to Paris to assist Livingston in the purchase of New Orleans and the Floridas; or afterward to Madrid, if the purchase could best be made there. And it so happened that an appointee stood ready in the person of James Monroe, then retiring as governor of Virginia.

Certainly if James Monroe were not ready for this task, two letters from Jefferson would have made him so. "I shall tomorrow," he wrote on January 10, "nominate you to the Senate for an extraordinary mission to France, and the circumstances are such as to render it impossible to decline; because the whole public hope will be rested on you." And again on the 13th, "All eyes," he said, "all hopes are fixed on you; and were you to decline, the chagrin would be universal, and would shake under your feet the high ground on which you now stand. Indeed, I know nothing which would produce such a shock, for on the event of this mission depends the future of this republic. . . . I am sensible of the measures you have taken for getting into a different line of business, that it will be a great sacrifice on your part, and presents from the season and other circumstances serious difficulties. But some men are born for the public. Nature by fitting them for the service of the human race on a broad scale, has stamped them with the evidence of her destination and their duty."[7]

"Some men are born for the public." Any student of Monroe's long and famous career knows that this was the chord that would always have to be touched if one wished him to perform a disagreeable or expensive or difficult task. All his life, he asked only to be of service: and in this demand, honorable as it was, there were only the two disadvantages that he might on occasion make public service his grand object, rather than the ends to which public service was to be put; or else, although as disinterested a man as it was possible to find in public life, that he might expect, as a matter of course, that the acclaim bestowed upon him should be equal to the demand he made of himself. He was, in his honest way, avid for fame; nor was his appetite in this respect tempered by any trace of humor. He was neither vain nor mean, but he was proud and sensitive, and might prove an awkward colleague to a man who was also in search of fame, if their paths, instead of merely converging, happened at any point to cross each other.

Monroe accepted the nomination which the Senate had approved on January 13, and which the House had implemented on January 11 with an appropriation of $2,000,000. The purpose of the nomination, said Jefferson, was to give aid to Livingston and Pinckney "in enlarging and more effectually securing our rights and interests in the river Mississippi and the territories eastward thereof"; the purpose of the appropriation, said the House, was "to defray any expenses which may be incurred in relation to the intercourse between the United States and foreign nations."[8]

Madison's instructions to Monroe and Livingston, first written on January 31, but finally dated March 2, were as follows: they were to treat with the French Government on the subject of "the Mississippi and the Territories Eastward thereof and without the limits of the United States. The object in view is to procure by just and satisfactory arrangements, a Cession to the United States of New Orleans and of West and East Florida, or as much thereof as the actual proprietor can be prevailed to part with." The price was left to the discretion of the two Americans, except that it was not to go above $9,375,000 (50,000,000 livres), including the $2,000,000 authorized by Congress. In the annexed draft of a proposed treaty, Madison suggested that the territory east of the Mississippi should be made to comprehend the two Floridas, the island of New Orleans and the islands lying to the north and east of that channel of the Mississippi commonly called the South Pass, and all such islands as appertained to the Floridas: "*France*," he added, "*reserving to herself all the Territory on the west side of the Mississippi.*"[9]

III

Livingston would have been somewhat more or somewhat less than human if he had received the news of the Monroe appointment with pleasure. He had already experienced, in the unofficial "mission" of Pierre Du Pont de

Nemours, a high-minded intermeddler, the mischievous side of the President's passion for special envoys: how much, he now asked himself, could be expected from this official colleague? It was not that he did not respect Mr. Monroe, with whom he had for years conducted a most cordial correspondence: what he was feeling was nothing more or less than personal chagrin. It was all very well for the Secretary of State to write, in his kindliest manner, that the mission implied no reflection whatsoever upon his abilities—and, indeed, the weakness of Pinckney at Madrid had been uppermost in Jefferson's and Madison's minds: a reflection upon his abilities was what Livingston saw in it.[10] "I shall do everything in my power to pave the way for him," he replied to Madison's letter of January 18, 1803, "and sincerely hope it may be attended with the desired effect. It will, however, cut off one resource on which I greatly relied; because I had established a confidence which it will take Mr. Monroe some time to inspire on what regards personal interest and had made arrangements for satisfying them which I must now relinquish. Enclosed is a letter addressed to the First Consul himself and sent him before I heard of Mr. Monroe's appointment."[11]

By "personal interest," in this instance, he did not refer to his efforts to tempt the Bonapartes with "liberal pots du vin"; what he had in mind, one ventures to think, was something rather more delicate. Monroe had been minister to France between 1794 and 1796, and in the course of his ministry had behaved in a manner which some people thought more becoming to a demagogue than to a minister. He was still known as a leader of what one might today call the left wing of the Republican party: and this leadership, while honorable to Monroe, was likely to prove a distinct disadvantage in any dealings with Napoleon Bonaparte. If there was one person whom the First Consul disliked at this stage in his career, that person was an avowed and enthusiastic democrat. It was because he had concealed his democratic inclinations behind the plain but statuesque façade of a Hudson River magnate that Livingston believed himself to be popular with Bonaparte.

And then there was another consideration. Whatever the diplomatic purposes of Monroe's appointment might be, in a domestic sense it was intended to quiet the passions of the West. Writing to Rufus King on March 23, Livingston said that he believed the appointment to be necessary in the United States, but that in Paris "it has greatly embarrassed my operations."[12] And the next day, he told James Madison that a recent dispatch from Pichon had informed the French Government that Monroe's appointment had "tranquillized everything." The result was that the French were inclined to wait and see "whether the storm would blow over, in which case they will treat with more advantage."[13] His whole case for cessions of territory west as well as east of the Mississippi now depended for success, he thought, upon one factor: and that was the threat that the West might take matters into its own hands. If Monroe's appointment diminished this threat, how were the French to be brought to terms?

He was not aware that a dispatch from Pichon received in Paris on March 28 absolutely contradicted what had been said in the previous one. "The crisis," Pichon now insisted, "grows greater every day, and we cannot push it into the distant future."[14] There rarely has been a more subtle combination of intellects than Jefferson's as President with Madison's as Secretary of State. While the President insisted upon the tranquilizing effect of Monroe's appointment, Madison consistently urged upon Pichon the thought that the West might refuse to be tranquilized. A correspondingly subtle transformation had taken place in the public character of Monroe, now tossing upon the Atlantic: the French could not tell whether he came waving an olive branch or brandishing a sword. One presumes to guess that this is exactly what Jefferson and Madison intended, that the game they were playing with the French was a huge but delicate bluff, and that it might have been better if they had confided in their resident minister.

Nor is the image of Monroe upon the wild Atlantic itself inappropriate. The historical circumstances through which he was passing on his way to Paris were stormy indeed: the whole Western World was, once again, hideously tottering on the edge of war. On March 12, at Madame (Josephine) Bonaparte's drawing room, the Consul went the usual round of the ladies and then passed into the room where the diplomats were assembled. He spoke a few words to Livingston and a few to the Danish Minister and then, passing to the end of the room, confronted Lord Whitworth, the British Ambassador. "I find, my Lord," he said abruptly, "your nation wants war again." "No, sir," replied Whitworth, "we wish for peace." After a few more very strong terms, so Livingston told Rufus King, "invoking the vengeance of heaven upon those who broke the treaty [of Amiens] he concluded—Malta must be evacuated or war. The prefet of the palace then told him that Madame B. & the ladies in the next room expected him. He then retired."[15] The agitated Lord Whitworth moved over to Livingston and confided to him exactly what had happened, and Livingston, returning at once to his cabinet, wrote to warn Jefferson. "Within a few days, the alarm spread through Europe," writes Henry Adams, "and the affairs of St. Domingo were forgotten."[16] This incident must be noticed in due time: it is sufficient to say here that when Monroe arrived in Paris, the Peace of Amiens, so brief and so inconclusive, was visibly drawing to its close.

In the meantime, as the Spanish blockade of New Orleans remained unbroken, the Federalists in Congress were moving to the attack. On January 15, Senator James Ross, of Pennsylvania, had moved to give the President authority to raise fifty thousand troops for the seizure of New Orleans; and it was only after a long and violent debate, lasting for many weeks, that the administration was able to get a gentler form of words substituted for the Ross resolution. Officially, Madison deprecated the Ross speech, for Ross was a Federalist and Madison was a pacifist: he said that it delegated an unconstitutional power to the executive. Privately, however, he warned Pichon that "it was true that the nation was in a ferment, especially in the West; that it felt its strength and needed all the confidence it had in the government to prevent it from acting. That this circumstance had made the United States itself examine the national disposition, and to conclude that it held the balance in the new world and could decide it at any moment."[17]

In Paris, Livingston, on April 8, received a copy of the New York *Chronicle,* which contained the full text of Senator Ross's resolution. Here perhaps was the thunderbolt he had been hoping for, and he hastened to send it to Talleyrand. On the same day, James Monroe and his family landed at Le Havre.[18]

IV

Monroe's letter, announcing his arrival, reached Paris on April 10, 1803, and did not add much to the Minister's peace of mind. Livingston felt that his own negotiation was on the verge of some denouement, he could not quite tell what, but that Talleyrand was now more hostile than ever, he could not quite tell why: with the coming of Monroe, would not everything have to be done over again?

Dear Sir [he wrote], I congratulate you on your safe arrival, and have long and anxiously wished for you. God grant that your mission may answer yours and the public expectations. War may do something for us—nothing else would. I have paved the way for you, and if you could add to my means an assurance that we were now in possession of New Orleans, we should do well; but I detain Mr. Benthelow who is impatient to fly to the arms of his wife— I have apprized the Minister of your arrival; and told him you would be here on Tuesday or Wednesday—present my Compts &c. to Mrs. Munroe, and believe me &c.[19]

This letter was only in part an accurate one. It was by no means the case that Livingston had long and anxiously wished for Monroe: but it was true that he had paved the way for him.

V

Indeed, everything and a great deal more than everything that Livingston had asked for was now, as if shaken from some cornucopia, to be lavished upon the two Americans and their countrymen. On April 10, Bonaparte, after hearing Easter Mass at St. Cloud, summoned Barbé-Marbois, his Minister of Finance, and Denis Decrès, his Minister of Marine, and told them that he feared England would seize Lousiana as her first act in the impending war. "I think," he said in his peremptory manner, "of ceding it to the United States. I can scarcely say that I cede it to them, for it is not yet in our possession. If, however, I leave the least time to our enemies [*pour peu que je laisse de temps à nos ennemis*], I shall only transmit an empty title to those republicans whose friendship I seek. They ask of me only one town in Louisiana; but I already consider the colony as entirely lost; and it appears to me that in the hands of this growing power it will be more useful to the policy and even to the commerce, of France than if I should attempt to keep it."[20]

Marbois, who had lived so long in America, who had once been intendant at Santo Domingo, who had married an American, was quite in favor of the cession. The astounded Decrès, who was thinking of naval bases, was totally opposed to it. Agreement or opposition meant nothing to Bonaparte once his mind was made up. The next morning, April 11, he summoned Marbois to his presence and told him: "I renounce Louisiana. It is not only New Orleans that I cede; it is the whole colony without reserve. I know the price of what I abandon. I have proved the importance I attach to this province, since my first diplomatic act with Spain had the object of recovering it. I renounce it with the greatest regret [*avec un vif déplaisir*]; to attempt obstinately to retain it would be folly. I direct you to negotiate this affair. Do not even wait for the arrival of Mr. Monroe: have an interview this very day with Mr. Livingston."[21]

So ran the memories of Barbé-Marbois, when in his old age he committed them to his *Histoire de la Louisiane*. He does not explain how the negotiation, thus apparently committed to him, still remained in the hands of M. Talleyrand. But it is quite certain that on April 11 Talleyrand asked Livingston to call at his headquarters in the Rue du Bac, and there, casually, even lightly, asked him whether the United States wished to have the whole of Louisiana. For a moment, Livingston lost his presence of mind. For months, he had been repeating, in that same room, his demands for West Florida, for New Orleans, for Louisiana above the Arkansas; for months, Talleyrand had listened in an imperturbable, a skeptical, a faintly derisive silence, into which each demand had dropped like a pebble into a still pool, causing only an exquisite ripple before it disappeared forever. Now the Foreign Minister was offering him the whole province.

In his report to Madison, written the same day, Livingston (who as yet had no idea of what had happened at St. Cloud) spoke with all the solemnity of one who had somehow converted M. Talleyrand. Under the circumstances, he could hardly have come to any other conclusion. But to the actual offer, he wrote,

I told him no, that our wishes extended only to New Orleans & the Floridas, that the policy of France however should dictate (as I had shown in an official note delivered to him) to give us the country above the river Arkansa[s] in order to place a barrier between them & Canada. He said that if they gave New Orleans the rest would be of little value & that he would wish to know what we would give for the whole? I told him that it was a subject I had not thought of but that I supposed we should not object to 20,000,000 [livres] provided our citizens were paid—He told me that this was too low an offer & that he would be glad if I would reflect upon it & tell him tomorrow. I told him that as Mr. Munroe wd. be in town in two days I would delay any further offer until I had the pleasure of introducing him. He added however that he did not speak from authority but that the idea had struck him.[22]

By the next day, Livingston had recovered from his astonishment, and haunted the office in the Rue du Bac, hoping, and it was only human, to gather some laurels for himself before Monroe's post chaise deposited that unwished-for emissary at the door of his Paris hotel. Talleyrand had become, in the meantime, somewhat more his old evasive self. "He . . . thought it proper," Livingston wrote to Madison on the 13th, "to declare that his proposition was only personal, but still requested me to make an offer; and upon my declining to do so, as I expected Mr. Munroe the next day, he shrugged up his shoulders and changed the conversation." At length, Livingston brought him back to the eccentric proposition he had attempted to advance in an informal note. Why not send General Bernadotte to Washington with dispatches from Livingston which should explain that Talleyrand, "in reply to my various notes," had been charged to ask him to present some particular proposition. After this, said Livingston, "we could work to mature the treaty even before the formal reception of Mr. Monroe. I will profit by his advice and he will appear as a contracting party before the treaty is concluded." He did not, of course, give the substance of this note to Madison: he merely mentioned his "informal note which contained a request grounded upon my apprehension of the consequence of sending out Genl. Bernadotte without enabling him to say a treaty was begun."

Talleyrand, at any rate, replied that he could answer only evasively "because Louisiana was not theirs." Livingston said that he smiled at this assertion, saying that he had seen the treaty recognizing it, that he knew the Consul had appointed officers to govern the country, and that Talleyrand himself had told him that General Victor was to take possession. Talleyrand still persisted that "they had it in contemplation to obtain it but had it not." If they did not have it, Livingston retorted, he would (if Mr. Monroe agreed) advise his government immediately to take New Orleans by force from Spain. "He seemed," he continued, "alarmed at the boldness of the measure" and said that he would answer the note, but would be forced to answer it evasively. At this, Livingston reported, he replied that he and Mr. Monroe were "not disposed to triffle," that he was sure the instructions Monroe was bringing with him would call for "precise & prompt notice," and that he feared that his government would think him but an indolent negotiator. Talleyrand laughed and said "that he would give me a certificate that I was the most importunate he had yet met with." "There is something so extraordinary in all this," Livingston wrote, "that I did not detail it to you till I found some clue to the labirinth, which I have done as you will find before I finish the letter."[23]

VI

Livingston had indeed discovered a clue to a labyrinth, but not quite the right labyrinth: so that, before finishing his letter, it becomes necessary to look ahead a week or so to an extraordinary scene in the bosom of the Bonaparte family which sounded like the opening of a palace revolution.

This scene is so famous, and has been distilled by Henry Adams with such extraordinary felicity out of the memoirs of Lucien Bonaparte, that it should not receive here more than the most summary relation. In brief, it is to the effect that Lucien Bonaparte, coming home to dress for the theater, where Talma was to appear in a new role, found his brother Joseph waiting for him with the dreadful news that the First Consul proposed to sell all of Louisiana. Filled with patriotic zeal, the two brothers repaired the next morning to the Tuileries, were admitted to the First Consul's presence, and found the great man soaking himself in a bath of scented water. There were passages of towering recrimination, in which Lucien and Joseph sought to restrain their brother from an act they thought so injurious to France: and the culmination was reached when Joseph, advancing to the edge of the bath, shouted: "I tell you, General, that you, I, and all of us, if you do what you threaten, may prepare ourselves soon to go and join the poor innocent devils whom you so legally, humanely, and especially with such justice, have transported to Sinnamary." Napoleon half started out of his bath. "You are insolent," he screamed, "I ought—" And he threw himself back with such force as to drench his two brothers with a mass of perfumed water.

The dripping Lucien had the wit to strike a theatrical pose and recite the words which Virgil gave to Neptune when he reproved the waves:

> *"Quos ego—! sed motos praestat componere fluctus:*
> *post mihi non simili poena commissa luetis."**

Whereupon the Bonapartes recovered their tempers, Bonaparte's valet fell into a swoon, Joseph left to change his clothes, and Lucien remained to continue the quarrel until his brother threatened to break him like the snuffbox which he flung violently upon the floor.[24]

The modern reader of this exemplary tale is conscious, however, that all is not quite as it seems. In the first volume of C. D. Yonge's *Life and Administration of Robert Banks, Second Earl of Liverpool,* published in 1868, there is a passage that escaped the attention of Henry Adams. It tells of an understanding between Lord Whitworth, the British Ambassador, and Joseph Bonaparte, in which, for a consideration of £100,000 and perhaps more, Joseph would undertake to make Napoleon Bonaparte change his mind about Malta. Whitworth had approached Joseph after his scene with Bonaparte on March 12. Whether Lucien was involved in this affair is less certain; but Talleyrand eventually was brought in, and Whitworth began to talk of £100,000 or even £2,000,000 as a sacrifice that would be cheap, considering the object it would obtain. When Talleyrand moved in, men invariably increased their bribes. No money actually changed hands; but it is quite certain that from the middle of March until the end of April, a group of influential men, tempted by this offer of British gold, was working to bring the First Consul into a peaceful frame of mind. Obviously, if he could be persuaded not to sell Louisiana to the Americans, he would be less likely to go to war with England over Malta.[25]

In the light of Yonge's revelations, the scene in the bath undergoes a significant transformation, and, instead of two patriotic brothers and one

---

* "Whom I—! But better it is to calm the troubled waves: hereafter it is not with a penalty like this that you will pay for your misdeeds." *Aeneid*, I, 135, 136.

bemused dictator, we find three Corsican bandits, all gifted, and one of them touched with genius, disputing very much at cross-purposes over the kind of spoil they could extract from the country which had adopted them. It is not surprising, surely, that Joseph should have ceased to be Livingston's intermediary or that Talleyrand should have intervened in the Louisiana negotiations, on April 11, for the sole purpose of clouding them with evasions.

VII

To return to Livingston's dispatch of April 13, Monroe passed the early afternoon of the 12th (it says) in the Rue Trudon, examining Livingston's papers. The two then sat down to dinner with several gentlemen, and, while they were still dining, Marbois was observed, walking in the Legation garden. "I sent out Col. Livingston to him. He told him he would return when we had dined—When we were taking coffee he came in, and after being some time in the room we strolled into the next room when he told me he had learned I had been at his house two days before when he was at St. Cloud. . . . I saw that this was meant as an opening to one of those free conversations I had frequently had with him." Livingston accordingly related the extraordinary conduct of Talleyrand. "He told me that this led to something important that had been currently mentioned to him at St. Cloud but as my house was full of company he thought I had better call upon him at any time before 11 that night—He went away & a little after when Mr. Monroe took leave I followed him."

There followed that momentous conversation between Livingston and Marbois, at the end of which half a continent began to pass into the hands of the United States. Marbois told Livingston that "he wished me to repeat what I had said relative to Mr. Talle[y]rand's requesting a proposition from me as to the purchase of Louisiana. I did so & concluded with the extreme absurdity of his evasions of that day." Marbois then explained that the First Consul, after making his announcement on the 10th that he intended to sell Louisiana, had remarked that the London papers said something about $2,000,000 being disposed among the people about him in order to bribe them. Later on, walking in the garden, the Consul was supposed to have said: "Well, you have charge of the Treasury, let them give you one hundred millions, pay their own claims and take the whole country." In other words, the American claims being estimated at twenty millions, Louisiana could be purchased for a hundred and twenty-five million francs or $22,500,000.

Here Marbois was acting like a minister of Finance with an empty treasury. Napoleon had made no such demand. On Easter Sunday, April 10, he had mentioned fifty million francs as a suitable price. As for Livingston, while he now realized (he said) that Talleyrand had been removed from the negotiation because of his propensity for taking bribes, and that Marbois had been substituted because of his known integrity, yet he was astounded at the enormous price he was being asked to pay. This was the greatest offer in the history of the modern world; and Livingston approached it in the spirit of one who, on an infinitely smaller scale, was accustomed from his youth to transactions in real estate. He began by professing that the United States had no interest in the west bank of the Mississippi: "that of course we would not give any great sum for the purchase—that he was right in his idea of the extreme exorbitancy of the demand—that however we would be ready to purchase provided the sum was reduced to reasonable limmits." At length, Marbois was induced to say that "if I would name 60 millions & take upon us the American claims to the amt. of 20 more, he wd. try how [it] would be accepted."

Livingston replied that it was vain to ask for a sum so greatly beyond the means of the United States; that if the government paid it, it would certainly lose the next election; that the Consul should be reminded of the ease with which Louisiana could pass to Great Britain in the event of a war; that he should also be told of the "ardour of the Americans to take it by force & the difficulty with which they were restrained by the prudence of the President"; that the war party in America would be strengthened by the news that France was on the verge of war with England. In short, he tried anything and everything: but Marbois was obdurate. Livingston then asked if, in the event of a purchase, France would stipulate that she would never possess the Floridas, but would aid the United States to procure them; and if the negotiation, should there be one, could be put into the hands of someone "who had more leisure than the Minister for Foreign Affairs." Marbois assented to both propositions; and even went so far as to say that Bonaparte knew of their personal friendship, and that there would be no difficulty "when the negotiation was somewhat advanced to have the management of it put into his hands." It was now midnight, and Livingston, still protesting that neither he nor Monroe could possibly agree to pay eighty million francs, left the Treasury and hurried home to write his dispatch to Madison.

Thus Sir you see [the dispatch triumphantly ended] a negotiation is fairly opened & upon grounds that I confess I prefer to all others—commercial priviledges are always troublesome, a simple money transaction is infinitely preferable—as to the quantum I have yet made up no opinion—

The field opened to us is infinitely larger than our instructions contemplate—the revenues increasing & the lands more than adequate to sink the capital shd. we ever go to the length proposed by Marbois—Nay I persuade myself that the whole sum may be raised by the sale of the territory west of the Mississippi with the right of sovereignty to some power in Europe whose vicinity we should not fear. I speak without reflection & without having seen Mr. Munroe as it was midnight when I left the Treasury office & is now near three O'Clock—it is so very important that you shd. be apprized that a negotiation is actually opened even before Mr. Munroe has been presented in order to calm the tumult which the news of war will renew that I have lost no time in communicating it. We shall do all we can to cheapen the purchase but my present sentiment is that we shall buy.[26]

VIII

It was not to be supposed that Monroe would sound the note of triumph that can be heard in every paragraph of this dispatch. On April 15, on the contrary, he wrote in confidence to complain of his treatment. On his arrival, he told Madison, Mr. Fulwar Skipwith, the American Consul General, informed him that Livingston had been doing everything in his power "to turn the occurrences in America and even my mission to his account"; that he had pressed the French Government on every point to show that everything so far had been accomplished without Monroe's aid, "and perhaps also that my mission had put in hazard what might otherwise have been easily obtained." His official correspondence itself—for Monroe, of course, had been given Livingston's dispatches to read—"sufficiently proves that he did not abstain, even on hearing that I was on my way, from the topics entrusted to us jointly." Skipwith, moreover, had been one of the guests at that famous dinner party on the 12th, and he remembered Livingston's telling him privately "he regretted his misfortune in my arrival, since it took from him the credit of having brought everything to a proper conclusion without my aid." And surely it was only a plausible pretext, a point of etiquette (that Marbois could not treat with Monroe until he had been formally presented) too strictly urged, that had kept Monroe away from the conference at the Treasury where the price for Louisiana had first been discussed.[27]

Thus the paths of the two ministers, instead of harmoniously converging, had crossed each other from the start. It was scarcely to be expected that they would do otherwise. Livingston knew all too well that Monroe was the government's official spokesman; that he had only to set foot in Paris for all eyes to be turned upon him; that the credit for a triumph, for which he himself had worked so persistently and in the face of such manifold discouragements, would probably go to the man who had done nothing but arrive in Paris. Monroe knew that Livingston would be bound to think in this way. He himself had come at great trouble and expense (for as envoy extraordinary he was given a salary but no outfit) in order to perform a public service; and he proposed to extract from it all the credit that he conceived to be his due. Was not the mission itself the reason for this sudden and unlooked-for offer? On the whole, he thought, he was being placed in the odd dilemma of having to negotiate, not only with the French Government, but with his colleague as well.[28]

It was difficult in those days for an American to think transcontinent-ally. It had strained Livingston's imagination to the utmost to make the suggestion that America should be granted the territory above the Arkansas. Monroe, until he reached Paris, thought only of cessions on the eastern bank of the Mississippi. The Secretary of State himself had ex-pressly excluded from his project of a treaty all lands west of that river. One can only suppose that the magnificence of Bonaparte's offer dawned slowly upon the minds of the two ill-matched colleagues.

The course of the negotiation can be traced in Monroe's "Journal and Memoranda" and in the dispatches and drafts of Livingston.[29] Thus we know that on April 14, Monroe was presented to Talleyrand, that on April 15, the two Americans were prepared to go as high as fifty million livres, but publicly offered no more than forty million; that when this was made known to Bonaparte at St. Cloud on April 16, he was said (by Marbois) to have received the news very coldly; and that Marbois believed that the negotiation had now been taken out of his hands. Monroe and Livingston then hastened to the Rue du Bac, but Talleyrand was inaccessi-ble. That afternoon, they dined with the Second Consul, and in the evening Marbois again appeared, to be told that the Americans would now go as high as fifty million livres. He retorted that if nothing came of this bid when he presented it to Bonaparte at St. Cloud on the 17th, they would have to assume that the offer of Louisiana was withdrawn. If Livingston and Monroe felt that there was any danger in tampering with the patience of a dictator, they never admitted it. "We resolved," said Livingston, "to rest for a few days upon our oars."[30]

As a matter of fact, Monroe had fallen ill; and for the next ten days the negotiations languished with him. Livingston was obliged to do alone such work as could be done: and one finds him writing on the 22nd and the 23rd in Monroe's name and his own to Marbois to discuss two *projets* for a treaty which Marbois had submitted. The first note shows them as still far apart, the second as drawing nearer: what held them apart was the excessive French demand as regards price and commercial advantages.[31] On April 24, Marbois was given the powers of a minister plenipotentiary to treat with Livingston and Monroe.[32] On April 27, the three gentlemen met informally at Monroe's apartment, with Monroe reclining on a sofa throughout the proceedings. The Frenchman had two *projets* with him: one drawn up by Bonaparte, which (Marbois admitted) was "hard and unreasonable"; the other was his own production, and he thought he could get Bonaparte to agree to it.[33]

Livingston had some qualms about the American claims, which he thought should be settled first; but he was overruled by Monroe and Marbois; and the two Americans spent the rest of the day in working over Marbois's *projet*, and in drawing up, very loosely, a claims convention of their own.[34] On April 29, Monroe was well enough to go with Livingston to the Treasury, where they presented their revised *projet*, and made an offer of fifty million livres to France and twenty million for the satisfaction of the American claims. Marbois insisted that he could proceed no farther with the discussion unless the price agreed upon was eighty millions: that is to say, sixty millions ($11,250,000) for Louisiana and twenty millions ($3,750,000) for the American claims. By this time, the two Americans had grasped, in all its magnificence, the nature of the diplomatic feat they were being asked to perform. They agreed to the eighty millions, and Marbois took their *projet*, with the understanding that he was to show it to the First Consul in the morning.[35]

On the next day, Livingston and Monroe addressed themselves privately to the question of the Floridas. It had been assumed all along that these had not been ceded to France; and in a draft of the *projet* submitted to Marbois on the 27th, a draft in Livingston's handwriting and doubtless representing his own views, it was suggested that the first article of the proposed purchase treaty should contain the following language from the third article of the Treaty of St. Ildefonso:

His Catholic Majesty promises and engages on his part to cede to the French Republic six months after the full and entire execution of the conditions and Stipulations herein relative to his Royal Highness the Duke of Parma, the Colony or Province of Louisiana with the Same Extent that it now has in the hands of Spain, & that it had when France possessed it; and Such as it Should be after the Treaties subsequently entered into between Spain and other States.

These words, now as famous as debate can make them, had only recently been made known to the Americans, who had been aware of the terms of the Treaty of St. Ildefonso, but not of its exact wording. Pedro

Cevallos, in Madrid, did not, in fact, communicate them to Pinckney until March 31, and Pinckney, forwarding them to Livingston on April 4, said "this is the first acknowledgement in writing I have been able to get since I arrived of the cession of Louisiana agreeably to its antient limits."[36] Livingston at first wished to add to these words the following rider: "It is further agreed that in case florida shd. by treaty by conquest or in any other way fall into the hands of france that they will transfer the same to the United States it being the object of this treaty to place the respective parties there in such a situation as to have in future no subjects for collision. And as a further proof of friendship and liberality the first consul agrees to aid the United States in acquiring from Spain such cessions within the said province of florida as may aid the commerce of the United States."[37] Marbois was willing to make a verbal stipulation to that effect, but never to put it in writing. By April 30, however, Livingston seems to have changed his mind. He now believed that the wording of the third article of the Treaty of St. Ildefonso could be construed as including at least West Florida in the retrocession. He wished the words to remain in the first article, without any mention of the Floridas.

Monroe, temperamentally a far more cautious personage, did not much care for this.

I own [he wrote] . . . adding the article of the treaty [of St. Ildefonso] as given us by him [Marbois] and the minister of Spain to the end of the treaty [to be] a preferable mode of expressing the object. . . . If the insertion of the art: to the treaty gives us a claim, or the sanction of France to such a claim, to W. Florida, which without it we shd. not have, the effect in that respect will also be the same in either case. My earnest wish, as I believe yrs., is, to make the instrument as concise, clear & distinct as possible, to have no words in it, not necessary. . . . However we must not lose time.[38]

We must not lose time. Now, with the great object almost accomplished, everyone was in a hurry. The treaty was drawn up in haste, the claims convention was loosely worded: the whole transaction was so momentous that neither side, it seems, dared to indulge in reflection. On May 1, Monroe was presented at the Tuileries, and, for the first time, the tall rawboned solemn Virginian confronted the First Consul. Their conversation was constrained, and devoted entirely to trivialities. At dinner, taken with the Consul, nothing was said about Louisiana, except that the business should be settled.[39] But Monroe had now been formally received, and on the next day,

May 2, we actually signed the treaty and convention for the sixty millions of Francs to France in the French language, but our copies in English not being made out we could not sign in our language. They were, however, prepared and signed two or three days afterwards. The convention respecting American claims took more time, and was not signed till about the 8th or 9th.[40]

IX

A student of Livingston's career would certainly be wanting in respect to his subject if he did not recite these incidents, famous though some of them already are. Yet there is a question of far more importance, both as regards Livingston himself and as regards the Louisiana Purchase made on May 2. What was Bonaparte's motive in parting with the great province, and when did he decide to make the sacrifice?

The conventional view—and conventional views are not to be lightly dismissed—used to be that Bonaparte was forced to sell Louisiana because of the imminence of war with England. "It is not difficult," writes Edward Channing, "to apportion the credit for this transaction. Napoleon, for reasons having nothing to do with the United States, suddenly determined to get whatever he could for whatever title to Louisiana he had. He threw the province, so to speak, at Livingston, Monroe, Madison and Jefferson; and they share between them—equally—whatever credit there was in catching it and holding it—that is all."[41] In other words, as soon as war broke out with England, Louisiana was lost. Or, as Talleyrand put it in a note to Decrès: ". . . the empire of circumstance, the foresight of the future, and the intention to compensate by an advantageous arrangement the inevitable loss of a country that war was going to place at the mercy of another nation . . ."—these were the motives.[42]

It would be idle to deny that these found their place in a great complex of motives. But it has always been the contention here that Livingston was conducting his later but still somewhat solitary campaign for claims and concessions against a background of dissolving empire. The crisis came on January 7, when Bonaparte learned that Leclerc had died in Santo Domingo and that his army had virtually ceased to exist. His expedition under General Victor was ice-bound in Holland. He pretended that when the ice relented he would still launch it, partly against Santo Domingo, partly toward the occupation of Louisiana. But the pictures which he had been making, when he issued his fatal decree for slavery in Guadeloupe, had now, through the valiant resistance of the Negroes of Santo Domingo, and the terrible carrying powers of Aëdes aegypti, totally disintegrated: just as, years later at Waterloo, his dreams of easy victory disappeared when the advance elements of Blücher's army clouded the horizon. Santo Domingo was lost, and although he continued to talk of employing Victor's expedition, he did so as a salve to his self-respect. The Floridas, moreover, had not been wrested from Carlos IV and the Prince of the Peace. Without Santo Domingo and the Floridas, Louisiana, as the seat of his western empire, was useless. He did not wait long. On January 30, there appeared that fateful article in the *Moniteur*, in which Colonel Sébastiani discussed the ease with which Egypt might be reconquered and expatiated upon the popularity of the French in the East.[43]

The British instinct in these matters was infallible. The expedition to Santo Domingo and the retrocession of Louisiana had made them nervous enough: now they perceived that Bonaparte had turned his attention from America to India. They resolved that nothing would induce them to hand Malta over to the French. On March 11, it was obvious to Rufus King that a British fleet of observation would soon be sent into the Channel to see that General Victor's fleet remained in port. It was no longer a West Indian or an American fleet; but it might be an invasion one. On March 12, Bonaparte hurled at Lord Whitworth, a petrified image of shocked politeness, his accusation that England was getting ready to fight France: one is unhappily familiar enough with the methods of modern dictators to be able to assume, with some confidence, that Bonaparte was getting ready to fight England. On March 18, King wrote that it was known in London that the expedition to Louisiana had been countermanded and that war, in his opinion, was now inevitable.[44]

It is the contention here that Bonaparte really lost interest in Louisiana between January 7 and January 30, between the news of Leclerc's death and the publication of Sébastiani's article in the *Moniteur*. If he afterward maintained the resemblance of an interest in it, that was for the sake of semblances only. The pressure to release it, meanwhile, was mounting week by week. In his February 24 memorial to the First Consul, Livingston insisted that the West would take New Orleans by force if it were not granted every satisfaction concerning deposit and navigation. In early March, he repeated this theme in every conversation with Talleyrand. On March 28, there appeared Pichon's dispatch, the happy fruit of Jefferson's and Madison's maneuvers, which insisted that a crisis was near at hand. It might, therefore, be maintained—and here is maintained—that Bonaparte did not give up Louisiana because of the imminence of war with England, but that the war with England was due to his losing interest in Louisiana.

The Monroe mission itself, which was known in Paris toward the end of February, measurably increased these pressures by adding to the uncertainty of events. Was he coming in a peaceful or in a belligerent mood? The bluff, for bluff it was, was consummated by the dispatch of Pichon.

And Monroe arrived on the same day that Livingston communicated to Bonaparte the angry resolution of Senator Ross.

But why did he offer the *whole* of Louisiana? The Americans would have been satisfied with New Orleans; indeed, at a pinch, they would have been content with a written promise to restore the rights of deposit and of navigation. It is also arguable that the British, who were by no means ardent colonizers in 1803, would have had no use for Louisiana without New Orleans, and with the Floridas in the hands of Spain. One can assert that Livingston's memorial "Is it advantageous to France to take possession of Louisiana?" made little impression on Bonaparte when it first came under his eyes, because he was then convinced that he had conquered Santo Domingo: but it was an extremely able paper, Bonaparte had a most retentive memory, and it would be wrong to suppose that it did not, eventually, leave its mark. And certainly Livingston's reiterated suggestion that it would be wise to give the United States all of Louisiana above the Arkansas was the first to come from any American, and first advanced the seminal idea that the United States would be willing to move westward of the Mississippi. Even his insistence on the payment of American debts, which wrung from Bonaparte a promise to settle them, had its place in the scheme. It came at a time when the First Consul was in a state of great tension, when he was meditating his change from West to East, when he was preparing for his lifelong task—the decimation of the youth of France and of Europe. It was like a gentle turn of the thumbscrew, a slight but perceptible stretching of the rack.

No event is due to a single cause: and, unless we dismiss the theory of causation altogether, the cession of Louisiana can be ascribed to a complex of successive or simultaneous pressures. There was the deathless resistance of the Negroes at Santo Domingo; there was the obstinancy of Carlos IV and Godoy; there was the failure of the Victor expedition to clear from Holland before the ice set in; there was the death of Leclerc; there was the fury of the West after the closing of the port of New Orleans; there was the subtle and successful bluff of Jefferson and Madison; there was the ambiguity of the Monroe mission; and, last of all, there was the importunate presence of Minister Livingston.

Last of all, but hardly least of all. The man who, persistently, without losing his self-respect, in the face of evasions and of sneers, with inadequate instructions and small support, put forth day in and day out his demand for territorial cessions certainly played a most creative part in that great event. It is only justice to remark upon the fortunate choice of President Jefferson when, in February, 1801, he offered the French mission to a somewhat too privileged gentleman from the banks of the Hudson.

CHAPTER FIVE

A month after the signing of the treaty, one finds Livingston writing a long letter to President Jefferson. It is midnight, he has just left Marbois, and he is writing in great agitation of spirit. The passport to Mr. Augustus Jay, who is to carry the ratified treaty to Washington, has not been delivered, and:

They have been this two days past in Council & principally basting Mr. Marbois on the subject of the treaty for it seems that the consul is less pleased with it since the ratification than before—& I am persuaded that if he could conveniently gett off he would. He says that the whole debt does not exceed four millions & that we have got 20. That delivering the ratifications to us was contrary to all form & that they must be recalled & given to Mr. Pichon to exchange & to this I believe we must consent as it is certainly regular tho' we shall first keep copies of the ratifications. He insists that if the stock is not delivered in the time prescribed the treaty is void. . . . In short he appears to wish the thing undone.

The villain in this piece, Livingston continues, is M. Talleyrand, who has made every "objection and insinuation" in order to disgust Bonaparte with the treaty. As we know now, Lord Whitworth had been tempting Talleyrand with gold; and although hostilities had been declared in May, and Lord Whitworth had departed, the offer was still good. Livingston, who knew nothing of this, supposed that Talleyrand was jealous of Marbois and angry because, through Marbois's honesty, "the proffits that might have resulted from the debt and the treaty is [sic] unexpectedly snatched from their hands."[1] But these last words he deleted.

And on June 3, he wrote to Madison to say that they have had a great deal of trouble since the ratification in Paris, and that he must earnestly press him to get it accomplished in Washington as quickly as possible. Again, on June 25, he wrote: "I hope in God that nothing will prevent your immediate ratification . . . be persuaded that France is sick of this bargain & that Spain is much dissatisfied & the slightest pretence will lose you the treaty."[2]

The effect of his letter upon Jefferson, when it was received in August, was to make the President revise his ideas. He had from the beginning doubted that the purchase was constitutional ("the Constitution has made no provision for our holding foreign territory"), and had hoped to make it so by constitutional amendment. It had then occurred to him that he might accomplish the ratification first, and call for the amendment afterward. Congress in any event was to be summoned into special session on October 17, but now "a letter [Livingston's] received yesterday," he wrote on August 18, "shows that nothing must be said on that subject which may give pretext for retracting." On September 7, he went even farther. "Our peculiar security," he wrote to W. C. Nicholas, "is in the possession of a written Constitution. Let us not make it a blank paper by construction. I say the same to those who consider the grant of the treaty-making power as boundless. If it is, then we have no Constitution. . . . If, however, our friends shall think differently, certainly I shall acquiesce with satisfaction, confiding that the good sense of our country will correct the evil of construction when it shall produce good effects."[3] This sudden reversal in the very middle of an argument might be laid to Jefferson's declared belief that "the law of self-preservation overrules the laws of obligations"; or to his faith in the purity of the Republican party; or to his knowledge that the nation had profited immeasurably through his boldness and vision: but the fact remains that he had acquiesced in making the Constitution a blank paper by construction and that Livingston's urgent letter had had something to do with it.[4]

To so magnificent an event as the Louisiana Purchase, a magnificent disregard for the Constitution was, perhaps, appropriate: and Jefferson's un-Jeffersonian behavior has justly been greeted with more applause than alarm or condemnation. It was not by grand errors but by shrill ghosts that the purchase was haunted: for haunted it was. Like other great events in human history, its aftermath was an embittered one. It was distressed by the quarrels and complaints of the principal actors, by acute misunderstandings and discreditable recriminations; in short, by an all-too-human failure to accept without glossing the accomplishment of success.

II

In the first place, no American was able to define just what it was that had been purchased; no Frenchman was willing to do so; no Spaniard would admit that the purchase was valid. The Americans knew that they had bought the west bank of the Mississippi from the Lake of the Woods to the island of New Orleans: beyond that, they had acquired a huge but unknown western domain. Today, we may assert that the purchase as a whole embraced the territory now within the borders of Arkansas, Missouri, Iowa, Nebraska, and South Dakota, almost all of Oklahoma and Kansas, and large portions of what is now North Dakota, Montana, Wyoming, Minnesota, Colorado, and Louisiana. From the Spanish attitude in 1817, it is more than likely that Texas could have been claimed as well. But could it be that West Florida, as far as the Perdido, or at least as far as the Mobile, was included in the purchase? To the negotiators, no less than to their superiors in Washington, this became of the first importance. Livingston and Monroe were not likely to forget that they had been instructed to purchase the east bank of the Mississippi, but had bought the west bank instead.

It became Livingston's object, therefore, to revert to his previous thinking on the matter, and to make the happy discovery that (the words are Henry Adams's) "France had actually bought West Florida without knowing it, and had sold it to the United States without being paid for it."[5] This, after some feverish research among old maps and documents, he believed he had been able to do: and the gaps in his argument, which was certainly an able one, were with equal ability mended by Monroe.[6] The French, however, were determined only to be mysterious. If there were not already an uncertainty as to the extent of the purchase, Bonaparte thought, it would have been necessary to put one there:[7] and for years afterward, he used the Floridas as a diplomatic bait in his more questionable dealings with the United States. "You have made a noble bargain for yourselves" was all that Talleyrand could be brought to say, "and I suppose you will make the most of it."[8] As for the Spaniards, they repeated the fact that Gouvion de St. Cyr, in July, 1802, had promised in the Consul's name that France would never alienate Louisiana; and they added that, since neither Russia nor Great Britain had been persuaded to recognize the Kingdom of Etruria, the terms of the Treaty of St. Ildefonso had not been fulfilled, and France had never possessed Louisiana at all. In 1817, they were still repeating these arguments. Livingston, having once convinced himself that the United States had purchased West Florida at least as far as the Perdido River, was usually for the simple solution of taking it by force.[9] This solution, achieved in a more subtle way during the administration of James Madison, is among the less creditable events in that great man's career.

But if there were flaws in the Louisiana Purchase Treaty, there was a tragic laxity in one of the conventions that accompanied it. Although Livingston at first took some credit for framing the claims convention, it was in fact "hastily, loosely and inaccurately constructed."[10] On second thought, he admitted that the primary intention had been to secure Louisiana and that "I considered the convention as a trifle compared with the other great object and as it had already delayed us many days, I was ready to take it under any form."[11] Everybody had been in a hurry because everybody was anxious to get the purchase ratified before war broke out. And so, the preamble of the claims convention was permitted to state that its purpose was to secure payment of the sums due to American citizens under the second and fifth articles of the convention of September 30, 1800. But, alas, the claims mentioned in the second article of that convention, as a hasty reference to its history might have shown, had first been postponed and then abandoned—abandonment being the *quid pro quo,* the fair equivalent, which the French had demanded in return for giving up the obligations due them under the treaties of 1778.[12]

Then again, while Monroe and Livingston were correct in saying that they had obtained twenty million livres in order to satisfy the debts due under the fifth article of the convention of 1800, the fact remained, as Fulwar Skipwith quite correctly pointed out, that the claims convention of 1803 was "a convention of exceptions to the one of 1800."[13] And these exceptions seriously restricted the valid claims. Nor were the exceptions all that was wrong. It was provided, for example, that the court of last appeal in deciding the validity of contested claims should be, not the American, but the French Treasury: considering the jobbery that flourished with such verdure among French official circles, this was a most improvident provision.[14] And lastly, the sum of twenty million livres "fell far below the amount of claims admitted in principle."[15]

As for the second convention, which concerned the financing of the purchase itself, this stated that the $11,250,000 was to be paid by creating United States 6-per-cent stock, which should be irredeemable for fifteen years.[16] Albert Gallatin, the Secretary of the Treasury, while delighted with the purchase itself, was seriously disturbed by these terms. He believed that the stock should have been redeemable in a shorter time, which would have saved the nation the payment of several millions of interest; nor did he much care for the price at which the Dutch banking house of Hope and Company and the British house of Baring had agreed to take the stock from the French. Seventy-eight and a half, he thought, did not reflect either favorably or accurately on the state of American public credit.[17] Compared to the flaws in the claims convention and their consequences, however, those in the purchase convention were relatively inconsequential: except, of course, to the houses of Hope and Company and of Baring, who cleared a handsome profit.

III

To the observer of Livingston's career, however, other considerations, whether of more or of less importance, are bound to make themselves more felt. "We have lived long," he said, after he had signed the treaty of cession, "but this is the noblest work of our lives."[18] Triumph of this kind is not the easiest of burdens. What consequences might it not have for an American who—like all Americans in public life, in those days perhaps even more than in ours—was not devoid of political ambitions! It has been one of the endeavors of this study to show that Livingston was by no means the insatiable politician which contemporary accounts and subsequent commentaries have held him to be. But to have been instrumental in buying a large slice of the New World, and to see—as he believed he saw—the laurels being filched from his brow by an impeccable hand . . . that was almost more than a man of spirit could bear.

It was clear from the beginning that James Monroe, in his own way, was about to take the credit for the Louisiana Purchase. And Monroe's way was not that of an ordinary public servant, far from it. It was not merely that Monroe had dedicated himself to the public service, it was also that he was transparently a good man. The present narrator has had occasion, in another place,* to make this statement and to mean it. Now there is in goodness a low as well as a high intensity; and the intensity of Monroe's goodness in the days that followed the signing of the Louisiana treaty was of the former discription. He did not arrogate to himself any of the credit for what had been done. But he was the spokesman of the government, the confidant of Jefferson, a Virginian known to be a coming man in the innermost circles of Republican life. He modestly admitted that he had had little to do with what had occurred; he also admitted that Livingston had been without influence: all was due to the policies of the government. In such a representation of the state of affairs, the government's representative was, as it were by default, bound to reap the credit. And, throughout his life, Monroe was popular in the West because of the part he had, in fact, not been permitted to play in the Louisiana Purchase.

Livingston's character was as unlike Monroe's as a character could well be. He had his share of virtues and his moments of vanity; but his display of virtue was usually more opaque than perspicuous, and his vanity was not modest or even-tempered or simple in its way of expressing itself.

* George Dangerfield, *The Era of Good Feelings*, New York, 1952, 326.

Livingston was a creature of impulse; a child of privilege, accustomed to having his own way in private life. In the political world, to be sure, he had become used to disappointment, and the edge of his appetite in this respect had long since been dulled. Now that it was whetted again upon the fine-grained, the monumental rock of the recent purchase, one can hardly blame him if he resented the belated appearance of Monroe, and his modest disclaimer, for Livingston as well as himself, of any real agency in the great deed. Of such disclaimers one is always tempted to ask who is to benefit by them: and it was clear from the beginning that the benefit would not be Livingston's.

The effect of this ferment or torment upon his thinking was unfortunate but predictable. All his fantasy rose to meet it; his imagination and his reason were, for the time being, banished from their seats. In his communication to Madison of April 13, he readily admitted that Bonaparte's decision to sell Louisiana had been made on April 10; but it afterward occurred to him that people might find some direct relation between Monroe's arrival on the 8th and Bonaparte's decision on the 10th. This, indeed, was Monroe's impeccable, exasperating, and fundamentally ungenerous position. It was not he, it was not the previous work of Livingston, it was his *arrival* alone, bearing with it all the weight of the foreign policy of Jefferson, that had turned the scale in America's favor. But supposing Bonaparte had made his decision on the morning of the 8th, some hours before Monroe's arrival at Le Havre? This alternative had scarcely suggested itself to Livingston than he began to adopt it. With a characteristic insouciance, he interpolated the date into a letter to Madison of May 12th, and then on May 28th tried it out upon Monroe. He drew up a draft for a joint letter to Charles Pinckney, announcing the purchase and containing the sentence: "On the 8th Apl the Consul announced to his Council at St. Cloud his determination to sell the whole of Louisiana as he had held it under the treaty with Spain to the United States." Monroe, however, strange to say, did not agree with this draft. He preferred, Livingston wrote on it, "not to have it so particular," and therefore a more general one was sent.[19] But, having once begun on this singular course, Livingston was hardly the man to stop short. He began to rewrite in his mind the final history of the purchase. If Bonaparte made his decision on the 8th, then Talleyrand made his first proposal on the 9th, and his second and very evasive answer on the 10th: it was under the influence of the gloom engendered by this answer that Livingston had written his somewhat despondent welcoming note of the same date to Monroe; but on the same day, he dispatched a letter to Talleyrand, telling him that some decision as to Louisiana would have to be reached before Monroe's arrival. Except for the welcoming letter to Monroe, each one of these events and communications was dated two days back. Livingston carried his fantasy so far as to attempt to change the date of his letter to Talleyrand in his letter book: one finds that he has superimposed a zero over the two in twelve.[20]

In the course of time, letters began to find their way to friends in America, in which they were informed that Bonaparte had conveniently decided to sell on the eighth; Livingston seems by this time to have persuaded himself that it was true.[21] And indeed, but for his own early admission to Madison that the tenth had been the date,[22] the single other authority would have been Barbé-Marbois's *Histoire de la Louisiane*, a book written in Marbois's old age and by no means trustworthy in all respects. Livingston usually insisted, as well, that the fulcrum that really turned the lever was his extraction from Bonaparte of a firm promise to pay the American claims. It would be most inaccurate to say that the vice-presidency, or the succession to the presidency in any form, occupied any but the farthest and airiest corner of his mind, but it would be true to say that he was preoccupied with the governorship of New York, a state in which so many of the American claimants resided. With Ambrose Spencer's letter in his files, and the great purchase an accomplished fact, it would have been astonishing if he had not been.

The torrent of his letters suddenly dried up on September 1, 1803, with an immense and detailed story written to General John Armstrong. It appeared again, sporadically, not least in a letter to Marbois of December 23: but the fantasy, none the less, had clearly worn itself out.[23] After all, there are two conditions that permit one to rewrite history entirely to suit oneself. One must have control of the public archives and one must have control of the public mind. Livingston could not retrieve his letter to Madison from the files of the State Department, nor could he summon back from the French archives his letter to Talleyrand, with its correct date of April 12. At this point, one can register the wish that he had never made such an attempt, or that one did not have to record it: for even if the story had been true, it would have made no difference to the great work he had actually performed in preparing for the Louisiana Purchase. As it is, one can merely assert that his public services to America have been neither dimmed nor diminished by the private disservice he has done himself.

The public mind, of course, was equally available to the administration, on the one hand, and the opposition, on the other: there was no controlling the press, where the news of the purchase had been thoroughly ventilated, from both points of view, before the end of June. An attempt was also made upon it when, between July 1 and July 20, a somewhat garbled version of Livingston's memorial on the disadvantages of Louisiana to France, sometimes with a laudatory covering letter from an American in Paris, was printed in the Boston, Washington, Philadelphia, and New York papers.[24] The administration was naturally upset.

You will find in the gazettes [Madison wrote to Monroe on July 30] a letter from Paris understood to be from Swan inclosing a copy of his [Livingston's] memorial representing it as the primary cause of the cession, praising the patriotism which undertook so great a service without authority, and throwing your agency out of any real merit while by good fortune it snatched the ostensible merit. . . . Another letter from Paris has been published which makes him Magnus Apollo. The publication of the memorial is so improper and in reference to the writer invites such strictures that a sanction by him is not to be presumed.[25]

And to Livingston he wrote that he trusted he would "trace the indiscretion to its author."[26] Livingston eventually replied, on November 15, that he was indeed sorry that a bad translation should have appeared in the papers: "the zeal of our friends," said the impenitent Minister, "often carries them too far." Yet surely (he added) it was only natural for them to attempt to do him justice. And had not Monroe's friends circulated a copy of that private letter to Monroe of April 10, in which Monroe had been welcomed in such despondent terms? He could only hope that Monroe would as sincerely lament this act as Livingston did that of "the gentleman that I suspect to have occasioned the publication that you so justly blame."[27]

The accusation against Monroe was quite true. On May 25, 1803, he had written a letter addressed "To Virginia Senators," and endorsed "To Genl. Mason, Col. W. C. Nicholas & John Breckenridge—private," in which he stated that:

The decision to offer us the territory by sale was not the effect of any management of mine, for it took place before I reached Paris; nor of my colleague or it would have taken place sooner. . . . I enclose a copy of a letter from Mr. Livingston bearing date the 10th of April, in answer to one from me of the 8th announcing my arrival, which establishes the above facts. I communicate this letter to you as a measure of precaution, that you may not only know that the above facts exist but the nature of the evidence which supports them. . . . If my mission produced any effect it was altogether owing to the motive which induced the President to nominate me, that is, the pronounced character which I had in reference to the object in question, & a belief that I would bring the affair promptly to an issue.[28]

Thus Livingston and Monroe promoted each his own cause. Had they not been antipathetic from the start? But let us admit that while the purchase was in the process of being made, from April 13 to May 2, they pocketed their differences and worked together for the public good; and that the tribute which each paid to the other's zeal during these crucial days was neither undeserved nor insincere.

IV

The other, and far more serious, train of errors and misunderstandings to appear in the wake of the Louisiana Purchase had to do with the American claims on France. According to Article VI of the claims convention, the Ministers Plenipotentiary of the United States were to name three persons who should act "for the present and provisionally." These commissioners were to examine all the accounts of claims already "liquidated" by the French bureaus, in order to see whether or not they belonged to the class of debts admitted by the convention; they were to examine the claims prepared for verification; and they were to examine the claims that were not yet prepared for liquidation.[29] If they passed the claims already liquidated or already verified for liquidation, then the claimants, by Article III, were entitled to receive orders on the American Treasury, payable sixty days after the exchange of ratifications, and bearing interest at 6 per cent. These orders were to be drawn by Livingston.[30] It was also stipulated in Article X that the Commercial Agent of the United States at Paris (Mr. Fulwar Skipwith) should assist in these examinations, and if he should think some claim should not have been admitted, but if, notwithstanding his opinion, the French bureaus should insist on admitting it, then he was to transmit his observations to the commissioners, who should transmit theirs to Livingston, who should in turn transmit *his* to the French Treasury, which was to make the final decision.[31]

The mischief latent in these complicated provisions was further increased by the fact that Skipwith acted as a private agent for certain claimants, that one of them was Livingston's brother, the merchant John R. Livingston, and that James Swan, the most insistent and enterprising of the claimants, was apparently excluded by Article V from receiving any money at all. Did not Article V declare that "it is the express intention of the contracting parties not to extend the benefit of the present convention to reclamations of American citizens, who shall have established houses of commerce in France, England, or other countries than the United States, in partnership with foreigners"?[32] And Livingston's son-in-law and unofficial private secretary, Robert L. Livingston, the husband of the beautiful Margaret Maria, was privately the agent for his uncle John, together with Fulwar Skipwith, with whom, however, John R. Livingston was soon to quarrel.[33] What a cautious minister he would have to be who could tread unscathed through these congregated delicacies: and what little likelihood there was that Robert R. Livingston would be such a man!

Moreover, the choice of the board of three commissioners, though clearly limited, was certainly unfortunate. Two of the three—Colonel James Mercer and Mr. William McClure—were Virginians, who were warmly attached to Monroe, and Mercer had already put himself on record as saying that Livingston was taking all the credit for the Louisiana Purchase. The third commissioner was Isaac Cox Barnet, of New Jersey.[34] On July 7, they appointed Nathaniel Cutting, of Massachusetts, their secretary.

Meanwhile, Monroe had left for England, on July 12, to replace Rufus King near the Court of St. James's. The atmosphere he left behind him had not been lightened by Livingston's private efforts to get the negotiations concerning Florida removed from Madrid to Paris; and, with the Channel between them, the two men managed to create quite a disturbance over Monroe's somewhat imprudent offer to guarantee, before the ratification of the Louisiana treaty in Washington, an advance of some ten million livres from Hope and Company to France. Livingston had raised endless difficulties, and had only yielded for the sake of appearances.[35] Monroe, however, could afford to endure such things: he had left behind him in Paris, in the persons of the two Virginian commissioners, a source of irritation which was bound to repay Livingston in some measure for all the pretensions and all the difficulties that he had raised.

Livingston had nothing to do until the Commissioners got to work. One finds him traveling to Lyons and on to Switzerland to see the glaciers. On his return, he had time to sketch out a scheme for "ambulating kitchens" for the use of troops on the march, and to send it to General Berthier. His reward would be "that you will baptize the machine with my name."[36] By the beginning of October, however, the Commissioners had swung into action, or, rather, inaction. When McClure, who had been delayed in England, at length took his seat on September 1, he found his colleagues deep in trouble over the "conjectural note" or list of claims, which had been annexed to the convention in accordance with Article II.[37] First, it was observed that the note had no dates; and when the dates were received from the French Commission de la Comptabilité

Intermédiaire, the supporting documents were insufficient or had been detained. Today, one regards the conjectural note with consternation: it bears every sign of looseness and disorder. The Minister, of course, who felt that he had pledged himself to prompt action in March, and who was besieged by the importunities of the creditors, was anxious to begin drawing money in September. The Commissioners demurred; they now doubted, they said, that they had the right to take *any* positive action until they had received the news that the treaty and conventions had been ratified in Washington.[38] On October 8, Livingston wrote to Monroe to complain that the Commissioners had stopped passing accounts, that McClure was at the bottom of it all, and to intimate that Monroe had influenced McClure. He sent a letter to Madison on October 14, saying that he was really surprised at Monroe; for when he had left France for England, that gentleman had been convinced of the necessity of getting the capital into the hands of the claimants as soon as possible and thus ridding the Treasury of the burden of interest. Could it be that their disagreement over the guarantee had made Monroe act in this unaccountable fashion?[39]

From London, meanwhile, the Federalist Christopher Gore, a claims commissioner in that city, was writing to Rufus King to say that "it is pretty evident that a portion of the followers of the present Government intend to ruin L[ivingston]. The gentleman here [Monroe] assumes no merit himself but ascribes all to the superior wisdom and discernment of the President, whose plans they very humbly executed." And Monroe, said Gore, had taken for his temporary secretary that very Thomas Sumter who had been Livingston's Secretary of Legation.[40] Livingston—it was the effect of a happy childhood—was always unaffectedly kind to young people; and when young Mr. Sumter fell in love with the bewitching Mademoiselle Delarge, his traveling companion to France, he had gone to endless trouble to get the marriage solemnized in spite of the maddening obstacles set up by the French law. But Sumter was a proud and humorless young gentleman, the Minister was a vigilant administrator, and when the Secretary demanded that he should be allowed to prescribe the nature and limits of his own duties, it was clear that their relationship could not be a long or a happy one.[41] At length, the Minister, by way of a jest, threatened that if Sumter did not behave himself, he would call in the private claims agent, Major J. C. Mountflorence—a gentleman who might have stepped out of the pages of Thackeray—as his assistant secretary. Sumter rose to the bait, and, after writing a letter of shocked pomposity, addressed as from one equal and independent power to another, shook the dust of Paris from his feet.[42] It was not exactly tactful of Monroe to employ him.

Christopher Gore, of course, was delighted with these signs of Republican disquiet, and his letters must be read with caution. None the less, with Sumter making what mischief he could in London, and McClure behaving with undue independence in Paris, it was not likely that the differences between Livingston and Monroe—or between Livingston and the Administration—would be rendered any less acute.

The climax of the argument between the Board of Commissioners and the Minister came on October 29, when McClure, Mercer, and Barnet addressed a letter to Livingston, calling him "an individual unconnected with the board," and asserting that "only to the Administration of the United States do we consider ourselves responsible." No one was more sensitive than Livingston where questions of status were concerned; Article X of the claims convention certainly conferred on him a measure of responsibility for the acts of the Commission; so that this was a declaration of war *à outrance*. He had already appealed to Monroe, and Monroe only made matters worse when he replied in his stiffest manner on October 29 that the Commissioners "are responsible for their own conduct, not we. . . . A contrary construction would degrade them into nothing."[43]

As one studies these obscure, unhappy records, which stand out like a set of dusty thumbprints on the fair margins of the Louisiana Purchase, one thing seems to be clear. If the Commissioners had not been so stiff-necked and so obstinate, the Minister would have co-operated with them, and the fate of the claimants might perhaps have been an easier one. But Livingston was never reasonable where his pride was concerned, and the effect of the Commission's insults was to make him take the one course most likely to exasperate them, and that was to appear friendly to the cause of James Swan.

Livingston, it is true, had drawn up, after several days of close and arduous work with James Monroe, that very convention which, by its fifth article, seemed expressly to exclude Swan from its benefits. It could be argued, however, that while Article V excluded Swan from claiming as an agent of the French Government, or as a partner in a partly French concern, he *could* claim for cases where he had traded on his own account. This was Livingston's position, and it was the correct one; so that while it would have been more becoming in him not to have shown a bias toward any particular set of claimants, there was certainly no suggestion of personal jobbery in the bias which he did show. From the beginning to the end of this affair, he was entirely above that kind of thing, as his papers prove. What he did propose to extract was adulation. He was nothing if not personal. He began to act more and more toward Swan and his associates as a Maecenas toward his clients: and Swan and his associates, some of whom had perfectly legitimate claims, replied in kind.[44] When at length, toward the third week in December,[45] the great news arrived in Paris of the exchange of ratification of the treaty and the conventions in Washington on October 21, the claimants headed a Committee of American Citizens in Paris who proposed to give a dinner to the Minister: and this event actually took place at the Hôtel de Fleury in the Rue Notre Dame des Champs on January 4. At this dinner, Livingston told Du Ponceau, the Commissioners and Skipwith, strange to relate, were the only Americans not present.[46]

Meanwhile, into the midst of these festivities there fell a letter from the Secretary of State, written on November 9 and received on January 1. The Secretary repeated his information of October 22 that the treaty and conventions had been ratified and the ratifications exchanged; and then went on to say that, since difficulties had arisen concerning the true construction of the claims convention, the President desired Livingston to ask the French Government's consent to the suspension of payments to creditors until it was ascertained whether the twenty million livres would be sufficient or not.[47] It was as if Madison had reiterated blow upon blow, each from a different angle. Livingston believed that to ask for a suspension was to bring the convention itself into discredit, and with it the treaty; he disliked, as a patron, being forced to tell his clients that a suspension was now ordered; and he held the position that the twenty million was sufficient for all claims and that, if it were not, one government or the other would have to take up the difference. He immediately wrote to Madison to explain the delicate position in which he was placed. Suppose the French Treasury were to pass such accounts as had been presented to it for liquidation, that the necessary certificates were given, and the parties applied to him for bills. What answer was he to give? And was it not evident that the President and Mr. Madison were obtaining their information through channels unfriendly to their minister? As Madison's letter left him no discretion, he would, of course, obey the order; but "my heart bleeds for the distress that it will occasion to many here," and, since the affair of the Floridas had passed beyond his control or been laid aside, "I beg you sir to present to the President my request to be replaced by the 15th. day of April next."[48]

V

One need not look for political motives in all this. Livingston's letters home at this time are in a distinctly wistful mood: he did not rate his political prospects very highly. Nor is the reason for this hard to find. Since Ambrose Spencer's letter, not one word of encouragement had been received from a Clintonian; and Ambrose Spencer's letter was nearly a year and a half old. The family still continued to write concerning one or another of the offices in which he was supposed to be interested—the governorship, which he had really wanted, and the vice-presidency, the subject of an occasional, transient speculation. But the family had received a severe setback when Edward Livingston was obliged to resign both as federal district attorney and as mayor of New York. It would take strong Clintonian support to revive the Minister's hopes, and as this became conspicuously lacking, as his hopes grew dim, he concentrated his energies more and more upon his differences with the Board of Commissioners.

Differences or duels—in that mass of correspondence, so full of unveiled insults and open animosities, of charges and countercharges and appeals to Washington, it would be hard to distinguish the one from the other. The Commissioners were unduly rigid and obstructive in their interpretation of the convention; the Minister, although he displayed an excessive laxity toward such as Mr. Swan, sincerely believed that by pressing the claims of one set of creditors he would be assisting the claims of all. Nor, once he had thought the matter over, was he opposed to prorating the twenty million livres among all the claimants if, as after all seemed likely, the twenty million would prove insufficient to meet their demands in full: the idea that he was against proration, because it would hurt his brother John R. Livingston, is somewhat out of order.[49]

As for any particular climax, in a correspondence so very climactic from beginning to end, perhaps one might be discerned around the third week of March, when the Board, in an immense letter, accused the Minister of assuring those "whose claims it is our duty to reject" that, the final appeal being with him and the French Treasury, "all our mischief will be remedied." The Minister repelled their charges in a letter no less immense. "As I do not think it necessary," he ended, "to reply to reports, sarcasms, professions etc, that occupy so great a part of your letter, or to reasonings upon points that are not contested, I presume you will not consider this a satisfactory answer." Nor did they. They returned at once with the accusation that a member of the Minister's family had been, with his knowledge and approval, making applications to the French Treasury behind their backs. The Minister replied that his son-in-law Colonel Livingston had merely asked at the Treasury a technical question—what form was to be adopted to enable the holder of a liquidation certificate to receive the final order? "It is not, Gentlemen," he declared, "by insinuations like this that you can wound the feelings of a man conscious of his integrity or hurt the character of one who has served his country in high & trustworthy offices for more than thirty years successively." And, indeed, the insinuation had been a most unworthy one.[50]

Possibly, as one authority puts it, one should hesitate before assigning blame to one side or the other. "[The Commissioners'] differences with Livingston were sometimes due to the fact that the latter, for the purpose of accomplishing the end for which the Convention was designed, was willing to go further than the commissioners in what might be called the creative interpretation of it."[51] This reasonable interpretation, needless to say, would have found no contemporary support. In Washington, when the mass of correspondence eventually descended upon the President and the Secretary of State, Jefferson abandoned his usual kindly approach to human frailty. "A more disgusting correspondence between men of sense," he said, had never come to his attention. As for Livingston, "he has quarreled with every public agent . . . with his colleague Monroe, his secretary of legation, Sumter, our consul at Paris, Skipwith, with the commissioners, and his letters to the Department of State have been rising in the arrogance of their style, till that of May 3* is such as, had he not been coming away, would have justified our informing him that we should make no further use of his services."[52]

Whether Livingston had quarreled with Monroe or Monroe with Livingston could be matter for a stupefying debate; but certainly Sumter had first fallen out with his chief; the Commissioners also had made the first breach, and Skipwith's dismissal as John R. Livingston's agent could not exactly have made him an impartial bystander. In short, the administration, ever since that unhappy publication of the Louisiana memorial, had

---

* In the letter of May 3, Livingston said that in Madison's letter to him of January 31, there was a passage "so repugnant to my feelings" that he trusted he had misunderstood it—*i.e.*, a passage which seemed to say that in case the whole sum of twenty million livres should not be absorbed by the awards of the Board, the Treasury would not be liable beyond the amount awarded. This seemed to mean, said Livingston, "that you are willing that justice should be done if it costs you nothing, but if after having made a bargain which you acknowledge to be a good one you can still make a saving out of the purchase money at the expense of the just claims of our fellow citizens or of france by setting up the unjust & illiberal constructions of the board, I must adhere to such construction." RRLP*.

not been disposed to do justice to Livingston; their predilection for James Monroe had done the rest; and, if anything remained undone, all that was arrogant, peremptory, privileged, and impulsive in Livingston's character had taken care of it. His genuine deserts, his valiant and creative labors had been undervalued, and he was in the sad position of a minister, who, while not officially disavowed, had been quietly consigned to the limbo of those who have fallen out of favor. And to all this, a letter from Mercer to Monroe adds its melancholy and somewhat disgraceful coda. "In my colleagues and Mr. Skipwith," says the righteous Virginian, "I have met nothing but integrity, independence and propriety. . . . In him [Livingston] I have witnessed only imbecility of mind and a childish vanity mixed with a considerable portion of duplicity." Such a charge, wrote Henry Adams, only injured the credit of Mercer's government.[53]

In the end, when the Commissioners had done their work and closed their books, it was found that they had directed 324 claims to be liquidated, had rejected 142 more, and that only five remained to be decided. But few prize cases had come before them—the majority were still pending before the Council of Prizes or the claimants were still vainly trying to determine the financial situation of the captors.[54] The obscure language of the convention—which everyone had accepted—was to have the last word. The final disposition of the claims was undertaken by the French Government, no full payment was made by the U.S. Treasury, and such payments as *were* made were so clouded by charges of corruption aimed at the French bureaus that every reputation was unjustly stained by them. "Livingston's diplomatic career," says Henry Adams, who admired him, "was poisoned by quarrels over this money." But he was innocent of every misdemeanor except one—that of endeavoring, in certain instances and under great provocation, to behave more like a Maecenas than a minister.

VI

One curious and characteristic adventure took place as a result of the dispute with the Board, the anxieties of the administration, and the mysterious behavior of the French. In April, the French became very uneasy about the slowness of the Board of Commissioners; and Livingston began to think that it might be a good idea, until he could get more positive instructions from Washington, if he should himself disappear. This, at any rate, was the reason he gave for making a trip to England in the middle of May.[55]

His printed Louisiana memorial, with its attacks on British pretensions, had been the subject of embarrassing protests in Washington.[56] His unprinted "Thoughts" on British and French seapower, which had accompanied the memorial when it was first presented to the First Consul, and which had suggested the terms upon which France and America could weaken the carrying trade of Great Britain, had been, from a British point of view, unprintable.[57] He had recently been foremost in accusing Mr. Francis Drake, the British Minister at Munich, of connivance in a plot to assassinate Bonaparte.[58] He was also considered to be, not merely an Anglophobe, but a stern and fanatical republican. Officially, he could not have set foot in a country where he was likely to be more unpopular.

Where his own plans were concerned, Livingston was not disposed to be tactful; and considerations of unpopularity would not have deterred him from gratifying a lifelong curiosity. Moreover, the influx of Whig visitors to Paris in the summer and fall of 1802 must have had something to do with his choice: for the Whigs had a tendency to be pro-American; they were now in opposition; and the thought that a visit from Livingston might at any rate be mischievous could not have escaped them. No written invitation has survived; nor need there have been one. It could have been enough for Charles James Fox, for example, to suggest during his visit to Paris how welcome Mr. Livingston would be if he happened to pay them a call. Nor could the Tory Government have ventured on a breach with neutral America by turning him away. The result was that, when he arrived in the middle of May, he was supposed to be the bearer of peace offers from Napoleon Bonaparte.

VII

He landed at Southampton on May 16, 1804, and was obliged to linger there for two days until his passports returned from London: the first news he heard was that Pitt had become head of the government.[59] On May 17, one of the directors of the Bank of England told George Rose (soon to be paymaster general under Pitt) that "Mr. Livingstone [*sic*] was arrived with powers to treat of peace." On the next day—the day that Napoleon was proclaimed emperor in Paris—Mr. Rose hurried round to Mr. Pitt, and told him that Mr. Fox's friends would use this inconvenient visitor to suggest that, if Mr. Fox had been secretary of State, a fruitful peace negotiation might have been the result. "The character of Mr. Livingstone," Pitt is made to say in Rose's memoirs, "(as a violent Republican, hating this country) would induce all right thinking people to rejoice that we had escaped the dangerous consequences of a negotiation between two such men as Mr. Livingstone and Mr. Fox."[60]

The newspapers then took up the tale. On May 18, the *Courier* of London announced that at the close of the market on the 17th, the funds rose "considerably" from a rumor that Mr. Livingston had arrived, bearing pacific proposals. On May 19, the *Times* doubted that he had arrived at all. On May 21, the *Courier* had tracked him to Monroe's residence on Wimpole Street and thence to Blake's Hotel in Jermyn Street. On May 24, the *Times* believed that he might have been instructed to "feel the pulse of the country"; while the *Courier* was quite sure that "our Ministry would not be very much inclined to listen to any pacific proposals coming through such a channel." On May 25, the *Times* was saddened to learn that "Mr. Fox has dined with Mr. Livingston": and felt called upon to express its horror at the thought that party spirit could be carried to such lengths. And so it went.[61] It seems that he was held to have bestowed upon Mr. Drake, and, by inference, the British Government the character of assassin and barbarian.

Livingston was by no means disturbed by these attentions. He seems, indeed, to have been privately delighted by them. "My arrival," he later wrote to his brother Edward, "made as much noise & speculation as if I had been the Cham of Tartary or prester John. The ministerial papers abused [me] because I had expressed in common with every other minister here my detestation of Drake's abominable correspondence." The Opposition had shown him every possible attention, and "near 200 of the nobility & gentry visited me." Such was his introduction to Whig society.[62]

For a few weeks he was thrown into the heart of this society, "the most agreeable society," it has been said, "England has ever known." The Whigs were a governing class, too luxurious for their own good, yet too earthy to be undone by luxury, refined, sensual, exuberant, a trifle amateur, a little philistine, but able to throw over every occasion the glow of an unmatched vitality and the iridescence of an extraordinary charm. In 1804, though politically indefinite and frustrated and out of power, they were still at their best as a social group.

The kindliest critic would not call Livingston an inspired letter writer. His communications are full of facts and observations—he is keenly interested in the world around him—but it would be difficult to extract any juice from what he has to say. Occasionally—a street scene in Paris; a handsome working girl on the banks of the Loire—he will write a vivid sketch: but Whig society, with a mixture of the casual and the elaborate, the simple and the ornate, was beyond his powers of description, as it would be beyond those of almost anyone. One is forced to allow it to speak for itself. "Dear Sir," Fox writes from 9 Arlington Street on May 20, "I am going out of town tomorrow for a few days, and shall be obliged to you if before I go you would fix a day for taking a mutton Chop with Mrs. Fox and me the latter end of the week—Either Friday or Saturday I shall be disengaged but the former would suit me best. . . . I am dear Sir yours ever C. J. Fox."[63] He arrived on Friday, and found that he was to share his mutton chop with General Fitzpatrick, Lord Lauderdale, Mr. Ponsonby, and "several other members of the House of Commons." As he was leaving, Mr. Fox begged him to wait, because he was expecting the Duchess of Devonshire and had promised her to present him; and just then she came in.

"She is a fine showy woman whose manners are extremely pleasing" is all that Livingston can say of this wonderful creature. "The Duchess in particular—" says a modern master—"lovely, exuberant, her whole personality flushed with a glowing sweetness which no heart could resist—seemed born to get and to give pleasure."[64] In her cooing, ecstatic voice she asked Livingston to a breakfast that she was to give at a villa she had near London and pressed him so hard that it was difficult to say no; but he had promised to go with Count Bentinck to inspect Lord Cholmondeley's country house that day, the steward had been advised to prepare beds and dinner, and he had to refuse, though it was an occasion "I should like of all things to be at." He then left Mr. Fox's for Lady Clare's, where among "a prodigious assembly of the gay and the great," he saw the Prince of Wales and the Duke of Cambridge, the latter of whom, "a very hansome man," sang three songs to the pianoforte, most agreeably, while the First Gentleman, who seemed to be on familiar terms with everyone, was all engaging manners and affable smiles.[65] He was, needless to say, in opposition to his father. Livingston, himself a fine figure of a man, courted, flattered, and pleased, attended party after party: but he was deaf, he could not catch all the subtleties of that refined, articulate, gossipy world: and evening after evening, he would steal away just as they sat down to supper.[66]

Mr. Monroe showed a characteristic side of himself to the man whom he thought perhaps a rival, certainly no friend: he was all goodness and consideration. Together, they visited the Abbey and St. Paul's, Greenwich Hospital, the House of Commons—"hardly equal . . . to our own House of Assembly at Albany"—and once, in Hyde Park, which "shone in gay equipages," the two tall Revolutionaries caught a glimpse of George III and the royal family driving in three carriages among their guards. He visited Bedlam with Lord Lauderdale and Sir Charles Blagden. He was taken to Drury Lane by Mr. Alexander Baring, and was much impressed by Mrs. Dorothea Jordan in *The Soldier's Daughter*. He went to the opera with Lord and Lady Cholmondeley, where the house was filled with splendidly dressed personages, but the ballet, the *Judgment of Paris*, was not nearly so good as anything one saw in Paris. He was much struck by a "lanskip by Reubens" on a visit to Lord Henry Petty at Lansdowne House. He dined with the eccentric Margravine of Anspach at Branden-burg House in Hammersmith, and with a Mr. Alljohn, a City merchant, who seemed to think that the French lived exclusively on mushrooms and frogs and that their peasantry were starved and half naked.[67]

But the great sights in England, for him, were the ones he was not permitted to see. As a landowner, he was profoundly interested in the improvements of the leading English agriculturalists: and on Sunday, May 28, he was to set off, by way of Lord Cholmondeley's country seat, to attend a sheepshearing at Thomas William Coke's vast estate at Holk-ham in Norfolk, the very center of progressive agriculture in England. The horses were at the door, he waited two hours for passports, when a note was received from "Mr. Reeves, who conducts the alien office," that they could not be granted without consulting Lord Hawkesbury: and, this being Sunday, Lord Hawkesbury could give no answer. Since Livingston had to be home by Saturday, in order to dine with the Portuguese Minister, he was obliged to give up the whole journey. And thus the Tory Government had a small revenge.[68]

VIII

Mr. Fox was not unmindful of the political amusement that he could obtain from the presence of the man to whom he was showing such marked attention. On June 5, he and Mr. Charles Grey called on Mr. Pitt to say that Mr. Livingston had been with them, and had told them that, while he had no authority to make any overture, he was convinced that the French Government wished to make peace. The neutrality of Malta in return for a French evacuation of Holland and Switzerland would be, he was persuaded, their idea of a fair exchange. Pitt replied that no good could come of such communications because, if the French had serious intentions of putting an end to the war, the Emperor would have chosen someone less exceptionable than the man who had made such accusations against Mr. Francis Drake. Besides, Mr. Livingston's public character at Napoleon's court made him a most unfitting intermediary.[69]

So runs the diary of Mr. George Rose. In Lord Stanhope's *Life* of

Pitt, however, it appears that Mr. Fox hinted that Livingston would have said a great deal more if he had found the government composed "as he perhaps expected when he left France"—that is, if he had found Mr. Fox at the Foreign Office. In an idle moment, it seems, Mr. Fox hoped to use the American visitor as a piece in some game he was playing for coalition with his formidable adversary: or perhaps he was simply amusing himself.

Nobody could assert that Livingston, when he left France for England, did *not* bear peace overtures: the Stanhope *Life* has Fox admitting that Livingston's opinions were founded upon a conversation with Joseph Bonaparte, to whom, as we know, peace could have been profitable. On the other hand, he may have said nothing that was attributed to him; or, which is much the same thing, may have said it only after he had read the newspapers or had been prompted by Mr. Fox, the most delightful of Whigs and a master of cajolery. In any or either event, the overture, in Lord Stanhope's words, "was only, I conceive, a *Will of the Wisp*."[70] But it was precisely the sort of adventure that would have delighted the fantastic element in Livingston's character. As for the *Times*, it continued to thunder long after he had gone.

IX

He returned to Paris in the middle of June—to Paris, where everything was on a much grander scale, where even his own Legation on the Rue Trudon was larger, he thought, than St. James's Palace—to Paris, with its shows and splendors and its now inevitable anticlimaxes.[71] Until he should receive new credentials, he could not be presented to the Emperor: as a diplomatist, he had less standing than heretofore.[72] The quarrel with the Board of Commissioners had not been abated by his absence; but since the French bureaus had as yet taken no steps on the liquidations presented to them, it had not been intensified either. He continued to press for West Florida, as being a part of the cession; and in a letter to Talleyrand suggested that, if Spain proved obdurate about delivering it to the Americans, the result would only be an alliance between the United States and Great Britain, the terms of which would be the lease to the former of the latter's unused warships, and its object the emancipation of the Spanish colonies. This extraordinary prediction shows, at any rate, to what length he was still prepared to go to fulfill his and Monroe's instructions to obtain the east bank of the Mississippi as well as the west one.[73]

On August 27, he heard from Madison that General Armstrong, his brother-in-law, had been appointed in his place: ever since his request for recall, he had been waiting for news of a replacement, and the appointment of one of his family could not have been displeasing.[74] From then on, he was simply marking time. He made plans for a tour of Italy, as soon as Armstrong should arrive; then he would set sail for America in the spring of 1805.

If he had had any thoughts of returning at an earlier date, they had already been dissipated by letters from home. Some of these letters had arrived, one must assume, long before he left for London: they showed— as, for example, one from John Armstrong, of February 7, and another, from William Cutting, of February 20—that Governor Clinton had decided to run for the vice-presidency, and that Chief Justice Morgan Lewis was to be the Republican candidate for governor. On March 18, 1804, John R. Livingston wrote to say that neither Tillotson nor Brockholst Livingston, "a weathercock" in spite of his professions of friendship for the Minister, had behaved well in the matter, but that "you will be better off" as a private gentleman, full of honors.

He already knew that his brother Edward had been obliged to resign as federal district attorney of New York and as mayor of that city. In June, 1803, it was discovered that money collected for customs-house bonds sent to Edward Livingston's office by the U.S. Treasury was missing, and in July, the government decided to remove him from his post as district attorney. Edward himself was entirely innocent; the money had been filched by a subordinate without his knowledge; but he was officially responsible. In the autumn of 1803, yellow fever raged in New York City; Edward, as mayor, gallantly stayed at his post, doing what he could for the sick; and eventually and inevitably caught the fever himself. When he recovered, his affairs had become so exceedingly deranged that he resigned the mayor's office as well (which De Witt Clinton seized at once), pledged all his private fortune to make up for his subordinate's defalcations, and went to seek the recovery of his ruined career in New Orleans.[75]

The news of the fall of his brother, followed by that of the nomination of his brother-in-law, produced much sympathy and not a word of recrimination from the Minister: his political ambitions had died with the new year. "For myself," he had written in March, 1804, before the news of Lewis's nomination could have reached him, "I expect or solicit nothing —I have done too much to hope to be permitted to do more."[76] He was now quite content to rest on his laurels. Before Armstrong arrived, he moved his family from the Legation in the Rue Trudon to a house in the Rue Chaumartin; and after having been permitted, as a special favor—for he still lacked the credentials—to present Armstrong to the Emperor, he left for Italy with his daughter and son-in-law.[77] His letters from Italy and Germany are singularly carefree. From politics, at long last, he was completely released: in spite of the sporadic and serious promptings of his ambition, this is where, all his life, he had most wished to be.

The family sailed from Nantes on May 26, 1805, and, after a short and stormy voyage, arrived in New York on the morning of June 29.[78] How much had passed since their sailing from that port in October, 1801 —how many triumphs and how many mistakes! Only one thing is certain: considering the great part he had played in the Louisiana Purchase, the man who landed that morning deserved conspicuously well of his countrymen.

CONCLUSION

MONOPOLY AND HUSBANDRY

Ἔσπερε πάντα φέρων, ὅσα φαίνολις ἐσκέδασ' αὔως,
    φέρεις ὄϊν,
φέρεις αἶγα, φέρεις ἀπὺ Fὸν μάτερι παῖδα.——SAPPHO

Evening star that bringest back all that the light of dawn had scattered, thou bringest the sheep, thou bringest the goat, thou bringest her child home to the mother.

CHAPTER ONE

On the subject of Chancellor Livingston [Albert Gallatin, Secretary of the Treasury, wrote to De Witt Clinton on May 13, 1805] . . . I can only say that I think his reception ought to be cordial, without being marked with those extraordinary testimonies of public approbation to which he does not seem to me to be entitled. What his views and feelings may be I know not; and the course he may, on his arrival, pursue is uncertain: but if there be any dissatisfaction either on his part or on that of the administration, none had been publicly expressed.[1]

Gallatin had never much cared for the Hudson River landlords since the days when he had taken a trip through New York State west of that river. He had thought the land poor and overpriced. Writing to his wife from Catskill Landing, he had thanked his good fortune that "in Pennsylvania not only we have neither Livingstones nor Rensselaers, but from the suburbs of Philadelphia to the banks of the Ohio, I do not know of a single family that has any extensive influence."[2] When Edward Livingston's shortages had become known, Gallatin was inclined to take the severest view of them.[3] Such sentiments, coming from a man of undoubted integrity, may be laid to the purity of his republicanism: but when he spoke of Chancellor Livingston's not being entitled to more than a "cordial" reception in New York, he undoubtedly spoke for the administration as well as for himself. Livingston was not to be forgiven for his memorial, for his feud with the Commissioners, for his abrupt and tactless language to James Madison, for his rivalry with Monroe: but the administration was unwilling to announce its dissatisfaction publicly. By the same token, its satisfaction with his services, if any, would be pronounced *sotto voce*. Great as this particular administration was, and valuable as its alliance with New York might prove to be, it was unlikely to provide a happy home for exceptional New Yorkers.

II

Although the years that remained to him were to be some of the most active of his whole career, Livingston's future course was not to be a political one: neither Gallatin nor Clinton had anything to fear. And it must be admitted that, in deciding to retire once and for all from politics, he had chosen as good a time as any in which to do so.

He himself had experienced a quite predictable change of feeling during his service as minister to France.

The basis of every democratic government [he wrote to his brother-in-law Thomas Tillotson on May 29, 1803], must be landed property to which the citizen is in some sort tied & it is for this reason that I have always doubted the policy of our laws of succession when they related only to a single farm—which after having been a succession of generations in a family becomes a sort of penates or household god from which the pious citizen will never fly & which he will defend with his life. The monied man has no home no country, gain is his god & it is indifferent to him how or where he is worshipped—In your large commercial cities this evil is unavoidable & it is for this reason that a large trading city is unfriendly to democracy. To introduce it into the heart of your country [he was writing against Tillotson's scheme for a new bank at Albany] is to give a new object to the enterprise of your farming citizen, to facilitate his changes of property & his means of extravagance. It is to make him despise the slow acquisitions of daily industry, to stimulate false hopes & to urge him to pursuits ruinous of his peace & of his virtue.

This kind of agrarian thinking, except for its friendly reference to "democracy," might have been held by his father, the Judge; and, except for its criticism of "our laws of succession," would not have come amiss from any sound contemporary Jeffersonian. It shows, once again, that Livingston's original conversion to the Republican church had been by no means entirely opportunistic. But what follows is somewhat different.

As to eradicating Aristocracy from a single district, I consider it as no moment [he continued], nay I do not know whether its existence is not rather an advantage than an evil, it serves as a bond of union among the republicans—it serves as a centinel upon their actions & discovers errors that they would otherwise overlook—It is not without design that God suffers the existence of a devil[.] Without the dread of this power & his seductions the priest would be much less sedulous in his attendance on the altar.[4]

Any student knows that the idea of natural aristocracy and the doctrines of the Jeffersonian schoolmen were not necessarily incompatible: but this is aristocracy in a new and puzzling form—both as a sentinel and as a devil's advocate, both as something useful and as something to be dreaded. But Livingston's jocosity does not conceal his real preference; as minister, he had begun to forget his borrowed character of ardent Jacobin and extreme

Republican—a character that was so very uncharacteristic—and was beginning to see himself once more as a landed aristocrat with a quasi-feudal
tenantry.

It so happened that, when he arrived in New York, its state government
was ostensibly in the hands of the Livingston family and its connections.
Morgan Lewis had become governor in 1804, Thomas T. Tillotson was
secretary of state, Brockholst Livingston and Smith Thompson (a connection by marriage) were justices of the State Supreme Court; while in the
city of New York, Maturin Livingston, Lewis's son-in-law, was recorder.
As long as Morgan Lewis could command a majority in the Council of
Revision, he disposed of a large patronage: the State Government, if the
Council wielded its powers of dismissal as well as its powers of appointment, could be used to create a state machine. The only trouble, and it
was a serious one, was that the (Clinton) state machine already existed.

And if it existed, Morgan Lewis was not the man to be able to alter
it to suit his purposes or promote his survival. Livingston said that his
brother-in-law was an imprudent man, who would not take advice.[5] By
imprudent, he meant, no doubt, Lewis's support, in 1805, of a charter for
the Merchant's Bank: Livingston himself, in spite of his maneuvers in
favor of the Manhattan Company, was at heart suspicious of banks. Moreover, since De Witt Clinton opposed the Merchant's Bank, this really
meant the end of the Livingston-Clinton alliance.[6] It had never amounted
to anything, except in terms of expediency.

The truth was that Lewis, a respectable, dignified man, who prided
himself on his aristocratic connections, was quite unfit for the governorship.
He had been elected at a favorable time: a time when the Livingstons had
distinguished themselves at home and abroad, as able judges and in
the field of diplomacy. But he suffered—if one accepts Livingston's description of him: that he was imprudent and would not take advice—from
the pride which goeth before a fall, the pride of the amateur. Tillotson,
who had probably given far more thought to the arts of government than
Lewis had, suffered, it would seem, from another kind of pride. He was
disposed to be haughty. He would not attend the Council of Appointment
as its secretary, as he was supposed to do.[7] And Maturin Livingston was
unpopular in his manners but fashionable and expensive in his habits.[8]
Here surely, in the shortcomings of these men, was the paradigm of aristocratic failure to suit itself to the demands of popular government.

Even Edward Livingston, who had behaved with such memorable
courage and unselfishness as mayor when the yellow fever struck New
York, had been so careless about the details of his district attorney's office

that he had allowed an assistant to rob it of a relatively huge sum of money. Nor did he know how to plead his case. When he went to Washington, after the defalcation came to light, he could not bring himself to enter into an explanation with Gallatin at the Treasury.[9] Thus he lost, one might say through pride, his one slim chance of administrative sympathy. He was the most brilliant member of the family and its connected group: but if he had survived into the reign of Lewis, would he have given his brother-in-law the strength he needed? Or would he have been too wayward? In any event, he had gone to New Orleans, where he was endeavoring to mend his fortunes; Brockholst Livingston had ascended to the United States Supreme Court in 1806; Smith Thompson was totally nonpolitical; and the former Chancellor, the head of the family and its most famous representative, had retired.

Somehow one cannot imagine any Livingston administration, even if every member of the family had been available and all had held office, as capable of victory in a battle with De Witt Clinton. An aristocratic group in government commonly vanishes from the scene from economic causes or because its historical roots do not go deep enough: one cannot assert with confidence that these were not factors in the defeat of the Livingstons. Certainly the growth of fee-simple farming, since the Revolution, could be held to have doomed them as a landed interest. But there was another and—who can say?—perhaps a more compelling reason: and it was a psychological one. It was a reluctance, as politics grew more popular, to condescend to the demands of popular politics.

"Were I even to entertain different sentiments," Livingston wrote, when asked in 1809 why he had gone into retirement, "I should find myself ill-calculated to take a lead among men rendered fastidious by too much courtship, to intrigue with little men, to carry little measures & to hold out lures for the ambition of every scoundrel that had smoked & drank himself into the honourable station of village chieftain."[10] This was the position, or it was analogous to the position, he had held when he reluctantly attempted to advise the Revolutionary Assembly of New York State: but it no longer carried any trace of affectation. It was the calculated statement of a philosophy; and, whether the philosophy was creditable or not, two things were obvious about it: it was not popular, and it was not Clintonian. It sums up, with laconic brevity, the failure and the death of a historical party.

For, under Lewis, the party failed and died. One need not rehearse in detail a familiar story. In January, 1806, Clinton attempted a reunion with the old Burrite group—its leaders were Colonel Swartwout, Peter

Irving, and M. L. Davis—at the house of his supporter General Theo-
dorus Bailey: or so it was alleged.[11] In January, too, after the Governor's
speech to the Legislature had drawn a good deal of ridicule for demanding
experienced drummers for the state militia—"the drum," he said, as a
former quartermaster general, "is all important in the day of battle"—a
Clintonian Council of Appointment had been nominated, and had proceeded
to dismiss Maturin Livingston and Thomas T. Tillotson.[12] In February,
there was another meeting of Clintonians and Burrites at Dyde's Hotel,
near New York, where toasts were said to have been drunk to the anticipated union.[13] This stirred up the energies of the non-Clintonian Republicans; and the April elections were in favor of Lewis: but they did not
pass without being faintly illuminated by a somewhat paradoxical incident
in Columbia County. There, the Clermont Livingstons had resorted to the
dubious expedient of voting the Federalist ticket in order to defeat the
Clinton-Burrite combination. For the members of an aristocratic party, such
a choice was as obvious as it was ominous; and the result, even locally, was
not altogether successful.

With the federalists opposed to us [wrote Martin Van Buren, at the time a
"jacobinical" supporter of Clinton], we reduced the Federal majority for
Assembly from 134 to 45, elected our representative to Congress, & for
the first time in many years obtained a majority for our Senator. The late
Chancellor attended the poll, quarreled with Colonel Ten Broeck, declared
our ticket to be a factious one, but when he came to vote he only voted the
Senator ticket, notwithstanding his son in law, Judge [Dr. William Wilson,
now a county judge], & Tenants voted the Federal ticket.[14]

The Livingstons were chiefly interested in the election of a Federalist
assemblyman, since it was with the help of the Federalists in the Assembly
that Governor Lewis proposed to regain control of the Council of Appointment: but the Chancellor, with his relatives and his tenants for once in
political agreement, could not quite bring himself to support his own
family party when it abandoned Republicanism in this forthright manner.
He was, in effect, no longer interested in political leadership: but his
desertion was suggestive.

When the new Legislature met in January, 1807, Lewis, aided by the
eighteen Federalists in the Assembly, was again in command of the Council
of Appointment. But his hour of doom was upon him. He reinstated his
son-in-law Maturin Livingston and his relative Dr. Tillotson: and at the
same time he wildly dismissed Clinton from his office of mayor of New
York. Many things could be alleged against Clinton: but also "it could be
said even then that his name was associated with every great enterprise

for the public good."[15] To treat him in this cavalier fashion was a fatal mistake; the mysterious passions of New York City were aroused; and a majority of the Republicans, "guided by the deposed Mayor," nominated Daniel D. Tompkins for governor. In the April election, he defeated Lewis by a 4,085 majority.[16] When a Council of Appointment was nominated in February, 1808, Tillotson and Livingston were dismissed once again; Marinus Willett surrendered the mayoralty to Clinton; and within a year, every officeholder open to removal and suspected of Livingston sympathies had been dismissed from office.[17] At times thereafter, a Livingston might be elected to a state senatorship or become a member of the Assembly: once there was a Livingston speaker, and once a lieutenant governor: but it might be said of the family, with perfect justice, that after 1808 they abstained from any *direct* attempt to control the state. The party had expired.

The former Chancellor, although family piety required him to denounce the Clinton maneuvers as "mad demagogism," decided after the Tompkins victory (so he told James Madison) that he would acquiesce in the verdict of the Republican party.[18] His feelings where state politics were concerned had become, in fact, almost, if not quite, completely atrophied. His imagination and his energies were absorbed in other matters: in the consummation of his dreams as a landholder, on the one hand; in the complexities of the steamboat, on the other.

CHAPTER TWO

I fear that you will laugh at me when I mention it [Livingston wrote to Thomas T. Tillotson from Paris on November 12, 1802], but I give you leave to do so provided you by no means neglect to execute [a commission] this session of the legislature thro' some of my friends—You know my passion for steam boats & the money I have expended on that object—I am not yet discouraged & tho all my old partners have given up the pursuit I have found a new one in Robert Fulton a most ingenious young man the inventor of the diving boat which made so much noise in Europe—We are now actually making experiments upon a large scale upon the Seine[.] Shd they succeed it would be mortifying to have any other competitor for the advantages—I have therefore drawn a short petition which I hope you will reduce to the form of law[,] coppying the old one only substituting Fulton's name & mine & reducing the size of the boat to one of twenty tons instead of thirty.[1]

II

Robert Fulton was about thirty-six years old when he made the acquaintance of Livingston. The two men had something in common. Both had some of the hardness of the entrepreneur; both displayed the vivid, tenacious, and imaginative spirit of the inventor. There the likeness ceased. Livingston, although he had an extensive knowledge of the principles of mechanics,[2] was always the amateur: always in search of something novel, and impatient with what had been tried. Fulton was a professional. He had been born into the artisan class; tools had been his familiars since he was a child; with tools he had been obliged to make his living—the tools of the gunsmith, the locksmith, the carpenter; the tools of the painter; of the draughtsman. From the beginning, he enjoyed a tremendous advantage over his aristocratic partner; and Livingston, though he never abandoned his dreams for a mercurial engine, recognized at once that in Fulton he had found a master.

Fulton's genius, for genius indeed he had, lay first in the faculty for combining into workable form the discarded or impracticable ideas of others; and secondly in an intense and, in its way, a statesmanlike vision. It was his destiny, in the realm of technical ideas, to find a commotion and turn it into a revolution. He was born in Lancaster County, Pennsylvania, in 1765. Lancaster County was the home of gunmaking during the Revolution; and, as a boy, he became an expert gunsmith. Later on, he went to Philadelphia to make his fortune; which, as a self-taught painter and draughtsman, he did to such good effect that he was able to purchase a farm for his widowed mother. He then went abroad, to London, to study under Benjamin West. He did not return for twenty years.

He was a competent painter, and numbered many artists among his friends, but painting became in time only an avocation. His vision was soon absorbed with the vital problems of inland navigation; with canals and canalboats, and all that they could mean to the economy of a nation. "In 1794 he was in correspondence with Boulton & Watt concerning the purchase of a suitable steam-engine for boat propulsion."[3] The dredging machine, or power shovel; the cast-iron aqueduct; the double inclined plane, for taking canalboats out of the canal and transporting them overland by rail at points where canal construction became prohibitive—these inventions or innovations owed much to his teeming brain. He wrote pamphlets and corresponded with eminent men; powerful noblemen like the Duke of Bridgewater and Lord Stanhope took him up; but he was no slavish Anglophile. Far from it. He began to dream about submarine mines, torpedoes, submarines: of all devices, the most inimical to British seapower. In 1799, he had an audience with the French Directory, who would have nothing to do with him; but the Consulate was more hospitable, and appointed a commission to examine his schemes. It was with this encouragement that he perfected his submarine to the extent of constructing a boat in which he and three mechanics, with the help of air from a compressed-air tank, could remain under water as deep as twenty-five feet for as long as four and a half hours. With this vessel—half contraption, half tomb—he was daring enough to reconnoiter the French seacoast, before the Peace of Amiens, in search of British warships: his reward was to be in proportion to the size of the ship destroyed, and would have gone as high as four hundred thousand francs.[4] He never overtook a British vessel; if he had done so, the history of naval warfare and the destinies of maritime nations might have been somewhat different. The Consulate lost interest; the British became curious, as well they might; and since, in 1804, Fulton was as eager to do to the French invasion fleet at Boulogne what he had tried to do to the British navy in 1801, one might perhaps venture to call him a cosmopolitan American.

In Paris, Fulton had become friends with another cosmopolitan— Joel Barlow, the poet and former Connecticut Wit, who combined an

aptitude for vaguely questionable business ventures with the sincere profession of high Jeffersonian principles. It was through Barlow that Fulton
was first brought to the attention of Minister Livingston. It was the meeting of flint and steel; the sparks, no more than dormant in the Minister's
composition since his failure in 1800, began to fly once more at the first
contact with the overwhelming personality of the handsome, dark, self-
confident Fulton. The two men were nothing if not American in their
outlook. What they had in mind, of course, was a revolution in national
transport and economy. The country was rich in magnificent waterways
—rivers, like the Mississippi, almost divine—down which the populace and
its produce floated to homestead or to market. But, in a sense, these
were only semiwaterways; for neither populace nor produce could float
up again; and even on so splendid a stream as the Hudson, the problem
of commercial sailing presented certain toilsome difficulties. And Livingston
and Fulton foresaw immense profits for themselves if they could corner
the market in steamboat transportation.

The two men signed a legal agreement on October 10, 1802, to con-
struct a steamboat for the purpose of navigating the Hudson between
New York and Albany; and on November 12, Livingston wrote the
letter to Tillotson which was the first step toward his monopoly on the
New York waters. He already had an agreement with Stevens and
Roosevelt, but this, he assumed, had been extinguished.[5]

III

Fulton did not believe that the usefulness of an invention consisted in its
ability to set oars, paddles, wheels, or resisting chains in motion by a
steam engine: "all these things," he said, "being governed by the laws
of nature, the real invention is to find them." To him, it was all a matter
of exact proportions, of nicely calculated relations. For example, to determine the resistance of water, he made use of Colonel Mark Beaufroy's
newly published experiments which, since they applied to solids pulled
under water, had not attracted the attention of naval architects.[6]

Barlow, who was completely in Fulton's confidence and who had some
knowledge of mechanics, encouraged him in his experiments with a model
boat, but was not sure that Livingston was the man to back him. He felt
for the Minister an odd mixture of veneration and suspicion. He could
write with admiration of the dignity and energy with which Livingston, at
one of his own dinners in the Rue Trudon, before "a flock of ambassadors,
etc.," could support Fulton's concept of a submarine, saying that, since

modern wars were commercial wars and were activated by navies, he was convinced that the submarine would put an end to warfare and was therefore humane. In this, he was supported by the great Comte de Volney: but the diplomatists present seem to have been discreetly silent.[7] Yet when it came to financing, Barlow preferred Daniel Parker: perhaps he thought that Livingston, as an inveterate projector, was not to be trusted with Fulton's secrets.[8] Fulton, however, did not care for Parker; and so the great combination was formed; and an experimental boat, financed by Livingston, was built and launched upon the Seine. This was in the spring of 1803; but the first boat, overcome by the weight of the machinery, broke in two and sank.[9] It was not until August 9, 1803, that a new and stronger boat had been built and launched before a large crowd of idle onlookers and a select committee of *savants* from the Institut National des Sciences et des Arts. The invention, wrote Bonaparte, "may change the face of the world": and the committee was to report upon the soundness or otherwise of this tentative but inspired prediction. A little apart stood "a tall man," writes John Marshall's biographer, "of distinguished bearing, whose powerful features, bold eyes, aggressive chin, and acquisitive nose indicated a character of unyielding determination, persistence, and hopefulness."[10] The portrait is a portrait, as it were, of one side of Livingston: of the projector, not of the politician. The Louisiana Purchase, recently concluded, had been in many respects a visionary project with him: he had pursued it with a matchless tenacity; and so it was with that revolutionary phenomenon the steamboat. For the French *savants*, although the boat made as much as two and three-quarters miles per hour upstream and fully twice that speed going down, although it maneuvered well and showed no disposition to sink, were not enthusiastic. They reported unfavorably to the Consul, who thereupon decided that the face of the world could best be changed by artillery. But Livingston and Fulton were undeterred. As their experimental boat moved up and down the Seine, an improbable, a well-nigh impossible object, but an object in motion, they saw nothing in it but the changing future of America. They agreed at once that Fulton should, as soon as possible, proceed to England and attempt to get an engine made there by Boulton & Watt, which could be shipped in due time to the United States.

IV

Fulton did not return to America until the winter of 1806. He had intended to go home in 1804; and there is among the Chancellor's papers for the spring of that year a letter to his brother Edward, which was to be delivered by Fulton in person, and in which he is described as

a very estimable young man & very distinguished for his treatise on cannels [sic] & his diving boat &c. You will find him a man of science in every line particularly in mathematicks & the fine arts & what is much better a most estimable man in every view.[11]

Fulton, however, lingered in England, hoping for permission to build a submarine that should create consternation and havoc among the French ships at Boulogne: the conservative British, after careful deliberation, and the expenditure of some £15,000, decided not to encourage such a fateful innovation. While he was in England, he succeeded in getting an engine made to his specifications by Boulton & Watt, and, what is more, in getting it shipped out of the country. For six months, it lay unnoticed at the customhouse in New York; it was not until April 23, 1807, that he claimed it; by then, the hull of his new steamboat was taking shape in the yards of Charles Browne at Paulus Hook; and Livingston, determined as ever, had got a new act passed through the State Legislature, extending his time limit for two more years.[12]

As the work proceeded, Livingston—who seems to have financed it by the sale of his New Jersey lands—found that he was seriously overspending himself; his brother-in-law John Stevens, when applied to for funds, answered not with capital but with criticism; but Fulton, using all his powers of persuasion, managed to squeeze a few thousands out of some gentlemen who begged to remain anonymous for fear of being ridiculed for lending themselves to so foolish a loan.[13]

At length, on August 9, Fulton got his craft to the river and was able to tell Livingston that, although the paddle wheels were not complete, she was already making three miles per hour and would certainly, "when in complete order, run up to my full calculations." On August 17, 1807, *The Steamboat* (as she was then called) was ready to make her maiden voyage to Albany.[14]

V

Cousin Chancellor has a wonderful new boat [wrote Helen Livingston to her mother], which is to make the voyage up the Hudson some day soon. It will hold a good many passengers and he has, with his usual kindness, invited us to be of the party. He says it will be something to remember all our lives. He says we need not trouble ourselves about provisions, as his men will see to all that.[15]

Livingston had invited the more closely related members of the clan to move into the future with himself and Fulton. It was a pioneering adventure, if ever there was one: but the Livingstons, as a group, scarcely presented the appearance of pioneers. The men (in the language of James Thomas Flexner's informed and felicitous book on the steamboat) "were elegant in spotless ruffles and professionally arranged hair"; the ladies "dimpled charmingly from under a correct bonnet, from over a stylish dress." Nor (Mr. Flexner thinks) did they display either the apprehension or the excitement appropriate to so novel an event: on the contrary, they "gave off an air of sophisticated disdain. . . . Unlike Fitch's common and slightly drunken friends, they had no vision, they did not believe."[16]

Certainly *The Steamboat*, as it lay at its berth on the North River near the state's prison, was not an object calculated to excite admiration. It was more like a raft than a river vessel. It was long and narrow—one hundred and fifty feet by thirteen; it drew two feet of water and displaced one hundred tons; its flat deck rose a few feet above the river. It had no curves: its bow and stern were cut off at an angle to form a point. There was a small mast at the stern; and from the mast to the tall fat chimney at the center, the machinery stood in stark, unseemly, unsightly nakedness. The unguarded paddle wheels and flywheels, the walking beam, the cylinder, the valves and pipes defied affection. Only the boiler, set in masonry, was covered: by a house like that of a canalboat, which contained, as well, an apartment for the officers. *The Steamboat* was also decked for a short distance from stem to stern: it was but a grudging accommodation for that privileged group which included, besides the variously related Livingstons, the ingenious Dr. Samuel Latham Mitchill and the Very Reverend the Dean of Ripon, who had been invited to Clermont, and who chose this novel method of arriving there. Never had the decanal gaiters and apron graced a more singular scene.[17]

Fulton got up steam; the fuel, a dry white-pine wood, sent up columns of flame and sparks from the mouth of the tall stack; the passengers were invited aboard; *The Steamboat* got under way. She had scarcely started before she stopped. Fulton asked for half an hour's grace from the manifestly skeptical passengers; and in half an hour, he had her on her way again. From then onward, she performed excellently—one would have said perfectly, except that "perfection" sounds more than usually extravagant when used in relation to that fiery, clanking, splashing, sooty object. As they passed through the Highlands by night, the passengers, now partly converts, were said to have sung—it was a tribute to the ancestry of some of them—"Ye banks and braes o' bonny Doon." The candles had been lit, and soon the ladies were bunked down on improvised cots in the cabin: the gentlemen got what rest they could on the deck. As *The Steamboat*, a plangent volcano, passed on her way through the night, one terrified rustic is said to have rushed home, locked the doors, and shouted that the devil was going up to Albany in a sawmill.[18]

At one in the afternoon of August 18, she put in at the Clermont landing, where the Chancellor and some of his guests were to disembark. Before going ashore, Livingston held up his hand for silence and announced the engagement of Robert Fulton and Harriet Livingston,* to which he had already given his blessing, but which he prudently refrained from acknowledging until *The Steamboat* had proved successful. He also took occasion to prophesy that before the end of the century, steamboats would be traveling to Europe. At this, his brother John R. Livingston, not as yet a convert, although afterward an investor, is said to have remarked, by no means in a whisper, that "Bob has had many a bee in his bonnet before now, but this steam folly will prove the worst yet."[19]

VI

You will learn with pleasure [Livingston wrote his son-in-law Robert L. Livingston, who was in France], that our Steamboat has succeeded wonderfully well, she came up last week [he was writing on September 2] to my house against the wind (what little there was) in twenty two hours[.] the next morning I got on board & reached Albany the weather being calm in 8 hours, which was exactly six miles an hour, we had however the tide, tho' not strong, for about six hours—She returned to New York from Albany in thirty hours the wind, tho light, all the time against her, at Hudson, & indeed at every publick landing, the sight was amusing[.] All the people of the town were upon the hills that bound the river—Upwards of twenty boats filled with men & women came to meet us, having seen us at a great distance coming down, & tho there was a number of five oard barges double manned, they could not by all their efforts keep near us more than ten minutes. She has exceeded Fulton's, & fully justified my calculations, that is, she goes at a mean, with & against the tide five miles an hour & this without making the engine work its full power. She has since her last trip been fitting up for passengers. She leaves town this morning, & will be here by daybreak tomorrow. It now only remains to see whether she will have such a number of passengers as to defray our expenses, & make the proffit we expect. If she does, I shall now have nothing left to wish for, but your speedy return, with my dear children.[20]

* Harriet Livingston was the daughter of Walter Livingston, and sister-in-law to the Chancellor's younger daughter, Margaret Maria.

In a pecuniary point of view [he wrote to the same correspondent on November 11], it [the fact that she made her voyages three times a week in thirty-three hours] is an important object & I think we may set down her clear profit at $3500 a year to each of us [*i.e.*, to Livingston and Fulton]. I design a fifth of mine for you & as much for Edward[.] There is a prospect of her more than doubling that estimate particularly as we design to build another boat. . . . Your Mother is very well having just returned from New York[.] She went down with the steam boat which is indeed the most fashionable mode of travelling.[21]

And again, on January 4, 1808, he told his daughter in France that Fulton was to spend the winter at Clermont with his bride in order to supervise the rebuilding of *The Steamboat* at Red Hook; that the boat had become a great favorite with the public; that it had met with some accidents owing to the use of "bad iron (a defect we shall remedy)"; and that "it generally carryed every trip upwards of 50 & sometimes 70 passengers & made 3 trips a week."[22]

The accidents were not entirely due to bad iron. The steamboat had caused a great deal of superstitious alarm among the pious dwellers by the banks of the Hudson; but it had also caused a great deal of anger. The captains of the sailing boats on that great river, an unduly prescient group of men, at once foresaw in the strange contraption the ruin of their own profession; and they took every chance that offered to run foul of her unguarded wheels. What with human as well as mechanical obstacles, therefore, she often broke down: but Fulton had surmounted every difficulty, had placed heavy guards around the paddle wheels, and was prepared, with his rebuilt boat, to face the year 1808 with an undiminished, indeed with an increased and buoyant, confidence.

VII

None the less, the year 1807 was the only serene year for the two partners. One finds among Livingston's papers, dated January, 1808, a lengthy fragment of a drafted letter to his brother-in-law John Stevens—the complete letter was actually sent on January 13—from which it appears that Stevens, relying on a United States patent, was preparing to navigate New York waters with a steamboat of his own devising. Livingston's letter, humming and exploding with a variety of legal arguments, confines itself primarily to two contentions.

In the first place, he contends that the Livingston-Fulton steamboat does not infringe Stevens's patent rights.

A long boat, & wheels, was not with us the result of mere reasoning a priori but of expensive & numerous experiments, upon an enlarged scale [he writes]. In the many years that this subject has occupied your thoughts, neither of these entered into your plans—on the contrary, sculls, & smoke [jack] wheels have occupied you for five years, nor did you ever after we had told you of our intention to use wheels,* manifest any faith in them, on the contrary you refused to come into partnership with us, though we repeatedly requested it, & communicated to you the result of our experiments at Paris because you believed our propelling power more defective than your own.[23]

And it is true that since 1802 Stevens had been experimenting with a small high-pressure engine, a marvelously compact device, but one that he had already found unsuitable for transportation on a large scale. He was now preparing to build his *Phoenix*, with a low-pressure engine similar to the one that Watt had built for Fulton, and with paddle wheels over the side, but broader than *The Steamboat* (or *The North River Steamboat*, as she was now called in the advertisements), and having certain other differences as regards engine braces, air pump, valves, and so forth. The second argument, therefore, to which Livingston addressed himself was to the effect that Stevens could not put this boat upon the river without coming into conflict with the Livingston-Fulton monopoly, as granted to him and his partner by act of the New York State Legislature. He had always been willing, he was still willing, to make Stevens a partner in the enterprise if Stevens would conform to the specifications of the Fulton boat. Was he not essentially a kindhearted man? To quarrel with his wife's brother and his old friend could only have been a grief to him; and he was always uneasily aware that there existed an agreement between him, Stevens, and Nicholas J. Roosevelt which may or may not have been ended by their inability to conform to the act of 1798. What he and Fulton wanted, in effect, was that Stevens should support their monopoly by admitting the superiority of their invention; so that the argument was not only one among three entrepreneurs, which might have been settled by compromise, but also one among three inventors, to whom fame, profitless fame, was a matter of grave importance. In such arguments, compromise is reached with difficulty.

In the ensuing correspondence, as it is outlined by Stevens's biographer, and in so far as it can be rescued from Livingston's papers, the basic disagreement is obvious enough. Stevens maintains that the Livingston-Fulton monopoly was in violation of the commerce clause of the Consti-

* Nicholas J. Roosevelt, however, could have claimed the paddle wheel: see J.H.B. Latrobe in *Maryland Historical Society Fund-Publication*, No. 5, 13-14.

tution; Livingston says that where a power is given to Congress which might have been exercised by the state prior to the forming of the Constitution, then, unless there is a prohibitory clause, Congress and the state have concurrent jurisdiction. It was not until 1824 that the Supreme Court, in the great case of *Gibbons* vs. *Ogden,* directly through the mouth of Justice William Johnson, and indirectly in the verdict of Chief Justice John Marshall, supported the contention of John Stevens.[24]

In the meantime, the state monopoly remained in all its rigor. As Livingston put it, in his communication to Stevens, he and Fulton had an exclusive right "to construct, make and use etc." all vessels moved by steam or fire in all creeks, rivers, bays, or waters whatsoever in the territory or jurisdiction of New York. If any person not licensed by Livingston and Fulton were to infringe upon this right, such a person must pay £100 for every offense and forfeit the boat and engine as well: and any court in the state had jurisdiction over the offense. Within a few weeks, on April 11, 1808, a new law was enacted by the New York Legislature, providing that, for every new boat established on New York waters by Livingston and Fulton and their associates, they should be entitled "to five years prolongation of their grant or contract with this state," up to but not exceeding thirty years. Everyone else was forbidden to navigate the waters of New York without a license from the monopolists, and every unlicensed vessel, "together with the engine, tackle and apparel thereof" was to be forfeited to them.[25] Once upon a time, before *The Steamboat* had proved successful, the Chancellor might have had (said "a very sensible member" of the New York Legislature) a grant for as many years as he wanted, "as the navigation by steam was thought to be much on footing as to practicability as the navigation by the Reindeer in the Chancellor's park." Now, with success, the limitation was fixed unalterably at thirty years: the monopoly was all the more formidable for this faint touch of kindness.[26]

In a modern point of view, nothing good can be said for such a monopoly; and it would be, therefore, merely redundant to repeat the customary recriminations. And there were recriminations enough, in those days as well as in these. The alternative to a private monopoly—that the state should have bought out Livingston and Fulton and established some efficient monopoly of its own—was of course quite unthinkable in the first decade of the nineteenth century. Another alternative has been suggested: that Fulton should have offered to serve as engine-builder to the nation, charging only for his services: but this is to ask that Livingston and Fulton should have been two other people, that they should have undergone a metamorphosis into individuals with a marked and somewhat morbid leaning toward self-sacrifice.[27] In the early nineteenth century, in the technological world, such personages were rare; and they have never been common at any time. As it was, Fulton was able to claim that "although the prospect of personal emolument has been some induce-ment to me, yet I feel infinitely more pleasure in reflecting on the numerous advantages my country will derive from the invention."[28] Livingston, to whom privilege came naturally, never saw the state monopoly as anything other than his just deserts: but he, too, conceived of himself less as an entrepreneur than as a public benefactor, who had expended a large portion of his capital in perfecting a useful invention, and who was entitled to the thanks and not the abuse of his countrymen. The real trouble was, of course, lack of capital. If the steamboat business had been thrown open to the economic and physical battering of an unrestricted competition, the Livingston-Fulton partnership could not have survived: for this reason, the monopoly was created, and the development of the steamboat was re-tarded for many years. In itself the very symbol of democracy, it was cer-tainly caught in an odd grip.

To judge from his papers, Livingston's enthusiasm for the steamboat steadily declined. He had an unconditional admiration for Robert Fulton; and he had to admit that Fulton, not he, was the partner responsible for the steamboat's technical virtues. He had, it is true, supplied vision and capital, each an indispensable element of success. But Fulton had taken the ideas of other men, every one of them embodied in some item of ma-chinery in his steamboat, and had combined them in harmonious and workable proportions. Although proportions were excluded from the patent law, it was upon proportions and tables that he really founded his patent, when at length he obtained one in 1809. His whole theory of "plus pressure" and "minus pressure," hull resistance and engine power, as set forth in his specifications, is in itself a remarkable discussion, but, being only theoretical, could hardly be called a patent. As early as 1808, he was declaring that neither John Stevens nor any other man had a right to use a steamboat whose length should be more than five times its breadth, "because I am the first to show the necessity of laying the weight in length upon the water."[29] Livingston, though his understanding of me-chanical principles was invaluable in the drawing up of legal papers and patent arguments, could only contribute his old notion of a mercurial engine, which was never tried, presumably because it would have been too expensive.[30]

But if his enthusiasm gradually declined, his tenacity no less steadily increased. It was, he declared, at least *morally* certain that no man would engage in an undertaking requiring much time, thought, and money if, after all his toil and all the hazards he had incurred, people could step in—the very people "who were laughing at his folly & considering him a visionary during its progress"—and deprive him of his profits. The state, he maintained, had made its grant and contract with him at a time when there was no prospect of any other person's engaging in such a venture without such encouragement: and even with it, few would have made the effort, and fewer still have completed the object. "It is then to what has falsely been called a monopoly that the state owes the incalculable advantage & honor of steamboats."[31]

Moreover, now that the practicability of steamboats had been proved, and entrepreneurs might venture upon building them with some assurance of success, would not a *multiplicity* of steamboats be injurious? Three steamboats were all that traffic upon the Hudson would bear. Should six more be built (and if there were no exclusive privilege, that number certainly *would* be built by "unthinking men who had not calculated the expense or profit of the undertaking"), then either these boats must be inferior or else they must consume a great deal of capital which could better be employed in other ventures. In short, he relied upon three arguments: that a state could restrain a United States patent from being put to use within its borders; that his own exclusive grant was also a contract (as in the wording of the act of 1808 it was) and was morally justifiable on any terms; and that unrestricted competition in steamboats would be wasteful. The states rights argument was supported, said Fulton after a visit to Washington, by no less an authority than James Madison: the rest of Livingston's argument was a convinced, an unabashed appeal to economic and political privilege.[32]

John Stevens ignored the claims of Livingston and Fulton and, in 1808, completed a steamboat of his own, which he called the *Phoenix* and which, while it employed a low-pressure engine and paddle wheels, did not follow Fulton's narrow design. (Fulton, rebuilding his boat in the winter of 1807-1808, had to some extent abandoned this design.) The *Phoenix* sailed from Perth Amboy to Paulus Hook, in defiance of the monopoly; for the monopoly's writ, marvelous to relate, ran in all the waters of the bay and the Hudson up to the low-water mark on the Jersey shore. About August of that year, also, she sailed from Perth Amboy to New Brunswick, "which proved her to be so imperfect," wrote Fulton, "that she was laid up for alterations."[33]

The partners did not attempt to enforce their monopoly against Stevens, partly because he did not as yet take on passengers, partly because Livingston always hoped to reach some compromise with him. The relations between the two men at this time, says Stevens's biographer, were "an odd mixture of personal affection and professional animosity."[34] Livingston had written for James Alexander Stevens, his nephew, what the boy's mother called a "chaste, correct and elegant" commencement address— "my friend," wrote the sister-in-law, "you have not forgotten how to write [like a young man] nor to feel like one, nor do I believe you ever will."[35] Indeed, in the previous winter, the uncle and nephew had been partners in building an iceboat at Clermont which went between sixteen and eighteen miles an hour, though they could not bring her to lie close to the wind.[36] One can imagine, too, that Mary Stevens Livingston added her influence toward creating a more fraternal atmosphere between her husband and her brother.

At any rate, a compromise was reached in December, 1809. It was, naturally enough, neither written nor reached in a very friendly manner. The preamble gave the distinct impression that all the inventions were Fulton's; and Livingston inserted a proviso that Stevens should, for himself, his heirs and representatives, fully and absolutely recognize not only the right of the Livingston-Fulton partnership to all inventions and improvements specified in their 1809 United States patent, but also their New York grant in all its unmajestic majesty.[37] Stevens could not bring himself to sign this agreement, but he allowed his name to stand upon it. According to its terms, he could construct and navigate steamboats upon the river and bay of Delaware, Chesapeake Bay, the Santee, Savannah, and Connecticut rivers, and the waters that led from Rhode Island.[38] Eventually, he decided to establish a line of steamboats on the Delaware between Philadelphia and Wilmington, and on the Chesapeake between Baltimore and the Head of Elk: the subscribers list, printed on November 18, 1810, shows that Fulton, Livingston, John R. Livingston, and De Witt Clinton were all down for ten shares apiece at $100 a share. The total capitalization was to be $75,000; and Stevens pledged the whole of his proportion of the revenues until half of this sum had been reimbursed.[39]

VIII

A contentious atmosphere thus surrounded the steamboat almost from the beginning. What else could be expected? Did not the steamboat promise to be a "very profitable speculation"; and, since Fulton had married the daughter of Livingston's second cousin, a girl whose brother had married Livingston's daughter, might not one say, with some justice, that the monopoly had been granted to a single family and its connections? When *The North River Steamboat* was being rebuilt, it was hoped that she would contain "beds for upwards of 70 people all laying single & four very hansome cabbins," besides a kitchen, a larder, a pantry, and a steward's room, "so that she will afford at once the most expeditious, & most commodious mode of travelling ever invented."[40] In the end, the number of cabins was reduced to three and the number of berths to fifty-four; the full fare from New York to Albany was $7.00, the minimum fare was $2.00; and the boat, with her proportions so changed as almost to make her a new vessel, was far more efficient. None the less, the more popular she became, the more the traveling public—it was really most ungrateful—complained that the rooms were overcrowded, the air offensive, the meals (at fifty cents apiece) inadequate, and so on and so on. If the price of wood went up in Albany, it was laid to the existence of a "vicious monopoly"—that is, to the amount of wood consumed by *The North River Steamboat* and her sisters.[41]

For sisters she had. In 1809, the *Car of Neptune* was built, in 1810 the *Paragon*. In 1809, the Mississippi Steamboat Company was founded, with Nicholas J. Roosevelt as both one of the founders and company agent to build the first boat at Pittsburgh. Roosevelt's affairs were in hopeless disorder: but he had some claim to be the inventor of paddle wheels; so that from either point of view, his own or the partners', the new arrangement was likely to produce a certain peace of mind. Roosevelt's first duty was to explore the possibilities of direct navigation, and with his gallant and beautiful wife, who was pregnant, he made the long voyage in a flatboat from Pittsburgh to New Orleans.[42]

The monopoly, in short, had decided that it must attempt to control, not only the waters around New York and up to Albany, but also the waters around New Orleans and up to Natchez. Two of the most vital commercial waterways in the United States would thus come within its power. It was no light matter to fall into the grip of the Livingston-Fulton monopoly. When John R. Livingston decided to build a boat, in 1809, he was granted a license on condition that he pay the monopoly one-sixth of his gross proceeds.[43] (He took his revenge by monopolizing the monopoly's workmen while his boat was building, and generally by making an infernal nuisance of himself.[44] When his boat, the *Raritan*, sailed from New Brunswick, he refused to allow John Stevens's passengers, who had disembarked at Trenton and made the trip to New Brunswick overland, to re-embark in her. It might be said of him that he was a natural monopolist.)

In the Territory of Orleans, however, the monopoly got its way without too much difficulty. On April 19, 1811, an act was passed by the Legislature which gave the Livingston-Fulton partnership even more exclusive privileges than those conferred upon it by New York statute: every operator of an unlicensed steamboat was to pay $5,000 and forfeit the boat and equipment.[45] In the autumn of 1811, Nicholas Roosevelt and his wife, in the *New Orleans*, slid over the Falls of the Ohio at Louisville, and, in a portentous season of earthquakes and other strange phenomena, threaded their way past snags and fresh shoals and through newly formed channels down to New Orleans. Thereafter, the *New Orleans* plied between New Orleans and Natchez, potentially a source of enormous earnings: in 1814, she is said to have cleared $20,000 on a capitalization of $40,000.[46]

Could the same be said of the New York steamboats? In 1812, one finds Fulton writing to Livingston that his estimate of clear profit for the following year was as follows:

North River Steamboats	$50,000
Steam Ferry Boat	2,000
Mississippi Boat	14,000
	$60,000
R. R. Livingston	33,000
½ profits Firefly (not yet built)	1,000
R. R. Livingston	$34,000

"With such immense profits in perspective," he adds, "you surely can send me a bill for 4000 which I can get discounted in the New York Bank."[47]

The sum of $34,000 was hardly "immense" when one considered how much of the profits had to be plowed back into the business: while what was left over, if anything, had to be expended in litigation. As John Stevens put it, as early as 1808:

Another projector has placed a wheel or paddles between two long boats— and on the platform between them he has a horse walk—He tried the machinery some days ago and with eight men. It is stated in the papers that the passage between Powles [Paulus] hook and New York was performed in 15 minutes a distance of 1¼ miles, or at the rate of five miles per hour. Thus you see *you have roused a spirit of interprise* and you are likely to have a host of competitors to contend with besides your Hum. Sevt.[48]

It is no wonder that Fulton complained in 1812 that "I am as poor as Jobe[,] pressed by my Bills in the Bank and children looking for bread."[49] In 1811, Livingston had already admitted that the public complained that "we will neither exert ourselves nor let others do it, without ourselves or our connections having all the boats."[50] The monopoly not only aroused the spirit of enterprise, which involved the partners in a tangle of lawsuits, but also the spirit of resentment. The New York act of April 19, 1811, for example, which provided that Livingston and Fulton could take over any rival boat just as if it had been stolen from them, excited, although it was primarily aimed at the New Jersey Legislature, a great deal of ill feeling among the citizens of New York.[51]

The partners could hardly have abandoned their public monopoly or divested themselves, in private, of their disguise of public benefactors: considering their natures, either course would have been unnatural. Their only remedy was to go to law and to do so in a spirit of righteous indignation. But this presented its difficulties. The various acts of the State Legislature permitted them to exact a fine for every infringement of their grant and also to seize the offending boat. But how did one extract these damages? An action for debt might extract the fine; an action for trover might be maintained for the boat: but it promised to be, in either case, a complicated business.[52] The best course, or the most obvious one, was to proceed by way of injunction; and this they were soon obliged to do in a most spectacular way, in Livingston's former Court of Chancery, and before a liberal chancellor, John Lansing.

For, eventually, and the event came very soon, a deadly and intransigent competition appeared upon the Hudson. The offenders were twenty-one enterprising gentlemen of Albany, who built a steamboat called the *Hope* during the winter of 1810-1811, which (after a successful trial run from Albany to New York) began taking passengers on May 1, 1811; and which was to have a sister ship, rather aptly to be named the *Perseverance*. Suit had already been brought in the United States Circuit Court in New York, praying that Livingston and Fulton should be "quieted in the possession"—that is, in their exclusive right to navigate the Hudson by steam; but Associate Supreme Court Justice Brockholst Livingston, in April, dismissed the bill for want of jurisdiction. The partners then sued their Albany competitors in the New York Court of Chancery, praying that they should be enjoined from operating their boat, because of the acts of 1808 and 1811. Much to their consternation, on November 18, 1811, the injunction was denied by Chancellor Lansing.[53]

Lansing denied the injunction, not because the two monopoly acts violated the commerce clause of the Constitution, but because they were opposed to the *jus publicum*. Had not Justinian laid down in his *Institutes* that the air, running water, the sea, and so on, are given to mankind in common by the law of Nature? Bridges and ferries were a mere modification of the *jus publicum:* but an exclusive right of navigation, granted to particular persons or vessels of a particular construction, was contrary to it. Moreover, the complainants' claim was not founded on an original invention. And in any event, since the common law had been the law of all the states at the time the Constitution was adopted, it became a serious matter whether or not a state could detract from privileges and immunities incapable of annihilation or restraint, common to all at the time of adoption, and regulated by principles which shielded them from every species of private appropriation. If the monopoly acts were valid, could not the state grant an exclusive right also in vessels impelled by wind or oars? And if it could, where was the line to be drawn? For surely such exclusive grants would be an abridgment of common rights? The former Chancellor's answer to this was that every new law was in some measure an abridgment of common rights; and that Chancellor Lansing's decision had failed to explain how the state could legally build a bridge, or grant a ferry, or incorporate a turnpike company. The reigning Chancellor had already answered this by maintaining that there was a difference between a *modification* and a denial of natural rights: his opinion was essentially a liberal attack on monopolies as such. The monopoly had only one recourse, which it immediately took, and that was to lodge an appeal with the state's Court for the Trial of Impeachments and the Correction of Errors.[54]

In the meantime, the climate of opinion—in Albany at least—was distinctly ugly. "We have all Albany against us," wrote Andrew Bartholomew, master of *The North River Steamboat* in August, 1811. It was, he thought, better to persuade the citizens of the justice of the monopoly by newspaper articles than to attempt to keep them away from the *Hope* by force. "The people of this country cannot be *drove* into any measures whatever," he remarked sagely, "but if you start right they will be led by the Nose to almost anything." At the moment, the *North River*, although far more comfortable in her appointments, was distinctly bug ridden; and the people were being led by the nose into the *Hope*, where the berths were "better fit for a coffin than to sleep in." In short, the *Hope* was full, while the *North River* had no more than twenty passengers, less than one-third of her capacity.[55] If the *Perseverance* came on the scene, the monopoly would be doomed, unless the Court of Errors stepped in to save it.

Fortunately for Livingston and Fulton, Justices Joseph C. Yates and Smith Thompson were extreme states rights men, while Chief Justice James Kent was "defending a law which, in a sense, was his own child"—he had been a justice of the State Supreme Court, and therefore a member of the Council of Revision that had passed upon and approved the original act of 1798 before it became law. The Court of Errors was composed of the justices of the State Supreme Court and the State senators, but the opinions of the justices, even in such an absurdly constituted court, would still be paramount. On March 12, 1812, the Court of Errors reversed the decree of Chancellor Lansing, and the injunction against the *Hope* was made permanent. Thus the monopoly was saved.[56]

Chief Justice Kent's opinion "was the source of all arguments thereafter used in defense of the steamboat monopoly." He maintained that the people of New York had not alienated to the national government the power to grant exclusive privileges; that the legislative power in a single independent government extended to every proper object of power, and was limited only by its own constitutional provisions, by the fundamental principles of all government, and by the unalienable rights of mankind. The steamboat monopoly violated none of these restrictions, since every man could freely use the waters of New York in the same manner that he had done before the monopoly came into being. "It interfered with no man's property . . . [there was] no violation of first principles."

Nor did the New York steamboat acts violate the national Constitution. When national and state laws are aimed at each other, the state laws must yield. This was not the case here, since all commerce within the state is exclusively within the power of that state, except that a state may not make treaties or lay tonnage import or export duties. Indeed, said Kent, the only safe rule to follow was this: "If any given power was originally vested in this State, if it has not been exclusively ceded to Congress, or if the exercise of it has not been prohibited to the States, we may then go on in the exercise of the power until it comes practically in collision with the actual exercise of some congressional power." This had been Livingston's position from the beginning.[57]

Livingston had spent that winter at Albany, where his lawyers were so busy with other matters that "I was compelled," he told James Mease, "to rub up the law which for the past twelve years I have been forgetting & to be the counsel to my counsellors." Nor were his lawyers the only source of worry. "If you can conveniently spare the money," he wrote his brother Edward in March, "I should be glad of it as our boats brought little last year owing to the opposition, & our expenses in law suits & new boats have been great."[58] And the valiant "Albanians," although defeated in the Court of Errors, did not by any means cease from troubling. In June, 1812, they presented a petition to the Legislature, requesting that they should be allowed to continue running their boats, and that the proceeds should be put into the hands of a receiver appointed by Chancellor Lansing, there to abide the event of a lawsuit they intended to bring before the United States courts. If the Legislature had accepted this scheme, the litigation might have been endless; and in the Legislature, said Edward P. Livingston, the "Jacobinical spirit" had been so aroused against the monopoly that there was every chance that the committee appointed to consider the petition would report in its favor.[59] There was nothing for it but for Livingston to come up from Clermont to use his influence. In this he was successful; and Fulton, in New York, was able to congratulate him on the news that "by your exertions and the good sense of the committee the Pickaroons have been defeated in their infamous Project." Such "violations of mental property," he declared, ought to be made an example of.[60]

Livingston's letters do not breathe this kind of triumph: all he seems to have felt was relief. The "Albanians" were not to be prosecuted to the full extent of the law—"popularity," said Fulton, "and to occupy all points by which to create support is now a principal object with us"—but were to be offered a compromise.[61] A purchaser had been found for the *Hope;* the purchase money was to be used to defray the legal expenses of both sides; the *Hope* was to run on the James River in Virginia; and the "Albanians" were to be offered a whole or a part of the state and patent rights on Lake Champlain. They could build a good boat there and move the machinery from the *Perseverance* into her; and the rights on the lake would be assured them for twenty-six years.[62] What their answer to this offer was is not known.

It is clear from all this and from the tone of his surviving letters that the monopoly was little more than the source of much weariness of the spirit to Livingston. Financially, it was as yet fruitless: although the three Hudson River boats grossed $110,511 in 1812, with a net profit of $32,271, Livingston in December had bills due or becoming due in the Manhattan Bank to the extent of at least $15,000.[63] But that was not all or nearly all. For it had never offered him those nonmaterial rewards which, at heart, he craved more than anything else. To Fulton, the steamboat was a child which he was prepared to defend with everything he had; but his imagination was preoccupied with steam warships and with torpedoes; and he was —whether hailed as a great engineer or derided as a great monopolist—

already a famous man. He had all the self-absorption of genius, but little of its sensitivity; "our prospects are brilliant," he wrote; overworked, in poor health, comparatively penniless, he was still on his way upward.[64] But Livingston had never been able to separate fame from status: and the fulfillment of his steamboat visions had brought none of the elevation which he believed to be his due. He had not emerged, in the public eye, as a public benefactor. On the contrary, he had received little praise and much recrimination; he had been identified with those grasping parvenus, those new moneyed men, for whom, as a landowner and an aristocrat, he had an instinctive contempt. He had fought his battles with all a projector's tenacity; but the projects themselves, now visible and triumphant upon the Hudson and the Mississippi, he knew to be technically the work of Fulton. The privilege had been great, but not the reward; and from 1808 onward, he had been turning in spirit more and more toward the shades, the charms, the duties, and the projects of Clermont itself, as a wayfarer turns toward home.

CHAPTER THREE

Clermont was celebrated by Horatio Gates Spafford in his 1813 *Gazetteer of New-York*, from notes taken when Mr. Spafford visited it in the autumn of 1810. The older mansion was then occupied by the Chancellor's elder daughter, Elizabeth, and her husband, Edward P. Livingston. The newer one, in which the Chancellor resided until his death, was devised in his will upon his younger daughter, Mrs. Robert L. Livingston.[1]

In Mr. Spafford's opinion, the newer Clermont was one of the largest and most commodious houses in the whole state. Its river front measured one hundred and four feet, it was ninety-one feet in depth, and to its main body of two stories and four pavilions, "surmounted with a balustrade of remarkable beauty," there had been added on the south front a greenhouse "with bathing-rooms and offices adjoining; over these is a large elegant breakfast room, and 4 bedrooms." This front overlooked the former Chancellor's pleasure grounds, which yielded in turn to a fine grassy vale, very carefully tended, edged by flowering shrubberies, and backed on the south side by an extensive and various orchard. The north front faced a lawn, bounded on the north by a stone building with a steeple and the gardens of Edward P. Livingston, and skirted on the east by "a beautiful wood on a bank raised about 10 feet, terminating in a second lawn, from the rear of which springs, precipitately, a rocky ridge covered with shrubs, trees and evergreens, affording a fine rich background. This is balanced on the opposite [west] side of the lawn by a beautiful avenue of locust trees, planted irregularly, through which winds the road to the House." Between the branches of these locusts, one could see the Hudson, "crowded with shipping"; and as one gazed westward from the front steps of the house, the great river was partially visible through the clumps of trees on its bank, where the Chancellor had made a shady walk. Beyond, on the far side of the river, there rose up from the farms, fields, and woods at their feet the thunderous Catskills—"a mass of interesting, picturesque and sublime objects," observes Mr. Spafford, "no where exceeded in this country." To the rear of the mansion, beyond the wooded ridge, lay the

Chancellor's park, once famous for its elk, but now dedicated to the care and breeding of merino sheep. The interior of the house had been much embellished with French tapestries and furniture since his return from Paris; and one of its four pavilions housed his library of four thousand books.[2]

II

Clermont had become a monument to the survival of the old New York aristocracy, and to such changes in taste as accompany the earliest emergence of a leisure class. The new house was rather grander than the colonial Livingstons could have desired or afforded: but it retained, no doubt, at least some of the simplicities upon which Strickland had remarked in 1794. The Chancellor still rose at five every morning, read or walked until breakfast, supervised his farm, spent long hours with his gun and dog or his fishing rod, examined into the details of the economy of his wide estates. In 1806, his bailiff, Dr. William Wilson, complained that he was asking too much of his rents. Had he not requested, when he left for Paris, that Wilson should not be too hard upon the poorer tenants?[3] But Paris had cost Livingston a good deal of money over and above his salary and outfit; the steamboat threatened to devour every spare dollar in cash and credit; and he was not, at his first return, in a mood to be a kindly landlord. However, he was anything but close-fisted by nature; he and Wilson soon came to an understanding; and one may suppose that by 1808, when Clermont was becoming a retreat from the problems of the steamboat, he was ready to be as generous as the way of a New York landlord permitted him to be. At any rate, when rent wars troubled his kinsman Henry Livingston at Ancram, and slew a neighboring landlord in the Hardenburgh Patent, he was never disturbed by them.[4]

William Wilson was a Scottish doctor, who arrived in America in 1784, settled near Clermont on the Chancellor's advice, and, besides physicking the neighborhood, became in the course of the years a county judge and the founder of the Columbia County Agricultural Society. He also found time, not only to supervise Henry Livingston's tumultuous affairs, but to manage the Chancellor's Clermont, Dutchess County, and Hardenburgh Patent estates as well. One gets the impression from his letters of an honest, vigorous, well-educated man, devoted to his patrons but with a mind of his own, and possessed, above all, of a genuine curiosity about his fellow men. It was curiosity mixed with kindness, but without admiration: the Chancellor's Hardenburgh Patent tenants, struggling heroically in the wilderness, were only "beggers" to him. As a bailiff, he delighted in his weird summer circuit of these various lands: from Esopus to the Neversink River, and then through "Westfield" to the Delaware, up the Delaware to its west branch, along the west branch as far as Delhi, across the mountains to Schohary Kill, and so down to Catskill. He described it as "a ride of 200 miles, thro' mountains, rivers rocks roots & beggars." The land was often, in its way, horrendous. "Westfield," near the present Roscoe and Rockland in Sullivan County, was almost inaccessible, "at present the most abominable place on the face of God's creation"; but the country as a whole—this was in 1802—was settling more rapidly than could have been expected. "We meet with Dutch men & Irish men—Frenchmen & Scotch—and when there they cannot well get away."[5] Here he was wrong; some did get away: but enough remained to cultivate the land and even to pay their rents irregularly: as long as they showed a disposition to pay, they were never expected to be regular. It was, indeed, dangerous to be too hard on them. When Gerard Hardenburgh, in 1808, ejected several families from his lands in the Neversink Valley, the "stubborn and intemperate old man" was murdered; and his heirs discreetly and quickly came to a compromise with the killers.[6]

It is not recorded that Livingston ever visited these inherited lands of his across the Hudson, beyond an occasional winter jaunt over the frozen river to his grandfather's pet project at Woodstock, a settlement of some nine hundred and fifty souls (in 1813), where there were two churches, two glass factories, and some vague hopes of coal.[7] These patrimonial lands were funds which would rise in price the sooner they were opened and settled: settlement, therefore, rather than the punctual discharge of rents, was what interested him. In 1803, one finds him telling Henry Willard that, of his "several tracts of land" between the Hudson and the Delaware, the greater part is fully or partly settled; but that he is willing to sell his two remaining unsettled tracts to a settlement project for $2.50 an acre or $30,000 apiece, one-fifth down and the rest upon legal interest until it is convenient to pay. He had clearly overpriced his wild land, since no more was heard from Mr. Willard: but the offer shows that he was willing to *sell* only where a sale would guarantee the settlement of a large tract, which would in turn raise the value of all his other lands. As for the conditions of leasehold, "I have a variety of tracts," he told Mr. Willard, "which are partly settled but where there are still many vacant farms." These he was willing to rent to tenants who could pay $15 for every hundred acres upon taking possession, then no rent for five years, then ten bushels of wheat for two years, then twenty-five bushels per hundred acres "for ever."

If the tenant disposes of his lease, he must first get the landlord's permission, and then pay one-eighth—the hated "quarter-sale"—of the purchase price.[8]

In a conversation with Joseph Bonaparte, concerning Jerome Bonaparte, who had married the spectacular Elizabeth Patterson and was fearful about returning to France, he said that for a gentleman of Jerome's rank to live "*honnêtement*" in America, it would be necessary for him to have a town house and a country house, "which I estimated at $55,000," and a regular income of not less than $15,000.[9] Was this, as it were, a *self-portrait*? It is impossible to estimate Livingston's income at any period, since his surviving account books offer only fragmentary evidence: but, considering Dr. Wilson's description of the Hardenburgh Patent when he rode through it in 1802, one can well believe the Minister when he told Joseph Bonaparte that American landed gentlemen did not expect more than a 3-per-cent revenue from their estates. They received, he said, a much greater interest from the rise in the value of land. In 1806, Dr. Wilson estimated the Clermont rents—that is, the rent from the actual Clermont estate, with its eighty leased and fairly prosperous farms—at $5,000 a year, and the Chancellor put them at $3,000: the wide difference in estimate was due to the fact that they were disputing over the amount Wilson should receive as his 5 per cent for collecting these particular rents.[10] Obviously, since most of these rents were paid in kind, much depended on the wheat market: but one cannot suppose that even a great landowner, although he commanded a large credit, was ever too well off for cash. The steamboat venture strained Livingston to the limit, forced him to sell lands, obliged him to fight tooth and nail for his monopoly: nor did the steamboat begin to pay until the monopoly was established by the Court of Errors and Appeals in 1812, less than one year before Livingston's death. It was little but a source of worry, grief, and disappointment to him, though not to his legatees.

III

Indeed, the old landed aristocracy of New York, although it lived in state and dispensed a profuse and apparently boundless hospitality, was surrounded by change in visible and uncontrollable forms. The opening up of western New York was one of these forms. It reduced the value of the older lands, except the fertile flats, and its political influence was most distressing to a conservative mind. The New York Society for the Improvement of Agriculture, Arts and Manufactures, which was reincorporated in 1804 as the New York Society for Useful Arts, while it retained its character as a status society, a gathering of gentlemen, was always directed toward combating the influence of the newer lands. And it did so by attacking change in another of its forms: in the tendency of the older eastern lands, especially where they were subjected to leasehold, to become sterile through constant cropping. Livingston disputed with Judge Richard Peters, of Pennsylvania, the Revolutionary patriot, the claim to be the first to introduce gypsum as a fertilizer: and as early as 1793, he was urging the members of the Society to sow grass seed, particularly clover, and to "put wheat on a clover clay, instead of an expensive fallow."[11] Within twenty years, the marvelous effect of clover on worn-out fields had convinced everyone who was at all interested in conservation: but had it convinced the small farmer?

The small farmer, whether he was a tenant farmer or whether he owned his own land, was expected to be too many people all at once. In 1796, for example, in return for a cash income estimated at $30 to $36 a year, he was farmer, carpenter, mason, lumberman, toolmaker, and handy man; while his rude home was dominated by that symbol of relentless family toil, the spinning wheel. Under these circumstances, and especially where the Jeffersonian incentive of ownership was lacking, could one expect him to respond eagerly to the exhortations of some gentlemanly society, or some aristocratic landlord? The striking increase in the use of gypsum shows that he was not totally deaf to them: but it was altogether beyond his capacity—that is to say, beyond his desire—to consider such relative abstractions as a more scientific method of crop rotation. As for politics, the tenant farmer was apt to be guided by an inherited or innate aversion to the opinions of his landlord.

IV

Livingston himself had foreseen, or at least anticipated, the possible danger to the old landlords in the constant depletion of their soils—a depletion that might have been attributed, quite apart from the damaging presence of leasehold, to the fact that eastern New York was not really suited to an extensive production of grain. He had long been interested in the breeding of sheep; when he was minister to France he had turned his attention to the possibility of exporting merinos to the United States; and the merino became, in the course of time and from a personal point of view, the most successful and the most consoling of all his projects.

A "project" it was, in the special sense that it appealed to his imagination, that it was distinctly novel, and that he expected it to contribute to his wealth, his status, and his fame.

From some experiments I have made [he wrote in 1806 to his former secretary, M. Mouchette], I have convinced myself & am trying to convince others that we can make fine cloths [from merino wool] at half the price at which they are furnished by England. . . . I have a thousand other projects in which you would take an important part were you here but which I relinquish because I have no one here with whom to converse about them. La Bigarre [Delabigarre] is again in New Orleans. . . . I can say of him as Prince Hen^y did of Falstaff, "I could have better spared a better man."[12]

For Delabigarre had followed Edward Livingston into his self-imposed exile: and his enthusiastic mind, the mind of some fevered participant in a high-flown contemporary Eclogue, was no longer at the Chancellor's service.

From the steamboat to the merino might seem, in scope no less than in promise, an earthy transition: but Livingston took a serious delight in husbandry. To live in the country was a necessity to him, to improve it an obsession. Before he left for Paris, he seems to have rented his house in New York, and never to have returned to it again. His traditional way of life, from which there was no escape, had already condemned him to extract an income from the system of leasehold, and therefore to close his eyes to the system's disadvantages: but were there not other ways in which valuable improvements could be achieved? The allurements of fame are many and strange. Had he not once written that the American who could introduce clover into general use "will perhaps be better entitled to a Statue than any other man in America—that one only excepted whose civil & military virtues have afforded us the means of pursuing in peace our agricultural pursuits—You will judge from my exertions that I am not unambitious of that honor?"[13] Hyperbole this may have been, but it was heartfelt: he had never been more sincere.

As for the merino, "Good sheep are getting in great demand among us," John R. Livingston wrote to Paris in 1802, "and as the breed may be much improved, would it not be advisable to endeavor to find out a Ram or two? Perhaps you might secure the Spanish [merino] breed by a little management. Your park is so admirably calculated to keep them that I think that you ought not to neglect it, particularly as it is of consequence to your Country." This latter consideration would certainly have been enough to excite Livingston's imagination; but, as it happened, he seems to have anticipated his brother. Early in the year, before he had received John R. Livingston's letter, he had inspected the "royal" flock at Rambouillet, which had originated in a gift from a king of Spain to a king of France; had chosen two rams and two ewes; and had persuaded the French Government to allow him to export them to America. This was, in itself, no mean feat: the French Government made as many difficulties about exporting the sheep of Rambouillet as the British Government did about exporting the steam engines of Watt.[14]

The merino sheep, even the merinos of Rambouillet, did not reveal their virtues to the uninstructed or the unimaginative eye. Originally bred by the Moors during their occupation of Spain, they were small and ill-shaped, and their wool appeared to be very short. Actually, it was so closely curled that its real length could be appreciated only by stretching it out. It was much greasier than that of other sheep, and when on the sheep seemed yellowish or even appeared to be of a dirty brown color: but when it was cleaned, it was extremely white, and so much finer and softer in texture than the common wool as to bear no comparison with it. The merino's appearance, therefore, bore no relation to its value.

Livingston's merinos arrived in America toward the end of July, 1802.[15] In the same year, Colonel David Humphreys, recalled by Jefferson as minister to Spain, had brought his seventy-five merino ewes and twenty-one merino rams across Spain and Portugal, loaded them on to his sloop *Perseverance*, and carried them over the Atlantic and up the Housatonic to Derby, Connecticut. Colonel Humphreys was not indisposed to regard this feat as a patriotic one: and, in one of his many marmoreal letters, offered himself to the praise of his countrymen for having accomplished it.[16] Livingston was of the same mind. His original idea, he said in 1809, had been to render himself "yet more extensively useful, by suggesting and enforcing such improvements in agriculture as might add to the wealth of individuals, and, by forming the basis of manufactures, to the independence of our country."[17] One need not, indeed, one should not, be unduly disturbed by such language; it was written at a time when the consequences and benefits of any innovation were quite incalculable; and when a "philosopher" not unnaturally saw himself as a benefactor to his country. It is perhaps needless to add that among the individuals who would become wealthier by the importation of merinos, Livingston numbered himself: and he was much disturbed, when he returned from France in 1805, to find that not one of Colonel Humphreys' sheep had been purchased in New York, and that the existence of his own merinos had gone quite unnoticed. He also discovered, to his horror, that a flock of one hundred half-bred and three-quarter-bred merinos, raised from a ram sent out by M. Delessert to his farm near Kingston, had actually been sold off at a price lower than that of common sheep. "I knew the importance of the object," he wrote, "and I resolved to leave no means unessayed to convince my fellow-citizens of it." The first step, therefore, was to buy up the scattered remnants of Delessert's flock, wherever they could be found, and at prices which astonished the owners.[18]

The next step was to procure, if possible, further exports. There exists, among his papers, the copy of an order from Jean-Baptiste Champagny, Napoleon's Minister of the Interior, authorizing the export of five rams, through the agency of M. Jacques Le Ray de Chaumont. Only one of these—it came either from Rambouillet or from the Empress's flock at Malmaison—actually arrived, in July, 1807; M. de Chaumont had, with more prudence than was quite seemly, left the others behind to enrich his own flock.[19] Livingston had already written to the Delesserts in France, saying that his original four merinos had now increased to seven full-breds and forty of mixed blood, and that he would set no limit to the price he would pay for superior rams and ewes, if only permission could be obtained to export them.[20] Nothing came of this: indeed, except for six merinos from the Prince of Hesse-Cassel's flock, which arrived in Philadelphia in 1807, and for General Armstrong's importation of nineteen rams and ewes on his return from France in 1809, there were no significant importations until 1810. The American breeders had to proceed on their own, and to hope that some "vital impulse"—as Colonel Humphreys put it—would somehow or other be given to the demand for finer wool.[21] This vital impulse was contributed by something which, elsewhere in the agrarian world, was considered a very devitalizing event; and that event was the embargo of 1807, the splendid but austere climax of Jefferson's and Madison's peaceful foreign policy.

V

As has been indicated, Livingston was far from popular with the administration on his return from France. He himself was not much given to nursing grudges—the break with Jay is the great exception—and he soon forgave the administration for displaying (so he thought, and not without reason) a certain favoritism toward Monroe in the matter of the Louisiana Purchase. Indeed, the purchase itself soon vanished into the farther recesses of his memory; his fertile and sanguine mind was too preoccupied with present ventures to worry vainly about the past; except for an occasional dig at Monroe, there is no trace of Louisiana in his surviving papers after his return; and only in a singular request to be sent abroad on some vague mission to Napoleon or to the King of Holland does he show, on the one hand, that he continued to pride himself upon his diplomatic gifts and, on the other, that he believed that he retained the confidence of the administration.[22] The belief was even more singular than the request; but then, Livingston was never the man to underestimate himself. Although President Jefferson was no longer popular with the Clermont Livingstons, because he had, in his official capacity, dispossessed Edward Livingston of some valuable lands in the neighborhood of New Orleans, the Chancellor always maintained a friendly correspondence with him. And he still continued, when occasion offered, to tender his advice to James Madison. The replies were invariably courteous, invariably noncommittal.

Events in Europe were now moving rapidly toward the total immersion of the United States in the Napoleonic Wars. British orders in council and French decrees threatened either to denationalize American neutral commerce or to drive it from the ocean. In December, 1807, therefore, the administration made the supreme gesture in its policy of peaceful coercion; it steered the great Embargo Act through Congress. The embargo was essentially a self-blockade. No American ship could leave for foreign ports; "U.S. ships in the coastal trade were required to post bond double the value of the craft and cargo as a guarantee that the goods would be relanded at a U.S. port"; and while foreign vessels were not prohibited from entering American ports, they were virtually outlawed by the provision that they could carry no goods out of them.[23]

The New York agriculturalist, no less than the New York merchant, was sadly crippled by this ascetic legislation. The farmer in the eastern part of that state was not even able to take his revenge upon it by illegally smuggling produce into Canada. The price of farm goods, and with it the value of land, plunged downward. But the former Chancellor was not in the least dismayed. As early as July 15, 1807, he had written to Madison to suggest the advisability of an embargo. It would, he thought, strengthen the hands of our envoys abroad, because they could more easily show the evils that America could bring upon Great Britain. Were not Canada and Nova Scotia virtually within our grasp? Could not Spain wrest from the British the conquests they so highly valued in South America? A measure like an embargo, because it would bespeak the energy of the American Government, would certainly deter the British Government from making war. Such were his arguments.[24]

They were not entirely altruistic. In February, 1806, before the passage of the Nicholson Non-Importation Act, which prohibited the importation of certain essential goods from England as a retaliation for British infringement of American rights on the high seas, he had written to Albert Gallatin, advocating the mild expedient of an additional 6-per-cent duty on British "cottons, woolens, silks, paper, linnens, glass—and all such other articles as we may manufacture for ourselves or buy in other markets."[25] A state of war in Europe, combined with a relatively free neutral commerce for America, suited the landowner: it could only raise the price of produce, and therefore enhance the value of his lands and rents. In 1806, Livingston professed to believe that really stern measures against England would be inadvisable, because England would be convinced that America was simply bluffing.

Between February, 1806, when he wrote suggesting a mild corrective, and July, 1807, when he was asking for the rigors of an embargo, he had reached the conclusion that only stern measures would, after all, convince the British that America was serious. This reversal in his thinking certainly could not have been occasioned by British orders in council; for rumors of really sweeping orders did not reach America until the middle of December, and it was the confirmation of these rumors that urged the administration into an embargo.[26]

Somehow, therefore, Livingston had reached the conclusion that an embargo—the bane of the farmer—would be an advisable measure; and he had reached this conclusion on his own. The reason for this was visible and pastoral: it could be found in the merino sheep, peacefully feeding in his park. An embargo would not only teach Great Britain that America was serious about the preservation of her neutral rights; it would also force America into manufacturing on her own, and there would be at last an incentive for the manufacture of those fine woolen goods which were normally imported from Great Britain. The embargo would have the double advantage of being both patriotic and profitable.

As long as the embargo remained in all its terrible majesty, and it remained for two years, Livingston gave it his unqualified support. It was, he told James Madison, a "wise and prudent measure."[27] "At all events," he said in a letter to his son-in-law in France, "we shall lay the foundation for manufactures which will render us less dependent upon commerce than we have been."[28] He described it, to Tench Coxe, as "the temporary restraints that we are compelled to put upon our commerce."

Nor [he continued optimistically], will the privations be half so great as the fears or the interests of many represent them to be. Flax, hemp, leather, wool will increase in value. [Illegible word] & barley will retain their original price. Wheat beef & pork may fall but they will still find a market on such terms as ought to satisfy the farmer when he considers that he is laying the foundation for an increased & regular demand & adding to the number of staple commodities—as well as opening new fields for the industry of his children. He may not be able to give them all farms, but he can make any number of them manufacturers.[29]

By the end of 1808, his full-bred and mixed merinos numbered one hundred and forty-five, and the profit on them, after deducting their keep, came to $2,366.[30] Early in 1809, James Madison wrote to congratulate him on his "patriotic zeal" as a breeder of merinos; and he was able to tell Simeon De Witt that all his lambs had been "spoken for this year" and some already for 1810, and that a fifteen-sixteenths lamb would fetch $125 and a seven-eighths lamb $50. "I am convinced," he wrote Dr. Samuel Bard, in February, 1809, "that our country is ripe for the manufacture of woolens & rather for fine woolens because the relative value of the labour is greater upon coarse." If only the farmer would do his duty and furnish the fleece and fine wool, the poor man would eat his bread in comfort and "if he chooses clothe him in purple & fine linnen." In July, he was told by James Mease that in the opinion of the Cattle Society of Philadelphia, "none of us had ever seen such beautiful samples" as the specimens of wool from the Clermont full-blooded merinos. The staple was double the length of Colonel Humphreys' ram and "had a silkiness and wavy appearance the other was entirely deficient in." Did not this refute the common opinion of Europe that European animals tended to degenerate when introduced into America? All in all, the embargo and its aftermath brought nothing but gratification to the sheep breeder at Clermont.[31]

Although in an article he wrote reluctantly for the Edinburgh Encyclopaedia at some time in 1812, he made a plea for "protecting duties" for manufactures, this was the only occasion on which he did so.[32] Perhaps if he had lived until 1816, he would have supported James Madison in his tariff system, as he had supported Jefferson throughout the embargo. But, in general, he never strayed, during the embargo or after it, from the position that Jefferson had come to hold, and which he afterward set forth in a famous letter to Benjamin Austin. "Experience has taught me," wrote Jefferson, "that manufactures are now as necessary to our independence as to our comfort; and if those who quote me as of a different opinion, will keep pace with me in purchasing nothing foreign where an equivalent of domestic fabric can be obtained, without regard to difference of price, it will not be our fault if we do not have a supply at home equal to our demand."[33] "Without regard to difference of price" . . . a measure of self-sacrifice was required, since the price of domestic fabrics was bound for a while to be higher than that of imported ones. Livingston, also, expected the farmer during the embargo to sacrifice his immediate interests to the future of household manufactures: but that he ever looked forward to any other system than a primitive one of household manufactures seems extremely doubtful. His agrarian thinking had been altered to this extent: he no longer held to the position that had certainly been his when he was minister to France, namely that the ideal American economy consisted in an exchange of raw materials for manufactured goods. He now perceived, with Jefferson, that manufactures were essential to the independence of America: whether the facts of history or the future of merino had brought him to this conclusion is scarcely a difficult question to answer. The merino had become a sacred object.

VI

The climactic moment in every year at Clermont had now become the Chancellor's sheepshearing. Elkanah Watson has left a brief record of this event.

> In 1810 [he writes], I attended his famous sheep-shearing, which attracted much attention, and acquired subsequently great newspaper notoriety. . . . The large company was entertained with the most elegant and sumptuous hospitality. At a public sale on this occasion, sheep were bought with great avidity, at prices varying from fifty to one thousand dollars. . . . There was an animated competition, and there were some earnest disputes for securing the purchase of select animals. . . . Dr. Mitchill produced a brilliant description of the festival, and, always classical and erudite, gave as a toast, "The modern Argonautic expedition, whereby our Jason has enriched his country with the invaluable treasure of the golden fleece."

As it happened, there was another Jason present on that memorable occasion; and "Chancellor Livingston and Colonel Humphreys disputed the merit of having first introduced the Merino sheep into the United States."[34]

Useful, benevolent, prosperous, dispensing hospitality and advice, a rural magnate, who had placed his learning and his ability entirely at the service of agriculture—here at last, fully released, stands the aristocratic self-image which had always beckoned Livingston away from the ambitions and the battles of the political world. One can imagine him, genial, carefree, with the rather loud voice of the very deaf man, disputing happily with Colonel Humphreys before a well-dined audience of his friends and neighbors; and disputing about a project that had proved to be eminently successful from every point of view—as a source of personal affluence no less than of public service—and that was quite beyond and above criticism.

For the merino sheep, although its popularity disappeared as suddenly as it had arisen within a few years of Livingston's death, did in fact, says Arthur H. Cole, impart "an appreciable improvement in quality" to the country's flocks. Livingston would have expected more than this—his expectations were never small—but this would not have dissatisfied him.[35]

VII

Livingston's contributions to the *Transactions* of the two New York agricultural societies are well-reasoned, thorough, and anything but amateur. But the wide and various learning, for which he was known in his day, does not appear in them any more than it does in the mass of his surviving letters. It is only in his *Essay on Sheep*, as in an occasional letter to Jefferson, that he allows a free rein to his speculative gifts. Much of the essay, which was written in 1806, and rewritten and enlarged in 1809, is highly technical: but in its early pages, he gives a curious account of what he believes to have been the beginnings of society.

By 1809, the steamboat having conspicuously failed to gratify the demands of his self-image, the sheep had come to occupy a central place in his imagination: it was quite in keeping with his habitual enthusiasm that he should now see this somewhat uninspiring animal as the founder of civilization. He asks himself how the sheep, so helpless and defenseless, could have survived the attacks of its powerful carnivorous enemies before it was domesticated by man. He believes that it must originally have been a quadruped possessed of great strength; and, like Buffon and other naturalists, has come to the conclusion that the domestic sheep must have been descended from the Muflon Musman found in parts of Europe, in Siberia, and in Kamchatka. Travelers have described this sheep: how the young are easy to catch and to tame, whereas the mature wild sheep is a match for its natural enemies. If, he argues, the sheep was one of the first creatures to be domesticated, if the domestication of the bull, the horse, and the camel are subsequent events, then it is to the sheep that we are indebted for the conversion of men from wild and wandering savages to mild and gentle shepherds.

This is how it all began.

The female savage [Livingston writes] that followed her husband to the chase snatched it [the young mouflon] from its bleeding dam, pressed it to her bosom, and became its mother; it sported with her children, and taught them to love a race which they had hitherto pursued only to destroy. A slight ray of reason must have shown the savage how much less precarious his subsistence would be, if he could only draw it from an animal that fed at the door of his hut, than if he was compelled to seek it in the chase. He would extend his flock; he would cease to trespass on the hunting grounds of others.

In this way, he thinks, larger tribes were formed for mutual benefit and common defense; the rights of property made themselves known; nations came into being where only wandering tribes had existed; and all this because of the domestication of sheep. "The cradle of music and poetry was rocked by the shepherd of Arcadia." By what simple means does Providence produce the greatest good!

He follows this enthusiastic hypothesis with a detailed account of sheep in various parts of the world, from Africa to Iceland, and with a discussion of the possible effects of climate and transportation, soil and fodder upon their size and the quality of their wool. His method is as scholarly, scientific, and comprehensive as it could be with the information he possessed; and it is clear that he had made extraordinary efforts, at home and abroad, to increase his knowledge of his subject. The merinos of Spain receive, of course, the chief part of his consideration: he describes in detail how they are raised; how they differ from region to region; their seasonal migrations, involving about twenty-five thousand shepherds and five million sheep; how their wool, incidentally, had provided the Spanish kings with an immense income. He traces their history in Spain up from the days of the Romans, the Goths, and the Moors; and then, for the rest of the book, plunges into a mass of technical data, of tabulated statistics, of detailed examinations into every phase of the care and breeding of sheep. It is a remarkable performance, still held to be useful, and it offers, in the flights of its speculation no less than in its marshaling of fact, an admirable example of the thinking of the American Enlightenment.[36]

The New York Legislature, in 1809, readily agreed to print a thousand copies of the *Essay on Sheep*. The author's name was presented as follows: "By Robert R. Livingston, LL.D., President of the Society for the Promotion of Useful Arts, Member of the American Philosophical Society, President of the American Society of Fine Arts,[37] Corresponding Member of the Agricultural Society of the Seine, Honorary Member of the Agricultural Society of Dutchess County." No mention of former chancellor or former minister: here, in this list of titles, was the mirror that now returned the image he most wished to see. And the image emerged in another and surprising shape. In 1810, in the *Port Folio* magazine, there appeared a review of the *Essay*, which, on the basis of a few paragraphs, deliberately misinterpreted, managed to dismiss it as nothing more than a pretentious literary effort. "This puffing, strutting little book," said the

Port Folio.[38] Livingston, as usual, leaped to his own defense in an immense letter, which, as was also not uncommon with him, he then decided not to send. If the critic of "Mr. Livingston's book" had had his way, the draft ended, Virgil would never have adorned the *Georgics* with beautiful figures, interesting episodes, "and those theological & philosophical digressions that make the delight of less discerning readers than our critic. For alas! Virgil writes of rural affairs, not merely as a farmer, but as a poet, a theologian, a philosopher & as a courtier."[39] As once, long ago, in his correspondence with General Montgomery, so now, in his last years, he saw himself ideally as the inhabitant of a Virgilian world: a gentleman's world, the world of the library and the farm.

In due time, the *Essay* made its appearance at Monticello. An "excellent" book, said Thomas Jefferson, writing—it is the last letter of his to be found in the Livingston papers—as a "farmer . . . a brother agriculturalist." "I mark with a white bean," were his final words, "the days on which I hear from my old friends and shall always be happy to learn from yourself, particularly that you enjoy health, with all the comforts which can cheer the evening of our days."[40]

VIII

But in his refuge at Clermont, Livingston was not to be free from the perpetual demands of the steamboat, and the galling abuse which beset him as the proprietor of a grinding monopoly. In the end, the steamboat proved to be too much for him. During the winter of 1811-1812, he had been forced to put forth all his old legal energies in preparing his case for his successful appeal from Chancellor Lansing's decision; nor, as has been shown, did the gentlemen from Albany cease from troubling him until June of 1812. To a man of Livingston's sensibilities, the legal and political battles in Albany had been acutely distasteful, profoundly wearisome. His daughter reported that in July he had become so listless and broken that even the children ceased to interest that most indulgent of grandparents; and that he spent many hours alone with his Bible. He had gone to Lebanon, New Jersey, vainly searching for health. He returned to Clermont in the early fall; and at Clermont, in November, he suffered his first paralytic stroke. He made a partial recovery; and his sister Mrs. Freeborn Garretson was able to tell Edward Livingston that his brother, whose religion or lack of religion had caused her the greatest misgivings for the past twenty-five years, was a changed man. Mrs. Garretson had married a Methodist clergyman, and had built her own church near Clermont: for many years, she had been industriously saving souls, and her letters and conversations had been devoted to things not of this world. The Chancellor, on the other hand, like most men of science in his day, had drifted into an easy deism; and was disposed—as his letters from France and Italy often show—to regard all formal religion with a detached, tolerant, amused curiosity. Now the immediate members of his family were astonished and delighted to find the stricken man discoursing on Christianity, "in such a strain of Heavenly eloquence," wrote Mrs. Garretson, "that every Eye was streaming with tears, and every Heart raised in gratitude to Heaven. Betsy [Mrs. Edward P. Livingston, his elder daughter] clapped her hands and shouted out thank God, who has heard my prayers for my dear Father." The entrance of Dr. Bard, who prescribed quiet, put an end to this scene.[41]

The Chancellor lingered on all winter, and in February he suffered a second stroke. "I have always shared what I had with my friends," he murmured before he became speechless, to Dr. Wilson, "there is one thing that I wish I could share." "What is that, sir?" said Dr. Wilson. "The peace that I feel."[42]

What else could the observer of today deduce from this fragmentary evidence than that his innately conservative spirit had willingly, indeed instinctively, returned to the simple pietism of his father, the Judge? All his life, through its many political changes, its speculative adventures, even its diplomatic triumphs, he seems always to have remained an exemplar of his colonial past. Now the patriarchal, the aristocratic self-image was at last complete. He died on February 25, 1813. Three days later, his body was carried to the family vault. It was accompanied, wrote his sister, " 'tis said by near a Thousand persons"—a vast concourse for that part of the world.[43]

A BIBLIOGRAPHICAL NOTE

NOTES

GENEALOGICAL CHART

INDEX

A Bibliographical Note

The Robert R. Livingston Papers in the New-York Historical Society's manuscript collection constitute the foundation of this book. Although silent, or nearly so, on Livingston's childhood and early youth, the collection is remarkably rich for every other phase of his life, both in incoming and outgoing letters. Except during his ministry to France, Livingston did not keep letter books, but preserved his drafts; and these, where it has been possible to compare them with the originals, indicate that the drafts varied little if at all from the final versions. Such things as deleted sentences give the reader the advantage, sometimes not an inconsiderable one, of knowing his first thoughts. It was his custom to mark the drafts "not sent," or words to that effect, when this was the case; one may assume, therefore, that drafts not so marked represent letters that were actually dispatched. I have not attempted to change his somewhat irregular punctuation and spelling, except when absolutely necessary, and I have given the same treatment to all other letters, English and French, quoted directly from manuscript. Changes or additions are always indicated, as [.], and so forth.

Related papers are the Livingston Family Papers in the New York Public Library and the Miscellaneous Livingston Manuscripts in the New-York Historical Society; a microfilmed set of the great Livingston-Redmond Papers at the Franklin Delano Roosevelt Library, Hyde Park, N.Y., is also in the New-York Historical Society. The Duane Papers in the New-York Historical Society are rich for the family background, and in references to Livingston himself. The Wilson Family Papers in the William L. Clements Library, University of Michigan, chiefly concerned with the voluminous and varied business of that rural genius Dr. William Wilson, Livingston's bailiff and physician, are not so strong in references to Livingston himself as one might have hoped; but they are none the less indispensable; and for a general picture of the activities of Columbia County from the late 1780's onward, they are priceless. The Livingston-Bancroft Transcripts in the New York Public Library carry Livingston through the Revolution; where these were transcribed (as many of them were) from letters now in the Robert R. Livingston Papers, the reader notices that they are often selections from individual letters, concerned only with matters of general history, and that personal and family matters are customarily omitted. The Schuyler Papers in the New York Public Library are also useful for Livingston's colonial and Revolutionary career. The Wainwright Autograph Collection in the Princeton University Library has several items of great interest both for family background and for some phases of Livingston's life. The Jay Papers and the De Witt Clinton Papers in the Columbia University Libraries' Special Collections have certain very illuminating letters on (as to the first collection) Livingston's early Revolutionary career and (as to the second) his Anti-Federalist and later career. The Sir Henry Clinton Papers in the William L. Clements Library are necessary for the burning of Kingston and the Clermont mansion and farm. The John Lamb Papers in the New-York Historical Society are useful for Livingston's role in the New York Constitutional Convention. The Robert Fulton Papers in the New-York Historical Society have much to offer concerning the early steamboat experiments but, oddly enough, do not cover the later and successful ones. But the chief reliance, so far as manuscript sources go, has been placed upon the Robert R. Livingston Papers, that vast and invaluable repository.

This is a biographical study which has, as its central theme, the interplay between a man brought up in the atmosphere of a privileged colonial aristocracy, on the one hand, and the emergence of popular government, on the other. It does not pretend, and should not pretend, to give a conspectus of the general history surrounding each phase of its subject's career. I have listed in this Note, therefore, only those books and articles that were particularly useful for a special inquiry.

For the New York colonial period of this book, there are two printed collections of primary material without which one would be lost indeed: E. B. O'Callaghan, ed., *Documentary History of the State of New York* (4 vols., Albany, 1849-1851) and E. B. O'Callaghan and Berthold Fernow, eds., *Documents Relative to the Colonial History of the State of New York* (15 vols., Albany, 1856-1887). Other primary material is printed in *Journal of the Legislative Council of the Colony of New York, 1691-1775* (2 vols., Albany, 1861); *Journal of the Votes and Proceedings of the General Assembly of the Colony of New York, 1691-1765* (2 vols., New York, 1746-1766); and *Colonial Laws of New York from the Year 1664 to the Revolution* (5 vols., Albany, 1894-1896). The Cadwallader Colden *Letters and Papers . . . 1711-1775* in New-York Historical Society *Collections,* L-LVI, LXVII-LXVIII (1918-1937) offer many valuable insights into this period; and *The Correspondence of General Thomas Gage with the Secretaries of State, 1763-1775,* Clarence E. Carter, ed., (2 vols., New Haven, 1931) is also useful for what might be called anticolonial thinking. For a general picture, there is the valuable *Historical Memoirs from 16 March 1763 to 9 July 1776 of William Smith, Edited, with an Introduction, Biography, and Notes, from the Previously Unpublished Manuscript in the New York Public Library,* William H. Sabine, ed., (New York, 1956). The resolutions of the Stamp Act Congress are in *Proceedings of the Congress at New York* (Annapolis, 1766) reprinted in Hezekiah Niles, *Principles and Acts of the Revolution* (Baltimore, 1822). For secondary sources, I am deeply indebted for information concerning the Livingston background to Dr. Milton M. Klein's brilliant doctoral dissertation, "The American Whig: William Livingston of New York," unpublished (Columbia University, 1954) and to his "Democracy and Politics in Colonial New York," *New York History*, XL, No. 3 (July, 1959), which offers fresh insights into the structure of the Livingston and De Lancey parties, although the *nature* of their politico-economic disputes still offers a field for exploration. One cannot manage without Carl L. Becker, *History of Political Parties in the Province of New York, 1760-1776* (Madison, 1909), although this seminal work treats the party disputes as being determined chiefly by personal ties—a point of view which will sooner or later be revised, as Dr. Klein indicates, as does also Beverly McAnear in his very suggestive "Mr. Robert R. Livingston's Reasons Against a Land Tax," *Journal of Political Economy*, XLVIII, No. 1 (February, 1940). Dorothy R. Dillon, *The New York Triumvirate* (New York, 1949) is a useful introduction to these obscure party struggles. Alexander C. Flick, ed., *History of the State of New York* (10 vols., New York, 1933-1937), Vol. II is important. For the agrarian wars and riots in the period there is Irving Mark's admirable *Agrarian Conflicts in Colonial New York, 1711-1775* (New York, 1940). Oscar M. Handlin, "The Eastern Frontier of New York," *New York History*, XVIII, No. 1 (January, 1937) is also very helpful. For the Stamp Act, there is Edmund S. and Helen M. Morgan, *The Stamp Act Crisis* (Chapel Hill, 1953), a most admirable conspectus. Also Beverly McAnear, "The Albany Stamp Act Riots," *William and Mary Quarterly*, 3rd Series, No. 4 (1947), which brings the riots home to the landlords. More generally, there is O. M. Dickerson, *The Navigation Acts and the American Revolution* (Philadelphia, 1951).

For the Livingston family background, there is Edwin Brockholst Livingston's family history, *The Livingstons of Livingston Manor* (New York, 1910), a superior example of books of this kind. Lawrence H. Leder, ed., "The Livingston Indian Records," *Pennsylvania History*, XXIII, No. 1 (January, 1956) is useful for this family background: it is to be regretted that Leder's work on Robert Livingston, first Lord of the Manor, had not made its appearance while this book was being written. For the way of life of the colonial aristocracy, there is George W. Schuyler's *Colonial New York: Philip Schuyler and His Family* (2 vols., New York, 1885) from which one gets the impression that it was a relatively simple way of life, as it would have to be before the emergence of a leisure class. Ann Grant, *Memoirs of an American Lady* (New York, 1903), a delightful book, confirms this, as it also does the impression that it was more simple in its environment than in its pride. Another charming account is Marquise de la Tour du Pin, *Journal d'une Femme de Cinquante Ans, 1778-1813* (2 vols., Paris, 1925), although she deals with the immediate post-Revolutionary period. Her portrait of

Talleyrand in his American exile is most illuminating. The idea of a simple, though highly privileged, aristocracy also emerges from any perusal of the family letters at this time. The introduction in Ross J. S. Hoffman, *Edmund Burke, New York Agent* (Philadelphia, 1956) gives many insights into the relations between the upper classes and the Provincial Government, although Burke himself played a very small role in provincial affairs. For the way of life of the merchant aristocracy, one must consult Carl Bridenbaugh, *Cities in the Wilderness: The First Century of Urban Life in America, 1625-1742* (New York, 1955) and *Cities in Revolt: Urban Life in America, 1743-1776* (New York, 1955), two rich storehouses of information, although Professor Bridenbaugh's method precludes him from giving a profile of individual cities. For a conspectus of merchant politics and economics, there is Arthur Meyer Schlesinger's classic *The Colonial Merchants and the American Revolution* (New York, 1957 ed.). Philip L. White, *The Beekmans of New York* (New York, 1956) is a fine evocation of a single merchant family. For Livingston's college background, there is *A History of Columbia University, 1754-1904* (New York, 1904), Vol. I., *King's College and Columbia College,* by John Howard Van Amringe, especially Appendix B. Also Frank Monaghan, *John Jay* (New York, 1935), a careful and scholarly biography. Paul M. Hamlin, *Legal Education in Colonial New York* (New York, 1939) is essential for Livingston's legal background.

In the Revolutionary period, the Robert R. Livingston Papers become voluminous, and are the chief source for any interpetation of Livingston. The essential printed documents for his public career are, of course, *Journals of the Provincial Congress, Provincial Convention, etc., of the State of New York (1775-1777),* (2 vols., Albany, 1842) and *Journals of the Continental Congress, 1774-1789,* W. C. Ford *et al.,* eds. (34 vols., Washington, 1904-1937). *Calendar of Historical Manuscripts Relating to the War of the Revolution in the Office of the Secretary of State, Albany, New York* (2 vols., Albany, 1868) is useful for the early phases. Among the printed collections of letters, etc., *The Correspondence and Public Papers of John Jay,* Henry P. Johnston, ed. (4 vols., New York, 1890-1893), is especially applicable to Robert R. Livingston. As to secondary works, there is a valuable account of the entrance of New York into the Revolution in Curtis P. Nettels' vivid and learned *George Washington and American Independence* (Boston, 1951). Becker's *History of Political Parties* is indispensable for preliminaries up to 1776, as is Lawrence H. Gipson, *The Coming of the Revolution, 1763-1775* (New York, 1954). For the military events, early and late, which infrequently intrude upon Livingston's career, Douglas Southall Freeman, *George Washington* (6 vols., New York, 1948-1954) was gratefully used; also Christopher Ward, *The War of the Revolution,* John Richard Alden, ed. (2 vols., New York, 1952), and a most useful small work, *The War for Independence,* by Howard Peckham (Chicago, 1958). More generally, there was John Richard Alden,

The American Revolution, 1775-1783 (New York, 1954). The chapters on the American Revolution in R. R. Palmer's superb *The Age of the Democratic Revolution* (Princeton, 1959) seem to me to be essential to any attempt to understand this period.

For the New York State Constitution there is, as secondary material, Flick, *History of the State of New York,* IV; E. Wilder Spaulding, *New York in the Critical Period, 1783-1789* (New York, 1932), who includes in his study this earlier event; D. L. Colvin, *Bicameral Principle in the New York Legislature* (New York, 1913); Clinton Rossiter, *Seedtime of the Republic* (New York, 1953), who offers an illuminating discussion of early constitutional principles and expectations.

For Livingston's nationalism in Congress there is E. C. Burnett, ed., *Letters of Members of the Continental Congress* (8 vols., Washington, 1921-1936), and his excellent *Continental Congress* (Washington, 1941). For insights into the condition of New York State itself, there are Thomas C. Cochran, *New York in the Confederation: An Economic Study* (Philadelphia, 1932) and Allan Nevins, *American States During and After the Revolution* (New York, 1924), two works that time has not robbed of their vigor, usefulness, and pertinence.

For Livingston's career as Secretary for Foreign Affairs, there is Francis Wharton, ed., *Revolutionary Diplomatic Correspondence of the United States* (6 vols., Washington, 1889), a quintessential work, particularly when correlated with and enriched by Livingston's correspondence in the Robert R. Livingston Papers; also Henri Doniol's classic *Histoire de la Participation de la France à l'Établissement des États-Unis d'Amérique* (5 vols., Paris, 1886-1892); Samuel Flagg Bemis, *Diplomacy of the American Revolution* (New York, 1935, and Bloomington, 1957), an indispensable authority; Vincent T. Harlow, *The Founding of the Second British Empire, 1763-1793* (London, 1952), especially useful for the peace negotiations in Paris and London. For Livingston himself as secretary, there is Milledge L. Bonham, Jr., "Robert R. Livingston," in Samuel Flagg Bemis, ed., *The American Secretaries of State and Their Diplomacy* (10 vols., New York, 1927-1929), Vol. I, a very favorable discussion; and Gaillard Hunt, *The Department of State* (Washington, 1893), also favorable.

For Livingston's career during the "critical period" (*i.e.,* as a Federalist), the greatest reliance was placed upon the information in his private papers. For his activities as Chancellor, there are the *Minutes of the Court of Chancery* in the Hall of Records, New York City, a detailed record of all cases— mortgage, guardianship, insolvency, insanity, divorce, etc.—beginning June 11, 1785. None of the Chancellor's opinions was recorded: the *Minutes* give a digest of the briefs, and the names of counsel. Livingston's "Rules and Orders," dated December 28, 1797, are also in these *Minutes.* Certain of the Chancellor's opinions emerge from 1 Caines, *Cases Argued and Determined in the Court for the Trial of Impeachments and Correction of Errors in the State of New York* (2 vols., New York, 1883) and 1 Johnson, *New York Common Law Reports, Coleman and Caines Cases* (New York, 1883). Alfred B. Street, *The Council of Revision of the State of New York* (Albany, 1859) presents examples of his legal and constitutional thinking. For his practices as a landlord, "R. R. Livingston's Account Book, Clermont, N. Y.: Great Patent Memorandum," and "R. R. Livingston's Great Patent Account Book, Middletown, New York" (both in New-York Historical Society), while incomplete, are most illuminating. Also, "List of Money Rents in Clermont for 1799," Wilson Family Papers, although of a later date, is exceedingly useful for comparative purposes. For Livingston's—to my mind, essentially agrarian —dabbling in a land-bank scheme, there is Bray Hammond, *Banks and Politics in America* (Princeton, 1957), in general a most stimulating book; also Merrill Jensen, *The New Nation* (New York, 1950), useful for the whole "critical period" as well. For the boundary dispute, the Duane Papers were more rewarding than the Livingston Papers, and there is Dixon Ryan Fox's very lively *Yankees versus Yorkers* (New York, 1940); also *Report of the Regents of the University of the State of New York,* Senate Document 71 (Albany, 1883).

For the New York ratifying convention, the Robert R. Livingston Papers have many scattered notes, but these do not amplify what can be read in the best printed source, Francis Childs, *The Debates and Proceedings of the Convention of the State of New-York* (New York, 1788), which do not give the student all he would ideally ask, but which are full enough to enable him to follow the debates with clarity. Childs is weakest at the end, and here he may be supplemented by Gilbert Livingston's manuscript notes in the New-York Historical Society. Secondary works are E. Wilder Spaulding, *New York in the Critical Period,* already mentioned, and valuable for the whole period; Forrest McDonald, *We the People: The Economic Origins of the Constitution* (Chicago, 1958), which offers some very interesting theory; Charles Beard, *An Economic Interpretation of the Constitution of the United States* (New York, 1944 ed.), although this classic ascribes to Livingston, for example, a fondness for public paper which he did not have; and the relevant locations in Henry C. Lodge, ed., *The Works of Alexander Hamilton* (12 vols., New York, 1904), in Nathan Schachner, *Alexander Hamilton* (New York, 1946), and in Broadus Mitchell, *Alexander Hamilton* (New York, 1957). Mitchell is particularly to be consulted on the Hamiltonian aspect of the debates.

For the Anti-Federalist phase of Livingston's career, much, as usual, depended upon such interpretations as seemed to emerge from a close study of the Robert R. Livingston Papers. The politics of New York are anything but luminous at this period. One still depends for instruction upon those two standbys, Jabez D. Hammond, *The History of Political Parties in the State of New-York* (2 vols., Albany, 1842), a history which, in addition to its many solid virtues, has for the student of Livingston a certain poignancy because

Hammond was a youthful contemporary of the Chancellor's, and D. S. Alexander, *A Political History of New York, 1774-1882* (3 vols., New York, 1906-1909), a book with many shrewd insights. For the Jay Treaty, there is Samuel Flagg Bemis's masterful *A Diplomatic History of the United States* (New York, 1936 and 1942), which the student fails to consult at his peril. There is also the same author's *Jay's Treaty: A Study in Commerce and Diplomacy* (New York, 1923), for a thorough exegesis and analysis. Monaghan's *Jay* does its very good best for Jay.

For the Chancellor as landlord and agricultural reformer at this period, the essential material is in the New York Society for the Promotion of Agriculture, Arts and Manufactures, *Transactions,* I (1792-1799), Parts 1 and 2. These articles show the amount of solid information and serious thought which Livingston brought to his life as an agriculturalist. That the articles were of his own composition is proved by the fact that the drafts of them have almost all survived in his papers—these drafts being, of course, in his own hand and with his own corrections.

For his early steamboat experiments, there is a good deal of information in the Fulton Papers, especially as regards his somewhat stormy relations with Nicholas J. Roosevelt; and a great deal in his own papers. The Stevens Papers, Stevens Institute, might be made more accessible; but there is, among the secondary sources, A. D. Turnbull's admirable *John Stevens: An American Record* (New York, 1928), which would have been all the more admirable if the dating of the letters in it had been more consistent. There is Rear-Admiral George Henry Preble's useful *A Chronological History of the Origin and Development of Steam Navigation* (Philadelphia, 1883). And there is James Thomas Flexner, *Steamboats Come True* (New York, 1944), an intelligent, thorough, and most felicitous examination of the history of early steamboating in this country. The general problem is also well handled in Richard Shelton Kirby, Sidney Withington, Arthur Burr Darling, and Frederick Gridley Kilgour, *Engineering in History* (New York, 1956).

For the Manhattan Company, the authority is now Beatrice G. Reubens, "Burr, Hamilton and the Manhattan Company," *Political Science Quarterly,* LXXII, No. 4 (December, 1957) and LXXIII, No. 1 (March, 1958). The letters of Robert Troup to Rufus King in the Rufus King Papers, New-York Historical Society, somewhat lighten the darkness of New York politics at this time. For the maneuvers preceding the election of Thomas Jefferson in the House of Representatives, I consulted particularly Irving Brant's brilliant and succinct reconstruction in *James Madison: Secretary of State, 1800-1809* (Indianapolis and New York, 1953).

For Livingston's career as minister to France, the Robert R. Livingston Papers—correspondence, drafts, and letter books—are, of course, very illuminating in any study of the Louisiana Purchase, where he played such a leading part. The relevant letter books are also extremely useful for the negotiation concerning the American claims. The material has to be collated with the two chief printed but incomplete primary sources: *American State Papers, Foreign Relations*, Vol. II, *France and Spain—Louisiana* (Washington, 1833), and the very nearly identical *State Papers and Correspondence Bearing upon the Purchase of the Territory of Louisiana*, 57 Cong., 2 Sess., HR Doc. No. 431. The few additions to the latter collection are all Monrovian. Transcripts of the *Archives des Affaires Étrangères, Correspondence Politique, États-Unis* are in the Division of Manuscripts, Library of Congress. There is also Edward Alexander Parsons, ed., *The Original Letters of Robert R. Livingston* (New Orleans, 1953), which contains certain letters from Livingston to King not elsewhere available.

For secondary sources, one begins, inevitably, with Henry Adams, *History of the United States of America During the Administration of Thomas Jefferson* (New York, 1930 ed.), Vols. I and II. Naturally, much information has come to light since this masterpiece was written; but anyone attempting an account of the Louisiana Purchase would, I should think, instinctively call Adams master. E. Wilson Lyon, *Louisiana in French Diplomacy* (Norman, 1934) is the best modern study in a far from extensive literature. François de Barbé-Marbois, *Histoire de la Louisiane* (Paris, 1829) is still one of the source books for these transactions: it was translated as *History of Louisiana, Translated from the French by an American Citizen* (Philadelphia, 1830). No doubt, one reads it with caution: but it is certain that without its account one would know nothing about Bonaparte's admitted—as compared to his real—reasons for selling; and, since Marbois was the Frenchman most nearly involved in the final negotiations, what he says has weight. F-P. Renaut, *La Question de la Louisiane, 1796-1806* (Paris, 1918) is interesting if, for the negotiations, conventional. The Louisiana Purchase is also thoroughly treated in Brant, *James Madison: Secretary of State*, already mentioned. Brant has studied the Robert R. Livingston Papers for this period, but his account is so heavily biased against Livingston as virtually to caricature him. The vexed subject of the boundaries of Louisiana is well handled in Richard R. Stenberg, "The Boundaries of the Louisiana Purchase," *Hispanic American Historical Review*, XIV, No. 1 (February, 1934). The same author's "Napoleon's Cession of Louisiana: A Suggestion," *Louisiana Historical Quarterly*, XXI, No. 1 (January, 1938), stresses Spain's refusal to yield the Floridas to France as the main cause of the cession of Louisiana to the United States. Lyon, mentioned above, certainly, after the most careful analysis, supports the contention that it was not simply the approaching war with Great Britain that decided Bonaparte to cede Louisiana. For the British effort to bribe Joseph Bonaparte and Talleyrand, there is Carl Ludwig Lokke, "Secret Negotiations to Maintain the Peace of Amiens," *American Historical Review*, XLIX, No. 1 (October, 1943). The terms of the purchase are carefully and thoroughly handled in J. E. Winston and R. W. Colomb, "How the Louisiana Purchase Was Financed," *Louisiana Historical Quarterly*, XII, No. 2 (April, 1929), which underscores the fact that the terms of the financing were hastily arranged. The final treaty and the two accompanying conventions are in *American State Papers, Foreign Relations,* Vol. II, *France and Spain—Louisiana.* For the American claims, there is an immense correspondence between the Claims Commissioners and Livingston in the Robert R. Livingston Papers; and the letters of Christopher Gore to Rufus King in the Rufus King Papers throw some light on the personal relations involved. J. B. Moore, ed., *History and Digest of the International Arbitrations to Which the United States Has Been a Party* (6 vols., Washington, 1898), Vol. V gives a very succinct and impartial account of the claims controversy as between the Commissioners and Livingston. Brant's account in *James Madison: Secretary of State* shows, as is the case throughout his masterly biography of Madison, a gift for significant research; but here he seems altogether too anxious to destroy the reputation of Livingston to be considered an even remotely impartial analyst.

For Livingston's visit to London, there is a great deal of material in the Livingston Papers, since he wrote regularly to his wife in Paris. For the reaction to it in the London *Times* and *Courier,* I am grateful to Dr. Bradford Perkins, of the University of California at Los Angeles, for providing me with the list of dates to consult: the two newspapers consulted can be found in the New York Public Library's newspaper collection. *The Diaries and Correspondence of the Right Honourable George Rose* (2 vols., London, 1860), Vol. II, and Earl Stanhope, *Life of William Pitt* (3 vols., London, 1879), Vol. III, show, in some detail, to what extent he fluttered the official dovecotes.

For the last phases of Livingston's life, the works of Alexander and Hammond, already mentioned, are useful for the governorship of Morgan Lewis. Also Dixon Ryan Fox, *The Decline of Aristocracy in the State of New York* (New York, 1919), for the governorship of Morgan Lewis, and for Fox's insights in general, although he deals only with the Federalist aristocracy, and dismisses the Livingstons' Republicanism as a mere deviation from a Federalist norm.

For the steamboat monopoly, the works of Flexner, Turnbull, and Preble, already mentioned, were sufficient: also Alice Crary Sutcliffe's charming *Robert Fulton and the Clermont* (New York, 1909), was useful. C. B. Todd, *Life and Letters of Joel Barlow* (New York, 1886) contains essential information on Fulton and Livingston in Paris. The *Minutes of the Court of Chancery* in the New York City Hall of Records yielded the exact date of Chancellor Lansing's opinion in *Fulton and Livingston* vs. *Van Ingen et al.:* which is more than 1 Paine *Circuit Court Reports* (New York, 1827) does for Justice Brockholst Livingston's decision, giving only "April Vacation" for the date. Albert J. Beveridge, *The Life of John Marshall* (4 vols., Boston, 1916-1919), Vol. IV gives an excellent and scholarly account of the steamboat monopoly and of the legislation and litigation connected with it.

For the final agricultural phase, the important secondary sources were: David M. Ellis, *Landlords and Farmers in the Hudson-Mohawk Region, 1790-1850* (Ithaca, 1946), an invaluable study; New York Society for the Promotion of Useful Arts, *Transactions*, II (1807); Arthur H. Cole, *The American Wool Manufacture* (2 vols., Cambridge, 1926), Vol. I, quite essential for an understanding of the merino and of the technical problems involved in early manufacture from its wool; Chester W. Wright, *Wool-Growing and the Tariff* (Cambridge, 1910), also useful for the merino; and, of course, P. W. Bidwell and J. I. Falconer's magistral *History of Agriculture in the Northern United States, 1620-1860* (Washington, 1925, New York, 1941). Robert R. Livingston's *Essay on Sheep* (New York, 1809) not only contains solid information on the merino, but is a rare example of the scope and thoroughness of his thinking, and of his scholarly habit of mind.

Notes

I have used abbreviations sparingly in the notes; those used are:

AAE,EU: Archives des Affaires Étrangères, Correspondence Politique, États-Unis
ASPFR II: *American State Papers, Foreign Relations,* Vol. II, *France and Spain—*
    Louisiana
DAB: Dictionary of American Biography
Doc. Hist. NY: Documentary History of the State of New York
Docs. Rel. Col. Hist. NY: Documents Relative to the Colonial History of the State of
    New York
JCC: Journals of the Continental Congress, 1774-1789
JPC: Journals of the Provincial Congress, Provincial Convention, etc., of the State
    of New York 1775-1777
LC: Library of Congress
NYHS: New-York Historical Society
NYPL: New York Public Library
RRL: Chancellor Robert R. Livingston
RRLP: Robert R. Livingston Papers, in the New-York Historical Society
RRLP*: See note on page 503
RRLP(P): See note on page 503
SPAC: State Papers and Correspondence Bearing upon the Purchase of the Territory
    of Louisiana
TOLRRL: See note on page 503

PART ONE, CHAPTER ONE

1. The Strickland Journal is in the manuscript collection of the New-York Historical Society. As regards slavery, it will be noticed in the *DAB* (1946 ed., XI, 323) that Chancellor Livingston opposed the 1785 bill to abolish slavery in New York. This needs a little amplification. In Alfred B. Street, *The Council of Revision of the State of New York,* 268, the Chancellor is shown as having opposed the bill in the Council of Revision because its last clause enacted that no Negro, mulatto, or mustee should have a legal vote in any case whatsoever. They cannot, said the Chancellor, "be deprived of those essential rights [of holding office and voting] without shocking the principle of equal liberty which every page in that Constitution labors to enforce." He added that the creation of an order of citizens who are to have no legal or representative share in the government "necessarily lays the foundation of an aristocracy of the most dangerous and malignant kind, rendering power permanent and hereditary in the hands of persons who deduce their origins from white ancestors only; though these at some future period, should not amount to a fiftieth part of the people." This opinion is dated March 21, 1785, and was given at New York. As was the Livingston custom, the Chancellor manumitted in his will "all my Slaves, that chuse it who have attained the age of thirty years within two years after my de-

cease or as much earlyer as may be convenient to my dear wife." This will was signed September 16, 1796: it was the will of which administration was granted to Mary Stevens Livingston, the executrix named in it, by James Vanderpool, Surrogate of the County of Columbia, at Kinderhook on June 3, 1813, RRLP. Any study of the various Livingston Papers would convince any reader that the Livingstons regarded slavery as, at best, an unpleasant necessity wished upon them by fate.

PART ONE, CHAPTER TWO

1. For the portrait of Robert Livingston, see New-York Historical Society *Quarterly*, XLIII, No. 3 (July, 1958), 283.
2. Joel Munsell, *Collections on the History of Albany* (10 vols., Albany, 1850-1859), III, 108, 121, IV, 215. G. W. Schuyler, *Colonial New York: Philip Schuyler and His Family* (2 vols., Albany, 1885), I, 243-44.
3. John R. Brodhead, *History of the State of New York* (2 vols., New York, 1853, 1871), II (1664-1691), 287.
4. I am greatly indebted to Dr. Milton M. Klein for permission to read his unpublished doctoral dissertation, "The American Whig: William Livingston of New York" (Columbia University, 1954), which contains much information on the origins of the Livingstons in New York.
5. Lawrence H. Leder, ed., "The Livingston Indian Records," *Pennsylvania History*, XXIII, No. 1 (January, 1956), 5-11.
6. *Ibid.*, 7. *Doc. Hist. N.Y.*, III, 633-34.
7. *DAB* (1946 ed.), Coote, Richard, IV, 419.
8. Leder, *loc. cit.*, 7-9. E. B. O'Callaghan, ed., *Documentary History of the State of New York* (4 vols., Albany, 1849-1851), III, 377 ff.
9. E. B. O'Callaghan and Berthold Fernow, eds., *Documents Relative to the Colonial History of the State of New York* (15 vols., Albany, 1856-1887), IV, 251, 720.
10. *Doc. Hist. NY*, III, 367, 369.
11. *Ibid.*, III, 615-16.
12. Patent of August 27, 1685, *ibid.*, III, 617-22.
13. Patent of July 22, 1686, *ibid.*, III, 622-27.
14. Oscar M. Handlin, "The Eastern Frontier of New York," *New York History*, XVIII, No. 1 (January, 1937), 53-54. Irving Mark, *Agrarian Conflicts in Colonial New York, 1711-1775* (New York, 1940), 32-33.
15. Attorney General of New York in New York Assembly, *Reports of the Attorney General*, No. 59 (Albany, 1853). *People of the State of New York* vs. *Herman Livingston* (Albany, 1853). Handlin, *loc. cit.*, 54.
16. *Docs. Rel. Col. Hist. NY*, III, 675.
17. Bellomont to Lords of Trade, January 2, 1701, *Doc. Hist. NY*, III, 629. Cf. *Docs. Rel. Col. Hist. NY*, IV, 822-23, VII, 795 ff.
18. A Court Leet had jurisdiction over crimes committed within the manor; a Court Baron had jurisdiction in civil actions arising within the manor.
19. *Docs. Rel. Col. Hist. NY*, V, 180. *Doc. Hist. NY*, III, 662, 667, 669, 672, 674, 682-86. Walter Allen Knittle, *Early Eighteenth Century Palatine Emigration* (Philadelphia, 1936), 160, 167-69. Mark, *op. cit.*, 34.
20. Leder, *loc. cit.*, 8. *Doc. Hist. NY*, III, 685, 690-702.
21. For the act of 1699, see *Journal of the Legislative Council of the Colony of New York, 1691-1775* (2 vols., Albany, 1861), I, 137. For the repealing act of 1702, see *Docs. Rel. Col. Hist. NY*, V, 21-26. See also Mark, *op. cit.*, 26, quoting *Acts of the Privy Council*, Col. Series, II, 553. For Cadwallader Colden in this instance see Mark, *op. cit.*, 43.

22. Curtis P. Nettels, *The Roots of American Civilization* (New York, 1938), 393.

23. Tryon to Lord Hillsborough, April 11, 1772, *Docs. Rel. Col. Hist. NY*, VIII, 293-94.

24. Handlin, *loc. cit.*, 54, quoting *General Court, Acts and Resolves, Public and Private, of the Province of Massachusetts Bay*, XIV, App. IX, 241, 263, 379, 453, 476, 543.

25. Handlin, *loc. cit.*, 58 ff. Mark, *op. cit.*, 118-19, 122-23, 126.

26. By an order in council of 1764, Great Britain asserted that the eastern boundary of New York was the western bank of the Connecticut River. This order had no teeth in it, and did not affect the maneuvers of New Hampshire. Dorothy R. Dillon, *The New York Triumvirate* (New York, 1949), 173.

27. Handlin, *loc. cit.*, 58 ff.

28. *Montressor Journals*, New-York Historical Society *Collections* (1881), 366, entry for May 17, 1766; and 375-76, entry for June 28, 1766. Mark, *op. cit.*, 141-43.

29. Beverly McAnear, "The Albany Stamp Act Riots," *William and Mary Quarterly*, 3rd Series, No. 4 (1947), 486-98.

30. Edmund S. and Helen M. Morgan, *The Stamp Act Crisis* (Chapel Hill, 1953), 184, quoting Howenburgh to J. T. Kemp, no date, Sedgwick Papers, Massachusetts Historical Society. See also General Gage to Secretary Henry Seymour Conway, December 21, 1765, and June 24, 1766, in Clarence E. Carter, ed., *The Correspondence of General Thomas Gage with the Secretaries of State, 1763-1775* (2 vols., New Haven, 1931), I, 79, 95. Gage said that the lawyers, the bench, the merchants and finally "the Rich and Powerfull People" in the province had stirred up the Stamp Act riots and that therefore the antirent rebellion was no more than their just due.

31. Leder, *loc. cit.*, 11. Philip L. White, *The Beekmans of New York* (New York, 1956), 163-64. See also Arthur H. Buffinton, "The Policy of Albany and English Westward Expansion," *Mississippi Valley Historical Review*, VIII, No. 4 (March, 1922), 360-61; Milton M. Klein, "Democracy and Politics in Colonial New York," *New York History*, XI, No. 3 (July, 1959), 225.

32. Governor Clinton was so incensed over Philip Livingston's patenting of the Canajoharie tract—the Indians said that "Mr. Livingston murdered us asleep"—that he wrote, "It is a vile family." A land patent, even one so questionable that Philip's heirs agreed to hand the land back to the Indians, would not alone have provoked this extreme language. Further blackened by Livingston's support of De Lancey, it might well have done so. Clinton to Newcastle, November 18, 1745, *Docs. Rel. Col. Hist. NY*, VI, 286.

33. Beverly McAnear, "Mr. Robert R. Livingston's Reasons Against a Land Tax," *Journal of Political Economy*, XLVIII (February, 1940), 63-90.

34. Dillon, *op. cit.*, 84. William Livingston's *A Review of the Military Operations in North America* was dated 1756, and was doubtless written with the assistance of Scott and Smith.

35. McAnear, "Mr. Robert Livingston's Reasons Against a Land Tax," 71-72, quoting Peter R. Livingston to Robert Livingston, Jr. (third Lord of the Manor), New York, April 20, 1770, Livingston-Redmond Papers.

36. Robert Livingston, Jr., to James Duane, March 9, 1772, Duane Papers, NYHS.

37. McAnear, "Mr. Robert R. Livingston's Reasons Against a Land Tax," 70-71.

PART ONE, CHAPTER THREE

1. Will of Robert Livingston, first Lord of the Manor of Livingston, a transcript, RRLP. The estate—variously spelled "Claremount," "Claremont," etc., and by Chancellor Livingston always "ClerMont"—was said to have been called Clermont

after the French town of that name. George W. Schuyler, *Colonial New York: Philip Schuyler and His Family,* I, 243-91.

2. Janet L. Montgomery, "Note," transcribed from the original once in the possession of Mrs. Lewis Livingston of Rhinebeck, N. Y., Miscellaneous Livingston Manuscripts, NYHS. Harold Donaldson Eberlein, *The Manors and Historic Homes of the Hudson Valley* (Philadelphia, 1924), 72.

3. Robert R. Livingston, Sr., to Robert Livingston, New York, April 12, 1766, RRLP.

4. Janet L. Montgomery, "Note."

5. Catharine Livingston Garretson to George Bancroft, Rhinebeck, September 22, 1843, Livingston-Bancroft Transcripts, NYPL, III, "Transcripts and Originals," 98.

6. RRL to the Rev. William Gordon, Clermont, November 27, 1778, *ibid.,* 82.

7. For Robert R. Livingston, Sr.'s mercantile activities, see Robert R. Livingston, Sr., to Robert Livingston, New York, April 17, 1750: "I am in hopes your privateers will do pretty well. . . . Grifeth is not hanged yet but has sent in a Dutch schooner & with two other privateers has taken two Dutch sloops. What we shall make of them I know not." See also Robert R. Livingston, Sr., to Robert Livingston, New York, July 23, 1750. The accounts of cash received and paid from May, 1758, to June 28, 1759, show that Robert R. Livingston, Sr., had dealings in flour, boards, sugar, coffee, and prizes brought in by privateers. See also Robert R. Livingston, Sr., to Robert Livingston, New York, July 20, 1760: "Flower is dull I can't sell." All in RRLP.

8. Dorothy R. Dillon, *The New York Triumvirate,* 57 ff.

9. *DAB* (1946 ed.), Livingston, Robert R. (August, 1718-December 9, 1775), XI, 319.

10. *Ibid.* Her mother was a daughter of a nephew of the first Lord of the Manor and of Margaretta Schuyler.

11. *Abstract of Wills on File in the Surrogate's Office, City of New York,* New-York Historical Society *Collections,* 1903, XII (New York, 1904), 342-43. Margaret Beekman Livingston was left in fee simple all Henry Beekman's property outside Dutchess County: the remainder she was to hold as tenant for life, with an authorization to her and to her husband to convey these lands to their children as they thought fit; all unconveyed at her death to be equally divided. For the character of Gertruyd Van Cortlandt, see Janet L. Montgomery "Note," no doubt a prejudiced account, since Mrs. Montgomery detested her Step-Dame, as she called her. Lord Cornbury, according to Mrs. Montgomery, "because of a vow, obliged himself for a month to wear woman's clothing. He was a large man, wore a hoop and a headdress and with a fan in his hand was seen frequently at night upon the ramparts." He fell in love with his wife, she says, because she had a beautiful ear, though otherwise plain; and when the beauty of her ear failed to move him any longer, he reduced her to such penury that she would borrow, and neglect to return, anything that caught her fancy on her visits to her neighbors in New York City. When the roll of her carriage wheels was heard, the cry was, "Here comes my lady—hide this, take that." Gertruyd Van Cortlandt was one of this lady's unofficial maids in waiting, who did her "serving work—for who could refuse their daughter to my lady." Miscellaneous Livingston Manuscripts, NYHS, and Livingston-Bancroft Transcripts, NYPL, III, 138.

12. The portrait, by John Wollaston, is reproduced in Philip L. White, *The Beekmans of New York,* facing page 19. Fragments of Margaret Beekman Livingston's diaries are in the Wainwright Autograph Collection, Princeton University Library.

13. Robert R. Livingston, Sr., to Robert Livingston, New York, March 17, 1762, RRLP.

14. Robert Livingston, Jr., to James Duane, November 30, 1765, Duane Papers, NYHS.

15. Anne Grant, *Memoirs of an American Lady* (New York, 1903), 171.

16. Janet L. Montgomery, "Note." The Colonel's father came from Esopus, or Kingston, in Ulster County. When his wife, Gertruyd Van Cortlandt Beekman, boasted of the many fine gentlemen who had courted her when she was in the entourage of Lady Cornbury, Colonel Beekman used to say, laconically, "And yet you took up at last with an Esopus farmer."

17. Margaret Beekman Livingston to Anne Home Shippen Livingston, 1788. Ethel Armes, ed., *Nancy Shippen, Her Journal Book* (Philadelphia, 1935), 262.

18. Dillon, *op. cit.*, 72-73.

19. Robert R. Livingston, Sr., to Governor Monckton, New York, January 26, 1765, Livingston Family Papers, NYPL.

20. Robert R. Livingston, Sr., to Robert Livingston, October 19, 1765, Livingston-Bancroft Transcripts, NYPL, III, 15.

21. Dillon, *op. cit.*, 81. Also Cadwallader Colden, *Letter Books*, NYHS *Collections* (New York, 1877-1878), IX, 415, 436-39, 455, 462. Colden's position was that Kempe had betrayed his trust by supporting the Supreme Court, and that Livingston sat on cases where his own family was directly concerned. Robert R. Livingston, Sr., to Robert Livingston, October 19, 1765, cited in 20 *supra*, adds: "It does not appear that our agent knew the affair was depending in Council, for at the very time he was assured by the Secretary of the Board of Trade that the instructions to Sir Harry Moore would be so altered as to put an end to the controversy."

22. Colden to Lords of Trade, November 7, 1764, *loc. cit.*, I, 469-70.

23. *Idem.*

24. Irving Mark, *Agrarian Conflicts in Colonial New York, 1711-1775* (New York, 1940), 106.

25. *Ibid.*, 91.

26. Robert R. Livingston, Sr., to Robert Livingston, New York, June 7, 1764, RRLP. "Lord Stirling told me yesterday that one Gilliland expects a number of Irish families here who are able to pay their Passage & settle themselves but not able to buy Lands. That he wants to procure a very large tract where they may settle on a perpetual Rent. I will try today or on Monday whether I can make a Bargain with him of 10,000 Acres in Number Four [in the Hardenburgh Patent]. I am thinking to offer such a Piece in a square 10/-per hundred for the first 7 years 20/-for the second & 30/-for ever after."

27. Robert R. Livingston, Sr., to Robert Livingston, New York, April 10, 1765, RRLP. The proposal, as he heard it, was "to take of [off] all the Quitrents & to lay half that sum that is to say 1/3 or 1/6 on all Lands in general." Quitrents were at 2/6 per hundred acres in 1765, but they were rarely paid at all, and never in full. A general land tax of 1/6 per hundred acres, strictly enforced—although strict enforcement was doubtless impossible—would have been a heavy burden on the landed proprietor, and an intolerable one if he was also a speculator.

28. Beverly McAnear, "Mr. Robert R. Livingston's Reasons Against a Land Tax," *Journal of Political Economy*, XLVIII (February, 1940), 63-90. Dr. McAnear is inclined to the belief that this undated manuscript in the William Smith, Jr., Papers, NYPL, was written in or about the year 1752. He adds that it might have been written in or about the years 1764-1765, when there was much public discussion of wild lands, because of the rumor of an impending parliamentary levy. Judge Livingston's letter to his father, quoted in 27 *supra*, together with some remarks in an earlier letter ("It appears plainly that the design of the Ministry is to

burden us with the whole expence of the Army and that the duties are only the beginning of evils. . . . They talk too of a Land Tax & to us the Ministry appear to have run mad." Robert R. Livingston, Sr., to Robert Livingston, June 17, 1764, RRLP, seems to me to place this manuscript in the period 1764-1765. The quotation is from Juvenal, *Satires,* I, 18, 19.

29. Robert R. Livingston, Sr., to John Sargent, New York, December 20, 1765, Livingston-Bancroft Transcripts, NYPL, III, 40.

30. Edmund S. and Helen M. Morgan, *The Stamp Act Crisis,* 107-09. O. M. Dickerson, *The Navigation Acts and the American Revolution* (Philadelphia, 1951), 190.

31. Robert R. Livingston, Sr., to Robert Livingston, October 17, 1765, Livingston-Bancroft Transcripts, NYPL, III, 15. The Congress opened October 7, and adjourned October 25. The New York delegation was the Assembly's Committee of Correspondence.

32. Morgan and Morgan, *op. cit.,* pp. 114-15, argue that the Congress did not confine its constitutional objections to internal taxes alone. The fourteen resolutions may be found in *Proceedings of the Congress at New York* (Annapolis, 1766), reprinted in Hezekiah Niles, *Principles and Acts of the Revolution,* 451 ff. The New York delegates were John Cruger, Philip Livingston, William Bayard, Leonard Lispenard, Robert R. Livingston, Sr. Carl L. Becker, *History of Political Parties in the Province of New York, 1760-1776* (Madison, 1909), 27. Robert R. Livingston's limitation of unconstitutional taxes to "internal" taxes is shown explicitly in Robert R. Livingston, Sr., to Robert Livingston, November 2, 1765, Livingston-Bancroft Transcripts, NYPL, III, "Transcripts and Originals," 25. Dillon, *op. cit.,* 94, maintains that William Livingston was of the same mind.

33. Gage to Secretary Henry Seymour Conway, October 12, 1765, *The Correspondence of General Thomas Gage with the Secretaries of State, 1763-1775,* I, 69.

34. Becker, *op. cit.,* 29.

35. Gage to Conway, December 21, 1765, and January 16, 1776, *Correspondence,* I, 78-79, 80-83. Cadwallader Colden to Conway, November 9, 1765, *Docs. Rel. Col. Hist. NY,* VII, 773, declares that the lawyers were behind it all. For accusations in Parliament, see Dickerson, *op. cit.,* 194.

36. Robert R. Livingston, Sr., to Robert Livingston, November 2, 1765, Livingston-Bancroft Transcripts, NYPL III, "Transcripts and Originals," 25. Robert R. Livingston, Sr., to former Governor Monckton, November 8, 1765, Livingston Family Papers, NYPL.

37. Morgan and Morgan, *op. cit.,* 199.

38. Robert R. Livingston, Sr., to former Governor Monckton, cited in 36 *supra.*

39. "I can't possibly describe to you the manner in which People here are affected on this occasion. One will wear nothing but Homespun another will drink no wine because it must pay a duty another proposes to dress in Sheepskin with the wool on all express their resentment. . . . In short so general is the resentment of all ranks that if they should carry the taxing of us into Execution and a French army *should land in America* of only three thousand men, I doubt whether they would meet with any opposition from the Inhabitants. I hope this account will rather divert than trouble your Repose in your Retirement. We shall do as well as our neighbors & the God in Heaven whom we serve will sanctify all things to those that love him and strive to serve him." Robert R. Livingston, Sr., to Robert Livingston, June 17, 1764, RRLP. This was written after the Sugar Act and while the Stamp Act was still merely talked of. Compare this with Robert R. Livingston, Sr., to John Sargent, December 20, 1765, Livingston-Bancroft Transcripts, NYPL, III, 41: "If you enforce [the Stamp Act] bid farewell to all the profitable trade you have hitherto had with North America, for you may be assured that we shall be contented with our home spun and that we will either go in sheepskins &

goatskins than buy a rag of your manufactures[.] but if you should attempt to enforce it and not succeed! In either case Britain will have been at the apex of her Glory and in the last America must go through terrible convulsions. Were matters left on the old footing, both would be happy and Britain the envy of the old world." For the colony united in disaffection, see this letter also.

40. "Actually the lower classes probably had little to lose by the Stamp Act. They might feel some concern over the restriction of trial by Jury, but they did not commonly engage in the legal business transactions which required a stamp. They would not have worried about the extra cost of matriculating at a University or entering a corporation or alienating a piece of land. They might have worried about the stamps on dice, playing cards and newspapers, but they probably read newspapers supplied by the management in their local coffee house, and a pair of dice will last a long time." Morgan and Morgan, *op. cit.*, 187.

41. *Ibid.*, 184. Robert Livingston, Sr., to former Governor Monckton, New York, November 8, 1765, Livingston Family Papers, NYPL.

42. Robert R. Livingston, Sr., to Robert Livingston, March 18, 1766, RRLP.

43. Robert R. Livingston, Sr., to John Sargent, New York, May 2, 1766. In this letter, also, he thanks his correspondent, who had been appointed the Assembly's special agent to bring about the repeal of the Stamp Act (since the regular agent, Robert Charles, would not move in the matter), for his letter of February 23, giving news of the repeal of the act. He says that they had had accounts before, but that these had come by way of Ireland and only in a newspaper. So also Robert R. Livingston, Sr., to Moses Franks, New York, May 2, 1766, thanking him for his letter of February 22, which "brings the best news imaginable. . . . You make me also happy in thinking that my letter was in some way influential in removing the intended delay on the grand question." Both in Livingston-Bancroft Transcripts, NYPL, III, 51, 55.

44. Robert R. Livingston, Sr., to Robert Livingston, New York, September 18, 1767, RRLP.

45. Robert R. Livingston, Sr., to John Sargent, cited in 43 *supra*.

46. Peter R. Livingston to Philip Schuyler, New York, January 16, 1769, Schuyler Papers, NYPL.

47. Jay to RRL, (January) 1769, RRLP.

48. Peter R. Livingston to Philip Schuyler, New York, February 27, 1769, Schuyler Papers, NYPL. He says that the Judge lost because all the tenants of Robert C. Livingston and Colonel Beekman voted against him.

49. Becker, *op. cit.*, 60. Philip Livingston was a merchant: the cry was aimed at William Livingston, who, though not a candidate, was the mainspring of the party, and against John Morin Scott. Dr. Milton M. Klein, "Democracy and Politics in Colonial New York," *New York History*, XL, No. 3 (July, 1959), 230-31, says that the secret ballot was never an issue with the tenants, and that a great proprietor like Henry Beekman, so far from assuming that his tenants would follow his lead, actually courted them with free food and drink before an election. Dr. Klein must always be listened to with attention. But when he says that Robert Livingston, Jr., "could not guarantee the political adherence of his tenants unless they were paid for their votes," it must be noted that the instance Klein cites is the advice Livingston gave to his friend Abraham Yates, Jr., who was running for the Assembly seat in Albany County in the crucial election year of 1761; that he is advising Yates to buy the votes of the people in the camps, who would not otherwise bother to attend the polls; that the people in the camps were outside Livingston's own pocket borough in the Manor; and that Livingston seems to have no fear for the votes in the Manor.

50. Becker, *op. cit.*, 60.

51. Mark, *op. cit.*, 106.
52. Robert Livingston, Jr., to James Duane, May 28, 1768, Duane Papers, NYHS.
53. Mark, *op. cit.*, 153, quoting "Philanthropos," "A Few Observations on the Conduct of the General Assembly of New York for some Years Past, Addressed to the Freemen and Freeholders of the City and Province."
54. Ross J. S. Hoffman, *Edmund Burke, New York Agent* (Philadelphia, 1956), Chapter III.
55. Robert R. Livingston, Sr., to Margaret Beekman Livingston, January 11, 1771, RRLP.
56. Same to same, December 24, 1770, Livingston Family Papers, NYPL.
57. The course of this controversy of the manor seat may also be traced in the following correspondence.

    1. Robert R. Livingston, Sr., to Robert Livingston, New York, October 23, 1769, RRLP. He says that the Assembly is to meet on November 21, and that he does not know whether or not he is to be admitted. He says that Governor Moore (who died September, 1769) had had a severe reprimand from the Ministry for not resenting the excluding resolution.

    2. Robert R. Livingston, Sr., to former Governor Monckton, New York, December 4, 1769, Livingston Family Papers, NYPL. He says that people in many parts of the province highly resent the Assembly's resolution, which he himself regards as an attack upon the prerogative of the Crown and the liberties of the people, since it is a universal practice throughout the colonies for one or more judges to be chosen representatives.

    3. Robert R. Livingston, Sr., to Margaret Beekman Livingston, January 11, 1771. Miscellaneous Livingston Manuscripts, NYHS. This is the letter in which he says that Edmund Burke, whom he believes to be the author of the Junius letters, has been appointed agent, to the consternation of Lord Dunmore.

    4. Edmund Burke to Robert R. Livingston, Sr., undated, "in answer to his dated 2d. April 1771." "I scarcely know what your parties are, and I am sure that when I become better acquainted with them, I shall be as little disposed, as I am now qualified, to enter into the passions of any of them. . . . I must therefore beg leave to decline an opinion upon a matter so interesting to yourself and so delicate to the public, as that which makes the subject of your letter."

    5. Edmund Burke to James De Lancey, Beaconsfield, June 9, 1771. Here Burke tells De Lancey that the matter of the disqualifying resolution is one of great difficulty. In England, judges do not sit in the Commons, but this is a matter of "mere usage. . . . It is not the judicial character which creates the disability. I make no doubt the supposed reason was their attendance on the House of Lords." He tells De Lancey that he (De Lancey) is the best judge, with his friends, "whether it will be your interest to push that affair"—the exclusion of Livingston —"to the utmost which on the whole is not likely to be supported by any body of people here,—as being contrary to the principles of some, and perhaps to the politics of all." 4 and 5 are from Burke's New York Letter-Book, quoted in Hoffman, *op. cit.*, 194-98.

    6. Robert Livingston, Jr., third Lord of the Manor, to James Duane, February 17, 1772, Duane Papers, NYHS. "The Honourable House of Assembly have again in their great wisdom and Plenitude of their Power objected to the Judge. [I] am in no ways obliged to them as it will give me the trouble to go to the place of Election again in this cold weather: for my vote he shall have if no other Freeholder will have him." If Livingston is elected and if the Assembly will still not receive him, it will oblige "the majority of the freeholders to attend their house in person to give their assent, or desent, to all Bills, orders, & Resolves that

may be offer'd; for represented we will be as having a right by Law." He is sure that the "lovers of liberty . . . will take us into their houses & give us Lodgings for one month in the year as the sessions are seldom longer."

7. Robert R. Livingston, Sr., to RRL, Calendar House, February 17, 1772, RRLP. "Yesterday morning I came here and brought Cousin Robert [Robert Livingston, Jr., the Third Lord] his Letters. He is determined to return me again. the Election is appointed next Friday. I wish an Article of this kind put in the news. The Freeholds of the manor of Livingston are highly exasperated at the ill usage they have received in being for above two years deprived of the most valuable rights of Englishmen." He adds that they will appear in person if their representative is not admitted, as they will not submit to be governed by the votes of a majority—"the worst kind of Tyranny that can be erected."

8. Robert R. Livingston, Sr., "To The Freeholders of the Manor of Livingston," February 22, 1772, thanks them for having re-elected him. "I am very sorry that the Floods prevented my meeting you at the Election, and making my acknowledgments personally for the Honour you have done me," RRLP.

9. Robert Livingston, Jr., to James Duane, April 6, 1772, Duane Papers, NYHS, complains of the part "some folks, & those your friends [John Watts, John Cruger, James De Lancey] have done us in every session since," and hopes that a final dissolution will come soon, as otherwise he will sell his estate in New York and move elsewhere, "where laws govern and not the will of Tyrants."

The Assembly's Exclusion Act was not well received in England, and was repealed. The way in which this repeal was negated, in New York, was simply by not presenting it to the Assembly. Such was the Council's advice to Lord Dunmore as appears in Robert R. Livingston, Sr., to Margaret Beekman Livingston, December 24, 1770, Livingston Family Papers, NYPL.

PART ONE, CHAPTER FOUR

1. Mrs. Catharine Livingston Garretson, "Memoir," Wainwright Autograph Collection, Princeton University Library. She describes the Judge as having, till the day of his death, neither wrinkles nor gray hair. His face was dignified and benign and he had a smile of uncommon sweetness. He was, she says, a little above the medium size, and neither slender nor corpulent. Mrs. Catharine L. Garretson to George Bancroft, Rhinebeck, September 22, 1843, Livingston-Bancroft Transcripts, III, 98.

2. Frank Monaghan, *John Jay* (New York, 1935), 26, gives these requirements for 1760. They were not changed until 1763, *A History of Columbia University, 1754-1904*, I, *King's College and Columbia College*, by John Howard Van Amringe, 451.

3. King's College stood about one hundred and fifty yards from the Hudson, "on the west side of the Broadway in the West Ward of the City of New York fronting easterly to Church Street between Barclay Street and Murray Street." It was on a slight eminence, commanding a fine view of New York, Long Island, Staten Island, and New York Bay. For the curriculum established March 1, 1763, and the rules for student behavior ("Body of Laws") recommended and adopted at the same time, see *A Historia of Columbia University*, cited above, I, App. B, 450-56. For the college diet, see *ibid*, I, 27. The President when RRL first entered college was Dr. Samuel Johnson; he resigned in February, 1763, and was succeeded by the Rev. Myles Cooper, M.A. and Fellow of Queen's College, Oxford. *Idem*. The building was designed by Robert Crommelin, who had also planned St. George's Chapel, and it was said by a visiting Englishman to be "the

most beautifully situated of any college . . . in the world." Carl Bridenbaugh, *Cities in Revolt* (New York, 1955), 22. Nathaniel Du Bois, Jr., to RRL, September 17, 1763, RRLP, describes RRL as a "very Proteus in Love. . . ."

4. RRL to Catharine Livingston, Belvedere, February 10, 1775, Livingston Family Papers, NYPL. "For my own part I love to have my passions agitated: & were it not for a spice of melancholy in my composition which I love to indulge—& a certain Flirtability (there's a Lady's word) by which (when with the girls) I cheat myself into spirits I shd half wish to bustle into town again."

5. Jay to RRL, October 31, 1765, Monaghan, *op. cit.*, 36. Jay to RRL, Rye, March 4, 1766, RRLP.

6. Monaghan, *op. cit.*, 37.

7. New York *Gazette*, May 27, 1765, quoted in Livingston-Bancroft Transcripts, NYPL, I, 20. Mrs. Catharine Livingston Garretson, "Memoir," makes St. George's Chapel the scene of the exercise. She recalls that RRL, "rising gracefully from the Front of the Gallery in St. George's Chapel and bowing to the audience, said In Laudem Libertatis." "It was thought," she adds, "this first exhibition did him much credit." The *Gazette* gives the place as Trinity Church and says that the speech was in English. The Schuyler present was the son of Colonel John Schuyler, of New Jersey.

8. Paul M. Hamlin, *Legal Education in Colonial New York* (New York, 1939), 42, 43, 65. The first volume of Blackstone made its appearance in the province in 1765, the fourth in 1769. The earliest American edition was in four volumes, printed by Robert Bell of Philadelphia, 1771-1772.

9. Monaghan, *op. cit.*, 44: "From the receipts of clerks' fees that have survived it is clear that Messrs. Jay, Livingston & Co. was formed in 1768. Their connection was not entirely dissolved until 1772, though they were not active as partners after 1770. Their first recorded case was that of 'Capt. Pride vs. Peter Du Bois,' begun in September vacation, 1768." See also Dorothy R. Dillon, *The New York Triumvirate*, 22. The Supreme Court on May 1, 1767, ruled that attorneys were not to be admitted to practice in that court without a five years' apprenticeship, to be shortened by two years if the candidate possessed a degree of Bachelor of Arts. By this ruling, Livingston, if he began his apprenticeship in the summer of 1765, would have been eligible for qualification in the summer of 1768. An understanding of January 5, 1764, had previously provided that a youth must have spent two years in college before commencing the study of the law, and must serve a clerkship of five years, for which he paid at the outset a fee of £200, before petitioning for a qualifying examination. Hamlin, *op. cit.*, 38. RRL appears to have suggested an eventual partnership in March, 1765, possibly the March 29 which Jay particularly notices. Jay to RRL, April 12, 1765, RRLP.

10. Hamlin, *op. cit.*, 97 and App. IX. The first session of The Moot was on November 30, 1770. Dillon, *op. cit.*, 27, n 14.

11. RRL to Governor Tryon, "Plan Proposed to his Excellency Gov. Tryon," undated, RRLP.

12. William H. Sabine, ed., *Historical Memoirs from 16 March 1763 to 9 July 1776 of William Smith, Edited, with an Introduction, Biography, and Notes, from the Previously Unpublished Manuscript in the New York Public Library* (New York, 1956), 129, 130, 132. "At all events," Smith writes, "the Young Fellows [Jay and Livingston] free themselves from public censure."

13. *Ibid.*, 154-55.

14. Undated draft in RRLP. The "glorious and disinterested" Assembly of 1768 was the one which met after the Livingstons had been defeated in that year. It was hostile to the government because it would not accept the Quartering Act without

some relaxation of British legislation against colonial paper money. The Assembly of 1769, by accepting a compromise, and with it the act which required it to vote money for the subsistence of the royal troops, provoked much wrath among the radicals, particularly against the De Lancey party, then controlling the Assembly.

15. Hamlin, *op. cit.*, 97. For more convivial occasions, he was a member of the Social Club, which met every Saturday evening at Fraunces' Tavern, at the corner of Broad and Dock Streets, in the winter, and in the summer at the clubhouse at Kip's Bay. Monaghan, *op. cit.*, 43, and John Brett Langstaff, *Dr. Bard of Hyde Park* (New York, 1942), 110.

16. Robert Livingston, Jr. (Third Lord), to James Duane, February 17, 1772, Duane Papers, NYHS. Also same to same, March 9, 1772. The third Lord of the Manor particularly mentions "Mr. Watts, Cruger, Walton & DeLancey" as Duane's particular friends.

17. Monaghan, *op. cit.*, 46. Also Thomas Jones, *History of New York During the Revolutionary War* (New York, 1879), II, 223. Robert R. Livingston, Sr., to Robert Livingston, September 18, 1767, RRLP: "Our Governor seems rather too much taken up with Trifles. The Grand Object with him is the building of a Play House tho nothing he could think of would give greater offence to People but he will have it guarded by the Army."

18. Janet L. Montgomery, "Memoirs," Livingston-Bancroft Transcripts, NYPL, III, 142 ff.

19. RRL, Draft of an Address to Governor Tryon, "written when I was Recorder of N. Y.," April, 1774, RRLP, offers the warmest wishes for the re-establishment of his health. Tryon actually left to consult with the authorities about the various disorders in his province.

20. Robert R. Livingston, Sr., to RRL, Clermont, April 9, 1774, RRLP. "I expected you here before this. Your House is far from being finished. Duey who is a very idle Fellow and has much neglected your business all winter has now brought two Hands Wch with himself and two Prentices makes five. He talks of finishing in a month but it will cost I suppose not less than two months."

PART TWO, CHAPTER ONE

1. Robert R. Livingston, Sr., to Robert Livingston (of Clermont), New York, April 22, 1775, RRLP. Carl L. Becker, *History of Political Parties in the Province of New York, 1760-1776*, 192. The delegates were Isaac Low, James Duane, Philip Livingston, John Jay, and John Alsop, from New York City; Henry Wisner and John Haring, from Orange; William Floyd, from Suffolk; Simon Boerum, from King's; and Peter Schuyler, George Clinton, Lewis Morris, Francis Lewis, and RRL. Of these fourteen, Low and Haring withdrew, Haring's reasons being held satisfactory. Low said that he did not consider himself a member.

2. RRL to Jay, Clermont, December 29, 1775, Jay Papers, Columbia University Libraries' Special Collections.

3. Robert R. Livingston, Sr., to RRL, New York, May 5, 1775, Livingston-Bancroft Transcripts, NYPL, III, 69.

4. RRL to the Rev. William Gordon, Clermont, November 27, 1778, *ibid.*, III, 82. Becker, *op. cit.*, 190. *Calendar of Historical Manuscripts Relating to the War of the Revolution in the Office of the Secretary of State, Albany, New York* (2 vols., Albany, 1868), I, 41, gives the precincts as Rhinebeck, North-East, Amenia, and Rondout. The three delegates were RRL, Morris Graham, and Egbert Benson.

5. Robert R. Livingston, Sr., to RRL, June 19, 1775, Livingston-Bancroft Transcripts, NYPL, I, 73. "Ye Mannor people" presumably means the 10th Regiment, Albany

County, Manor of Livingston District, of which Peter R. Livingston was colonel and Henry Livingston major. RRL was also commissioned a major in this regiment on October 2, 1775. *Calendar of Historical Manuscripts*, I, 173.

6. RRL to Jay, Belvedere, July 17, 1775, Jay Papers, Columbia University Libraries' Special Collections.

7. *Idem.*

8. Robert Livingston, Jr. (Third Lord), to James Duane, April 15, 1775; and to Mary (or Maria) Livingston Duane, May 9, 1775, Duane Papers, NYHS.

9. Robert R. Livingston, Sr., to Gen. Richard Montgomery, Rhinebeck, November 27, 1775, Livingston-Bancroft Transcripts, NYPL, I, 65.

10. RRL to Catharine Livingston, Belvedere, March 26, 1775, Livingston Family Papers, NYPL.

11. Robert R. Livingston, Sr., to RRL, Clermont, May 18, 1775, Livingston-Bancroft Transcripts, NYPL, III, 71.

12. John Richard Alden, *The American Revolution, 1775-1783* (New York, 1954), 29.

13. RRL to Jay, Belvedere, July 17, 1775, Jay Papers, Columbia University Libraries' Special Collections. Dr. John Jones to James Duane, New York, July 13, 1775, Duane Papers, NYHS, complains that "the wretched contemptible policy of this Province in general, & our friends in particular relative to the present interesting dispute, renders it almost impossible for a stranger of liberal spirit & genuine Patriotism to pass his time agreeably among us. . . . In the disposal of officers particularly in the military department the most shameful partiality prevails, all or most of the inferior commissioned officers being selected from the creatures & absolute dependents of the governing party, indeed the conduct of our gentry & principal people have rendered this vile arrangement almost inevitable." Jones was a patriot and a friend of George Washington, whether at this time or later. *DAB* (1946 ed.), Jones, John, X, 181. By "governing party," Jones means the radicals, who were encouraged by the moderation of the gentry.

14. Robert Livingston, of Clermont, to Robert R. Livingston, Sr., Woodstock, January 11, 1766, Livingston-Bancroft Transcripts, NYPL, III, 41.

15. Catharine L. Garretson to George Bancroft, Rhinebeck, September 22, 1843. Janet L. Montgomery, "Memoirs." Both in Livingston-Bancroft Transcripts, NYPL, III, 98, 142.

16. Janet L. Montgomery to Edward Livingston, undated, *ibid.*, III, 128.

17. Same to same, undated, *ibid.*, I, opp. p. 26.

18. Richard Montgomery to RRL, New York, June 3, 1775, *ibid.*, I, 33.

19. Same to same, Albany, August 6, 1775, *ibid.*, I, 41.

20. Same to same, "In Camp near St. John's," October 5, 1775, *ibid.*, I, 55.

21. Gouverneur Morris to RRL, October, 1775, *ibid.*, I, 49.

22. Robert R. Livingston, Sr., to Richard Montgomery, Rhinebeck, November 15, 1775, Livingston Family Papers, NYPL.

23. Richard Montgomery to Robert R. Livingston, Sr., "Headquarters before Quebec," December 16, 1775, Livingston-Bancroft Transcripts, NYPL, I, 81 ff.

24. *Idem.*

25. Alden, *op. cit.*, 58.

26. Richard Montgomery to RRL, "Headquarters before Quebec," December 17, 1775, Livingston-Bancroft Transcripts, NYPL, I, 83.

27. Richard Montgomery to Robert R. Livingston, Sr., cited in 23 *supra*. Same to same, Montreal, November 13, 1775, Wainwright Autograph Collection, Princeton University Library: "I send Harry with my dispatches which gives him an opportunity of going to Philadelphia."

28. *JCC*, III, 476, 477, 479, 484. His argument was that you cannot make war without money, and how can you make money without maintaining commercial relations of some kind with England? "We are between the hawk and the buzzard; we puzzle ourselves between commercial and warlike opposition."

29. RRL, note dated October 27, 1775, RRLP.

30. Alden, *op. cit.*, 43 ff.

31. RRL to Jay, Fort George, November 27, 1775, Jay Papers, Columbia University Libraries' Special Collections.

32. RRL to Richard Montgomery, Ticonderoga, November 29, 1775, Livingston-Bancroft Transcripts, NYPL, I, 73. The appeal to the Canadians, contained in this draft, suggests that they should choose a provincial convention which would eventually send delegates to Congress.

33. RRL, draft of a letter from the committee to Richard Montgomery, Ticonderoga, November 30, 1775, *ibid.*, I, 75.

34. *Idem.* Also see 32 *supra*.

35. RRL to Jay, Albany, December 6, 1775, Jay Papers, Columbia University Libraries' Special Collections.

36. Catharine L. Garretson to George Bancroft, cited in 15 *supra*. RRL to Jay, Clermont, December 29, 1775, Jay Papers, Columbia University Libraries' Special Collections.

37. RRL to Viscount Ranelagh, Manor of Livingston, February 3, 1776, RRLP.

38. RRL to James Duane, February 16, 1776, Livingston-Bancroft Transcripts, NYPL, I, 125.

39. RRL to Jay, Clermont, March 20, 1776, *The Correspondence and Public Papers of John Jay*, I, 48.

40. Jay to RRL, Philadelphia, March 4, 1776, *ibid.*, I, 43.

41. RRL to James Duane, February 16, 1776, cited in 38 *supra*.

PART TWO, CHAPTER TWO

1. Lawrence H. Gipson, *The Coming of the Revolution, 1763-1775* (New York, 1954), 231.

2. Carl L. Becker, *History of Political Parties in the Province of New York, 1760-1776*, 229-35.

3. *Ibid.*, 243.

4. *Ibid.*, 247-49. Curtis P. Nettels, *George Washington and American Independence* (Boston, 1951), 202-13.

5. Nettels, *op. cit.*, 284-85.

6. *Ibid.*, 284-87. Becker, *op. cit.*, 247-53.

7. RRL to James Duane, February 16, 1776, Livingston-Bancroft Transcripts, NYPL, I, 125.

8. Nettels, *op. cit.*, 221.

9. James Duane to RRL, Philadelphia, March 20, 1776, Livingston-Bancroft Transcripts, NYPL, I, 139. Cf. Dr. John Jones to James Duane, New York, April 14, 1776, Duane Papers, NYHS: "Mr. Livingstone [*i.e.*, Philip Livingston] who is lately returned from you informs me that Congress really expects commissioners— if they come quickly and offer you Carte Blanche, perhaps we may have peace upon that footing of reconciliation, otherwise, from the rising spirit of the people, I presume you will be under the necessity of declaring yourselves The High & Mighty States of the Thirteen United Colonies." Dr. Jones clearly expected little of the commissioners.

10. C. F. Adams, ed., *The Works of John Adams* (10 vols., Boston, 1856), II (Diary), 347.

11. *Docs. Rel. Col. Hist. NY*, VIII, 663-81. RRL to Jay, Clermont, February 15, 1776, Jay Papers, Columbia University Libraries' Special Collections.

12. Becker, *op. cit.*, 267, quoting *American Archives*, Peter Force, ed., Fourth Series, 1774-1776 (6 vols., Washington, 1837), VI, 840, 895, 994.

13. Robert R. Livingston, Sr., to Robert Livingston, of Clermont, New York, January 11, 1711, RRLP: "Cousin Robert is quite unfortunate in his children. His first son [Peter R. Livingston] goes up in the spring to live at the Manor & his good and generous Father will be obliged to advance eleven thousand pounds for him after which he will not be worth one groat." Same to Margaret Beekman Livingston, June 20, 1771, Livingston Family Papers, NYPL. As regards "poor Peter's affair . . . it is better that the Manor be incumbered and he reduced to live on the produce of a single farm" than that he should compound with his creditors. From this indebtedness, he never escaped. Peter R. Livingston was president of the New York Congress which voted July 8, 1776, to approve the Declaration of Independence. He did not approve and did not cast a vote, although he afterward identified himself with the patriot cause.

14. RRL to Jay, Philadelphia, May 17, 1776, *The Correspondence and Public Papers of John Jay*, I, 58.

15. *Idem.* Duane to Jay, Philadelphia, May 18, 1776, *The Correspondence and Public Papers of John Jay*, I, 61.

16. *JCC*, V, 388, 391, 426.

17. Delegates to New York Congress, June 8, 1776 (draft by RRL), Livingston-Bancroft Transcripts, NYPL, I, 185. *The Writings of Thomas Jefferson*, Paul Leicester Ford, ed. (10 vols., New York, 1892-1899), I, 21 ff.

18. Becker, *op. cit.*, 271, quoting *American Archives*, Fourth Series, VI, 814. RRL to Nathaniel Odle, Esq., Philadelphia, June 17, 1776, Livingston-Bancroft Transcripts, NYPL, I, 189.

19. Alexander C. Flick, ed., *History of the State of New York*, IV, 153. Becker, *op. cit.*, 267, 272. The Mechanics' Committee also requested that the delegates at Philadelphia should be given the power to vote for independence. To this the Congress replied, May 29, that they were determined "patiently to await and firmly to abide by whatever a majority of that august body shall think needful." *Ibid.*, 270, quoting *American Archives*, Fourth Series, VI, 614, 1362-63.

20. *The Writings of Thomas Jefferson*, I, 32. Becker, *op. cit.*, 272. Nettles, *op. cit.*, 288, 294, and 295, quoting Washington to Congress, June 30, 1776, *The Writings of George Washington*, J. C. Fitzpatrick, ed. (39 vols., Washington, 1931-1941), V, 203.

21. *The Writings of Thomas Jefferson*, I, 28.

22. Livingston-Bancroft Transcripts, NYPL, I, 188.

23. *The Writings of Thomas Jefferson*, I, 28 n.

24. No Loyalists voted in this election. For Dutchess County, it was a simple matter of arrangement. On May 29, Jay wrote RRL from New York to say that he believed a resolution would be taken to secure additional members; "and should my conjectures prove right, I shall inform the members of Dutchess of your readiness to serve, and advise them to elect you." *The Correspondence and Public Papers of John Jay*, I, 65. On June 11, he wrote to RRL: "I have settled matters with James Livingston, that if no other of the present members should resign, he will in order to make room for you. I have written Benson on the subject." Becker, *op. cit.*, 275.

25. RRL to Jay, Philadelphia, July 6, 1776, Jay Papers, Columbia University Libraries' Special Collections.

26. "Immersed in . . . local defense" means that he had just attended at Poughkeepsie, on August 1, a meeting of the Secret Committee of the State of New York (present: Gilbert Livingston, William Paulding, RRL) and had received instructions to proceed to New York City to confer with General Washington on the defense of the state, and give him all the assistance in his power: for which purpose he was vested with all the powers of the committee. Gilbert Livingston Correspondence in Livingston-Redmond Papers, Franklin Delano Roosevelt Library.

PART TWO, CHAPTER THREE

1. Margaret Beekman Livingston to RRL, July 6, 1776, Livingston Family Papers, NYPL.
2. Wesley Frank Craven, *The Legend of the Founding Fathers* (New York, 1956), 55, quoting Jay to the Reverend Samuel Miller, February 28, 1800, in Princeton University Library.
3. *JPC*, I, 532.
4. Frank Monaghan, *John Jay*, 85. Alexander C. Flick, ed., *History of the State of New York*, IV, 155.
5. Henry Beekman Livingston to RRL, Fort Constitution, May 29, 1776, Livingston-Bancroft Transcripts, NYPL, I, 177, on the condition of Fort Constitution [Fort Lee] and Fort Montgomery at that time. Washington to James Duane, New York, August 8, 1776, *ibid.*, I, 193, on the weak condition of the army—a total of 17,225 men, of which 10,514 were fit for duty.
6. The committee was composed of John Jay, John Sloss Hobart, William Smith, William Duer, Gouverneur Morris, RRL, John Broome, John Morin Scott, Abraham Yates, Henry Wisner, Samuel Townsend, Charles Dewitt, and Robert Yates. James Duane was added in September. Flick, *op. cit.*, IV, 153.
7. *Ibid.*, IV, 155.
8. *JPC*, I, 566, 593. Robert Yates was chairman of the secret committee on fortifications, according to *Calendar of Historical Manuscripts . . .*, I, 425-26. John Jay, Christopher Tappen, and Gilbert Livingston were the other members.
9. *JPC*, I, 599, 627.
10. RRL to Edward Rutledge, Fishkill, October 10, 1776, Livingston-Bancroft Transcripts, NYPL, I, 229, tells of these letters to Washington.
11. Washington to RRL, "Mr. Lowe's," October 20, 1776, *ibid.*, I, 259.
12. Douglas Southall Freeman, *George Washington*, IV, 236-38, gives a most eloquent description of this state of affairs.
13. Tench Tilghman to RRL, Headquarters White Plains, November 6 and 8, 1776; RRL to Tench Tilghman, November 9, 1776, Livingston-Bancroft Transcripts, NYPL, I, 267, 271, 275. The committee was appointed September 17, 1776; and its members were William Allison, William Duer, RRL, and Henry Wisner. *JPC*, I, 627. The first letter was written by William Duer to Tench Tilghman, September 22, 1776. RRL to Tench Tilghman, Fishkill, October 10, 1776, says that even a defeat at New York, though dispiriting, would not matter if proper magazines were laid up for the defense of the Highlands. Tench Tilghman to RRL and William Duer, October 13, 1776, replies that "the General thinks so well of your hint of laying up magazines beyond the Highlands, that he has ordered his Commissary General to attend immediately to it." RRL to Tench Tilghman, Fishkill, December 9, 1776, says: "Tho' we are constantly employed in the detection of Treasons, yet Plots multiply upon us daily, and we have every reason to dread an open rebellion." In this letter, he says that cavalry should be raised; and that their not having been raised must be set down "in the same chapter of ignorance and

error in which our contempt for military discipline is written." For some idea of the treasons which this committee detected, see William Duer to Tench Tilghman, Fishkill, September 28, October 1, 3, 8, and 10, 1776. The last mentions the fear of an immediate Tory uprising in Dutchess County. All these letters are in William Duer Papers, NYHS.

14. *JPC*, I, 633, 635, 638, 684, 719, 721, 726, 727. *Calendar of Historical Manuscripts . . .* , I, 504-09, 512, 525, gives details of the committee appointed to cooperate with General Schuyler. In *ibid.*, I, 505, will be found the action taken regarding an insurrection believed to be imminent in the Manor of Livingston, where the militia who could be relied upon were few and badly armed. The Committee of the Manor of Livingston was requested to form and equip a company of Rangers to be kept in readiness for immediate service. Lieutenant Colonel Henry Livingston, a son of Robert Livingston, Jr., the third Lord of the Manor, was to be sent a copy of this resolve. Edward Rutledge to RRL, Philadelphia, October 21, 1776, Livingston-Bancroft Transcripts, NYPL, I, 217, describes RRL as "riding about the country in counteracting the schemes of the Tories."

15. Edward Rutledge to RRL, Philadelphia, September 23, 1776, Livingston-Bancroft Transcripts, NYPL, I, 213.

16. RRL to Philip Schuyler, Fishkill, October 2, 1776, Schuyler Papers, NYPL, saying "what he alludes to I cannot positively say tho' I can in part guess—I have not yet seen Jay but have little hopes of his being prevailed upon to go, as his wife is now here and very unwell. With respect to myself I have such a variety of publick & private reasons to detain me that I cannot as yet leave this." RRL to Edward Rutledge, October 10, 1776, Livingston-Bancroft Transcripts, NYPL, I, 229.

17. For the New York Constitution see *JPC*, I, 834-98; Flick, *op. cit.*, IV, 153-67; E. Wilder Spaulding, *New York in the Critical Period, 1783-1789*, 87-95; Jay to RRL and Gouverneur Morris, April 29, 1777, in *The Correspondence and Public Papers of John Jay*, I, 128-36; D. L. Colvin, *Bicameral Principle in the New York Legislature*, 30 ff.; Clinton Rossiter, *Seedtime of the Republic*, 402-39.

18. *A History of Columbia University 1754-1904*, I, 451.

19. Rossiter, *op. cit.*, 360, for Blackstone; 358-59, for Locke and Montesquieu.

20. John Adams claimed that Jay took this disquisition—it was in the form of a letter to George Wythe—home with him to study for the New York Constitution. His claim is substantial (*The Works of John Adams*, III, 59), and in the light of RRL's letter to Rutledge (see 16 *supra*), it is difficult to resist. From this letter, too, it appears that RRL studied Algernon Sidney.

21. Monaghan, *op. cit.*, 94.

22. The Reverend J. H. Livingston to RRL, Albany, February 28, 1777, is for "all sects upon an equal and proper footing"; but on April 8, 1777, same to same, he would exclude papists from religious tolerance. Same to same, March 17, 1777, writes of "Foolish Deism." All in RRLP.

23. *JPC*, I, 910.

24. Hamilton to RRL, Headquarters Morristown, May 19, 1777, RRLP. The letter is full of interest to students of Hamilton. Hamilton also says (1) The executive lacks vigor, nor should his election be trusted to "the people at large." (The £100 freeholders!) (2) He believes that there should have been *one* chamber, not two, and that this should have been elected "really and not nominally by the people"— as the Assembly was, in his opinion. (3) "The complexity of your Legislature will occasion delay." On the whole, except for 1, a distinctly radical opinion!

25. *JPC*, I, 910.

26. Monaghan, *op. cit.*, 99. *The Correspondence and Public Papers of John Jay*, I, 137. RRL to William Duer, June 12, 1777, RRLP.

27. Henry Beekman Livingston to RRL, Fort Constitution, May 29, 1776, Livingston-Bancroft Transcripts, NYPL, I, 177, says that two New England men have declared on oath that Schuyler has a general's commission in the "regular," *i.e.*, British, army. "God grant it may be no more than a malicious lie."

28. *DAB* (1946 ed.), Scott, John Morin, XVI, 495. *The Works of John Adams*, II, 349. Flick, *op. cit.*, IV, 168.

29. The returns for this election are incomplete. Monaghan, *op. cit.*, 99, suggests a close race, with the soldier vote deciding the issue. Clinton was elected lieutenant governor as well, which office he resigned.

30. Flick, *op. cit.*, IV, 168. Spaulding, *op. cit.*, 97.

31. Flick, *op. cit.*, IV, 171, 172.

32. *The Correspondence and Public Papers of John Jay*, I, 147. Gouverneur Morris to RRL, Kingston, October 8, 1777, RRLP.

33. Hamilton to RRL, Headquarters Morristown, July 6, 1777. John Carter to Walter Livingston, Albany, July 23, 1777. Both in RRLP.

34. John Carter to Walter Livingston, Albany, July 7, 9, 14, 23, August 10, 1777, RRLP.

35. Walter Livingston to John Carter, Teviotdale, August 11, 1777, Walter Livingston Letter Books, RRLP.

36. An extensive account of Henry Beekman Livingston's quarrel with McDougall will be found in the McDougall Papers, NYHS. The court-martial and reprimand of Livingston are in *Calendar of Historical Manuscripts . . .*, II, 153-59. Also Henry Beekman Livingston to RRL, Peekskill, June 30, 1777, RRLP. In this letter, there is enclosed a copy of Washington to Henry Beekman Livingston, Headquarters Middle Brook, June 1, 1777, in which Washington says that differences between officers are always disagreeable, but "when they happen between those for whom I have a regard they are doubly so."

37. RRL to William Duer, June 12, 1777, RRLP. It is a safe assumption that RRL did not confide these views to Duer alone.

38. Letter of the Committee on Insurrection at Rhinebeck and Livingston Manor, RRL, Chairman, May 9, 1777, *JPC*, I, 918.

39. RRL to John Hancock, Kingston, June 11, 1777, RRLP.

40. Freeman, *op. cit.*, IV, 444.

41. Washington to RRL, Camp at the Clove, July 18, 1777, RRLP.

42. *JPC*, I, 997, 1014.

43. Hamilton to RRL, Camp at the Cross Roads, August 10, 1777, RRLP.

44. John R. Livingston to RRL, Clermont, August 29, 1777, RRLP: "This day Harry Livingston dined with us and . . . assured me that if a man had twenty thousand pounds to lay out [at Boston] that we should clear a vast deal of money . . . now what I mean to propose is that you should give me leave to draw upon you at four days sight for ten thousand pounds to be laid out on our joint account. . . . You need not borrow the money until I draw for it . . ." Walter Livingston to Mrs. Catharine Schuyler, August 16, 1777, Walter Livingston Letter Books, RRLP.

45. Henry Beekman Livingston to RRL, Camp near Stillwater, October 1, 1777. Also same to same, October 4 and 5, 1777. Also same to same, Saratoga, October 14, 1777: "In the last engagement my regiment was the first that entered the enemies lines, and I believe I can safely affirm that I was the first man in there next to Genl Arnold who was on Horse Back." All in RRLP.

46. Gouverneur Morris to RRL, Kingston, October 13, 1777, RRLP.

47. General John Vaughan to General Sir Henry Clinton, On Board the Friendship off Esopus, October 17, 1777, Clinton Papers, Clements Library.

48. Same to same, Livingston's Manor, Sunday, October 19, 1777, *ibid.*

49. *JPC*, I, 1005. Mrs. Catharine L. Garretson, "Memoir," Wainwright Autograph Collection, Princeton University Library, says that Captain Montgomery was a prisoner from Burgoyne's army; and that his surgeon wished to save Clermont by keeping Montgomery in bed; but that RRL would not allow this, and sent them off into safekeeping elsewhere. "Our House and my Br's were then consume[d] houses, barns, stocks, Mills, everything." Actually, RRL was not present on this unhappy occasion: or so it would appear from RRL to Pierre Van Cortlandt, Salisbury, October 28, 1777: "I thought it improper when the enemy came up the river to leave this side of the water, which was unfortunate, in wanting both yours and the Governor's direction. I therefore remained with the militia till the enemy left us. I am just now arrived at this place in order to inquire into the situation of my family, which has hitherto been left to shift for themselves. . . ." Quoted in Edwin Brockholst Livingston, *The Livingstons of Livingston Manor* (New York, 1910), 284. RRL to Viscount Ranelagh, Salisbury, November 2, 1777, says: "Gen'l Vaughan [came] up Hudsons [River] at the head of a considerable body of troops —In which . . . he acquired Laurels of a very modern growth by burning about 200 farm houses & barns & a few country seats among them my mother's and mine (which being at the waters edge and [under] cover of the british shiping were destroyed . . .)." Words in parentheses were deleted from the draft. RRLP.

50. General John Vaughan to Sir Henry Clinton, October 19, 1777. Clinton Papers, Clements Library.

51. Same to same, October 26, 1777, *ibid.*

52. General Horatio Gates to Sir Henry Clinton, Ship Mercury, October 31, 1777, RRLP. This is in Henry Beekman Livingston's handwriting. A slightly different version is in the Clinton Papers, Clements Library. Vaughan's list of what he burned is on the back of this version, with Clinton's comments. In RRL's handwriting there is in RRLP a draft of a letter of protest from the New York Legislature to Congress, undated, which contains the following deleted passage: "We wish the enemy to be informed that for every [one] of our countrymen who has starved in jails one of them shall die on the Gibbet—That for every house or barn unnecessarily fired a certain number of their [*unfinished*]."

53. Gouverneur Morris to RRL, Bounton, December 1, 1777, RRLP.

PART TWO, CHAPTER FOUR

1. RRL to John Alsop, Manor of Livingston, December 19, 1777, RRLP. According to "R. R. Livingston's Account Book, Clermont N.Y.," NYHS, the amount was £2,291/1/4: *i.e.*, "July 13, 1777 sent by Marshal to Mr. Alsop which refused to receive-£2291-1-4."

2. Egbert Benson to RRL, Red Hook, December 3, 1777, RRLP. Italics inserted.

3. His commission, so dated and at Marble Town, is in RRLP.

4. RRL to Jay, Rhinebeck, February 2, 1779, RRLP.

5. RRL to Gouverneur Morris, Rhinebeck, January 29, 1778. RRL to Philip Schuyler, Poughkeepsie, March 29, 1778. RRL to Gouverneur Morris, Manor of Livingston, June 13, 1778. All in RRLP.

6. RRL to Gouverneur Morris, Manor of Livingston, April 6, 1778, RRLP.

7. Same to same, Manor of Livingston, June 13, 1779, RRLP.

8. RRL to William Duer, Rhinebeck, January 29, 1778, RRLP. So also RRL to Washington, Manor of Livingston, January 12, 1778, RRLP: Public credit is "stretched beyond all bounds. Certificates which are the only cash of the Quartermasters forage masters and Commissaries have now lost their credit, but force alone affords a scanty supply to the Army." See also Livingston-Bancroft Transcripts, NYPL, II, 87.

9. RRL to Gouverneur Morris, Rhinebeck, January 29, 1778, RRLP.
10. Same to same, January, 1778, RRLP.
11. Washington to RRL, Valley Forge, March 11, 1778, RRLP. In this letter, Washington says of General Putnam that the inquiry into the loss of Fort Montgomery will probably afford just grounds for his removal, "but whether it does or not, the prejudices of all ranks in that quarter against him are so great that it would be impolitic for him to return."
12. RRL to Gouverneur Morris, Manor of Livingston, April 6, 1778, RRLP.
13. RRL to William Duer, Clermont, July 3, 1778, RRLP.
14. RRL to Gouverneur Morris, Clermont, July 27, 1778, RRLP.
15. RRL to Jay, Poughkeepsie, March 4, 1779, RRLP. RRL says that this bill was defeated in the Senate, which showed that party spirit was dying down, and that "other little squibs have miscarried."
16. RRL to Gouverneur Morris, Manor of Livingston, June 13, 1778: "At present I have dipped my hands in mortar in spite of the want of leisure, of materials, & workmen. I have such strong attachments to Claremont that I find myself at home nowhere else—And am now laying out as much in building a paltry farm house as would formerly have built me a palace." And Governor George Clinton to RRL, Poughkeepsie, April 16, 1778: "I have not granted any exemptions to workmen employed by the people who were burned out last fall nor do I think it would be prudent until the drafts for filling up the Continental battalion are compleated. When that is done I will chearfully furnish you & Mrs. Livingston with your full Proportion." Both in RRLP.
17. Gouverneur Morris to RRL, Philadelphia, January 21, 1779, RRLP.
18. Jay to RRL, Philadelphia, February 16, 1779, RRLP.
19. RRL to William Duer, Clermont, July 3, 1778, RRLP.
20. RRL to Jay, Rhinebeck, January 25, 1779, RRLP.
21. Henry Beekman Livingston to RRL, Say Brook, September 24, 1776, says he has carried off 3,129 sheep and about 400 cattle. "Oliver Delancey in the character of Brigadier General has been very Busy. I am proscribed a reward of £500 is set upon my Head I have great reason to think through his means." Also same to same, August or September, 1776. He had been to Long Island with his detachment and part of Colonel Richmond's regiment of Rhode Islanders. "I should at this time have broke up Master Oliver's Brigade but was opposed by the Rhode Islanders officers who declared they would not continue in so dangerous a situation any longer." He received a letter of approbation from Governor Jonathan Trumbull. Both in RRLP.
22. Henry Beekman Livingston to RRL, Tiverton, August 8, 1778; Camp Rhode Island, August 19, 1788; Tiverton, August 31, 1788. Henry was a volunteer on furlough, and was given command of the Light Corps, which, in the battle of August 29, beat back "the Grenadiers and the Anspachers." He says, indeed, that he had the "Honor to turn the Fate of the Day." Christopher Ward, *The War of the Revolution*, II, 592, says that "their [*i.e.*, that part of Sullivan's army under fire] spirit and resolution was without fault." Livingston adds that he was thanked by General Sullivan in orders, "but he has made his thanks so general that I conceive the Honour is much lessened." He writes to RRL, Boston, September 15, 1778, that his Light Corps consisted of 270 Continentals and 70 militia. All in RRLP.
23. Henry Beekman Livingston to RRL, Camp at White Marsh, November 30/ December 1, 1777: "How can we hang men for desertion when we starve them with cold?" Same to same, Valley Forge, December 24, 1777, complains of the mismanagement of our commissaries, "who are treading in the paths of our Quartermasters and Forrage Masters who have already starved our Horses."

He adds that all the soldiers and officers are lousy, and that there is no liquor, no tea, no sugar, and no vegetables. "Poor Jack has been necessitated to make up his Blanket into a vest and Breeches. If I did not fear starving to death I would do the same." Same to same, Valley Forge, March 25, 1778: "We have a Prussian Lieutenant General (arrived in camp) and Knight of the Black Eagle which he wears made of lead tied to his button holes. He is an agreeable man about fifty-five and talks English pretty well, French and German as far as I am capable of judging very well. . . ." All in RRLP.

24. Asked by RRL as to this—RRL to Washington, Manor of Livingston, December 8, 1777—Washington replies, Headquarters Valley Forge, December 27, 1777, RRLP: "The only dispute that has come to my knowledge is that between him and Col° Cortlandt, and, in that, I must say Col° Cortlandt has in my opinion an undoubted right to the precedency, upon principles of strict justice." He adds: "I have a high opinion of him [Henry Beekman Livingston] and shall not be forgetful of him."

25. Henry Beekman Livingston to Henry Laurens, Philadelphia, November 19, 1778, RRLP.

26. Gouverneur Morris to RRL, Philadelphia, January 21, 1779, RRLP.

27. Henry Beekman Livingston to RRL, Boston, September 5, 1778, RRLP.

28. John R. Livingston to RRL, Boston, October 17, 1776, RRLP

29. Same to same, Rhinebeck, January 25, 1779, RRLP.

30. Same to same, Rhinebeck, January 13, 1780, RRLP.

31. Same to same, Boston, March 29, 1780, RRLP. Morris said that one should not trade with one's enemies and that Dr. Franklin would not grant a permit.

32. Same to same, Boston, November 15, 1780, RRLP.

33. Same to same, Clermont, August 27, 1780, RRLP.

34. Jay to RRL and Gouverneur Morris, Philadelphia, September 29, 1779, RRLP, says that he has suggested their names to Governor Clinton as delegates "in order to settle our New England and Vermont" disputes. So Jay to Governor Clinton, Philadelphia, September, 1779, in E. C. Burnett, ed., *Letters of Members of the Continental Congress* (8 vols., Washington, 1921-1936), IV, 460-61. See also Nathaniel Scudder to Richard Henry Lee, Philadelphia, November 16, 1779, *ibid.*, IV, 520.

35. JCC, XV, 1293. His credentials were dated October 15, 1779.

36. Henri Doniol, *Histoire de la Participation de la France à l'Établissement des États-Unis d'Amérique*, IV, 333. Description in *Rapport fort étendu de la Luzerne*, 11 February, 1780 (*AAE, EU*, Tom 11, No. 53). Irving Brant, *James Madison: The Nationalist, 1780-1787* (Indianapolis and New York, 1948), 31.

37. John Sloss Hobart to RRL, Sharon, November 19, 1779; Philip Schuyler to RRL, Morristown, December 7, 1779, RRLP.

38. George Clinton to RRL, Poughkeepsie, January 7, 1780, RRLP.

39. Thomas C. Cochran, *New York in the Confederation: An Economic Study* (Philadelphia, 1932), 46-47.

40. Margaret Beekman Livingston to RRL, Clermont, December 30, 1779, RRLP.

41. Same to same, Clermont, February, 1780, RRLP.

42. RRL to George Clinton, May 21, 1780, RRLP.

43. George Clinton to RRL, Poughkeepsie, July 7, 1780, RRLP: "I soon discovered from the Temper of a majority of both Houses & the Reluctance with which they engaged in any business but such as was immediately calculated for forwarding the operations of the present Campaign that an Application at this time would at least have been fruitless if not Injurious." The Governor, it would seem, writes not without irony.

44. See 34 *supra*. See Egbert Benson to RRL, January 3, 1780, RRLP, where Benson tells RRL that he is mistaken if he thinks he can leave when Duane and Scott arrive. He was elected to settle "the Boundary business."

45. James Duane to RRL, Manor Livingston and Albany, January 18, 1780, RRLP.

46. RRL to George Clinton, Philadelphia, November 30, 1779. The line he suggested was to be "extended from the northwest corner of Pennsylvania to the Lake Ontario our western boundary, and from thence along the northwest shore of Lake Ontario and the river St. Lawrence to the bounds of Canada, and from thence along those boundaries to the State of New Hampshire. This will secure Niagara to us, and the navigation of Lake Ontario. It will put our old claim out of dispute, enable Congress and us to apply our lands to countersecure our money." Burnett, *op. cit.*, IV, 530. Governor Clinton to RRL, Poughkeepsie, January 7, 1780, RRLP: "It may be to our interest to give up a part of our western lands; if by this we may be able to enjoy the Remainder free from every claim. —On this condition I would for my own Part be contented with the Boundary described in your letter."

47. Nathanael Greene to Moore Furman, January 4, 1780, quoted in Douglas Southall Freeman, *George Washington*, V, 144.

48. Washington to Joseph Reed, May 28, 1780, *ibid.*, V, 166-67.

49. Washington to Joseph Jones, May 31, 1780, *ibid.*, V, 167.

50. RRL and delegates to Governor Clinton, Philadelphia, March 20, 1780, RRLP.

51. E. C. Burnett, *Continental Congress* (Washington, 1941), 442 ff. *JCC*, XVI, 36, 38.

52. Philip Schuyler to RRL, Morristown, December 7, 1779: "If the Board of War should be reorganized on your plan and that appointment be offered as you wish It will be necessary to give more ample powers than the board at present possesses." Same to same, Saratoga, December 10, 1779: "I have very seriously and with much attention reflected on the proposition you were so obliging [as] to make before I left Philadelphia. . . . If objection should be made to Invest me solely with the power intended for the board of war, and to let the gentlemen now on that board remain and be considered deputy secretaries, Congress may if they please appoint me Secretary at War and president of the board of war, deciding what powers shall be invested in the Secretary, and what he shall enjoy in conjunction with the board at which he is to preside." Both in RRLP. RRL to Philip Schuyler, Philadelphia, December 20, 1779: "Greene has offered his resignation which at the present we have refused all eyes are fixed upon you Wd to God you could be persuaded to take it with [y]our former rank," Burnett, *Letters of Members of the Continental Congress*, IV, 543.

53. Burnett, *Continental Congress*, 446.

54. *Ibid.*, 447. Washington to James Duane, May 14, 1780, Burnett, *Letters of Members of the Continental Congress*, V, 140. Philip Schuyler to James Duane, May 13, 1780, Duane Papers, NYHS.

55. Brant, *op. cit.*, 35.

56. RRL to Philip Schuyler, Philadelphia, June 9, 1870, Burnett, *Letters of Members of the Continental Congress*, V, 202.

57. RRL to James Duane, Valley Lebanon, May 2, 1780, Duane Papers, NYHS.

58. Nathaniel Peabody to Josiah Bartlett, August 6, 1780: "I once read of a people who were at times led by a cloud; and I have known of a people whose Grand Multiformed Sanhedrin were often times in the midst of a Fog," Burnett, *Continental Congress*, 465.

59. Burnett, *ibid.*, 458, believes that the undated report in *JCC* for October 3, 1780,

dates from *circa* June 19, when RRL was chairman of the committee appointed on Luzerne's memorial of June 18, and that the report emanates from this committee. It could also have emanated from the committee appointed to consider Luzerne's memorial of May 17, and RRL's remark as to "the grand business" (RRL to Philip Schuyler, Philadelphia, May 26, 1780, Burnett, *Letters of Members of the Continental Congress*, V, 170) possibly refers to these resolutions. His report was presented May 24, 1780 (see Francis Wharton, ed., *The Revolutionary Diplomatic Correspondence of the United States*, III, 699-701) and the "grand design" may also be an allusion to this report.

60. Burnett, *Continental Congress*, 485.
61. Brant, *op. cit.*, 41.
62. Philip Schuyler to RRL, Philadelphia, April 23, 1780, RRLP.
63. John Mathews to RRL, Philadelphia, April 24, 1780, Burnett, *Letters of Members of the Continental Congress*, V, 123.
64. Marbois to RRL, Philadelphia, May 9, 1780, RRLP.
65. RRL to Governor Clinton, Philadelphia, May 18, 1780, Burnett, *Letters of Members of the Continental Congress*, V, 150.
66. New York delegates to Governor Clinton, Philadelphia, May 21, 1780, *ibid.*, V, 161.
67. Burnett, *Continental Congress*, 475.
68. Carl Van Doren, *Secret History of the American Revolution* (New York, 1941), 172.
69. Washington to RRL, Ramapo, June 29, 1780, RRLP. Washington to Reed, October 18, 1780, *Writings*, J. C. Fitzpatrick, ed., XX, 214.
70. William Wallace, *Traitorous Hero* (New York, 1954), 229. Van Doren, *op. cit.*, 304, quoting Hannah Arnold to Arnold, September 4, 1780, in Tomlinson Collection, NYPL.
71. RRL to Gouverneur Morris, Clermont, November 20, 1780, RRLP.
72. Margaret Beekman Livingston to John R. Livingston, Clermont, January 21, 1781, RRLP.

PART TWO, CHAPTER FIVE

1. Thomas C. Cochran, *New York in the Confederation: An Economic Study*, 48, 49.
2. Walter Livingston Letter Books, Manor Resolutions of January 5, 1781, RRLP.
3. RRL to Washington, Clermont, January 8, 1781, RRLP.
4. RRL to Gouverneur Morris, Clermont, January 10, 1781, RRLP.
5. Walter Livingston to Captain Jacob Bogardus of the Oblong, January, 1781, Walter Livingston Letter Books, RRLP. These letter books show also that the manor committee was composed of John Livingston, Walter Livingston, and Samuel Ten Broeck—two leading men and one substantial one—and that the chair was taken by Captain Jacob Shaver, a small farmer. See also Walter Livingston to RRL, Manor of Livingston, January 7, 1781, RRLP.
6. *Idem.*
7. RRL to Gouverneur Morris, cited in 4 *supra*.
8. Washington to RRL, New Windsor, January 31, 1781, RRLP.
9. RRL to Marbois, Clermont, June 4, 1781, RRLP: "I was fortunate enough to discover a Plott among a number of people in my neighborhood to go off to the enemy westward & plunder the houses of the leading Whigs & as some say escorte me to Niagara—seven or eight of them I took & committed to jail but about 20 escaped on finding they were discovered and among them one of my own domesticks who had been a british soldier."

10. RRL to Gouverneur Morris, Clermont, April 3, 1781, RRLP.

11. *Idem:* "The misled people are recovering their senses I shall aid them to more advantage hereafter when not involved in the disgraces that I see are soon to fall upon their present leaders." For an example of RRL's lack of influence with the Legislature, there is in RRLP the draft of an address from the Legislature of New York to their constituents, in RRL's handwriting, with amendments by other hands, which shows that it was prepared by RRL at the request of several members of both houses and that it was so amended in joint committee as—Egbert Benson certifies on the back—no longer to be considered the work of RRL. His references to a system of taxation which left "but too much room for the prejudices and partiality of those employed in collecting them to work upon" and to "the inequality of the assessments of provision & forage" were deleted. He was particularly irritated when, in his sentence "The extraordinary powers given to Commissioners for defeating conspiracies may at least be palliated if not justified by our peculiar situation," the words *at least be palliated if not* were deleted. The draft shows that RRL's strictures against excessive taxation did not differ materially from those of the Manor meeting of January 5. What he objected to was the holding of a meeting at all.

12. Marbois to RRL, Philadelphia, January 2, 1781, RRLP.

13. RRL to Marbois, Clermont, February 18, 1781, RRLP.

14. James Lovell to Samuel Adams, February 16, 1781: "We are to discuss next Sat'day the Proposition for appointing a Resident with his official powers to go to France, instead of a Sec'y to the Embassy. This will dignify the place enough for R. R. Livingston. And I am somewhat inclined to think our Affairs here make several wish to be away from the fatigue which they cause. I do not like the scale of influence abroad should have weights from New York rather than from some other State. But I shall not be inclined to stand against R.R.L. in the Nomination for the new office . . . ," Francis Wharton, *Revolutionary Diplomatic Correspondence of the United States*, V, 40. Marbois to RRL, Philadelphia, May 9, 1780, RRLP: "*Il n'avoit qu'un Seul cas où nous aurions pu nous applaudir de votre départ; c'est celui où les circonstances vous auroient mis à portée de Servir votre patrie en Europe et de consolider le même tems les liens qui unissent nos deux nations. Je suis persuadé que le Congrès ne peut faire qu'un bon Choix, et cependant je fais des voeux pour que ce choix ne se fasse pas avant que vos amis vous ayent determiné à revenir ici. Tout paroît dépendre du suffrage des Jerseys.*" Gouverneur Morris to RRL, Philadelphia, February 21, 1781, RRLP: "You desire to know in what quality Lawrence [sic] is gone to France. I answer he is gone in consequence of a Plan to remove Franklin indirectly a Thing which for obvious reasons could not be done directly. I believe he means well and I really love him as an agreeable sensible young man but I fear he will do mischief. If so the Blood be upon their Heads who sent him."

15. RRL to Gouverneur Morris, Clermont, June 4, 1781, RRLP.

16. RRL to James Duane, Clermont, November 12, 1780, Duane Papers, NYHS: "Have you done anything with the report for arranging the departments? This is called for on all hands. I hope the Committee of Ways and Means have reported at least as much as we agreed upon before I left you."

17. Irving Brant, *James Madison: The Nationalist, 1780-1787* (Indianapolis and New York, 1948), 122-24.

18. Gouverneur Morris to RRL, Philadelphia, February 21, 1781: "Lee, Maddison and yourself are in nomination. I believe you will be appointed." Nearly a month later —Gouverneur Morris to RRL, Philadelphia, March 14, 1781—Morris says that he believes that the duties of secretary for Foreign Affairs will be annexed to the secretaryship of Congress. That overtures were being made from the

other side is suggested in RRL to Samuel Adams, Clermont, March 18, 1781: where RRL asks Adams to give him "a transient view of what is doing behind the curtain. I only mean so much of it as a mere spectator may be indulged—tho as an old actor with a call to the stage in his pocket I might perhaps ask more— Your friend Mr. Otis did me the favor to pass a week with us." Gouverneur Morris to RRL, Philadelphia, May 7, 1781. RRL to Marbois, Clermont, July 7, 1781: "I am sorry to hear that Mr. Madison & I have been pitted against each other. . . . As we have one interest it should not be split. . . . Shd the choice fall on Mr. M—my esteem for him would leave no room for the mortification I might otherwise feel on such an occasion." All in RRLP.

19. Marbois to RRL, Philadelphia, March 27, 1781, RRLP: "*Nous évitons même de laisser paroître en faveur de qui nous faisons nos voeux; car avec certaines personnes ce seroit un motif d'exclusion.*"
20. Marbois to RRL, Philadelphia, June 29, 1781, RRLP: "*Je sais que votre État par des considérations particulières pourra former quelques objections à ce qui passera; et néanmoins je desire que les délégués soient présens. . . . Plus qu'il aura d'hommes éclairés en Congrès plus la conduite et le désintéressement du Roi auroient de Témoins et d'approbateurs.*"
21. For the Instructions, see Wharton, *op. cit.*, IV, 504-05.
22. Samuel Flagg Bemis, *Diplomacy of the American Revolution* (1957 ed.), 181-82, cites the memoir of February, 1781, in *AAE,EU*, XV, 269-78.
23. *Ibid.*, 184-85.
24. "Report of a Conference with the French Minister, Luzerne," in Congress, May 28, 1781; Luzerne to the President of Congress, Philadelphia, May 25, 1781, Wharton, *op. cit.*, IV, 453-57, 434.
25. Luzerne to Vergennes, June 11, 1781, *AAE,EU*, XVII. B. Fay, *Esprit Révolutionnaire en France et aux États-Unis à la Fin du XVIIIᵉ Siècle* (Paris, 1925), 88.
26. *Rapport du Ier Novembre*, 1781. Henri Doniol, *Histoire de la Participation de la France à l'Établissement des États-Unis d'Amérique*, V, 65 *n*.
27. Arthur Lee to Samuel Adams, August 13, 1781, E. C. Burnett, *Letters of Members of the Continental Congress*, VI, 176 *n*.
28. New York delegates to Governor Clinton, Philadelphia, August 10, 1781. James Mitchell Varnum to Washington, August 20, 1781: "We have been so fortunate at last as to elect a Minister of Foreign Affairs." Both in Burnett, *ibid.*, VI, 175, 191.
29. For a most illuminating account of the attitude of the *Philosophes* toward America, see Durand Echeverria, *Mirage in the West: A History of the French Image of American Society to 1815* (Princeton, 1957), Chapters I and II.
30. Thomas McKean to RRL, August 11, 1781. RRL to Marbois, Clermont, August 24, 1781. However, RRL to Gouverneur Morris, Clermont, August 24, 1781, says: "I feel I shd have been mortified at being passed by on this occasion, & yet I experience more pain than pleasure at the appointment." RRL to Thomas McKean, Clermont, August 24, 1781. Thomas McKean to RRL, Philadelphia, September 6, 1781. RRL to Thomas McKean, Clermont, September 23, 1781. All in RRLP. For the location of RRL's house in Philadelphia, see "The Autobiography of Peter Stephen Du Ponceau," *Pennsylvania Magazine of History and Biography*, LXII, No. 2 (April, 1939), 341.
31. RRL to Charles Thomson, Secretary of Congress, May 7, 1782; RRL to John Hanson, President of Congress, May 8, 1782, RRLP. The seating plan of the banquet shows RRL, as master of ceremonies, seated opposite the President; but Congress had first to correct its journals to show that the Secretary for Foreign Affairs was to invite in the name of Congress the heads of departments, the

President and Council of Pennsylvania, and any other whom he thought proper. Samuel Flagg Bemis, ed., *The American Secretaries of State and their Diplomacy*, I, 130. James Duane to RRL, Philadelphia, October 2, 1781, RRLP.

32. RRL, "Draft on the Present State of Europe, Not Sent," December, 1781, RRLP. RRL to the President of Congress, January 25, 1782, in Gaillard Hunt, *The Department of State*, 20-23.

33. "The Autobiography of Peter Stephen Du Ponceau," *loc. cit.*, LXIII, No. 3 (June 3, 1939), 337-38. For location of the office, see Bemis, *The American Secretaries of State*, I, 120, where the house is said to have been only twelve feet in width.

34. "Regulations for the Department of Foreign Affairs," In Congress, February 22, 1782, Wharton, *op. cit.* V, 199-201. *Secret Journals of the Acts and Proceedings of Congress, from the first meeting thereof to the Dissolution of the Confederation, by adoption of the Constitution of the United States* (4 vols., Boston, 1820-1821), III, 254. JCC, XXII, 87. For salary, *JCC*, XXI, 855. Walter Stone's name is mentioned in a Department of Foreign Affairs list, February, 1783, in RRLP. Exactly when Têtard joined the Department cannot be determined. Têtard's letter of December 10, 1781, is in RRLP.

35. Samuel Osgood to John Adams, Annapolis, December 7, 1783; Arthur Lee to Francis Dana, Philadelphia, July 6, 1782, Burnett, *Letters of Members of the Continental Congress*, VII, 380, VI, 225.

36. *JCC,* XXIII, 586-89.

37. RRL to Franklin, Philadelphia, September 5, 1782, Wharton, *op. cit.*, V, 696.

38. Franklin to RRL, Passy, December 6, 1782, *ibid.*, VI, 110-11.

39. RRL to Jay, Philadelphia, October 20, 1781, RRLP. The words "memorial, his ridiculous" were deleted in the draft, so that the letter (which is not in Wharton) reads: "His display of his public character."

40. RRL to John Adams, Philadelphia, November 20, 1781 (with passage deleted), RRLP. See also Wharton, *op. cit.*, IV, 850.

41. John Adams to RRL, Amsterdam, February 14, 1782, Wharton, *op. cit.*, V, 163.

42. Same to same, Amsterdam, February 21, 1782, *ibid.*, V, 196-97.

43. Bemis, *The American Secretaries of State*, I, 168. Francis Dana to John Adams, July 29, 1783, Wharton, *op. cit.*, VI, 617.

44. RRL to Jay, Philadelphia, April 20, 1782, RRLP.

45. Luzerne to Vergennes, November 1, 1781, Doniol, *op. cit.*, V, 65 *n.*

46. *Ibid.*, V, 64-65: "*Aussitôt entré officiellement en fonctions, il tint pour admises les instructions complémentaires, et, dans la prévision que la défaite eprouvée par l'Angleterre allait imprimer de rapidité aux démarches, il indiqua à Franklin la série des prétentions excessives qui avait eu cours antérieurement comme étant désormais la doctrine du Congrès. Ses instructions developpèrent abondamment, sur la question des limites, sur celle de la pêche, sur celles des biens confisqués aux loyalistes, la sophistique qui avait déployée avec insistence à tant de reprises.*"

47. The whole letter, RRL to Franklin, Philadelphia, February 7, 1782, is in Wharton, *op. cit.*, V, 87-94. In RRLP, only one page of the draft of this letter remains.

48. RRL to Gouverneur Morris, Clermont, January 10, 1781, RRLP. Brant, *op. cit.*, 152.

49. Doniol, *op. cit.*, V, 66 *n.*

50. RRL to Franklin, Philadelphia, February 13, 1782, Wharton, *op. cit.*, V, 160.

51. Frank Monaghan, *John Jay*, 176.

52. Clarence L. Ver Steeg, *Robert Morris: Revolutionary Financier* (Philadelphia, 1954), 112-14.

53. *Ibid.*, 133 and n 3.

54. *Ibid.*, 134 and n 4. RRL to Philip Schuyler, Philadelphia, February 13, 1782, RRLP.
55. RRL to Lafayette, Philadelphia, February 14, 1782, RRLP.
56. Bemis, *The Diplomacy of the American Revolution*, 202, cites Jared Sparks ed., *The Writings of George Washington* (10 vols., Boston, 1834-1837), VIII, 297.
57. *Idem*. RRL to the Governors of the States, May 2, 1782; Luzerne to RRL, In Congress, May 28, 1782, Wharton, *op. cit.*, V, 393, 445. See also Washington to RRL, August 14, 1782, RRLP.
58. Bemis, *The Diplomacy of the American Revolution*, 204, gives the credit to Vergennes. Vincent T. Harlow, *The Founding of the Second British Empire, 1763-1793* (London, 1952), 261 n, declares that "with Franklin and the British Ministers in agreement about a separate negotiation, Vergennes had no choice in the matter. Franklin had won the first round in his 'America first' policy." A reading of Professor Bemis, the ranking authority in America, along with Professor Harlow, is recommended as a stimulating and provocative experience.
59. Jay to RRL, Bordeaux, June 14, 1782, RRLP.

PART TWO, CHAPTER SIX

1. Marbois to Vergennes, Philadelphia, March 13, 1782, Francis Wharton, *Revolutionary Diplomatic Correspondence of the United States*, V, 238-39. RRL to Jay, Philadelphia, December 30, 1782: "As to the letter of Marbois, I am by no means surprised at it. He always endeavored to persuade us that our claim to the fisheries was inadmissable. . . . This letter . . . and the conduct of the court marks the distinction between a great politician and a short-sighted one. . . . I wish you had in a private letter to me in cipher informed me how you got the letter . . . and how it happened to be copied in English. I more particularly wish to know whether it passed through the hands of either British commissioners. If it has, it will be of consequence to see the original; for though true on the whole, yet it may have been colored in the translation." (Wharton, VI, 175.) This final suggestion was as far as RRL cared to go; he was quite convinced (from personal experience) that Marbois meant what he said. In Wharton, there is the following passage from the same letter: "I know not how far 583-485-6-388-497 may merit your confidence. You are the best judge of his conduct. I ought, however, in justice to him, to mention that he has steadily in his letters recommended an adherence to our western claims and to the fisheries, assuring us that they were both attainable if we were firm." From the draft in RRLP one finds that 583-485-6-388-497 is the cipher for Lafayette. This draft (dated January 3, 1783) represents an intermediate version of the dispatch to Jay. Wharton (VI, 173-76) has one version dated December 30, 1782, and (VI, 176-180 n) another dated January 4, 1783. The instructions sent by RRL in any of these versions would, by their Francophile attitude, have been seriously embarrassing to Jay if they had arrived during the negotiations. The idea that the Marbois letter was spurious, advanced by Wharton in V, 241-42 n, has been disproved by the discovery in the French archives of a quintuplicate. Bemis, *The American Secretaries of State and their Diplomacy*, I, 220 n, adds that Marbois later admitted its authenticity, and that there is a copy of it in British Government, Record Office, C.O., 5/40.
2. Bemis, *op. cit.*, 222, quoting *The Correspondence of George III* (6 vols., London, 1927-1928), VI, 125.
3. Vincent T. Harlow, *The Founding of the Second British Empire, 1763-1793*, 282.
4. Washington to RRL, Verplank's Point, September 19, 1782, RRLP.

5. Jay to RRL, Paris, September 18, 1782, Wharton, *op. cit.*, V, 740.
6. Harlow, *op. cit.*, 279.
7. Jay to the President of Congress, St. Ildefonso, October 3, 1781, Wharton, *op. cit.*, IV, 738-65.
8. RRL to Jay, Philadelphia, April 27, 1782, Wharton, *op. cit.*, V, 332-35. Congress's resolution is in *ibid.*, V, 380.
9. RRL to Jay, April 28, 1782, RRLP.
10. RRL to Franklin, Philadelphia, August 9, 1782; RRL to Jay, Philadelphia, August 8, 1782, RRLP.
11. "Congressional Action on Engagements with France," Wharton, *op. cit.*, V, 645-51, especially 650.
12. Jay to RRL, Madrid, April 28, 1782: ". . . can it be wise to instruct your commissioners to speak only as the French ministers shall give them utterance? Let whatever I write about the French and their Ambassador here by all means be kept secret. Marbois gleans and details every scrap of news," Wharton, *op. cit.*, V, 373.
13. John Adams to RRL, Paris, October 31, 1782, Wharton, *op. cit.*, V, 839.
14. Same to same, Paris, November 6, 1782, *ibid.*, V, 855.
15. E. C. Burnett, *Letters of Members of the Continental Congress*, VII, v-vii.
16. Wharton, *op. cit.*, VI, 282.
17. For the text of the preliminary articles see Bemis, *op. cit.*, App., 259-64.
18. Adams, Jay, Franklin, and Laurens to RRL, Paris, December 14, 1782: "As we had reason to imagine that the articles respecting the boundaries, the refugees, and the fisheries did not correspond with the policy of this court, we did not communicate the preliminaries to the minister until after they were signed, and not even then the *separate article*. We hope that these considerations will excuse our having so far deviated from the spirit of our instructions," Wharton, *op. cit.*, VI, 133. Laurens took part only in the final stages, and made no suggestion except a provision for the return of captured slaves.
19. "Madison's Report of Debates in Congress," March 12, 13, 14, 15, 1783, Wharton, *op. cit.*, VI, 282-84. And for March 18, *ibid.*, VI, 317-25.
20. Wharton, *op. cit.*, VI, 283.
21. Bemis, *op. cit.*, 240-41.
22. RRL to Washington, Philadelphia, March 12, 1783; RRL to the President of Congress, Office of Foreign Affairs, March 18, 1783, Wharton, *op. cit.*, VI, 291, 313-16.
23. Vergennes to Luzerne, Versailles, December 19, 1782 (transcription), Wharton, *op. cit.*, VI, 150-52.
24. RRL to Peace Commissioners, Philadelphia, March 25, 1782, Wharton, *op. cit.*, VI, 338-40.
25. John Adams to RRL, Paris, July 9, 1783, Wharton, *op. cit.*, VI, 529-30.
26. Jay to RRL, Paris, July 19, 1783, RRLP.
27. RRL to President of Congress, Philadelphia, December 2, 1782, Wharton, *op. cit.*, VI, 100.
28. The first mention of dissatisfaction is Egbert Benson to RRL, Poughkeepsie, February 28, 1782. Benson says that some question will be raised in the Legislature as to whether, having accepted office as secretary for Foreign Affairs, the Chancellor had not rendered his office of chancellor *ipso facto* void. (*I.e.*, the Chancellor could legally be a delegate to Congress only when on a special mission; and it was questionable whether or not he could hold any office other than that of delegate.) RRL received permission from President John Hanson to visit his state, and in the middle of March was at Poughkeepsie, where the Legislature unanimously declared that he was still chancellor. So RRL to Robert Morris,

Poughkeepsie, March 18, 1782. The real trouble began in November, when Morgan Lewis, the Chancellor's brother-in-law, told him that "very vigorous exertions are making to deprive you of the Chancery. . . . You will scarcely think it possible but Jn—e H—t [John Sloss Hobart] is warmly ranged against you and is not without Hopes of becoming your successor. . . . His reasons are that it is an Imposition on them to be obliged to do your business in the Council of Appointment [sic]." Morgan Lewis to RRL, Albany, November 5, 1782. Same to same, Albany, December 21, 1782, begs RRL to attend the next session of the Legislature at Kingston. "The Chancery has become a matter of very great speculation. . . . I think it indisputable that your friend Jemmy [James Duane] will put every spring in motion." Ephraim Paine wrote to RRL from Kingston on February 25, 1783, to say that the House was prepared to vote the Chancery vacant, and was only waiting for the Council of Appointment to convene. Richard Morris wrote on the same day to say that a committee of the whole House and Senate, with General Ten Broeck in the chair, held that RRL was no longer Chancellor, and that he expected a resolution to be passed to that effect and a recommendation from the House to send the resolution to the Council of Appointment. Morgan Lewis wrote from Albany on March 8, 1783, and reported that John Morin Scott had asked the Senate at Kingston for its sense on the vacancy, saying that he did not desire the office for himself. He was seconded by James Duane. "Mr. Scott," wrote Lewis, "made some illiberal comments on the Chancellor's character as a man of Integrity." He says that RRL was defended by Abraham Yates. He adds that some members thought that RRL should be impeached, others that Governor Clinton should be impeached. It is noteworthy that throughout this controversy RRL was supported by Governor Clinton. If he had not been, he might have lost his office. The controversy died down toward the end of March, 1783, but it was always latent and was certainly a factor in RRL's decision to leave Philadelphia. All letters above are in RRLP.

29. RRL asked Governor Clinton (Philadelphia, July 31, 1782) to help procure him a loan for $2,000, "on my private credit, for which I am willing to allow such interest as you judge reasonable. I suppose there is no prospect of obtaining from the State the money they owe me which would prevent the necessity which the detention of that & the expense of my present office lays me under of troubling your Excellency." Clinton replied (Poughkeepsie, August 5, 1782) that he had lately executed a bond with a friend for £1,000 for his private use, "the whole of which (having lately sold my farm at New Windsor) I shall not have immediate use for and I believe it will therefore be in my power . . . to assist you with the greater part if not the whole of the sum you want." As early as February 23, 1782, RRL told Clinton that he might resign "the next week," both because he longed to return to New York State and because Congress, while making some changes in his office at his request, had thought it proper to deprive him of the power of appointing his own secretary. All in RRLP. Luzerne gave these reasons to Vergennes (Philadelphia, January 2, 1783) for RRL's resignation: "*M. Livingston, homme estimable par sa caractère et par ses talents, n'a pas eu occasion de déployer beaucoup d' habilité. . . . Sa vanité ne lui à point permis de vivre ici sans éclat, et la dépendence où il étoit a achevé de lui rendre ses fonctions désagréables . . . il ne doit dans les affaires essentielles rien déterminer que de l'aveu du Congrès,*" Henri Doniol, *Histoire de la Participation de la France à l'Établissement des États-Unis d'Amérique,* V, 303-04.

30. Irving Brant, *James Madison: The Nationalist, 1780-1787* (Indianapolis and New York, 1948), 260: "To publish such a preference for state office, Madison argued, tended to degrade the United States."

31. RRL to Francisco Rendon, Philadelphia, March 6, 1782; RRL to Luzerne, Office of Foreign Affairs, November 6, 1781, Wharton, *op. cit.*, V, 226; IV, 832.

32. Bemis, *op. cit.*, I, 165.

33. Draft entitled "Thoughts on the Department of Foreign Affairs, submitted to the Committee for Making the Arrangements for a Peace establishment," April 29, 1783, RRLP. This report is divided into two parts. In the first, concerning the Secretary for Foreign Affairs, he says it would be advisable to add "so far to the dignity of this minister as to show that he is at the head of the diplomatic corps and thence to give a greater weight with our own ministers to his instructions and procure him more respect from the ministers of other powers." He should not be considered, as he is at present, the last of the "great executive officers of the United States." He should have the power to nominate, if not to appoint, all "secretaries to embassies, agents, & Vice Consuls at places where they may be found necessary without the jurisdiction of any particular Consul, as Madeira, the Canaries, &c." He did not, however, venture to suggest that his communications to ministers abroad should be free of the scrutiny of Congress. The report, rather, reflects how deeply he had been affronted by the lack of dignity and of patronage in the Department of Foreign Affairs. The second part of the report deals with diplomatic agents abroad. He says (1) that ministers should be of the second or third orders—ministers plenipotentiary and ministers. He would keep ministers plenipotentiary near the courts of Versailles and of Madrid; but at London, Lisbon, and The Hague, he believed that only ministers were required. (2) With the northern courts and the princes of Italy, he believed only consuls at the principal ports to be necessary. "The day is not very far distant," he said, however, "when we shall find from men of fortune of our own Country persons properly qualified to accept embassies to Rome, Naples, Florence, Turin & Venice —with very little expense & much honor as well as utility to the United States." (3) Consuls, in the present state of U.S. finances, must be permitted to trade. (4) To control them, the minister should be consul-general in the Kingdom where he resides, with power to suspend. Vice-consuls should be able to draw on the minister for sums expended in the national service, and the minister should have credit upon the U.S.A. for limited sums to answer their drafts. (5) Salaries of ministers should depend on their character and situation. *I.e.*, a minister plenipotentiary to France or Spain, $10,000; a minister to England, Portugal, and Holland, $7,000. These salaries to be inclusive of house hire and all contingent expenses, except the purchase of public prints and newspapers, where they should not economize. Allowance made to a secretary of Legation should never exceed $900. (6) The expenses of the Department of Foreign Affairs, including the salaries of under secretaries, clerks, office rent, stationery, etc., at present comes to about $8,000. This sum should be raised to $10,000 to put him on a footing with ministers at foreign courts. Out of this he should defray all contingent expenses, so as to avoid the trouble of keeping and settling accounts.

34. RRL to President of Congress, June 14, 1783, RRLP. This sentence does not occur in Wharton's version of this letter (*op. cit.*, VI, 477-78), and it must be assumed that RRL deleted it, possibly because it represented a little too clearly his thinking on this subject.

35. See Stephen Higginson to Samuel Adams, Philadelphia, June 10, 1783: "The event [of RRL's departure] I think a very agreable One. . . . I wish for one other removal and then I think Congress would be free of dangerous influence and might with much more safety be entrusted with the power of assessing and collecting Moneys in the States, or of imposing and collecting Duties . . . ," Burnett, *op. cit.*, VII, 184.

36. Charles Thomson, Secretary of Congress, to RRL, June 4, 1783: "I am extremely sorry to find that the public must be deprived of the benefit of your experience. . . . I am the more mortified as I am persuaded . . . that you would have continued in the office had your salary only be made equal to your necessary expenses. . . . I rejoice in the honorable testimonial Congress has given of your ability, zeal, and fidelity. I wish the next who fills the office may give us as much satisfaction"; RRL to the President of Congress, Valley Lebanon, June 14, 1783, makes acknowledgment to Congress "for their polite resolution of the 2d. instant," Wharton, *op. cit.*, VI, 475, 487-88.

37. RRL to Marbois, Clermont, July 18, 1783, writes of the "desire which has this moment seized me, upon the news of the arrival of the definitive treaty to be permitted to sign it as secretary pro tempore. . . ." Hamilton to RRL, Princeton, July 23, 1783, writes of his consultation with Madison. RRL to Hamilton, Clermont, August 30, 1783. All in RRLP.

38. RRL to Marbois, Clermont, September 5, 1783, shows that he had not quite given up the idea of secretary pro tempore. "If I should be disappointed, I shall submit to the disappointment with all resignation and acknowledge myself justly mortified for not having renounced (according to my baptismal vow) the 'pomps & vanities of this wicked world.'" RRL to Marbois, Clermont, October 9, 1783, thinks that Congress may come to New York and that therefore "I almost wish I had not ['so hastily' deleted] quited a station which made a connection between our families a duty as it always will be a pleasure . . . but perhaps after all I can be more useful in my present station . . . particularly if I can aid in introducing a spirit of moderation in the government which I think suffers in its reputation by too cruel a triumph over a vanquished foe." Both in RRLP.

PART THREE, CHAPTER ONE

1. RRL to Dr. John Bard, Clermont, June 26, 1784, RRLP: "I send by the bearer . . . your Cavallo on electricity. I have been told that Miss de Normandy has received great benefit from its use & am anxious to know how she applied it. Suffering a current of the electric fluid to pass thro' my ears as you directed seems to have been of no service, but rather injurious to my hearing."

2. William Kent, *Memoirs and Letters of James Kent* (Boston, 1898), 292-95. "The case I allude to was the following. Chancellor Livingston claimed lands lying on the south bounds of the lower manor of Livingston, and the claim was large in the amount of property. . . ." Philip Livingston to Gilbert Livingston, Albany, March 23, 1743/4, Miscellaneous Livingston Manuscripts, NYHS, refers to "the tryall between Brother Robert [Robert Livingston, of Clermont] & hoffman." Morgan Lewis to RRL, New York, August 10, 1775, RRLP, shows that Hamilton, having lost the motion for a new trial, issued a writ of error in form. RRL to Robert Livingston, Jr. (third Lord), Clermont, August 9, 1786, Livingston-Redmond Papers, Franklin Delano Roosevelt Library, shows that the Chancellor, in compliance with what he believed to be Robert Livingston's wish, submitted the case to arbitrators. "Should I fail, those who have trampled on the grave of our common ancestors must remain in possession & the stigma on their characters continue." Precisely when the compromise was effected is not known. It is first mentioned in 4 *Laws of the State of New York* (Albany, 1886), 347, Act of March 23, 1799, referring to the boundaries of Columbia County as "the line settled and established between Robert R. Livingston and Zachariah Hoffman and others, as their mutual boundary, so far as respects them individually."

3. *Minutes of the Court of Chancery*, Hall of Records, New York City, beginning June 11, 1785. From Livingston's correspondence, it appears that some Chancery business was transacted throughout the Revolution, but of this there is no record. The act of April 18, 1785 (2 *Laws of the State of New York*, Albany, 1886, 124), gives the Chancellor's fees as follows: "For the seal to every common writ—three shillings; for exemplifications—twenty shillings; for every decree—two pounds; for every opinion or order on a petition or motion, controverted and argued in court—twenty shillings; appointing a guardian—ten shillings." A pound in New York was then equal to two and a half dollars.

4. The recorded decisions in cases on appeal are in I Caines, *Cases Argued and Determined in the Court for the Trial of Impeachments and Correction of Errors in the State of New York*, iii ff. *Herman Le Roy et al., Appellants* vs. *Peter Servis et al., Respondents*. Case heard February, 1801, before John Lansing, Jr., C. J., Morgan Lewis, J., Egbert Benson, J., James Kent, J., Jacob Radcliff, J., President of Senate and Senators. The court does not sustain the decree of Chancellor Livingston in this case, and gives its reasons. The Chancellor had permitted demurrers to the whole of the complainants' bill, on the grounds that the bill blended relief with a prayer for discovery: but the Court of Errors ruled that the complainants were properly before the court on the point of discovery, and that the defendents were bound to answer this part of the bill: and so the demurrer to the whole was not well taken. Again, in 2 Caines, 344, in the case of *William Laight et al., Appellants,* vs. *John Morgan et al. Respondants,* a very similar case to the above, James Kent, J., gave the court's decision reversing Chancellor Livingston's decree in the Court of Chancery, and said that there was an established and convenient rule of pleading in Chancery, to the effect that you may meet a complainant's bill by several modes of defense: you may demur to one part, answer to another, plead to a third, and disclaim to a fourth. So in a bill, as the bill now under review, which seeks for a discovery and also for relief, consequential to such a discovery, the bill being good for one object, without affidavit, and not for the other, the defendent ought to meet the sound part of the bill by an answer, and be allowed to use his own option whether or not he demurred to the other. No authoritative rule can be found for declaring that a bill, bad in one part only and good in other parts, can be dismissed by a general demurrer. Therefore the decree of the Court of Chancery, allowing the demurrer of the respondant, must be reversed. The same reason for reversal is given in *Munro et al.* vs. *Allaire et al.,* 2 Caines, 195. In 2 Caines, 299-300, *Charles Newkerk and Gertryd, his wife, executrix of Peter Schuyler, deceased, Appellants* vs. *Edward S. Willett, Respondant,* the decision of Chancellor Livingston to dissolve the injunction against Willett was upheld by the court, as the appellants were not entitled to a discovery of the facts. See also I Johnson, *New York Common Law Reports, Coleman and Caines Cases.*

5. RRL to Jefferson, New York, December 10, 1790, RRLP.

6. Luzerne to RRL, Paris, February 15, 1785 (in English, in secretary's hand); RRL to Luzerne, Clermont, June 2, 1785, RRLP.

7. Charles Pinckney to RRL, New York, August 28, 1785, RRLP, says that Rutledge declines going to The Hague, and that he is giving him (RRL) the earliest intimation, so that he can inform his friends in Congress, "should the same intentions of going to Europe exist, as when I last saw you at the Baron's. . . . I hope it is unnecessary to assure you that was not a gentleman [Ralph Izard] from our State a candidate for this office, I know of no one who would more warmly meet my support, and approbation than yourself." RRL to Charles Pinckney, Clermont, September 11, 1785, RRLP.

8. Margaret Beekman Livingston to RRL, Clermont, December 22, 1781, RRLP.

9. Margaret Beekman Livingston to Catharine Livingston, Rhinebeck, May 21, 1779, Miscellaneous Livingston Manuscripts, NYHS.

10. John R. Livingston to RRL, Rhinebeck, January 25, 1779, RRLP.

11. Armes, ed., *Nancy Shippen*, 114-15.

12. RRL to John R. Livingston, Manor of Livingston, April 11, 1778, Miscellaneous Livingston Manuscripts, NYHS: "Mama left us this morning to return to Clare Mount where she has put up a hut & spent great part of last week—It made me extreamly melancholy a day or two ago to see the ruins. I can hardly describe my sensations at seeing the top of the chimney over the hill, an object which allways excited the most pleasing emotions as it was an earnest of the joys of that once social fire side. . . . When I cam down the hill I saw Mama in her garden, tending with solitary care those plants her hands had reared in happier times Good Gods what a flood of tender thoughts burst in upon me—I felt what you may conceive but what I know not how to describe—I was too much unmaned to speak to her for some time. We get strange attatchments to inanimate things. I have done all I can to wean Mama from this object but in vain—She has no pleasure any were else, or in any conversation but the mode of rebuilding & improving this place. She wanders about like the gost that reluctantly quits the body which was once the vehicle of its joys—nor can I wonder at it, I have scarce lamented the loss of my own house, but gaze with all the luxury of sorrow on the ruins of the old building—I mark out the several ruins & each recals some pleasing or some tender scene to my imagination."

13. "R. R. Livingston's Account Book, Clermont, N. Y.," NYHS, contains "Great Patent Memorandum," which gives a picture of the Hardenburgh leases. "List of Money Rents in Clermont for 1799," Wilson Family Papers, Clements Library.

14. *Ibid.* RRL to John R. Livingston, Clermont, May 18, 1779, RRLP, says that on May 17 he made a partial division of the Great Patent, laying out from eighteen thousand to twenty thousand acres to a share—each girl to have a twelfth and each boy a twelfth and a twenty-fourth. Since John R. had already chosen ten thousand acres, he is to take "nine thousand in addition to it & adjoining in an oblong square not having more than one half its brea[d]th on the river which will be a much better allotment than any of us has made—Your other half lott or twenty fourth is part of Lott 22 & 23 consisting of about 20,000 acres between you & Edward—We shall come to a further division on my return [from Phildephia]." See also Catharine L. Garretson, "Memoir," Wainwright Autograph Collection, Princeton University. In a memorandum, undated, but written before his mother's death in 1800, RRLP, RRL says that he divided "three hundred thousand acres of Land among my brothers & sisters." The location of these lands is to be found in the Clermont and Middletown Account Books, NYHS.

15. Robert Livingston, Jr., to James Duane, Manor Livingston, January, 1781, Miscellaneous Livingston Manuscripts, NYHS, complains that Colonel Hay has sent a number of soldiers "into my Maner" and billeted them until the people have threshed all their wheat, and then sent the wheat to be ground in Dutchess County, which (he contends) is contrary to law—"but this is not regarded nor is any law in this state. I sincerely wish it was in my power to move out of it, but that's not possible. I must tarry & be ruined, unless a speedy peace takes place." In this same letter, he says he wishes Henry Livingston would return with the money for the two barrels of sugar which he sold, "to enable me to pay off my workmen, for have none left all is out of my hands & the poor men unpaid, it is not in my power to help you, nor him, nor John, nor myself." Colonel Udney Hay to James Duane, Poughkeepsie, December 2, 1781, complains that Colonel Livingston [Robert Livingston, Jr.]

has refused to deliver to Mr. Roosevelt certain vouchers for flour, which Colonel Livingston paid for taxes. Robert Livingston, Jr., to James Duane, January 14, 1783, declares that taxes have "reduced me almost to a state of want. . . . For want of money my negros and stock must next go." He adds that the people who owe him money, owing to its scarcity, cannot pay their debts, "which has prevented me from blowing my furnace for these three years." Both in Duane Papers, NYHS.

16. Margaret Beekman Livingston to RRL, Clermont, June 4, 1782, RRLP: "Yesterday morning the Genl. and his Lady left Clermont & returned to headquarters after calling upon harry on his way down—we happened to have Mr. & Mrs. Provost to dine with us when news was brought that ye Genl. and Gover. were at the Landing—the whole soon after entered to my great joy—the Genl. said he was going with the Govr. to Albany and would leave his Lady with me till his return which he did the next day at Ten o'Clock—he admired the place and Mrs. Washington seemed pleased we went to the Manor spent a day with peter & the next morning returned home after loging at Walters. red hook Church was crowded to see Mrs. Washn. Dr. Livingston preached she was here eight days. . . ."

17. Washington to RRL, Newburgh, March 19, 1783; RRL to Washington, April 9, 1783, RRLP.

18. RRL to Hamilton, Clermont, August 30, 1783, RRLP.

PART THREE, CHAPTER TWO

1. Margaret Beekman Livingston to RRL, Clermont, April 30, 1783. Andrew Elliot to RRL, New York, April 14, 1783. Elliot was a Loyalist who had friends in the New York Legislature, and who therefore asked if he could put his horses in Mrs. Livingston's stable. He says in this letter that Colonel Crosbie, the Barrack Quartermaster General, had occupied the house for two years and was about to embark for England. Elliot also wanted to sell his own house in the Bowery with twenty acres of land. RRL replied, April 18, 1783, that if his mother's house has been used by the Crown, she may hope to receive the customary allowance made in such cases; and wishes to invest it in Colonel Crosbie's coach and furniture, her own having been destroyed. He thinks some difficulty may arise as to the disposal of Elliot's Bowery house, for although Elliot's friends in the Legislature prevented his estates being confiscated, yet a new law—which he has not yet seen—may possibly change this. Also, there is an old law of the state which makes all bargains void which are arrived at while the British are still in possession of the city. He will, however, use "what little interest I have," to obtain permission from the Legislature for Elliot to sell; and would like, himself, to become the purchaser. "Should I become a purchaser I should have more hopes of being able to obtain a confirmation of this bargain than if it passed into other hands." (This correspondence gives some idea of the ease and freedom of communication between occupied New York and patriot New York at this time.) John R. Livingston to RRL, Boston, April 21, 1783, says that he has lately been in New York, with letters from Governor John Hancock and General Howe, and that Sir Guy Carleton received him with every possible politeness and said that "my name was a sufficient inducement for him to do everything in his power to serve me." All in RRLP. Robert Cambridge Livingston to James Duane, May 30, 1783, explains that he has been to New York, "a disagreeable place," to discover the state of his father's (Robert Livingston, Jr.'s) property, but that it was inaccessible. But James Duane's house, lodge, "glass-houses," fishpond, farmhouse, and other buildings were in good repair, having been occupied by some "great person."

Henry Livingston to James Duane, Manor Livingston, July 16, 1783, says that the occupant was Admiral Digby. Both in Duane Papers, NYHS.

2. Hamilton to RRL, August 13, 1783, RRLP. Henry Livingston to James Duane, New York, September 6, 1783. Mary Duane (daughter) to James Duane, Manor Livingston, August 30, 1783, says "Uncle Hary is gone down to N York he is grown the most busy creature in the world all day in the store measuring Ells of Muslin and calico to the Country People." Robert Livingston, Jr., to James Duane, September 12, 1783, and March 22, 1784. All in Duane Papers, NYHS.

3. RRL to Hamilton, Clermont, August 30, 1783. RRL to Elias Boudinot, Clermont, September 27, 1783. RRL to Marbois, October 8, 1783. All in RRLP.

4. Jay to RRL, September 12, 1783, RRLP.

5. Washington to RRL, Poughkeepsie, November 15, 1783. RRL to Marbois, New York, December 18, 1783. Peter S. Du Ponceau to RRL, Philadelphia, December 3, 1783, congratulates him on being a member of the Temporary Council. All in RRLP. James Duane to Mary Livingston Duane, New York, December 4, 1783, says that in spite of the prediction of disorder and ruin, following upon George Washington's entry, New York has been in a state of "perfect Tranquillity." "You will readily conclude," he adds, "that all who staid behind are *very* civil." James Duane to Mary Livingston Duane, New York, December 22, 1783, says that the houses in Fly Market and King Street, "which we possess through your Father's goodness, are in miserable condition. . . . They really look as if they had been inhabited by savages or wild beasts." Both in Duane Papers, NYHS. As for predictions of disorder, see Colonel W. Malcolm to James Duane, Montgomery, July 20, 1783, Duane Papers, NYHS: "It is true I fear this entry into York and the consequences to be apprehended more than any thing during the war."

6. RRL to Marbois, April 4, 1784, RRLP: "Three days ago some heated people took up one Hoby who commanded a privateer & distinguished himself by his success & his cruelty & in carting him about the town they unfortunately met with Capt. Muir a british officer who not being in uniform but wearing a cockade they mistook for an American in the british service (of whom we have several in our streets & coffee houses) they placed him on the cart & were proceeding to shew him Cunninghams gallows & then as they say to turn them out of the State [hang them]— The Governor & myself came up in time to rescue them and to seize the principal offenders whom we committed to gaol—they have been indicted and will be tried this term."

7. RRL to Reverend Samuel Provoost, New York, January 14, 1784, RRLP, describes this controversy. He says that on January 13, it was unanimously decided that Provoost should be chosen rector at a meeting of the trustees and a great number of Whig churchmen—at any rate that the trustees and members should enter into engagement that he should have post as soon as the Trinity charter was organized by the Legislature so as to conform to the present constitution. "Both Mr. Duane & myself have ventured to assert that we are sufficiently acquainted with your political principles & with your regard to the church" to believe that he would submit them to no further embarrassments. Provoost, a confirmed Whig, was then living in Dutchess County; and his wife had been ill. RRL none the less begs him to come up at once, over the snowy roads, by sled—a carpenter can make such a covering with blankets as will preserve her from the least harm. Under these circumstances, the fifth rector and future bishop came back to New York.

8. RRL to Jay, Clermont, April 20, 1779, RRLP: "Never was there a greater compound of folly, avarice & injustice than our confiscation bill owing to Benson's compromising genious [what follows is deleted: 'and Scott's desire to satisfy the ship carpenters of Poughkeepsie']." Alfred B. Street, *The Council of Revision of*

the State of New York, 219-26, shows that the Council vetoed on March 14, 1779, "An Act for forfeitures and confiscations &c"; and that the Chancellor reported its objections: That the bill was repugnant to plain and immutable laws of justice; that it was obscure and contradictory; that it tended to deprive well-affected inhabitants of the state of their just rights; that the clause allowing only one month for the payment of money for purchase of forfeited estates will do great harm to "many of the industrious farmers and others who have not had it in their power to accumulate money during the war," and that therefore "the price of the lands will be diminished and the whole confiscated property be vested in a few monopolizers and merchants in this and the neighboring states." This veto was overruled in the Assembly but not in the Senate. However, later enactments of March 27, April 1, June 30, and October 9, affected precisely what RRL had objected to on March 14. E. Wilder Spaulding, *New York in the Critical Period, 1783-1789* (New York, 1932), 70, 121, 122.

9. RRL to Jay, New York, January 25, 1784, RRLP. Also, RRL to Charles De Witt, Clermont, May 8, 1784, RRLP, describes the radical party as "so jealous of power as to endeavour to exclude property & abilities from the weight that they must and will have in every society."

10. RRL to P. J. Van Berckel, New York, January 24, 1784. P. J. Van Berckel to RRL, Philadelphia, January 27, 1784, says that he entirely approves of RRL's scheme but has already joined with Robert and Gouverneur Morris in a similar scheme. Why not write to them, or allow him (Van Berckel) to break the matter to them? RRL to P. J. Van Berckel, New York, February 1, 1784, replies that his objects and those of Robert and Gouverneur Morris may be dissimilar. Theirs may be confined to lands, whereas RRL's "center merely in houses & lotts & estates upon this Island having already as much improved and unimproved Land in other parts of the State as will satisfy my wishes." But if the Morrises and Van Berckel are willing to go into a scheme for acquiring houses and estates, he will allow the three of them a half-interest and himself the other half. All in RRLP. For his request of Jay to establish a credit, see RRL to Jay in 9 *supra*.

11. Thomas T. Tillotson to RRL, New York, June 15, 1784, RRLP: "The pews at St. Paul's have been sold at public vendue. . . . I have got the large square one of Oliver Delancey's for you & me. . . . Those near the Pulpit sold high, particularly ours, from its superior advantage to others." For RRL's befriending of Rivington, there are bills rendered by the latter in RRLP which show that extensive purchases of books, especially law books, were made in 1784, 1785, and 1787.

12. "Robert R. Livingston Argument against commercial banks, or the defects of monied banks." "Observations on the establishment of a land bank." RRLP. The first dated 1784, the second undated, but must be 1784. The prospectus for this land bank appeared in *The Independent Gazette; or the New-York Journal Revived*, February 12, 1784. Subscriptions to shares (750 all told) at $1,000 each were to be received by Stephen Sayre and John Stevens at No. 6 Wall Street. Whether this John Stevens was RRL's father-in-law or his brother-in-law is not certain. See also Broadus Mitchell, *Alexander Hamilton*, 346 and n 5, and 347 ff. Bray Hammond, *Banks and Politics in America*, 65; Merrill Jensen, *The New Nation*, 232-233; Hamilton to John B. Church, March 10, 1784, *The Works of Alexander Hamilton*, IX, 396 ff.

13. Marbois to RRL, Philadelphia, April 27, 1784; RRL to Marbois, July 6, 1784, RRLP.

14. *Journal of the New York Assembly*, 7 Sess., 1784 (February 21). Mitchell, *op. cit.*, 347, 353.

15. Robert R. Livingston, "Observations . . ." cited in 12 *supra*.

16. Margaret Beekman Livingston to RRL, Clermont, April 30, 1783, RRLP. The elections were held "yesterday. . . . I hope for Clinton but fear pain [Ephraim Paine, who, with Schuyler, ran against Clinton] will git in altho' some say there is no fear."

17. Thomas T. Tillotson to RRL, New York, May 1784, RRLP. The state tariff was imposed by an act of November 18, 1784. This act to amend an act imposing certain duties on certain goods, wares, and marchandise imported into New York was vetoed in the Council of Revision on March 12, 1785. John Sloss Hobart, Jr., presented the Council's objections. RRL was present and approved Hobart's objections. They were, however, overruled in the Legislature. Street, *op. cit.*, 267-68.

18. "State of New York in Senate, November 17, 1784," RRLP. RRL and Egbert Benson to be "counsellors and agents" for New York; to repair to Trenton by December 1; and there to assist in the appointment of a federal court to settle the controversy. James Duane, "Journal of Proceedings of the law appointing James Duane, John Jay, Robert R. Livingston, Egbert Benson and Walter Livingston agents for vindicating the State of New York against the claims of the Commonwealth of Massachusetts," RRLP. *JCC*, XXVI, 663, shows that he presented his credentials, December 7, 1784. He told Luzerne in 1785 that he was only led to resume his seat in Congress because of the Massachusetts controversy, and could give little attention to the other business before the Congress (RRL to Luzerne, Clermont, June 2, 1785, RRLP). In *JCC* XXVIII, 7, 8, 25, 26 n, 30, 65, 73, 90, 103, 130 n, 154, 165 n, 173, 174, 222, 227, 242, 247, are the evidence of his activities in Congress other than in the Massachusetts case. He left at the end of April, 1785. The Duane Papers for 1784 and 1785 have pertinent references to this controversy, but they are brief. On June 9, 1785, it is agreed between New York agents and Massachusetts agents that Samuel Jones and Alexander Hamilton be appointed counsellors and solicitors for New York. On September 7, 1786, the Massachusetts agents declared themselves ready to settle the controversy otherwise than by a federal court; and lists of agents on this occasion show King out of the Massachusetts list and Jay, W. Livingston, and Egbert Benson out of the New York list, with R. Benson, Haring, Yates, Smith, and Lansing substituted. According to James Duane to Peter S. Curtenius, State Auditor, February 15, 1788, the commissioners were allowed eight dollars a day. On November 1, 1786, RRL to James Duane, Clermont, the Chancellor asked Duane, "if you make a draft to defray your expenses to Hardford," to include £50 for him, "as I can command no specie here for the purpose." Both in Duane Papers, NYHS.

19. Dixon Ryan Fox, *Yankees versus Yorkers*, 185. Thomas C. Cochran, *New York in the Confederation: An Economic Study*, 96, quoting *Report of the Regents of the University of the State of New York*: Sen. Docs. 71 (Albany, 1883), 411-14.

20. Spaulding, *op. cit.*, 182, quoting *Messages from the Governors*, II, 263.

21. Fox, *op. cit.*, 186.

22. Elias Boudinot to RRL, Princeton, October 23, 1783; RRL to Boudinot, Clermont, November 1, 1783, RRLP.

23. RRL to Luzerne, Clermont, June 2, 1785; RRL to Charles De Witt, Clermont, June 25, 1784, RRLP. RRL, "Thoughts on emitting bills of Credit," March, 1786, RRLP, shows that the bill was referred to him (*i.e.*, the bill passed by the Assembly, March 6, 1786) and that he expressed total opposition. The bill was amended in the Senate to £150,000, and then, after struggle with the Assembly, the £200,000 was restored and the bill became law on April 18, 1786. Spaulding, *op. cit.*, 149.

24. RRL to Marbois, Clermont, May 27, 1786. RRL, "Articles in the Treaty of

Commerce with G. Britain, proposed by Mr. Livingston, which are not the same with those in the Treaty with France," 1783. Both in RRLP.

25. RRL to Luzerne, New York, April 24, 1787, RRLP.

26. Alexander McDougall to RRL, July 6, 1784, informs RRL that he was elected an honorary member of the Society of the Cincinnati. Peter S. Du Ponceau to RRL, Philadelphia, November 5, 1783: "Some people say the Cincinnati must become extremely dangerous or extremely ridiculous, in general it [the society] has alarmed very few persons. The first general meeting is to be in May next." Both in RRLP.

27. New York State Society of the Cincinnati, at a meeting held at the Coffee House, July 15, 1786, request RRL to deliver an oration in honor of the independence of the United States at its next anniversary (Robert Pemberton, Secretary, to RRL, New York, July 15, 1786). RRL to Baron von Steuben, October 26, 1786, says he will not have sufficient time to prepare an oration for next July 4, but that he will be a delegate to the general convention of the Cincinnati at Philadelphia. Samuel B. Webb, R. Platt, Marinus Willett to RRL, June 23, 1787, gives program for the meeting of the Cincinnati on July 4, 1787. Baron von Steuben to RRL, June 27, 1787, says that the convention of the Cincinnati at Philadelphia went off very pleasantly—evidently RRL did not attend this convention out of prudence —and then tells him that he cannot and must not give up the plan for delivering an oration to the New York Society of the Cincinnati on July 4. All in RRLP.

28. Robert R. Livingston, "Draft of Oration to the Society of the Cincinnati given, New York, July 4, 1787," RRLP.

PART THREE, CHAPTER THREE

1. E. Wilder Spaulding, *New York in the Critical Period, 1783-1789*, 189, 217 n.

2. Hamilton to Washington, July 3, 1788, in Broadus Mitchell, *Alexander Hamilton*, 403. Baron von Steuben to RRL, New York, June 29, 1788, RRLP.

3. RRL to Robert Livingston, Jr., Clermont, October 4, 1779, Duane Papers, NYHS. Peter R. Livingston to Peter Sylvester, Manor Livingston, October 18, 1780, Livingston-Redmond Papers, Franklin Delano Roosevelt Library. Brockholst Livingston to Henry Livingston, Elizabeth Town, October 8, 1783, Duane Papers, NYHS.

4. Hamilton's opinion, dated Albany, November 3, 1783, is in the Duane Papers, NYHS.

5. Henry Livingston to Walter Livingston, Manor Livingston, April 24, 1785. Henry Livingston to RRL, Manor Livingston, March 13, 1787. Morgan Lewis to RRL, New York, August 10, 1785. All in RRLP. Robert Livingston, Jr., to James Duane, April 25, 1785, Duane Papers, NYHS.

6. RRL to James Duane, draft dated "1784," RRLP.

7. Same to same, undated draft, presumably 1784, RRLP.

8. Robert Livingston, Jr., to James Duane, March 31, 1788, Duane Papers, NYHS: "Mr. Patterson is going down to New York. He has discoursed with the Chancellor on the subject of the mills & will tell you all of it on his arrival. I do really wish you could & would take an active part in this essential business to clear my Estate agreeable to my honord Grandfather's Will from this covetous troublesome man, as I now am determined to go to the bottom & End if please God I am spard so long in the land of the living and I will pay you in Cash what I am to pay Mr. Hamilton or more[.] I think I have had Mr. Broc. Livingstons opinion on this cause but I know not where it is if he has given it let him be imployd too, Mr. Lansingh [John Lansing, Jr.] I purpose to fee also as I have his opinion."

9. Philip Schuyler to RRL, Albany, March 29, 1788; William Wilson to RRL, March 13, 1788, RRLP.

10. Spaulding, *op. cit.*, 192-99. Robert Livingston, Jr., to James Duane, March 31, 1788, Duane Papers, NYHS: ". . . among which is Ten Broeck the Deputy Sheriff of Columbia . . . They do considerable mischief among the Ignorant."

11. Forrest McDonald, *We the People: The Economic Origins of the Constitution,* (Chicago, 1958), 186. Spaulding, *op. cit.*, 200. Beard, *An Economic Interpretation of the Constitution of the United States* (New York, 1944 ed.), 92.

12. Richard Varick, Recorder *et al.*, May 29, 1788, certifies that John Jay, Richard Morris, John Sloss Hobart, Alexander Hamilton, Robert R. Livingston, Isaac Roosevelt, James Duane, Richard Harison, and Nicholas Low are elected delegates from the City and County of New York to meet in convention at the Court House at Poughkeepsie in Dutchess County on the third Tuesday in June. Duane Papers, NYHS.

13. RRL to Governor Clinton, Clermont, February 20, 1787, RRLP.

14. Robert Livingston, Jr., to James Duane, March 30, 1784, Duane Papers, NYHS. Robert Livingston, Jr., to Walter Livingston, Manor Livingston, February 4, 1785, RRLP.

15. McDonald, *op. cit.*, 295-96, gives a lucid exposition of this. However, in 296 n 138, he seems to think that New York yeomen farmers were economically literate, indeed to the astounding extent that they could foretell the effects of Clinton's financial measures.

16. De Witt Clinton to Governor Clinton, April 25, 1788, Spaulding, *op. cit.*, 213-14.

17. Charles Tillinghast to John Lamb, Poughkeepsie, June 21, 1788, Lamb Papers, NYHS.

18. Spaulding, *op. cit.*, 213.

19. Charles Tillinghast to John Lamb, cited in 17 *supra.*

20. Francis Childs, *The Debates and Proceedings of the Convention of the State of New-York.* Of all the extant reports, this is by far the most complete, though Childs himself apologized for its deficiencies. Chancellor Livingston left a somewhat scattered account; but it does not differ in any important respect from Childs's account and is far less complete. In the Clements Library, there is a printed copy of the Constitution, with RRL's notes; but these are notes of the amendments made chiefly by the opposition, and are quite cursory. Gilbert Livingston's notes, manuscript, NYPL, cover the last period, where Childs is weakest, but in clarity are not in any way equal to the earlier Childs. The McKesson Papers, NYHS (John McKesson was secretary to the Convention) may also be consulted as a supplement to Childs. *The Journal of the Convention of the State of New York . . . Printed by Nicholas Power* (Poughkeepsie, 1788), gives no speeches, but provides all the other information. I have followed Childs, since he covers RRL's most typical speeches. RRL's first speech of June 19 is in Childs, 6-11. RRL left among his papers the text of this speech. Lansing's answer of June 20 is in Childs, 11-15.

21. Charles Tillinghast to John Lamb, cited in 17 *supra*: "Morgan Lewis asked me this morning who wrote Mr. Williams's Speech (with which he opened the Convention today) I told him I had no doubt it was his own composition[.] he said he was not equal to it. Greswold who was standing by said that he had compiled it from York News Papers—I replied if so, he had as much credit with me as Mr. Hamilton, for retailing in Convention *Publius*—this silenced the gentleman."

22. Childs, *op. cit.*, 38-39, June 21, 1788.

23. *Ibid.*, 42, June 21, 1788.

24. *Ibid.*, 52-53.

25. *Ibid.*, 43, speech of Saturday, June 21, 1788.
26. Clinton to John Lamb, Poughkeepsie, June 21, 1788, Lamb Papers, NYHS.
27. Childs, *op. cit.*, 128-29, speech of July 1, 1788.
28. *Ibid.*, 132-33, speech of July 2, 1788. "Verdill" is the Rev. John Vardill, Loyalist and spy. For Vardill's opinion of RRL: "elegant . . . persuasive . . . desirous of honours & wealth chiefly to enjoy them in *Pleasures*," see B. F. *Stevens Facsimiles* (London, 1885-1895), No. 438.
29. *Ibid.*, 133, speech of July 2, 1788.
30. *Ibid.*, 134, speech of July 2, 1788.
31. De Witt Clinton to Charles Tillinghast, Poughkeepsie, July 2, 1788, Lamb Papers, NYHS.
32. Childs, *op. cit.*, 136, speech of July 2, 1788.
33. The news from New Hampshire was known on June 24. On June 25, RRL said that "the Confederation . . . was now dissolved." To which Melancton Smith replied that he had always expected nine states to ratify, so that the news which had "such a solemn effect" upon RRL did not alter his feelings or wishes. Childs, *op. cit.*, 85, 86. The news from Virginia was known on July 2. Ezra L'Hommedieu believed that since the adoption by New Hampshire and Virginia, a great change in sentiment had taken place among the opposition. Ezra L'Hommedieu to John Smith, New York, July 20, 1788, John Smith Papers, NYHS. This was the opinion of George Mason, of Virginia. Spaulding, *op. cit.*, 261. McDonald says, *op. cit.*, 284: "Only after the convention learned that New Hampshire and Virginia had ratified was their [the Anti-Federalists'] resistance broken." I believe that it had effectually, though not formally or openly, been broken long before. See 40 *infra*.
34. Mitchell, *op. cit.*, 456, quoting *The Works of Alexander Hamilton*, IX, 437-38. Hamilton to Madison, Poughkeepsie, July 5, 1788. *Idem*, quoting J. C. Hamilton, ed., *Life of Alexander Hamilton* (2 vols., New York, 1834; Philadelphia, 1840), I, 465, James Madison to Alexander Hamilton [July (13), 1788].
35. Childs, *op. cit.*, 142.
36. *Journal of the Convention*, 67.
37. *Ibid.*, 68.
38. *Ibid.*, 70.
39. *Ibid.*, 76. Childs, *op. cit.*, 143. The Convention's thirty-two amendments to the Constitution were arranged and embodied in a circular letter to the states, urging a second convention in order to adopt necessary amendments. This circular letter was agreed to on July 26, and facilitated the final vote. As to this final vote of 30 to 27, Spaulding (267 n) shows that other Clintonians would have voted aye if necessary.
40. Spaulding, *op. cit.*, 254-55, says that the idea of the secession of the commercial part of the state had been aired before the Convention, quoting Jay to Washington, May 29, 1788, *The Correspondence and Public Papers of John Jay*, II, 334 ff. He says that it was occasionally referred to in the newspapers of other states and infrequently in the New York press. P. L. Ford in his Introduction to *The Federalist* (New York, 1898), xxvi, says that Hamilton wrote to Madison that the surrounding states would attempt to detach the southern counties in case of a rejection. Spaulding adds that the *Pennsylvania Gazette* of June 11 printed an address to the New York Convention in which it was suggested that a rejection would force Staten Island to secede to New Jersey, and New York and Long Island to Connecticut, thus closing the mouth of the Hudson, and ruining the foreign trade of the rest of the state. Late in July, he says, the New Haven *Gazette* learned that New York, Richmond, Kings, Queens, Suffolk, and Westchester were ready to secede and form a distinct state in case of rejection. And he quotes General S. B.

Webb's letter to Miss Hogeboom of July 6 (W. C. Ford, ed., *Correspondence . . . of Samuel Blachley Webb*, 3 vols., New York, 1894, III, 111) that should the Convention refuse to ratify " 'tis more than probable there will be a separation of the State." McDonald, *op. cit.*, 288 n 124, holds this view. I maintain, also, that separation was in any case unbearable.

41. Carl N. Dreger, *Out of our Past* (New York, 1959), 90 n 7, points out with admirable force and clarity the dangers of employing terms like "radical" and "conservative" "to cover what actually amount to congeries of ideas instead of a single attitude. . . ."

PART FOUR, CHAPTER ONE

1. Jay to RRL, August 18, 1784, RRLP. Frank Monaghan, *John Jay*, 230
2. RRL to Jay, Kingston, October 6, 1779. *The Correspondence and Public Papers of John Jay*, I, 245-46. John Jay to RRL, Martinique, December 24, 1779, and Madrid, October 6, 1780, RRLP.
3. RRL to Luzerne, Trenton, December 12, 1784, RRLP.
4. Monaghan, *op. cit.*, 273-75.
5. RRL to James Duane, New York, April 3, 1786, RRLP.
6. Monaghan, *op. cit.*, 274. The guest was Mrs. William Smith, only daughter of John Adams.
7. RRL to Jay, New York, January 25, 1784, RRLP.
8. RRL to Henry Livingston, undated, RRLP. The internal evidence shows that this letter was written either late in 1786 or in 1787.
9. Chief Justice William Smith to Peter R. Livingston, Quebec, January 2, 1790, Livingston-Redmond Papers, Franklin Delano Roosevelt Library.
10. RRL to Peter Van Schaack, New York, January 20, 1790, Livingston Family Papers, NYPL.
11. RRL to Washington, New York, October 21, 1788, RRLP.
12. RRL to Marbois, New York, April 1, 1789. Cf. John Armstrong to Alida Livingston Armstrong, New York, March 31, 1789. "Joanna [Joanna Livingston, the Chancellor's sister and Armstrong's sister-in-law] has written to you. . . . I have just left her and Mrs. [Morgan] Lewis exacting tarts, nuts and fruits and making themselves very merry with Beaux & Belles, and the old Congress and the new, and the federal hall and the fireworks, and everything else that this grave Town holds most venerable and sacred. Note: They are to have all the world with them on Wednesday night at a concert which is now the fashionable entertainment. . . ." Both in RRLP.
13. Margaret Beekman Livingston to RRL, Clermont, April, 1789, RRLP. She says she was "so unsuccessful in my application among your Tenants when I last applyed to them that I have givin up all thoughts of going among them. . . ."
14. John C. Fitzpatrick, ed., *The Diaries of George Washington* (4 vols., Boston, 1925), IV, 7. David Gelston to John Smith, New York, April 27, 1789, John Smith Papers, NYHS. RRL to Washington, New York, May 2, 1789, RRLP.
15. Rufus W. Griswold, *The Republican Court* (New York, 1867), 139-41.
16. *Ibid.*, 145.
17. Washington to RRL, New York, May 31, 1789, RRLP.
18. Janet L. Montgomery to RRL, July 22(?), 1789, RRLP.
19. Janet L. Montgomery to RRL, undated, RRLP. Internal evidence points to its having been written between July 27 and August 3, 1789.
20. *The Diaries of George Washington*, IV, 62.
21. Hamilton to Walter Livingston, May 18, 1789, RRLP. It should be remembered that Walter had also married a Schuyler.

22. RRL to John Stevens, Jr., Clermont, July 18, 1789, RRLP.
23. John R. Livingston to RRL, Boston, April 30, 1783, RRLP. He invested £10,000 at 8/- for 20/-. Although a successful merchant in later life, John R. did not make a fortune out of the Revolution: his correspondence shows that he was always in difficulties. William Duer and Walter Livingston "in agreement with" Royal Flint, March 15, 1790, RRLP.
24. RRL to Janet L. Montgomery, January 15, 1790, RRLP.
25. RRL, "To the Printer" (1792) and "Thoughts on the . . . Election of 1792" (1792). RRL to Morgan Lewis, New York, January 27, 1791. All in RRLP.
26. Morgan Lewis to RRL, Philadelphia, January 24, 1791, RRLP.
27. RRL to Morgan Lewis, New York, January 27, 1791, RRLP.
28. Janet L. Montgomery to RRL, Tullaghan, July 19, 1790, RRLP.
29. Henry Livingston to Walter Livingston, November 28, 1790. Margaret Beekman Livingston to RRL, Clermont, December 15, 1790. Mrs. Livingston attended the funeral because Robert Livingston, Jr., was, after all, her late husband's closest friend. To be more accurate, she did not wait for the other brothers to confide in her, but left the manor house before they returned from the funeral. What happened was that she "saw none of the Gentn. as I came away before they returned. I have visited Peter who says he is disinherited." Both in RRLP.
30. Margaret Beekman Livingston to RRL, cited *supra*.
31. RRL to Edward Livingston, Clermont, June 5, 1791, RRLP.
32. John Livingston to Walter Livingston, Manor Livingston, November 13, 1791, and March 7, 1792, RRLP.
33. Same to same, Manor Livingston, February 16, 1792, RRLP.
34. William Duer, Agreement with Walter Livingston, February 18, 1792. William Duer to Walter Livingston, New York, March 23, 1792, and March 26, 1792. William S. Livingston to Walter Livingston, New York, April 10, 1792, congratulates him on having fled New York. Walter Livingston to Philip H. Livingston, Manor Livingston, April 17, 1792. All in RRLP.
35. "Thoughts on the . . . Election of 1792" (1792), RRLP.
36. "To Mr. M——," March 27, 1792, RRLP.
37. Irving Brant, *James Madison: Father of the Constitution, 1787-1800* (Indianapolis and New York, 1950), 339-40.
38. RRL to Edward Livingston, Clermont, October 1, 1792, RRLP: "If the choice is to fall upon a man that I like better, I will support him, if not, the little weight I have shall be thrown into A———'s scale."

PART FOUR, CHAPTER TWO

1. RRL, "To Mr. M—— representative for Herkimer County," RRLP. New York *Daily Advertiser*, February 27, 1792.
2. New York *Daily Advertiser*, March 31, 1792.
3. New York *Journal, Extraordinary*, March 31, 1792.
4. RRL, "To the Printer" (1792), RRLP.
5. This appeared in the New York *Journal*, April 4, 1792.
6. Thomas T. Tillotson to RRL, New York, June 3, 1792, RRLP.
7. Quoted in Frank Monaghan, *John Jay*, 334. Clinton submitted the legal aspects of the Otsego, Tioga, and Clinton ballots to Rufus King and Aaron Burr. King considered that the former sheriff of Otsego was still *de facto* sheriff, and that the canvassers should have counted the votes. Burr held that the sheriff, his commission having expired, was no longer *de jure* the sheriff and that the votes were invalid. Precedents were against Burr.

8. Jay is quoted in Monaghan, *op. cit.*, 336. RRL to Edward Livingston, Clermont, June 19, 1792. RRL, "Election Squib" on the canvassers (1792). Both in RRLP.

9. Morgan Lewis to RRL, Johnstown, July 4, 1792, RRLP.

10. Edward Livingston to RRL, New York, July 4, 1792, RRLP. There were many other names for the Anti-Federalist party: the Livingstons always called themselves Republicans, with or without the capital R. Federalist is also a convenient rather than an established name for the administration party at this time, which the Livingstons, writing to one another, often designated as "the party" or "the ministerialists" or "the court party," etc. RRL to Edward Livingston, Clermont, July 20, 1792, RRLP.

11. D. S. Alexander, *A Political History of New York, 1774-1882* (3 vols., New York, 1906-1909), I, 62. The Council was composed of Philip Schuyler, Zina Hitchcock, Selah Strong, and Reuben Hopkins. The latter was a Republican. Jabez D. Hammond, *The History of Political Parties in the State of New-York* (2 vols., Albany, 1842), I, 81. Thomas T. Tillotson told RRL that Strong and Hitchcock "have a proper mixture of ignorance and obstinacy to answer the purposes of the Sachem [Schuyler]." Thomas T. Tillotson to RRL, Albany, January 11, 1793, RRLP.

12. Monaghan, *op. cit.*, 349.

13. RRL, "Reflections on Monarchy" (1792). RRL to Monroe, Clermont, January 4, 1794. RRL to Edward Livingston, Clermont, November 11, 1793. All in RRLP.

14. RRL to Edward Livingston, Albany, January 21, 1794, RRLP.

15. RRL to Monroe, Clermont, January 4, 1794. Also, RRL to Monroe, New York, March 10, 1794. In this letter he maintains that the detention or capture of neutral vessels while in the exercise of natural rights, except when they are transporting contraband, is a direct violation of the law of nations. RRL to Monroe, Clermont, April 8, 1794, says, "I have laid it down long since that if war was to be avoided at all it wd. be by pursuing measures that would convince the world that you neither dreaded or was unprepared for the event and that in every case it would be important to strike the first blow which often decided the fate of nations." He believed that the administration had now stolen something of a march on the Republicans—"you have suffered yourselves to be anticipated in . . . every . . . war measure by yr. antagonists." He believed at this point that Great Britain was prepared to make concessions and that it was to be regretted that we had laid no claim to the gratitude of France. He complained that "Mr. Jefferson's concessions on the subject of the right of neutral bottoms will be severely felt. They destroy our claim of compensation from Britain & they together with the treaty give a right to France to resort to us for the damage they have sustained by our neglect to protect their property." RRL to James Monroe, New York, May 15, 1794, says that we should connive at the fitting out of privateers under French colors by giving such a construction to the Treaty of 1778 as it could be made to bear. RRL to Dr. James M. Adair, Clermont, February 2, 1794. All in RRLP.

16. The order in council of June 8, 1793, ordered all British naval commanders to bring in neutral ships bound for French ports with corn, flour, or meal. The second order in council of November 6, 1793, directed them to bring in all ships laden with goods that were the produce of any colony belonging to France, or carrying provisions or supplies for the use of such colonies. This order was not made public until the naval vessels reached the Caribbean; and the result was the sudden capture of three hundred American vessels trading with the French islands, which had been thrown open to American trade since the beginning of

the war. A third order of January 8, 1794, modified the second order, in line with the Rule of 1756, which forbade neutral trade in time of war which had been forbidden in time of peace, and also with the well-established right to seize enemy goods from neutral ships. It also ordered the capture of all vessels laden in whole or in part with military or naval stores (but did not define what such contraband was) bound for an enemy port under blockade. Blockade was not rigidly defined either. Samuel Flagg Bemis, *A Diplomatic History of the United States,* 99-100.

17. RRL to Jay, May (11), 1794; Jay to RRL, "Sunday night 11 May 1794," RRLP.

18. RRL to Monroe, Clermont, April 8, 1794; RRL to Sir John Temple, Clermont, April 8, 1794, RRLP. Walter Livingston said, "I like the appointment of Mr. Jay he will make an able & faithful servant." Walter Livingston to Philip S. Livingston, Manor Livingston, April 24, 1794, Walter Livingston Letter-Books, NYHS. John Livingston, Walter's brother, wrote him on the same day that he was sorry Jay was going to England, that he suspected that he would not do the U.S.A. the justice it ought to have from "that imperious nation." "I hope to hear a war is declared before he can get to Billy Pitt—& that he may be taken prisoner—" John Livingston to Walter Livingston, April 24, 1794, RRLP. In the election of 1798, John Livingston was said to be a supporter of Jay. John Smith to William Wilson, Poughkeepsie, March 24, 1798, Wilson Family Papers, Clements Library. The manor Livingstons were never politically consistent in these years, even after the feud with Clermont had been settled.

19. Washington to RRL, Philadelphia, April 29, 1794: "Dear Sir, Circumstances have rendered it expedient to recall Mr. Gouverneur Morris from his Mission to the Republic of France—Would it be convenient and agreeable to you to supply his place? An affirmative answer, would induce an immediate nomination of you, for this appointment to the Senate, and the significance of your sentiments, relatively thereto, as soon as your determination is formed would oblige me; particularly as it is not expected that that body will remain much longer in Session. —With very great esteem & regard I am—Dear Sir your Obed. Hble Servt." RRL replied, New York, May 10, 1794, that he could not make immediate arrangements for permanent residence abroad and was therefore compelled to decline the honor. "Permit me however sir to assure you that I have recd this mark of your attention with infinite sensibility since it affords me the convincing proof that my enemies have been less successful than I imagined in depriving me of your favorable opinion which I always have & always shall estimate far above the honors & emoluments of office—" Washington wrote again on May 14, saying that he was "desirous of accomodating you in point of time, as far as the puplic service will permit—If therefore such an accomodation will remove your objections; I shall be glad to be informed on the return of mail, what will be the shortest time necessary for your preparation. Your answer will immediately decide me." RRL replied, New York, May 15, 1794, that he was flattered by this new proof of the President's friendly attention, but could not make his arrangements "within any time which would consist with the public interest . . . without making such important personal sacrifice as your kindness for me would not permit you to exact." His letter to Monroe setting forth his real reasons was dated New York, May 15, 1794. The family's opinion is in Morgan Lewis to RRL, New York, May 1, 1794. All in RRLP. Also Georges-Pierre LeBlanc to RRL, "20 Floreal 2d yr" (May 9, 1794), RRLP. In this letter, LeBlanc assures RRL that the appointment of Brockholst Livingston, which RRL had evidently suggested, would not do, or could not be hoped for.

20. RRL to William Wilson, New York, January 25, 1795, says that Yates is "of the

class of people that will be most agreeable to the common people," but that if Wilson could contrive to have a meeting at Hudson or Kingston "it would compel them to take me up & you can easily see that I must not appear to have any agentcy in this business." But by February 1, he was writing that the Republicans in the Assembly will almost certainly fix on Yates, though they profess to have little confidence in him: but they have been persuaded "that he has immense interest to the north. For my part I am perfectly indifferent to the thing myself." RRL to William Wilson, New York, February 1, 1795. Both in Wilson Family Papers, Clements Library. In his letter to Wilson of January 25, RRL says that he has heard that the western posts were not to be evacuated until June, 1796; rumors, and not inaccurate ones, concerning Jay's treaty arrived in America well ahead of the treaty itself. In the letter of February 1, he expatiates more widely on the terms of the treaty.

21. Monaghan, *op. cit.*, 405 ff.

22. Edward Livingston to RRL, New York, July 6, 1795, RRLP.

23. Claude G. Bowers, *Jefferson and Hamilton* (Boston and New York, 1925), 271.

24. Bemis, *op. cit.*, 103. Professor Bemis has written a famous full-length study, *Jay's Treaty: A Study in Commerce and Diplomacy.* If its findings have been superseded, I do not know by whom.

25. RRL to Washington, Clermont, July 8, 1795, RRLP. In this long letter he inveighed against Articles XXIV and XXV, which he felt spoke for themselves; but he also called his attention to Article VII, which expressly admits that enemy property on board a neutral vessel is liable to capture; and Article XII, where the question is to be revived again within two years after the termination of war. Does not this show, he argued, a "fixed determination" to aid Great Britain even at our own expense and that of the French Republic? And Article XVIII left British definitions of siege and blockade untouched, or, rather, undefined; and of course acquiesced in their absurd and unlimited construction of these terms, while enabling them to renew their attempt to starve France and her colonies. In our treaty with France of 1778, tar, turpentine, cordage, sails, masts, etc. are expressly declared not to be contraband; yet in Jay's Treaty they are declared contraband. Upon what principle will France suppose we entered upon this stipulation? Surely Great Britain is our "secret enemy" and France "a most certain ally." A war with France would be the signal for a civil war among ourselves. Washington did not reply until August 20 (To RRL, Philadelphia, August 20, 1795, RRLP). He said that RRL's of July 8 had been received on the day preceding his departure for Mount Vernon, "from whence I intended to acknowledge the receipt of it; but so many letters of a public nature were poured upon me at that place, and the urgency of the business in which I have since been engaged, have prevented my doing it until now. . . . The opinions & reasonings of enlightened men are particularly acceptable: but, as it happens, in other matters, so in this, they are extremely varient. —You deem the treaty palpably defective, & pregnant with evils: others think it contains substantial good. —For myself, I freely own that I cannot discern in it the mischief you anticipate: on the contrary, altho' it does not rise to all our wishes, yet it appears to me calculated to procure to the United States such advantages as entitle it to our acceptance. —My final act, of course, conforms to this opinion." Maturin Livingston, RRL's nephew, on hearing that Washington had signed the treaty wrote: "The original compact between the people & the government is broken—There is no Constitution nor are any bound to obey." Maturin Livingston to RRL, New York, August 17, 1795, RRLP. Also RRL to Samuel Adams, Clermont, July 10, 1795, and RRL to James Monroe, Clermont, August 25, 1795, and New York, December 13, 1795. All in RRLP.

26. The "Cato" articles appeared on these dates in the *Argus*: Cato No. 1, July 15, 1795; Cato No. 2, July 17; Cato No. 3, July 22; Cato No. 4, July 25; Cato No. 5, July 31; Cato No. 6, August 7; Cato No. 7, August 11; Cato No. 8, August 17; Cato No. 9, August 22; Cato No. 10, August 26; Cato No. 11, August 29; Cato No. 12, September 2; Cato No. 13, September 10; Cato No. 14, September 16; Cato No. 15, September 23; Cato No. 16, September 30. The indefatigable writer says in 16 that several articles remain to be discussed, but that the "present unhappy situation of the city" (the yellow fever) compelled him to lay aside his pen. "When these circumstances cease to operate, I may again resume it." He never did.

27. Edward Livingston to Margaret Beekman Livingston, New York, July 20, 1795, RRLP.

28. He is, at any rate, alleged to have described the Treaty as "an execrable one," the work of "an old woman." This came by way of Talleyrand to Volney to Jefferson: scarcely an impartial route. If Hamilton did say these things, he was ungrateful. The treaty at least saved his financial structure. Monaghan, *op. cit.*, 389. Bemis, *op. cit.*, 103.

29. Alexander, *op. cit.*, I, 80.

30. RRL to De Witt Clinton, New York, February 19, 1798, De Witt Clinton Papers, Columbia University Libraries' Special Collections.

31. William Wilson to RRL, March 1, 1798, RRLP: "In that vile place the Camp they held a meeting & declared for Jay & [the] present lieut govr. . . . I trust your friends are more numerous & respectable than has been supposed."

32. De Witt Clinton to RRL, Albany, March 2, 1798, De Witt Clinton Papers, Columbia University Libraries' Special Collections.

33. RRL to De Witt Clinton, New York, March 7, 1798, *ibid.*

34. As, for example, RRL to William Wilson, April 13, 1798, concerning the vote at Saugerties and Kingston, Wilson Family Papers, Clements Library.

35. Alexander, *op. cit.*, I, 75, 76.

PART FOUR, CHAPTER THREE

1. *Minutes of the Court of Chancery*, entry for January 27, 1787, and Chancellor's "Rules and Orders" (Rule No. 26), established December 28, 1797.

2. Jabez D. Hammond, *The History of Political Parties in the State of New-York*, I, 108.

3. Nathan Pendleton to RRL, New York, September 22, 1797; Aaron Burr to RRL, August 26, 1799, RRLP. *Minutes* for 1799 and 1800.

4. Thomas Tillotson to RRL, Albany, February 27, 1799; "There is much grumbling about your and [Morgan] Lewis's absenting yourselves from what they call your duty." Thomas Tillotson to RRL, Albany, Thursday, March 15, 1799, says that it seems "a subject of animadversion" that he and Lewis should be absent the whole winter except for perhaps a week each. Both in RRLP.

5. RRL to John R. Livingston, Clermont, May 18, 1785, RRLP.

6. *Minutes*, entry for April 24, 1786. Edward Livingston, to be sure, according to these *Minutes*, was examined for fitness by his kinsman Brockholst Livingston and his brother-in-law Morgan Lewis. On the other hand, it was not until October 13, 1787, that the Chancellor ordered that solicitors of the court must serve two years in that capacity before they could become counselors: so that in 1786, there was no reason why he should not be admitted solicitor and counsel on the same day. For Edward Livingston's capacities as a lawyer, see DAB (1946 ed.), Livingston, Edward, XI, 311, where Sir Henry Maine is quoted as de-

scribing him as "the first legal genius of his time." As regards Edward Livingston's legal standards and somewhat aristocratic attitude toward his profession, see Edward Livingston to RRL, Clermont, June 7, 1789, RRLP, where, asking for his brother's influence in obtaining for him an under secretaryship of State—no one knew then that the Livingstons had ceased to have any influence with Washington— he says: "The vile crowd of Indigent & therefore dishonest Practitioners that dishonor our Profession have cast a Stygma on the Practice." Edward Livingston's portrait, from an engraving by E. Wellmore after a drawing by J. B. Longacre, is in Claude G. Bowers, *Jefferson and Hamilton* (Boston and New York, 1925), facing page 148. Needless to say, there are others. In 1794, RRL was much opposed to Edward Livingston's running for election. In New York City, he wrote, "the tories make a powerful party & I find the mechanicks and cartmen are on their side." RRL to Edward Livingston, Clermont, April 18, 1794, RRLP.

7. Bowers, *op. cit.*, 290, quoting Oliver Wolcott in Henry Adams, *The Life of Albert Gallatin* (Philadelphia, 1879), 152. In RRL's references to the French Revolution, scattered through his letters in RRLP, he had nothing but good to say of it. On the other hand, he was disturbed by what he called "the madness of the young Jacobins or Maratists" in 1792: "All I dread is that the people may be wearied out & seek in tyranny a permanent refuge from anarchy." RRL to John Stevens in A. D. Turnbull, *John Stevens: An American Record*, 114. By 1795, he was reassured: "the system of blood" was not to be restored and things in France were all that "the most sanguine Republican could wish." RRL to John Stevens, Jr., Clermont, August 30, 1795, *ibid.*, 124.

8. RRL to Edward Livingston, Clermont, October 30, 1795, RRLP.

9. Walter Livingston to Henry W. Livingston, May 28, 1792, RRLP, says that he was liable for $375,000 by Duer's failure, though he believes that what ruined him and forced him to confine himself in the manor was the failure of Alexander McComb, Richard Platt, John Dewhurst, and others, by which he became liable for another $100,000.

10. These maneuvers can be followed in the Walter Livingston Letter-Books, RRLP. The method seems to have been a confession by Walter Livingston of judgments in favor of Henry Livingston, Philip Henry Livingston, and John Rutson Van Rensselaer for debts which—in the opinion of Walter Livingston's creditors— were nonexistent. They said, for example, that the judgment in favor of Philip Henry was for notes left with Walter as escrows, for which Philip Henry never paid anything. For the Chancellor's unfavorable attitude toward Henry Livingston's deed obtained from Walter Livingston, see Henry Livingston to Walter Livingston, New York, February 13, 1793. See also Brockholst Livingston to Walter Livingston, New York, April 14, 1793, for judgment in favor of Henry Livingston, who (said the creditor) did not owe Walter "a shilling." Both in RRLP. Walter Livingston to Guilian Ver Planck, President of the Bank of New York, Manor Livingston, June 30, 1794, explains that he has taken steps to effect the sale of Duer's lands by virtue of his judgment against Duer's estate for (he now says) $400,000; and that Duer's friends have prevented execution by injunctions obtained from Chancery. Walter Livingston to Brockholst Livingston, July 1, 1794, says: "You write to me that the Chancellor knew nothing of the present injunction." Both in Walter Livingston Letter-Books, RRLP. Brockholst Livingston replies, New York, July 5, 1794, RRLP, that the clerks in chancery always grant injunctions "without the Chancellor's knowledge." Walter Livingston to Philip Schuyler Livingston, Manor Livingston, August 29, 1794: "The Chancellor dissolved the injunction so far as to permit the Sheriff to sell on advertising again. Mr. Bay applied to him for an order on the Clerk in Chancery

not to grant any more injunctions. He replied when they see this and know that I have twice dissolved them they will not grant any more." Walter Livingston to Brockholst Livingston, September 2, 1794: "Mr. Bay attended and the Chancellor readily Dissolved the injunction, and ordered the amount of the sales to be paid into the Bank—That will prevent me from bidding, and the lands will be sold under value to my great prejudice." Both in Walter Livingston Letter-Books, RRLP. The order of the Court of Chancery, "held in the Chancellor's Chambers in Clermont," on August 27, dissolving the injunction in the cause of William Duer and Walter Livingston *adversus* George Stacey, on the motion of Mr. Bay on behalf of Mr. Brockholst Livingston, "of Council for Walter Livingston, one of the defendants," is in RRLP. It must be repeated that the Chancellor judged this cause on its merits, and did no favors to Walter.

11. Walter Livingston to RRL, Manor Livingston, August 23, 1794, Walter Livingston Letter-Books, RRLP. RRL to Walter Livingston, Clermont, August 23, 1794, RRLP. It was Walter's embarrassing conveyance to his relatives that started a new turbulence among the manor (not the Clermont) tenants, which may be traced in his letter books in RRLP and in the Wilson Family Papers, Clements Library.

12. See 10 *supra*.

13. RRL to Walter Livingston, Clermont, April 7, 1795. This letter was in reply to a letter of Walter's of April 2, in which Walter asks if RRL will sell his right to the building of a sawmill at the mouth of Roeliff Jansen Kill. "Not being possessed of our ancestor's will I am not perfectly acquainted with the rights bequeathed to your grandfather." *I.e.*, the first offers of an accommodation, according to this sentence, were made from the manor, not from Clermont. Both in Walter Livingston's Letter-Books, RRLP. In 1797, as evidence of the new cordiality, we find a poem from the Chancellor to Mrs. Henry W. Livingston, Walter's daughter-in-law, beginning: "So Mary midst the seasons gloom / By Henry's care like Spring you bloom. . . ." It is dated February, 1797, RRLP.

14. The Reverend Robert G. Wetmore, "Minister of the Epis: Church," certifies that at Clermont on June 10, 1798, "Mr. Robert L. Livingston and Miss Margaret Livingston were legally married by me according to the due and prescribed Order of the Protestant Episcopal Church in presence of divers respectable witnesses." Since both Henry Livingston and John Stevens wrote on July 9 and July 10 respectively to say how sorry they were not to be able to attend this ceremony, their invitations having been issued on June 20 and June 30, one can only suppose that Mr. Wetmore had misdated his certificate. Henry Livingston to Robert L. Livingston, Ancram House, July 9, 1798. John Stevens to RRL, Hoboken, July 10, 1798, says that, owing to difficulties in obtaining a sloop and to unfavorable winds when he did get one, "I was obliged to give up all thoughts of getting up in time for the wedding." Both in RRLP.

15. RRL to Samuel L. Mitchell, Clermont, September 17, 1792: "all the plans I had projected of agricultural improvement for this year have been frustrated by the care of building a country house." His Clermont Account Book, NYHS, shows that the house was completed in 1793; on December 20, 1793, he gives a certain Mr. Hathaway, "in consideration of his fidelity in finishing my house," £100 beyond what has been already advanced. His agreement with Ebenezer White was made on June 15, 1794.

16. As regards "harshness," distraint, while very infrequent, revealed how harsh both conditions of life and legal actions could be. When Henry Walter, a Clermont tenant, was distrained for being $600 in arrears, in October, 1799, his possessions and their appraisal values were as follows: 1 Negro Wench— $62.50; 180 bushels of corn—$90; 2 feather beds and bedding—$19; 1 cup-

board—$3.75; 3 Tables—$10.75; 1 Horse—$60; 1 Cow—$13.75; 1 Sleigh—$17; 1 Plough—$2; 1 Wagon—$22.50; 1 Set harness—$7.50; 3 loads Hay—$9; 7 Hogs—$31.37½." Wilson Family Papers, Clements Library.

17. 3 *Laws of the State of New York* (Albany, 1887), 467-68. RRL was president; John Sloss Hobart, vice-president; Samuel Jones, treasurer; Samuel L. Mitchell and Samuel Jones, Jr., secretaries. John Jay was among its original members. David M. Ellis, *Landlords and Farmers in the Hudson-Mohawk Region, 1790-1850*, 98.

18. As, for example, RRL in *Transactions of the Society Instituted in the State of New York for the Promotion of Agriculture, Arts and Manufactures*, I (1792-1799), Part I, 2-54 (on gypsum) and Part II, 65-91 (on lucerne). For other writings, see *ibid.*, Part II, 47-63 (An Address), 92-94, 140-41 (Excretion Duct of the Feet of Sheep), 223-28 (Effects of Shade Trees on Vegetation); Part IV (1799), 20-29 (Vetches), 60-66 (Manures), 80-83 (Elk and Moose), 153-60 (Flour Mills), 174-78 (Bot Worms).

19. Ellis, *op. cit.*, 79, says that the farmers of eastern New York between 1791 and 1801 were, for better or for worse, entering upon the phase of commercial farming. Some part of the landlords' support of the federal Constitution had been predicated upon such an event.

20. RRL to Arthur Young, Clermont, January 11, 1794, RRLP.

21. RRL to Samuel L. Mitchell, Clermont, February 14, 1800, RRLP, where he explains how he first discovered the potentialities of conserva.

22. *New York: A Guide to the Empire State* (New York, 1940), American Guide Series, 610.

23. Pierre Delabigarre to RRL, New York, June 30, 1794, RRLP.

24. RRL to Samuel L. Mitchill, Clermont, September 17, 1792, RRLP.

25. RRL to Simeon De Witt, September 8, 1799, RRLP.

26. RRL to Timothy Pickering, Clermont, September 4, 1799. U.S. Patent, dated Philadelphia, October 28, 1799. John Stevens to RRL, Hoboken, August 28, 1799. Pierre Delabigarre to RRL, Poughkeepsie, July 25, 1800. All in RRLP.

27. Turnbull, *op. cit.*, 113.

28. RRL to Nicholas J. Roosevelt, New York, December 8, 1797. RRL to Nicholas J. Roosevelt, New York, December 22, 1797; Albany, January 12, 1798; Clermont, January 18, 1798; Clermont, January 20, 1798; Albany, January 23, 1798; New York, February 20, 1798; New York, February 22, 1798; New York, March 2, 1798; New York, March 15, 1798; New York, March 18, 1798; and Clermont, April 6, 1798, when at last an agreement was reached. Roosevelt was to have 12/100 not only in any patent right but in the right RRL had under the New York law: but RRL excludes any right in boats on "my ferry or Mr. Stevens"—*i.e.*, in ferries running to Stevens and Livingston-Stevens property in the Amboys, which were part of the Stevens estate—though Roosevelt could claim 12/100 in any new ferry established to the Jersey shore. All in Fulton Papers, NYHS.

29. Act of March 27, 1798, 4 *Laws of the State of New York*, 382-83. RRL to Nicholas J. Roosevelt, December 7, 1797, Fulton Papers, NYHS. Turnbull, *op. cit.*, 131. James T. Flexner, *Steamboats Come True* (New York, 1944), 262.

30. Charles Standinger to Nicholas J. Roosevelt, December 18, 1797, Fulton Papers, NYHS. Standinger so spells his name. Stevens spelled it "Stoudinger"; Roosevelt, "Standinger."

31. Nicholas J. Roosevelt to RRL, Second River, September 8, 1798, Fulton Papers, NYHS: "I would therefore recommend that we throw two wheels of wood over the sides fastened to the axes of the flys with 8 arms or paddles . . . and that we navigate the vessel with these until we can obtain an engine of proper size." Turnbull, *op. cit.*, 134.

32. As early as June 25, RRL writes to Roosevelt from Clermont: "I shall anxiously expect the fruit of our Labour in seeing you arrive here at the rate of about five miles an hour on the day you have set—Mr. Delabigarre has prepared his battery to give you a salute as you pass Red Hook." On August 17, he writes to Roosevelt from Albany to express his mortification at the steamboat's failure, to accuse the engine, not the wheel, of being responsible for the failure, to say that Roosevelt must be responsible for any pecuniary loss, and to suggest that he should get other workmen. He apologized in a letter written from Clermont on August 22, and Roosevelt accepts this apology in a letter written on August 27. On the back of the draft of this letter is the notation: "Dt. Robt R. Livingston . . . on the pretext of his wishing to throw the whole expense on me after the failure of his wheel." All in Fulton Papers, NYHS.

33. After a further exchange of letters, faintly acrimonious on both sides, and dealing with various possible improvements, RRL tells Roosevelt from Clermont that "I say nothing on the subject of wheels over the sides." RRL to Nicholas J. Roosevelt, Clermont, September 18, 1798. That the boat was equipped with RRL's horizontal wheel seems indicated by Nicholas J. Roosevelt to RRL, Second River, October 21, 1798. "The Spanish Minister was on hand the day we made the last experiment . . . during our sail he at the time the tide & wind favour us supposed we went at the rate of 6 miles an hour—but I think the delight he felt at the novelty of the voyage was the cause of this mistake—I have at present a better opinion of your plans than ever and would wish them to be contrasted with Mr. Stevens plan or wheels over the sides." Both in Fulton Papers, NYHS. Rear-Admiral George Henry Preble, *A Chronological History of the Origin and Development of Steam Navigation*, 32, says this boat was equipped with a system of paddles, resembling a horizontal chain pump.

34. RRL to Nicholas J. Roosevelt, Clermont, October 28, 1798, Fulton Papers, NYHS.

35. Same to same, Clermont, November 19, 1798, *ibid.*

36. Beatrice G. Reubens, "Burr, Hamilton and the Manhattan Company," *Political Science Quarterly*, LXXII, No. 4 (December, 1957), 578-607, and LXXIII, No. 1 (March, 1958), 100-25.

37. Reubens, *loc. cit.*, 600. Bray Hammond, *Banks and Politics in America*, 152.

38. Alfred B. Street, *The Council of Revision in the State of New York*, 425.

39. *Idem.* Robert Troup to Rufus King, June 5, 1799, Rufus King Papers, NYHS. Troup seems to have confused the governor's voting powers in the Council of Revision with those in the Council of Appointment, where the governor possessed only a casting vote. For the Chancellor's appearance at the Council of Revision, see 38 *supra.*

40. RRL to Nicholas J. Roosevelt, Clermont, April 17, 1799, Fulton Papers, NYHS.

41. Reubens, *loc. cit.*, 103.

42. New York *Commercial Advertiser*, May 16, 1799. There were ten interrogatories in all, but the Chancellor's vote in the Council was not mentioned. "Socrates's" contention was that the business of the Manhattan Company was bound to come before the Chancery Court.

43. Reubens, *loc. cit.*, 596, citing *A Collection of Rare Autographs Commemorating the 120th Anniversary of the Bank of the Manhattan Company, 1799-1919* (New York, 1919). De Witt Clinton was down for one thousand shares; so that there can certainly be observed in this "a definitely political allocation of power."

44. Of course, to promote a banking institution in the teeth of the majority of "the most respectable mercantile & monied interest of the city," who, according to Troup, were against it in April 1799, would not be displeasing to an enemy

of the whole moneyed interest. Robert Troup to Rufus King, April 15, 1799. Rufus King Papers, NYHS.

45. Reubens, *loc. cit.*, 104.

46. The two hundred forty were handed over to Brockholst Livingston, possibly as collateral for moneys advanced to RRL. Aside from his large interest in the Livingston-Fulton monopoly, the only shares besides these two hundred forty owned by RRL at his death were two hundred shares in the Middle District Bank, valued at $5 apiece, some turnpike shares, and a few shares in two manufacturing concerns—the Hamilton Manufacturing (Glass House) Society and the Oriskany Manufacturing Society. "An Inventory of the Goods, Chattels and Credits of Robert R. Livingston . . ." taken September 30, 1813, RRLP. As has been well stated, Livingston's name, like Swartwout's and De Witt Clinton's, was "unfamiliar on the rosters of corporate stockholders." Reubens, *loc. cit.*, 597.

47. Hammond, *op. cit.*, 156.

48. "Politicus" (James Cheetham), *An Impartial Enquiry* . . . (New York, 1806), 8. Reubens, *loc. cit.*, 579.

49. "R. R. Livingston's Account Book, Clermont, N. Y.," NYHS, shows that he drew checks on the Bank of New York in 1799. The bank discounted his notes for steamboat purposes, but RRL to John Stevens, Clermont, October 25, 1799, RRLP, shows that it was sometimes hesitant.

50. My contention—that the Chancellor should have disqualified himself from voting in the Council—was apparently not a contemporary one. He himself could have eased his conscience, if it pricked him, by telling himself with perfect truth that a water company was in itself a good project. He offered the Manhattan Company a steam engine gratis, if it would use one for pumping purposes— it was, to him, a kind of laboratory in that respect. RRL to Gentlemen of the Committee for Supplying Water, Clermont, September 2, 1799, RRLP. His brother-in-law John Stevens was a member of this committee until July 4, 1800; he was also a member of the board of directors, and had subscribed in advance for one thousand shares. Turnbull, *op. cit.*, 148. The Manhattan Company supplied water, though most inefficiently, for many years: but its inefficiency could not have been predicted, and as for the union of a public-improvements corporation with banking, it took America forty years to learn how dangerous that could be.

51. RRL to Nicholas J. Roosevelt, Clermont, April 17, 1799, Fulton Papers, NYHS: "You find by the list of laws that the one you wished has passed granting the priviledge for 20 years."

52. The correspondence is all in RRLP. It was concluded amicably, as far as RRLP are concerned, on April 3, 1800, in a letter from John Stevens to RRL. Whether the paddle wheels were to be in the stern—John Stevens to RRL, July 15, 1799— an early approach to the propeller—or over the sides, cannot be determined. RRL had, at any rate, abandoned his horizontal wheel, and was devoting most of his thinking to the engine: *i.e.*, the rotatory motion and the mercury principle. Nicholas J. Roosevelt to RRL, New York, April 13, 1801, talks of commencing a new experiment. The rest is silence.

53. RRL to Benjamin De Witt, Clermont, October 8, 1799. James Watt to Dr. Robertson, Glasgow, October 25, 1800. Just when this letter reached RRL cannot be determined: it may have been, of course, before experiments were abandoned in 1801. Both in RRLP.

54. RRL to John Armstrong, Paris, March 31, 1804, RRLP, says that if Burr considers among the good things he has done the change brought about in the politics

of New York by the establishment of the Manhattan Company, "he will hardly be so hardy to deny that he received the whole plan & the first hint from me."

55. RRL to Nicholas J. Roosevelt, Clermont, February 5, 1799, quoted in Turnbull, *op. cit.*, 137-38.

56. RRL to Joseph Priestley, Clermont, December 30, 1799, RRLP.

57. Jefferson to RRL, Philadelphia, February 23, 1799, RRLP.

58. RRL to Sir John Sinclair, President of the Board of Agriculture, Albany, March 15, 1799, RRLP.

59. Washington to RRL, Philadelphia, February 10, 1793, praises the "patriotic characters" who have instituted and supported the New York Society. RRL to Washington, New York, February 2, 1795, enclosing second part of the Society's "proceedings"; with some remarks on the importance of lucerne to the Southern states. Washington to RRL, Philadelphia, Febuary 16, 1795, says that he wishes there were more societies like the New York Society; that he will read RRL's article on lucerne with edification and pleasure; that he has long been impressed with the value of that grass, especially if it can be "cultivated in broad cast to advantage"; and that he sends a pamphlet on the culture of potatoes from the shoots. All in RRLP. RRL was referring to his article on lucerne in *Transactions*, I, Part II, 65-91.

60. RRL to Jefferson, Clermont, March 14, 1801, RRLP. This seems to be an elaborate answer to Jefferson to RRL, Washington, December 14, 1800, first paragraph: the rest of the letter concerned the offer of the secretaryship of the Navy and had long since been answered (January 7, 1801), *The Writings of Thomas Jefferson*, Paul Leicester Ford, ed., IX, 150-51.

PART FOUR, CHAPTER FOUR

1. Henry Adams, *History of the United States of America During the Administration of Thomas Jefferson*, I, 112, 113.

2. *Ibid.*, I, 230.

3. *DAB* (1946 ed.), Clinton, De Witt, IV, 221 ff.

4. RRL to Edward Livingston, New York, December 31, 1797, and Clermont, January 25, 1799, RRLP.

5. *The Writings of Thomas Jefferson*, Paul Leicester Ford, ed., IX, 152-53.

6. Irving Brant, *James Madison: Secretary of State, 1800-1809* (Indianapolis and New York, 1953), 26.

7. Burr to RRL, New York, December 9, 1800, RRLP.

8. Irving Brant, *James Madison: Secretary of State, 1800-1809*, 26.

9. Edward Livingston to RRL, Washington, December 16, 1800, RRLP.

10. RRL to Jefferson, New York, May 8, 1800, RRLP.

11. RRL to Edward Livingston, Clermont, December 1, 1800, RRLP.

12. RRL to Aaron Burr, January 1, 1801, RRLP.

13. Edward Livingston to RRL, January 29, 1801; RRL to Gouverneur Morris, Clermont, February 7, 1801; RRL to Edward Livingston, New York, February 20, 1801, RRLP.

14. Edward Livingston to RRL, New York, April 11, 1800, RRLP.

15. Gouverneur Morris to RRL, Washington, January 23, 1801, RRLP.

16. Jabez D. Hammond, *The History of Political Parties in the State of New-York*, I, 138.

17. RRL to Gouverneur Morris, Clermont, February 7, 1801, RRLP.

18. Peter W. Yates to RRL, Albany, October 26, 1800, RRLP.

19. Henry Livingston to William Wilson, Ancram, July 27, 1797, Wilson Family Papers, Clements Library.
20. Jefferson to RRL, Washington, February 18 and 24, 1801, *The Writings of Thomas Jefferson,* IX, 182, 187.
21. Louis André Pichon to RRL, Washington, April 2, 1801, RRLP.
22. RRL to Edward Livingston, Clermont, August 23, 1801, RRLP.
23. D. S. Alexander, *A Political History of New York, 1774-1882,* I, 117.

PART FIVE, CHAPTER ONE

1. RRL to Edward Livingston, *Boston* Frigate, "43.3 N. Long. 54.23W.," October 20, 1801, RRLP, where RRL says that he is now five days out.
2. Richard Somers, USN, to Captain William J. Keen, September 28, 1801, Item 205, Parke-Bernet 1683.
3. Margaret Beekman Livingston to RRL, New York, December 31, 1793, RRLP.
4. Note by Margaret L. Tillotson, Wainwright Autograph Collection, Princeton University Library: which says that she died on July 1, 1800. "She arose in her usual health and spirits, walked in her ga[rden and at] 9 at night was called from the bosom of her family."
5. Will of Col. Henry Beekman in *Abstract of Wills on File in the Surrogate's Office, City of New York,* New-York Historical Society *Collections, 1903,* XII (New York, 1904), 342-43.
6. RRL to Margaret L. Tillotson, Nantes, December 3, 1801, RRLP.
7. RRL to Joanna Livingston, Nantes, November 23, 1801, RRLP.
8. RRL, Note on the Minister's Reception, Sunday, December 6, 1801, RRLP.
9. Madame de Staël, *Oeuvres* (17 vols., Paris, 1821), XV, 47-48.
10. G. Lacour-Gayet, *Talleyrand* (4 vols., Paris, 1934), II, 106-07.
11. *Ibid.,* IV, 50.
12. *Ibid.,* II, 45, 103.
13. *Ibid.,* II, 55.
14. *Ibid.,* IV, 53.
15. Talleyrand to Moreau de Saint Méry, February 17, 1797, *ibid.,* IV, 51.
16. Comte de Las Cases, *Mémorial de Sainte-Hélène,* Marcel Dunan, ed. (2 vols., Paris, 1951), I, 499.
17. Madison to RRL, September 28, 1801, *ASPFR* II, 510-11.
18. Vincent T. Harlow, *The Founding of the Second British Empire, 1763-1793,* 312-407.
19. Henry Adams, *History of the United States During the Administration of Thomas Jefferson,* I, 339-40.
20. E. Wilson Lyon, *Louisiana in French Diplomacy* (Norman, 1934), 106-07.
21. The convention is printed in Hunter Miller, ed., *Treaties and Other International Acts of the United States of America* (Washington, 1931), II, 457-82.
22. RRL to Margaret L. Tillotson, Nantes, December 3, 1801, RRLP.

PART FIVE, CHAPTER TWO

Livingston's drafts, papers, and letter books—he maintained a set of letter books only during his term of service as minister to France—have been used as the source material for this and subsequent Louisiana chapters: but I have compared them with the printed material in *American State Papers, Foreign Relations,* Vol. II, *France and Spain—Louisiana,* 506-83. Very nearly the identical material can also be found in *State Papers and Correspondence Bearing upon the Purchase of the*

Territory of Louisiana, 57 Cong., 2 Sess., HR Doc. No. 431. Livingston's papers usually match this printed material exactly; where the printed material presents only extracts, the extracts represent all in any given note or dispatch which is relevant to the Louisiana Purchase. Where excisions have been made, they have almost invariably been with regard to Livingston's wistful remarks on the necessity of bribes in dealing with French officials. If a note or dispatch from or to Livingston does *not* appear in the printed material cited above, I have marked it with an asterisk. Private letters, merely for the sake of clarity, are marked (P). The reader is also referred to *The Original Letters of Robert R. Livingston,* Edward Alexander Parsons, ed., which contains certain letters from Livingston to Rufus King which do not appear in the drafts or letter books in RRLP. This collection is abbreviated as TOLRRL.

1. RRL to A. J. Dallas, Paris, December 30, 1801. RRL to Angelica Schuyler Church, Paris, February 27, 1802. Both in RRLP(P).
2. RRL to Dr. Samuel Bard, Paris, May 28, 1802, RRLP(P).
3. RRL to Mrs. James Fairlie, Paris, December 26, 1801. Livingston was a great admirer of French women in all walks of society. "Beauty is much more rare than in America," he writes his sister Joanna, "but . . . grace & manners supply so well the place of beauty that you hardly ask whether a woman is handsome or not," RRL to Joanna Livingston, Paris, March 28, 1802. Both in RRLP(P).
4. RRL to Alida L. Armstrong, Paris, February 28, 1802, RRLP(P).
5. RRL to Gouverneur Morris, Paris, January 14, 1802, RRLP(P).
6. RRL to Gouverneur Morris, May 22, 1802, RRLP(P).
7. RRL to Brockholst Livingston, May 13, 1802, RRLP(P).
8. RRL to Madison, Paris, December 30, 1801, RRLP*. For some reason this pertinent material was edited out of *ASPFR* II, 513. RRL to Madison, January 15, 1802, *ASPFR* II, 513. RRL to Madison, Paris, March 22, 1802, RRLP*.
9. RRL to Talleyrand, March 16, 1802: where he apologizes for his "harsh" language, and adds that "if ever there was a moment when it becomes a Minister to speak with freedom, it is when he feels that the dearest interests of his country are at stake." RRLP and *ASPFR* II, 548-49.
10. 34 Cong. 1 Sess. Senate Ex. Doc. No. 87, "Report of the Secretary of State . . ." 8, 10.
11. Madison to RRL, Department of State, March 14, 1802, RRLP(P): "Mr. Gerard is a very respectable merchant & citizen of the U. States, and feels so strongly both the justice & importance of his claims, as to depute Mr. Curwan to Paris for the purpose of supporting them. He has expressed an anxiety also that they should be particularly recommended to your patronage. . . ." It appears from the "Report" quoted in 10 *supra,* that Girard's claim for the *Betsey,* because of an embargo, was eventually admitted, and that two others were denied. How much Mr. Girard eventually received is, to the best of my knowledge, unknown.
12. RRL to Madison, Paris, December 12 and 10, 1801, RRLP and *ASPFR* II, 512.
13. RRL to Madison, Paris, January 15, 1802, RRLP and *ASPFR* II, 513. In RRLP*, Livingston goes on to say that the French "seem to know little or care little about public faith or credit." Their whole system of finance reduces itself "to plans not for the payment but for the extinguishment of the debt."
14. Rufus King to RRL, London, January 16, 1802, RRLP and (in part) in TOLRRL, 24.
15. Bonaparte to Toussaint L'Ouverture, November 18, 1801, quoted in Henry Adams, *History of the United States of America During the Administration of Thomas Jefferson,* I, 393-94.
16. *Ibid.,* 396.

17. RRL to Talleyrand, Paris, February 20, 1802, RRLP and *ASPFR* II, 513-14. For Talleyrand's reply, see Lyon, *Louisiana in French Diplomacy*, 158-59.
18. Rufus King to RRL, April 1, 1802, RRLP*.
19. RRL to Madison, April 24, 1802, RRLP and *ASPFR* II, 515-16.
20. Rufus King to RRL, April 25, 1802, RRLP*.
21. RRL to Talleyrand, April 28, 1802, RRLP*.
22. RRL to Madison, Paris, May 28, 1802, RRLP and *ASPFR* II, 518: in which RRL says that he "waits impatiently some further instructions from you."
23. RRL to D'Azara, May 28, 1802; D'Azara to RRL, June 2, 1802, RRLP and *ASPFR* II, 518, 519.
24. RRL to Madison, Paris, July 3, 1802, RRLP*: "I think I collected from him that at least West Florida was not yet theirs."
25. Rufus King to RRL, July 12, 1802, RRLP*.
26. Charles Pinckney to RRL, Madrid, July 20, 1802, RRLP*.
27. Jefferson to RRL, Washington, April 18, 1802, *SPAC*, 15-18.
28. Madison to RRL, Washington, May 1, 1802, *ASPFR* II, 516.
29. RRL, "Is it advantageous to France to take possession of Louisiana?" RRLP and *ASPFR* II, 520-24. Enclosed in a letter to Madison of August 10, 1802. At much the same time, he prepared and submitted to the French government, but did not print, his "Thoughts on the Relative Situation of France, Britain and America, as Commercial and Maritime Nations," which suggested that more liberal trade agreements among the U.S.A., France, and other nations would undermine Great Britain's maritime power. RRLP and *ASPFR* II, 578-81.
30. Irving Brant, *James Madison: Secretary of State, 1800-1809*, 95, quoting report of Thomas Sumter, Jr., October 1803, in Monroe Papers. It should be added that Sumter was an *ex parte* witness, having quarreled with RRL in the previous year and resigned his post.

PART FIVE, CHAPTER THREE

1. RRL to Madison, Paris, September 1, 1802, RRLP and *ASPFR* II, 525.
2. E. Wilson Lyon, *Louisiana in French Diplomacy*, 133.
3. See 1 *supra*.
4. RRL to Talleyrand, October 19, 1802, RRLP*.
5. RRL to Jefferson, October 28, 1802, RRLP and *ASPFR* II, 525-26.
6. F-P. Renaut, *La Question de la Louisiane, 1796-1806*, 111.
7. RRL to Edward Livingston, Paris, November 10, 1802, RRLP(P). John Bernard Trotter, *Memoirs of the Latter Years of Charles James Fox* (London, 1811), 265.
8. RRL to Morgan Lewis, Paris, December 7, 1802, RRLP(P).
9. RRL to John R. Livingston, Paris, December 24, 1802, RRLP(P).
10. RRL to Janet L. Montgomery, Paris, January 16, 1802, RRLP(P).
11. RRL to John Armstrong, Paris, January 18, 1802, RRLP(P).
12. Draft of a note to Joseph Bonaparte, undated, RRLP*.
13. *Idem*.
14. RRL to Joseph Bonaparte, undated, RRLP*. There is also in RRLP* a "Note not delivered & translation." If French would provide for the payment of the American debt in 5-per-cent stock, and wish to convert the American stock, created in order to pay for territorial cessions, into cash to supply their present demands, RRL will find a person who will make a contract for the whole amount of the American stock, and promise (with security) not to sell it below a price fixed by RRL at about 80 per cent, in consideration of the depreciation which must occur in the creation of a new stock. The contractor shall be at liberty to pay half this

sum, payable by U.S., in 5-per-cent French stock, so that, coming into the market to purchase this, he will raise its price, nor will France object to receiving her own stock, bearing the same interest, in return for the stock of a foreign nation. For the remaining half, the American contractor shall pay in French money at eighty livres for every one hundred livres, in six payments, one payment every two months. Upon this operation little is to be gained; the profit comes from the purchase of French stock. RRL will guarantee that Joseph Bonaparte will receive, as his part of the deal, two million livres in French stock or one and a half million in specie. No wonder this note was never delivered! RRL clearly had this scheme in mind when he wrote his letter of December 24 (see 16 *infra*). The date on the draft, January 7, represents the day when it was actually put into writing, and perhaps the day, too, when it was abandoned. No more is heard of it.

15. RRL to Joseph Bonaparte, "2d. note," undated, RRLP. In *ASPFR* II, 534, this is cited as "No. 2 to ———." This clearly preceded the note in 16 *infra*.

16. RRL to Joseph Bonaparte, "Third Note to Joseph Bonaparte," December 24, 1802, in RRLP, but in *ASPFR* II, 530, it is cited as "Mr Livingston to ———, No. 4." The problem of numbering in *ASPFR* II is perhaps due to the fact that the existence of the note in 12 and 13 *supra* was not then known.

17. RRL to Joseph Bonaparte (17 Nivoise, An 11), January 7, 1803, RRLP, and *ASPFR* II, 536-37, where it is designated as No. 3.

18. Joseph Bonaparte to RRL, January 11, 1803, RRLP.

19. RRL to Talleyrand, January 10, 1803, RRLP and *SPAC*, 89-92.

20. Whitworth to Lord Hawkesbury, January 4, 1803, in Oscar Browning, ed., *England and Napoleon in 1803: Being the dispatches of Lord Whitworth and Others* (London, 1887), 37.

21. RRL to Talleyrand, January 10, 1803, cited in 19 *supra*.

22. Whitworth to Lord Hawkesbury, Paris, February 7, 1803, in Browning, *op. cit.*, 60.

23. RRL to Madison, February 18, 1803, RRLP, and *ASPFR* II, 533.

24. RRL to "Citizen Bonaparte, First Consul of France & President of the Italian Republic," February 24, 1803, Fair Copy dated February 27, 1803, RRLP, and *ASPFR* II, 538-40.

25. Talleyrand to RRL, March 10, 1803, RRLP, and *ASPFR* II (19 Ventose An 11), 545.

26. RRL to Madison, Paris, March 11, 1803, RRLP, and *ASPFR* II, 545.

27. Irving Brant, *James Madison: Secretary of State, 1800-1809*, 113.

28. Ambrose Spencer to RRL, Hudson, July 27, 1802. RRL to Ambrose Spencer, Paris, January 13, 1803. RRL tells Spencer in this letter that he has received his letter only "a few days ago." Both in RRLP(P). He also mentions Spencer's offer in a letter to his brother-in-law John Armstrong, Paris, January 18, 1803, RRLP(P).

29. John R. Livingston to RRL, New York, December 30, 1802, RRLP(P): "I know Swan well and am very much afraid of his schemes."

30. RRL to Joseph Bonaparte, January 7, 1803, RRLP, and *ASPFR* II, 536-37. RRL to Talleyrand, Paris (5 Ventose, An 11), February 24, 1803, RRLP*: here RRL says that there is no middle way between a rupture and such a declaration from the French Government as will satisfy the Americans concerning their right of deposit; and adds that Monroe's instructions will be "precise & positive." He is asking for Talleyrand's intervention with the First Consul so that such a quieting declaration may be made at once. He acknowledges the news officially in RRL to James Madison, Paris, March 3, 1803, RRLP and *ASPFR* II, 545. Rufus

King to RRL, London, February 23, 1803, TOLRRL, 42, says he has just heard of Monroe's appointment.

PART FIVE, CHAPTER FOUR

1. Rufus King to RRL, London, April 25, 1802, RRLP*.
2. Jefferson to RRL, Washington, October 10, 1802. *Writings*, Ford, ed., IX, 396-97.
3. Edward Channing, *A History of the United States* (6 vols., New York, 1905-1925), IV, 326.
4. E. Wilson Lyon, *Louisiana in French Diplomacy*, 170. And Pichon to Talleyrand, *AAE,EU*, LV, October 30 and November 4, 1802.
5. Henry Adams, *History of the United States of America During the Administration of Thomas Jefferson*, I, 427.
6. Jefferson to Monroe, January 13, 1803, *Writings*, Ford, ed., IX, 418.
7. Jefferson to Monroe, January 10 and 13, 1803, *ibid.*, IX, 416, 419-20.
8. *Annals of Congress*, 7 Congress, 2 Session, 371-74.
9. *ASPFR* II, 539-44. Italics inserted.
10. Madison to RRL, Department of State, January 18, 1803, *ASPFR* II, 529.
11. RRL to Madison, Paris, March 3, 1803, *ASPFR* II, 537.
12. RRL to Rufus King, Paris, March 23, 1803, RRLP and TOLRRL, 108-09.
13. RRL to Madison, March 24, 1803, RRLP and *ASPFR* II, 549.
14. Irving Brant, *James Madison: Secretary of State, 1800-1809*, 117.
15. RRL to Rufus King, Paris, March 15, 1803, RRLP and TOLRRL, 106. A slightly different version is in RRL to Jefferson, March 12, 1803, *ASPFR* II, 547.
16. Adams, *op. cit.*, II, 19.
17. Brant, *op. cit.*, 120.
18. *Ibid.*, 122.
19. Monroe to RRL, April 8, 1803; RRL to Monroe, April 10, 1803, RRLP.
20. François de Barbé-Marbois, *Histoire de la Louisiane*, 287.
21. *Ibid.*, 298. The words "Do not even wait for the arrival of Mr. Monroe" can be stretched, not altogether unnaturally, to mean that Bonaparte wished Livingston to have the credit for this transaction.
22. RRL to Madison, April 11, 1803, RRLP and *ASPFR* II, 552.
23. Same to same, April 13, 1803, RRLP and *ASPFR* II, 552-53.
24. Adams, *op. cit.*, II, 33-39.
25. Carl Ludwig Lokke, "Secret Negotiations to Maintain the Peace of Amiens," *American Historical Review*, XLIX, No. 1 (October, 1943), 55-64. C. D. Yonge, *Life and Administration of Robert Banks, Second Earl of Liverpool* (2 vols., London, 1868), I, 106-17.
26. RRL to Madison, April 13, 1803, cited in 23 *supra*.
27. Monroe to Madison, April 15, 1803, *SPAC*, 164-65.
28. *Idem.*
29. The "Journal and Memoranda" is to be found in *SPAC*, 165 ff.
30. RRL to Madison, Paris, April 17, 1803, RRLP and *ASPFR* II, 554.
31. RRL to Marbois, April 22 and 23, 1803, drafts in RRLP (appearing in Letter Book D as Letter No. 1 and Letter No. 2), RRLP*.
32. A copy of Marbois's powers, so dated from St. Cloud, appears in Letter Book D, RRLP*.
33. *SPAC*, 165.
34. *Idem.*
35. *SPAC*, 168.

36. Pedro Cevallos to Pinckney, Madrid, March 31, 1803; Pinckney to RRL, Madrid, April 4, 1803, RRLP*.
37. Draft, undated, in RRLP*.
38. Monroe to RRL, April 30(?), 1803, RRLP*.
39. Adams, *op. cit.*, II, 42.
40. Monroe's "Journal and Memoranda," *SPAC*, 170-81. The treaty and the two conventions are in *ASPFR* II, 507-09. See also *Treaties and Conventions Between the United States and Other Powers* (Washington, 1889), 331-38.
41. Channing, *op. cit.*, IV, 319.
42. Lyon, *op. cit.*, 203. Talleyrand to Decrès, May 24, 1803 (4 Prairial, An 11), *AAE,EU*, LV.
43. H.A.L. Fisher, *A History of Europe* (London, 1936), 841.
44. Rufus King to RRL, London, March 11, 1803, RRLP and TOLRRL, 44. Same to same, London, March 18, 1803, RRLP*.

PART FIVE, CHAPTER FIVE

1. RRL to Jefferson, Paris, June 2, 1803, RRLP*.
2. RRL to Madison, Paris, June 3 and 25, 1803, RRLP and *ASPFR* II, 563, 566.
3. Jefferson to Madison, August 18, 1803; Jefferson to W. C. Nicholas, September 7, 1803; in Henry Adams, *History of the United States of America During the Administration of Thomas Jefferson*, II, 86, 89. Article III of the treaty would also have seemed most unconstitutional to a supporter of states rights.
4. Adrienne Koch, *Jefferson and Madison* (New York, 1950), 239-41.
5. Adams, *op. cit.*, II, 68.
6. RRL to Monroe, May 23, 1803, RRLP. Irving Brant, *James Madison: Secretary of State, 1800-1809*, 147-48.
7. "*Si l'obscurité n'y était pas, il serait peut-être d'une bonne politique de l'y mettre.*" François de Barbé-Marbois, *Histoire de la Louisiane*, 312.
8. Adams, *op. cit.*, II, 72.
9. For example, RRL to Madison, Paris, May 20, 1803, RRLP and *ASPFR* II, 561.
10. J. B. Moore, ed., *History and Digest of International Arbitrations to Which the United States Has Been a Party*, V, 4440.
11. Adams, *op. cit.*, II, 46.
12. *Treaties and Conventions Between the United States and Other Powers*, 331-34.
13. *ASPFR* VI, 187; Moore, *op cit.*, V, 4441.
14. *Treaties and Conventions*, 338.
15. Adams, *op. cit.*, II, 47.
16. *Treaties and Conventions*, 335.
17. Raymond Walters, Jr., *Albert Gallatin*, 154.
18. Marbois, *op. cit.*, 333. "*Nous avons long-temps vécu,*" he is made to say by Marbois, "*et voilà la plus belle oeuvre de toute notre vie. Le traité que nous venons de signer n'a point été surpris par la finesse ou dicté par la force; également avantageux aux deux contractants, il changera des vastes solitudes en des pays florissants. C'est aujourd'hui que les États-Unis sont au nombre des puissances du premier rang. . . .*" ("We have lived a long time, and this is the noblest work of our lives. The treaty we have just signed has not been obtained by guile or dictated by force; equally beneficial to both contracting parties, it will change vast solitudes into flourishing countries. Today, the United States take their place among the powers of the first rank.") Without putting an undue trust in Marbois's memory, we may assume that RRL made a speech to this effect.
19. This draft is in RRLP*.

20. Letter Book B, 26, No. 11. The original, dated April 12, 1803, is in *AAE,EU*, Supp. VII, 340.

21. For example, RRL to Horatio Gates, Paris, June 8, 1803; RRL to Elkanah Watson, Paris, June 25, 1803; RRL to John Graham (in Madrid), Paris, July 10, 1803; RRL to Samuel L. Mitchill, Paris, July 23, 1803; RRL to John Armstrong, Paris, September 1, 1803. All in RRLP(P). RRL to Rufus King, Paris, May 7, 1803, TOLRRL, 59-60, goes farther and says that "about ten days before Mr. Monroe arrived the decision was taken and Talleyrand pressed me to conclude."

22. RRL to Madison, Paris, April 11, 1803, says that he believed the decision to sell had been made on "Saturday"—*i.e.*, Saturday, April 9. RRL to Madison, Paris, April 13, 1803, mentions "Sunday . . . (the day on which, as I told you, the determination had been taken to sell). . . ." Both in RRLP and *ASPFR* II, 552, 553.

23. RRL to John Armstrong, Paris, September 1, 1803, cited in 21 *supra*; RRL to Marbois, December 23, 1803, RRLP(P).

24. For example, the Philadelphia *Aurora* carried it on July 7, 1803; the Philadelphia *Gazette of the United States* on July 15, 1803; on July 8, 1803, the Washington *National Intelligencer*; the Boston *New England Palladium* carried it on July 1, 1803; the Boston *Columbia Centinel* on July 2, 1803; the New York *Daily Advertiser* on July 6, 1803; the New York *American Citizen* on July 7, 1803; the New York *Chronicle* on July 7, 1803; the New York *Herald* on July 20, 1803. No doubt a great many others printed it.

25. Madison to Monroe, July 30, 1803, *SPAC*, 226.

26. Madison to RRL, July 29, 1803, RRLP and *ASPFR* II, 566.

27. RRL to Madison, Paris, November 15, 1803, *SPAC*, 268.

28. Monroe to Virginia Senators, May 25, 1803, *The Writings of James Monroe*, S. M. Hamilton, ed. (New York, 1898-1903), IV, 32.

29. *Treaties and Conventions*, 337.

30. *Ibid.*, 336.

31. *Ibid.*, 338.

32. Skipwith's correct attitude toward a conflict of interest in his case will be found in Skipwith to RRL, Paris, August 10, 1803, RRLP. John R. Livingston's claim for hides delivered at Havre and Brest in 1795—a total of 330,786 livres-12-0—will be found in *Treaties and Conventions*, 339, *i.e.*, in the conjectural note. He had other and larger claims outside the note. *Treaties and Conventions*, 337.

33. John R. Livingston to RRL, Red Hook, August 2, 1803, RRLP(P).

34. RRL and Monroe to Marbois, Paris, June 8, 1803, RRLP*.

35. RRL to Marbois, Paris, September 1, 1803; RRL to Monroe, September 13, 1803, RRLP*.

36. RRL to Pierre-Alexandre Berthier, Paris, September 26, 1803, RRLP(P).

37. For the conjectural note see *Treaties and Conventions*, 339-42.

38. Moore, *op. cit.*, 4440.

39. RRL to Monroe, Paris, October 8, 1803; RRL to Madison, Paris, October 14, 1803, RRLP*.

40. Christopher Gore to Rufus King, London, September 6, 1803, Rufus King Papers, NYHS.

41. Sumter was married in March, 1802. RRL to Madison, Paris, March 22, 1802. The efforts to get him married are described in RRL to Janet L. Montgomery, Paris, May 9, 1802. Their disagreements, originated by Sumter, are detailed in Sumter to RRL, September 27, 1802: this exchange of notes gives an interesting picture of the routine of the Legation in 1802. All in RRLP(P).

42. Sumter to RRL, October 24, 1802, RRLP(P).

43. Commissioners to RRL, October 29, 1803. Monroe to RRL, London, October 29, 1803. RRLP*.

44. Creditors to RRL, November 4, 1803; RRL to Creditors, November 4, 1803, RRLP(P).
45. RRL to Charles Pinckney, Paris, December 21, 1803: "You have learned that our treaty has been ratified." RRLP*. Madison to RRL, November 9, 1803, says that in a previous letter of October 22 he told RRL of the exchange of ratifications. *ASPFR* II, 572.
46. Committee to RRL, December 29, 1803; RRL to Peter Stephen Du Ponceau, Paris, January 11, 1804, RRLP(P).
47. Madison to RRL, Department of State, November 9, 1803, as in 45 *supra*.
48. RRL to Madison, Paris, January 1, 1804, RRLP*.
49. RRL to Madison, June 19, 1804, RRLP*, is for proration.
50. Commissioners to RRL, March 22, 1804; RRL to Commissioners, March 22, 1804, RRLP (Letter Book D). Commissioners to RRL, March 26, 1804; RRL to Commissioners, March 26, 1804, RRLP*.
51. Moore, *op. cit.*, V, 4440.
52. Jefferson to Madison, August 18, 1804, quoted in Brant, *op. cit.*, 226.
53. Adams, *op. cit.*, II, 48.
54. Moore, *op. cit.*, V, 4444-45.
55. RRL to Madison, Paris, May 4, 1804, RRLP*, says he will go to England to prevent "any application from this government which will force me to draw bills."
56. Madison to RRL, Department of State, March 31, 1804, RRLP*: "Mr. Merry has formed complaint of the expression in your printed memorial which was construed into ill will toward Great Britain and an undue partiality to the French Government[.] he said he was expressly instructed by his Government to make this complaint[,] that the memorial was viewed in a very serious light." The letter appears in *ASPFR* II, 575-78, but all reference to Merry's complaint has been stricken out.
57. Madison to RRL, *ut supra*. Merry clearly had this second memorial also in mind when he dwelt further on "the notoriety of its author and on its tendency as an ostensible evidence of the spirit and views of so important and so *maritime* a power as the U.S. to excite animosity in other nations against Great Britain to wound her essential interests."
58. See 62 *infra*.
59. RRL to Mary Stevens Livingston, Southampton, May 16, 1804, RRLP(P).
60. *The Diaries and Correspondence of the Right Honourable George Rose* (2 vols., London, 1860), II, 136. Rose believed that peace was essential to the well-being of Great Britain, and was therefore disposed to take Livingston's arrival very seriously.
61. I am deeply indebted to Dr. Bradford Perkins, University of California at Los Angeles, for listing these dates: the newspapers consulted were in the NYPL collection.
62. RRL to Edward Livingston, Paris, July 30, 1804, RRLP(P).
63. Charles James Fox to RRL, 9 Arlington Street, May 20, 1804, RRLP(P).
64. Lord David Cecil, *Melbourne* (London, 1954 ed.), 53.
65. RRL to Mary Stevens Livingston, London, May 25, 1804, RRLP(P).
66. Same to same, London, May 27, 1804, RRLP(P).
67. *Idem.*, and RRL to Mary Stevens Livingston, London, May 22, 1804, RRLP(P): "Mr. Monroe recd. me in the most friendly manner."
68. William Count Bentinck to RRL, Lynn, May 25, 1804; Earl of Cholmondeley to RRL, Piccadilly, Thursday (May 26), 1804: has written to Houghton to order dinner and beds, and his bailiff will take RRL over his farm and then to Holkham. "P.S. Bentinck is a good man but a very bad Politician." RRL to Mary Stevens Livingston, London, May 28, 1804, RRLP(P).

69. *The Diaries and Correspondence of the Right Honourable George Rose,* II, 152.
70. Earl Stanhope, *Life of William Pitt* (3 vols., London, 1879), III, 249-51. To support the notion that RRL did bring peace overtures there is a letter in RRLP from Sir Charles Blagden, written four years later, in which Sir Charles regrets "that your pacific efforts did not meet with a better return. . . . Even those with whom you conversed here confidentially have not since all held the same language as they did then. Indeed both parties in the state seem now almost equally disinclined to peace." Blagden to RRL, London, May 21, 1811.
71. RRL to Edward Livingston, Paris, July 30, 1804, RRLP(P).
72. The *Corps Diplomatique* had been notified on 28/29 April 1804, that Napoleon had been invested with the imperial dignity, RRLP*.
73. RRL to Talleyrand, August 23, 1804, RRLP*.
74. RRL to Madison, Paris, August 28, 1804, RRLP*, says he has received the announcement "yesterday" in Madison's letter of June 26.
75. John Armstrong to RRL, February 7, 1804. William Cutting to John R. Livingston (forwarded), February 20, 1804. John R. Livingston to RRL, March 18, 1804. John R. Livingston to RRL, Red Hook, September 18, 1804. Peter W. Yates to RRL, November 12, 1804. P. Delabigarre to RRL, November 4, 1804. Edward Livingston to RRL, December 24, 1804. John R. Livingston to RRL, New York, January 12, 1804, says that Edward's public debts amounted to $50,000 and his private ones to $21,000. All in RRLP(P).
76. RRL to Thomas T. Tillotson, March 12, 1804, RRLP(P).
77. John Armstrong to RRL, Paimboeuf, October 11, 1804, RRLP(P), announces arrival with "your sisters Joanna and Alida, with a whole regiment of nephews." Talleyrand to RRL, Paris, October 27, 1804, RRLP*.
78. RRL to Madison, New York, June 29, 1805, RRLP(P).

CONCLUSION, CHAPTER ONE

1. Albert Gallatin to De Witt Clinton, Washington, May 13, 1805, Columbia University Libraries' Special Collections.
2. Raymond Walters, Jr., *Albert Gallatin* (New York, 1957), 134.
3. Albert Gallatin to De Witt Clinton, Washington, June 17, 1803, Columbia University Libraries' Special Collections.
4. RRL to Thomas T. Tillotson, Paris, May 29, 1803, RRLP.
5. RRL to Edward Livingston, Clermont, April 13, 1806: says that Lewis lacks prudence and steadiness and will not take advice. So also RRL to John Armstrong, Clermont, April 8, 1806: "The Govr. is, as you know, little calculated to guide a vessel in a storm. He acts precipitately & without advice." Both in RRLP.
6. D. S. Alexander, *A Political History of New York, 1774-1882,* I, 150.
7. Lewis's most statesmanlike measure was to recommend, on February 5, 1805, that the net proceeds of the first five hundred thousand acres of state land should be appropriated as a permanent fund in support of common schools. The bill was passed April 2, 1805. Jabez D. Hammond, *The History of Political Parties in the State of New-York,* I, 217. RRL to John Armstrong, Clermont, April 8, 1806, RRLP, says that Tillotson, contrary to practice, has exercised the duty of secretary to the Council of Appointment by deputy. This is ascribed to pride.
8. Maturin Livingston was "unpopular in his manners, deficient in a knowledge of law, without industry, and given to pleasure rather than business." Alexander, *op. cit.,* I, 147-48.
9. So Albert Gallatin to De Witt Clinton, cited in 3 *supra.* See also Raymond Walters, Jr., *op. cit.,* 165. Walters adds that the deficiency had now been found

to approximate $100,000, of which all but $40,000 was covered by property Edward Livingston left behind.

10. RRL to John Armstrong, Clermont, December 29, 1809, RRLP.
11. A meeting of January 24, 1806: so Hammond, *op. cit.*, I, 228. So also RRL to John Armstrong, Clermont, April 8, 1806, RRLP.
12. Hammond, *op. cit.*, I, 234.
13. *Ibid.*, I, 230-31.
14. Martin Van Buren to De Witt Clinton, May 4, 1806, De Witt Clinton Papers, Columbia University Libraries' Special Collections.
15. Hammond, *op. cit.*, I, 238. Alexander, *op. cit.*, I, 155.
16. Hammond, *op. cit.*, I, 246. Alexander, *op. cit.*, I, 155.
17. Alexander, *op. cit.*, I, 165.
18. RRL to Edward Livingston, New York, May 6, 1807; RRL to Madison, Clermont, May 17, 1807, RRLP.

CONCLUSION, CHAPTER TWO

1. RRL to Thomas T. Tillotson, Paris, November 12, 1802, RRLP.
2. For example, New York Society for the Promotion of Agriculture, Arts and Manufactures, *Transactions*, Part IV, 89-93.
3. *DAB* (1946 ed.), Fulton, Robert, VII, 69.
4. *Ibid.*, 70.
5. James Thomas Flexner, *Steamboats Come True*, 286. Tillotson's efforts resulted in the act of April 5, 1803, *Laws of New York, 1802-4* (Albany, 1804), 323-24.
6. Flexner, *op. cit.*, 281-82.
7. Barlow to Ruth Barlow and Robert Fulton [1802], C. B. Todd, *Life and Letters of Joel Barlow*, 190.
8. Flexner, *op. cit.*, 284.
9. *DAB* (1946 ed.), VII, 71.
10. Albert J. Beveridge, *The Life of John Marshall* (4 vols., Boston, 1916-1919), IV, 398-99.
11. RRL to Edward Livingston, Paris, April 25, 1804, RRLP.
12. Flexner, *op. cit.*, 317. Act of April 16, 1807, *Laws of New York, 1807-09* (Albany, 1809), 213-14.
13. Flexner, *op. cit.*, 318.
14. Flexner, *op. cit.*, 319, shows that Fulton in all documents called the boat the *North River Steamboat of Clermont*, the *North River Steamboat*, or the *North River*. (All references to it in RRLP bear this out.) On its first voyage, it seems simply to have been *The Steamboat*. Flexner also quotes the *Hudson Bee*, May 13, 1810, which stated that *The North River Steamboat* "has lately been known by the name *Clermont*, that is in books."
15. Alice Crary Sutcliffe, *Robert Fulton and the Clermont*, 209.
16. Flexner, *op. cit.*, 321.
17. Sutcliffe, *op. cit.*, 210-11.
18. Flexner, *op. cit.*, 322-23.
19. Sutcliffe, *op. cit.*, 212-13.
20. RRL to Robert L. Livingston, Clermont, September 2, 1807, RRLP.
21. Same to same, Clermont, November 11, 1807, RRLP.
22. RRL to Margaret L. Livingston, Clermont, January 4, 1808, RRLP.
23. RRL to John Stevens, fragment of a draft, dated January, 1808, RRLP. Stevens Papers, Doc. 985. A. D. Turnbull, *John Stevens: An American Record*, 240 ff.
24. 9 *Wheaton*, 3 ff.
25. *Laws of New York, 1807-09*, 407-08.

26. Talbot Hamlin, *Benjamin Henry Latrobe* (New York, 1955), 408.
27. Flexner, *op. cit.*, 347.
28. *Ibid.*, 326. Sutcliffe, *op. cit.*, 235.
29. Robert Fulton to RRL, July, 1808, Turnbull, *op. cit.*, 259.
30. Charles Standinger to RRL, New York, November 28, 1808, RRLP.
31. "My Essay on Steamboats . . ." undated, probably 1811, RLP.
32. Robert Fulton to RRL, Calorama, Washington, July 12, 1808, RRLP.
33. H. W. Dickinson, *Robert Fulton, Engineer and Artist* (London, 1913), 243. Fulton's note on the back of John Stevens to RRL, Hoboken, July 23, 1808, RRLP, says, "About August . . . the Boat made one trip to Brunswick." Actually, the boat succeeded in making a journey to the Delaware over one hundred fifty miles of ocean. Flexner, *op. cit.*, 335.
34. Turnbull, *op. cit.*, 261.
35. Rachel Cox Stevens to RRL, April 16, 1808, RRLP.
36. Turnbull, *op. cit.*, 261.
37. Fulton's first U.S. patent was granted February 11, 1809; practically the whole claim is for the right proportioning of the engine to the boat, and for the combination of the parts. A second patent was granted February 9, 1811. Dickinson, *op. cit.*, 241-42.
38. Draft of this agreement, in RRL's handwriting, is in RRLP. Turnbull, *op. cit.*, 283-84.
39. In Turnbull, *op. cit.*, facing p. 262, there is a facsimile list of the first subscribers, followed by Stevens's pledge.
40. RRL to Margaret L. Livingston, Clermont, February 14, 1808, RRLP.
41. Sutcliffe, *op. cit.*, opp. p. 268, gives a Prospectus. Flexner, *op. cit.*, 338.
42. Hamlin, *op. cit.*, 371-72.
43. These terms appear in John R. Livingston to RRL, New York, January 10, 1810. See also John R. Livingston to RRL, New York, July 28, 1809: "I am fearful the gross Sixth will weigh all proffits out of our scale." Both in RRLP.
44. Robert Fulton to RRL, January 4, 1810, RRLP: "He pushed himself into our enterprise[,] occupied our workmen[,] caused us to loosse 4 to 5000 dollars by retarding the finish of our boat. . . ."
45. *Acts of the Territory of Orleans, 1811* (New Orleans, 1811), 112-18.
46. Hamlin, *op. cit.*, 373, 376 n.
47. Robert Fulton to RRL, New York, June 12, 1812, RRLP.
48. John Stevens to RRL, Hoboken, June 17, 1808, RRLP.
49. Robert Fulton to RRL, cited in 47 *supra*.
50. Turnbull, *op. cit.*, 305.
51. *Idem.* Dickinson, *op. cit.*, 246, says that New Jersey, January 25, 1811, passed a law granting her citizens full and equal right to navigate in waters between New Jersey and New York.
52. Cadwallader D. Colden's opinion in *Fulton and Livingston* vs. *Lake Champlain Boat*, RRLP. Thomas Addis Emmet, consulted by the monopoly, said that, in his opinion, no state legislature had any authority to grant an exclusive right: but that if the state law was valid, then the forfeited property could be seized without any preceding process of law, if it could be done without a breach of the peace. Dickinson, *op. cit.*, 245.
53. Beveridge, *op. cit.*, IV, 405. Justice Livingston's decision will be found in 1 *Paine's Circuit Reports* (New York, 1827), 45-46. Paine gives the date simply as being in the April vacation. The *Minutes of the Court of Chancery*, entry for November 27, 1811, give the date of Chancellor Lansing's opinion as November 18, 1811.

54. John Lansing, Jr., "Decree and Opinion," with RRL's marginal notes, undated, is in RRLP.

55. Andrew Bartholomew to RRL, August 17, 1811, RRLP.

56. Beveridge, *op. cit.*, IV, 406.

57. For Chief Justice Kent's opinion see 9 Johnson, *Reports of Cases Argued and Determined in the Supreme Court . . . in the State of New-York* (20 vols., New York, 1808-23), 573 ff.

58. RRL to James Mease, New York, March 24, 1812; RRL to Edward Livingston, Clermont, March 19, 1812, RRLP.

59. Edward P. Livingston to RRL, Albany, June 12, 1812, RRLP.

60. Robert Fulton to RRL, New York, June 16, 1812, RRLP.

61. Same to same, New York, September 24, 1812, RRLP.

62. RRL to Messrs. Parker, Lansing, Winne, and Townsend, Clermont, September 5, 1812. The letter is not in his handwriting, RRLP.

63. Robert Fulton to Robert L. Livingston, New York, December 12, 1812, RRLP.

64. Robert Fulton to Edward P. Livingston and Robert L. Livingston, April 6, 1813. In his letter of December 12, he told the two brothers-in-law that his mind and time were engaged in the following projects: two boats about to be built for the Mississippi, one for the James River, one to run from Washington to "Potomac Creek (?)," one Sound boat, "Cutting's two ferry boats," the monopoly's second North River ferry boat, and negotiations going on for two boats on the Ohio. (It appears from Harriet L. Fulton to RRL, New York, July 19, 1812, asking for RRL's half of the patentee's rights, since her husband had promised her all the rights for pin money, that the first North River ferry was running in 1812. RRL gave her his half—$1,580.50—on July 16, 1812, so that Harriet Fulton's letter appears to have been misdated for June 20.) In August, Fulton writes, "The Boats are doing extraordinary well, our establishment is Vast and, this year all paid, we shall feel the clear gain of a large acquired capital." Again in September, he writes, "We have now not only the best works but the best prospects in the United States." Robert Fulton to Edward P. and Robert L. Livingston, New York, August 12, and New York, September 1, 1813. On October 2, 1813, "Robert L. Livingston and Edward P. Livingston in account with Robert Fulton" shows that the balance due Fulton at that time was $17,083.52. All in RRLP.

CONCLUSION, CHAPTER THREE

1. After the Chancellor's death, the newer Clermont was known as Arryl House: Harold Donaldson Eberlein, *The Manors and Historic Homes of the Hudson Valley* (Philadelphia, 1924), 76. Eberlein says that "it was built from a design by Bunel, inspired, it is said, by the Château of Beaumarchais."

2. Horatio Gates Spafford, *Gazetteer of New-York* (Albany, 1813), 164-65.

3. William Wilson to RRL, Clermont, June 16, 1806, Wilson Family Papers, Clements Library.

4. P. Delabigarre to RRL, Tivoli Box, July 5, 1802, says: "Your tenants . . . all wish for your return & ask me eagerly whether you would not come back this fall; your absence, without any flattery, has thrown a dark veil all around." So Edward P. Livingston to RRL, New York, December 11, 1802, written after EPL's return from Paris: "Your tenants flocked to us to hear news of you, and all appeared anxious for your return—those who lived near you, and always found a ready market for their Produce, at your house, feel the loss very much indeed, and are now less punctual in paying than the others." The portrait of a landlord whose in-

clinations were toward benevolence does seem to emerge from these statements. Both in RRLP.

5. William Wilson to RRL, Clermont, July 15, 1802; William Wilson to Edward P. Livingston, Clermont, July 6, 1802, RRLP.

6. David M. Ellis, *Landlords and Farmers in the Hudson-Mohawk Region, 1790-1850* (Ithaca, 1946), 62.

7. Spafford, *op. cit.*, 331.

8. RRL to Henry Willard, Paris, February 25, 1803, RRLP. However, William Wilson, in his letter to Edward P. Livingston cited above, says that the price of lands in the Hardenburgh Patent had not fallen, in spite of the European peace, although peace in Europe usually produced that effect. It is doubtful if RRL would have been willing to sell if his ministry to France had not cost him a good deal of money in mere living expenses. As for the rents being "for ever," an account of his rents in the Woodstock and Shandaken area, on the edge of the patent, show that they were always "for three lives," not forever, and that here, at any rate, there was no tenant mobility.

9. RRL to [James Madison], March 12, 1804, RRLP.

10. William Wilson to RRL, Clermont, June 16, 1806; RRL to William Wilson, Clermont, June 25, 1806, Wilson Family Papers, Clements Library.

11. Ellis, *op. cit.*, 94-99. *Memoirs*, Philadelphia Agricultural Society (Philadelphia, 1808), I, 158, quoted in Lyman Carrier, *The Beginnings of Agriculture in America* (New York, 1923), 270-71, where Peters makes 1771 the date of his first experiment in gypsum. New York Society for the Promotion of Agriculture, Arts and Manufactures, *Transactions*, I (1792-1799), Part 2, 63, for RRL on clover; see also RRL in Edinburgh Encyclopaedia, I, 335. For RRL on gypsum see New York Society *Transactions*, I, Part 1, 25-54.

12. RRL to M. Mouchette, Clermont, June 8, 1806. RRL to Albert Gallatin, Clermont, February 2, 1809, describes Mouchette as having "lived many years with me as my Secretary in America." He went with RRL to France, and acted as his translator, since "Mr. Sumter had not understood french and I had no such facility in it as to write it with ease and elegance." Mouchette stayed behind in France to become the director of a school at Thouars: so RRL to Messrs. Delessert, Clermont, November 4, 1806. All in RRLP.

13. Draft of an address in RRLP dated 1794.

14. John R. Livingston to RRL, New York, January 10, 1802. RRL to John R. Livingston, Paris, May 9, 1802, in answer, says that he is sending a ram and two ewes. Arthur H. Cole, *The American Wool Manufacture*, 6, says that he sent two pairs.

15. John R. Livingston to RRL, Red Hook, July 30, 1802, RRLP.

16. Cole, *op. cit.*, I, 74-75.

17. RRL, *Essay on Sheep* (New York, 1809), 6.

18. Cole, *op. cit.*, I, 74-75. Chester W. Wright, *Wool-Growing and the Tariff* (Cambridge, 1910), 15.

19. Copy of an order dated July 10, 1806; RRL to Margaret L. Livingston, July 12, 1807, RRLP.

20. RRL to Messrs. Delessert, Clermont, November 4, 1806.

21. Wright, *op. cit.*, 15.

22. RRL to Madison, Clermont, March 22, 1807, RRLP.

23. *Encyclopedia of American History,* Richard B. Morris, ed., Henry Steele Commager, chief consultant ed. (New York, 1953), 136.

24. RRL to Madison, Clermont, July 15, 1807, RRLP.

25. RRL to Albert Gallatin, Clermont, February 16, 1806, RRLP.

26. John Bach McMaster, *A History of the People of the United States* (8 vols., New York, 1883-1913), III, 275.

27. RRL to Madison, Clermont, January 8, 1808, RRLP.
28. RRL to Robert L. Livingston, Clermont, February 3, 1808, RRLP.
29. RRL to Tench Coxe, Clermont, May 24, 1808, RRLP.
30. This account is in RRLP.
31. Madison to RRL, Washington, January 11, 1809. RRL to Simeon De Witt, Clermont, March 1, 1809. RRL to Dr. Samuel Bard, Clermont, February 25, 1809. James Mease to RRL, Philadelphia, July 20, 1809. He told George Washington Parke Custis that his top lambs "were all bespoke a year in advance at $150 each & many more demanded of the full blood than I can as yet supply." Custis had written offering him a pair of Arlington Long Wooled Sheep, as to "a brother, labouring in the same patriotic cause, you will therefore accept these as a national tribute." RRL to G. W. P. Custis, Clermont, July 20, 1807. Custis to RRL, Arlington House, May 18, 1809. A small fine was imposed on the sale of the Arlington produce for the benefit of the Arlington Institute; RRL, however, was not interested in long-wooled sheep, except for a few ewes to cross with his merinos and to act as nurses. One also finds in RRL to James Mease, Clermont, August 2, 1809, that the chief obstacle to the household manufacture of merino wool, the difficulty of carding it by hand, had been obviated by the setting up of two carding mills with fine cards in his neighborhood, "and a third is erecting." In consequence, the price of wool has gone up, and instead of the household manufacturers asking for one year's credit, they now pay half the price down and the rest in eight months. Private families even advanced money to his overseer three months before the sheep were shorn to secure a preference. All in RRLP. For difficulties in carding see Cole, *op. cit.*, I, 99, and Wright, *op. cit.*, 16.
32. Joseph Delaplaine to RRL, Philadelphia, November 24, 1811, asks him to reconsider his letter of November 18, and write the article for the American edition of the Edinburgh Encyclopaedia, on "Agriculture." "A considerable number of patrons of the Encyclopaedia felt a strong desire, and were assured, that the article would come from your pen." What a pity that it should not be written, he said, "by one who possesses all the moral and physical advantages in so eminent a degree." RRLP. RRL did reconsider, and his article, which must have been written before he became ill in July, 1812, will be found in the Edinburgh Encyclopaedia, first American edition (Philadelphia, 1832), I, 332-41, and his plea for protecting duties on p. 341.
33. Thomas Jefferson to Benjamin Austin, Monticello, January 9, 1816. *Writings*, Ford, ed., XI, 500-05.
34. *Men and Times of the Revolution, or Memoirs of Elkanah Watson* (New York, 1857), 394. "The Chancellor," Watson says, "was a very useful and benevolent man, a scholar of profound erudition, an ardent patriot, and a prompt and decided promoter of all the essential interests of the country. His name should be cherished as that of one of her best benefactors; and may his memory long live in the gratitude of his country." *Ibid.*, 397.
35. Cole, *op. cit.*, I, 85.
36. Robert R. Livingston, *Essay on Sheep . . . Printed by order of the Legislature of the State of New York* (New York, 1809).
37. For the American Society of Fine Arts, originally the New York Society of Fine Arts, see RRL to Janet L. Montgomery, Paris, August 1, 1802, RRLP, where he says that he has just returned from a "board of artists" which was making arrangements to send copies of statues to New York. He is sending a Laocoön, a "Venus of the capital . . . as you expect a fine lady from France I will order her to be smoothed off for you," an Apollo, "I wish I had your directions as to the fig-leaf for he is as naked as Adam before the fall & what makes it the more shameful in him is that he has his robe over his arm . . . I should regret, however,

making any alteration in him," two fighting gladiators, and a very fine Germanicus. These, he thought, would be quite sufficient "to open your galery." Among the members of the Society was the Emperor Napoleon. Bonaparte to Edward Livingston, Malmaison, April 11, 1804, accepts with pleasure a membership in "*votre Academie* [des Arts de New York]," RRLP.

38. *Port Folio*, IV (December 10, 1810), 565-73.
39. Undated draft in RRLP.
40. Jefferson to RRL, Monticello, April 20, 1812, RRLP.
41. Catharine L. Garretson to Edward Livingston, Rhinebeck, November 25, 1812, Miscellaneous Livingston Manuscripts, NYHS.
42. Catharine L. Garretson to Edward Livingston, Rhinebeck, March 3, 1813 (a copy), Wainwright Autograph Collection, Princeton University Library.
43. The exact hour and date of his death—6:00 P.M., February 25—is in the Wilson Family Papers, Clements Library. Catharine L. Garretson to Edward Livingston, Rhinebeck, March 3, 1813, Wainwright Autograph Collection, Princeton University Library.

Index